JEWISH NEW TESTAMENT

JEWISH NEW TESTAMENT

A translation of the New Testament
that expresses its Jewishness

by

David H. Stern

"For out of Tziyon shall come forth *Torah*
and the Word of *Adonai* from Yerushalayim."
— Yesha'yahu 2:3

JEWISH NEW TESTAMENT PUBLICATIONS, INC.
Post Office Box 615, Clarksville, Maryland 21029 USA

Bible.   N.T.   English.   Stern.   1989
    Jewish New Testament: a translation of the New Testament that expresses
its Jewishness / by David H. Stern. — 1st ed. — Jerusalem, Israel;
Clarksville, Md., USA : Jewish New Testament Publications, Inc., ©1989.

    xxxi, 391 p.:ill. ; 21 cm.

    I. Stern, David H., 1935-   II. Title.
BS2095.S8   1989   225.5'209—dc20   89-84606
                                                          AACR 2 MARC
    Library of Congress

Published by
JEWISH NEW TESTAMENT PUBLICATIONS, INC.
P. O. Box 615, Clarksville, Maryland 21029 U.S.A.

Publishing History;
First paperback edition, May 1989
Second printing, November 1989
Third printing, July 1990
Fourth printing, April 1994
Fifth printing, September 1995
Sixth printing, November 1996
Seventh printing, June 1997
Eighth printing, March 1998

First hardback edition, June 1991
Second printing, February 1995
Third printing, June 1997
Fourth printing, May 1998

Cover illustration by Mickey Klugman Caspi
Typeset in Times Roman by Barry Segal International, Jerusalem, Israel
Printed in the United States of America

ISBN 965-359-003-0 (paperback)
ISBN 965-359-006-5 (hardback)
ISBN 965-359-014-6 (blue leatherette)
ISBN 965-359-010-3 (red leatherette)

Library of Congress Catalog Card Number: 89-84606

ברוך אתה יהוה אלהינו מלך העולם אשר נותן תורת-אמת
ובשורת-ישועה לעמו ישראל ולכל העמים על-ידי בנו ישוע
המשיח אדוננו.

Praised are you, *Adonai* our God, King of the universe, who
gives the *Torah* of truth and the Good News of salvation to his
people Israel and to all the peoples through his son Yeshua the
Messiah, our Lord.

CONTENTS

INTRODUCTION

BOOKS OF THE NEW TESTAMENT

GLOSSARIES, INDEXES AND MAPS

INTRODUCTION

I WHY THE *JEWISH NEW TESTAMENT*?

Why is this New Testament different from all other New Testaments? Because the *Jewish New Testament* expresses its original and essential Jewishness. Nearly all other English translations of the New Testament — and there are literally hundreds — present its message in a Gentile-Christian linguistic, cultural and theological framework.[1]

And what is wrong with that? Nothing! For although the Gospel is Jewish in origin, it is not only for Jews but also for Gentiles. The New Testament itself makes this very clear,[2] so it is appropriate that its message be communicated to non-Jews in ways that impose on them a minimum of alien cultural baggage.[3] And this approach has been successful: millions of Gentiles have come to trust in the God of Avraham, Yitzchak and Ya'akov and in the Jewish Messiah, Yeshua.[4]

The New Testament is a Jewish Book. However, the time has come to restore the Jewishness of the New Testament. For the New Testament is in fact a Jewish book — by Jews, mostly about Jews, and for Jews as well as Gentiles. It is all very well to adapt a Jewish book for easier appreciation by non-Jews, but not at the cost of suppressing its inherent Jewishness. The *Jewish New Testament* evidences

---

1   Exceptions: *The Book of Life* (Nashville: Thomas Nelson, 1982) and *The Living Bible: Messianic Edition* (Wheaton, Illinois: Tyndale House, 1984), by the Messianic Jews Sid Roth and David Bronstein, Jr., are adaptations of existing English versions. *The Original New Testament* (San Francisco: Harper & Row, 1985) is Hugh Schonfield's revision of his earlier translation, *The Authentic New Testament* (1955); Schonfield accepted Yeshua as the Messiah in his youth but reneged in later years. A translation by the Messianic Jew, H. W. Cassirer, is scheduled for publication.
2   Romans 1:16, 3:29-30, 10:12.
3   See 1 Corinthians 9:19-23.
4   These are the Hebrew names of Abraham, Isaac, Jacob and Jesus. Brief definitions of Semitic names and terms used on each two-page spread of this Introduction appear at the bottom of each right-hand page. For pronunciation and more information see the Pronouncing Explanatory Glossary beginning on page 358; also refer to section VIII of this Introduction.

Av·ra·ham — Abraham   Ye·shu·a — Jesus
Ya·'a·kov — Jacob   Yitz·chak — Isaac

this Jewishness in its very name, which, like the name "Jews for Jesus", unites two ideas that some consider incompatible and would rather separate.

But such separation cannot be. For the central figure of the New Testament, Yeshua the Messiah, was a Jew who was born to Jews in Beit-Lechem, grew up among Jews in Natzeret, ministered to Jews in the Galil, and died and rose from the grave in the Jewish capital, Yerushalayim — all in *Eretz-Israel*, the Land which God gave to the Jewish people. Moreover, Yeshua is still a Jew, since he is still alive, and nowhere does Scripture say or suggest that he has stopped being Jewish. His twelve closest followers were Jews. For years all his *talmidim* were Jews, numbering "tens of thousands" in Yerushalayim alone.[5] The New Testament was written entirely by Jews (Luke being, in all likelihood, a proselyte to Judaism); and its message is directed "to the Jew especially, but equally to the Gentile."[6] It was Jews who brought the Gospel to non-Jews, not the other way around. Sha'ul, the chief emissary to the Gentiles, was a lifelong observant Jew, as is evident from the book of Acts.[7] Indeed the main issue in the early Messianic Community ["Church"] was not whether a Jew could believe in Yeshua, but whether a Gentile could become a Christian without converting to Judaism.[8] The Messiah's vicarious atonement is rooted in the Jewish sacrificial system.[9] The Lord's Supper is rooted in the Jewish Passover. Immersion [baptism] is a Jewish practice. Yeshua said, "Salvation is from the Jews."[10] The New Covenant itself was promised by the Jewish prophet Jeremiah.[11] The very concept of a Messiah is exclusively Jewish. Indeed the entire New Testament completes the *Tanakh*, the Hebrew Scriptures which God gave to the Jewish people; so that the New Testament without the Old is as impossible as the second floor of a house without the first, and the Old without the New as unfinished as a house without a roof.

Moreover, much of what is written in the New Testament is incomprehensible apart from its Jewish context. Here is an example, only one of many.[12] Yeshua says in the Sermon on the Mount,[13] literally, "If your eye be evil, your whole body will be dark."[14] What is an evil eye? Someone not knowing the Jewish background might suppose Yeshua was talking about casting spells. However, in Hebrew, having an *'ayin ra'ah*, an "evil eye", means being stingy; while having an *'ayin tovah*, a "good eye", means being generous. Yeshua is simply urging

---

5   Acts 21:20.
6   Romans 1:16.
7   See Acts 16:3, 17:2, 18:18, 20:16, 21:23-27, 23:7, 25:8, 28:17.
8   See Acts 15:1-29 and the whole book of Galatians.
9   See especially Leviticus 17:11, and compare Messianic Jews [Hebrews] 9:22.
10 Yochanan [John] 4:22.
11 Jeremiah 31:30-34.
12 For others, consult David Bivin and Roy Blizzard, Jr., *Understanding the Difficult Words of Jesus* (Austin, Texas: Center for Judaic-Christian Studies, 1984). See also the *Jewish New Testament Commentary* (in preparation) and Section VI below.
13 Mattityahu [Matthew] 5 — 7.
14 Mattityahu [Matthew] 6:23.

generosity against stinginess. And this understanding fits with the surrounding verses: "Where your wealth is, there your heart will be also.... You can't be a slave to both God and money."[15]

But the best demonstration of the New Testament's Jewishness is also the most convincing proof of its truth, namely, the number of *Tanakh* prophecies — all of them centuries older than the New Testament events — which are fulfilled in the person of Yeshua from Natzeret. The probability that anyone could satisfy dozens of prophetic conditions by mere chance is infinitesimal. No pretender to Messiahship, such as Shim'on Bar-Kokhva[16] or Shabtai Tzvi[17], has fulfilled more than a few of them. Yeshua fulfilled every one of the prophecies intended to be fulfilled at his first coming; Section VII below lists fifty-two. The rest of the prophecies he will fulfill when he returns in glory.

Thus the *Jewish New Testament* aims at making it normal to think of the New Testament as Jewish.

But there are three additional areas in which the *Jewish New Testament* can aid in *tikkun-ha'olam* ["fixing up the world"]: Christian antisemitism, Jewish failure to receive the Gospel, and separation between the Church and the Jewish people.

Christian Antisemitism. First, a vicious circle of Christian antisemitism feeds on the New Testament. The New Testament itself contains no antisemitism; but since the early days of the Church, antisemitism has misused the New Testament to justify itself and infiltrate Christian theology. Translators of the New Testament, even though not themselves antisemites, absorb that antisemitic theology, and produce anti-Jewish translations. Readers of these translations acquire attitudes which are anti-Jewish and alien to Judaism. Some of these readers become theologians who further refine and develop the antisemitic character of Christian theology (they may be unaware of the built-in anti-semitism); while others become antisemitic activists who persecute Jews, thinking that by so doing they are serving God. This vicious circle must be broken. The *Jewish New Testament*, by removing centuries-old antisemitic theological biases and positively stressing Jewishness, is an attempt to do so.

Jewish Misgivings About the Gospel. Second, while there are some 100,000 Messianic Jews in English-speaking countries, it is obvious that most Jewish people do not accept Yeshua as the Messiah. While the reasons include Christian

---

15 Mattityahu [Matthew] 6:21, 24.
16 Died 135 C.E. (see footnote 36).
17 1626-1676.

'a·yin ra·'ah — "evil eye", stinginess
'a·yin to·vah — a "good eye", generosity
Beit-Le·chem — Bethlehem
E·retz-Is·ra·el — the Land of Israel
the Ga·lil — Galilee
Na·tze·ret — Nazareth
Sha·'ul — Saul (Paul)

tal·mi·dim — disciples
Ta·nakh — Hebrew Scriptures, "Old Testament"
tik·kun-ha·'o·lam — "fixing up the world"
Ye·ru·sha·la·yim — Jerusalem
Ye·shu·a — Jesus

persecution of Jews, secular worldviews that allow little place for either God or a Messiah, and refusal to turn from sin, a major cause is the perception by Jews that the Gospel is irrelevant to them. This perceived irrelevancy arises partly from the way Christianity presents itself, but also from the alienation induced by most New Testament translations. With their Gentile Christian cultural trappings and their anti-Jewish theological underpinnings, they lead many Jews to see the New Testament as a Gentile book about a Gentile god. The Jesus portrayed therein seems to bear little relationship to Jewish life. It becomes hard for a Jew to experience Yeshua the Messiah as who he really is, namely, a friend to every Jewish heart. While the *Jewish New Testament* cannot eliminate all the barriers between every Jew and faith in his Messiah, it does remove some of the linguistic, cultural and theological obstacles. A Jewish person reading the *Jewish New Testament* can experience Yeshua as the Messiah promised by the *Tanakh* to the Jewish people; he can see that the New Testament is for Jews as much as for Gentiles; and he is confronted with the message of the Bible as a whole, both testaments together, as true, important and worthy of acceptance, the key to both his own and Jewish national salvation.

Separation Between the Messianic Community and the Jewish People. Finally, centuries of Jewish rejection of Yeshua and Christian rejection of Jews has produced a situation today in which it is commonly supposed that Christianity is Christianity, and Judaism is Judaism, and never the twain shall meet. Moreover, many Jews and Christians are satisfied with this arrangement. But it was not God's will that there be two separate peoples of God. Gentile Christians who recognize that they have joined Israel, not replaced it, and Messianic Jews who identify fully with both the Jewish people and the Jewish Messiah, Yeshua, must work together to heal the greatest schism in the history of the world, the split between the Church and the Jewish people. The *Jewish New Testament* has a part to play in this great task of bringing the two together in a way that preserves the identity of the Jewish people within the Messianic Community, as both Jews and Gentiles honor God and his Messiah according to the *Tanakh* and the New Testament.

Contents of Rest of Introduction. In the remainder of this Introduction, Sections II and III contain an orientation to the Bible in general and the New Testament in particular. Sections IV-VII relate to what distinguishes the *Jewish New Testament* from other versions. Section VIII explains the features of the *Jewish New Testament*, so that the reader can use it efficiently.

II THE BIBLE

The Central Message of the Bible. In telling about God, his people Israel, and their Messiah Yeshua, the Bible's constant theme is that man needs to be saved and God provides salvation. The purpose of life and the meaning of history is that God will deliver humanity from the misery of sin and restore the conditions that enable individuals and nations to relate rightly with him. Morality and happiness are inseparably linked with salvation.

The *Tanakh*. For according to the *Tanakh*[18] [the Old Testament], God created man in his image to be in intimate, loving and obedient fellowship with him.[19] But man rebelled, chose his own way instead of God's[20] — and still does.[21] The name for such rebellion is sin, and the penalty for sin is death[22] — not only cessation of life but everlasting separation from God.[23] However, God, who is merciful as well as just, wills to save man from what he has earned and deserves. To this end God chose one person, Avraham, and through him brought forth a people, the Jews, commissioning them to "be a blessing" and "a light to the nations."[24] Through Moshe he gave them a *Torah* making known his standards for righteousness. Through judges, kings and prophets he encouraged them, disciplined them and promised that final salvation would come to them and the other peoples through an "anointed one" (Hebrew *mashiach*, English "Messiah," which means the same as Greek *christos*, English "Christ").

The New Testament and Yeshua. Continuing this chronicle the New Testament proclaims that the Messiah of Israel prophesied in the *Tanakh* is Yeshua, a real, historical person who, like others, was born, lived and died. However, unlike others, he did not die simply because his life ended but in order to redeem us from our sins. Also unlike others he was resurrected from the dead, is alive now "at the right hand of God"[25] and will come a second time to rule as King of Israel and bring peace to the world. In explaining why he alone was qualified to be the final sacrifice for sins the New Testament calls him both Son of Man and Son of God. The first term, taken from the *Tanakh*,[26] means that he is fully and ideally human, sinless, "a lamb without blemish."[27] Since he did not owe his life for his own sins, he could be "God's lamb...taking away the sin of the world."[28] The second term,

---

18 The word *Tanakh* is an acronym made from the first letters of the three main divisions of the Hebrew Bible: *Torah* (the "Law", Pentateuch), *Neviim* (Prophets) and *K'tuvim* (Writings). See glossary entry on page 374.
19 Genesis 1:26 — 2:25.
20 Genesis 3:1-19.
21 I Kings 8:46, Ecclesiastes 7:20, Romans 3:23.
22 Genesis 2:17, 5:5; Romans 6:23.
23 Genesis 3:22-24, Isaiah 59:1-2.
24 Genesis 12:1-3, Isaiah 49:6.
25 Psalm 110:1, Acts 7:56, and throughout Messianic Jews [Hebrews].
26 Daniel 7:13.
27 Exodus 12:5, Leviticus 1-6, 1 Kefa [1 Peter] 1:19.
28 Yochanan [John] 1:29, 36.

Av·ra·ham — Abraham
ma·shi·ach — Messiah
Mo·she — Moses

Ta·nakh — Hebrew Bible, "Old Testament"
To·rah — Teaching, "Law"
Ye·shu·a — Jesus

hinted at in the *Tanakh*,[29] means that "in him, bodily, lives the fullness of all that God is;" so that he is uniquely able to express God's love to humanity.[30]

The Messianic Community. The New Testament also describes formative events among the early Jewish and Gentile followers of Yeshua and explains how this new Messianic Community or "Church" is related to the Jewish people. Unlike much Christian theology, the New Testament does not say that the Messianic Community replaces the Jews as God's people. Nor does it say that the Messianic Community stands alongside the Jews as a second eternal people of God with a separate destiny and separate promises. Rather, the relationship is more complex: Gentiles are grafted as "wild olive branches" into a Jewish "cultivated olive tree," some of whose branches "fell off" but will one day be "grafted back into their own olive tree," so that in the end, "all Israel will be saved."[31] It is on this basis that unity will be restored between the Messianic Community and the Jewish people.

Breadth of Vision. The Bible's concept of salvation is both individual and corporate, so that the *Tanakh* and the New Testament speak to the full range of human activity — family life, class struggle, social concerns, commerce, agriculture, the environment, national identity, government, justice, interpersonal relationships, worship, prayer, physical health, emotional well-being and the inner life of the spirit. In all of these areas the Bible informs us that a right response to God's initiatives will bring salvation to every part of our lives — individually, socially, communally, nationally and universally.

Two Testaments, One Bible. The two parts of the Bible, the *Tanakh* and the New Testament, deal with parallel material in complementary ways. History, having commenced with the creation of heaven and earth and the sinless paradise of Eden in the first two chapters of the Old Testament, ends with the sinless paradise of "a new heaven and a new earth"[32] in the last two chapters of the New Testament. The New Testament, continuing the salvation history set forth in the *Tanakh* on the basis of covenants made with Noach, Avraham, Moshe and David, presents itself as encompassing the "new covenant" which God promised to make "with the house of Israel and the house of Y'hudah"[33] and presents Yeshua as consummating the systems of kings, prophets, priests and sacrifices described in the *Tanakh*, and as being himself the sum and substance of the *Torah*. Thus the New Testament apart from the Old is heretical, and the Old Testament apart from the New is incomplete — two testaments, one Bible.

Testaments and Covenants, New and Old. The term "testament" reflects a tension between the Hebrew language of the *Tanakh* and the Greek of the New Testament. The Hebrew word *b'rit* means "covenant, contract". The Greek word for "covenant" or *"b'rit"* is *"diathêkê"*. But *"diathêkê"* can also mean "testament"

---

29   Isaiah 9:5-7, Zechariah 12:10, Psalms 2:7, Proverbs 30:4.
30   Colossians 2:9, Yochanan [John] 3:16.
31   Romans 11:16-26.
32   Isaiah 65:17, Revelation 21:1.
33   Jeremiah 31:30-34.

in the sense of "will".[34] The Hebrew words *"b'rit chadashah"* mean "new covenant". But the set of texts translated here, called the *B'rit Chadashah* in Hebrew, is known in English as the New Testament because of the influence of Greek *diathêkê* — even though what Jeremiah foretold was a new foundational contract between God and the Jewish people, not a will: a covenant, not a testament.

Moreover, a "new" covenant implies an "old" one, in this case the Mosaic Covenant made by God with the Jewish people at Mount Sinai.[35] The New Testament makes this explicit at Messianic Jews [Hebrews] 8:6-13, where, in context, "old" does not imply "bad" but merely "earlier". Since the *Tanakh*, in which the Mosaic Covenant is pivotal, dates from between 1500 and 300 B.C.E.,[36] it is called the Old Testament, distinguishing it from the first-century C.E writings which constitute the New Testament.

III THE NEW TESTAMENT

Contents of the New Testament. The New Testament consists of twenty-sever. documents called "books" written in the first century of the Common Era by at least eight authors.[37]

- **The Gospels.** The first four books, known as the Gospels, are four views of Yeshua's life and purpose in "salvation history" (the record of God's involvement in human history for the purpose of saving mankind). The first and fourth Gospels are understood to have been written by two of Yeshua's twelve *talmidim*, Mattityahu and Yochanan. The second is attributed to Mark, who accompanied another of Yeshua's *talmidim*, Kefa. The author of the third was Luke, an associate of Sha'ul.

   The old English word "gospel" means "good news". Therefore, in a significant sense there are not four gospels but one, namely, the Good News of who Yeshua is and what he has done. But each of the four Gospels presents this Good News in its own way, just as four honest witnesses to an event will each have his own version of what happened. Broadly speaking, one may say

---

34   Messianic Jews [Hebrews] 9:16-17.

35   Exodus 19-24.

36   B.C.E. stands for "Before the Common Era"; C.E. for "Common Era". Modern Jewish literature uses these abbreviations instead of "B.C." and "A.D."

37   The following material concerning the historicity of the New Testament events and the authorship and dating of the New Testament documents is based on mainstream conservative New Testament scholarship. See the discussion of tradition and scholarship near the end of this section.

Av·ra·ham — Abraham
b'rit — covenant
b'rit cha·da·shah — new covenant
Ke·fa — Peter
Mat·tit·ya·hu — Matthew
Mo·she — Moses
No·ach — Noah

Sha·'ul — Saul (Paul)
tal·mi·dim — disciples
Ta·nakh — Hebrew Bible, "Old Testament"
To·rah — Teaching, "Law"
Ye·shu·a — Jesus
Y'hu·dah — Judah
Yo·cha·nan — John

that Mattityahu has a Jewish readership in mind, while it seems that Luke is writing for Gentiles.[38] Mark's version is fast-paced and filled with human-interest details. Yochanan's never loses sight of Yeshua's heavenly origin, portraying him clearly as not only Son of Man but Son of God.

The first three are known as the Synoptic Gospels (the word "synoptic" means "same viewpoint"), since many of the same incidents are reported in two or three of them, often in similar or even identical language. Scholars have attempted to explain the differences and similarities in the Synoptics, often by postulating that one writer copied from another, or, more sophisticatedly, that two or all three of them had direct or indirect access to some of the same oral or written sources.

- **Acts.** Luke is also the author of "The Acts of the Emissaries", which could as well be called "Luke, Part II" (see the opening verses of both Luke and Acts). This book, in which Yeshua's emissaries [apostles] Kefa and Sha'ul are the chief protagonists, describes the history of the early Messianic Community from about 30 C.E. to 65 C.E., first in Yerushalayim, where New Testament faith was entirely an internal Jewish matter, and then as the Gospel spread to "Y'hudah, Shomron, indeed to the ends of the earth,"[39] that is, to Rome, the pagan antithesis of Yerushalayim. A major purpose of the book of Acts is to prove that Gentiles can become Messianic without converting to Judaism. (It is ironic that today popular opinion requires a reverse application of the book of Acts to show that Jews can become Messianic without "converting" to what has become identified as a different religion, Christianity.)

- **Sha'ul's Letters.** The rest of the New Testament, except for the last book, consists of letters. The first thirteen are by Sha'ul, the "emissary to the Gentiles".[40] Five are to Messianic communities which he founded in Greece — in Corinth (2 letters), Philippi and Thessalonica (modern Salonika, 2); two to communities he founded in what is now Turkey — in Galatia and Ephesus; and two to communities established by others — Colosse (near Ephesus), and Rome. These nine letters deal with issues of behavior and belief which arose in the several congregations. Of the remaining four, known as the Pastoral Letters, three are to his trainees Timothy (2) and Titus; and one, to a friend named Philemon, requests him to welcome back as a free brother a slave who ran away.

- **The General Letters.** Next is "A Letter to a Group of Messianic Jews", otherwise known as "To the Hebrews". Although sometimes attributed to Sha'ul, Apollos or Priscilla and Aquila, its authorship is uncertain. Addressing a Messianic Jewish readership, it relates the new dispensation brought by Yeshua to the themes of the *Tanakh*. Following are a letter from Ya'akov, the brother of Yeshua and leader of the Messianic community in Yerushalayim; two letters from Kefa; three from Yochanan; and one from

---

38 His emphasis on the universality of salvation and his addressing his book to "Theophilos" (Greek for "lover of God") suggest that he is writing for the broadest possible audience.
39 Acts 1:8.
40 Romans 11:13, Galatians 2:7-9.

Y'hudah, another brother of Yeshua. As a group these are called the General Letters and are concerned with matters of faith and practice.

• **Revelation.** The final book of the New Testament is "The Revelation of Yeshua the Messiah to Yochanan", containing descriptions of visions revealed by the resurrected and glorified Messiah to the emissary Yochanan (or, according to some, to another Yochanan). It is also known as the Apocalypse, since it describes "apocalyptic" events, that is, end-time disasters and interventions of God in history connected with the final judgment of mankind. Containing over five hundred quotations from and allusions to the *Tanakh*, more than any other New Testament book, it resembles and draws on the visions of such writers as Isaiah, Ezekiel, Zechariah and Daniel. Some consider it to be speaking of what today is still in the future, others regard it as describing the age of history which began two thousand years ago, and still others believe its primary reference is to first-century events. Its figurative language gives room for such different interpretive approaches or for a combination thereof.

Language of the New Testament. While the *Tanakh* was written largely in Hebrew (portions of Ezra and Daniel are in a related Semitic language, Aramaic), most of the early manuscripts of the New Testament are in Greek — not the classical language of Homer or Plato, but *koinê* ["common"] Greek, the *lingua franca* of everyday affairs throughout the Eastern Mediterranean and Middle East during the first century.

Nevertheless, a number of scholars, not necessarily a majority, believe that portions of the New Testament were written in Hebrew or Aramaic, or drew upon source materials in those languages; this case has been made for all four Gospels, Acts, Revelation and several of the General Letters. Moreover, Sha'ul, whose letters were composed in Greek, clearly drew on his native Jewish and Hebraic thought-forms when he wrote. In fact, as shown earlier, some phrases in the New Testament manuscripts make no sense unless one reaches through the Greek to the underlying Hebrew expressions.[41]

Dating. The earliest New Testament books, such as Shaul's letters to the Galatians, Thessalonians and Corinthians, and probably the letter of Ya'akov, were written around 50 C.E., some twenty years after Yeshua's death and resurrection. Sha'ul's other letters date from the 50's and 60's, the Gospels and Acts in their essentially final form from between 65 and 85, and the other General Letters and Revelation from between 65 and 100. Some scholars believe that some New Testament books underwent final editing in the early second century.

---

41   See analysis of Mattityahu 6:23 in Section I, also footnote 12.

Ke·fa — Peter
Sha·'ul — Saul (Paul)
Shom·ron — Samaria
Ta·nakh — Hebrew Scriptures, "Old Testament"

Ya·'a·kov — Jacob
Ye·ru·sha·la·yim — Jerusalem
Ye·shu·a — Jesus
Y'hu·dah — Judea, Jude
Yo·cha·nan — John

The Canon. Besides the documents which now form the New Testament, there were written other versions of the Good News, other histories of events in the early Messianic Community, other discussions of doctrine and practice and other apocalypses.[42] It was the early Messianic Community which exercised the spiritual discernment necessary to decide which books truly brought God's message to humanity and which were lesser creations, perhaps of historical or spiritual value but not God-breathed. Quotations from New Testament books are found already in the non-canonical "Teaching of the Apostles" (80-100 C.E.), but the first list including New Testament books was made by the heretic Marcion around 150 C.E. This product of error surely stimulated the development of an orthodox canon, such as appears in the Muratorian Fragment at the end of the second century. But the earliest known enumeration of exactly the twenty-seven books constituting today's New Testament, with neither additions nor omissions, is in the Thirty-Ninth Paschal Letter of Athanasius (367 C.E.). Though the list is late, the books themselves were used in Messianic congregations from the time they were written, just as the books of the *Tanakh* were an integral part of Judaism centuries before its canon was authoritatively determined in the Council of Yavneh (c. 90 C.E.) by Rabbi Yochanan Ben-Zakkai and his colleagues.

Tradition and Scholarship. The above introductory material reflects mainstream conservative New Testament scholarship, which confirms most of the traditional views on these subjects. But during the past two centuries all the authorships have been challenged, likewise all the datings and the historicity of most of the events (one should note that the *Tanakh* has been similarly questioned).

The debate continues, but facts should impose limits on it — to give but one example, there are handwritten manuscripts of portions of the New Testament from as early as the first half of the second century, disproving the more extreme suggestions that the New Testament was written two, three or four hundred years after Yeshua. Also some of the criticism is based on presuppositions which, though presenting themselves as objective, are actually religious in character but opposed to the claims of the Bible; so that they determine negative conclusions *a priori* — *e.g.*, a world-view of doubt or "scientism" that precludes the possibility of miracles, or a disbelief in the ability of the ancient writers to distinguish between real and imaginary events, or a too willing confidence that the early Messianic communities altered reports to fit their wishes.

Although there is no lack of unanswered questions, many respected scholars nevertheless believe that the traditional authors are in fact the authors, that the early datings are correct, and, most importantly, that Yeshua really lived, "died for our sins,... and... was raised on the third day, in accordance with what the *Tanakh* says."[43]

---

42 See Edgar Hennecke, *New Testament Apocrypha* (Philadelphia: The Westminster Press, 1965).

43 1 Corinthians 15:3-4.

IV HOW THE *JEWISH NEW TESTAMENT* EXPRESSES THE NEW TESTAMENT'S JEWISHNESS

Three Ways of Bringing Out the Jewishness of the New Testament. This translation highlights Jewishness in three somewhat overlapping ways — cosmetically (or superficially), culturally and religiously, and theologically.

- **Cosmetically.** Cosmetic changes from the usual renderings are the most frequent and obvious. The names "Jesus", "John", "James" and "Peter" never appear, only "Yeshua", "Yochanan", "Ya'akov" and "Kefa". The terms "immersion", "emissary", "execution-stake" and "Messianic community"(or "congregation") replace "baptism", "apostle", "cross" and "church". Semitic terms which belong to "Jewish English" (see below) substitute for certain English words — for example, *"talmid"* instead of "disciple" and "do *tzedakah"* instead of "give to charity". Many of these alterations replace "church language"(in which Christian stimuli produce automatic responses) with neutral terminology that encourages the reader to think. Although any one of these changes is superficial, the sheer quantity of them impresses on the reader that the New Testament is indeed a Jewish book, and this true and genuine effect is not superficial.

- **Culturally and Religiously.** Cultural and religious changes strengthen the reader's awareness of the Jewish cultural or religious context in which New Testament events took place. One example is at Mattityahu 9:20, where the lady seeking to be healed touches not merely the "fringe" or "edge" of Yeshua's robe, but his *"tzitzit"*, the ritual tassel which the *Torah* instructs Jewish men to wear on the corners of their garments as a reminder to obey all of God's commandments.[44] Another is at Acts 20:7, where the meeting of Sha'ul with the believers in Ephesus "on the first day of the week" was probably held not on Sunday evening but, reflecting the Jewish, biblical way of organizing the calendar, on *"Motza'ei-Shabbat"*, that is, Saturday night.

- **Theologically.** Theological changes are the most penetrating, since New Testament translating has been thoroughly permeated by Gentile-Christian theologies which de-emphasize the Jews as still God's people, the *Torah* as still valid, and God as still One. An example of such a change is at Messianic Jews [Hebrews] 8:6, where the Greek word *nenomothetêtai* means not merely that the New Covenant "has been enacted" on the basis of better

---

44   Numbers 15:37-41.

===

Ke·**fa** — Peter
Mat·tit·ya·hu — Matthew
Mo·tza·'ei-Shab·bat — Saturday night
Sha·'ul — Saul (Paul)
tal·mid — disciple
Ta·nakh — Hebrew Bible, "Old Testament"

do *tze·da·kah* — give to charity
tzi·tzit — ritual fringe
Ya·'a·kov — Jacob
Ye·shu·a — Jesus
Yo·cha·nan — John

promises, but on those promises "has been made *Torah*." Another is at Romans 10:4, where the word *telos* does not mean that the Messiah terminates the Law, but that he is "the goal at which the *Torah* aims." Theological implications of these and some other *Jewish New Testament* renderings are discussed in Section VI below.

"Jewish English". Besides systematically using the original Semitic names for persons and places in and near the Land of Israel the *Jewish New Testament* draws on "Jewish English", defined as Hebrew and Yiddish expressions which English-speaking Jews incorporate into everyday speech. While meant to bring the Jewishness of the New Testament into clearer focus, some readers may find this aspect of the translation unfamiliar or anachronistic and therefore exhausting or jarring; or they may take exception to particular decisions — for example, to using the word *"shalom"* instead of "peace", or *"talmid"* instead of "disciple", or the Yiddish word *"tsuris"* instead of "troubles" — or to generally *not* using *"Mashiach"* in place of "Messiah". Such objection is expected because "Jewish English" is an *ad hoc* concept, so that each English-speaking Jew creates his own version of it. Some are unaware of these speech patterns. Some regard certain phrases as second nature but are unacquainted with others. Some who know the expressions may find them uncongenial in a Bible, while others may tire from seeing too many unfamiliar terms scattered through the book. But since "Jewish English" in its manifold variety is widely used, an appeal is made for tolerance of those elements included in the *Jewish New Testament*.

Jewish New Testament Commentary. As the *Jewish New Testament* goes to press, approaching completion is a verse-by-verse commentary in which controversial renderings are defended and additional background of interest to both Jews and Christians is provided. The *Jewish New Testament Commentary* deals with questions Jewish people have about the New Testament, Yeshua and Christianity; questions Christians have about Judaism and the Jewish roots of their faith, and questions Messianic Jews have about their own identity and role in God's plan for human history. Passages which are problematical from a Jewish viewpoint are treated, such as Mattityahu 27:25 ("His blood is on us and on our children!") and Yochanan's remarks in his gospel about "the Jews" (in this translation frequently "the Judeans"). Likewise, present-day points of friction between Jews and Christians are discussed at some appropriate place — for instance, the issue of whether evangelizing Jews is in principle unethical is treated in the context of 2 Corinthians 4:2 ("We refuse to make use of shameful underhanded methods, employing deception or distorting God's message."). It is hoped that the commentary can be published soon. In the meantime, Section VI deals briefly with a few topics of this kind.

V TRANSLATION ISSUES

Among the philosophical points raised in translation are formal versus dynamic equivalence ("literal translations" versus "paraphrases") and the degree to which a translator's interpretation of a text's meaning should be reflected in his translation.

"Literal Translations" Versus "Paraphrases". There is a scale on which translations can be measured. At one end of the scale are "literal" translations, which reproduce in the receptor language (English) the grammatical forms of the source language (Greek); translators call these "formally equivalent translations". The King James Version, the Revised Standard Version, the New American Standard Version and the 1917 Jewish Publication Society version of the Hebrew Bible are examples; an interlinear version (or "pony"), which renders the Greek text word by word, is the ultimate literal translation. At the other end of the scale are "dynamically equivalent translations", which aim at reproducing in the receptor language not the grammatical forms of the source language but the meanings that the original readers would have understood. Popularly these are sometimes called "paraphrases", although that term ought to be reserved for documents in which the source and receptor languages are the same (for example, a paraphrase of Hamlet's soliloquy might begin, "My problem is whether or not to go on living...."). The Today's English Version ("Good News Bible") and the New Jerusalem Bible (Roman Catholic) are examples of dynamically equivalent translations. The New English Bible, the New International Version, and the modern Jewish Publication Society edition fall somewhere between.

On this scale the *Jewish New Testament* tends toward the dynamically equivalent end of the scale. And at certain points especially related to the issue of Jewishness it becomes militantly so. For example, in other versions the Greek phrase *upo nomon* is usually translated "under the law". But because this rendering has been used to buttress anti-*Torah* Christian theology, the *Jewish New Testament* spells out the meaning of these two Greek words in thirteen English words: "in subjection to the system which results from perverting the *Torah* into legalism".[45]

The Translator and His Interpretations. Which raises the question of whether the translator should "inject his opinions" into his translation. The *Jewish New Testament* cautiously answers in the affirmative, on the ground that it inevitably happens anyhow, so that the translator who supposes he "maintains neutrality", merely channeling ideas from the source language to the receptor language without influencing the result, deludes both himself and his readers. For necessarily every decision as to how to render a Greek word or phrase into English expresses the translator's opinion. A translator ideologically committed to not intruding his opinions does so in spite of himself, but without taking responsibility for it.

Therefore, a translator should decide what a word or phrase means (in his opinion!) and then convey that meaning as clearly as possible. For example, in the case of *upo nomon*,[46] precisely because wrong meanings have been conveyed in the past, the translator of the *Jewish New Testament* considers it his

---

45 For more on this topic, see Section VI below.
46 Discussed above and in Section VI.

Ma·shi·ach — Messiah	*To·rah* — Teaching, "Law"
Mat·tit·ya·hu — Matthew	*tsu·ris* — trouble
sha·lom — peace	Ye·shu·a — Jesus
tal·mid — disciple	Yo·cha·nan — John

responsibility to convey what he believes to be the one and only correct meaning in as unmistakable a way as possible. Even when a Greek expression seems vague, capable of more than one interpretation, the translator should not transfer the ambiguity into English but should decide on *one* of the possible interpretations and render that one well. (In editions that supply alternative readings, the ambiguity can be discussed in a marginal note.)

On the other side of the picture, this approach opens the door to abuse. Therefore it must be stressed that the fact that the translator's opinions will necessarily be reflected in his translation does not mean that he should exploit his role, illegitimately swaying his readers toward a partisan position.

Greek Text Used for This Translation. There are more than five thousand ancient manuscripts of all or part of the New Testament, more than for any other document from antiquity. Due to scribal errors and other factors they do not agree with each other at every point. Textual criticism, which sets out to determine the correct reading of a text from imperfect or disagreeing sources, is far beyond the competence of most New Testament translators, including this one. Fortunately there exist critical editions of the Greek text of the New Testament, wherein specialists have investigated, compared and judged the accuracy of the differing textual readings found in the manuscripts. The *Jewish New Testament* is based primarily on the United Bible Societies' *The Greek New Testament:*[47] a number of English and Hebrew versions and commentaries were consulted for reference.

VI   REASONS FOR CERTAIN RENDERINGS

Several *Jewish New Testament* renderings differ from those found in most versions and have significant implications for theology. While there is not space in this edition to defend all the controversial renderings and outline their theological implications, the following material is intended to demonstrate that such defenses exist and constitutes a preview of the forthcoming *Jewish New Testament Commentary.* Until its publication something of the translator's overall rationale can be gleaned from his book, *Messianic Jewish Manifesto,* or its abridgement, *Restoring the Jewishness of the Gospel.*[48]

Did Yeshua Fill or Fulfill the *Torah*? The common Greek word *plerôsai* means "to fill". At Mattityahu 5:17 most translations render it "to fulfill". The theological implications often drawn are that Yeshua fulfilled all the prophecies of the *Tanakh* pertaining to the Jews, so that none remain for them now; and that he kept the *Torah* perfectly, so that no one need obey it today. But these conclusions do not follow logically, and in fact they contradict Yeshua's immediately preceding statement that he did *not* come to abolish (or destroy) the

---

47   3rd Edition (New York: American Bible Society, 1975).
48   David H. Stern, *Messianic Jewish Manifesto* and *Restoring the Jewishness of the Gospel* (Jerusalem, Israel: Jewish New Testament Publications, 1988).

Torah. More fundamental for translation, however, is the question of whether *plerôsai* in this verse should be rendered "to fulfill" at all. The translator's view[49] is that Yeshua came to *fill* the *Torah* and the ethical pronouncements of the Prophets *full* with their *complete meaning*, so that everyone can know all that obedience entails. For this reason the *Jewish New Testament* says that Yeshua came "not to abolish but to complete." In fact, this is the subject of the entire Sermon on the Mount;[50] and Mattityahu 5:17, understood in this way, is its theme sentence. Interestingly, this understanding is concordant with Jewish tradition, which says that when the Messiah comes, he will both explain obscure passages of *Torah* and actually change it.

Binding and Loosing: Who Has the Authority to Determine *Halakhah*?
At Mattityahu 18:18 the Greek words usually rendered "bind" and "loose" are translated "prohibit" and "permit". This reflects the first-century Jewish application of these concepts to their leaders, who were understood as having authority from God to decide what practices should be followed by the community, *i.e.*, to determine *halakhah* (a term which dates from a later period). In verses 18-20 the Messiah transfers this power from the rabbis to his own *talmidim*. This authority was not assumed instantaneously,[51] nor was it assumed later when it should have been. But the fact that Messianic Jews and Gentiles have hitherto made little use of Yeshua's far-reaching grant of authority does not cancel it.

Does the Messiah Bring the *Torah* to an End, or Is He Its Goal? At Romans 10:4 the King James Version gives a translation typical of most versions: "For Christ is the end of the law for righteousness to everyone that believeth." But Greek *telos*, which gives us the English word "teleology", usually means "goal, purpose, consummation", not "termination". The Messiah did *not* bring the *Torah* to an end. Rather, as the *Jewish New Testament* renders it, "the goal at which the *Torah* aims is the Messiah, who offers righteousness to everyone who trusts." This is the point which Sha'ul is making in Romans 9:30-10:13. For this reason the Greek word *de* at the beginning of Romans 10:6 is rendered as a continuative, "moreover", rather than as an adversative, "but"; for the latter word would imply that there are two paths to righteousness — through deeds (*i.e.*, obeying the *Torah* apart from faith, verse 5) and through faith (verses 6-10). However, Sha'ul's point throughout the passage, and indeed throughout Romans, is that for Jews and Gentiles alike there has never been more than one

---

49 See Section V.
50 Mattityahu [Matthew] 5 — 7.
51 See Mattityahu [Matthew] 23:2.

===

ha·la·khah — "way of walking," Jewish law/custom
Mat·tit·ya·hu — Matthew
Sha·'ul — Saul (Paul)
tal·mi·dim — disciples

Ta·nakh — Hebrew Scriptures, "Old Testament"
To·rah — Teaching, "Law"
Ye·shu·a — Jesus

route to righteousness, namely, trusting God; so that the *Torah* is built on trusting God and from beginning to end has always required faith.[52]

The New Testament Has Been Given as *Torah*. At Messianic Jews [Hebrews] 8:6 most translations inform us that the New Covenant "has been enacted" on the basis of better promises. This would be an adequate translation were the subject matter Athenian legislation or Roman decrees. But the Greek word used here, *nenomothetêtai*, is a compound of *nomos*, which can mean "law" generally but in the book of Messianic Jews *always* means the *Torah* specifically, and *tithêmi*, a common word meaning "put" or "place". The only other appearance of *nenomothetêtai* in the New Testament is a few verses earlier, at 7:11, where all agree that it refers to the giving of the *Torah* on Mount Sinai, as do the related words *nomothesia* (Romans 9:4) and *nomothetês* (Ya'akov 4:12). Therefore the *Jewish New Testament* says that the New Covenant "has been given as *Torah* on the basis of better promises." This not only strengthens the theological contention that the *Torah* remains in force, but makes the New Covenant given through Yeshua *Torah* in the same sense as is the Sinaitic Covenant given through Moshe.

"Works of the Law" and "Under the Law": Is the *Torah* Legalistic? The Greek phrases *erga nomou* and *upo nomon* were coined by Sha'ul and used by him in three of his letters — Romans, Galatians and 1 Corinthians; each appears ten times in the New Testament. They are usually translated "works of the law" and "under the law" respectively. This often causes the reader to infer that keeping the *Torah* is bad, and that being within the framework of *Torah*-observance is bad. The *Jewish New Testament*, following the lead of Cranfield,[53] takes these phrases as referring not to the *Torah* itself but to man's legalistic perversion of it. Therefore *erga nomou* is rendered: "legalistic observance of *Torah* commands" and *upo nomon*, "in subjection to the system which results from perverting the *Torah* into legalism". The reader can then infer, correctly, that according to the New Testament teaching of Sha'ul, legalism — whether Jewish, Christian or other — is bad, but living according to God's *Torah* is good.

***Kurios*, Lord and *Y-H-V-H*.** In the New Testament the Greek word *kurios* is frequently ambiguous. It can mean "sir", "lord" (as in "lord of the manor"), "Lord" (with divine overtones), and *"Y-H-V-H"* ("Jehovah", God's personal name, for which Judaism substitutes the word *"Adonai"* and many translations substitute "LORD"). Most translations, by always rendering *kurios* "Lord", finesse the issue of when it means *"Y-H-V-H"*. The *Jewish New Testament* does not — in keeping with the principle stated in Section V above that translators should decide the true meaning of a word and render that meaning clearly, rather than transfer vagueness from one language to another. In several places this approach brings into bold relief a key theological issue separating Messianic from

---

52   Romans 1:16-17. For more on this, see Daniel P. Fuller, *Gospel and Law: Contrast or Continuum?* (Grand Rapids, Michigan: Eerdmans, 1980), as well as Chapter V of *Messianic Jewish Manifesto*, mentioned above (footnote 48).

53   C. E. B. Cranfield, *International Critical Commentary: The Epistle to the Romans* (Edinburgh: T. & T. Clark, Ltd., 1979), p. 853.

traditional Judaism, namely, whether the concept of *Adonai* can include Yeshua the Messiah and/or the Holy Spirit. Philippians 2:10-11 informs us that the day is coming when "every knee will bow...and every tongue will acknowledge that Yeshua the Messiah is *Adonai.*" Since this passage quotes Isaiah 45:23, where it is explicit that every knee will bow to *Adonai*, *kurios* is here translated *"Adonai"*. 2 Corinthians 3:16-18 quotes Exodus 34:34, "whenever someone turns to *Adonai*, the veil is taken away," then explicitly points out that *"'Adonai'* in this text means the Spirit," and uses the phrase, *"Adonai* the Spirit".

The Land of Israel in the New Covenant. The Greek phrase *ē gē* is usually translated "the earth", but eighteen times in the New Testament it refers to the Land of Israel. Two are explicit — Mattityahu 2:20-21 calls the Holy Land *"Eretz-Israel"*. Four are citations from the *Tanakh* — Mattityahu 5:5 (Psalm 37:11), Mattityahu 24:30 and Revelation 1:7 (Zechariah 12:10, 14), and Ephesians 6:3 (Deuteronomy 5:17). Five are based on the *Tanakh* — Luke 4:25 and Ya'akov 5:17-18 (1 Kings 17:1; 18:1, 41-45), Messianic Jews 11:9 (Genesis 12, 13, 15, 20, 23), and Revelation 20:9 (Ezekiel 38-39). The remaining eight are implied by the context — Mattityahu 5:13, 10:34, 27:45; Mark 15:33; Luke 12:51, 21:23, 23:44; and Revelation 11:10. In an age when many Christian theologians use "replacement theology" (which asserts that the Church has replaced the Jews as God's people) in an attempt to prove that the Land of Israel is no longer promised by God to the Jewish people, it is important to see that the physical Land of Israel plays a significant role in the New Testament's portrayals of God's plan for the Jews in particular and for humanity in general, past, present and future.

VII *TANAKH* PROPHECIES FULFILLED BY YESHUA THE MESSIAH

Following is a partial list of the *Tanakh* prophecies pertaining to Yeshua's first coming, along with the New Testament locations reporting their fulfillment by him.

Space does not permit showing why each of these prophecies should be understood as referring to Yeshua the Messiah. Many books discuss this subject in detail, mentioning other *Tanakh* prophecies which point to Yeshua.[54]

---

54 See Appendix IX of *The Life and Times of Jesus the Messiah*, 2nd ed. (New York: Anson D. F. Randolph and Company, 1884), by the Messianic Jew Alfred Edersheim, in which a list of 456 *Tanakh* passages messianically applied in ancient rabbinic writings is supported by 558 quotations from those writings. Also see J. Barton Payne, *Encyclopedia of Biblical Prophecy* (New York: Harper & Row, 1973).

A·do·nai — the LORD, Jehovah
E·retz-Is·ra·el — the Land of Israel
Mat·tit·ya·hu — Matthew
Sha·'ul — Saul (Paul)

Ta·nakh — Hebrew Bible, "Old Testament"
To·rah — Teaching, "Law"
Ya·'a·kov — Jacob
Ye·shu·a — Jesus

Besides prophecies there are incidents in the *Tanakh* which function as pictures in advance, or "types", of Yeshua. What is known in Judaism as the *akedah* ["binding"], the near-sacrifice of Yitzchak by Avraham, is explicitly called a type of Yeshua the Messiah at Messianic Jews [Hebrews] 11:17-19. The life of Yosef provides another example: his brothers tried to kill him, but in the end he saved them from death, even though they did not recognize him at first. This does not mean that Genesis 22 contains a "prophecy" that Yeshua would be raised from the dead, or that Genesis 37-45 states that the Jewish people, as a nation, would initially reject their Savior. Rather it shows that God's salvation plan unfolding itself in history has a unity determined by him from the beginning to be consummated in Yeshua the Messiah. Indeed Yeshua himself explained it this way to two of his *talmidim*.[55]

PROPHECY: THE MESSIAH MUST...	SOURCE IN THE *TANAKH*	FULFILLMENT IN THE NEW TESTAMENT
Be the "seed of the woman" that would "bruise" or "crush" the serpent's "head"	Genesis 3:15	Galatians 4:4 1 Yochanan 3:8
Be the "seed of Avraham"	Genesis 12:3	Mattityahu 1:1; Acts 3:25 Galatians 3:16
Be the "seed of Yitzchak"	Genesis 17:19, 21:12	Mattityahu 1:2, Luke 3:34, Messianic Jews 11:17-19
Be the "seed of Ya'akov" and the "star out of Ya'akov" who will "have dominion"	Genesis 28:14; Numbers 24:17, 19	Mattityahu 1:2, Luke 3:34, Revelation 22:16
Be a descendant of Y'hudah	Genesis 49:10	Mattityahu 1:2-3, Luke 3:33, Messianic Jews 7:14
Be a descendant of David and heir to his throne	2 Samuel 7:12-13; Isaiah 9:6(7), 11:1-5; Jeremiah 23:5	Mattityahu 1:1, 6; Acts 13:23; Romans 1:4
Have eternal existence	Micah 5:1(2)	Yochanan 1:1, 14; 8:58; Ephesians 1:3-14; Colossians 1:15-19; Revelation 1:18
Be the Son of God	Psalm 2:7; Proverbs 30:4	Mattityahu 3:17, Luke 1:32

---

55   Luke 24:25-27.

PROPHECY: THE MESSIAH MUST...	SOURCE IN THE *TANAKH*	FULFILLMENT IN THE NEW TESTAMENT
Have God's own name, *Y-H-V-H* *(Adonai)*, applied to him	Isaiah 9:5-6(6-7), Jeremiah 23:5-6	Romans 10:9, Philippians 2:9-11
Come at a specific time, namely, 69 x 7 years (483 years) after the rebuilding of the wall of Yerushalayim	Daniel 9:24-26	Mattityahu 2:1, 16, 19; Luke 3:1, 23
Be born in Beit-Lechem, in Y'hudah	Micah 5:1(2)	Mattityahu 2:1, Luke 2:4-7
Be born of a virgin	Isaiah 7:14[56]	Mattityahu 1:18 — 2:1, Luke 1:26-35
Be adored by great persons	Psalm 72:10-11	Mattityahu 2:1-11
Be preceded by one who would announce him	Isaiah 40:3-5, Malachi 3:1	Mattityahu 3:1-3; Luke 1:17, 3:2-6
Be anointed with the Spirit of God	Isaiah 11:2, 61:1; Psalm 45:8(7)	Mattityahu 3:16, Yochanan 3:34, Acts 10:38
Be a prophet like Moshe	Deuteronomy 18:15, 18	Acts 3:20-22
Have a ministry of binding up the brokenhearted, proclaiming liberty to the captives and announcing the acceptable year of the Lord	Isaiah 61:1-2	Luke 4:18-19
Have a ministry of healing	Isaiah 35:5-6, 42:18	Mattityahu 11:5; throughout the Gospels
Have a ministry in the Galil	Isaiah 8:23—9:1 (9:1-2)	Mattityahu 4:12-16

56   The Hebrew word *'almah* in Isaiah 7:14 means "young woman", and in the *Tanakh* always
"a young woman of unsullied reputation", which is why the Jewish translators of the
Septuagint, the Greek version of the *Tanakh* prepared 200 years before Yeshua's birth, rendered this word into Greek as *parthenos*, "virgin"; this is the word used at Mattityahu 1:23.

A·do·nai — the LORD, Jehovah	*tal·mi·dim* — disciples
a·ke·dah — binding	*Ta·nakh* — Hebrew Bible, "Old Testament"
'al·mah — young woman, virgin	Ya·'a·kov — Jacob
Av·ra·ham — Abraham	Ye·ru·sha·la·yim — Jerusalem
Beit-Le·chem — Bethlehem	Ye·shu·a — Jesus
Da·vid — David	Y'hu·dah — Judah, Judea
the Ga·lil — Galilee	Yitz·chak — Isaac
Ke·fa — Peter	Yo·cha·nan — John
Mat·tit·ya·hu — Matthew	Yo·sef — Joseph
Mo·she — Moses	

PROPHECY: THE MESSIAH MUST...	SOURCE IN THE *TANAKH*	FULFILLMENT IN THE NEW TESTAMENT
Be tender and compassionate	Isaiah 40:11, 42:3	Mattityahu 12:15, 20; Messianic Jews 4:15
Be meek and unostentatious	Isaiah 42:2	Mattityahu 12:15-16, 19
Be sinless and without guile	Isaiah 53:9	1 Kefa 2:22
Bear the reproaches due others	Isaiah 53:12, Psalm 69:10	Romans 15:3
Be a priest	Psalm 110:4	Messianic Jews 5:5-6, 6:20, 7:15-17
Enter publicly into Yerushalayim on a donkey	Zechariah 9:9	Mattityahu 21:1-11, Mark 11:1-11
Enter the Temple with authority	Haggai 2:7-9, Malachi 3:1	Mattityahu 21:12 — 24:1; Luke 2:27-38, 45-50; Yochanan 2:13-22
Be hated without cause	Isaiah 49:7, Psalm 69:5(4)	Yochanan 15:24-25
Be undesired and rejected by his own people	Isaiah 53:2, 63:3; Psalm 69:9(8)	Mark 6:3; Luke 9:58; Yochanan 1:11, 7:3-5
Be rejected by the Jewish leadership	Psalm 118:22	Mattityahu 21:42, Yochanan 7:48
Be plotted against by Jews and Gentiles together	Psalm 2:1-2	Acts 4:27
Be betrayed by a friend	Psalm 41:9, 55:13-15(12-14)	Mattityahu 26:21-25, 47-50; Yochanan 13:18-21; Acts 1:16-18
Be sold for 30 pieces of silver	Zechariah 11:12	Mattityahu 26:15
Have his price given for a potter's field	Zechariah 11:13	Mattityahu 27:7
Be forsaken by his *talmidim*	Zechariah 13:7	Mattityahu 26:31, 56
Be struck on the cheek	Micah 4:14(5:1)	Mattityahu 27:30
Be spat on	Isaiah 50:6	Mattityahu 26:67, 27:30
Be mocked	Psalm 22:8-9(7-8)	Mattityahu 26:67-68; 27:31, 39-44
Be beaten	Isaiah 50:6	Mattityahu 26:67; 27:26, 30

PROPHECY: THE MESSIAH MUST...	SOURCE IN THE *TANAKH*	FULFILLMENT IN THE NEW TESTAMENT
Be executed by crucifixion, by having his hands and feet pierced	Psalm 22:17(16)[57] Zechariah 12:10	Mattityahu 27:35; Luke 24:39; Yochanan 19:18, 34-37; 20:20-28; Revelation 1:7
Be thirsty during his execution	Psalm 22:16(15)	Yochanan 19:28
Be given vinegar to quench that thirst	Psalm 69:22(21)	Mattityahu 27:34
Be executed without having a bone broken	Exodus 12:46, Psalm 34:21(20)	Yochanan 19:33-36
Be considered a transgressor	Isaiah 53:12	Mattityahu 27:38
Be "cut off, but not for himself."	Daniel 9:24-26	Romans 5:16, 1 Kefa 3:18
Be the one whose death would atone for sins of mankind	Isaiah 53:5-7, 12	Mark 10:45; Yochanan 1:29, 3:16; Acts 8:30-35
Be buried with the rich when dead	Isaiah 53:9	Mattityahu 27:57-60
Be raised from the dead	Isaiah 53:9-10; Psalms 2:7, 16:10	Mattityahu 28:1-20; Acts 2:23-36, 13:33-37; 1 Corinthians 15:4-8
Ascend to the right hand of God	Psalms 16:11, 68:19(18), 110:1	Luke 24:51; Acts 1:9-11, 7:55, Messianic Jews 1:3
Exercise his priestly office in heaven	Zechariah 6:13	Romans 8:34, Messianic Jews 7:25 — 8:2
Be the cornerstone of God's Messianic Community	Isaiah 28:16, Psalm 118:22-23	Mattityahu 21:42, Ephesians 2:20, 1 Kefa 2:5-7
Be sought after by Gentiles as well as Jews	Isaiah 11:10, 42:1	Acts 10:45
Be accepted by the Gentiles	Isaiah 11:10, 42:1-4, 49:1-12	Mattityahu 12:21, Romans 15:10

---

57   The Septuagint (see footnote 56) has: "They pierced my hands and my feet," implying the Hebrew word *karu* in its source text. The Masoretic Hebrew text, accepted as standard in traditional Judaism, has *k'ari*, and the line reads, "Like a lion, my hands and my feet."

k·'a·ri — like a lion
ka·ru — they pierced
Ke·fa — Peter
Mat·tit·ya·hu — Matthew

tal·mi·dim — disciples
Ta·nakh — Hebrew Bible, "Old Testament"
Ye·ru·sha·la·yim — Jerusalem
Yo·cha·nan— John

VIII   USING THE *JEWISH NEW TESTAMENT*

Tanakh **References.** In order to highlight the connection between the New Testament and the *Tanakh* on which it builds, *Tanakh* quotations in the *Jewish New Testament* are printed in **boldface** and their sources given in footnotes at the bottom of each column of text. The chapter-and-verse numberings and the order of the books of the *Tanakh* within a given footnote are those found in Hebrew editions of the Bible (and some Jewish-sponsored English versions). Where the Christian versions (and some Jewish ones) have a different chapter and verse, these are given afterwards in parentheses, *e.g.*, Joel 3:1-5(2:28-32), Psalm 69:9(8). The *Index of Tanakh References* on pages 384-388 lists every citation of a *Tanakh* verse in the text of the *Jewish New Testament*.

Semitic Terms and Names. Hebrew, Aramaic and Yiddish terms (including names of God) appear in italics *(bat-kol, Adonai)*, but Semitic names of persons and places (including spiritual "places") do not (Shlomo, Ashdod, Gey-Hinnom).

Three glossaries and two maps help the reader find his way among some 400 Semitic names and terms found in the *Jewish New Testament*.

- **Pronouncing Explanatory Glossary.** On pages 358-378 is a comprehensive glossary of Hebrew, Aramaic and Yiddish words and names used in the *Jewish New Testament*. Pronunciation rules are found on page 358. The definitions and explanations vary in length from one line to a paragraph.

- **Page-by-Page Glossaries.** At the bottom of each right-hand page of text is a brief glossary of the Semitic words and names used on that page and on the facing left page. This does not replace the glossary at the end of the book but offers a time-saving brief definition.

- **"Reverse" Glossary.** Readers acquainted with the New Testament in other English versions may wish to know what the *Jewish New Testament* substitutes for terms familiar to them. In the Reverse Glossary on pages 379-383 one may look up words such as "crucify" and "Mary" to find their equivalents (in this case, "execute on a stake" and "Miryam").

- **Maps.** On pages 390-391 are two maps — *"Eretz-Israel* in the Time of Yeshua" and "The Eastern Mediterranean and Near East in the Second Temple Period". The map index on page 389 lists both the *Jewish New Testament* names and the usual English names of all places mentioned in the New Testament. Several other locations are also shown for reference.

Textual Notes. In this edition of the *Jewish New Testament* discussion of textual issues is kept to a minimum. About twenty passages regarded as inauthentic by most scholars, none more than two verses in length, are absent from the text and placed in starred footnotes (*) at the bottom of the column. Three passages — Mattityahu 6:13b, Mark 16:9-20 and Yochanan 7:53-8:11 — are included in the text but given a starred footnote briefly explaining the textual problem. This edition does not offer textual variants or alternative readings.

Translator's Interpolations. In a very few places explanatory interpolations by the translator corresponding to nothing in the original text are placed in brackets (*e.g.*, at Mattityahu 1:21, 6:23). Explanations of a similar character found in the original text usually appear in parentheses (*e.g.* at Mattityahu 1:23). Certain words or phrases in the original Greek are represented by "expanded" renderings,[58] but for philosophical reasons[59] these are not distinguished from the rest of the translation.

---

58 See, for example, the discussions of *upo nomon* and *erga nomou* in Sections V and VI.
59 See Section V.

A·do·nai — the LORD, Jehovah
bat-kol — voice from heaven
E·retz-Is·ra·el — the Land of Israel
Gey-Hin·nom — Gehenna, hell

Mat·tit·ya·hu — Matthew
Shlo·mo — Solomon
Ta·nakh — Hebrew Bible, "Old Testament"
Yo·cha·nan — John

THE GOOD NEWS OF YESHUA THE MESSIAH, AS REPORTED BY

MATTITYAHU (MATTHEW)

1 [1]This is the genealogy of Yeshua the Messiah, son of David, son of Avraham:

[2] Avraham was the father of Yitzchak, Yitzchak was the father of Ya'akov, Ya'akov was the father of Y'hudah and his brothers, [3] Y'hudah was the father of Peretz and Zerach (their mother was Tamar), Peretz was the father of Chetzron, Chetzron was the father of Ram, [4] Ram was the father of Amminadav, Amminadav was the father of Nachshon, Nachshon was the father of Salmon, [5] Salmon was the father of Bo'az (his mother was Rachav), Bo'az was the father of Oved (his mother was Rut), Oved was the father of Yishai, [6] Yishai was the father of David the king.

David was the father of Shlomo (his mother was the wife of Uriyah), [7] Shlomo was the father of Rechav'am, Rechav'am was the father of Aviyah, Aviyah was the father of Asa, [8] Asa was the father of Y'hoshafat, Y'hoshafat was the father of Yoram, Yoram was the father of Uziyahu, [9] Uziyahu was the father of Yotam, Yotam was the father of Achaz, Achaz was the father of Chizkiyahu, [10] Chizkiyahu was the father of M'nasheh,

M'nasheh was the father of Amon, Amon was the father of Yoshiyahu, [11] Yoshiyahu was the father of Y'khanyahu and his brothers at the time of the Exile to Babylon.

A·chaz	— Ahaz
Am·mi·na·dav	— Amminadab
A·mon	— Amon
A·sa	— Asa
A·vi·yah	— Abijah
Av·ra·ham	— Abraham
Bo·'az	— Boaz, Boöz
Chetz·ron	— Hezron, Esrom
Chiz·ki·ya·hu	— Hezekiah, Ezekias
Da·vid	— David
M'na·sheh	— Manasseh, Manasses
Nach·shon	— Nahshon, Naasson
O·ved	— Obed
Pe·retz	— Perez, Phares
Ra·chav	— Rahab
Ram	— Ram, Aram
Re·chav·'am	— Rehoboam
Rut	— Ruth
Sal·mon	— Salmon
Shlo·mo	— Solomon
Ta·mar	— Tamar
U·ri·yah	— Uriah, Urias
U·zi·ya·hu	— Uzziah, Ozias
Ya·'a·kov	— Jacob
Ye·shu·a	— Jesus
Y'ho·sha·fat	— Jehoshaphat, Josaphat
Y'hu·dah	— Judah
Yi·shai	— Jesse
Yitz·chak	— Isaac
Y'khan·ya·hu	— Jeconiah, Jehoiachin
Yo·ram	— Jehoram, Joram, Jorim
Yo·shi·ya·hu	— Josiah, Josias
Yo·tam	— Jotham
Ze·rach	— Zerah, Zara, Zarah

¹² After the Babylonian Exile,
  Y'khanyahu was the father of
    Sh'altiel,
  Sh'altiel was the father of Z'rubavel,
¹³ Z'rubavel was the father of Av'ichud
  Av'ichud was the father of Elyakim,
  Elyakim was the father of Azur,
¹⁴ Azur was the father of Tzadok,
  Tzadok was the father of Yakhin,
  Yakhin was the father of El'ichud,
¹⁵ El'ichud was the father of El'azar,
  El'azar was the father of Mattan,
  Mattan was the father of Ya'akov,
¹⁶ Ya'akov was the father of Yosef, the
    husband of Miryam,
  From whom was born the Yeshua
    that was called the Messiah.

¹⁷ Thus there were fourteen generations
    from Avraham to David,
  fourteen generations from David to
    the Babylonian Exile,
  and fourteen generations from the
    Babylonian Exile to the Messiah.

¹⁸ Here is how the birth of Yeshua the Messiah took place. When his mother Miryam was engaged to Yosef, before they were married, she was found to be pregnant from the *Ruach-HaKodesh.* ¹⁹ Her husband-to-be, Yosef, was a man who did what was right; so he made plans to break the engagement quietly, rather than put her to public shame. ²⁰ But while he was thinking about this, an angel of *Adonai* appeared to him in a dream and said, "Yosef, son of David, do not be afraid to take Miryam home with you as your wife; for what has been conceived in her is from the *Ruach-HaKodesh.* ²¹ She will give birth to a son, and you are to name him Yeshua, [which means *'Adonai* saves',] because he will save his people from their sins."

²² All this happened in order to fulfill what *Adonai* had said through the prophet,

²³ **"The virgin will conceive and bear a**
    son,
  and they will call him Immanu'el."[a]

(The name means, "God is with us.")

²⁴ When Yosef awoke he did what the angel of *Adonai* had told him to do — he took Miryam home to be his wife, ²⁵ but he did not have sexual relations with her until she had given birth to a son, and he named him Yeshua.

2 ¹ After Yeshua was born in Beit-Lechem in the land of Y'hudah during the time when Herod was king, Magi from the east came to Yerushalayim ² and asked, "Where is the newborn King of the Jews? For we saw his star in the east and have come to worship him."

³ When King Herod heard of this he became very agitated, and so did everyone else in Yerushalayim. ⁴ He called together all the head *cohanim* and *Torah*-teachers of the people and asked them, "Where will the Messiah be born?" ⁵ "In Beit-Lechem of Y'hudah," they replied, "because the prophet wrote,

⁶ **'And you, Beit-Lechem in the land of**
    Y'hudah,
  are by no means the least among the
    rulers of Y'hudah;
  for from you will come a Ruler
  who will shepherd my people
    Israel.'[b]

⁷ Herod summoned the Magi to meet with him privately and asked them exactly when the star had appeared. ⁸ Then he sent them to Beit-Lechem with these instructions: "Search carefully for the child; and when you find him, let me know, so that I too may go and worship him."

⁹ After they had listened to the king,

---

a Isaiah 7:14   *b* Micah 5:1(2)

they went away; and the star which they had seen in the east went in front of them until it came and stopped over the place where the child was. ¹⁰When they saw the star, they were overjoyed. ¹¹Upon entering the house, they saw the child with his mother Miryam; and they prostrated themselves and worshipped him. Then they opened their bags and presented him gifts of gold, frankincense and myrrh. ¹²But they had been warned in a dream not to return to Herod, so they took another route back to their own country.

¹³After they had gone, an angel of *Adonai* appeared to Yosef in a dream and said, "Get up, take the child and his mother and escape to Egypt, and stay there until I tell you to leave. For Herod is going to look for the child in order to kill him." ¹⁴So he got up, took the child and his mother, and left during the night for Egypt, ¹⁵where he stayed until Herod died. This happened in order to fulfill what *Adonai* had said through the prophet,

"Out of Egypt I called my son."ᶜ

¹⁶Meanwhile, when Herod realized that the Magi had tricked him, he was furious and gave orders to kill all the boys in and around Beit-Lechem who were two years old or less, calculating from the time the Magi had told him. ¹⁷In this way were fulfilled the words spoken through the prophet Yirme-yahu,

¹⁸ **"A voice was heard in Ramah,**
   sobbing and lamenting loudly.
   It was Rachel sobbing for her
      children
   and refusing to be comforted,
   because they are no longer alive."ᵈ

¹⁹After Herod's death, an angel of

Adonai appeared in a dream to Yosef in Egypt ²⁰and said, "Get up, take the child and his mother, and go to *Eretz-Israel*, for those who wanted to kill the child are dead." ²¹So he got up, took the child and his mother, and went back to *Eretz-Israel*. ²²However, when he heard that Archelaus had succeeded his father Herod as king of Y'hudah, he was afraid to go there. Warned in a dream, he withdrew to the Galil ²³and settled in a town called Natzeret, so that what had been spoken by the prophets might be fulfilled, that he will be called a *Natzrati*.

A·do·nai — the LORD, Jehovah
Av·'i·chud — Abiud
Av·ra·ham — Abraham
A·zur — Azor
Beit-Le·chem — Bethlehem
co·ha·nim — priests
Da·vid — David
El·'a·zar — Eleazar
El·'i·chud — Eliud
El·ya·kim — Eliakim
E·retz-Is·ra·el — the Land of Israel
the Ga·lil — Galilee
Im·ma·nu·'el — Immanuel
Ma·gi — leaders, sages
Mat·tan — Matthan
Mir·yam — Miriam, Mary
Na·tze·ret — Nazareth
Natz·ra·ti — person from Natzeret, Nazarene
Ra·chel — Rachel
Ra·mah — Ramah
Ru·ach-Ha·Ko·desh — Holy Spirit
Sh·'al·ti·el — Shealtiel, Salathiel
To·rah-teachers — scribes
Tza·dok — Zadok, Sadoc
Ya·'a·kov — Jacob
Ya·khin — Achim
Ye·ru·sha·la·yim — Jerusalem
Ye·shu·a — Jesus
Y'hu·dah — Judah, Judea
Yir·me·ya·hu — Jeremiah, Jeremias
Y'khan·ya·hu — Jeconiah, Jehoiachin
Yo·sef — Joseph
Z'ru·ba·vel — Zerubbabel, Zorobabel

---

c Hosea 11:1   d Jeremiah 31:14(15)

3 ¹It was during those days that Yochanan the Immerser arrived in the desert of Y'hudah and began proclaiming the message, ²"Turn from your sins to God, for the Kingdom of Heaven is near!" ³This is the man Yesha'yahu was talking about when he said,

"The voice of someone crying out:
'In the desert prepare the way of
Adonai!
Make straight paths for him!'"*e*

⁴Yochanan wore clothes of camel's hair with a leather belt around his waist, and his food was locusts and wild honey. ⁵People went out to him from Yerushalayim, from all Y'hudah, and from the whole region around the Yarden. ⁶Confessing their sins, they were immersed by him in the Yarden River.

⁷But when Yochanan saw many of the *P'rushim* and *Tz'dukim* coming to be immersed by him, he said to them, "You snakes! Who warned you to escape the coming punishment? ⁸If you have really turned from your sins to God, produce fruit that will prove it! ⁹And don't suppose you can comfort yourselves by saying, 'Avraham is our father'! For I tell you that God can raise up for Avraham sons from these stones! ¹⁰Already the axe is at the root of the trees, ready to strike; every tree that doesn't produce good fruit will be chopped down and thrown in the fire! ¹¹It's true that I am immersing you in water so that you might turn from sin to God; but the one coming after me is more powerful than I — I'm not worthy even to carry his sandals — and he will immerse you in the *Ruach HaKodesh* and in fire. ¹²He has with him his winnowing fork; and he will clear out his threshing floor, gathering his wheat into the barn but burning up the straw with unquenchable fire!"

¹³Then Yeshua came from the Galil to the Yarden to be immersed by Yochanan. ¹⁴But Yochanan tried to stop him. "You are coming to me? I ought to be immersed by you!" ¹⁵However, Yeshua answered him, "Let it be this way now, because we should do everything righteousness requires." Then Yochanan let him. ¹⁶As soon as Yeshua had been immersed, he came up out of the water. At that moment heaven was opened, he saw the Spirit of God coming down upon him like a dove, ¹⁷and a voice from heaven said, "This is my Son, whom I love; I am well pleased with him."

4 ¹Then the Spirit led Yeshua up into the wilderness to be tempted by the Adversary. ²After Yeshua had fasted forty days and nights, he was hungry. ³The Tempter came and said to him, "If you are the Son of God, order these stones to become bread." ⁴But he answered, "The *Tanakh* says,

'Man does not live on bread alone,
but on every word that comes
from the mouth of *Adonai*'"*f*

⁵Then the Adversary took him to the holy city and set him on the highest point of the Temple. ⁶"If you are the Son of God," he said, "jump! For the *Tanakh* says,

'He will order his angels to be
responsible for you.
They will support you with their
hands,
so that you will not hurt your feet
on the stones.'"*g*

⁷Yeshua replied to him, "But it also says,'Do not put *Adonai* your God to the test.'"*h*

---

e Isaiah 40:3

f Deuteronomy 8:3   *g* Psalm 91:11-12
h Deuteronomy 6:16

⁸ Once more, the Adversary took him up to the summit of a very high mountain, showed him all the kingdoms of the world in all their glory, ⁹ and said to him, "All this I will give you if you will bow down and worship me." ¹⁰ "Away with you, Satan!" Yeshua told him, "For the *Tanakh* says,

> 'Worship *Adonai* your God,
> and serve only him.'"^{*i*}

¹¹ Then the Adversary let him alone, and angels came and took care of him.

¹² When Yeshua heard that Yochanan had been put in prison, he returned to the Galil; ¹³ but he left Natzeret and came to live in K'far-Nachum, a lakeshore town near the boundary between Z'vulun and Naftali. ¹⁴ This happened in order to fulfill what Yesha'yahu the prophet had said,

¹⁵ "Land of Z'vulun
and land of Naftali,
toward the lake,
beyond the Yarden,
Galil-of-the-*Goyim* —
¹⁶ The people living in darkness
have seen a great light;
upon those living in the region,
in the shadow of death,
light has dawned."^{*j*}

¹⁷ From that time on, Yeshua began proclaiming, "Turn from your sins to God, for the Kingdom of Heaven is near!"

¹⁸ As Yeshua walked by Lake Kinneret, he saw two brothers who were fishermen — Shim'on, known as Kefa, and his brother Andrew — throwing their net into the lake. ¹⁹ Yeshua said to them, "Come after me, and I will make you fishers for men!" ²⁰ At once they left their nets and went with him.

²¹ Going on from there, he saw two other brothers — Ya'akov Ben-Zavdai and Yochanan his brother — in the boat with their father Zavdai, repairing their nets; and he called them. ²² At once they left the boat and their father and went with Yeshua.

²³ Yeshua went all over the Galil teaching in their synagogues, proclaiming the Good News of the Kingdom, and healing people from every kind of disease and sickness. ²⁴ Word of him spread throughout all Syria, and people brought to him all who were ill, suffering from various diseases and pains, and those held in the power of demons, and epileptics and paralytics; and he healed them. ²⁵ Huge crowds followed him from the Galil, the Ten Towns, Yerushalayim, Y'hudah, and Ever-HaYarden.

A·do·nai — the LORD, Jehovah
Av·ra·ham — Abraham
E·ver-Ha·Yar·den — beyond the Jordan
the Ga·lil — Galilee
Ga·lil-of-the-*Go·yim* — Galilee of the Gentiles (nations)
Ke·fa — Peter
K'far-Na·chum — Capernaum
Lake Kin·ne·ret — the Sea of Galilee
Naf·ta·li — Naphtali, Nephthalim
Na·tze·ret — Nazareth
P'ru·shim — Pharisees
Ru·ach-Ha·Ko·desh — Holy Spirit
Sa·tan — The Adversary, the Accuser, the Devil
Shim·'on — Simon
Ta·nakh — Hebrew Bible, "Old Testament"
Tz'du·kim — Sadducees
Ya·'a·kov Ben-Zav·dai — James the son of Zebedee
Yar·den — Jordan
Ye·sha'·ya·hu — Isaiah
Ye·shu·a — Jesus
Ye·ru·sha·la·yim — Jerusalem
Y'hu·dah — Judea
Yo·cha·nan — John
Yo·cha·nan the Immerser — John the Baptist
Zav·dai — Zebedee
Z'vu·lun — Zebulun, Zabulon

---

i Deuteronomy 6:13   *j* Isaiah 8:23-9:1(9:1-2)

5 ¹Seeing the crowds, Yeshua walked up the hill. After he sat down, his *talmidim* came to him, ²and he began to speak. This is what he taught them:

³ "How blessed are the poor in spirit!
for the Kingdom of Heaven is theirs.

⁴ "How blessed are those who mourn!
for they will be comforted.

⁵ "How blessed are **the meek!**
for they **will inherit the Land!** *k*

⁶ "How blessed are those who hunger
and thirst for righteousness!
for they will be filled.

⁷ "How blessed are those who show
mercy!
for they will be shown mercy.

⁸ "How blessed are the pure in heart!
for they will see God.

⁹ "How blessed are those who make
peace!
for they will be called sons of God.

¹⁰ "How blessed are those who are
persecuted because they pursue
righteousness!
for the Kingdom of Heaven is theirs.

¹¹"How blessed you are when people insult you and persecute you and tell all kinds of vicious lies about you because you follow me! ¹²Rejoice, be glad, because your reward in heaven is great — they persecuted the prophets before you in the same way.

¹³"You are salt for the Land. But if salt becomes tasteless, how can it be made salty again? It is no longer good for anything except being thrown out for people to trample on.

¹⁴"You are light for the world. A town built on a hill cannot be hidden. ¹⁵Likewise, when people light a lamp, they don't cover it with a bowl, but put it on a lampstand, so that it shines for everyone in the house. ¹⁶In the same way, let your light shine before people, so that they may see the good things you do and praise your Father in heaven.

¹⁷"Don't think that I have come to abolish the *Torah* or the Prophets. I have come not to abolish but to complete. ¹⁸Yes indeed! I tell you that until heaven and earth pass away, not so much as a *yud* or a stroke will pass from the *Torah* — not until everything that must happen has happened. ¹⁹So whoever disobeys the least of these *mitzvot* and teaches others to do so will be called the least in the Kingdom of Heaven. But whoever obeys them and so teaches will be called great in the Kingdom of Heaven. ²⁰For I tell you that unless your righteousness is far greater than that of the *Torah*-teachers and *P'rushim,* you will certainly not enter the Kingdom of Heaven!

²¹You have heard that our fathers were told, **'Do not murder,'** *l* and that anyone who commits murder will be subject to judgment. ²²And I tell you that anyone who even nurses anger against his brother will be subject to judgment; that whoever calls his brother, 'You good-for-nothing!' will be brought before the *Sanhedrin;* that whoever says, 'Fool!' incurs the penalty of burning in the fire of Gey-Hinnom! ²³So if you are offering your gift at the Temple altar and you remember there that your brother has something against you, ²⁴leave your gift where it is by the altar, and go, make peace with your brother. Then come back and offer your gift. ²⁵If someone sues you, come to terms with him quickly, while you and he are on the way to court; or he may hand

---

k Psalm 37:11

l Exodus 20:13, Deuteronomy 5:17

you over to the judge, and the judge to the officer of the court, and you may be thrown in jail! ²⁶ Yes indeed! I tell you, you will certainly not get out until you have paid the last penny.

²⁷"You have heard that our fathers were told, **'Do not commit adultery.'**ᵐ ²⁸And I tell you that a man who even looks at a woman with the purpose of lusting after her has already committed adultery with her in his heart. ²⁹If your right eye makes you sin, gouge it out and throw it away! Better that you should lose one part of you than have your whole body thrown into Gey-Hinnom. ³⁰And if your right hand makes you sin, cut it off and throw it away! Better that you should lose one part of you than have your whole body thrown into Gey-Hinnom.

³¹"It was said, **'Whoever divorces his wife must give her a get.'**ⁿ ³²But I tell you that anyone who divorces his wife, except on the ground of fornication, makes her an adulteress; and that anyone who marries a divorcee commits adultery.

³³"Again, you have heard that our fathers were told, **'Do not break your oath,'** and **'Fulfill what you have sworn to Adonai.'**ᵒ ³⁴And I tell you not to swear at all — not 'by **heaven,'** because it is God's **throne;** ³⁵not 'by the **earth,'** because it is his **footstool;**ᵖ and not 'by Yerushalayim,' because it is **the city of the Great King.**ᵈ ³⁶And don't swear by your head, because you can't make a single hair white or black. ³⁷Just let your 'Yes' be a simple 'Yes,' and your 'No' a simple 'No;' anything more than this has its origin in evil.

³⁸"You have heard that our fathers were told, **'Eye for eye and tooth for tooth.'**ʳ ³⁹But I tell you not to stand up against someone who does you wrong. On the contrary, if someone hits you on the right cheek, let him hit you on the left cheek too! ⁴⁰If someone wants to sue you for your shirt, let him have your coat as well! ⁴¹And if a soldier forces you to carry his pack for one mile, carry it for two! ⁴²When someone asks you for something, give it to him; when someone wants to borrow something from you, lend it to him.

⁴³"You have heard that our fathers were told,**'Love your neighbor**ˢ — and hate your enemy,' ⁴⁴But I tell you, love your enemies! Pray for those who persecute you! ⁴⁵Then you will become children of your Father in heaven. For he makes his sun shine on good and bad people alike, and he sends rain to the righteous and the unrighteous alike. ⁴⁶What reward do you get if you love only those who love you? Why, even tax-collectors do that! ⁴⁷And if you are friendly only to your friends, are you doing anything out of the ordinary? Even the *Goyim* do that! ⁴⁸Therefore, be perfect, just as your Father in heaven is perfect.

---

r Exodus 21:24, Leviticus 24:20, Deuteronomy 19:21   s Leviticus 19:18

A·do·nai — the LORD, Jehovah
the Ga·lil — Galilee
get — divorce document
Gey-Hin·**nom** — Gehenna, hell
Go·yim — Gentiles, nations, pagans
mitz·vot — commandments
P'ru·shim — Pharisees
San·hed·rin — Jewish religious court
tal·mi·dim — disciples
To·rah — Teaching, "Law", Pentateuch
To·rah-teachers — scribes
Ye·ru·sha·la·yim — Jerusalem
Ye·shu·a — Jesus
Y'hu·dah — Judea
yud — smallest letter in the Hebrew alphabet

---

m Exodus 20:13(14), Deuteronomy 5:18
n Deuteronomy 24:1   o Leviticus 19:12
  Numbers 30:3(2)
p Isaiah 66:1   q Psalm 48:2

6 [1]"Be careful not to parade your acts of *tzedakah* in front of people in order to be seen by them! If you do, you have no reward from your Father in heaven. [2]So, when you do *tzedakah*, don't announce it with trumpets to win people's praise, like the hypocrites in the synagogues and on the streets. Yes! I tell you, they have their reward already! [3]But you, when you do *tzedakah*, don't even let your left hand know what your right hand is doing. [4]Then your *tzedakah* will be in secret; and your Father, who sees what you do in secret, will reward you.

[5]"When you pray, don't be like the hypocrites, who love to pray standing in the synagogues and on street corners, so that people can see them. Yes! I tell you, they have their reward already! [6]But you, when you pray, go into your room, close the door, and pray to your Father in secret. Your Father, who sees what is done in secret, will reward you.

[7]"And when you pray, don't babble on and on like the pagans, who think God will hear them better if they talk a lot. [8]Don't be like them, because your Father knows what you need before you ask him. [9]You, therefore, pray like this:

'Our Father in heaven!
May your Name be kept holy.
[10]May your Kingdom come,
 your will be done on earth as in heaven.
[11]Give us the food we need today.
[12]Forgive us what we have done wrong, as we too have forgiven those who have wronged us.
[13]And do not lead us into hard testing, but keep us safe from the Evil One.
*For kingship, power and glory are yours forever. *Amen.*'

---

* The latter half of verse 13 is not found in the oldest manuscripts.

[14]For if you forgive others their offences, your heavenly Father will also forgive you; [15]but if you do not forgive others their offences, your heavenly Father will not forgive yours.

[16]"Now when you fast, don't go around looking miserable, like the hypocrites. They make sour faces so that people will know they are fasting. Yes! I tell you, they have their reward already! [17]But you, when you fast, wash your face and groom yourself, [18]so that no one will know you are fasting — except your Father, who is with you in secret. Your Father, who sees what is done in secret, will reward you.

[19]"Do not store up for yourselves wealth here on earth, where moths and rust destroy, and burglars break in and steal. [20]Instead, store up for yourselves wealth in heaven, where neither moth nor rust destroys, and burglars do not break in or steal. [21]For where your wealth is, there your heart will be also. [22]'The eye is the lamp of the body.' So if you have a 'good eye'[that is, if you are generous] your whole body will be full of light; [23]but if you have an 'evil eye'[if you are stingy] your whole body will be full of darkness. If, then, the light in you is darkness, how great is that darkness! [24]No one can be slave to two masters; for he will either hate the first and love the second, or scorn the second and be loyal to the first. You can't be a slave to both God and money.

[25]"Therefore, I tell you, don't worry about your life — what you will eat or drink; or about your body — what you will wear. Isn't life more than food and the body more than clothing? [26]Look at the birds flying about! They neither plant nor harvest, nor do they gather food into barns; yet your heavenly Father feeds them. Aren't you worth more than they are? [27]Can any of you

by worrying add a single hour to his life?

²⁸ "And why be anxious about clothing? Think about the fields of wild irises, and how they grow. They neither work nor spin thread, ²⁹ yet I tell you that not even Shlomo in all his glory was clothed as beautifully as one of these. ³⁰ If this is how God clothes grass in the field — which is here today and gone tomorrow, thrown in an oven — won't he much more clothe you? What little trust you have!

³¹ "So don't be anxious, asking, 'What will we eat?', 'What will we drink?' or 'How will we be clothed?' ³² For it is the pagans who set their hearts on all these things. Your heavenly Father knows you need them all. ³³ But seek first his Kingdom and his righteousness, and all these things will be given to you as well. ³⁴ Don't worry about tomorrow — tomorrow will worry about itself! Today has enough *tsuris* already!

7 ¹ "Don't judge, so that you won't be judged. ² For the way you judge others is how you will be judged — the measure with which you measure out will be used to measure to you. ³ Why do you see the splinter in your brother's eye but not notice the log in your own eye? ⁴ How can you say to your brother, 'Let me take the splinter out of your eye,' when you have the log in your own eye? ⁵ You hypocrite! First, take the log out of your own eye; then you will see clearly, so that you can remove the splinter from your brother's eye!

⁶ "Don't give to dogs what is holy, and don't throw your pearls to the pigs. If you do, they may trample them under their feet, then turn and attack you.

⁷ "Keep asking, and it will be given to you; keep seeking, and you will find; keep knocking, and the door will be opened to you. ⁸ For everyone who keeps asking receives; he who keeps seeking finds; and to him who keeps knocking, the door will be opened. ⁹ Is there anyone here who, if his son asks him for a loaf of bread, will give him a stone? ¹⁰ or if he asks for a fish, will give him a snake? ¹¹ So if you, even though you are bad, know how to give your children gifts that are good, how much more will your Father in heaven keep giving good things to those who keep asking him!

¹² "Always treat others as you would like them to treat you; that sums up the teaching of the *Torah* and the Prophets.

¹³ "Go in through the narrow gate; for the gate that leads to destruction is wide and the road broad, and many travel it; ¹⁴ but it is a narrow gate and a hard road that leads to life, and only a few find it.

¹⁵ "Beware of the false prophets! They come to you wearing sheep's clothing, but underneath they are hungry wolves! ¹⁶ You will recognize them by their fruit. Can people pick grapes from thorn bushes, or figs from thistles? ¹⁷ Likewise, every healthy tree produces good fruit, but a poor tree produces bad fruit. ¹⁸ A healthy tree cannot bear bad fruit, or a poor tree good fruit. ¹⁹ Any tree that does not produce good fruit is cut down and thrown in the fire! ²⁰ So you will recognize them by their fruit.

²¹ "Not everyone who says to me, 'Lord, Lord!' will enter the Kingdom of Heaven, only those who do what my Father in heaven wants. ²² On that Day, many will say to me, 'Lord, Lord!

A · men — Amen, so be it
Shlo · mo — Solomon
To · rah — Teaching, "Law", Pentateuch
tsur · is — troubles
tze · da · kah — righteousness, charity

9

Didn't we prophesy in your name? Didn't we expel demons in your name? Didn't we perform many miracles in your name?' ²³ Then I will tell them to their faces, 'I never knew you! **Get away from me, you workers of lawlessness!**'[t]

²⁴ "So, everyone who hears these words of mine and acts on them will be like a sensible man who built his house on bedrock. ²⁵ The rain fell, the rivers flooded, the winds blew and beat against that house, but it didn't collapse, because its foundation was on rock. ²⁶ But everyone who hears these words of mine and does not act on them will be like a stupid man who built his house on sand. ²⁷ The rain fell, the rivers flooded, the wind blew and beat against that house, and it collapsed — and its collapse was horrendous!"

²⁸ When Yeshua had finished saying these things, the crowds were amazed at the way he taught, ²⁹ for he was not instructing them like their *Torah*-teachers but as one who had authority himself.

8 ¹ After Yeshua had come down from the hill, large crowds followed him. ² Then a man afflicted with a repulsive skin disease came, kneeled down in front of him and said, "Sir, if you are willing, you can make me clean." ³ Yeshua reached out his hand, touched him and said, "I *am* willing! Be cleansed!" And at once he was cleansed from his skin disease. ⁴ Then Yeshua said to him, "See that you tell no one; but as a testimony to the people, go and let the *cohen* examine you, and offer the sacrifice that Moshe commanded."

⁵ As Yeshua entered K'far-Nachum, a Roman army officer came up and pleaded for help. ⁶ "Sir, my orderly is lying at home paralyzed and suffering terribly!" ⁷ Yeshua said, "I will go and heal him." ⁸ But the officer answered, "Sir, I am unfit to have you come into my home. Rather, if you will only give the command, my orderly will recover. ⁹ For I too am a man under authority. I have soldiers under me, and I say to this one, 'Go!' and he goes; to another, 'Come!' and he comes; to my slave, 'Do this!' and he does it." ¹⁰ On hearing this Yeshua was amazed and said to the people following him, "Yes! I tell you, I have not found anyone in Israel with such trust! ¹¹ Moreover, I tell you that many will come from the east and from the west to take their places at the feast in the Kingdom of Heaven with Avraham, Yitzchak and Ya'akov. ¹² But those born for the Kingdom will be thrown outside in the dark, where people will wail and grind their teeth!" ¹³ Then Yeshua said to the officer, "Go; let it be for you as you have trusted." And his orderly was healed at that very moment.

¹⁴ Yeshua went to Kefa's home and there saw Kefa's mother-in-law sick in bed with a fever. ¹⁵ He touched her hand, the fever left her, and she got up and began helping him.

¹⁶ When evening came, many people held in the power of demons were brought to him. He expelled the spirits with a word and healed all who were ill. ¹⁷ This was done to fulfill what had been spoken through the prophet Yesha'yahu,

> **"He himself took our weaknesses and bore our diseases"**[u]

¹⁸ When Yeshua saw the crowd around him, he gave orders to cross to the other side of the lake. ¹⁹ A *Torah*-teacher approached and said to him,

---

t Psalm 6:9(8)

u Isaiah 53:4

"Rabbi, I will follow you wherever you go." ²⁰ Yeshua said to him, "The foxes have holes, and the birds flying about have nests, but the Son of Man has no home of his own." ²¹ Another of the *talmidim* said to him, "Sir, first let me go and bury my father." ²² But Yeshua replied, "Follow me, and let the dead bury their own dead."

²³ He boarded the boat, and his *talmidim* followed. ²⁴ Then, without warning, a furious storm arose on the lake, so that waves were sweeping over the boat. But Yeshua was sleeping. ²⁵ So they came and roused him, saying, "Sir! Help! We're about to die!" ²⁶ He said to them, "Why are you afraid? So little trust you have!" Then he got up and rebuked the winds and the waves, and there was a dead calm. ²⁷ The men were astounded. They asked, "What kind of man is this, that even the winds and sea obey him?"

²⁸ When Yeshua arrived at the other side of the lake, in the Gadarenes' territory, there came out of the burial caves two men controlled by demons, so violent that no one dared travel on that road. ²⁹ They screamed, "What do you want with us, Son of God? Have you come here to torture us before the appointed time?" ³⁰ Now some distance from them a large herd of pigs was feeding. ³¹ The demons begged him, "If you are going to drive us out, send us into the herd of pigs." ³² "All right, go!" he told them. So they came out and went into the pigs, whereupon the entire herd rushed down the hillside into the lake and drowned. ³³ The swineherds fled, went off to the town and told the whole story, including what had happened to the demonized men. ³⁴ At this, the whole town came out to meet Yeshua. When they saw him, they begged him to leave their district.

9 ¹ So he stepped into a boat, crossed the lake again and came to his own town. ² Some people brought him a paralyzed man lying on a mattress. When Yeshua saw their trust, he said to the paralyzed man, "Courage, son! Your sins are forgiven." ³ On seeing this, some of the *Torah*-teachers said among themselves, "This man is blaspheming!" ⁴ Yeshua, knowing what they were thinking, said, "Why are you entertaining evil thoughts in your hearts? ⁵ Tell me, which is easier to say — 'Your sins are forgiven' or 'Get up and walk'? ⁶ But look! I will prove to you that the Son of Man has authority on earth to forgive sins." He then said to the paralyzed man, "Get up, pick up your mattress, and go home!" ⁷ And the man got up and went home. ⁸ When the crowds saw this, they were awestruck and said a *b'rakhah* to God the Giver of such authority to human beings.

⁹ As Yeshua passed on from there he spotted a tax-collector named Mattityahu sitting in his collection booth. He said to him, "Follow me!" and he got up and followed him.

¹⁰ While Yeshua was in the house eating, many tax-collectors and sinners came and joined him and his *talmidim* at the meal. ¹¹ When the *P'rushim* saw this, they said to his *talmidim*, "Why

---

Av·ra·ham — Abraham
b'ra·khah — blessing
co·hen — priest
Ke·fa — Peter
K'far-Na·chum — Capernaum
Mat·tit·ya·hu — Matthew
Mo·she — Moses
P'ru·shim — Pharisees
tal·mi·dim — disciples
To·rah-teacher — scribe
Ya·'a·kov — Jacob
Ye·sha'·ya·hu — Isaiah
Ye·shu·a — Jesus
Yitz·chak — Isaac

does your rabbi eat with tax-collectors and sinners?" [12] But Yeshua heard the question and answered, "The ones who need a doctor aren't the healthy but the sick. [13] As for you, go and learn what this means: '**I want compassion rather than animal-sacrifices.**'[v] For I didn't come to call the 'righteous', but sinners!"

[14] Next, Yochanan's *talmidim* came to him and asked, "Why is it that we and the *P'rushim* fast frequently, but your *talmidim* don't fast at all?" [15] Yeshua said to them, "Can wedding guests mourn while the bridegroom is still with them? But the time will come when the bridegroom is taken away from them; then they will fast. [16] No one patches an old coat with a piece of unshrunk cloth, because the patch tears away from the coat and leaves a worse hole. [17] Nor do people put new wine in old wineskins; if they do, the skins burst, the wine spills and the wineskins are ruined. No, they pour new wine into freshly prepared wineskins, and in this way both are preserved."

[18] While he was talking, an official came in, kneeled down in front of him and said, "My daughter has just died. But if you come and lay your hand on her, she will live." [19] Yeshua, with his *talmidim*, got up and followed him.

[20] A woman who had had a hemorrhage for twelve years approached him from behind and touched the *tzitzit* on his robe. [21] For she said to herself, "If I can only touch his robe, I will be healed." [22] Yeshua turned, saw her and said, "Courage, daughter! Your trust has healed you." And she was instantly healed.

[23] When Yeshua arrived at the official's house and saw the flute-players, and the crowd in an uproar, [24] he said,

"Everybody out! The girl isn't dead, she's only sleeping!" And they jeered at him. [25] But after the people had been put outside, he entered and took hold of the girl's hand, and she got up. [26] News of this spread through all that region.

[27] As Yeshua went on from there, two blind men began following him, shouting, "Son of David! Take pity on us!" [28] When he entered the house, the blind men came up, and Yeshua said to them, "Do you believe that I have the power to do this?" They replied, "Yes, sir." [29] Then he touched their eyes and said, "Let it happen to you according to your trust;" [30] and their sight was restored. Yeshua warned them severely, "See that no one knows about it." [31] But instead, they went away and talked about him throughout that district.

[32] As they were going, a man controlled by a demon and unable to speak was brought to Yeshua. [33] After the demon was expelled the man who had been mute spoke, and the crowds were amazed. "Nothing like this has ever been seen in Israel," they said. [34] But the *P'rushim* said, "It is through the ruler of the demons that he expels demons."

[35] Yeshua went about all the towns and villages, teaching in their synagogues, proclaiming the Good News of the Kingdom, and healing every kind of disease and weakness. [36] When he saw the crowds, he had compassion on them because they were harried and helpless, like sheep without a shepherd. [37] Then he said to his *talmidim*, "The harvest is rich, but the workers are few. [38] Pray that the Lord of the harvest will send out workers to gather in his harvest."

10 [1] Yeshua called his twelve *talmidim* and gave them authority to drive out unclean spirits and to heal every kind of disease and weakness.

---

v Hosea 6:6

12

² These are the names of the twelve emissaries:

First, Shim'on, called Kefa,
and Andrew his brother,
Ya'akov Ben-Zavdai
and Yochanan his brother,
³ Philip
and Bar-Talmai,
T'oma
and Mattityahu the tax-collector,
Ya'akov Bar-Chalfai
and Taddai,
⁴ Shim'on the Zealot,
and Y'hudah from K'riot,
who betrayed him.

⁵ These twelve Yeshua sent out with the following instructions: "Don't go into the territory of the *Goyim*, and don't enter any town in Shomron, ⁶ but go rather to the lost sheep of the house of Israel. ⁷ As you go, proclaim, 'The Kingdom of Heaven is near,' ⁸ heal the sick, raise the dead, cleanse those with skin diseases, expel demons. You have received without paying, so give without asking payment. ⁹ Don't take money in your belts, no gold, no silver, no copper; ¹⁰ and for the trip don't take a pack, an extra shirt, shoes or a walking stick — a worker should be given what he needs.

¹¹ "When you come to a town or village, look for someone trustworthy and stay with him until you leave. ¹² When you enter someone's household, say, '*Shalom aleikhem*!' ¹³ If the home deserves it, let your *shalom* rest on it; if not, let your *shalom* return to you. ¹⁴ But if the people of a house or town will not welcome you or listen to you, leave it and shake its dust from your feet! ¹⁵ Yes, I tell you, it will be more tolerable on the Day of Judgment for the people of S'dom and 'Amora than for that town!

¹⁶ "Pay attention! I am sending you out like sheep among wolves, so be as prudent as snakes and as harmless as doves. ¹⁷ Be on guard, for there will be people who will hand you over to the local *sanhedrins* and flog you in their synagogues. ¹⁸ On my account you will be brought before governors and kings as a testimony to them and to the *Goyim*. ¹⁹ But when they bring you to trial, do not worry about what to say or how to say it; when the time comes, you will be given what you should say. ²⁰ For it will not be just you speaking, but the Spirit of your heavenly Father speaking through you.

²¹ "A brother will betray his brother to death, and a father his child; children will turn against their parents and have them put to death. ²² Everyone will hate you because of me, but whoever holds out till the end will be preserved from harm. ²³ When you are persecuted in one town, run away to another. Yes

---

'A·mora — Gomorrah
Ba·'al-zib·bul — Beelzebul, Beelzebub (Satan)
Bar-Tal·mai — Bartholomew
Da·vid — David
Go·yim — Gentiles, nations, pagans
Ke·fa — Peter
Mat·tit·ya·hu — Matthew
P'ru·shim — Pharisees
San·hed·rin — Jewish religious court
S'dom — Sodom
sha·lom — peace
Sha·lom a·lei·khem! — Peace be upon you! (greeting)
Shim·'on — Simon
Shom·ron — Samaria
Tad·dai — Thaddeus
tal·mi·dim — disciples
T·'o·ma — Thomas
tzi·tzit — ritual fringe
Ya·'a·kov Bar-Chal·fai — James the son of Alpheus
Ya·'a·kov Ben-Zav·dai — James the son of Zebedee
Ye·shu·a — Jesus
Y'hu·dah from K'ri·ot — Judas Iscariot.
Yo·cha·nan — John

indeed; I tell you, you will not finish going through the towns of Israel before the Son of Man comes.

²⁴"A *talmid* is not greater than his rabbi, a slave is not greater than his master. ²⁵It is enough for a *talmid* that he become like his rabbi, and a slave like his master. Now if people have called the head of the house Ba'alzibbul, how much more will they malign the members of his household! ²⁶So do not fear them; for there is nothing covered that will not be uncovered, or hidden that will not be known. ²⁷What I tell you in the dark, speak in the light; what is whispered in your ear, proclaim on the housetops.

²⁸"Do not fear those who kill the body but are powerless to kill the soul. Rather, fear him who can destroy both soul and body in Gey-Hinnom. ²⁹Aren't sparrows sold for next to nothing, two for an assarion? Yet not one of them will fall to the ground without your Father's consent. ³⁰As for you, every hair on your head has been counted. ³¹So do not be afraid, you are worth more than many sparrows.

³²"Whoever acknowledges me in the presence of others I will also acknowledge in the presence of my Father in heaven. ³³But whoever disowns me before others I will disown before my Father in heaven.

³⁴"Don't suppose that I have come to bring peace to the Land. It is not peace I have come to bring, but a sword! ³⁵For I have come to set

> a man against his father,
> a daughter against her mother,
> a daughter-in-law against her mother-in-law,
> ³⁶ so that a man's enemies will be the members of his own house hold.ʷ

³⁷Whoever loves his father or mother more than he loves me is not worthy of me; anyone who loves his son or daughter more than he loves me is not worthy of me. ³⁸And anyone who does not take up his execution-stake and follow me is not worthy of me. ³⁹Whoever finds his own life will lose it, but the person who loses his life for my sake will find it.

⁴⁰"Whoever receives you is receiving me, and whoever receives me is receiving the One who sent me. ⁴¹Anyone who receives a prophet because he is a prophet will receive the reward a prophet gets, and anyone who receives a *tzaddik* because he is a *tzaddik* will receive the reward a *tzaddik* gets. ⁴²Indeed, if someone gives just a cup of cold water to one of these little ones because he is my *talmid* — yes! — I tell you, he will certainly not lose his reward!"

11 ¹After Yeshua had finished instructing the twelve *talmidim*, he went on from there to teach and preach in the towns nearby.

²Meanwhile, Yochanan the Immerser, who had been put in prison, heard what the Messiah had been doing; so he sent a message to him through his *talmidim*, ³asking, "Are you the one who is to come, or should we look for someone else?" ⁴Yeshua answered, "Go and tell Yochanan what you are hearing and seeing — ⁵**the blind are seeing again, the lame are** walking, people with skin diseases are being cleansed, **the deaf are hearing,**ˣ the dead are being raised,ʸ **the Good News is being told to the poor**ᶻ — ⁶and how blessed is anyone not offended by me!" ˈ

ʷ Micah 7:6

x Isaiah 35:5-6   y Isaiah 26:14
z Isaiah 61:1

[7] As they were leaving, Yeshua began speaking about Yochanan to the crowds: "What did you go out to the desert to see? Reeds swaying in the breeze? [8] No? then what did you go out to see? Someone who was well dressed? Well-dressed people live in kings' palaces. [9] *Nu*, so why did you go out? To see a prophet! Yes! and I tell you he's much more than a prophet. [10] This is the one about whom the *Tanakh* says,

> 'See, I am sending out my messenger ahead of you;
> he will prepare your way before you.'[a]

[11] Yes! I tell you that among those born of women there has not arisen anyone greater than Yochanan the Immerser! Yet the one who is least in the Kingdom of Heaven is greater than he! [12] From the time of Yochanan the Immerser until now, the Kingdom of Heaven has been suffering violence; yes, violent ones are trying to snatch it away. [13] For all the prophets and the *Torah* prophesied until Yochanan. [14] Indeed, if you are willing to accept it, he is Eliyahu, whose coming was predicted. [15] If you have ears, then hear!

[16] "Oh, what can I compare this generation with? They're like children sitting in the marketplaces, calling out to each other,

> [17] 'We made happy music,
> but you wouldn't dance!
> We made sad music,
> but you wouldn't cry!'

[18] For Yochanan came, fasting, not drinking — so they say, 'He has a demon.' [19] The Son of Man came, eating freely and drinking wine — so they say, 'Aha! A glutton and a drunkard! A friend of tax-collectors and sinners!' Well, the proof of wisdom is in the actions it produces."

[20] Then Yeshua began to denounce the towns in which he had done most of his miracles, because the people had not turned from their sins to God. [21] "Woe to you, Korazin! Woe to you, Beit-Tzaidah! Why, if the miracles done in you had been done in Tzor and Tzidon, they would long ago have put on sackcloth and ashes as evidence that they had changed their ways. [22] But I tell you it will be more bearable for Tzor and Tzidon than for you on the Day of Judgment! [23] And you, K'far-Nachum, will you be **exalted to heaven? No, you will be brought down to Sh'ol!**[b] For if the miracles done in you had been done in S'dom, it would still be in existence today. [24] But I tell you that on the Day of Judgment it will be more bearable for the land of S'dom than for you!"

[25] It was at that time that Yeshua said, "I thank you, Father, Lord of heaven

---

b Isaiah 14:13, 15

Ba·'al-zib·bul — Beelzebul, Beelzebub (Satan)
Beit-Tzai·dah — Bethsaida
E·li·ya·hu — Elijah
Gey-Hin·nom — Gehenna, hell
K'far-Na·chum — Capernaum
Ko·ra·zin — Chorazin
nu? — well?
S'dom — Sodom
Sh·'ol — Sheol, Hades, hell
tal·mid — disciple
tal·mi·dim — disciples
Ta·nakh — Hebrew Scriptures, "Old Testament"
To·rah — Teaching, "Law"; Pentateuch
tzad·dik — righteous man
Tzi·don — Sidon
Tzor — Tyre
Ye·shu·a — Jesus
Yo·cha·nan — John
Yo·cha·nan the Immerser — John the Baptist

---

a Malachi 3:1

and earth, that you concealed these things from the sophisticated and educated and revealed them to ordinary folks. ²⁶ Yes, Father, I thank you that it pleased you to do this.

²⁷ "My Father has handed over everything to me. Indeed, no one fully knows the Son except the Father, and no one fully knows the Father except the Son and those to whom the Son wishes to reveal him.

²⁸ "Come to me, all of you who are struggling and burdened, and I will give you rest. ²⁹ Take my yoke upon you and learn from me, because I am gentle and humble in heart, **and you will find rest for your souls.**^c ³⁰ For my yoke is easy, and my burden is light."

12 ¹ One *Shabbat* during that time, Yeshua was walking through some wheat fields. His *talmidim* were hungry, so they began picking heads of grain and eating them. ² On seeing this, the *P'rushim* said to him, "Look! Your *talmidim* are violating *Shabbat*!" ³ But he said to them, "Haven't you ever read what David did when he and those with him were hungry? ⁴ He entered the House of God and ate the Bread of the Presence, which was prohibited, both to him and to his companions — it is permitted only to the *cohanim.* ⁵ Or haven't you read in the *Torah* that on *Shabbat* the *cohanim* profane *Shabbat* and yet are blameless? ⁶ I tell you, there is in this place something greater than the Temple! ⁷ If you knew what **'I want compassion rather than animal-sacrifice'**^d meant, you would not condemn the innocent. ⁸ For the Son of Man is Lord of *Shabbat*!"

⁹ Going on from that place, he went into their synagogue. ¹⁰ A man there had a shriveled hand. Looking for a reason to accuse him of something, they asked him, "Is healing permitted on *Shabbat*?" ¹¹ But he answered, "If you have a sheep that falls in a pit on *Shabbat*, which of you won't take hold of it and lift it out? ¹² How much more valuable is a man than a sheep! Therefore, what is permitted on *Shabbat* is to do good." ¹³ Then to the man he said, "Hold out your hand." As he held it out, it became restored, as sound as the other one. ¹⁴ But the *P'rushim* went out and began plotting how they might do away with Yeshua. ¹⁵ Aware of this, he left that area.

Many people followed him; and he healed them all ¹⁶ but warned them not to make him known. ¹⁷ This was to fulfill what had been spoken through Yesha'yahu the prophet,

¹⁸ "Here is my servant, whom I have chosen,
my beloved, with whom I am well pleased;

I will put my Spirit on him,
and he will announce justice to the Gentiles.

¹⁹ He will not fight or shout,
no one will hear his voice in the streets;

²⁰ he will not snap off a broken reed
or snuff out a smoldering wick

until he has brought justice through to victory.
²¹ In him the Gentiles will put their hope."^e

²² Then some people brought him a man controlled by demons who was blind and mute; and Yeshua healed him, so that he could both speak and see. ²³ The crowds were astounded and asked, "This couldn't be the Son of David, could it?" ²⁴ But when the

---

c Jeremiah 6:16   d Hosea 6:6

e Isaiah 42:1-4

P'rushim heard of it, they said, "It is only by Ba'al-zibbul, the ruler of the demons, that this man drives out demons."

²⁵However, knowing what they were thinking, Yeshua said to them, "Every kingdom divided against itself will be ruined, and every city or household divided against itself will not survive. ²⁶If Satan drives out Satan, he is divided against himself; so how can his kingdom survive? ²⁷Besides, if I drive out demons by Ba'al-zibbul, by whom do your people drive them out? So, they will be your judges! ²⁸But if I drive out demons by the Spirit of God, then the Kingdom of God has come upon you!

²⁹"Or again, how can someone break into a strong man's house and make off with his possessions unless he first ties up the strong man? After that he can ransack his house.

³⁰"Those who are not with me are against me, and those who do not gather with me are scattering. ³¹Because of this, I tell you that people will be forgiven any sin and blasphemy, but blaspheming the *Ruach HaKodesh* will not be forgiven. ³²One can say something against the Son of Man and be forgiven; but whoever keeps on speaking against the *Ruach HaKodesh* will never be forgiven, neither in the *'olam hazeh* nor in the *'olam haba.*

³³"If you make a tree good, its fruit will be good; and if you make a tree bad, its fruit will be bad; for a tree is known by its fruit. ³⁴You snakes! How can you who are evil say anything good? For the mouth speaks what overflows from the heart. ³⁵The good person brings forth good things from his store of good, and the evil person brings forth evil things from his store of evil. ³⁶Moreover, I tell you this: on the Day of Judgment people will have to

give account for every careless word they have spoken; ³⁷for by your own words you will be acquitted, and by your own words you will be condemned."

³⁸At this some of the *Torah*-teachers said, "Rabbi, we want to see a miraculous sign from you." ³⁹He replied, "A wicked and adulterous generation asks for a sign? No! None will be given to it but the sign of the prophet Yonah. ⁴⁰For just as Yonah **was three days and three nights in the belly of the sea-monster,***ᶠ* so will the Son of Man be three days and three nights in the depths of the earth. ⁴¹The people of Nineveh will stand up at the Judgment with this generation and condemn it, for they turned from their sins to God when Yonah preached, but what is here now is greater than Yonah. ⁴²The Queen of the South will stand up at the Judgment with this generation and condemn it, for she came from the ends of the earth to hear the wisdom of Shlomo, but what is here now is greater than Shlomo.

⁴³"When an unclean spirit comes out of a person, it travels through dry

---

ᶠ Jonah 1:17

Ba·'al·zib·**bul** — Beelzebul, Beelzebub (Satan)
*co·ha·**nim*** — priests
Da·**vid** — David
Nin·e·**veh** — Nineveh
*'ol·am ha·**ba*** — the world/age to come
*'ol·am ha·**zeh*** — the world/age
*P'ru·**shim*** — Pharisees
Ru·ach-Ha-Ko·desh — Holy Spirit
Sa·**tan** — Satan, the Adversary
*Shab·**bat*** — the Sabbath
Shlo·**mo** — Solomon
*tal·mi·**dim*** — disciples
*To·**rah*** — Teaching, "Law"; Pentateuch
*To·**rah***-teachers — scribes
Ye·sha'·**ya**·hu — Isaiah
Ye·**shu**·a — Jesus
Yo·**nah** — Jonah

17

country seeking rest and does not find it. ⁴⁴Then it says to itself, 'I will return to the house I left.' When it arrives, it finds the house standing empty, swept clean and put in order. ⁴⁵Then it goes and takes with it seven other spirits more evil than itself, and they come and live there — so that in the end, the person is worse off than he was before. This is how it will be for this wicked generation."

⁴⁶He was still speaking to the crowd when his mother and brothers appeared outside, asking to talk with him.⁴⁷* ⁴⁸But to the one who had informed him he replied, "Who is my mother? Who are my brothers?" ⁴⁹Pointing to his *talmidim*, he said, "Look! Here are my mother and my brothers! ⁵⁰Whoever does what my Father in heaven wants, that person is my brother and sister and mother."

13 ¹That same day, Yeshua went out of the house and sat down by the lake; ²but such a large crowd gathered around him that he got into a boat and sat there while the crowd stood on the shore. ³He told them many things in parables:

"A farmer went out to sow his seed. ⁴As he sowed, some seed fell alongside the path; and the birds came and ate it up. ⁵Other seed fell on rocky patches where there was not much soil. It sprouted quickly because the soil was shallow; ⁶but when the sun had risen, the young plants were scorched; and since their roots were not deep, they dried up. ⁷Other seed fell among thorns, which grew up and choked the plants. ⁸But others fell into rich soil

and produced grain, a hundred or sixty or thirty times as much as had been sown. ⁹Those who have ears, let them hear!"

¹⁰Then the *talmidim* came and asked Yeshua, "Why are you speaking to them in parables?" ¹¹He answered, "Because it has been given to you to know the secrets of the Kingdom of Heaven, but it has not been given to them. ¹²For anyone who has something will be given more, so that he will have plenty; but from anyone who has nothing, even what he does have will be taken away. ¹³Here is why I speak to them in parables: they look without seeing and listen without hearing or understanding. ¹⁴That is, in them is fulfilled the prophecy of Yesha'yahu which says,

'You will keep on hearing but
  never understand,
and keep on seeing but never perceive,
¹⁵because the heart of this people
  has become dull —
with their ears they barely hear,
and their eyes they have closed,
so as not to see with their eyes,
hear with their ears,
understand with their heart,
and do *t'shuvah*,
so that I could heal them.'ᵍ

¹⁶"But you, how blessed are your eyes, because they see, and your ears, because they hear! ¹⁷Yes indeed! I tell you that many a prophet and many a *tzaddik* longed to see the things you are seeing but did not see them, and to hear the things you are hearing but did not hear them.

¹⁸So listen to what the parable of the sower means. ¹⁹Whoever hears the message about the Kingdom, but doesn't understand it, is like the seed

---

* Some manuscripts include verse 47: Some-one told him, "Your mother and brothers are standing outside, asking to talk with you."

---

g Isaiah 6:9-10

sown along the path — the Evil One comes and seizes what was sown in his heart. [20]The seed sown on rocky ground is like a person who hears the message and accepts it with joy at once, [21]but has no root in himself. So he stays on for a while; but as soon as some trouble or persecution arises on account of the message, he immediately falls away. [22]Now the seed sown among thorns stands for someone who hears the message, but it is choked by the worries of the world and the deceitful glamor of wealth, so that it produces nothing. [23]However, what was sown on rich soil is the one who hears the message and understands it; such a person will surely bear fruit, a hundred or sixty or thirty times what was sown."

[24]Yeshua put before them another parable. "The Kingdom of Heaven is like a man who sowed good seed in his field; [25]but while people were sleeping, his enemy came and sowed weeds among the wheat, then went away. [26]When the wheat sprouted and formed heads of grain, the weeds also appeared. [27]The owner's servants came to him and said, 'Sir didn't you sow good seed in your field? Where have the weeds come from?' [28]He answered, 'An enemy has done this.' The servants asked him, 'Then do you want us to go and pull them up?' [29]But he said, 'No, because if you pull up the weeds, you might uproot some of the wheat at the same time. [30]Let them both grow together until the harvest; and at harvest-time I will tell the reapers to collect the weeds first and tie them in bundles to be burned, but to gather the wheat into my barn.'"

[31]Yeshua put before them another parable. "The Kingdom of Heaven is like a mustard seed which a man takes and sows in his field. [32]It is the smallest of all seeds, but when it grows up it is larger than any garden plant and becomes a tree, so that the birds flying about come and nest in its branches."

[33]And he told them yet another parable. "The Kingdom of Heaven is like yeast that a woman took and mixed with a bushel of flour, then waited until the whole batch of dough rose."

[34]All these things Yeshua said to the crowds in parables; indeed, he said nothing to them without using a parable. [35]This was to fulfill what had been spoken through the prophet,

"I will open my mouth in parables, I will say what has been hidden since the creation of the universe."[h]

[36]Then he left the crowds and went into the house. His *talmidim* approached him and said, "Explain to us the parable of the weeds in the field." [37]He answered, "The one who sows the good seed is the Son of Man; [38]the field is the world. As for the good seed, these are the people who belong to the Kingdom; and the weeds are the people who belong to the Evil One. [39]The enemy who sows them is the Adversary, the harvest is the end of the age, and the harvesters are angels. [40]Just as the weeds are collected and burned up in the fire, so will it be at the end of the age. [41]The Son of Man will send forth his angels, and they will collect out of his Kingdom all the things that cause people to sin and all the people who are far from *Torah*; [42]and they will throw

---

[h] Psalm 78:2

---

tal·mi·dim — disciples
To·rah — Teaching, "Law"; Pentateuch
do t'shu·vah — repent, turn from sin to God
tzad·dik — righteous man
Ye·sha'·ya·hu — Isaiah
Ye·shu·a — Jesus

them into the fiery furnace, where people will wail and grind their teeth. ⁴³Then the righteous will shine forth like the sun in the Kingdom of their Father. Whoever has ears, let him hear!

⁴⁴"The Kingdom of Heaven is like a treasure hidden in a field. A man found it, hid it again, then in great joy went and sold everything he owned, and bought that field.

⁴⁵"Again, the Kingdom of Heaven is like a merchant on the lookout for fine pearls. ⁴⁶On finding one very valuable pearl he went away, sold everything he owned and bought it.

⁴⁷"Once more, the Kingdom of Heaven is like a net thrown into the lake, that caught all kinds of fish. ⁴⁸When it was full, the fishermen brought the net up onto the shore, sat down and collected the good fish in baskets, but threw the bad fish away. ⁴⁹So it will be at the close of the age — the angels will go forth and separate the evil people from among the righteous ⁵⁰and throw them into the fiery furnace, where they will wail and grind their teeth.

⁵¹"Have you understood all these things?" "Yes," they answered. ⁵²He said to them, "So then, every *Torah*-teacher who has been made into a *talmid* for the Kingdom of Heaven is like the owner of a home who brings out of his storage room both new things and old."

⁵³When Yeshua had finished these parables, he left ⁵⁴and went to his home town. There he taught them in their synagogue in a way that astounded them, so that they asked, "Where do this man's wisdom and miracles come from? ⁵⁵Isn't he the carpenter's son? Isn't his mother called Miryam? and his brothers Ya'akov, Yosef, Shim'on and Y'hudah? ⁵⁶And his sisters, aren't they all with us? So where does he get all

this?" ⁵⁷And they took offense at him. But Yeshua said to them, "The only place people don't respect a prophet is in his home town and in his own house." ⁵⁸And he did few miracles there because of their lack of trust.

14 ¹Around that time, Herod, the regional governor, heard of the fame of Yeshua ²and said to his attendants, "This must be Yochanan the Immerser. He has been raised from the dead; that is why these miraculous powers are at work in him."

³For Herod had arrested Yochanan, put him in chains and thown him in prison because of Herodias, the wife of his brother Philip; ⁴since Yochanan had told Herod, "It violates the *Torah* for you to have her as your wife." ⁵Herod had wanted to put Yochanan to death; but he was afraid of the people, in whose eyes Yochanan was a prophet. ⁶However, at Herod's birthday celebration, Herodias' daughter danced before the company and pleased Herod so much ⁷that he promised with an oath to give her whatever she asked. ⁸Prompted by her mother, she said, "Give me here on a platter the head of Yochanan the Immerser." ⁹The king became deeply upset; but out of regard for the oaths he had sworn before his dinner guests, he ordered that her wish be granted, ¹⁰and sent and had Yochanan beheaded in prison. ¹¹The head was brought on a platter to the girl, and she gave it to her mother. ¹²Yochanan's *talmidim* came, took the body and buried it; then they went and told Yeshua.

¹³On hearing about this, Yeshua left in a boat to be by himself in the wilderness. But the people learned of it and followed him from the towns by land. ¹⁴So when he came ashore, he saw a huge crowd; and, filled with compassion for them, he healed those of them who were sick.

[15] As evening approached, the *talmidim* came to him and said, "This is a remote place and it's getting late. Send the crowds away, so that they can go and buy food for themselves in the villages." [16] But Yeshua replied, "They don't need to go away. Give them something to eat, yourselves!" [17] "All we have with us," they said, "is five loaves of bread and two fish." [18] He said, "Bring them here to me." [19] After instructing the crowds to sit down on the grass, he took the five loaves and the two fish and, looking up toward heaven, made a *b'rakhah*. Then he broke the loaves and gave them to the *talmidim*, who gave them to the crowds. [20] They all ate as much as they wanted, and they took up twelve baskets full of the pieces left over. [21] Those eating numbered about five thousand men, plus women and children.

[22] Immediately, he had the *talmidim* get in the boat and go on ahead of him to the other side, while he sent the crowds away. [23] After he had sent the crowds away, he went up into the hills by himself to pray. Night came on, and he was there alone. [24] But by this time, the boat was several miles from shore, battling a rough sea and a headwind. [25] Around four o'clock in the morning, he came toward them, walking on the lake! [26] When the *talmidim* saw him walking on the lake, they were terrified. "It's a ghost!" they said and screamed with fear. [27] But at once Yeshua spoke to them. "Courage," he said, "it is I. Stop being afraid." [28] Then Kefa called to him, "Lord, if it is really you, tell me to come to you on the water." [29] "Come!" he said. So Kefa got out of the boat and walked on the water toward Yeshua. [30] But when he saw the wind, he became afraid; and as he began to sink, he yelled, "Lord! Save me!" [31] Yeshua immediately stretched out his hand, took hold of him, and said to him, "Such little trust! Why did you doubt?" [32] As they went up into the boat, the wind ceased. [33] The men in the boat fell down before him and exclaimed, "You really are God's son!"

[34] Having made the crossing, they landed at Ginosar. [35] When the people of the place recognized him, they sent word throughout the neighborhood and brought him everyone who was ill. [36] They begged him that the sick people might only touch the *tzitzit* on his robe, and all who touched it were completely healed.

15 [1] Then some *P'rushim* and *Torah*-teachers from Yerushalayim came to Yeshua and asked him, [2] "Why is it that your *talmidim* break the Tradition of the Elders? They don't do *n'tilat-yadayim* before they eat!" [3] He answered, "Indeed, why do *you* break the command of God by your tradition? [4] For God said, '**Honor your father and mother,**'[i] and '**Anyone who curses his father or mother must be put to death.**'[j] [5] But you say, 'If anyone says

---

i Exodus 20:12, Deuteronomy 5:16
j Exodus 21:17, Leviticus 20:9

---

b'ra·khah — blessing
Gi·no·sar — Gennesaret
Ke·fa — Peter
Mir·yam — Miriam, Mary
n'ti·lat-ya·da·yim — ritual handwashing
P'ru·shim — Pharisees
Shim·'on — Simon
tal·mi·dim — disciples
To·rah — Teaching, "Law"; Pentateuch
To·rah-teacher — scribe
tzi·tzit — ritual fringe
Ya·'a·kov — James
Ye·ru·sha·la·yim — Jerusalem
Ye·shu·a — Jesus
Y'hu·dah — Judas, Jude
Yo·cha·nan — John
Yo·cha·nan the Immerser — John the Baptist
Yo·sef — Joseph

to his father or mother, "I have promised to give to God what I might have used to help you," ⁶ then he is rid of his duty to honor his father or mother.' Thus by your tradition you make null and void the word of God! ⁷ You hypocrites! Yesha'yahu was right when he prophesied about you,

⁸ 'These people honor me with their lips,
but their hearts are far away from me.
⁹ Their worship of me is useless, because they teach man-made rules as if they were doctrines.'"ᵏ

¹⁰ Then he called the crowd to him and said, "Listen and understand this! ¹¹ What makes a person unclean is not what goes into his mouth; rather, what comes out of his mouth, that is what makes him unclean!"

¹² The *talmidim* came to him and said, "Do you know that the *P'rushim* were offended by what you said?" ¹³ He replied, "Every plant that my Father in heaven has not planted will be pulled up by the roots. ¹⁴ Let them be. They are blind guides. When a blind man guides another blind man, both will fall in a pit."

¹⁵ Kefa said to him, "Explain the parable to us." ¹⁶ So he said, "Don't you understand even now? ¹⁷ Don't you see that anything that enters the mouth goes into the stomach and passes out into the latrine? ¹⁸ But what comes out of your mouth is actually coming from your heart, and that is what makes a person unclean. ¹⁹ For out of the heart come forth wicked thoughts, murder, adultery and other kinds of sexual immorality, theft, lies, slanders.... ²⁰ These are what really make a person unclean, but eating without doing

---

k Isaiah 29:13

n'tilat-yadayim does not make a person unclean."

²¹ Yeshua left that place and went off to the region of Tzor and Tzidon. ²² A woman from Cana'an who was living there came to him, pleading, "Sir, have pity on me. Son of David! My daughter is cruelly held under the power of demons!" ²³ But Yeshua did not say a word to her. Then his *talmidim* came to him and urged him, "Send her away, because she is following us and keeps pestering us with her crying." ²⁴ He said, "I was sent only to the lost sheep of the house of Israel." ²⁵ But she came, fell at his feet and said, "Sir, help me!" ²⁶ He answered, "It is not right to take the children's food and toss it to their pet dogs." ²⁷ She said, "That is true, sir, but even the dogs eat the leftovers that fall from their master's table." ²⁸ Then Yeshua answered her, "Lady, you are a person of great trust. Let your desire be granted." And her daughter was healed at that very moment.

²⁹ Yeshua left there and went along the shore of Lake Kinneret. He climbed a hill and sat down; ³⁰ and large crowds came to him, bringing with them the lame, the blind, the crippled, the mute and many others. They laid them at his feet, and he healed them. ³¹ The people were amazed as they saw mute people speaking, crippled people cured, lame people walking and blind people seeing; and they said a *b'rakhah* to the God of Israel.

³² Yeshua called his *talmidim* to him and said, "I feel sorry for these people, because they have been with me three days, and now they have nothing to eat. I don't want to send them away hungry, because they might collapse on the way home." ³³ The *talmidim* said to him, "Where will we find enough loaves of bread in this remote place to satisfy so big a crowd?" ³⁴ Yeshua asked them,

"How many loaves do you have?" They said, "Seven, and a few fish." ³⁵ After telling the crowd to sit down on the ground, ³⁶ he took the seven loaves and the fish, made a *b'rakhah*, broke the loaves and gave them to the *talmidim*, who gave them to the people. ³⁷ Everyone ate his fill, and they took seven large baskets full of the leftover pieces. ³⁸ Those eating numbered four thousand men, plus women and children. ³⁹ After sending the crowd away, he got in the boat and went off to the region of Magadan.

16 ¹ Then some *P'rushim* and *Tz'dukim* came to trap Yeshua by asking him to show them a miraculous sign from Heaven. ² But his response was, "When it is evening, you say, 'Fair weather ahead,' because the sky is red; ³ and in the morning you say, 'Storm today!' because the sky is red and overcast. You know how to read the appearance of the sky, but you can't read the signs of the times! ⁴ A wicked and adulterous generation is asking for a sign? It will certainly not be given a sign — except the sign of Yonah!" With that he left them and went off.

⁵ The *talmidim*, in crossing to the other side of the lake, had forgotten to bring any bread. ⁶ So when Yeshua said to them, "Watch out! Guard yourselves against the *chametz* of the *P'rushim* and *Tz'dukim*," ⁷ they thought he said it because they hadn't brought bread. ⁸ But Yeshua, aware of this, said, "Such little trust you have! Why are you talking with each other about not having bread? ⁹ Don't you understand yet? Don't you remember the five loaves of the five thousand and how many baskets you filled? ¹⁰ Or the seven loaves of the four thousand and how many baskets you filled? ¹¹ How can you possibly think I was talking to you about bread? Guard yourselves from

the *chametz* of the *P'rushim* and *Tz'dukim*!" ¹² Then they understood — they were to guard themselves not from yeast for bread but from the teaching of the *P'rushim* and *Tz'dukim*.

¹³ When Yeshua came into the territory around Caesarea Philippi, he asked his *talmidim*, "Who are people saying the Son of Man is?" ¹⁴ They said, "Well, some say Yochanan the Immerser, others Eliyahu, still others Yirmeyahu or one of the prophets." ¹⁵ "But you," he said to them, "who do you say I am?" ¹⁶ Shim'on Kefa answered, "You are the *Mashiach*, the Son of the living God." ¹⁷ "Shim'on Bar-Yochanan," Yeshua said to him, "how blessed you are! For no human being revealed this to you, no, it was my Father in heaven. ¹⁸ I also tell you this: you are Kefa" [which means 'Rock'], and on this rock I will build my Community, and the gates of Sh'ol will not overcome it. ¹⁹ I will give you the keys of the Kingdom of Heaven.

---

b'ra·khah — blessing
Ca·na·'an — Canaan
cha·metz — leaven
Da·vid — David
E·li·ya·hu — Elijah
Ke·fa — Peter
Lake Kin·ne·ret — the Sea of Galilee
Ma·shi·ach — Messiah
n'ti·lat-ya·da·yim — ritual handwashing
P'ru·shim — Pharisees
Shim·'on Bar-Yo·cha·nan — Simon, son of John
Shim·'on Ke·fa — Simon Peter
Sh·'ol — Sheol, Hades, hell
tal·mi·dim — disciples
Tz'du·kim — Sadducees
Tzi·don — Sidon
Tzor — Tyre
Ye·sha'·ya·hu — Isaiah
Ye·shu·a — Jesus
Yir·me·ya·hu — Jeremiah
Yo·cha·nan the Immerser — John the Baptist
Yo·nah — Jonah

Whatever you prohibit on earth will be prohibited in heaven, and whatever you permit on earth will be permitted in heaven." ²⁰Then he warned the *talmidim* not to tell anyone that he was the Messiah.

²¹From that time on, Yeshua began making it clear to his *talmidim* that he had to go to Yerushalayim and endure much suffering at the hands of the elders, the head *cohanim* and the *Torah*-teachers; and that he had to be put to death; but that on the third day, he had to be raised to life. ²²Kefa took him aside and began rebuking him, "Heaven be merciful, Lord! By no means will this happen to you!" ²³But Yeshua turned his back on Kefa, saying, "Get behind me, Satan! You are an obstacle in my path, because your thinking is from a human perspective, not from God's perspective!"

²⁴Then Yeshua told his *talmidim*, "If anyone wants to come after me, let him say 'No' to himself, take up his execution-stake, and keep following me. ²⁵For whoever wants to save his own life will destroy it, but whoever destroys his life for my sake will find it. ²⁶What good will it do someone if he gains the whole world but forfeits his life? Or, what can a person give in exchange for his life? ²⁷For the Son of Man will come in his Father's glory, with his angels; and then he will repay everyone according to his conduct. ²⁸Yes! I tell you that there are some people standing here who will not experience death until they see the Son of Man coming in his Kingdom!"

17 ¹Six days later, Yeshua took Kefa, Ya'akov and his brother Yochanan and led them up a high mountain privately. ²As they watched, he began to change form — his face shone like the sun, and his clothing became as white as light. ³Then they looked and saw Moshe and Eliyahu speaking with him. ⁴Kefa said to Yeshua, "It's good that we're here, Lord. I'll put up three shelters if you want — one for you, one for Moshe and one for Eliyahu." ⁵While he was still speaking, a bright cloud enveloped them; and a voice from the cloud said, "This is my Son, whom I love, with whom I am well pleased. Listen to him!" ⁶When the *talmidim* heard this, they were so frightened that they fell face down on the ground. ⁷But Yeshua came and touched them. "Get up!" he said, "Don't be afraid." ⁸So they opened their eyes, looked up and saw only Yeshua by himself.

⁹As they came down the mountain, Yeshua ordered them, "Don't tell anyone what you have seen until the Son of Man has been raised from the dead." ¹⁰The *talmidim* asked him, "Then why do the *Torah*-teachers say that Eliyahu must come first?" ¹¹He answered, "On the one hand, Eliyahu is coming and will restore all things; ¹²on the other hand, I tell you that Eliyahu has come already, and people did not recognize him but did whatever they pleased to him. In the same way, the Son of Man too is about to suffer at their hands." ¹³Then the *talmidim* understood that he was talking to them about Yochanan the Immerser.

¹⁴As they came up to the crowd, a man approached Yeshua, kneeled down in front of him, ¹⁵and said, "Sir, have mercy on my son, because he is an epileptic and has such terrible fits that he often falls into the fire or into the water. ¹⁶I brought him to your *talmidim*, but they couldn't heal him." ¹⁷Yeshua answered, "Perverted people, without any trust! How long will I be with you? How long must I put up with you? Bring him here to me!" ¹⁸Yeshua rebuked the demon, and it came out of

the boy, so that from that moment he was healed.

[19] Then the *talmidim* went to him privately and said, "Why couldn't we drive it out?" [20] He said to them, "Because you have such little trust! Yes! I tell you that if you have trust as tiny as a mustard seed, you will be able to say to this mountain, 'Move from here to there!' and it will move; indeed, nothing will be impossible for you!" [21]*

[22] As they were going about together in the Galil, Yeshua said to them, "The Son of Man is about to be betrayed into the hands of people [23] who will put him to death, and on the third day he will be raised." And they were filled with sadness.

[24] When they came to K'far-Nachum, the collectors of the half-*shekel* came to Kefa and said, "Doesn't your rabbi pay the Temple tax?" [25] "Of course he does," said Kefa. When he arrived home, Yeshua spoke first. "Shim'on, what's your opinion? The kings of the earth — from whom do they collect duties and taxes? From their sons or from others?" [26] "From others," he answered. "Then," said Yeshua, "The sons are exempt. [27] But to avoid offending them — go to the lake, throw out a line, and take the first fish you catch. Open its mouth, and you will find a *shekel*. Take it and give it to them for me and for you."

18 [1] At that moment the *talmidim* came to Yeshua and asked, "Who is the greatest in the Kingdom of Heaven?" [2] He called a child to him, stood him among them, [3] and said, "Yes! I tell you that unless you change and become like little children, you won't even enter the Kingdom of Heaven! [4] So the greatest in the Kingdom is whoever makes himself as

humble as this child. [5] Whoever welcomes one such child in my name welcomes me; [6] and whoever ensnares one of these little ones who trust me, it would be better for him to have a millstone hung around his neck and be drowned in the open sea! [7] Woe to the world because of snares! For there must be snares, but woe to the person who sets the snare!

[8] So if your hand or foot becomes a snare for you, cut it off and throw it away! Better that you should be maimed or crippled and obtain eternal life than keep both hands or both feet and be thrown into everlasting fire! [9] And if your eye is a snare for you, gouge it out and fling it away! Better that you should be one-eyed and obtain eternal life than keep both eyes and be thrown into the fire of Gey-Hinnom. [10] See that you never despise one of these little ones, for I tell you that their angels in heaven are continually seeing the face of my Father in heaven. [11]*

[12] "What's your opinion? What would somebody do who has a hundred sheep, and one of them wanders away? Won't

---

* Some manuscripts include verse 11: For the Son of Man came to save the lost.

---

co·ha·nim — priests
E·li·*ya*·hu — Elijah
the Ga·*lil* — Galilee
Gey-Hin·*nom* —Gehenna, hell
Ke·*fa* — Peter
K'far-Na·*chum* — Capernaum
Mo·*she* — Moses
Sa·*tan* — Satan, the Adversary
she·kel — coin, about one-half ounce
tal·mi·dim — disciples
To·rah-teachers — scribes
Ya·'a·*kov* — James
Ye·ru·sha·*la*·yim — Jerusalem
Ye·*shu*·a — Jesus
Yo·cha·*nan* — John
Yo·cha·*nan* the Immerser — John

---

* Some manuscripts include verse 21: But this kind does not go out except through prayer and fasting.

he leave the 99 on the hillsides and go off to find the stray? ¹³ And if he happens to find it? Yes! I tell you he is happier over it than over the 99 that never strayed! ¹⁴ Thus your Father in heaven does not want even one of these little ones to be lost.

¹⁵ "Moreover, if your brother commits a sin against you, go and show him his fault — but privately, just between the two of you. ¹⁶ If he doesn't listen, take one or two others with you so that **every accusation can be supported by the testimony of two or three witnesses.**ᶥ ¹⁷ If he refuses to hear them, tell the congregation; and if he refuses to listen even to the congregation, treat him as you would a pagan or a tax-collector. ¹⁸ Yes! I tell you people that whatever you prohibit on earth will be prohibited in heaven, and whatever you permit on earth will be permitted in heaven. ¹⁹ To repeat, I tell you that if two of you here on earth agree about anything people ask, it will be for them from my Father in heaven. ²⁰ For wherever two or three are assembled in my name, I am there with them."

²¹ Then Kefa came up and said to him, "Rabbi, how often can my brother sin against me and I have to forgive him? As many as seven times?" ²² "No, not seven times," answered Yeshua, "but seventy times seven! ²³ Because of this, the Kingdom of Heaven may be compared with a king who decided to settle accounts with his deputies. ²⁴ Right away they brought forward a man who owed him many millions, ²⁵ and since he couldn't pay, his master ordered that he, his wife, his children and all his possessions be sold to pay the debt. ²⁶ But the servant fell down before him. 'Be patient with me,' he begged, 'and I will pay back every-

thing.' ²⁷ So out of pity for him, the master let him go and forgave the debt.

²⁸ "But as that servant was leaving, he came upon one of his fellow servants who owed him some tiny sum. He grabbed him and began to choke him, crying, 'Pay back what you owe me!' ²⁹ His fellow servant fell before him and begged, 'Be patient with me, and I will pay you back.' ³⁰ But he refused; instead, he had him thrown in jail until he should repay the debt. ³¹ When the other servants saw what had happened, they were extremely distressed; and they went and told their master everything that had taken place. ³² Then the master summoned his servant and said, 'You wicked servant! I forgave you all that debt just because you begged me to do it. ³³ Shouldn't you have had pity on your fellow servant, just as I had pity on you?' ³⁴ And in anger his master turned him over to the jailers for punishment until he paid back everything he owed. ³⁵ This is how my heavenly Father will treat you, unless you each forgive your brother from your hearts."

19 ¹ When Yeshua had finished talking about these things, he left the Galil and traveled down the east side of the Yarden River until he passed the border of Y'hudah. ² Great crowds followed him, and he healed them there.

³ Some *P'rushim* came and tried to trap him by asking, "Is it permitted for a man to divorce his wife on any ground whatever?" ⁴ He replied, "Haven't you read that at the beginning the Creator **made them male and female,**ᵐ ⁵ and that he said, **'For this reason a man should leave his father and mother and be united with his wife, and the two are to become one flesh'?**ⁿ

---

l Deuteronomy 19:15

m Genesis 1:27, 5:2   *n* Genesis 2:24

6 Thus they are no longer two, but one. So then, no one should split apart what God has joined together."

7 They said to him, "Then why did Moshe give the commandment that a man should **hand his wife a *get*** and divorce her?"[o] 8 He answered, "Moshe allowed you to divorce your wives because your hearts are so hardened. But this is not how it was at the beginning. 9 Now what I say to you is that whoever divorces his wife, except on the ground of sexual immorality, and marries another woman commits adultery!"

10 The *talmidim* said to him, "If that is how things are between husband and wife, it would be better not to marry!" 11 He said to them, "Not everyone grasps this teaching, only those for whom it is meant. 12 For there are different reasons why men do not marry — some because they were born without the desire, some because they have been castrated, and some because they have renounced marriage for the sake of the Kingdom of Heaven. Whoever can grasp this, let him do so."

13 Then children were brought to him so that he might lay his hands on them and pray for them, but the *talmidim* rebuked the people bringing them. 14 However, Yeshua said, "Let the children come to me, don't stop them, for the Kingdom of Heaven belongs to such as these." 15 Then, after laying his hands on them, he went on his way.

16 A man approached Yeshua and said, "Rabbi, what good thing should I do in order to have eternal life?" He said to him, 17 "Why are you asking me about good? There is One who is good! But if you want to obtain eternal life, observe the *mitzvot*." 18 The man asked him, "Which ones?" and Yeshua said, "**Don't murder, don't commit adultery, don't steal, don't give false testimony,**[p] 19 **honor father and mother,**[q] and **love your neighbor as yourself.**"[r] 20 The young man said to him, "I have kept all these; where do I still fall short?" 21 Yeshua said to him, "If you are serious about reaching the goal, go and sell your possessions, give to the poor, and you will have riches in heaven. Then come, follow me!" 22 But when the young man heard this, he went away sad, because he was wealthy.

23 Then Yeshua said to his *talmidim*, "Yes. I tell you that it will be very hard for a rich man to enter the Kingdom of Heaven. 24 Furthermore, I tell you that it is easier for a camel to pass through a needle's eye than for a rich man to enter the Kingdom of God." 25 When the *talmidim* heard this they were utterly amazed. "Then who," they asked, "can be saved?" 26 Yeshua looked at them and said, "Humanly, this is impossible; but with God everything is possible." 27 Kefa replied, "Look, we have left everything and followed you. So what will we have?" 28 Yeshua said to them, "Yes. I tell you that in the regenerated world, when the Son of Man sits on his glorious throne, you who have followed me will also sit on twelve thrones and judge the twelve tribes of Israel.

---

o Deuteronomy 24:1, 3

p Exodus 20:13(13-16), Deuteronomy 5:17-20

q Exodus 20:12, Deuteronomy 5:16

r Leviticus 19:18

---

the Ga·**lil** — Galilee
get — divorce document
Ke·**fa** — Peter
*mitz·**vot*** — commandments
Mo·**she** — Moses
*P'ru·**shim*** — Pharisees
*tal·mi·**dim*** — disciples
Yar·**den** — Jordan
Ye·**shu**·a — Jesus
Y'hu·**dah** — Judea

²⁹ Everyone who has left houses, brothers, sisters, father, mother, children or fields for my sake will receive a hundred times more, and he will obtain eternal life. ³⁰ But many who are first will be last, and many who are last will be first.

20 ¹"The Kingdom of Heaven is like a farmer who went out at daybreak to hire workers for his vineyard. ² After agreeing with the workers on a wage of one denarius, [the standard daily wage,] he sent them off to his vineyard. ³ Then, on going out at about nine in the morning, he saw more men standing around in the market-square doing nothing, ⁴ and said to them, 'You go to the vineyard too — I'll pay you a fair wage.' So they went. ⁵ At noon, and again around three in the afternoon, he did the same thing. ⁶ About an hour before sundown, he went out, found still others standing around, and asked them, 'Why have you been standing here all day, doing nothing?' ⁷ They said to him, 'Because no one hired us.' 'You too,' he told them, 'go to the vineyard.'

⁸ "When evening came, the owner of the vineyard said to his foreman, 'Call the workers and pay them their wages, starting with the last ones hired and ending with the first.' ⁹ The workers who came an hour before sunset each received a denarius, ¹⁰ so the workers who came first expected they would get more, but each of them also received just a denarius. ¹¹ On receiving their wages, they began grumbling to the farmer, ¹²'These latecomers have worked only one hour, while we have borne the brunt of the day's work in the hot sun, yet you have put them on an equal footing with us!' ¹³ But he answered one of them, 'Look, friend, I'm not being unfair with you. Didn't you agree to work today for a denarius? ¹⁴ Now take your pay and go! I choose to give the last worker as much as I'm giving you. ¹⁵ Haven't I the right to do what I want with what belongs to me? Or do you begrudge my generosity?' ¹⁶ Thus the last ones will be first and the first last."

¹⁷ As Yeshua was going up to Yerushalayim, he took the twelve *talmidim* aside by themselves and said to them, as they went on their way, ¹⁸"We are now going up to Yerushalayim, where the Son of Man will be handed over to the head *cohanim* and *Torah*-teachers. They will sentence him to death ¹⁹ and turn him over to the *Goyim*, who will jeer at him, beat him and execute him on a stake as a criminal. But on the third day, he will be raised."

²⁰ Then Zavdai's sons came to Yeshua with their mother. She bowed down, begging a favor from him. ²¹ He said to her, "What do you want?" She replied, "Promise that when you become king, these two sons of mine may sit, one on your right and the other on your left." ²² But Yeshua answered, "You don't know what you are asking. Can you drink the cup that I am about to drink?" They said to him, "We can." ²³ He said to them, "Yes, you will drink my cup. But to sit on my right and on my left is not mine to give, it is for those for whom my Father has prepared it."

²⁴ Now when the other ten heard about this, they were outraged at the two brothers. ²⁵ But Yeshua called them and said, "You know that among the *Goyim*, those who are supposed to rule them become tyrants, and their superiors become dictators. ²⁶ Among you, it must not be like that. On the contrary, whoever among you wants to be a leader must become your servant, ²⁷ and whoever wants to be first must be your slave! ²⁸ For the Son of Man did not come to be served, but to serve — and to give his life as a ransom for many."

²⁹ As they were leaving Yericho, a

large crowd followed Yeshua. ³⁰Two blind men sitting by the side of the road heard that he was passing by and shouted, "Son of David! Have pity on us!" ³¹The crowd scolded them and told them to be quiet, but they shouted all the louder, "Lord! Son of David! Have pity on us!" ³²Yeshua stopped, called them and said, "What do you want me to do for you?" ³³They said to him, "Lord, open our eyes." ³⁴Filled with tenderness, Yeshua touched their eyes; and instantly they received their sight and followed him.

21 ¹As they were approaching Yerushalayim, they came to Beit-Pagey on the Mount of Olives. Yeshua sent two *talmidim* ²with these instructions: "Go into the village ahead of you, and you will immediately find a donkey tethered there with its colt. Untie them and bring them to me. ³If anyone says anything to you, tell him, 'The Lord needs them;' and he will let them go at once." ⁴This happened in order to fulfill what had been spoken through the prophet,

5   **"Say to the daughter of Tziyon,
    'Look! Your King is coming to
    you,
    riding humbly on a donkey,
    and on a colt, the offspring of a
    beast of burden!'"ˢ**

⁶So the *talmidim* went and did as Yeshua had directed them. ⁷They brought the donkey and the colt and put their robes on them, and Yeshua sat on them. ⁸Crowds of people carpeted the road with their clothing, while others cut branches from trees and spread them on the road. ⁹The crowds ahead of him and behind shouted,

  "Please! Deliver us!"

to the Son of David;

  **"Blessed is he who comes in the
   name of *Adonai!*"**

  "You in the highest heaven! **Please!
   Deliver us!"ᵗ**

¹⁰When he entered Yerushalayim, the whole city was stirred. "Who is this?" they asked. ¹¹And the crowds answered, "This is Yeshua, the prophet from Natzeret in the Galil."

¹²Yeshua entered the Temple grounds and drove out those who were doing business there, both the merchants and their customers. He upset the desks of the money-changers and knocked over the benches of those who were selling pigeons. ¹³He said to them, "It has been written, '**My house will be called a house of prayer.'ᵘ** But you are making it into a **den of robbers!"ᵛ**

¹⁴Blind and lame people came up to him in the Temple, and he healed them. ¹⁵But when the head *cohanim* and *Torah*-teachers saw the wonderful things he was doing, and the children crying out in the Temple, "**Please deliver us!"ʷ** to the Son of David, they

---

t Psalm 118:25-26   *u* Isaiah 56:7
v Jeremiah 7:11   *w* Psalm 118:25

A·do·nai — the LORD, Jehovah
Beit-Pa·gey — Bethphage
co·ha·nim — priests
Da·vid — David
the Ga·lil — Galilee
Go·yim — Gentiles, nations, pagans
Na·tze·ret — Nazareth
tal·mi·dim — disciples
To·rah-teachers — scribes
Tzi·yon — Zion
Ye·ri·cho — Jericho
Ye·ru·sha·la·yim — Jerusalem
Ye·shu·a — Jesus
Zav·dai — Zebedee

---

s Zechariah 9:9

were furious. ¹⁶They said to him, "Do you hear what they're saying?" Yeshua replied, "Of course! Haven't you ever read,

> 'From the mouth of children and infants
> you have prepared praise for yourself'?"^x

¹⁷With that, he left them and went on outside the city to Beit-Anyah, where he spent the night.

¹⁸The next morning, on his way back to the city, he felt hungry. ¹⁹Spotting a fig tree by the road, he went up to it but found nothing on it except leaves. So he said to it, "May you never again bear fruit!" and immediately the fig tree dried up. ²⁰The *talmidim* saw this and were amazed. "How did the fig tree dry up so quickly?'' they asked. ²¹Yeshua answered them, "Yes! I tell you, if you have trust and don't doubt, you will not only do what was done to this fig tree; but even if you say to this mountain, 'Go and throw yourself into the sea!' it will be done. ²²In other words, you will receive everything you ask for in prayer, no matter what it is, provided you have trust."

²³He went into the Temple area; and as he was teaching, the head *cohanim* and the elders of the people approached him and demanded, "What *s'mikhah* do you have that authorizes you to do these things? And who gave you this *s'mikhah*?" ²⁴Yeshua answered, "I too will ask you a question. If you answer it, then I will tell you by what *s'mikhah* I do these things. ²⁵The immersion of Yochanan — where did it come from? From Heaven or from a human source?" They discussed it among themselves: "If we say, 'From Heaven,' he

will say, 'Then why didn't you believe him?' ²⁶But if we say, 'From a human source,' we are afraid of the people, for they all regard Yochanan as a prophet." ²⁷So they answered Yeshua, "We don't know." And he replied, "Then I won't tell you by what *s'mikhah* I do these things.

²⁸"But give me your opinion: a man had two sons. He went to the first and said, 'Son, go and work today in the vineyard.' ²⁹He answered, 'I don't want to;' but later he changed his mind and went. ³⁰The father went to his other son and said the same thing. This one answered, 'I will, sir;' but he didn't go. ³¹Which of the two did what his father wanted?" "The first," they replied. "That's right!" Yeshua said to them. "I tell you that the tax-collectors and prostitutes are going into the Kingdom of God ahead of you! ³²For Yochanan came to you showing the path to righteousness, and you wouldn't trust him. The tax-collectors and prostitutes trusted him; but you, even after you saw this, didn't change your minds later and trust him.

³³"Now listen to another parable. There was a farmer who planted a vineyard. He put a wall around it, dug a pit for the winepress and built a tower; then he rented it to tenants and left. ³⁴When harvest-time came, he sent his servants to the tenants to collect his share of the crop. ³⁵But the tenants seized his servants — this one they beat up, that one they killed, another they stoned. ³⁶So he sent some other servants, more than the first group, and they did the same to them. ³⁷Finally, he sent them his son, saying, 'My son they will respect.' ³⁸But when the tenants saw the son, they said to each other, 'This is the heir. Come, let's kill him and take his inheritance!' ³⁹So they grabbed him, threw him out of the

---

x Psalm 8:3(2)

vineyard and killed him. ⁴⁰Now when the owner of the vineyard comes, what will he do to those tenants?" ⁴¹They answered him, "He will viciously destroy those vicious men and rent out the vineyard to other tenants who will give him his share of the crop when it's due." ⁴²Yeshua said to them, "Haven't you ever read in the *Tanakh*,

> **'The very rock which the builders rejected
> has become the cornerstone!
> This has come from *Adonai*,
> and in our eyes it is amazing'?**ʸ

⁴³Therefore, I tell you that the Kingdom of God will be taken away from you and given to the kind of people that will produce its fruit!" ⁴⁴*

⁴⁵As the head *cohanim* and the *P'rushim* listened to his stories, they saw that he was speaking about them. ⁴⁶But when they set about to arrest him, they were afraid of the crowds; because the crowds considered him a prophet.

22 ¹Yeshua again used parables in speaking to them: ²"The Kingdom of Heaven is like a king who prepared a wedding feast for his son, ³but when he sent his slaves to summon the invited guests to the wedding, they refused to come. ⁴So he sent some more slaves, instructing them to tell the guests, 'Look, I've prepared my banquet, I've slaughtered my bulls and my fattened cattle, and everything is ready. Come to the wedding!' ⁵But they weren't interested and went off, one to his farm, another to his business; ⁶and the rest grabbed his slaves, mistreated

them and killed them. ⁷The king was furious and sent his soldiers, who killed those murderers and burned down their city.

⁸"Then he said to his slaves, 'Well, the wedding feast is ready; but the ones who were invited didn't deserve it. ⁹So go out to the streetcorners and invite to the banquet as many as you find.' ¹⁰The slaves went out into the streets, gathered all the people they could find, the bad along with the good; and the wedding hall was filled with guests.

¹¹"Now when the king came in to look at the guests, he saw there a man who wasn't dressed for a wedding; so he asked him, ¹²'Friend, how did you get in here without wedding clothes?' The man was speechless. ¹³Then the king said to the servants, 'Bind him hand and foot, and throw him outside in the dark!' In that place people will wail and grind their teeth, ¹⁴for many are invited, but few are chosen."

¹⁵Then the *P'rushim* went away and put together a plan to trap Yeshua with his own words. ¹⁶They sent him some of their *talmidim* and some members of Herod's party. They said, "Rabbi, we know that you tell the truth and really teach what God's way is. You aren't concerned with what other people think about you, since you pay no attention to a person's status. ¹⁷So tell us your

---

* Some manuscripts include verse 44: Whoever falls on this stone will be broken in pieces; but if it falls on him, he will be crushed to powder!

ʸ Psalm 118:22-23

A·do·nai — the LORD, Jehovah
Beit-An·yah — Bethany
co·ha·nim — priests
Da·vid — David
P'ru·shim — Pharisees
s'mi·khah — ordination, authorization
tal·mi·dim — disciples
Ta·nakh — Hebrew Scriptures, "Old Testament"
To·rah-teachers — scribes
Ye·shu·a — Jesus
Yo·cha·nan — John

opinion: does *Torah* permit paying taxes to the Roman Emperor or not?" ¹⁸ Yeshua, however, knowing their malicious intent, said, "You hypocrites! Why are you trying to trap me? ¹⁹ Show me the coin used to pay the tax!" They brought him a denarius; ²⁰ and he asked them, "Whose name and picture are these?" ²¹ "The Emperor's," they replied. Yeshua said to them, "*Nu*, give the Emperor what belongs to the Emperor. And give to God what belongs to God!" ²² On hearing this, they were amazed; and they left him and went away.

²³ That same day, some *Tz'dukim* came to him. They are the ones who say there is no such thing as resurrection, so they put to him a *sh'eilah*: ²⁴ "Rabbi, Moshe said, '**If a man dies childless, his brother must marry his widow and have children to preserve the man's family line.'** ᶻ ²⁵ There were seven brothers. The first one married and then died; and since he had no children, he left his widow to his brother. ²⁶ The same thing happened to the second brother, and the third, and finally to all seven. ²⁷ After them all, the woman died. ²⁸ Now in the Resurrection — of the seven, whose wife will she be? For they all married her."

²⁹ Yeshua answered them, "The reason you go astray is that you are ignorant both of the *Tanakh* and of the power of God. ³⁰ For in the Resurrection, neither men nor women will marry; rather, they will be like angels in heaven. ³¹ And as for whether the dead are resurrected, haven't you read what God said to you, ³² '**I am the God of Avraham, the God of Yitzchak and the God of Ya'akov'?** ᵃ He is God not of the dead but of the living!"

³³ When the crowds heard how he taught, they were astounded; ³⁴ but when the *P'rushim* learned that he had silenced the *Tz'dukim*, they got together, ³⁵ and one of them who was a *Torah* expert asked a *sh'eilah* to trap him: ³⁶ "Rabbi, which of the *mitzvot* in the *Torah* is the most important?" ³⁷ He told him, "'**You are to love *Adonai* your God with all your heart and with all your soul and with all your strength.'** ᵇ ³⁸ This is the greatest and most important *mitzvah*. ³⁹ And a second is similar to it, '**You are to love your neighbor as yourself.'** ᶜ ⁴⁰ All of the *Torah* and the Prophets are dependent on these two *mitzvot*."

⁴¹ Then, turning to the assembled *P'rushim*, Yeshua put a *sh'eilah* to them: ⁴² "Tell me your view concerning the Messiah: whose son is he?" They said to him, "David's." ⁴³ "Then how is it," he asked them, "that David, inspired by the Spirit, calls him '**Lord**', when he says,

⁴⁴ '***Adonai* said to my Lord,
    "Sit here at my right hand
    until I put your enemies under
    your feet"'?** ᵈ

⁴⁵ If David thus calls him '**Lord**', how is he his son?" ⁴⁶ No one could think of anything to say in reply; and from that day on, no one dared put to him another *sh'eilah*.

23 ¹ Then Yeshua addressed the crowds and his *talmidim*: ² "The *Torah*-teachers and the *P'rushim*," he said, "sit in the seat of Moshe. ³ So whatever they tell you, take care to do it. But don't do what they do, because they talk but don't act! ⁴ They tie heavy loads onto people's shoulders but won't lift a finger to help carry them. ⁵ Everything they do is done to be seen by

---

ᶻ Deuteronomy 25:5-6   ᵃ Exodus 3:6

ᵇ Deuteronomy 6:5   ᶜ Leviticus 19:18
ᵈ Psalm 110:1

others; for they make their *t'fillin* broad and their *tzitziyot* long, ⁶they love the place of honor at banquets and the best seats in the synagogues, ⁷and they love being greeted deferentially in the marketplaces and being called 'Rabbi'.

⁸"But you are not to let yourselves be called 'Rabbi'; because you have one Rabbi, and you are all each other's brothers. ⁹And do not call anyone on earth 'Father', because you have one Father, and he is in heaven. ¹⁰Nor are you to let yourselves be called 'leaders', because you have one Leader, and he is the Messiah! ¹¹The greatest among you must be your servant, ¹²for whoever promotes himself will be humbled, and whoever humbles himself will be promoted.

¹³"But woe to you hypocritical *Torah*-teachers and *P'rushim*! For you are shutting the Kingdom of Heaven in people's faces, neither entering yourselves nor allowing those who wish to enter to do so. ¹⁴*

¹⁵"Woe to you hypocritical *Torah*-teachers and *P'rushim*! You go about over land and sea to make one proselyte; and when you succeed, you make him twice as fit for Gey-Hinnom as you are!

¹⁶"Woe to you, you blind guides! You say, 'If someone swears by the Temple, he is not bound by his oath; but if he swears by the gold in the Temple, he is bound. ¹⁷You blind fools! Which is more important? the gold? or the Temple which makes the gold holy? ¹⁸And you say, 'If someone swears by the altar, he is not bound by his oath;

but if he swears by the offering on the altar, he is bound.' ¹⁹Blind men! Which is more important? the sacrifice? or the altar which makes the sacrifice holy? ²⁰So someone who swears by the altar swears by it and everything on it. ²¹And someone who swears by the Temple swears by it and the One who lives in it. ²²And someone who swears by heaven swears by God's throne and the One who sits on it.

²³"Woe to you hypocritical *Torah*-teachers and *P'rushim*! You pay your tithes of mint, dill and cumin; but you have neglected the weightier matters of the *Torah* — justice, mercy, trust. These are the things you should have attended to — without neglecting the others! ²⁴Blind guides! — straining out a gnat, meanwhile swallowing a camel!

²⁵"Woe to you hypocritical *Torah*-teachers and *P'rushim*! You clean the outside of the cup and the dish, but inside they are full of robbery and self-indulgence. ²⁶Blind *Parush*! First clean

=====

A·do·nai — the LORD, Jehovah
Av·ra·ham — Abraham
Da·vid — David
dav·ven·ing — praying
Gey-Hin·nom —Gehenna, hell
mitz·vah — commandment, principle
mitz·vot — commandments, principles
Mo·she — Moses
nu — so
Pa·*rush* — Pharisee
P'ru·shim — Pharisees
sh·'ei·lah — question
tal·mi·dim — disciples
Ta·nakh — Hebrew Scriptures,"Old Testament"
t'fil·lin — phylacteries
To·rah — Teaching, "Law"; Pentateuch
To·rah-teachers — scribes
Tz'du·kim — Sadducees
tzi·tzi·yot — ritual fringes
Ya·'a·kov — Jacob
Ye·shu·a — Jesus
Yitz·chak — Isaac

---

* Some manuscripts include verse 14: Woe to you hypocritical *Torah*-teachers and *P'ru-shim*! For you swallow up widows' houses while making a show of *davvening* at great length. Because of this your punishment will be all the worse!

the inside of the cup, so that the outside may be clean too.

²⁷"Woe to you hypocritical *Torah*-teachers and *P'rushim*! You are like whitewashed tombs, which look fine on the outside but inside are full of dead people's bones and all kinds of rottenness. ²⁸Likewise, you appear to people from the outside to be good and honest, but inwardly you are full of hypocrisy and far from *Torah*.

²⁹"Woe to you hypocritical *Torah*-teachers and *P'rushim*! You build tombs for the prophets and decorate the graves of the *tzaddikim*, ³⁰and you say, 'Had we lived when our fathers did, we would never have taken part in killing the prophets.' ³¹In this you testify against yourselves that you are worthy descendants of those who murdered the prophets. ³²Go ahead then, finish what your fathers started!

³³"You snakes! Sons of snakes! How can you escape being condemned to Gey-Hinnom? ³⁴Therefore I am sending you prophets and sages and *Torah*-teachers — some of them you will kill, indeed, you will have them executed on stakes as criminals; some you will flog in your synagogues and pursue from town to town. ³⁵And so, on you will fall the guilt for all the innocent blood that has ever been shed on earth, from the blood of innocent Hevel to the blood of Z'kharyah Ben-Berekhyah, whom you murdered between the Temple and the altar. ³⁶Yes! I tell you that all this will fall on this generation!

³⁷"Yerushalayim! Yerushalayim! You kill the prophets! You stone those who are sent to you! How often I wanted to gather your children, just as a hen gathers her chickens under her wings, but you refused! ³⁸Look! **God is abandoning your house to you, leaving it desolate.**ᵉ ³⁹For I tell you, from now

e Jeremiah 22:5

on, you will not see me again until you say, '**Blessed is he who comes in the name of Adonai.**'ᶠ

24 ¹As Yeshua left the Temple and was going away, his *talmidim* came and called his attention to its buildings. ²But he answered them, "You see all these? Yes! I tell you, they will be totally destroyed — not a single stone will be left standing!"

³When he was sitting on the Mount of Olives, the *talmidim* came to him privately. "Tell us," they said, "when will these things happen? And what will be the sign that you are coming, and that the *'olam hazeh* is ending?"

⁴Yeshua replied: "Watch out! Don't let anyone fool you! ⁵For many will come in my name, saying, 'I am the Messiah!' and they will lead many astray. ⁶You will hear the noise of wars nearby and the news of wars far off; see to it that you don't become frightened. Such things must happen, but the end is yet to come. ⁷For peoples will fight each other, nations will fight each other, and there will be famines and earthquakes in various parts of the world; ⁸all this is but the beginning of the 'birth-pains'. ⁹At that time you will be arrested and handed over to be punished and put to death, and all peoples will hate you because of me. ¹⁰At that time many will be trapped into betraying and hating each other, ¹¹many false prophets will appear and fool many people; ¹²and many people's love will grow cold because of increased distance from *Torah*. ¹³But whoever holds out till the end will be delivered. ¹⁴And this Good News about the Kingdom will be announced throughout the whole world as a witness to all the *Goyim*. It is then that the end will come.

¹⁵"So when you see the **abomination that causes devastation** spoken about

f Psalm 118:26

through the prophet Dani'el standing in the Holy Place"[g] (let the reader understand the allusion), [16]"that will be the time for those in Y'hudah to escape to the hills. [17]If someone is on the roof, he must not go down to gather his belongings from his house; [18]if someone is in the field, he must not turn back to get his coat. [19]What a terrible time it will be for pregnant women and nursing mothers! [20]Pray that you will not have to escape in winter or on Shabbat. [21]For their will be trouble then worse than there has ever been from the beginning of the world until now, and there will be nothing like it again![h] [22]Indeed, if the length of this time had not been limited, no one would survive; but for the sake of those who have been chosen, its length will be limited.

[23]"At that time, if someone says to you, 'Look! Here's the Messiah!' or, 'There he is!' don't believe him. [24]for there will appear false messiahs and false prophets performing great miracles — amazing things! — so as to fool even the chosen, if possible. [25]There! I have told you in advance! [26]So if people say to you, 'Listen! He's out in the desert!' don't go; or, 'Look! He's hidden away in a secret room!' don't believe it. [27]For when the Son of Man does come, it will be like lightning that flashes out of the east and fills the sky to the western horizon. [28]Wherever there's a dead body, that's where you find the vultures.

[29]But immediately following the trouble of those times,

the sun will grow dark,
the moon will stop shining,[i]

the stars will fall from the sky,
and the powers in heaven will be
shaken.[j]

[30]"Then the sign of the Son of Man will appear in the sky, **all the tribes of the Land will mourn,**[k] and they will see **the Son of Man coming on the clouds** of heaven with tremedous power and glory.[l] [31]He will send out his angels **with a great shofar;**[m] and they will gather together his chosen people from the four winds, from one end of heaven to the other.

[32]"Now let the fig tree teach you its lesson: when its branches begin to sprout and leaves appear, you know that summer is approaching. [33]In the same way, when you see all these things, you are to know that the time is near, right at the door. [34]Yes! I tell you that this people will certainly not pass away before all these things happen. [35]Heaven and earth will pass away, but my words will never pass away.

[36]"But when that day and hour will come no one knows — not the angels in heaven, not the Son, only the Father.

j Isaiah 34:4, Haggai 2:6, 21
k Zechariah 12:10, 14   l Daniel 7:13-14
m Isaiah 27:13

A·do·**nai** — the LORD, Jehovah
Da·ni·**'el** — Daniel
Gey-Hin·**nom** — Gehenna, hell
Go·**yim** — Gentiles, nations, pagans
He·**vel** — Abel
'ol·**am** ha·**zeh** — this world/age
P'ru·**shim** — Pharisees
Shab·**bat** — the Sabbath
sho·**far** — ram's horn, trumpet
tal·mi·**dim** — disciples
To·**rah** — Teaching, "Law"; Pentateuch
Tor·**rah**-teachers — scribes
tzad·di·**kim** — righteous men
Ye·ru·sha·**la**·yim — Jerusalem
Ye·**shu**·a — Jesus
Y'hu·**dah** — Judea
Z'khar·**yah** Ben-Be·rekh·**yah** — Zecharian the son of Berechiah

g Daniel 9:27, 11:31, 12:11
h Joel 2:2, Daniel 12:1
i Isaiah 13:10; Ezekiel 32:7; Joel 2:10, 3:4 (2:31), 4:15 (3:15)

³⁷ For the Son of Man's coming will be just as it was in the days of Noach. ³⁸ Back then, before the Flood, people went on eating and drinking, taking wives and becoming wives, right up till the day Noach entered the ark; ³⁹ and they didn't know what was happening until the Flood came and swept them all away. It will be just like that when the Son of Man comes. ⁴⁰ Then there will be two men in a field — one will be taken and the other left behind. ⁴¹ There will be two women grinding flour at the mill — one will be taken and the other left behind. ⁴² So stay alert, because you don't know on what day your Lord will come. ⁴³ But you do know this: had the owner of the house known when the thief was coming, he would have stayed awake and not allowed his house to be broken into. ⁴⁴ Therefore you too must always be ready, for the Son of Man will come when you are not expecting him.

⁴⁵ "Who is the faithful and sensible servant whose master puts him in charge of the household staff, to give them their food at the proper time? ⁴⁶ It will go well with that servant if he is found doing his job when his master comes. ⁴⁷ Yes, I tell you that he will put him in charge of all he owns. ⁴⁸ But if that servant is wicked and says to himself, 'My master is taking his time;' ⁴⁹ and he starts beating up his fellow servants and spends his time eating and drinking with drunkards; ⁵⁰ then his master will come on a day the servant does not expect, at a time he doesn't know; ⁵¹ and he will cut him in two and put him with the hypocrites, where people will wail and grind their teeth!

25 ¹ "The Kingdom of Heaven at that time will be like ten bridesmaids who took their lamps and went out to meet the groom. ² Five of them were foolish and five were sensible.

³ The foolish ones took lamps with them but no oil, ⁴ whereas the others took flasks of oil with their lamps. ⁵ Now the bridegroom was late, so they all went to sleep. ⁶ It was the middle of the night when the cry rang out, 'The bridegroom is here! Go out to meet him!' ⁷ The girls all woke up and prepared their lamps for lighting. ⁸ The foolish ones said to the sensible ones, 'Give us some of your oil, because our lamps are going out.' ⁹ 'No,' they replied, 'there may not be enough for both you and us. Go to the oil dealers and buy some for yourselves.' ¹⁰ But as they were going off to buy, the bridegroom came. Those who were ready went with him to the wedding feast, and the door was shut. ¹¹ Later, the other bridesmaids came. 'Sir! Sir!' they cried, 'Let us in!' ¹² But he answered, 'Indeed! I tell you, I don't know you!' ¹³ So stay alert, because you know neither the day nor the hour.

¹⁴ "For it will be like a man about to leave home for awhile, who entrusted his possessions to his servants. ¹⁵ To one he gave five talents [equivalent to a hundred years' wages]; to another, two talents; and to another, one talent — to each according to his ability. Then he left. ¹⁶ The one who had received five talents immediately went out, invested it and earned another five. ¹⁷ Similarly, the one given two earned another two. ¹⁸ But the one given one talent went off, dug a hole in the ground and hid his master's money.

¹⁹ "After a long time, the master of those servants returned to settle accounts with them. ²⁰ The one who had received five talents came forward bringing the other five and said, 'Sir, you gave me five talents; here, I have made five more.' ²¹ His master said to him, 'Excellent! You are a good and trustworthy servant. You have been

faithful with a small amount, so I will put you in charge of a large amount. Come and join in your master's happiness!' ²² Also the one who had received two came forward and said, 'Sir, you gave me two talents; here, I have made two more.' ²³ His master said to him, 'Excellent! You are a good and trustworthy servant. You have been faithful with a small amount, so I will put you in charge of a large amount. Come and join in your master's happiness!'

²⁴ "Now the one who had received one talent came forward and said, 'I knew you were a hard man. You harvest where you didn't plant and gather where you didn't sow seed. ²⁵ I was afraid, so I went and hid your talent in the ground. Here! Take what belongs to you!' ²⁶ 'You wicked, lazy servant!' said his master, 'So you knew, did you, that I harvest where I haven't planted? and that I gather where I didn't sow seed? ²⁷ Then you should have deposited my money with the bankers, so that when I returned, I would at least have gotten back interest with my capital! ²⁸ Take the talent from him and give it to the one who has ten. ²⁹ For everyone who has something will be given more, so that he will have more than enough; but from anyone who has nothing, even what he does have will be taken away. ³⁰ As for this worthless servant, throw him out in the dark, where people will wail and grind their teeth!'

³¹ "When the Son of Man comes in his glory, accompanied by all the angels, he will sit on his glorious throne. ³² All the nations will be assembled before him, and he will separate people one from another as a shepherd separates sheep from goats. ³³ The 'sheep' he will place at his right hand and the 'goats' at his left.

³⁴ "Then the King will say to those on his right, 'Come, you whom my Father has blessed, take your inheritance, the Kingdom prepared for you from the founding of the world. ³⁵ For I was hungry and you gave me food, I was thirsty and you gave me something to drink, I was a stranger and you made me your guest, ³⁶ I needed clothes and you provided them, I was sick and you took care of me, I was in prison and you visited me.' ³⁷ Then the people who have done what God wants will reply, 'Lord, when did we see you hungry and feed you, or thirsty and give you something to drink? ³⁸ When did we see you a stranger and make you our guest, or needing clothes and provide them? ³⁹ When did we see you sick or in prison, and visit you?' ⁴⁰ The King will say to them, 'Yes! I tell you that whenever you did these things for one of the least important of these brothers of mine, you did them for me!'

⁴¹ "Then he will also speak to those on his left, saying, 'Get away from me, you who are cursed! Go off into the fire prepared for the Adversary and his angels! ⁴² For I was hungry and you gave me no food, thirsty and you gave me nothing to drink, ⁴³ a stranger and you did not welcome me, needing clothes and you did not give them to me, sick and in prison and you did not visit me.' ⁴⁴ Then they too will reply, 'Lord, when did we see you hungry, thirsty, a stranger, needing clothes, sick or in prison, and not take care of you?' ⁴⁵ And he will answer them, 'Yes! I tell you that whenever you refused to do it for the least important of these people, you refused to do it for me!' ⁴⁶ They will go off to eternal punishment, but those who have done what God wants will go to eternal life."

26 ¹ When Yeshua had finished speaking, he said to his

No·ach — Noah

talmidim, ²"As you know, *Pesach* is two days away, and the Son of Man will be handed over to be nailed to the execution-stake."

³Then the head *cohanim* and the elders of the people gathered in the palace of Kayafa the *cohen hagadol.* ⁴They made plans to arrest Yeshua surreptitiously and have him put to death; ⁵but they said, "Not during the festival, or the people will riot."

⁶Yeshua was in Beit-Anyah, at the home of Shim'on, the man who had had the repulsive skin disease. ⁷A woman with an alabaster jar filled with very expensive perfume approached Yeshua while he was eating and began pouring it on his head. ⁸When the *talmidim* saw it, they became very angry. "Why this waste?" they asked. ⁹"This could have been sold for a lot of money and given to the poor." ¹⁰But Yeshua, aware of what was going on, said to them, "Why are you bothering this woman? She has done a beautiful thing for me. ¹¹The poor you will always have with you, but you will not always have me. ¹²She poured this perfume on me to prepare my body for burial. ¹³Yes! I tell you that throughout the whole world, wherever this Good News is proclaimed, what she has done will be told in her memory."

¹⁴Then one of the Twelve, the one called Y'hudah from K'riot, went to the head *cohanim* ¹⁵and said, "What are you willing to give me if I turn Yeshua over to you?" **They counted out thirty silver coins and gave them** to Y'hudah.*ⁿ* ¹⁶From then on he looked for a good opportunity to betray him.

¹⁷On the first day for *matzah,* the *talmidim* came to Yeshua and asked, "Where do you want us to prepare your *Seder?*" ¹⁸"Go into the city, to so-and-so," he replied, "and tell him that the

Rabbi says, 'My time is near, my *talmidim* and I are celebrating *Pesach* at your house.'" ¹⁹The *talmidim* did as Yeshua directed and prepared the *Seder.*

²⁰When evening came, Yeshua reclined with the twelve *talmidim;* ²¹and as they were eating, he said, "Yes, I tell you that one of you is going to betray me." ²²They became terribly upset and began asking him, one after the other, "Lord, you don't mean me, do you?" ²³He answered, "The one who dips his *matzah* in the dish with me is the one who will betray me. ²⁴The Son of Man will die just as the *Tanakh* says he will; but woe to that man by whom the Son of Man is betrayed! It would have been better for him had he never been born!" ²⁵Y'hudah, the one who was betraying him, then asked, "Surely, Rabbi, you don't mean me?" He answered, "The words are yours."

²⁶While they were eating, Yeshua took a piece of *matzah,* made the *b'rakhah,* broke it, gave it to the *talmidim* and said, "Take! Eat! This is my body!" ²⁷Also he took a cup of wine, made the *b'rakhah,* and gave it to them, saying, "All of you, drink from it! ²⁸For this is my blood, which ratifies the New Covenant, my blood shed on behalf of many, so that they may have their sins forgiven. ²⁹I tell you, I will not drink this 'fruit of the vine' again until the day I drink new wine with you in my Father's Kingdom."

³⁰After singing the *Hallel,* they went out to the Mount of Olives. ³¹Yeshua then said to them, "Tonight you will all lose faith in me, as the *Tanakh* says, **'I will strike the shepherd dead, and the sheep of the flock will be scattered.'**º ³²But after I have been raised, I will go ahead of you into the Galil." ³³"I will never lose faith in you," Kefa answered, "even if everyone else does." ³⁴Yeshua

ⁿ Zechariah 11:12

º Zechariah 13:7

said to him, "Yes! I tell you that tonight before the rooster crows, you will disown me three times!" 35 "Even if I must die with you," Kefa replied, "I will never disown you!" And all the *talmidim* said the same thing.

36 Then Yeshua went with his *talmidim* to a place called *Gat-Sh'manim* and said to them, "Sit here while I go over there and pray." 37 He took with him Kefa and Zavdai's two sons. Grief and anguish came over him, 38 and he said to them, "My heart is so filled with sadness that I could die! Remain here and stay awake with me." 39 Going on a little farther, he fell on his face, praying, "My Father, if possible, let this cup pass from me! Yet — not what I want, but what you want!" 40 He returned to the *talmidim* and found them sleeping. He said to Kefa, "Were you so weak that you couldn't stay awake with me for even an hour? 41 Stay awake, and pray that you will not be put to the test — the spirit indeed is eager, but human nature is weak."

42 A second time he went off and prayed. "My Father, if this cup cannot pass away unless I drink it, let what you want be done." 43 Again he returned and found them sleeping, their eyes were so heavy.

44 Leaving them again, he went off and prayed a third time, saying the same words. 45 Then he came to the *talmidim* and said, "For now, go on sleeping, take your rest.... Look! The time has come for the Son of Man to be betrayed into the hands of sinners. 46 Get up! Let's go! Here comes my betrayer!"

47 While Yeshua was still speaking, Y'hudah (one of the Twelve!) came, and with him a large crowd carrying swords and clubs, from the head *cohanim* and elders of the people. 48 The betrayer had arranged to give

them a signal: "The man I kiss is the one you want — grab him!" 49 He went straight up to Yeshua, said, "*Shalom*, Rabbi!" and kissed him. 50 Yeshua said to him, "Friend, do what you came to do." Then they moved forward, laid hold of Yeshua and arrested him.

51 At that, one of the men with Yeshua reached for his sword, drew it out and struck at the servant of the *cohen hagadol*, cutting off his ear. 52 Yeshua said to him, "Put your sword back where it belongs, for everyone who uses the sword will die by the sword. 53 Don't you know that I can ask my Father, and he will instantly provide more than a dozen armies of angels to help me? 54 But if I did that, how could the passages in the *Tanakh* be fulfilled that say it has to happen this way?"

55 Then Yeshua adressed the crowd: "So you came out to take me with swords and clubs, the way you would the leader of a rebellion? Every day I sat in the Temple court, teaching; and you didn't seize me then. 56 But all this has happened so that what the prophets

---

Beit-An·yah — Bethany
b'ra·khah — blessing
co·ha·nim — priests
co·hen ha·ga·dol — high priest
the Ga·lil — Galilee
Gat-Sh'ma·nim — Gethsemane
Hal·lel — psalms of praise
Ka·ya·fa — Caiaphas
Ke·fa — Peter
ma·tzah — unleavened bread
Pe·sach — Passover
Se·der — Passover eve meal
Sha·lom! — Peace! (greeting)
Shim·'on — Simon
tal·mi·dim — disciples
Ta·nakh — Hebrew Scriptures, "Old Testament"
Ye·shu·a — Jesus
Y'hu·dah — Judas
Y'hu·dah from K'ri·ot — Judas Iscariot
Zav·dai — Zebedee

wrote may be fulfilled." Then the *talmidim* all deserted him and ran away.

⁵⁷Those who had seized Yeshua led him off to Kayafa the *cohen hagadol,* where the *Torah*-teachers and elders were assembled. ⁵⁸Kefa followed him at a distance as far as the courtyard of the *cohen hagadol*; then he went inside and sat down with the guards to see what the outcome would be.

⁵⁹The head *cohanim* and the whole *Sanhedrin* looked for some false evidence against Yeshua, so that they might put him to death. ⁶⁰But they didn't find any, even though many liars came forward to give testimony. At last, however, two people came forward and said, ⁶¹"This man said, 'I can tear down God's Temple and build it again in three days.'" ⁶²The *cohen hagadol* stood up and said, "Have you nothing to say to the accusation these men are making?" ⁶³Yeshua remained silent. The *cohen hagadol* said to him, "I put you under oath! By the living God, tell us if you are the *Mashiach,* the Son of God!" ⁶⁴Yeshua said to him, "The words are your own. But I tell you that one day you will see **the Son of Man sitting at the right hand of** *HaG'vurah* and **coming on the clouds of heaven."**ᵖ ⁶⁵At this, the *cohen hagadol* tore his robes. "Blasphemy!" he said. "Why do we still need witnesses? You heard him blaspheme! ⁶⁶What is your verdict?" "Guilty," they answered. "He deserves death!" ⁶⁷Then they spit in his face and pounded him with their fists; and those who were beating him ⁶⁸said, "Now, you 'Messiah', 'prophesy' to us: who hit you that time?"

⁶⁹Kefa was sitting outside in the courtyard when a servant girl came up to him. "You too were with Yeshua from the Galil," she said. ⁷⁰But he

denied it in front of everyone — "I don't know what you're talking about!" ⁷¹He went out onto the porch, and another girl saw him and said to the people there, "This man was with Yeshua of Natzeret." ⁷²Again he denied it, swearing, "I don't know the man!" ⁷³After a little while, the bystanders approached Kefa and said, "You must be one of them — your accent gives you away." ⁷⁴This time he began to invoke a curse on himself as he swore, "I do not know the man!" — and immediately a rooster crowed. ⁷⁵Kefa remembered what Yeshua had said, "Before the rooster crows, you will disown me three times;" and he went outside and cried bitterly.

27 ¹Early in the morning, all the head *cohanim* and elders met to plan how to bring about Yeshua's death. ²Then they put him in chains, led him away and handed him over to Pilate the governor.

³When Y'hudah, who had betrayed him, saw that Yeshua had been condemned, he was seized with remorse and returned the thirty silver coins to the head *cohanim* and elders, ⁴saying, "I sinned in betraying an innocent man to death." "What is that to us?" they answered. "That's your problem." ⁵Hurling the pieces of silver into the sanctuary, he left; then he went off and hanged himself.

⁶The head *cohanim* took the silver coins and said, "It is prohibited to put this into the Temple treasury, because it is blood money." ⁷So they decided to use it to buy the potter's field as a cemetery for foreigners. ⁸This is how it came to be called the Field of Blood, a name it still bears. ⁹Then what Yirmeyahu the prophet spoke was fulfilled, **"And they took the thirty silver coins, which was the price the people of Israel had agreed to pay for him,**

---

p Daniel 7:13, Psalm 110:1

[10]and used them to buy the potter's field, just as the Lord directed me."[q]

[11]Meanwhile, Yeshua was brought before the governor, and the governor put this question to him: "Are you the King of the Jews?" Yeshua answered, "The words are yours." [12]But when he was accused by the head *cohanim* and elders, he gave no answer. [13]Then Pilate said to him, "Don't you hear all these charges they are making against you?" [14]But to the governor's great amazement, he did not say a single word in reply to the accusations.

[15]It was the governor's custom during a festival to set free one prisoner, whomever the crowd asked for. [16]There was at that time a notorious prisoner being held, named Yeshua Bar-Abba. [17]So when a crowd had gathered, Pilate said to them, "Whom do you want me to set free for you? Bar-Abba? or Yeshua, called 'the Messiah'?" [18]For he understood that it was out of jealousy that they had handed him over. [19]While he was sitting in court, his wife sent him a message, "Leave that innocent man alone. Today in a dream I suffered terribly because of him." [20]But the head *cohanim* persuaded the crowd to ask for Bar-Abba's release and to have Yeshua executed on the stake. [21]"Which of the two do you want me to set free for you?" asked the governor. "Bar-Abba!" they answered. [22]Pilate said to them, "Then what should I do with Yeshua, called 'the Messiah'?" They all said, "Put him to death on the stake! Put him to death on the stake!" [23]When he asked, "Why? What crime has he committed?" they shouted all the louder, "Put him to death on the stake!" [24]When Pilate saw that he was accomplishing nothing, but rather that a riot was starting, he took water, washed his hands in front of the crowd, and said, "My hands are clean of this man's blood; it's your responsibility." [25]All the people answered, "His blood is on us and on our children!" [26]Then he released to them Bar-Abba; but Yeshua, after having him whipped, he handed over to be executed on a stake.

[27]The governor's soldiers took Yeshua into the headquarters building, and the whole battalion gathered around him. [28]They stripped off his clothes and put on him a scarlet robe, [29]wove thorn-branches into a crown and put it on his head, and put a stick in his right hand. Then they kneeled down in front of him and made fun of him: "Hail to the King of the Jews!" [30]They spit on him and used the stick to beat him about the head. [31]When they had finished ridiculing him, they took off the robe, put his own clothes back on him and led him away to be nailed to the execution-stake.

[32]As they were leaving, they met a man from Cyrene named Shim'on; and they forced him to carry Yeshua's execution-stake. [33]When they arrived

---

Bar- Ab·ba — Barabbas
co·ha·nim — priests
co·hen ha·ga·dol — high priest
the Ga·lil — Galilee
Ha· G'vu·rah — the Power, God
Ka·ya·fa — Caiaphas
Ke·fa — Peter
Ma·shi·ach — Messiah
Na·tze·ret — Nazareth
San·hed·rin — Jewish religious court
Shim·'on — Simon
tal·mi·dim — disciples
Ta·nakh — Hebrew Scriptures, "Old Testament"
To·rah-teachers — scribes
Ye·shu·a — Jesus
Ye·shu·a Bar-Ab·ba — Jesus Barabbas
Y'hu·dah — Judas
Yir·me·ya·hu — Jeremiah

---

[q] Zechariah 11:12-13

at a place called Gulgolta (which means "place of a skull"), [34]they gave him wine mixed with bitter gall to drink; but after tasting it, he would not drink it. [35]After they had nailed him to the stake, they divided his clothes among them by throwing dice. [36]Then they sat down to keep watch over him there. [37]Above his head they placed the written notice stating the charge against him,

THIS IS YESHUA
THE KING OF THE JEWS

[38]Then two robbers were placed on execution-stakes with him, one on the right and one on the left. [39]People passing by hurled insults at him, **shaking their heads**[r] [40]and saying, "So you can destroy the Temple, can you, and rebuild it in three days? Save yourself, if you are the Son of God, and come down from the stake!" [41]Likewise, the head *cohanim* jeered at him, along with the *Torah*-teachers and elders, [42]"He saved others, but he can't save himself!" "So he's King of Israel, is he? Let him come down now from the stake! Then we'll believe him!" [43]"He **trusted God? So, let him rescue him — if he wants him!**[s] After all, he did say, 'I'm the Son of God'!" [44]Even the robbers nailed up with him insulted him in the same way.

[45]From noon until three o'clock in the afternoon, all the Land was covered with darkness. [46]At about three, Yeshua uttered a loud cry, "*Eli! Eli! L'mah sh'vaktani?* (My God! My God! Why have you deserted me?)"[t] [47]On hearing this, some of the bystanders said, "He's calling for Eliyahu." [48]Immediately one of them ran and took a sponge, soaked it in **vinegar**, put it on a stick and **gave** it

to him **to drink.**[u] [49]The rest said, "Wait! Let's see if Eliyahu comes and rescues him." [50]But Yeshua, again crying out in a loud voice, yielded up his spirit.

[51]At that moment the *parokhet* in the Temple was ripped in two from top to bottom; and there was an earthquake, with rocks splitting apart. [52]Also the graves were opened, and the bodies of many holy people who had died were raised to life; [53]and after Yeshua rose, they came out of the graves and went into the holy city, where many people saw them. [54]When the Roman officer and those with him who were keeping watch over Yeshua saw the earthquake and what was happening, they were awestruck and said, "He really was a son of God."

[55]There were many women there, looking on from a distance; they had followed Yeshua from the Galil, helping him. [56]Among them were Miryam from Magdala, Miryam the mother of Ya'akov and Yosef, and the mother of Zavdai's sons.

[57]Towards evening, there came a wealthy man from Ramatayim named Yosef, who was himself a *talmid* of Yeshua. [58]He approached Pilate and asked for Yeshua's body, and Pilate ordered it to be given to him. [59]Yosef took the body, wrapped it in a clean linen sheet, [60]and laid it in his own tomb, which he had recently had cut out of the rock. After rolling a large stone in front of the entrance to the tomb, he went away. [61]Miryam of Magdala and the other Miryam stayed there, sitting opposite the grave.

[62]Next day, after the preparation, the head *cohanim* and the *P'rushim* went together to Pilate [63]and said, "Sir, we remember that that deceiver said while he was still alive, 'After three days I will be raised.' [64]Therefore, order that the

---

r Psalm 22:8(7)   s Psalm 22:9(8)

t Psalm 22:2(1)

u Psalm 69:22(21)

grave be made secure till the third day; otherwise the *talmidim* may come, steal him away and say to the people, 'He was raised from the dead;' and the last deception will be worse than the first." ⁶⁵Pilate said to them, "You may have your guard. Go and make the grave as secure as you know how." ⁶⁶So they went and made the grave secure by sealing the stone and putting the guard on watch.

28 ¹After *Shabbat*, toward dawn on Sunday, Miryam of Magdala and the other Miryam went to see the grave. ²Suddenly there was a violent earthquake, for an angel of *Adonai* came down from heaven, rolled away the stone and sat on it. ³His appearance was like lightning, and his clothes were as white as snow. ⁴The guards were so terrified at him that they trembled and became like dead men. ⁵But the angel said to the women, "Don't be afraid. I know you are looking for Yeshua, who was executed on the stake. ⁶He is not here, because he has been raised — just as he said! Come and look at the place where he lay. ⁷Then go quickly and tell the *talmidim*, 'He has been raised from the dead, and now he is going to the Galil ahead of you. You will see him there.' Now I have told you."

⁸So they left the tomb quickly, frightened yet filled with joy; and they ran to give the news to his *talmidim*. ⁹Suddenly Yeshua met them and said, "*Shalom!*" They came up and took hold of his feet as they fell down in front of him. ¹⁰Then Yeshua said to them, "Don't be afraid! Go and tell my brothers to go to the Galil, and they will see me there."

¹¹As they were going, some of the guards went into the city and reported to the head *cohanim* everything that had happened. ¹²Then they met with the elders; and after discussing the matter, they gave the soldiers a sizeable sum of money ¹³and said to them, "Tell people, 'His *talmidim* came during the night and stole his body while we were sleeping.' ¹⁴If the governor hears of it, we will put things right with him and keep you from getting in trouble." ¹⁵The soldiers took the money and did as they were told, and this story has been spread about by Judeans till this very day.

¹⁶So the eleven *talmidim* went to the hill in the Galil where Yeshua had told them to go. ¹⁷When they saw him, they prostrated themselves before him; but some hesitated. ¹⁸Yeshua came and talked with them. He said, "All authority in heaven and on earth has been given to me. ¹⁹Therefore, go and make people from all nations into *talmidim*, immersing them into the reality of the Father, the Son and the *Ruach Ha-Kodesh*, ²⁰and teaching them to obey everything that I have commanded you. And remember! I will be with you always, yes, even until the end of the age."

A·do·nai — the LORD, Jehovah
co·ha·nim — priests
E·li! E·li! L' mah sh'vak·ta·ni? — My God! My God! Why have you left me?
E·li·ya·hu — Elijah
the *Ga·lil* — Galilee
Gul·gol·ta — Golgotha, Calvary
Mir·yam — Miriam, Mary
pa·ro·khet — curtain
Ra·ma·ta·yim — Arimathea
Ru·ach-Ha·Ko·desh — Holy Spirit
Shab·bat — the Sabbath
Sha·lom! — Peace! (greeting)
tal·mid — disciple
tal·mi·dim — disciples
To·rah-teachers — scribes
Ya·'a·kov — James
Ye·shu·a — Jesus
Yo·sef — Joseph
Zav·dai — Zebedee

THE GOOD NEWS OF YESHUA THE MESSIAH, AS REPORTED BY

MARK

1 ¹The beginning of the Good News of Yeshua the Messiah, the Son of God:

²It is written in the prophet Yesha'yahu,

> "See, I am sending my messenger
> ahead of you;
> he will prepare the way before
> you.*ᵃ*

³ "The voice of someone crying out:
> 'In the desert prepare the way for
> ***Adonai!***
> Make straight paths for him!'"*ᵇ*

⁴So it was that Yochanan the Immerser appeared in the desert, proclaiming an immersion involving turning to God from sin in order to be forgiven. ⁵People went out to him from all over Y'hudah, as did all the inhabitants of Yerushalayim. Confessing their sins, they were immersed by him in the Yarden River. ⁶Yochanan wore clothes of camel's hair, with a leather belt around his waist; he ate locusts and wild honey. ⁷He proclaimed: "After me is coming someone who is more powerful than I — I'm not worthy even to bend down and untie his sandals. ⁸I have immersed you in water, but he will immerse you in the *Ruach HaKodesh*."

⁹Shortly thereafter, Yeshua came from Natzeret in the Galil and was immersed in the Yarden by Yochanan. ¹⁰Immediately upon coming up out of the water, he saw heaven torn open and

the Spirit descending upon him like a dove; ¹¹then a voice came from heaven, "You are my Son, whom I love; I am well pleased with you."

¹²Immediately the Spirit drove him out into the wilderness, ¹³and he was in the wilderness forty days being tempted by the Adversary. He was with the wild animals, and the angels took care of him.

¹⁴After Yochanan had been arrested, Yeshua came into the Galil proclaiming the Good News from God:

¹⁵ "The time has come,
God's Kingdom is near!

Turn to God from your sins
and believe the Good News!"

¹⁶As he walked beside Lake Kinneret, he saw Shim'on and Andrew, Shim'on's brother, casting a net into the lake; for they were fishermen. ¹⁷Yeshua said to them, "Come, follow me, and I will make you into fishers for men!" ¹⁸At once they left their nets and followed him.

¹⁹Going on a little farther, he saw Ya'akov Ben-Zavdai and Yochanan, his brother, in their boat, repairing their nets. ²⁰Immediately he called them, and they left their father Zavdai in the boat with the hired men and went after Yeshua.

²¹They went into K'far-Nachum, and on *Shabbat* Yeshua went into the synagogue and began teaching. ²²They were amazed at the way he taught, for he did

---

a Malachi 3:1   *b* Isaiah 40:3

not instruct them like the *Torah*-teachers but as one who had authority himself.

²³ In their synagogue just then was a man with an unclean spirit in him, who shouted, ²⁴ "What do you want with us, Yeshua from Natzeret? Have you come to destroy us? I know who you are — the Holy One of God!" ²⁵ But Yeshua rebuked the unclean spirit, "Be quiet and come out of him!" ²⁶ Throwing the man into a convulsion, it gave a loud shriek and came out of him. ²⁷ They were all so astounded that they began asking each other, "What is this? A new teaching, one with authority behind it! He gives orders even to the unclean spirits, and they obey him!" ²⁸ And the news about him spread quickly through the whole region of the Galil.

²⁹ They left the synagogue and went with Ya'akov and Yochanan to the home of Shim'on and Andrew. ³⁰ Shim'on's mother-in-law was lying sick with a fever, and they told Yeshua about her. ³¹ He came, took her by the hand and lifted her onto her feet. The fever left her, and she began helping them.

³² That evening after sundown, they brought to Yeshua all who were ill or held in the power of demons, ³³ and the whole town came crowding around the door. ³⁴ He healed many who were ill with various diseases and expelled many demons, but he did not allow the demons to speak, because they knew who he was.

³⁵ Very early in the morning, while it was still dark, Yeshua got up, left, went away to a lonely spot and stayed there praying. ³⁶ But Shim'on and those with him went after him; ³⁷ and when they found him, they said, "Everybody is looking for you." ³⁸ He answered, "Let's go somewhere else — to the other villages around here. I have to proclaim the message there too — in fact this is why I came out." ³⁹ So he traveled all through the Galil, preaching in their synagogues and expelling demons.

⁴⁰ A man afflicted with a repulsive skin disease came to Yeshua and begged him on his knees, "If you are willing, you can make me clean." ⁴¹ Moved with pity, Yeshua reached out his hand, touched him and said to him, "I *am* willing! Be cleansed!" ⁴² Instantly the skin disease left him, and he was cleansed. ⁴³ Yeshua sent him away with this stern warning: ⁴⁴ "See to it that you tell no one; instead, as a testimony to the people, go and let the *cohen* examine you, and offer for your cleansing what Moshe commanded." ⁴⁵ But he went out and began spreading the news, talking freely about it; so that Yeshua could no longer enter a town openly but stayed out in the country, where people continued coming to him from all around.

2 ¹ After a while, Yeshua returned to K'far-Nachum. The word spread that he was back, ² and so many people

---

A·do·**nai** — the LORD, Jehovah
co·**hen** — priest
the Ga·**lil** — Galilee
K'far-Na·**chum** — Capernaum
Lake Kin·ne·ret — the Sea of Galilee
Mo·she — Moses
Na·**tze**·ret — Nazareth
Ru·ach-Ha·Ko·desh — Holy Spirit
Shab·bat — the Sabbath
Shim·'on — Simon
To·rah-teachers — scribes
Ya·'a·kov — James
Ya·'a·kov Ben-Zav·**dai** — James the son of Zebedee
Yar·den — Jordan
Ye·ru·sha·la·yim — Jerusalem
Ye·sha'·ya·hu — Isaiah
Ye·shu·a — Jesus
Y'hu·dah — Judea
Yo·cha·nan — John
Yo·cha·nan the Immerser — John the Baptist
Zav·dai — Zebedee

gathered around the house that there was no longer any room, not even in front of the door. While he was preaching the message to them, ³four men came to him carrying a paralyzed man. ⁴They could not get near Yeshua because of the crowd, so they stripped the roof over the place where he was, made an opening, and lowered the stretcher with the paralytic lying on it. ⁵Seeing their trust, Yeshua said to the paralyzed man, "Son, your sins are forgiven." ⁶Some *Torah*-teachers sitting there thought to themselves, ⁷"How can this fellow say such a thing? He is blaspheming! Who can forgive sins except God?" ⁸But immediately Yeshua, perceiving in his spirit what they were thinking, said to them, "Why are you thinking these things? ⁹Which is easier to say to the paralyzed man? 'Your sins are forgiven'? or 'Get up, pick up your stretcher and walk'? ¹⁰But look! I will prove to you that the Son of Man has authority on earth to forgive sins." He then said to the paralytic, ¹¹"I say to you: get up, pick up your stretcher and go home!" ¹²In front of everyone the man got up, picked up his stretcher at once and left. They were all utterly amazed and praised God, saying, "We have never seen anything like this!"

¹³Yeshua went out again by the lake. All the crowd came to him, and he began teaching them. ¹⁴As he passed on from there, he saw L'vi Ben Chalfai sitting in his tax-collection booth and said to him, "Follow me!" And he got up and followed him.

¹⁵As Yeshua was in L'vi's house eating, many tax-collectors and sinners were sitting with Yeshua and his *talmidim,* for there were many of them among his followers. ¹⁶When the *Torah*-teachers and the *P'rushim* saw that he was eating with sinners and tax-collectors, they said to his *talmidim,* "Why does he eat with tax-collectors and sinners?" ¹⁷But, hearing the question, Yeshua answered them, "The ones who need a doctor aren't the healthy but the sick. I didn't come to call the 'righteous' but sinners!"

¹⁸Also Yochanan's *talmidim* and the *P'rushim* were fasting; and they came and asked Yeshua, "Why is it that Yochanan's *talmidim* and the *talmidim* of the *P'rushim* fast, but your *talmidim* don't fast?" ¹⁹Yeshua answered them, "Can wedding guests fast while the bridegroom is still with them? As long as they have the bridegroom with them, fasting is out of the question. ²⁰But the time will come when the bridegroom is taken away from them; and when that day comes, they will fast. ²¹No one sews a piece of unshrunk cloth on an old coat; if he does, the new patch tears away from the old cloth and leaves a worse hole. ²²And no one puts new wine in old wineskins; if he does, the wine will burst the skins, and both the wine and the skins will be ruined. Rather, new wine is for freshly prepared wineskins."

²³One *Shabbat* Yeshua was passing through some wheat fields; and as they went along, his *talmidim* began picking heads of grain. ²⁴The *P'rushim* said to him, "Look! Why are they violating *Shabbat?*" ²⁵He said to them, "Haven't you ever read what David did when he and those with him were hungry and needed food? ²⁶He entered the House of God when Evyatar was *cohen gadol* and ate the Bread of the Presence, which is forbidden for anyone to eat but the *cohanim,* and even gave some to his companions." ²⁷Then he said to them, "*Shabbat* was made for mankind, not mankind for *Shabbat;* ²⁸so the Son of Man is Lord even of *Shabbat.*"

3 [1]Yeshua went again into a synagogue, and a man with a shriveled hand was there. [2]Looking for a reason to accuse him of something, people watched him carefully to see if he would heal him on *Shabbat*. [3]He said to the man with the shriveled hand, "Come up where we can see you!" [4]Then to them he said, "What is permitted on *Shabbat*? Doing good or doing evil? Saving life or killing?" But they said nothing. [5]Then, looking them over and feeling both anger with them and sympathy for them at the stoniness of their hearts, he said to the man, "Hold out your hand." As he held it out, it became restored. [6]The *P'rushim* went out and immediately began plotting with some members of Herod's party how to do away with him.

[7]Yeshua went off with his *talmidim* to the lake, and great numbers followed him from the Galil. [8]When they heard what he was doing, great numbers also followed him from Y'hudah, Yerushalayim, Idumea, the territory beyond the Yarden, and the Tzor-Tzidon area. [9]He told his *talmidim* to have a boat ready for him, so that he could escape the crush of the crowd if necessary, [10]for he had healed many people, and all the sick kept pressing forward to touch him. [11]Whenever the unclean spirits saw him, they would fall down in front of him and scream, "You are the Son of God!" [12]But he warned them strictly not to make him known.

[13]Then he went up into the hill country and summoned to himself those he wanted, and they came to him. [14]He appointed twelve to be with him, to be sent out to preach [15]and to have authority to expel demons:

[16] Shim'on, to whom he gave another name, "Kefa";

[17] Ya'akov Ben-Zavdai and Yochanan, Ya'akov's brother — to them he gave the name "B'nei-Regesh" (that is, "Thunderers");

[18] Andrew, Philip, Bar-Talmai, Mattityahu, T'oma, Ya'akov Ben-Chalfai, Taddai, Shim'on the Zealot,

[19] and Y'huda from K'riot, the one who betrayed him.

Then he entered a house; [20]and once more, such a crowd came together that they couldn't even eat. [21]When his family heard about this, they set out to take charge of him; for they said, "He's out of his mind!"

[22]The *Torah*-teachers who came down from Yerushalayim said, "He has Ba'alzibbul in him," and "It is by the

---

Ba-'al-zib-**bul** — Beelzebul, Beelzebub (Satan)
B'nei-**Re**-gesh — sons of tumult/rage, hot-tempered people.
Bar-Tal-**mai** — Bartholomew
co-ha-nim — priests
co-hen ga-dol — high priest
Da-**vid** — David
Ev-ya-**tar** — Abiathar
the Ga-**lil** — Galilee
Ke-**fa** — Peter
L'**vi** — Levi
L'**vi** Ben-Chal-**fai** — Levi the son of Alpheus
Mat-tit-**ya**-hu —Matthew
P'ru-shim — Pharisees
Shab-bat — the Sabbath
Shim-**'on** — Simon
Tad-**dai** — Thaddeus
tal-mi-dim — disciples
T'**o**-ma —Thomas
To-rah-teachers — scribes
Tzi-**don** — Sidon
Tzor — Tyre
Ya-'a-**kov** — James
Ya-'a-**kov** Ben-Chal-**fai** — James the son of Alpheus
Ya-'a-**kov** Ben-Zav-**dai** — James the son of Zebedee
Yar-**den** — Jordan
Ye-ru-sha-**la**-yim — Jerusalem
Ye-**shu**-a — Jesus
Y'hu-**dah** — Judea
Y'hu-**dah** from K'ri-**ot** — Judas Iscariot
Yo-cha-**nan** — John

ruler of the demons that he expels the demons." [23]But he called them and spoke to them in parables: "How can Satan expel Satan? [24]If a kingdom is divided against itself, that kingdom can't survive; [25]and if a household is divided against itself, that household can't survive. [26]So if Satan has rebelled against himself and is divided, he can't survive either; and that's the end of him. [27]Furthermore, no one can break into a strong man's house and make off with his possessions unless he first ties up the strong man. After that, he can ransack his house. [28]Yes! I tell you that people will be forgiven all sins and whatever blasphemies they utter; [29]however, someone who blasphemes against the *Ruach HaKodesh* never has forgiveness but is guilty of an eternal sin." [30]For they had been saying, "He has an unclean spirit in him."

[31]Then his mother and brothers arrived. Standing outside, they sent a message asking for him. [32]A crowd was sitting around him; and they said to him, "Your mother and your brothers are outside, asking for you." [33]He replied, "Who are my mother and my brothers?" [34]Looking at those seated in a circle around him, he said, "See! Here are my mother and my brothers! [35]Whoever does what God wants is my brother, sister and mother!"

4 [1]Again Yeshua began to teach by the lake, but the crowd that gathered around him was so large that he got into a boat on the lake and sat there, while the crowd remained on shore at the water's edge. [2]He taught them many things in parables. In the course of his teaching, he said to them: [3]"Listen! A farmer went out to sow his seed. [4]As he sowed, some seed fell alongside the path; and the birds came and ate it up. [5]Other seed fell on rocky patches where there was not much soil.

It sprouted quickly because the soil was shallow; [6]but when the sun rose, the young plants were scorched; and since their roots were not deep, they dried up. [7]Other seed fell among thorns, which grew up and choked it; so that it yielded no grain. [8]But other seed fell into rich soil and produced grain; it sprouted, and grew, and yielded a crop — thirty, sixty, even a hundred times what was sown." [9]And he concluded, "Whoever has ears to hear with, let him hear!"

[10]When Yeshua was alone, the people around him with the Twelve asked him about the parables. [11]He answered them, "To you the secret of the Kingdom of God has been given; but to those outside, everything is in parables, [12]so that

> they may be always looking but never seeing;
> always listening but never understanding.
> Otherwise, they might turn and be forgiven!" *c*

[13]Then Yeshua said to them, "Don't you understand this parable? How will you be able to understand any parable? [14]The sower sows the message. [15]Those alongside the path where the message is sown are people who no sooner hear it than the Adversary comes and takes away the message sown in them. [16]Likewise, those receiving seed on rocky patches are people who hear the message and joyfully accept it at once; [17]but they have no root in themselves. So they hold out for a while, but as soon as some trouble or persecution arises on account of the message, they immediately fall away. [18]Others are those sown among thorns — they hear the message; [19]but the worries of the world, the deceitful glamor of wealth and all the

---

c Isaiah 6:9-10

48

other kinds of desires push in and choke the message; so that it produces nothing. ²⁰But those sown on rich soil hear the message, accept it and bear fruit — thirty, sixty or a hundredfold."

²¹He said to them, "A lamp isn't brought in to be put under a bowl or under the bed, is it? Wouldn't you put it on a lampstand? ²²Indeed, nothing is hidden, except to be disclosed; and nothing is covered up, except to come out into the open. ²³Those who have ears to hear with, let them hear!"

²⁴He also said to them, "Pay attention to what you are hearing! The measure with which you measure out will be used to measure to you — and more besides! ²⁵For anyone who has something will be given more; but from anyone who has nothing, even what he does have will be taken away."

²⁶And he said, "The Kingdom of God is like a man who scatters seed on the ground. ²⁷Nights he sleeps, days he's awake; and meanwhile the seeds sprout and grow — how, he doesn't know. ²⁸By itself the soil produces a crop — first the stalk, then the head, and finally the full grain in the head. ²⁹But as soon as the crop is ready, the man comes with his sickle, because it's harvest-time."

³⁰Yeshua also said, "With what can we compare the Kingdom of God? What illustration should we use to describe it? ³¹It is like a mustard seed, which, when planted, is the smallest of all the seeds in the field; ³²but after it has been planted, it grows and becomes the largest of all the plants, with such big branches that the birds flying about can build nests in its shade."

³³With many parables like these he spoke the message to them, to the extent that they were capable of hearing it. ³⁴He did not say a thing to them without using a parable; when he was

alone with his own *talmidim* he explained everything to them.

³⁵That day, when evening had come, Yeshua said to them, "Let's cross to the other side of the lake." ³⁶So, leaving the crowd behind, they took him just as he was, in the boat; and there were other boats with him. ³⁷A furious windstorm arose, and the waves broke over the boat, so that it was close to being swamped. ³⁸But he was in the stern on a cushion, asleep. They woke him and said to him, "Rabbi, doesn't it matter to you that we're about to be killed?" ³⁹He awoke, rebuked the wind and said to the waves, "Quiet! Be still!" The wind subsided, and there was a dead calm. ⁴⁰He said to them, "Why are you afraid? Have you no trust even now?" ⁴¹But they were terrified and asked each other, "Who can this be, that even the wind and the waves obey him?"

5 ¹Yeshua and his *talmidim* arrived at the other side of the lake, in the Gerasenes' territory. ²As soon as he disembarked, a man with an unclean spirit came out of the burial caves to meet him. ³He lived in the burial caves; and no one could keep him tied up, not even with a chain. ⁴He had often been chained hand and foot, but he would snap the chains and break the irons off his feet, and no one was strong enough to control him. ⁵Night and day he wandered among the graves and through the hills, howling and gashing himself with stones.

⁶Seeing Yeshua from a distance, he ran and fell on his knees in front of him ⁷and screamed at the top of his voice,

---

Ru·ach-Ha·Ko·desh — Holy Spirit
Sa·tan — Satan, the Adversary
tal·mi·dim — disciples
To·rah-teachers — scribes
Ye·ru·sha·la·yim — Jerusalem
Ye·shu·a — Jesus

"What do you want with me, Yeshua, Son of God *HaElyon*? I implore you in God's name! Don't torture me!" ⁸For Yeshua had already begun saying to him, "Unclean spirit, come out of this man!" ⁹Yeshua asked him, "What's your name?" "My name is Legion," he answered, "there are so many of us;" ¹⁰and he kept begging Yeshua not to send them out of that region.

¹¹Now there was a large herd of pigs feeding near the hill, ¹²and the unclean spirits begged him, "Send us to the pigs, so we can go into them." ¹³Yeshua gave them permission. They came out and entered the pigs; and the herd, numbering around two thousand, rushed down the hillside into the lake and were drowned. ¹⁴The swineherds fled and told it in the town and in the surrounding country, and the people went to see what had happened. ¹⁵They came to Yeshua and saw the man who had had the legion of demons, sitting there, dressed and in his right mind; and they were frightened. ¹⁶Those who had seen it told what had happened to the man controlled by demons and to the pigs; ¹⁷and the people began begging Yeshua to leave their district.

¹⁸As he was getting into the boat, the man who had been demonized begged him to be allowed to go with him. ¹⁹But Yeshua would not permit it. Instead, he said to him, "Go home to your people, and tell them how much *Adonai* in his mercy has done for you." ²⁰He went off and began proclaiming in the Ten Towns how much Yeshua had done for him, and everyone was amazed.

²¹Yeshua crossed in the boat to the other side of the lake, and a great crowd gathered around him. ²²There came to him a synagogue official, Ya'ir by name, who fell at his feet ²³and pleaded desperately with him, "My little daughter is at the point of death.

Please! Come and lay your hands on her, so that she will get well and live!"

²⁴He went with him; and a large crowd followed, pressing all around him. ²⁵Among them was a woman who had had a hemorrhage for twelve years ²⁶and had suffered a great deal under many physicians. She had spent her life savings; yet instead of improving, she had grown worse. ²⁷She had heard about Yeshua, so she came up behind him in the crowd and touched his robe; ²⁸for she said, "If I touch even his clothes, I will be healed." ²⁹Instantly the hemorrhaging stopped, and she felt in her body that she had been healed from the disease. ³⁰At the same time, Yeshua, aware that power had gone out from him, turned around in the crowd and asked, "Who touched my clothes?" ³¹His *talmidim* responded, "You see the people pressing in on you; and still you ask, 'Who touched me?'" ³²But he kept looking around to see who had done it. ³³The woman, frightened and trembling, because she knew what had happened to her, came and fell down in front of him and told him the whole truth. ³⁴"Daughter," he said to her, "your trust has healed you. Go in peace, and be healed of your disease."

³⁵While he was still speaking, people from the synagogue official's house came, saying, "Your daughter has died. Why bother the rabbi any longer?" ³⁶Ignoring what they had said, Yeshua told the synagogue official, "Don't be afraid, just keep trusting." ³⁷He let no one follow him except Kefa, Ya'akov and Yochanan, Ya'akov's brother. ³⁸When they came to the synagogue official's house, he found a great commotion, with people weeping and wailing loudly. ³⁹On entering, he said to them, "Why all this commotion and weeping? The child isn't dead, she's just asleep!" ⁴⁰And they jeered at him. But

he put them all outside, took the child's father and mother and those with him, and went in where the child was. ⁴¹ Taking her by the hand, he said to her, "*Talita, kumi!*" (which means, "Little girl, I say to you, get up!"). ⁴² At once the girl got up and began walking around; she was twelve years old. Everybody was utterly amazed. ⁴³ He gave them strict orders to say nothing about this to anyone, and told them to give her something to eat.

6 ¹ Then Yeshua left and went to his home town, and his *talmidim* followed him. ² On *Shabbat* he started to teach in the synagogue, and many who heard him were astounded. They asked, "Where did this man get all this? What is this wisdom he has been given? What are these miracles worked through him? ³ Isn't he just the carpenter? the son of Miryam? the brother of Ya'akov and Yosi and Y'hudah and Shim'on? Aren't his sisters here with us?" And they took offense at him. ⁴ But Yeshua said to them. "The only place people don't respect a prophet is in his home town, among his own relatives, and in his own house." ⁵ So he could do no miracles there, other than lay his hands on a few sick people and heal them. ⁶ He was amazed at their lack of trust.

Yeshua went through the surrounding towns and villages, teaching. ⁷ He summoned the Twelve and started sending them out in pairs, giving them authority over the unclean spirits. ⁸ He instructed them, "Take nothing for your trip except a walking stick — no bread, no pack, no money in your belt. ⁹ Wear shoes but not an extra shirt. ¹⁰ Whenever you enter a house, stay there until you leave the place; ¹¹ and if the people of some place will not welcome you, and they refuse to hear you, then, as you leave, shake the dust off your feet as a warning to them."

¹² So they set out and preached that people should turn from sin to God, ¹³ they expelled many demons, and they anointed many sick people with oil and healed them.

¹⁴ Meanwhile, King Herod heard about this, for Yeshua's reputation had spread. Some were saying, "Yochanan the Immerser has been raised from the dead; that is why these miraculous powers are at work in him." ¹⁵ Others said, "It is Eliyahu!" and still others, "He is a prophet, like one of the old prophets." ¹⁶ But when Herod heard about it, he said, "Yochanan, whom I had beheaded, has been raised."

¹⁷ For Herod had sent and had Yochanan arrested and chained in prison because of Herodias, the wife of his brother Philip. Herod had married her, ¹⁸ but Yochanan had told him, "It violates the *Torah* for you to marry your brother's wife." ¹⁹ So Herodias had a grudge against him and wanted him put to death. But this she could not accomplish, ²⁰ because Herod stood in awe of Yochanan and protected him, for he knew that he was a *tzaddik*, a holy man. Whenever he heard him, he

E·li·ya·hu — Elijah
Ha·El·yon — Most High
Ke·fa — Peter
Mir·yam — Miriam, Mary
Shab·bat — the Sabbath
Shim·'on — Simon
ta·li·ta, ku·mi! — daughter, rise!
tal·mi·dim — disciples
To·rah — Teaching, "Law"; Pentateuch
tzad·dik — righteous man
Ya·'a·kov — James
Ya·'ir — Jairus
Ye·shu·a — Jesus
Y'hu·dah — Judas, Jude, Juda
Yo·cha·nan — John
Yo·cha·nan the Immerser — John the Baptist
Yo·si — "Joe" (diminutive of Yosef, "Joseph")

became deeply disturbed, yet he liked to listen to him.

[21] Finally, the opportunity came. Herod gave a banquet on his birthday for his nobles and officers and the leading men of the Galil. [22] The daughter of Herodias came in and danced, and she pleased Herod and his guests. The king said to the girl, "Ask me for whatever you want; I will give it to you;" [23] and he made a vow to her, "Whatever you ask me, I will give you, up to half my kingdom." [24] So she went out and said to her mother, "What should I ask for?" She said, "The head of Yochanan the Immerser." [25] At once the daughter hurried back to the king and announced her request: "I want you to give me right now on a platter the head of Yochanan the Immerser." [26] Herod was appalled; but out of regard for the oaths he had sworn before his dinner guests, he did not want to break his word to her. [27] So the king immediately sent a soldier from his personal guard with orders to bring Yochanan's head. The soldier went and beheaded Yochanan in the prison, [28] brought his head on a platter, and gave it to the girl; and the girl gave it to her mother. [29] When Yochanan's *talmidim* heard of it, they came and took the body and laid it in a grave.

[30] Those who had been sent out rejoined Yeshua and reported to him all they had done and taught. [31] There were so many people coming and going that they couldn't even take time to eat, so he said to them, "Come with me by yourselves to a place where we can be alone, and you can get some rest." [32] They went off by themselves to an isolated spot; [33] but many people, seeing them leave and recognizing them, ran ahead on foot from all the towns and got there first. [34] When Yeshua came ashore, he saw a huge crowd. Filled with compassion for them, because they were like sheep without a shepherd, he began teaching them many things.

[35] By this time, the hour was late. The *talmidim* came to him and said, "This is a remote place, and it's getting late. [36] Send the people away, so that they can go and buy food for themselves in the farms and towns around here." [37] But he answered them, "Give them something to eat, yourselves!" They replied, "We are to go and spend thousands on bread, and give it to them to eat?" [38] He asked them, "How many loaves do you have? Go and check." When they had found out, they said, "Five. And two fish." [39] Then he ordered all the people to sit down in groups on the green grass. [40] They sat down in groups of fifty or a hundred. [41] Then he took the five loaves and the two fish, and, looking up toward heaven, made a *b'rakhah*. Next he broke up the loaves and began giving them to the *talmidim* to distribute. He also divided up the two fish among them all. [42] They all ate as much as they wanted, [43] and they took up twelve baskets full of the broken pieces and fish. [44] Those who ate the loaves numbered five thousand men.

[45] Immediately Yeshua had his *talmidim* get in the boat and go on ahead of him toward the other side of the lake, toward Beit-Tzaidah, while he sent the crowds away. [46] After he had left them, he went into the hills to pray. [47] When night came, the boat was out on the lake, and he was by himself on land. [48] He saw that they were having difficulty rowing, because the wind was against them; so at around four o'clock in the morning he came toward them, walking on the lake! He meant to come alongside them; [49] but when they saw him walking on the lake, they thought

it was a ghost and let out a shriek; ⁵⁰for they had all seen him and were terrified. However, he spoke to them. "Courage," he said, "it is I. Stop being afraid!" ⁵¹He got into the boat with them, and the wind ceased. They were completely astounded, ⁵²for they did not understand about the loaves; on the contrary, their hearts had been made stonelike.

⁵³After they had made the crossing, they landed at Ginosar and anchored. ⁵⁴As soon as they got out of the boat, the people recognized him ⁵⁵and began running around throughout that whole region and bringing sick people on their stretchers to any place where they heard he was. ⁵⁶Wherever he went, in towns, cities or country, they laid the sick in the marketplaces. They begged him to let them touch even the *tzitzit* on his robe, and all who touched it were healed.

7 ¹The *P'rushim* and some of the *Torah*-teachers who had come from Yerushalayim gathered together with Yeshua ²and saw that some of his *talmidim* ate with ritually unclean hands, that is, without doing *n'tilat-yadayim*. ³(For the *P'rushim*, and indeed all the Judeans, holding fast to the Tradition of the Elders, do not eat unless they have given their hands a ceremonial washing. ⁴Also, when they come from the marketplace they do not eat unless they have rinsed their hands up to the wrist; and they adhere to many other traditions, such as washing cups, pots and bronze vessels.)

⁵The *P'rushim* and the *Torah*-teachers asked him, "Why don't your *talmidim* live in accordance with the Tradition of the Elders, but instead eat with ritually unclean hands?" ⁶Yeshua answered them, "Yesha'yahu was right when he prophesied about you hypocrites — as it is written,

'These people honor me with their lips,
but their hearts are far away from me.
⁷ Their worship of me is useless, because they teach man-made rules as if they were doctrines.'ᵈ

⁸"You depart from God's command and hold onto human tradition. ⁹Indeed," he said to them, "you have made a fine art of departing from God's command in order to keep your tradition! ¹⁰For Moshe said, 'Honor your father and your mother,'ᵉ and 'Anyone who curses his father or mother must be put to death.'ᶠ ¹¹But you say, 'If someone says to his father or mother, "I have promised as a *korban*"' (that is, as a gift to God) ""what I might have used to help you,"' ¹²then you no longer let him do anything for his father or mother. ¹³Thus, with your tradition which you had handed down to you, you nullify the Word of God! And you do other things like this."

ᵈ Isaiah 29:13
ᵉ Exodus 20:12, Deuteronomy 5:16
ᶠ Exodus 21:17, Leviticus 20:9

Beit-Tzai·**dah** — Bethsaida
b'ra·khah — blessing
the Ga·**lil** — Galilee
Gi·no·**sar** — Gennesaret
kor·ban — sacrifice
Mo·**she** — Moses
n'ti·lat-ya·da·yim — ritual handwashing
P'ru·shim — Pharisees
tal·mi·dim — disciples
To·rah — Teaching, "Law"; Pentateuch
To·rah-teachers — scribes
tzi·tzit — ritual fringe
Ye·ru·sha·la·yim — Jerusalem
Ye·sha'·ya·hu — Isaiah
Ye·shu·a — Jesus
Yo·cha·nan — John
Yo·cha·nan the Immerser — John the Baptist

¹⁴Then Yeshua called the people to him again and said, "Listen to me, all of you, and understand this! ¹⁵There is nothing outside a person which, by going into him, can make him unclean. Rather, it is the things that come out of a person which make a person unclean!" ¹⁶*

¹⁷When he had left the people and entered the house, his *talmidim* asked him about the parable. ¹⁸He replied to them, "So you too are without understanding? Don't you see that nothing going into a person from outside can make him unclean? ¹⁹For it doesn't go into his heart but into his stomach, and it passes out into the latrine." (Thus he declared all foods ritually clean.) ²⁰"It is what comes out of a person," he went on, "that makes him unclean. ²¹For from within, out of a person's heart, come forth wicked thoughts, sexual immorality, theft, murder, adultery, ²²greed, malice, deceit, indecency, envy, slander, arrogance, foolishness. ²³All these wicked things come from within, and they make a person unclean."

²⁴Next, Yeshua left that district and went off to the vicinity of Tzor and Tzidon. There he found a house to stay in and wanted to remain unrecognized, but keeping hidden proved impossible. ²⁵Instead, a woman whose little daughter had an unclean spirit in her came to him and fell down at his feet. ²⁶The woman was a Greek, by birth a Syrophoenician, and she begged him to drive the demon out of her daughter. ²⁷He said, "Let the children be fed first, for it is not right to take the children's food and toss it to their pet dogs." ²⁸She answered him, "That is true, sir; but even the dogs under the table eat the children's leftovers." ²⁹Then he said to her, "For such an answer you may go on home; the demon has left your daughter." ³⁰She went back home and found the child lying on the couch, the demon gone.

³¹Then he left the district of Tzor and went through Tzidon to Lake Kinneret and on to the region of the Ten Towns. ³²They brought him a man who was deaf and had a speech impediment and asked Yeshua to lay his hand on him. ³³Taking him off alone, away from the crowd, Yeshua put his fingers into the man's ears, spat, and touched his tongue; ³⁴then, looking up to heaven, he gave a deep groan and said to him, "*Hippatach!*" (that is, "Be opened!"). ³⁵His ears were opened, his tongue was freed, and he began speaking clearly. ³⁶Yeshua ordered the people to tell no one; but the more he insisted, the more zealously they spread the news. ³⁷People were overcome with amazement. "Everything he does, he does well!" they said. "He even makes the deaf hear and the dumb speak!"

8 ¹It was during that time that another large crowd gathered, and they had nothing to eat. Yeshua called his *talmidim* to him and said to them, ²"I feel sorry for these people, because they have been with me three days, and now they have nothing to eat. ³If I send them off to their homes hungry, they will collapse on the way; some of them have come a long distance." ⁴His *talmidim* said to him, "How can anyone find enough bread to satisfy these people in a remote place like this?" ⁵"How many loaves do you have?" he asked them. They answered, "Seven." ⁶He then told the crowd to sit down on the ground, took the seven loaves, made a *b'rakhah*, broke the loaves and gave them to his *talmidim* to serve to the people. ⁷They also had a few fish; making a *b'rakhah* over them he also

---

* Some manuscripts include verse 7:16: Anyone who has ears that can hear, let him hear!

ordered these to be served. [8] The people ate their fill; and the *talmidim* took up the leftover pieces, seven large basketsful. [9] About four thousand were there. [10] After sending them away, Yeshua got into the boat with his *talmidim* and went off to the district of Dalmanuta.

[11] The *P'rushim* came and began arguing with him; they wanted him to give them a sign from Heaven, because they were out to trap him. [12] With a sigh that came straight from his heart, he said, "Why does this generation want a sign? Yes! I tell you, no sign will be given to this generation!" [13] With that, he left them, got into the boat again and went off to the other side of the lake.

[14] Now the *talmidim* had forgotten to bring bread and had with them in the boat only one loaf. [15] So when Yeshua said to them, "Watch out! Guard yourselves from the *chametz* of the *P'rushim* and the *chametz* of Herod," [16] they thought he had said it because they had no bread. [17] But, aware of this, he said, "Why are you talking with each other about having no bread? Don't you see or understand yet? Have your hearts been made like stone? [18] You have eyes — don't you see? You have ears — don't you hear? And don't you remember? [19] When I broke the five loaves for the five thousand, how many baskets full of broken pieces did you collect?" "Twelve," they answered him. [20] "And when I broke the seven loaves for the four thousand, how many baskets full of broken pieces did you collect?" "Seven," they answered. [21] He said to them, "And you still don't understand?"

[22] They came to Beit-Tzaidah. Some people brought him a blind man and begged Yeshua to touch him. [23] Taking the blind man's hand, he led him outside the town. He spit in his eyes,

put his hands on him and asked him, "Do you see anything?" [24] He looked up and said, "I see people, but they look like walking trees." [25] Then he put his hands on the blind man's eyes again. He peered intently, and his eyesight was restored, so that he could see everything distinctly. [26] Yeshua sent him home with the words, "Don't go into town."

[27] Yeshua and his *talmidim* went on to the towns of Caesarea Philippi. On the way, he asked his *talmidim*, "Who are people saying I am?" [28] "Some say you are Yochanan the Immerser," they told him, "others say Eliyahu, and still others, one of the prophets." [29] "But you," he asked, "who do you say I am?" Kefa answered, "You are the *Mashiach*." [30] Then Yeshua warned them not to tell anyone about him. [31] He began teaching them that the Son of Man had to endure much suffering and be rejected by the elders, the head *cohanim* and the *Torah*-teachers; and that he had to be put to death; but that after three days, he had to rise again. [32] He spoke very plainly about it. Kefa took him aside and began rebuking him. [33] But, turning around and looking at his *talmidim*, he rebuked Kefa. "Get

---

Beit-Tzai·**dah** — Bethsaida
b'ra·khah — blessing
cha·metz — leaven
co·ha·nim — priests
Dal·ma·nu·ta — Dalmanutha
E·li·ya·hu — Elijah
Hip·pa·tach! — Be opened!
Ke·**fa** — Peter
Lake Kin·ne·ret — the Sea of Galilee
Ma·shi·ach — Messiah
P'ru·shim — Pharisees
tal·mi·dim — disciples
To·rah-teachers — scribes
Tzi·**don** — Sidon
Tzor — Tyre
Ye·shu·a — Jesus
Yo·cha·**nan** the Immerser — John the Baptist

behind me, Satan!" he said, "For your thinking is from a human perspective, not from God's perspective!"

³⁴ Then Yeshua called the crowd and his *talmidim* to him and told them, "If anyone wants to come after me, let him say 'No' to himself, take up his execution-stake, and keep following me. ³⁵ For whoever wants to save his own life will destroy it, but whoever destroys his life for my sake and for the sake of the Good News will save it. ³⁶ Indeed, what will it benefit a person if he gains the whole world but forfeits his life? ³⁷ What could a person give in exchange for his life? ³⁸ For if someone is ashamed of me and of what I say in this adulterous and sinful generation, the Son of Man also will be ashamed of him when he comes in his Father's glory with the holy

9 angels." ¹ "Yes!" he went on, "I tell you that there are some people standing here who will not experience death until they see the Kingdom of God come in a powerful way!"

² Six days later, Yeshua took Kefa, Ya'akov and Yochanan and led them up a high mountain privately. As they watched, he began to change form, ³ and his clothes became dazzlingly white, whiter than anyone in the world could possibly bleach them. ⁴ Then they saw Eliyahu and Moshe speaking with Yeshua. ⁵ Kefa said to Yeshua, "It's good that we're here, Rabbi! Let's put up three shelters — one for you, one for Moshe and one for Eliyahu." ⁶ (He didn't know what to say, they were so frightened.) ⁷ Then a cloud enveloped them; and a voice came out of the cloud, "This is my Son, whom I love. Listen to him!" ⁸ Suddenly, when they looked around, they no longer saw anyone with them except Yeshua.

⁹ As they came down the mountain, he warned them not to tell anyone what they had seen until after the Son of Man had risen from the dead. ¹⁰ So they kept the matter to themselves; but they continued asking each other, "What is this 'rising from the dead'?" ¹¹ They also asked him, "Why do the *Torah*-teachers say that Eliyahu has to come first?" ¹² "Eliyahu will indeed come first," he answered, "and he will restore everything. Nevertheless, why is it written in the *Tanakh* that the Son of Man must suffer much and be rejected? ¹³ There's more to it: I tell you that Eliyahu has come, and they did whatever they pleased to him, just as the *Tanakh* says about him."

¹⁴ When they got back to the *talmidim*, they saw a large crowd around them and some *Torah*-teachers arguing with them. ¹⁵ As soon as the crowd saw him, they were surprised and ran out to greet him. ¹⁶ He asked them, "What's the discussion about?" ¹⁷ One of the crowd gave him the answer: "Rabbi, I brought my son to you because he has an evil spirit in him that makes him unable to talk. ¹⁸ Whenever it seizes him, it throws him to the ground — he foams at the mouth, grinds his teeth and becomes stiff all over. I asked your *talmidim* to drive the spirit out, but they couldn't do it." ¹⁹ "People without any trust!" he responded. "How long will I be with you? How long must I put up with you? Bring him to me!" ²⁰ They brought the boy to him; and as soon as the spirit saw him, it threw the boy into a convulsion. ²¹ Yeshua asked the boy's father, "How long has this been happening to him?" "Ever since childhood," he said; ²² "and it often tries to kill him by throwing him into the fire or into the water. But if you can do anything, have pity on us and help us!" ²³ Yeshua said to him, "What do you mean, 'if you can'? Everything is possible to someone who has trust!" ²⁴ Instantly the father of the child

exclaimed, "I do trust — help my lack of trust!" 25 When Yeshua saw that the crowd was closing in on them, he rebuked the unclean spirit, saying to it, "You deaf and dumb spirit! I command you: come out of him, and never go back into him again!" 26 Shrieking and throwing the boy into a violent fit, it came out. The boy lay there like a corpse, so that most of the people said he was dead. 27 But Yeshua took him by the hand and raised him to his feet, and he stood up.

28 After Yeshua had gone indoors, his *talmidim* asked him privately, "Why couldn't we drive it out?" 29 He said to them "This is the kind of spirit that can be driven out only by prayer."

30 After leaving that place, they went on through the Galil. Yeshua didn't want anyone to know, 31 because he was teaching his *talmidim*. He told them, "The Son of Man will be betrayed into the hands of men who will put him to death; but after he has been killed, three days later, he will rise." 32 But they didn't understand what he meant, and they were afraid to ask him.

33 They arrived at K'far-Nachum. When Yeshua was inside the house, he asked them, "What were you discussing as we were traveling?" 34 But they kept quiet; because on the way, they had been arguing with each other about who was the greatest. 35 He sat down, summoned the Twelve and said to them, "If anyone wants to be first, he must make himself last of all and servant of all." 36 He took a child and stood him among them. Then he put his arms around him and said to them, 37 "Whoever welcomes one such child in my name welcomes me, and whoever welcomes me welcomes not me but the One who sent me."

38 Yochanan said to him, "Rabbi, we saw a man expelling demons in your name; and because he wasn't one of us, we told him to stop." 39 But Yeshua said, "Don't stop him, because no one who works a miracle in my name will soon after be able to say something bad about me. 40 For whoever is not against us is for us. 41 Indeed, whoever gives you even a cup of water to drink because you come in the name of the Messiah — yes! I tell you that he will certainly not lose his reward.

42 "Whoever ensnares one of these little ones who trust me — it would be better for him to have a millstone hung around his neck and be thrown in the sea. 43 If your hand makes you sin, cut it off! Better that you should be maimed but obtain eternal life, rather than keep both hands and go to Gey-Hinnom, to unquenchable fire! 44 * 45 And if your foot makes you sin, cut it off! Better that you should be lame but obtain eternal life, rather than keep both feet and be thrown into Gey-Hinnom! 46 * 47 And if your eye makes you sin, pluck it out! Better that you should be one-eyed but enter the Kingdom of God, rather than keep both eyes and be thrown into Gey-Hinnom,

---

* Some manuscripts include identical verses 9:44, 46: "Where their worm does not die, and the fire is not quenched." (Isaiah 66:24)

E·li·ya·hu — Elijah
the Ga·lil — Galilee
Gey-Hin·nom — Gehenna, hell
Ke·fa — Peter
K'far-Na·chum — Capernaum
Mo·she — Moses
Sa·tan — Satan, the Adversary
tal·mi·dim — disciples
Ta·nakh — Hebrew Scriptures, "Old Testament"
To·rah-teachers — scribes
Ya·'a·kov — James
Ye·shu·a — Jesus
Yo·cha·nan — John

⁴⁸ **where their worm does not die, and the fire is not quenched.**ᵍ

⁴⁹ Indeed, everyone is going to be salted with fire. ⁵⁰ Salt is excellent, but if it loses its saltiness, how will you season it? So have salt in yourselves — that is, be at peace with each other."

10 ¹ Then Yeshua left that place and went into the regions of Y'hudah and the territory beyond the Yarden. Again crowds gathered around him; and again, as usual, he taught them. ² Some *P'rushim* came up and tried to trap him by asking him, "Does the *Torah* permit a man to divorce his wife?" ³ He replied, "What did Moshe command you?" ⁴ They said, "Moshe allowed a man to **hand his wife a *get*** and divorce her."ʰ ⁵ But Yeshua said to them, "He wrote this commandment for you because of your hardheartedness. ⁶ However, at the beginning of creation, God **made them male and female.**ⁱ ⁷ **For this reason, a man should leave his father and mother and be united with his wife,** ⁸ **and the two are to become one flesh.**ʲ Thus they are no longer two, but one. ⁹ So then, no one should break apart what God has joined together." ¹⁰ When they were indoors once more, the *talmidim* asked him about this. ¹¹ He said to them, "Whoever divorces his wife and marries another woman commits adultery against his wife; ¹² and if a wife divorces her husband and marries another man, she too commits adultery."

¹³ People were bringing children to him so that he might touch them, but the *talmidim* rebuked those people. ¹⁴ However, when Yeshua saw it, he became indignant and said to them, "Let the children come to me, don't stop them; for the Kingdom of God belongs to such as these. ¹⁵ Yes! I tell you, whoever does not receive the Kingdom of God like a child will not enter it!" ¹⁶ And he took them in his arms, laid his hands on them, and made a *b'rakhah* over them.

¹⁷ As he was starting on his way, a man ran up, kneeled down in front of him and asked, "Good rabbi, what should I do to obtain eternal life?" ¹⁸ Yeshua said to him, "Why are you calling me good? No one is good except God! ¹⁹ You know the *mitzvot* — '**Don't murder, don't commit adultery, don't steal, don't give false testimony,**ᵏ **don't defraud, honor your father and mother,...**'ˡ ²⁰ "Rabbi," he said, "I have kept all these since I was a boy." ²¹ Yeshua, looking at him, felt love for him and said to him, "You're missing one thing. Go, sell whatever you own, give to the poor, and you will have riches in heaven. Then come, follow me!" ²² Shocked by this word, he went away sad; because he was a wealthy man.

²³ Yeshua looked around and said to his *talmidim*, "How hard it is going to be for people with wealth to enter the Kingdom of God!" ²⁴ The *talmidim* were astounded at these words; but Yeshua said to them again, "My friends, how hard it is to enter the Kingdom of God! ²⁵ It's easier for a camel to pass through a needle's eye than for a rich man to enter the Kingdom of God." ²⁶ They were utterly amazed and said to him, "Then who can be saved?" ²⁷ Yeshua looked at them and said, "Humanly, it is impossible, but not with God; with God, everything is possible." ²⁸ Kefa began saying to him,

---

ᵍ Isaiah 66:24   ʰ Deuteronomy 24:1, 3
ⁱ Genesis 1:27, 5:2   ʲ Genesis 2:24

ᵏ Exodus 20:13(13-16), Deuteronomy 5:17-20
ˡ Exodus 20:12, Deuteronomy 5:16

"Look, we have left everything and followed you." ²⁹ Yeshua said, "Yes! I tell you that there is no one who has left house, brothers, sisters, mother, father, children or fields, for my sake and for the sake of the Good News, ³⁰ who will not receive a hundred times over, now, in the 'olam hazeh, homes, brothers, sisters, mothers, children and lands — with persecutions! — and in the 'olam haba, eternal life. ³¹ But many who are first will be last, and many who are last will be first!"

³² They were on the road going up to Yerushalayim. Yeshua was walking ahead of them, and they were amazed — and those following were afraid. So again taking the Twelve along with him, he began telling them what was about to happen to him. ³³ "We are now going up to Yerushalayim, where the Son of Man will be handed over to the head cohanim and the Torah-teachers. They will sentence him to death and turn him over to the Goyim, ³⁴ who will jeer at him, spit on him, beat him and kill him; but after three days, he will rise."

³⁵ Ya'akov and Yochanan, the sons of Zavdai, came up to him and said, "Rabbi, we would like you to do us a favor." ³⁶ He said to them, "What do you want me to do for you?" ³⁷ They replied, "When you are in your glory, let us sit with you, one on your right and the other on your left." ³⁸ But Yeshua answered, "You don't know what you're asking! Can you drink the cup that I am drinking? or be immersed with the immersion that I must undergo?" ³⁹ They said to him, "We can." Yeshua replied, "The cup that I am drinking, you will drink; and the immersion I am being immersed with, you will undergo. ⁴⁰ But to sit on my right and on my left is not mine to give.

Rather, it is for those for whom it has been prepared."

⁴¹ When the other ten heard about this, they became outraged at Ya'akov and Yochanan. ⁴² But Yeshua called them to him and said to them, "You know that among the Goyim, those who are supposed to rule them become tyrants, and their superiors become dictators. ⁴³ But among you, it must not be like that! On the contrary, whoever among you wants to be a leader must be your servant; ⁴⁴ and whoever wants to be first among you must become everyone's slave! ⁴⁵ For the Son of Man did not come to be served, but to serve — and to give his life as a ransom for many."

⁴⁶ They came to Yericho; and as Yeshua was leaving Yericho with his talmidim and a great crowd, a blind beggar, Bar-Timai (son of Timai), was

---

Bar-Ti·mai — Bartimaeus
b'ra·khah — blessing
co·ha·nim — priests
get — divorce document
Go·yim — Gentiles, nations, pagans
Ke·fa — Peter
mitz·vot — commandments
Mo·she — Moses
Na·tze·ret — Nazareth
'o·lam ha·ba — the world/age to come
'o·lam ha·zeh — this world/age
P'ru·shim — Pharisees
tal·mi·dim — disciples
Ti·mai — Timaeus
To·rah — Teaching, "Law"; Pentateuch
To·rah-teachers — scribes
Ya·'a·kov — James
Yar·den — Jordan
Ye·ri·cho — Jericho
Ye·ru·sha·la·yim — Jerusalem
Ye·shu·a — Jesus
Y'hu·dah — Judea
Yo·cha·nan — John
Zav·dai — Zebedee

sitting by the side of the road. 47 When
he heard that it was Yeshua from
Natzeret, he started shouting, "Yeshua!
Son of David! Have pity on me!"
48 Many people scolded him and told
him to be quiet, but he shouted all the
louder, "Son of David! Have pity on
me!" 49 Yeshua stopped and said, "Call
him over!" They called to the blind
man, "Courage! Get up! He's calling
for you!" 50 Throwing down his blanket,
he jumped up and came over to Yeshua.
51 "What do you want me to do for
you?" asked Yeshua. The blind man
said to him, "Rabbi, let me be able to
see again." 52 Yeshua said to him, "Go!
Your trust has healed you." Instantly
he received his sight and followed him
on the road.

11 1 As they were approaching
Yerushalayim, near Beit-Pagey
and Beit-Anyah, by the Mount of
Olives, Yeshua sent two of his *talmidim*
2 with these instructions: "Go into the
village ahead of you; and as soon as
you enter it, you will find a colt tied
there that has never been ridden. Untie
it, and bring it here. 3 If anyone asks
you, 'Why are you doing this?' tell him,
'The Lord needs it,' and he will send it
here right away."

4 They went off and found a colt in
the street tied in a doorway, and they
untied it. 5 The bystanders said to them,
"What are you doing, untying that
colt?" 6 They gave the answer Yeshua
had told them to give, and they let them
continue. 7 They brought the colt to
Yeshua and threw their robes on it, and
he sat on it.

8 Many people carpeted the road
with their clothing, while others spread
out green branches which they had cut
in the fields. 9 Those who were ahead
and those behind shouted,

> **"Please! Deliver us!"**[m]
>
> **"Blessed is he who comes in the name of *Adonai*!"**[n]
>
> 10 "Blessed is the coming Kingdom of our father David!"

and,

> "You in the highest heaven! **Please! Deliver us!"**[o]

11 Yeshua entered Yerushalayim, went
into the Temple courts and took a good
look at everything; but since it was now
late, he went out with the Twelve to
Beit-Anyah.

12 The next day, as they came back
from Beit-Anyah, he felt hungry. 13 Spotting in the distance a fig tree in leaf, he
went to see if he could find anything on
it. When he came up to it, he found
nothing but leaves; for it wasn't fig
season. 14 He said to it, "May no one
ever eat fruit from you again!" And his
talmidim heard what he said.

15 On reaching Yerushalayim, he
entered the Temple courts and began
driving out those who were carrying on
business there, both the merchants and
their customers. He also knocked over
the desks of the money-changers, upset
the benches of the pigeon-dealers, 16 and
refused to let anyone carry merchandise
through the Temple courts. 17 Then, as
he taught them, he said, "Isn't it written
in the *Tanakh*, **My house will be called
a house of prayer for all the *Goyim***[p]
But you have made it into a **den of
robbers!"**[q] 18 The head *cohanim* and the
Torah-teachers heard what he said and
tried to find a way to do away with him;
they were afraid of him, because the
crowds were utterly taken by his teaching. 19 When evening came, they left the
city.

m Psalm 118:25 *n* Psalm 118:26
o Psalm 118:25 *p* Isaiah 56:7
q Jeremiah 7:11

²⁰In the morning, as the *talmidim* passed by, they saw the fig tree withered all the way to its roots. ²¹Kefa remembered and said to Yeshua, "Rabbi! Look! The fig tree that you cursed has dried up!" ²²He responded, "Have the kind of trust that comes from God! ²³Yes! I tell you that whoever does not doubt in his heart but trusts that what he says will happen can say to this mountain, 'Go and throw yourself into the sea!' and it will be done for him. ²⁴Therefore, I tell you, whatever you ask for in prayer, trust that you are receiving it, and it will be yours. ²⁵And when you stand praying, if you have anything against anyone, forgive him; so that your Father in heaven may also forgive your offenses." ²⁶*

²⁷They went back into Yerushalayim; and as he was walking in the Temple courts, there came to him the head *cohanim*, the *Torah*-teachers and the elders; ²⁸and they said to him, "What *s'mikhah* do you have that authorizes you to do these things? Who gave you this *s'mikhah* authorizing you to do them?" ²⁹Yeshua said to them, "I will ask you just one question: answer me, and I will tell you by what *s'mikhah* I do these things. ³⁰The immersion of Yochanan — was it from Heaven or from a human source? Answer me." ³¹They discussed it among themselves: "If we say, 'From Heaven,' he will say, 'Then why didn't you believe him?' ³²But if we say, 'From a human source,...'" — they were afraid of the people, for they all regarded Yochanan as a genuine prophet. ³³So they answered Yeshua, "We don't know." "Then," he replied, "I won't tell you by what *s'mikhah* I do these things."

12 ¹Yeshua began speaking to them in parables. "A man planted a vineyard. He put a wall around it, dug a pit for the wine press and built a tower; then he rented it to tenant-farmers and left. ²When harvest-time came, he sent a servant to the tenants to collect his share of the crop from the vineyard. ³But they took him, beat him up and sent him away empty-handed. ⁴So he sent another servant; this one they punched in the head and insulted. ⁵He sent another one, and him they killed; and so with many others — some they beat up, others they killed. ⁶He had still one person left, a son whom he loved; in the end, he sent him to them, saying, 'My son they will respect.' ⁷But the tenants said to each other, 'This is the heir. Come, let's kill him, and the inheritance will be ours!' ⁸So they seized him, killed him and threw him out of the vineyard. ⁹What will the owner of the vineyard do? He will come, destroy those tenants and give the vineyard to others! ¹⁰Haven't you read the passage in the *Tanakh* that says,

> **'The very rock which the builders rejected
> has become the cornerstone!**

A·do·nai — the LORD, Jehovah
Beit-An·yah — Bethany
Beit-Pa·gey — Bethphage
co·ha·nim — priests
Da·vid — David
Go·yim — Gentiles, nations, pagans
Ke·fa — Peter
Na·tze·ret — Nazareth
s'mi·khah — ordination
tal·mi·dim — disciples
Ta·nakh — Hebrew Scriptures, "Old Testament"
To·rah-teachers — scribes
Ye·ru·sha·la·yim — Jerusalem
Ye·shu·a — Jesus
Yo·cha·nan — John

---

* Some manuscripts include verse 11:26: But if you do not forgive, your Father in heaven will not forgive your offenses.

61

¹¹ **This has come from *Adonai*,**
and in our eyes it is amazing'?"ʳ

¹²They set about to arrest him, for they recognized that he had told the parable with reference to themselves. But they were afraid of the crowd, so they left him and went away.

¹³Next they sent some *P'rushim* and some members of Herod's party to him in order to trap him with a *sh'eilah*. ¹⁴They came and said to him, "Rabbi, we know that you tell the truth and are not concerned with what people think about you, since you pay no attention to a person's status but really teach what God's way is. Does *Torah* say that taxes are to be paid to the Roman Emperor, or not?" ¹⁵But he, knowing their hypocrisy, said to them, "Why are you trying to trap me? Bring me a denarius so I can look at it." ¹⁶They brought one; and he asked them, "Whose name and picture are these?" "The Emperor's," they replied. ¹⁷Yeshua said, "Give the Emperor what belongs to the Emperor. And give to God what belongs to God!" And they were amazed at him.

¹⁸Then some *Tz'dukim* came to him. They are the ones who say there is no such thing as resurrection, so they put to him a *sh'eilah*: ¹⁹"Rabbi, Moshe wrote for us that **if a man's brother dies and leaves a wife but no child, his brother must take the wife and have children to preserve the man's family line.**ˢ ²⁰There were seven brothers. The first one took a wife, and when he died he left no children. ²¹Then the second one took her and died without leaving children, and the third likewise, ²²and none of the seven left children. Last of all, the woman also died. ²³In the Resurrection, whose wife will she be? For all seven had her as wife."

²⁴Yeshua said to them, "Isn't this the reason that you go astray? because you are ignorant both of the *Tanakh* and of the power of God? ²⁵For when people rise from the dead, neither men nor women marry — they are like angels in heaven. ²⁶And as for the dead being raised, haven't you read in the book of Moshe, in the passage about the bush, how God said to him, '**I am the God of Avraham, the God of Yitzchak and the God of Ya'akov'?**ᵗ ²⁷ He is God not of the dead, but of the living! You are going far astray!"

²⁸One of the *Torah*-teachers came up and heard them engaged in this discussion. Seeing that Yeshua answered them well, he asked him, "Which is the most important *mitzvah* of them all?" ²⁹Yeshua answered, "The most important is,

'*Sh'ma Israel, Adonai Eloheynu, Adonai echad* [Hear, O Israel, the LORD our God, the LORD is one], ³⁰and you are to love *Adonai* your God with all your heart, with all your soul, with all your understanding **and with all your strength.'**ᵘ

³¹The second is this:

'You are to love your neighbor as yourself.'ᵛ

There is no other *mitzvah* greater than these." ³²The *Torah*-teacher said to him, "Well said, Rabbi; you speak the truth when you say that he is one, and that there is no other besides him; ³³and that loving him with all one's heart, understanding and strength, and loving one's neighbor as oneself, mean more than all the burnt offerings and sacrifices." ³⁴When Yeshua saw that he responded sensibly, he said to him,

---

ʳ Psalm 118:22-23   ˢ Deuteronomy 25:5-6

ᵗ Exodus 3:6   ᵘ Deuteronomy 6:4-5

ᵛ Leviticus 19:18

"You are not far from the Kingdom of God." And after that, no one dared put to him another *sh'eilah*.

³⁵ As Yeshua was teaching in the Temple, he asked, "How is it that the *Torah*-teachers say the Messiah is the Son of David? ³⁶ David himself, inspired by the *Ruach HaKodesh*, said,

> '*Adonai* said to my Lord,
> "Sit here at my right hand
> until I put your enemies under
> your feet."'ʷ

³⁷ David himself calls him 'Lord'; so how is he his son?"

The great crowd listened eagerly to him. ³⁸ As he taught them, he said, "Watch out for the kind of *Torah*-teachers who like to walk around in robes and be greeted deferentially in the marketplaces, ³⁹ who like to have the best seats in the synagogues and take the places of honor at banquets, ⁴⁰ who like to swallow up widows' houses while making a show of *davvening* at great length. Their punishment will be all the worse!"

⁴¹ Then Yeshua sat down opposite the Temple treasury and watched the crowd as they put money into the offering-boxes. Many rich people put in large sums, ⁴² but a poor widow came and put in two small coins. ⁴³ He called his *talmidim* to him and said to them, "Yes! I tell you, this poor widow has put more in the offering-box than all the others making donations. ⁴⁴ For all of them, out of their wealth, have contributed money they can easily spare; but she, out of her poverty, has given everything she had to live on."

13 ¹ As Yeshua came out of the Temple, one of the *talmidim* said to him, "Look, Rabbi! What huge stones! What magnificent buildings!"

² "You see all these great buildings?" Yeshua said to him, "They will be totally destroyed — not a single stone will be left standing!"

³ As he was sitting on the Mount of Olives opposite the Temple, Kefa, Ya'akov, Yochanan and Andrew asked him privately, ⁴ "Tell us, when will these things happen? And what sign will show when all these things are about to be accomplished?"

⁵ Yeshua began speaking to them: "Watch out! Don't let anyone fool you! ⁶ Many will come in my name, saying, 'I am he!' and they will fool many people. ⁷ When you hear the noise of wars nearby and the news of wars far off, don't become frightened. Such things must happen, but the end is yet to come. ⁸ For peoples will fight each other, and nations will fight each other, there will be earthquakes in various places, there will be famines; this is but the beginning of the 'birth pains'.

A·do·nai — the LORD, Jehovah
Av·ra·ham — Abraham
Da·vid — David
dav·ven·ing — praying
Ke·fa — Peter
mitz·vah — commandment, principle
Mo·she — Moses
P'ru·shim — Pharisees
Ru·ach-Ha·Ko·desh — Holy Spirit
sh'ei·lah — question
Sh'ma Is·ra·el, A·do·nai E·lo·hey·nu,
   A·do·nai e·chad — Hear, O Israel, the
   LORD our God, the LORD is one
tal·mi·dim — disciples
Ta·nakh — Hebrew Scriptures, "Old Testament"
To·rah — Teaching, "Law"; Pentateuch
To·rah-teacher — scribe
Tz'du·kim — Sadducees
Ya·'a·kov — James
Ye·shu·a — Jesus
Yitz·chak — Isaac
Yo·cha·nan — John

ʷ Psalm 110:1

[9]"But you, watch yourselves! They will hand you over to the local *sanhedrins*, you will be beaten up in synagogues, and on my account you will stand before governors and kings as witnesses to them. [10]Indeed, the Good News has to be proclaimed first to all the *Goyim*. [11]Now when they arrest you and bring you to trial, don't worry beforehand about what to say. Rather, say whatever is given you when the time comes; for it will not be just you speaking, but the *Ruach HaKodesh*. [12]Brother will betray brother to death, and a father his child; children will turn against their parents and have them put to death; [13]and everyone will hate you because of me. But whoever holds out till the end will be delivered.

[14]"Now when you see **the abomination that causes devastation**[x] standing where it ought not to be" (let the reader understand the allusion), "that will be the time for those in Y'hudah to escape to the hills. [15]If someone is on the roof, he must not go down and enter his house to take any of his belongings; [16]if someone is in the field, he must not turn back to get his coat. [17]What a terrible time it will be for pregnant women and nursing mothers! [18]Pray that it may not happen in winter. [19]For there will be **worse trouble** at that time **than there has ever been from the very beginning,** when God created the universe, **until now; and there will be nothing like it again.**[y] [20]Indeed, if God had not limited the duration of the trouble, no one would survive; but for the sake of the elect, those whom he has chosen, he has limited it.

[21]"At that time, if anyone says to you, 'Look! Here's the Messiah!' or, 'See, there he is!' — don't believe him!

[22]There will appear false messiahs and false prophets performing signs and wonders for the purpose, if possible, of misleading the chosen. [23]But you, watch out! I have told you everything in advance!

[24]"In those days, after that trouble,

**the sun will grow dark,
the moon will stop shining,**
[25] **the stars will fall from the sky,
and the powers in heaven will be shaken.**[z]

[26]Then they will see **the Son of Man coming in clouds** with tremendous power and glory.[a] [27]He will send out his angels and gather together his chosen people from the four winds, from the ends of the earth to the ends of heaven.

[28]"Now let the fig tree teach you its lesson: when its branches begin to sprout and leaves appear, you know that summer is approaching. [29]In the same way, when you see all these things happening, you are to know that the time is near, right at the door. [30]Yes! I tell you that this people will certainly not pass away before all these things happen. [31]Heaven and earth will pass away, but my words will certainly not pass away. [32]However, when that day and hour will come, no one knows — not the angels in heaven, not the Son, just the Father. [33]Stay alert! Be on your guard! For you do not know when the time will come.

[34]"It's like a man who travels away from home, puts his servants in charge, each with his own task, and tells the doorkeeper to stay alert. [35]So stay alert! for you don't know when the owner of the house will come, [36]whether it will be evening, midnight, cockcrow

---

x Daniel 9:27, 11:31, 12:11
y Joel 2:2, Daniel 12:1

z Isaiah 13:10, 34:4; Ezekiel 32:7; Joel 2:10, 3:4 (2:31), 4:15(3:15); Haggai 2:6, 21
a Daniel 7:13-14

or morning — you don't want him to come suddenly and find you sleeping! ³⁷ And what I say to you, I say to everyone: stay alert!"

14 ¹ It was now two days before Pesach (that is, the festival of Matzah), and the head cohanim and the Torah-teachers were trying to find some way to arrest Yeshua surreptitiously and have him put to death; ² for they said, "Not during the festival, or the people will riot."

³ While he was in Beit-Anyah in the home of Shim'on (a man who had had a repulsive skin disease), and as he was eating, a woman came with an alabaster jar of perfume, pure oil of nard, very costly, broke the jar and poured the perfume over his head. ⁴ But some there angrily said to themselves, "Why this waste of perfume? ⁵ It could have been sold for a year's wages and given to the poor!" And they scolded her. ⁶ But Yeshua said, "Let her be. Why are you bothering her? She has done a beautiful thing for me. ⁷ For you will always have the poor with you; and whenever you want to, you can help them. But you will not always have me. ⁸ What she could do, she did do — in advance she poured perfume on my body to prepare it for burial. ⁹ Yes! I tell you that wherever in the whole world this Good News is proclaimed, what she has done will be told in her memory."

¹⁰ Then Y'hudah from K'riot, who was one of the Twelve, went to the head cohanim in order to betray Yeshua to them. ¹¹ They were pleased to hear this and promised to give him money. And he began looking for a good opportunity to betray Yeshua.

¹² On the first day for matzah, when they slaughtered the lamb for Pesach, Yeshua's talmidim asked him, "Where do you want us to go and prepare your Seder?" ¹³ He sent two of his talmidim with these instructions: "Go into the city, and a man carrying a jar of water will meet you. Follow him; ¹⁴ and whichever house he enters, tell him that the Rabbi says, 'Where is the guest room for me, where I am to eat the Pesach meal with my talmidim?' ¹⁵ He will show you a large room upstairs, furnished and ready. Make the preparations there." ¹⁶ The talmidim went off, came to the city and found things just as he had told them they would be; and they prepared the Seder.

¹⁷ When evening came, Yeshua arrived with the Twelve. ¹⁸ As they were reclining and eating, Yeshua said, "Yes! I tell you that one of you is going to betray me." ¹⁹ They became upset and began asking him, one after the other, "You don't mean me, do you?" ²⁰ "It's one of the Twelve," he said to them, "someone dipping matzah in the dish with me. ²¹ For the Son of Man will die, just as the Tanakh says he will; but woe to that man by whom the Son of Man is betrayed! It would have been better for him had he never been born!"

²² While they were eating, Yeshua took a piece of matzah, made the

Beit-An·yah — Bethany
co·ha·nim — priests
Go·yim — Gentiles, nations, pagans
ma·tzah — unleavened bread
Pe·sach — Passover
Ru·ach-Ha·Ko·desh — Holy Spirit
san·hed·rin — Jewish religious court
Se·der — Passover eve meal
Shim·'on — Simon
tal·mi·dim — disciples
Ta·nakh — Hebrew Scriptures, "Old Testament"
To·rah-teachers — scribes
Ye·shu·a — Jesus
Y'hu·dah — Judea
Y'hu·dah from K'ri·ot — Judas Iscariot

b'rakhah, broke it, gave it to them and said, "Take it! This is my body." ²³ Also he took a cup of wine, made the *b'rakhah*, and gave it to them; and they all drank. ²⁴ He said to them, "This is my blood, which ratifies the New Covenant, my blood shed on behalf of many people. ²⁵ Yes! I tell you, I will not drink this 'fruit of the vine' again until the day I drink new wine in the Kingdom of God."

²⁶ After singing the *Hallel*, they went out to the Mount of Olives. ²⁷ Yeshua said to them, "You will all lose faith in me, for the *Tanakh* says,

> **'I will strike the shepherd dead, and the sheep will be scattered.'**[b]

²⁸ But after I have been raised, I will go ahead of you into the Galil." ²⁹ Kefa said to him, "Even if everyone else loses faith in you, I won't." ³⁰ Yeshua replied, "Yes! I tell you that this very night, before the rooster crows twice, you will disown me three times!" ³¹ But Kefa kept insisting, "Even if I must die with you, I will never disown you!" And they all said the same thing.

³² They went to a place called Gat-Sh'manim; and Yeshua said to his *talmidim*, "Sit here while I pray." ³³ He took with him Kefa, Ya'akov and Yochanan. Great distress and anguish came over him; ³⁴ and he said to them, "My heart is so filled with sadness that I could die! Remain here and stay awake." ³⁵ Going on a little farther, he fell on the ground and prayed that if possible, the hour might pass from him: ³⁶ "*Abba*!" (that is, "Dear Father!") "All things are possible for you. Take this cup away from me! Still, not what I want, but what you want." ³⁷ He came and found them sleeping; and he said to Kefa, "Shim'on, are you asleep?

Couldn't you stay awake one hour? ³⁸ Stay awake, and pray that you will not be put to the test — the spirit indeed is eager, but human nature is weak."

³⁹ Again he went away and prayed, saying the same words; ⁴⁰ and again he came and found them sleeping, their eyes were so very heavy; and they didn't know what to answer him.

⁴¹ The third time, he came and said to them, "For now, go on sleeping, take your rest.... There, that's enough! The time has come! Look! The Son of Man is being betrayed into the hands of sinners! ⁴² Get up! Let's go! Here comes my betrayer!"

⁴³ While Yeshua was still speaking, Y'hudah (one of the Twelve!) came, and with him a crowd carrying swords and clubs, from the head *cohanim*, the *Torah*-teachers and the elders. ⁴⁴ The betrayer had arranged to give them a signal: "The man I kiss is the one you want. Grab him, and take him away under guard." ⁴⁵ As he arrived, he went right up to Yeshua, said, "Rabbi!" and kissed him. ⁴⁶ Then they laid hold of Yeshua and arrested him; ⁴⁷ but one of the people standing nearby drew his sword and struck at the servant of the *cohen hagadol*, cutting off his ear.

⁴⁸ Yeshua addressed them: "So you came out to take me with swords and clubs, the way you would the leader of a rebellion? ⁴⁹ Every day I was with you in the Temple court, teaching, and you didn't seize me then! But let the *Tanakh* be fulfilled." ⁵⁰ And they all deserted him and ran away. ⁵¹ There was one young man who did try to follow him; but he was wearing only a nightshirt; and when they tried to seize him, ⁵² he slipped out of the nightshirt and ran away naked.

⁵³ They led Yeshua to the *cohen hagadol*, with whom all the head

[b] Zechariah 13:7

cohanim, elders and *Torah*-teachers were assembling. [54]Kefa followed him at a distance right into the courtyard of the *cohen hagadol*, where he sat down with the guards and warmed himself by the fire.

[55]The head *cohanim* and the whole *Sanhedrin* tried to find evidence against Yeshua, so that they might have him put to death, but they couldn't find any. [56]For many people gave false evidence against him, but their testimonies didn't agree. [57]Some stood up and gave this false testimony: [58]"We heard him say, 'I will destroy this Temple made with hands; and in three days I will build another one, not made with hands.'" [59]Even so, their testimonies didn't agree.

[60]The *cohen hagadol* stood up in the front and asked Yeshua, "Have you nothing to say to the accusations these men are making?" [61]But he remained silent and made no reply. Again the *cohen hagadol* questioned him: "Are you the *Mashiach, Ben-HaM'vorakh*?" [62]"I AM," answered Yeshua. "Moreover, you will see **the Son of Man sitting at the right hand of** *HaG'vurah* **and coming on the clouds of heaven.**"[c] [63]At this, the *cohen hagadol* tore his clothes and said, "Why do we still need witnesses? [64]You heard him blaspheme! What is your decision?" And they all declared him guilty and subject to the death penalty.

[65]Then some began spitting at him; and after blindfolding him, they started pounding him with their fists and saying to him, "Let's see you prophesy!" And as the guards took him, they beat him too.

[66]Meanwhile, Kefa was still in the courtyard below. One of the serving-girls of the *cohen hagadol* [67]saw Kefa warming himself, took a look at him, and said, "You were with the man from Natzeret, Yeshua!" [68]But he denied it, saying, "I haven't the faintest idea what you're talking about!" He went outside into the entryway, and a rooster crowed. [69]The girl saw him there and started telling the bystanders, "This fellow is one of them." [70]Again he denied it. A little later, the bystanders themselves said to Kefa, "You must be one of them, because you're from the Galil." [71]At this he began to invoke a curse on himself as he swore, "I do not know this man you are telling me about!" — [72]and immediately the rooster crowed a second time. Then Kefa remembered what Yeshua had said to him, "Before the rooster crows twice, you will disown me three times." And throwing himself down, he cried.

15 [1]As soon as it was morning, the head *cohanim* held a council meeting with the elders, the *Torah*-

---

Ab·ba — Dear Father, "Dad"
Ben-Ha M'vo·rakh — son of the Blessed One, i.e., son of God.
b'ra·khah — blessing
co·ha·nim — priests
co·hen ha·ga·dol — high priest
the Ga·lil — Galilee
Gat-Sh'ma·nim — Gethsemane
Ha·G'vu·rah — the Power, i.e., God
Hal·lel — psalms of praise
Ke·fa — Peter
Ma·shi·ach — Messiah
ma·tzah — unleavened bread
Na·tze·ret — Nazareth
san·hed·rin — Jewish religious court
Shim·'on — Simon
tal·mi·dim — disciples
Ta·nakh — Hebrew Scriptures, "Old Testament"
To·rah-teachers — scribes
Ya·'a·kov — James
Ye·shu·a — Jesus
Y'hu·dah — Judas
Yo·cha·nan — John

---

c   Daniel 7:13, Psalm 110:1

teachers and the whole *Sanhedrin.* Then they put Yeshua in chains, led him away and handed him over to Pilate. ² Pilate put this question to him: "Are you the King of the Jews?" He answered him, "The words are yours." ³ The head *cohanim* too made accusations against him, ⁴ and Pilate again inquired of him, "Aren't you going to answer? Look how many charges they are making against you!" ⁵ But Yeshua made no further response, to Pilate's amazement.

⁶ Now during a festival, Pilate used to set free one prisoner, whomever the crowd requested. ⁷ There was in prison among the rebels who had committed murder during the insurrection a man called Bar-Abba. ⁸ When the crowd came up and began asking Pilate to do for them what he usually did, ⁹ he asked them, "Do you want me to set free for you the 'King of the Jews'?" ¹⁰ For it was evident to him that it was out of jealousy that the head *cohanim* had handed him over. ¹¹ But the head *cohanim* stirred up the crowd to have him release Bar-Abba for them instead. ¹² Pilate again said to them, "Then what should I do with the man you call the King of the Jews?" ¹³ They shouted back, "Put him to death on the stake!" ¹⁴ He asked, "Why? What crime has he committed?" But they only shouted louder, "Put him to death on the stake!" ¹⁵ So Pilate, wishing to satisfy the mob, set Bar-Abba free for them; but he had Yeshua whipped and then handed over to be executed on the stake.

¹⁶ The soldiers led him away inside the palace (that is, the headquarters building) and called together the whole battalion. ¹⁷ They dressed him in purple and wove thorn branches into a crown, which they put on him. ¹⁸ Then they began to salute him, "Hail to the King of the Jews!" ¹⁹ They hit him on the head with a stick, spat on him and kneeled in mock worship of him. ²⁰ When they had finished ridiculing him, they took off the purple robe, put his own clothes back on him and led him away to be nailed to the execution-stake.

²¹ A certain man from Cyrene, Shim'on, the father of Alexander and Rufus, was passing by on his way in from the country; and they forced him to carry the stake. ²² They brought Yeshua to a place called Gulgolta (which means "place of a skull"), ²³ and they gave him wine spiced with myrrh, but he didn't take it. ²⁴ Then they nailed him to the execution-stake; and they divided his clothes among themselves, throwing dice to determine what each man should get. ²⁵ It was nine in the morning when they nailed him to the stake. ²⁶ Over his head, the written notice of the charge against him read,

THE KING OF THE JEWS

²⁷ On execution-stakes with him they placed two robbers, one on his right and one on his left. ²⁸* ²⁹ People passing by hurled insults at him, shaking their heads and saying, "Aha! So you can destroy the Temple, can you, and rebuild it in three days? ³⁰ Save yourself and come down from the stake!" ³¹ Likewise, the head *cohanim* and the *Torah*-teachers made fun of him, saying to each other, "He saved others, but he can't save himself!" ³² and, "So he's the Messiah, is he? The King of Israel? Let him come down now from the stake! If we see that, then we'll believe him!" Even the men nailed up with him insulted him.

---

* Some manuscripts include verse 15:28: And the passage from the *Tanakh* was fulfilled which says, **"He was counted with transgressors."** (Isaiah 53:12)

³³At noon, darkness covered the whole Land until three o'clock in the afternoon ³⁴At three, he uttered a loud cry, " *Elohi! Elohi! L'mah sh'vaktani?*" (which means, "My God! My God! Why have you deserted me?")*ᵈ* ³⁵On hearing this, some of the bystanders said, "Look! He's calling for Eliyahu!" ³⁶One ran and soaked a sponge in **vinegar**, put it on a stick and **gave** it to him **to drink**.*ᵉ* "Wait!" he said, "Let's see if Eliyahu will come and take him down." ³⁷But Yeshua let out a loud cry and gave up his spirit. ³⁸And the *parokhet* in the Temple was torn in two from top to bottom. ³⁹When the Roman officer who stood facing him saw the way he gave up his spirit, he said, "This man really was a son of God!"

⁴⁰There were women looking on from a distance; among them were Miryam from Magdala, Miryam the mother of the younger Ya'akov and of Yosi, and Shlomit. ⁴¹These women had followed him and helped him when he was in the Galil. And many other women were there who had come up with him to Yerushalayim.

⁴²Since it was Preparation Day (that is, the day before a *Shabbat*), as evening approached, ⁴³Yosef of Ramatayim, a prominent member of the *Sanhedrin* who himself was also looking forward to the Kingdom of God, went boldly to Pilate and asked for Yeshua's body. ⁴⁴Pilate was surprised to hear that he was already dead, so he summoned the officer and asked him if he had been dead awhile. ⁴⁵After he had gotten confirmation from the officer that Yeshua was dead, he granted Yosef the corpse. ⁴⁶Yosef purchased a linen sheet; and after taking Yeshua down, he wrapped him in the linen sheet, laid him in a tomb which had been cut out of the rock, and rolled a stone against the entrance to the tomb. ⁴⁷Miryam of Magdala and Miryam the mother of Yosi saw where he had been laid.

16 ¹¹When *Shabbat* was over, Miryam of Magdala, Miryam the mother of Ya'akov, and Shlomit bought spices in order to go and anoint Yeshua. ²Very early on Sunday, just after sunrise, they went to the tomb. ³They were asking each other, "Who will roll away the stone from the entrance to the tomb for us?" ⁴Then they looked up and saw that the stone, even though it was huge, had been rolled back already. ⁵On entering the tomb, they saw a young man dressed in a white robe sitting on the right; and they were dumbfounded. ⁶But he said, "Don't be so surprised! You're looking for Yeshua from Natzeret, who was executed on the stake. He has risen, he's not here! Look

Bar-Ab·ba — Barabbas
co·ha·nim — priests
E·li·ya·hu — Elijah
E·lo·hi! E·lo·hi! L'mah sh'vak·ta·ni — My God! My God! Why have you left me?
the Ga·lil — Galilee
Gul·gol·ta — Golgotha, Calvary
Ke·fa — Peter
Mir·yam — Miriam, Mary
Na·tze·ret — Nazareth
pa·ro·khet — curtain
Ra·ma·ta·yim — Arimathea
san·hed·rin — Jewish religious court
Shab·bat — the Sabbath
Shim·'on — Simon
Shlo·mit — Salome
tal·mi·dim — disciples
Ta·nakh — Hebrew Scriptures, "Old Testament"
To·rah-teachers — scribes
Ya·'a·kov — James
Ye·ru·sha·la·yim — Jerusalem
Ye·shu·a — Jesus
Yo·sef — Joseph
Yo·si — "Joe" (diminutive of Yosef, "Joseph")

d Psalm 22:2(1)   *e* Psalm 69:22(21)

at the place where they laid him. [7] But go and tell his *talmidim*, especially Kefa, that he is going to the Galil ahead of you. You will see him there, just as he told you." [8] Trembling but ecstatic they went out and fled from the tomb, and they said nothing to anyone, because they were afraid.

[*9] When Yeshua rose early Sunday, he appeared first to Miryam of Magdala, from whom he had expelled seven demons. [10] She went and told those who had been with him, as they were crying and mourning. [11] But when they heard that he was alive and that she had seen him, they wouldn't believe it.

[12] After that, Yeshua appeared in another form to two of them as they were walking into the country. [13] They went and told the others, but they didn't believe them either.

---

* Verses 16:9-20 are found in many ancient Greek manuscripts but not in the two oldest ones.

[14] Later, Yeshua appeared to the Eleven as they were eating, and he reproached them for their lack of trust and their spiritual insensitivity in not having believed those who had seen him after he had risen. [15] Then he said to them, "As you go throughout the world, proclaim the Good News to all creation. [16] Whoever trusts and is immersed will be saved; whoever does not trust will be condemned. [17] And these signs will accompany those who do trust: in my name they will drive out demons, speak with new tongues, [18] not be injured if they handle snakes or drink poison, and heal the sick by laying hands on them."

[19] So then, after he had spoken to them, the Lord Yeshua was taken up into heaven and **sat at the right hand of God**.[f] [20] And they went out and proclaimed everywhere, the Lord working with them and confirming the message by the accompanying signs.

---

f Psalm 110:1

THE GOOD NEWS OF YESHUA THE MESSIAH, AS REPORTED BY

LUKE

1 ¹Dear Theophilos:
Concerning the matters that have taken place among us, many people have undertaken to draw up accounts ²based on what was handed down to us by those who from the start were eyewitnesses and proclaimers of the message. ³Therefore, Your Excellency, since I have carefully investigated all these things from the beginning, it seemed good to me that I too should write you an accurate and ordered narrative, ⁴so that you might know how well-founded are the things about which you have been taught.

⁵In the days of Herod, King of Y'hudah, there was a *cohen* named Z'kharyah who belonged to the Aviyah division. His wife was a descendant of Aharon, and her name was Elisheva. ⁶Both of them were righteous before God, observing all the *mitzvot* and ordinances of *Adonai* blamelessly. ⁷But they had no children, because Elisheva was barren; and they were both well along in years.

⁸One time, when Z'kharyah was fulfilling his duties as *cohen* during his division's period of service before God, ⁹he was chosen by lot (according to the custom among the *cohanim*) to enter the Temple and burn incense. ¹⁰All the people were outside, praying, at the time of the incense burning, ¹¹when there appeared to him an angel of *Adonai* standing to the right of the incense altar. ¹²Z'kharyah was startled and terrified at the sight. ¹³But the angel said to him, "Don't be afraid, Z'kharyah; because your prayer has been heard. Your wife Elisheva will bear you a son, and you are to name him Yochanan. ¹⁴He will be a joy and a delight to you, and many people will rejoice when he is born, ¹⁵for he will be great in the sight of *Adonai*. He is never to drink wine or other liquor, and he will be filled with the *Ruach HaKodesh* even from his mother's womb. ¹⁶He will turn many of the people of Israel to *Adonai* their God. ¹⁷He will go out ahead of *Adonai* in the spirit and power of Eliyahu to **turn the hearts of fathers to their children**[a] and the disobedient to the wisdom of the righteous, to make ready for *Adonai* a people prepared."

---

[a] Malachi 3:23-24(4:5-6)

A·do·nai — the LORD, Jehovah
A·ha·ron — Aaron
A·vi·yah — Abijah, Abia
co·ha·nim — priests
co·hen — priest
E·li·she·va — Elizabeth, Elisabeth
E·li·ya·hu — Elijah
the Ga·lil — Galilee
Mir·yam — Miriam, Mary
mitz·vot — commandments, principles
Ru·ach-Ha·Ko·desh — Holy Spirit
Ya·'a·kov — James
Ye·shu·a — Jesus
Yo·cha·nan — John
Z'khar·yah — Zechariah, Zacharias

[18]Z'kharyah said to the angel, "How can I be sure of this? For I am an old man; my wife too is well on in years." [19]"I am Gavri'el," the angel answered him, "and I stand in the presence of God. I was sent to speak to you, to give you this good news. [20]Now, because you didn't believe what I said, which will be fulfilled when the time comes, you will be silent, unable to speak until the day these things take place."

[21]Meanwhile, the people were waiting for Z'kharyah; they were surprised at his taking so long in the Temple. [22]But when he came out unable to talk to them, they realized that he had seen a vision in the Temple; speechless, he communicated to them with signs. [23]When his period of Temple service was over, he returned home. [24]Following this, Elisheva his wife conceived, and she remained five months in seclusion, saying, [25]"Adonai has done this for me; he has shown me favor at this time, so as to remove my public disgrace."

[26]In the sixth month, the angel Gavri'el was sent by God to a city in the Galil called Natzeret, [27]to a virgin engaged to a man named Yosef, of the house of David; the virgin's name was Miryam. [28]Approaching her, the angel said, "Shalom, favored lady! Adonai is with you!" [29]She was deeply troubled by his words and wondered what kind of greeting this might be. [30]The angel said to her, "Don't be afraid, Miryam, for you have found favor with God. [31]Look! You will become pregnant, you will give birth to a son, and you are to name him Yeshua. [32]He will be great, he will be called Son of HaElyon. Adonai, God, will give him the throne of his forefather David; [33]and he will rule the House of Ya'akov forever — there will be no end to his Kingdom." [34]"How can this be," asked Miryam of the angel, "since I am a virgin?" [35]The angel answered her,

"The Ruach HaKodesh will come over you,
the power of HaElyon will cover you.
Therefore the holy child born to you
will be called the Son of God.

[36]You have a relative, Elisheva, who is an old woman; and everyone says she is barren. But she has conceived a son and is six months pregnant! [37] For with God, nothing is impossible." [38]Miryam said, "I am the servant of Adonai; may it happen to me as you have said."

[39]Without delay, Miryam set out and hurried to the town in the hill country of Y'hudah [40]where Z'kharyah lived, entered his house and greeted Elisheva. [41]When Elisheva heard Miryam's greeting, the baby in her womb stirred, Elisheva was filled with the Ruach HaKodesh [42]and spoke up in a loud voice,

"How blessed are you among women! And how blessed is the child in your womb!

[43]"But who am I, that the mother of my Lord should come to me? [44]For as soon as the sound of your greeting reached my ears, the baby in my womb leaped for joy! [45]Indeed you are blessed, because you have trusted that the promise Adonai has made to you will be fulfilled."

[46]Then Miryam said,

"My soul magnifies Adonai;
[47]**and** my spirit **rejoices in God, my Savior,**
[48]who **has taken notice of** his **servant-girl
in her humble position.**[b]

For — imagine it! — from now on, all generations will call me blessed!

b I Samuel 2:1, 1:11

[49] "The Mighty One has done great things for me!

Indeed, **his name is holy;**

[50] and in every generation

he has **mercy on those who fear him.**[c]

[51] "He has performed mighty deeds with his arm,

routed the secretly proud,

[52] brought down rulers from their thrones,

raised up the humble,

[53] filled the hungry with good things,

but sent the rich away empty.

[54] "He has taken the part of his servant Israel,

mindful of the mercy

[55] which he promised to our fathers,

to Avraham and his seed forever."

[56] Miryam stayed with Elisheva for about three months and then returned home.

[57] The time arrived for Elisheva to have her baby, and she gave birth to a son. [58] Her neighbors and relatives heard how good *Adonai* had been to her, and they rejoiced with her.

[59] On the eighth day, they came to do the child's *b'rit-milah*. They were about to name him Z'kharyah, after his father, [60] when his mother spoke up and said, "No, he is to be called Yochanan." [61] They said to her, "None of your relatives has that name," [62] and they made signs to his father to find out what he wanted him called. [63] He motioned for a writing tablet, and to everyone's surprise he wrote, "His name is Yochanan." [64] At that moment, his power of speech returned, and his first words were a *b'rakhah* to God. [65] All their neighbors were awestruck; and throughout the hill country of Y'hudah, people talked about all these

things. [66] Everyone who heard of them said to himself, "What is this child going to be?" For clearly the hand of *Adonai* was with him.

[67] His father Z'kharyah was filled with the *Ruach HaKodesh* and spoke this prophecy:

[68] "**Praised be *Adonai*, the God of Israel,**[d]

because he has visited and made a ransom to liberate his people

[69] by raising up for us a mighty Deliverer

who is a descendant of his servant David.

[70] It is just as he has spoken

through the mouth of the prophets from the very beginning —

[71] that we should be delivered from our enemies

and from the power of all who hate us.

[72] "This has happened so that he might show

the mercy promised to our fathers —

---

[d] Psalm 41:14(13), 72:18, 106:48

A·do·nai — the LORD, Jehovah
Av·ra·ham — Abraham
b'ra·khah — blessing
b'rit-mi·lah — ritual circumcision
Da·vid — David
E·li·she·va — Elizabeth, Elisabeth
the Ga·lil — Galilee
Gav·ri·'el — Gabriel
Ha·El·yon — the Highest, i.e., God
Mir·yam — Miriam, Mary
Na·tze·ret — Nazareth
Ru·ach-Ha·Ko·desh — Holy Spirit
Sha·lom! — Peace! (greeting)
Ya·'a·kov — James
Ye·shu·a — Jesus
Y'hu·dah — Judea
Yo·cha·nan — John
Yo·sef — Joseph
Z'khar·yah — Zechariah, Zacharias

---

[c] Psalms 111:9, 103:17

that he would remember his holy covenant,
^{73} the oath he swore before *Avraham avinu*
^{74} to grant us that we, freed from our enemies,
would serve him without fear,
^{75} in holiness and righteousness before him all our days.

^{76} "You, child, will be called a prophet of *HaElyon*;
you will **go before the Lord to prepare his way**^{e}
^{77} by spreading the knowledge among his people
that deliverance comes by having sins forgiven
^{78} through our God's most tender mercy,
which causes the Sunrise to visit us from Heaven,
^{79} to **shine upon those in darkness, living in the shadow of death,**^{f}
and to guide our feet into the paths of peace."

^{80} The child grew and became strong in spirit, and he lived in the wilderness until the time came for him to appear in public to Israel.

2 ^{1}Around this time, Emperor Augustus issued an order for a census to be taken throughout the Empire. ^{2}This registration, the first of its kind, took place when Quirinius was governing in Syria. ^{3}Everyone went to be registered, each to his own town. ^{4}So Yosef, because he was a descendant of David, went up from the town of Natzeret in the Galil to the town of David, called Beit-Lechem, in Y'hudah, ^{5}to be registered, with Miryam, to whom he was engaged, and who was pregnant. ^{6}While they were there, the time came for her to give birth; ^{7}and she gave birth to her first child, a son. She wrapped him in cloth and laid him down in a feeding trough, because there was no space for them at the inn.

^{8}In the countryside nearby were some shepherds spending the night in the fields, guarding their flocks, ^{9}when an angel of *Adonai* appeared to them, and the *Sh'khinah* of *Adonai* shone around them. They were terrified; ^{10}but the angel said to them, "Don't be afraid, because I am here announcing to you Good News that will bring great joy to all the people. ^{11}This very day, in the town of David, there was born for you a Deliverer who is the Messiah, the Lord. ^{12}Here is how you will know: you will find a baby wrapped in cloth and lying in a feeding trough." ^{13}Suddenly, along with the angel was a vast army from heaven praising God:

^{14} "In the highest heaven, glory to God!
And on earth, peace among people of good will!"

^{15}No sooner had the angels left them and gone back into heaven than the shepherds said to one another, "Let's go over to Beit-Lechem and see this thing that has happened, that *Adonai* has told us about." ^{16}Hurrying off, they came and found Miryam and Yosef, and the baby lying in the feeding trough. ^{17}Upon seeing this, they made known what they had been told about this child; ^{18}and all who heard were amazed by what the shepherds said to them. ^{19}Miryam treasured all these things and kept mulling them over in her heart. ^{20}Meanwhile, the shepherds returned, glorifying and praising God for everything they had heard and seen; it had been just as they had been told.

^{21}On the eighth day, when it was time for his *brit-milah*, he was given the name Yeshua, which is what the angel had called him before his conception.

---

e Malachi 3:1, Isaiah 40:3   *f* Isaiah 9:1(2)

²² When the time came for their purification according to the *Torah* of Moshe, they took him up to Yerushalayim to present him to *Adonai* ²³ (as it is written in the *Torah* of *Adonai,* "**Every firstborn male is to be consecrated to *Adonai*"**⁸) ²⁴ and also to offer a sacrifice of **a pair of doves or two young pigeons,**ʰ as required by the *Torah of Adonai.*

²⁵ There was in Yerushalayim a man named Shim'on. This man was a *tzaddik,* he was devout, he waited eagerly for God to comfort Israel, and the *Ruach HaKodesh* was upon him. ²⁶ It had been revealed to him by the *Ruach HaKodesh* that he would not die before he had seen the Messiah of *Adonai.* ²⁷ Prompted by the Spirit, he went into the Temple courts; and when the parents brought in the child Yeshua to do for him what the *Torah* required, ²⁸ Shim'on took him in his arms, made a *b'rakhah* to God, and said,

²⁹ "Now, *Adonai,* according to your word,
    your servant is at peace as you let him go;
³⁰ for I have seen with my own eyes your *yeshu'ah,*
³¹ which you prepared in the presence of all peoples —

³² a light that will bring revelation to the *Goyim*
    and glory to your people Israel."

³³ Yeshua's father and mother were marvelling at the things Shim'on was saying about him. ³⁴ Shim'on blessed them and said to the child's mother, Miryam,

"This child will cause many in Israel to fall and to rise,

he will become a sign whom people will speak against;
³⁵ moreover, a sword will pierce your own heart too.

All this will happen in order to reveal many people's inmost thoughts."

³⁶ There was also a prophet named Chanah Bat-P'nu'el, of the tribe of Asher. She was a very old woman — she had lived with her husband seven years after her marriage ³⁷ and had remained a widow ever since; now she was eighty-four. She never left the Temple grounds but worshipped there night and day, fasting and praying. ³⁸ She came by at that moment and began thanking God and speaking about the child to everyone who was waiting for Yerushalayim to be liberated.

³⁹ When Yosef and Miryam had finished doing everything required by the *Torah* of *Adonai,* they returned to the Galil, to their town Natzeret.

A·do·nai — the LORD, Jehovah
Av·ra·ham a·vi·nu — our father Abraham
Beit-Le·chem — Bethlehem
b'ra·khah — blessing
b'rit-mi·lah — ritual circumcision
Cha·nah Bat-P'nu·'el — Hannah (Anna) the daughter of Phanuel
Da·vid — David
the Ga·lil — Galilee
Go·yim — Gentiles, nations, pagans
Ha·El·yon — the Highest, i.e., God
Mir·yam — Miriam, Mary
Mo·she — Moses
Na·tze·ret — Nazareth
Ru·ach-Ha·Ko·desh — Holy Spirit
Shim'on — Simon
Sh'khi·nah — glorious Presence
To·rah — Teaching, "Law"; Pentateuch
tzad·dik — righteous man
Ye·ru·sha·la·yim — Jerusalem
Ye·shu·a — Jesus
ye·shu·'ah — salvation (word play on Yeshua)
Y'hu·dah — Judea
Yo·sef — Joseph

---

g Exodus 13:2, 12, 15   *h* Leviticus 12:8

⁴⁰The child grew and became strong and filled with wisdom — God's favor was upon him.

⁴¹Every year Yeshua's parents went to Yerushalayim for the festival of *Pesach*. ⁴²When he was twelve years old, they went up for the festival, as custom required. ⁴³But after the festival was over, when his parents returned, Yeshua remained in Yerushalayim. They didn't realize this; ⁴⁴supposing that he was somewhere in the caravan, they spent a whole day on the road before they began searching for him among their relatives and friends. ⁴⁵Failing to find him, they returned to Yerushalayim to look for him. ⁴⁶On the third day they found him — he was sitting in the Temple court among the rabbis, not only listening to them but questioning what they said; ⁴⁷and everyone who heard him was astonished at his insight and his responses. ⁴⁸When his parents saw him, they were shocked; and his mother said to him, "Son! Why have you done this to us? Your father and I have been terribly worried looking for you!" ⁴⁹He said to them, "Why did you have to look for me? Didn't you know that I had to be concerning myself with my Father's affairs?" ⁵⁰But they didn't understand what he meant.

⁵¹So he went with them to Natzeret and was obedient to them. But his mother stored up all these things in her heart.

⁵²And Yeshua grew both in wisdom and in stature, gaining favor both with other people and with God.

3 ¹In the fifteenth year of Emperor Tiberius' rule; when Pontius Pilate was governor of Y'hudah, Herod ruler of the Galil, his brother Philip ruler of Iturea and Trachonitis, and Lysanias ruler of Abilene, ²with Anan and Kayafa being the *cohanim g'dolim*; the word of God came to Yochanan Ben-Z'kharyah in the desert. ³He went all through the Yarden region proclaiming an immersion involving turning to God from sin in order to be forgiven. ⁴It was just as had been written in the book of the sayings of the prophet Yesha'yahu,

"The voice of someone crying out:
'In the desert prepare the way for
   Adonai!
Make straight paths for him!'"
⁵ Every valley must be filled in,
   every mountain and hill leveled off;
   the winding roads must be straightened
   and the rough ways made smooth.
⁶ Then all humanity will see
   God's deliverance.'"*i*

⁷Therefore, Yochanan said to the crowds who came out to be immersed by him, "You snakes! Who warned you to escape the coming punishment? ⁸If you have really turned from your sins, produce fruit that will prove it! And don't start saying to yourselves, 'Avraham is our father'! For I tell you that God can raise up for Avraham sons from these stones! ⁹Already the axe is at the root of the trees, ready to strike; every tree that doesn't produce good fruit will be chopped down and thrown in the fire!"

¹⁰The crowds asked Yochanan, "So then, what should we do?" ¹¹He answered, "Whoever has two coats should share with somebody who has none, and whoever has food should do the same." ¹²Tax-collectors also came to be immersed; and they asked him, "Rabbi, what should we do?" ¹³"Collect no more than the government assesses," he told them. ¹⁴Some soldiers asked him, "What about us? What should we do?" To them he said, "Don't intimidate

---

i Isaiah 40:3-5

anyone, don't accuse people falsely, and be satisfied with your pay."

¹⁵ The people were in a state of great expectancy, and everyone was wondering whether perhaps Yochanan himself might be the Messiah; ¹⁶ so Yochanan answered them all, "I am immersing you in water, but he who is coming is more powerful than I — I'm not worthy to untie his sandals! He will immerse you in the *Ruach HaKodesh* and in fire. ¹⁷ He has with him his winnowing fork to clear out his threshing floor and gather his wheat into his barn, but he will burn up the straw with unquenchable fire!"

¹⁸ And with many other warnings besides these he announced the Good News to the people.

¹⁹ But Yochanan also denounced Herod the regional governor for taking as his own wife Herodias, the wife of his brother, and for all the other wicked things Herod had done; ²⁰ whereupon Herod added this to the rest: he locked up Yochanan in prison.

²¹ While all the people were being immersed, Yeshua too was immersed. As he was praying, heaven was opened; ²² the *Ruach HaKodesh* came down on him in physical form like a dove; and a voice came from heaven, "You are my Son, whom I love; I am well pleased with you."

²³ Yeshua was about thirty years old when he began his public ministry. It was supposed that he was a son of the Yosef who was

of Eli,
²⁴ of Mattat,
of L'vi,
of Malki,
of Yannai,
of Yosef,
²⁵ of Mattityahu,
of Amotz,

of Nachum,
of Chesli,
of Naggai,
²⁶ of Machat,
of Mattityahu,
of Shim'i
of Yosef,
of Yodah,
²⁷ of Yochanan,
of Reisha,
of Z'rubavel
of Sh'altiel,
of Neri,

A·do·nai — the LORD, Jehovah
A·motz — Amos
A·nan — Annas
Av·ra·ham — Abraham
Ches·li — Esli
co·ha·nim g'do·lim — high priests
E·li — Heli
the Ga·lil — Galilee
Ka·ya·fa — Caiaphas
L'vi — Levi
Ma·chat — Maath
Mal·ki — Melchi
Mat·tat — Matthat
Mat·tit·ya·hu — Mattathias
Na·chum — Nahum
Nag·gai — Nagge
Na·tze·ret — Nazareth
Ne·ri — Neri
Pe·sach — Passover
Rei·sha — Rhesa
Ru·ach-Ha·Ko·desh — Holy Spirit
Sh'al·ti·el — Salathiel
Shim·'i — Semein
To·rah — Teaching, "Law"; Pentateuch
Yan·nai — Jannai, Janna
Yar·den — Jordan
Ye·ru·sha·la·yim — Jerusalem
Ye·sha'·ya·hu — Isaiah
Ye·shu·a — Jesus
Y'hu·dah — Judea
Yo·cha·nan — John; Joanan, Joanna
Yo·cha·nan Ben-Z'khar·yah — John the son of Zechariah (Zacharias)
Yo·dah — Joda, Juda
Yo·sef — Joseph, Josech
Z'ru·ba·vel — Zerubbabel, Zorobabel

²⁸ of Malki,
of Addi,
of Kosam,
of Elmadan,
of Er,
²⁹ of Yeshua,
of Eli'ezer,
of Yoram,
of Mattat,
of L'vi,
³⁰ of Shim'on,
of Y'hudah,
of Yosef,
of Yonam,
of Elyakim,
³¹ of Mal'ah,
of Manah,
of Mattatah,
of Natan,
of David,
³² of Yishai,
of Oved,
of Bo'az,
of Salmon,
of Nachshon,
³³ of Amminadav,
of Admin,
of Arni,
of Chetzron,
of Peretz,
of Y'hudah,
³⁴ of Ya'akov,
of Yitzchak,
of Avraham,
of Terach,
of Nachor,
³⁵ of Serug,
of Re'u,
of Peleg,
of Ever,
of Shelah
³⁶ of Keinan,
of Arpachshad,
of Shem,
of Noach,
of Lemekh,
³⁷ of Metushelach,

of Chanoch,
of Yered,
of Mahalal'el,
of Keinan,
³⁸ of Enosh,
of Shet,
of Adam,
of God.

4 ¹Then Yeshua, filled with the *Ruach HaKodesh*, returned from the Yarden and was led by the Spirit in the wilderness ²for forty days of testing by the Adversary. During that time he ate nothing, and afterwards he was hungry. ³The Adversary said to him, "If you are the Son of God, order this stone to become bread." ⁴Yeshua answered him, "The *Tanakh* says, '**Man does not live on bread alone.**'"ʲ

⁵The Adversary took him up, showed him in an instant all the kingdoms of the world, ⁶and said to him, "I will give you all this power and glory. It has been handed over to me, and I can give it to whomever I choose. ⁷So if you will worship me, it will all be yours." ⁸Yeshua answered him, "The *Tanakh* says, '**Worship *Adonai* your God and serve him** only.'"ᵏ

⁹Then he took him to Yerushalayim, set him on the highest point of the Temple and said to him, "If you are the Son of God, jump from here! ¹⁰For the *Tanakh* says,

> '**He will order his angels to be responsible for you**
> **and protect you.**
> ¹¹ **They will support you with their hands,**
> **so that you will not hurt your feet on the stones.'**"ˡ

ʲ Deuteronomy 8:3
ᵏ Deuteronomy 6:13-14   ˡ Psalm 91:11-12

[12] Yeshua answered him, "It also says, 'Do not put *Adonai* your God to the test.'"[m] [13] When the Adversary had ended all his testings, he let him alone until an opportune time.

[14] Yeshua returned to the Galil in the power of the Spirit, and reports about him spread throughout the countryside. [15] He taught in their synagogues, and everyone respected him.

[16] Now when he went to Natzeret, where he had been brought up, on *Shabbat* he went to the synagogue as usual. He stood up to read, [17] and he was given the scroll of the prophet Yesha'yahu. Unrolling the scroll, he found the place where it was written,

[18] "The Spirit of *Adonai* is upon me; therefore he has anointed me to announce Good News to the poor;

he has sent me to proclaim freedom for the imprisoned
and renewed sight for the blind,

to release those who have been crushed,
[19] to proclaim a year of the favor of *Adonai*."[n]

[20] After closing the scroll and returning it to the *shammash*, he sat down;

m Deuteronomy 6:16   *n* Isaiah 61:1-2, 58:6

A·dam — Adam
Ad·di — Addi
Ad·min — Admin
A·do·nai — the LORD, Jehovah
Am·mi·na·dav — Amminadab
Ar·ni — Arni
Ar·pach·shad — Arphaxad
Av·ra·ham — Abraham
Bo·'az — Boaz, Booz
Cha·noch — Enoch
Chetz·ron — Hezron, Esrom
Da·vid — David

E·li·'e·zer — Eliezer
El·ma·dan — Elmadam, Elmodam
El·ya·kim — Eliakim
E·nosh — Enos
Er — Er
E·ver — Eber, Heber
the Ga·lil — Galilee
Kei·nan — Cainan
Ko·sam — Cosam
L'vi — Levi
Le·mekh — Lamech
Ma·ha·lal·'el — Mahalaleel
Mal·'ah — Melea
Mal·ki — Melchi
Ma·nah — Menna
Mat·tat — Matthat
Mat·ta·tah — Mattatha
Me·tu·she·lach — Methuselah, Mathusala
Na·chor — Nahor, Nachor
Nach·shon — Nahshon, Naasson
Na·tan — Nathan
Na·tze·ret — Nazareth
No·ach — Noah, Noe
O·ved — Obed
Pe·leg — Peleg, Phalec
Pe·retz — Perez
Re·'u — Reu, Ragau
Ru·ach-Ha·Ko·desh — Holy Spirit
Sal·mon — Salmon
Se·rug — Serug, Saruch
Shab·bat — the Sabbath
sham·mash — attendant
She·lah — Shelah, Sala
Shem — Shem, Sem
Shet — Seth
Shim·'on — Simeon
Ta·nakh — Hebrew Scriptures, "Old Testament"
Te·rach — Terah, Thara
Ya·'a·kov — Jacob
Yar·den — Jordan
Ye·red — Jared
Ye·ru·sha·la·yim — Jerusalem
Ye·sha'·ya·hu — Isaiah
Ye·shu·a — Jesus; Joshua, Jose
Y'hu·dah — Judah, Juda
Yi·shai — Jesse
Yitz·chak — Isaac
Yo·nam — Jonan
Yo·ram — Jorim
Yo·sef — Joseph

and the eyes of everyone in the synagogue were fixed on him. ²¹He started to speak to them: "Today, as you heard it read, this passage of the *Tanakh* was fulfilled!" ²²Everyone was speaking well of him and marvelling that such appealing words were coming from his mouth. They were even asking, "Can this be Yosef's son?"

²³Then Yeshua said to them, "No doubt you will quote to me this proverb — "'Doctor, cure yourself!" We've heard about all the things that have been going on over in K'far-Nachum; now do them here in your home town!' ²⁴Yes!" he said, "I tell you that no prophet is accepted in his home town. ²⁵It's true, I'm telling you — when Eliyahu was in Israel, and the sky was sealed off for three-and-a-half years, so that all the Land suffered a severe famine, there were many widows; ²⁶but Eliyahu was sent to none of them, only to a widow in Tzarfat in the land of Tzidon. ²⁷Also there were many people with serious skin diseases in Israel during the time of the prophet Elisha; but not one of them was healed, only Na'aman the Syrian."

²⁸On hearing this, everyone in the synagogue was filled with fury. ²⁹They rose up, drove him out of town and dragged him to the edge of the cliff on which their town was built, intending to throw him off. ³⁰But he walked right through the middle of the crowd and went away.

³¹He went down to K'far-Nachum, a town in the Galil, and made a practice of teaching them on *Shabbat*. ³²They were amazed at the way he taught, because his word carried the ring of authority.

³³In the synagogue there was a man who had an unclean demonic spirit, who shouted in a loud voice, ³⁴"Yaah! What do you want with us, Yeshua from Natzeret? Have you come to destroy us? I know who you are — the Holy One of God!" ³⁵But Yeshua rebuked it: "Be quiet, and come out of him!" The demonic spirit threw the man down in the middle of the crowd and came out of him, having done him no harm. ³⁶They were all astounded and said to one another, "What kind of teaching is this? Why, he gives orders with power and authority to the unclean spirits, and they come out!" ³⁷And reports about him went out through the whole surrounding district.

³⁸Leaving the synagogue, he went to Shim'on's house. Shim'on's mother-in-law was suffering from a high fever, and they asked him to do something for her. ³⁹So, standing over her, he rebuked the fever; and it left her. She immediately got up and began helping them.

⁴⁰After sunset, all those who had people sick with various diseases brought them to Yeshua, and he put his hands on each one of them and healed them; ⁴¹also demons came out of many, crying, "You are the Son of God!" But, rebuking them, he did not permit them to say that they knew he was the Messiah.

⁴²When day had come, he left and went away to a lonely spot. The people looked for him, came to him and would have kept him from leaving them. ⁴³But he said to them, "I must announce the Good News of the Kingdom of God to the other towns too — this is why I was sent." ⁴⁴He also spent time preaching in the synagogues of Y'hudah.

5 ¹One day, as Yeshua was standing on the shore of Lake Kinneret, with the people pressing in around him in order to hear the word of God, ²he noticed two boats pulled up on the beach, left there by the fishermen, who were cleaning their nets. [3]He got into one of the boats, the one belonging to Shim'on, and asked him to put out a little way from shore. Then he sat down and taught the people from the boat.

[4]When he had finished speaking, he said to Shim'on, "Put out into deep water, and let down your nets for a catch." [5]Shim'on answered, "We've worked hard all night long, Rabbi, and haven't caught a thing! But if you say so, I'll let down the nets." [6]They did this and took in so many fish that their nets began to tear. [7]So they motioned to their partners in the other boat to come and help them; and they came and filled both boats to the point of sinking. [8]When he saw this, Shim'on Kefa fell at Yeshua's knees and said, "Get away from me, sir, because I'm a sinner!" [9]For astonishment had seized him and everyone with him at the catch of fish they had taken, [10]and likewise both Ya'akov and Yochanan, Shim'on's partners. "Don't be frightened," Yeshua said to Shim'on, "from now on you will be catching men — alive!" [11]And as soon as they had beached their boats, they left everything behind and followed him.

[12]Once, when Yeshua was in one of the towns, there came a man completely covered with a repulsive skin disease. On seeing Yeshua, he fell on his face and begged him, "Sir, if you are willing, you can make me clean." [13]Yeshua reached out his hand and touched him, saying, "I *am* willing! Be cleansed!" Immediately the skin disease left him. [14]Then Yeshua warned him not to tell anyone. "Instead, as a testimony to the people, go straight to the *cohen* and make an offering for your cleansing, as Moshe commanded." [15]But the news about Yeshua kept spreading all the more, so that huge crowds would gather to listen and be healed of their sicknesses. [16]However, he made a practice of withdrawing to remote places in order to pray.

[17]One day when Yeshua was teaching, there were *P'rushim* and *Tora*-teachers present who had come from various villages in the Galil and Y'hudah, also from Yerushalayim; and the power of *Adonai* was with him to heal the sick. [18]Some men came carrying a paralyzed man lying on a bed. They wanted to bring him inside and lay him in front of Yeshua, [19]but they couldn't find a way to get him in because of the crowd. So they went up onto the roof and lowered him on his mattress through the tiles into the middle of the gathering, right in front of Yeshua. [20]When Yeshua saw their trust, he said, "Friend, your sins are forgiven you." [21]The *Torah*-teachers and the *P'rushim* began thinking, "Who is this fellow that speaks such

A·do·**nai** — the LORD, Jehovah
co·**hen** — priest
E·**li**·sha — Elisha
E·li·**ya**·hu — Elijah
the Ga·**lil** — Galilee
K'far-Na·**chum** — Capernaum
Ke·**fa** — Peter
Lake Kin·**ne**·ret — the Sea of Galilee
Mo·she — Moses
Na·'a·**man** — Naaman
Na·**tze**·ret — Nazareth
P'ru·shim — Pharisees
Shab·bat — the Sabbath
Shim·'**on** — Simon
Ta·nakh — Hebrew Scriptures, "Old Testament"
To·rah-teachers — scribes
Tzar·**fat** — Zarephath
Tzi·**don** — Sidon
Ya·'a·**kov** — James
Ye·ru·sha·**la**·yim — Jerusalem
Ye·**shu**·a — Jesus
Y'hu·**dah** — Judea
Yo·cha·**nan** — John
Yo·**sef** — Joseph

blasphemies? Who can forgive sin except God?" ²²But Yeshua, knowing what they were thinking, answered, "Why are you turning over such thoughts in your hearts? ²³Which is easier to say? 'Your sins are forgiven you'? or 'Get up and walk'? ²⁴But look! I will prove to you that the Son of Man has authority on earth to forgive sins." He then said to the paralytic, "I say to you: get up, pick up your mattress and go home!" ²⁵Immediately, in front of everyone, he stood up, picked up what he had been lying on, and went home praising God. ²⁶Amazement seized them all, and they made a b'rakhah to God; they were awestruck, saying, "We have seen extraordinary things today."

²⁷Later Yeshua went out and saw a tax-collector named L'vi sitting in his tax-collection booth; and he said to him, "Follow me!" ²⁸He got up, left everything and followed him.

²⁹L'vi gave a banquet at his house in Yeshua's honor, and there was a large group of tax-collectors and others at the table with them. ³⁰The P'rushim and their Torah-teachers protested indignantly against his talmidim, saying, "Why do you eat and drink with tax-collectors and sinners?" ³¹It was Yeshua who answered them: "The ones who need a doctor aren't the healthy but the sick. ³²I have not come to call the 'righteous', but rather to call sinners to turn to God from their sins."

³³Next they said to him, "Yochanan's talmidim are always fasting and davvening, and likewise the talmidim of the P'rushim; but yours go on eating and drinking." ³⁴Yeshua said to them, "Can you make wedding guests fast while the bridegroom is still with them? ³⁵The time will come when the bridegroom will be taken away from them; and when that time comes, they will fast."

³⁶Then he gave them an illustration: "No one tears a piece from a new coat and puts it on an old one; if he does, not only will the new one continue to rip, but the piece from the new will not match the old. ³⁷Also, no one puts new wine into old wineskins; if he does, the new wine will burst the skins and be spilled, and the skins too will be ruined. ³⁸On the contrary, new wine must be put into freshly prepared wineskins. ³⁹Besides that, after drinking old wine, people don't want new; because they say, 'The old is good enough.'"

6 ¹One Shabbat, while Yeshua was passing through some wheat fields, his talmidim began plucking the heads of grain, rubbing them between their hands and eating the seeds. ²Some of the P'rushim said, "Why are you violating Shabbat?" ³Yeshua answered them, "Haven't you ever read what David did when he and his companions were hungry? ⁴He entered the House of God and took and ate the Bread of the Presence, which no one is permitted to eat but the cohanim. ⁵The Son of Man," he concluded, "is Lord of Shabbat."

⁶On another Shabbat, when Yeshua had gone into the synagogue and was teaching, a man was there who had a shriveled hand. ⁷The Torah-teachers and P'rushim watched Yeshua carefully to see if he would heal on Shabbat, so that they could accuse him of something. ⁸But he knew what they were thinking and said to the man with the shriveled hand, "Come up and stand where we can see you!" He got up and stood there. ⁹Then Yeshua said to them, "I ask you now: what is permitted on Shabbat? Doing good or doing evil? Saving life or destroying it?" ¹⁰Then, after looking around at all of them, he said to the man, "Hold out your hand." As he held it out, his hand was restored. ¹¹But the others were

filled with fury and began discussing with each other what they could do to Yeshua.

[12] It was around that time that Yeshua went out to the hill country to pray, and all night he continued in prayer to God. [13] When day came, he called his *talmidim* and chose from among them twelve to be known as emissaries —

[14] Shim'on, whom he named Kefa,
Andrew his brother,
Ya'akov,
Yochanan,
Philip,
Bar-Talmai,
[15] Mattityahu,
T'oma,
Ya'akov Ben-Chalfai,
Shim'on, the one called the Zealot,
[16] Y'hudah Ben-Ya'akov, and
Y'hudah from K'riot, who turned traitor.

[17] Then he came down with them and stood on a level place. A large crowd of his *talmidim* was there with great numbers of people from all Y'hudah, Yerushalayim and the coast around Tzor and Tzidon; they had come to hear him and be healed of their diseases. [18] Those who were troubled with unclean spirits were being healed; [19] and the whole crowd was trying to touch him, because power kept going out from him, healing everyone.

[20] He looked at his *talmidim* and said:

"How blessed are you poor!
for the Kingdom of God is yours.

[21] "How blessed are you who are hungry!
for you will be filled.

"How blessed are you who are crying now!
for you will laugh.

[22] "How blessed you are whenever people hate you and ostracize you and insult you and denounce you as a criminal on account of the Son of Man. [23] Be glad when that happens; yes, dance for joy! because in heaven your reward is great. For that is just how their fathers treated the prophets.

[24] "But woe to you who are rich,
for you have already had all the comfort you will get!

[25] "Woe to you who are full now,
for you will go hungry!

"Woe to you who are laughing now,
for you will mourn and cry!

[26] "Woe to you when people speak well of you, for that is just how their fathers treated the false prophets! [27] "Nevertheless, to you who are listening, what I say is this:

====================

Bar-Tal·**mai** — Bartholomew
b'ra·khah — blessing
co·ha·nim — priest
dav·ven·ing — praying
L'vi — Levi
Mat·tit·**ya**·hu — Matthew
P'ru·shim — Pharisees
Shab·bat — the Sabbath
Shim·'on — Simeon
tal·mi·dim — disciples
T·'o·ma — Thomas
To·rah-teachers — scribes
Tzi·don — Sidon
Tzor — Tyre
Ya·'a·kov — James
Ya·'a·kov Ben-Chal·**fai** — James son of Alphaeus
Ye·ru·sha·**la**·yim — Jerusalem
Ye·**shu**·a — Jesus
Y'hu·**dah** — Judea
Y'hu·**dah** Ben-Ya·'a·kov — Judas son of James
Y'hu·**dah** from K'ri·ot — Judas Iscariot
Yo·cha·**nan** — John

"Love your enemies!
Do good to those who hate you,
²⁸ bless those who curse you,
pray for those who mistreat you.

²⁹ "If someone hits you on one cheek,
offer the other too;
if someone takes your coat,
let him have your shirt as well.

³⁰ "If someone asks you for something,
give it to him;
if someone takes what belongs to
you,
don't demand it back.

³¹"Treat other people as you would like them to treat you. ³² What credit is it to you if you love only those who love you? Why, even sinners love those who love them. ³³ What credit is it to you if you do good only to those who do good to you? Even sinners do that. ³⁴ What credit is it to you if you lend only to those who you expect will pay you back? Even sinners lend to each other, expecting to be repaid in full. ³⁵ But love your enemies, do good, and lend expecting nothing back! Your reward will be great, and you will be children of *HaElyon*; for he is kind to the ungrateful and the wicked. ³⁶ Show compassion, just as your Father shows compassion.

³⁷ "Don't judge,
and you won't be judged.

Don't condemn,
and you won't be condemned.

Forgive,
and you will be forgiven.

³⁸ Give,
and you will receive gifts —
the full measure, compacted, shaken together and overflowing, will be put right in your lap. For the measure with which you measure out will be used to measure back to you!"

³⁹ He also told them a parable: "Can one blind man lead another blind man? Won't they both fall into a pit? ⁴⁰ A *talmid* is not above his rabbi; but each one, when he is fully trained, will be like his rabbi. ⁴¹ So why do you see the splinter in your brother's eye, but not notice the log in your own eye? ⁴² How can you say to your brother, 'Brother, let me remove the splinter from your eye,' when you yourself don't see the log in your own eye? You hypocrite! First take the log out of your own eye; then you will see clearly, so that you can remove the splinter from your brother's eye!

⁴³ "For no good tree produces bad fruit, nor does a bad tree produce good fruit. ⁴⁴ Each tree is recognized by its own fruit — figs aren't picked from thorn bushes, nor grapes from a briar patch. ⁴⁵ The good person produces good things from the store of good in his heart, while the evil person produces evil things from the store of evil in his heart. For his mouth speaks what overflows from his heart.

⁴⁶"Why do you call me, 'Lord! Lord!' but not do what I say? ⁴⁷ Everyone who comes to me, hears my words and acts on them — I will show you what he is like: ⁴⁸ he is like someone building a house who dug deep and laid the foundation on bedrock. When a flood came, the torrent beat against that house but couldn't shake it, because it was constructed well. ⁴⁹ And whoever hears my words but doesn't act on them is like someone who built his house on the ground without any foundation. As soon as the river struck it, it collapsed and that house became a horrendous wreck!"

7 ¹ When Yeshua had finished speaking to the people, he went back to K'far-Nachum. ² A Roman army officer there had a servant he regarded highly, who was sick to the point of death. 3 Hearing about Yeshua, the officer sent some Jewish elders to him with the request that he come and heal his servant. 4 They came to Yeshua and pleaded earnestly with him, "He really deserves to have you do this, 5 for he loves our people — in fact, he built the synagogue for us!" 6 So Yeshua went with them. He had not gone far from the house, when the officer sent friends who said to him, "Sir, don't trouble yourself. I'm not worthy to have you come under my roof — 7 this is why I didn't presume to approach you myself. Instead, just give a command and let my servant recover. 8 For I too am a man set under authority. I have soldiers under me; and I say to this one, 'Go!' and he goes; and to another, 'Come!' and he comes; and to my slave, 'Do this!' and he does it." 9 Yeshua was astonished at him when he heard this; and he turned and said to the crowd following him, "I tell you, not even in Israel have I found such trust!" 10 When the messengers got back to the officer's house, they found the servant in good health.

11 The next day Yeshua, accompanied by his *talmidim* and a large crowd, went to a town called Na'im. 12 As he approached the town gate, a dead man was being carried out for burial. His mother was a widow, this had been her only son, and a sizeable crowd from the town was with her. 13 When the Lord saw her, he felt compassion for her and said to her, "Don't cry." 14 Then he came close and touched the coffin, and the pallbearers halted. He said, "Young man, I say to you: get up!" 15 The dead man sat up and began to speak, and Yeshua **gave him to his mother.** *o* 16 They were all filled with awe and gave glory

to God, saying, "A great prophet has appeared among us," and, "God has come to help his people." 17 This report about him spread throughout all Y'hudah and the surrounding countryside.

18 Yochanan's *talmidim* informed him of all these things. Then Yochanan called two of his *talmidim* 19 and sent them to the Lord to ask, "Are you the one who is to come? Or should we look for someone else?" 20 When the men came to him, they said, "Yochanan the Immerser has sent us to you to ask, 'Are you the one who is to come? Or should we keep looking — for someone else?'" 21 Right then he was healing many people of diseases, pains and evil spirits, and giving sight to many who were blind. 22 So he answered them by saying, "Go, tell Yochanan what you have been seeing and hearing: **the blind are seeing again, the lame are** walking, people with skin diseases are being cleansed, **the deaf are hearing,** the dead are being raised, **the Good News is being told to the poor**_p_ — 23 and how blessed is anyone not offended by me!"

24 When the messengers from Yochanan had gone, Yeshua began speaking to the crowds about Yochanan: "What did you go out into the desert to see? Reeds swaying in the breeze? 25 No? then what did you go out to see? Someone who was well dressed? But

---

o 1 Kings 17:23

_p_ Isaiah 35:5-6, 26:14, 61:1

Ha·El·yon — the Highest, i.e., God
K'far-Na·**chum** — Capernaum
Na·'**im** — Nain
*tal·**mid*** — disciple
*tal·mi·**dim*** — disciples
Ye·**shu·a** — Jesus
Y'hu·**dah** — Judea
Yo·cha·**nan** — John
Yo·cha·**nan** the Immerser — John the Baptist

people who dress beautifully and live in luxury are found in kings' palaces. [26]*Nu,* so what did you go out to see? A prophet! Yes, and I tell you he's much more than a prophet. [27]This is the one about whom the *Tanakh* says,

'See, I am sending out my messenger ahead of you;
he will prepare your way before you.'[q]

[28]I tell you that among those born of women there has not arisen anyone greater than Yochanan the Immerser! Yet the one who is least in the Kingdom of Heaven is greater than he!"

[29]All the people who heard him, even the tax collectors, by undergoing Yochanan's immersion acknowledged that God was right; [30]but the *P'rushim* and the *Torah*-teachers, by not letting themselves be immersed by him, nullified for themselves God's plan.

[31]"Therefore," said the Lord, "how can I describe the people of this generation? What are they like? [32]They are like children sitting in the marketplaces, calling to one another,

'We made happy music,
but you wouldn't dance!
We made sad music,
but you wouldn't cry!'

[33]For Yochanan has come not eating bread and not drinking wine; and you say, 'He has a demon!' [34]The Son of Man has come eating and drinking; and you say, 'Aha! A glutton and a drunkard! A friend of tax-collectors and sinners!' [35]Well, the proof of wisdom is in all the kinds of people it produces."

[36]One of the *P'rushim* invited Yeshua to eat with him, and he went into the home of the *Parush* and took his place at the table. [37]A woman who lived in that town, a sinner, who was aware that he was eating in the home of the *Parush,* brought an alabaster box of very expensive perfume, [38]stood behind Yeshua at his feet and wept until her tears began to wet his feet. Then she wiped his feet with her own hair, kissed his feet and poured the perfume on them.

[39]When the *Parush* who had invited him saw what was going on, he said to himself, "If this man were really a prophet, he would have known who is touching him and what sort of woman she is, that she is a sinner." [40]Yeshua answered, "Shim'on, I have something to say to you." "Say it, Rabbi," he replied. [41]"A certain creditor had two debtors; the one owed ten times as much as the other. [42]When they were unable to pay him back, he canceled both their debts. Now which of them will love him more?" [43]Shim'on answered, "I suppose the one for whom he canceled the larger debt." "Your judgment is right," Yeshua said to him.

[44]Then, turning to the woman, he said to Shim'on, "Do you see this woman? I came into your house — you didn't give me water for my feet, but this woman has washed my feet with her tears and dried them with her hair! [45]You didn't give me a kiss; but from the time I arrived, this woman has not stopped kissing my feet! [46]You didn't put oil on my head, but this woman poured perfume on my feet! [47]Because of this, I tell you that her sins — which are many! — have been forgiven, because she loved much. But someone who has been forgiven only a little loves only a little." [48]Then he said to her, "Your sins have been forgiven." [49]At this, those eating with him began saying among themselves, "Who is this fellow that presumes to forgive sins?"

---

[q] Malachi 3:1

⁵⁰ But he said to the woman, "Your trust has saved you; go in peace."

8 ¹ After this, Yeshua traveled about from town to town and village to village, proclaiming the Good News of the Kingdom of God. With him were the Twelve, ² and a number of women who had been healed from evil spirits and illnesses — Miryam (called Magdalit), from whom seven demons had gone out; ³ Yochanah the wife of Herod's finance minister Kuza; Shoshanah; and many other women who drew on their own wealth to help him.

⁴ After a large crowd had gathered from the people who kept coming to him from town after town, Yeshua told this parable: ⁵ "A farmer went out to sow his seed. As he sowed, some fell along the path and was stepped on, and the birds flying around ate it up. ⁶ Some fell on rock; and after it sprouted, it dried up from lack of moisture. ⁷ Some fell in the midst of thorns, and the thorns grew up with it and choked it. ⁸ But some fell into rich soil, and grew, and produced a hundred times as much as had been sown." After saying this, he called out, "Whoever has ears to hear with, let him hear!"

⁹ His *talmidim* asked him what this parable might mean, ¹⁰ and he said, "To you it has been given to know the secrets of the Kingdom of God; but the rest are taught in parables, so that they may **look but not see, and listen but not understand.**ʳ

¹¹ "The parable is this: the seed is God's message. ¹² The ones along the path are those who hear, but then the Adversary comes and takes the message out of their hearts, in order to keep them from being saved by trusting it. ¹³ The ones on rock are those who, when they hear the word, accept it with

joy; but these have no root — they go on trusting for awhile; but when a time of testing comes, they apostatize. ¹⁴ As for what fell in the midst of thorns — these are the ones who hear; but as they go along, worries and wealth and life's gratifications crowd in and choke them, so that their fruit never matures. ¹⁵ But what fell in rich soil — these are the ones who, when they hear the message, hold onto it with a good, receptive heart; and by persevering, they bring forth a harvest.

¹⁶ "No one who has lit a lamp covers it with a bowl or puts it under a bed; no, he puts it on a stand; so that those coming in may see the light. ¹⁷ For nothing is hidden that will not be disclosed, nothing is covered up that will not be known and come out into the open. ¹⁸ Pay attention, then, to how you hear! For anyone who has something will be given more; but from anyone who has nothing, even what he seems to have will be taken away."

¹⁹ Then Yeshua's mother and brothers came to see him, but they couldn't get near him because of the crowd. ²⁰ It was reported to him, "Your mother and your brothers are standing outside and want to see you." ²¹ But he gave them this answer: "My mother and brothers

---

Ku·za — Chuza
Mir·yam (Mag·da·lit) — Mary Magdalene
nu — well
Pa·rush — Pharisee
P'ru·shim — Pharisees
Shim·'on — Simeon
Sho·sha·nah — Susanna
tal·mi·dim — disciples
Ta·nakh — Hebrew Scriptures, "Old Testament"
To·rah-teachers — scribes
Ye·shu·a — Jesus
Yo·cha·nah — Johanna
Yo·cha·nan — John
Yo·cha·nan the Immerser — John the Baptist

ʳ Isaiah 6:9

are those who hear God's message and act on it!"

²²One day Yeshua got into a boat with his *talmidim* and said to them, "Let's cross to the other side of the lake." So they set out; ²³and as they were sailing, he fell asleep. A windstorm came down on the lake, so that the boat began to fill up with water, putting them in great danger. ²⁴They went and woke him, saying, "Rabbi! Rabbi! We're about to die!" He woke up, rebuked the wind and the rough water; and they calmed down, so that it was still. ²⁵Then he said to the *talmidim*, "Where is your trust?" Awestruck, they marveled, asking one another, "Who can this be, that he commands even the wind and the water, and they obey him?"

²⁶They sailed on and landed in the region of the Gerasenes, which is opposite the Galil. ²⁷As Yeshua stepped ashore, a man from the town who had demons came to meet him. For a long time he had not worn clothes; and he lived, not in a house, but in the burial caves. ²⁸Catching sight of Yeshua, he screamed, fell down in front of him and yelled, "Yeshua! Son of God *HaElyon*! What do you want with me? I beg you, don't torture me!" ²⁹For Yeshua had ordered the unclean spirit to come out of the man. It had often taken hold of him — he had been kept under guard, chained hand and foot, but had broken the bonds and been driven by the demon into the desert. ³⁰Yeshua asked him, "What is your name?" "Legion," he said, because many demons had entered him. ³¹They begged Yeshua not to order them to go off into the Bottomless Pit.

³²Now there was a herd of many pigs, feeding on the hill; and the demons begged him to let them go into these. So he gave them permission. ³³The

demons came out of the man and entered the pigs, whereupon the herd rushed down the hillside into the lake and were drowned.

³⁴When the swineherds saw what had happened, they fled and told it in the town and in the country; ³⁵and the people came out to see for themselves. They came to Yeshua and found the man out of whom the demons had gone, sitting — dressed and in his right mind — at the feet of Yeshua; and they were frightened. ³⁶Those who had seen it told how the formerly demonized man had been delivered.

³⁷Then all the people of the Gerasene district asked him to leave them, for they had been seized with great fear. So he boarded the boat and returned. ³⁸The man from whom the demons had gone out begged that he might go with him; but Yeshua sent him away, saying, ³⁹"Go back to your home and tell how much God has done for you." He went away proclaiming throughout the whole town how much Yeshua had done for him.

⁴⁰When Yeshua got back, the crowd welcomed him; for they were all expecting him. ⁴¹Then there came a man named Ya'ir who was president of the synagogue. Falling at Yeshua's feet, he pleaded with him to come to his house; ⁴²for he had an only daughter, about twelve years old; and she was dying.

As he went, with the crowds on every side virtually choking him, ⁴³a woman who had had a hemorrhage for twelve years, and could not be healed by anyone, ⁴⁴came up behind him and touched the *tzitzit* on his robe; instantly her hemorrhaging stopped. ⁴⁵Yeshua asked, "Who touched me?" When they all denied doing it, Kefa said, "Rabbi! The crowds are hemming you in and jostling you!" ⁴⁶But Yeshua said, "Someone did touch me, because I felt power go out of me." ⁴⁷Seeing she could not escape notice, the woman, quaking with fear, threw herself down before him and confessed in front of everyone why she had touched him and how she had been instantly healed. ⁴⁸He said to her, "My daughter, your trust has saved you; go in peace."

⁴⁹While Yeshua was still speaking, a man came from the synagogue president's house. "Your daughter has died," he said. "Don't bother the rabbi any more." ⁵⁰But on hearing this, Yeshua answered him, "Don't be afraid! Just go on trusting, and she will be made well." ⁵¹When he arrived at the house, he didn't allow anyone to go in with him except Kefa, Yochanan, Ya'akov and the child's father and mother. ⁵²All the people were wailing and mourning for her; but he said, "Don't weep; she hasn't died, she's sleeping." ⁵³They jeered at him, since they knew she had died. ⁵⁴But he took her by the hand, called out, "Little girl, get up!" ⁵⁵and her spirit returned. She stood up at once, and he directed that something be given her to eat. ⁵⁶Her parents were astounded, but he instructed them to tell no one what had happened.

9 ¹Calling together the Twelve, Yeshua gave them power and authority to expel all the demons and to cure diseases; ²and he sent them out to proclaim the Kingdom of God and to heal. ³He said to them, "Take nothing for your trip — neither a walking stick nor a pack, neither bread nor money; and don't have two shirts. ⁴Whatever house you enter, stay there and go out from there. ⁵Wherever they don't welcome you, shake the dust from your feet when you leave that town as a warning to them." ⁶They set out and went through village after village, healing and announcing the Good News everywhere.

⁷Herod the governor heard about all that was going on and was perplexed, because it was said by some that Yochanan had been raised from the dead, ⁸by others that Eliyahu had appeared, and by others that one of the prophets of long ago had come back to life. ⁹Herod said, "I had Yochanan beheaded, so who is this about whom I keep hearing such things?" And he began trying to see him.

¹⁰On their return, the emissaries detailed to Yeshua what they had done. Then, taking them with him, he withdrew by himself to a town called Beit-Tzaidah. ¹¹But the crowds found out and followed him. Welcoming them, he went on to speak to them about the Kingdom of God and to heal those who needed to be healed.

¹²The day began to draw to a close. The Twelve came to him and said, "Send the crowd away, so that they can go and get lodging and food in the towns and farms around here, because where we are is a remote place." ¹³But he said to them, "Give them something to eat, yourselves!" They said, "We have no more than five loaves of bread and two fish — unless we ourselves are supposed to go and buy food for all these people!" ¹⁴(For there were about five thousand men.) He said to his *talmidim*, "Make them sit down in groups of about fifty each." ¹⁵They did what he told them and had them all sit

---

Beit-Tzai·**dah** — Bethsaida
Eli·**ya**·hu — Elijah
the Ga·**lil** — Galilee
Ha·**El**·*yon* — the Highest, i.e., God
Ke·**fa** — Peter
tal·*mi*·***dim*** — disciples
tzi·*tzit* — ritual fringe
Ya·'a·**kov** — James
Ya·'**ir** — Jairus
Ye·**shu**·a — Jesus
Yo·cha·**nan** — John

down. [16] Then he took the five loaves and the two fish and, looking up toward heaven, made a *b'rakhah*, broke the loaves and began giving them to the crowd. [17] Everyone ate as much as he wanted; and they took up what was left over, twelve baskets full of broken pieces.

[18] Once when Yeshua was praying in private, his *talmidim* were with him; and he asked them, "Who are the crowds saying I am?" [19] They answered, "Yochanan the Immerser; but others say Eliyahu, and others that some prophet of long ago has risen." [20] "But you," he said to them, "who do you say I am?" Kefa answered, "The *Mashiach* of God!" [21] However, he, warning them, ordered them to tell this to no one, [22] adding, "The Son of Man has to endure much suffering and be rejected by the elders, the head *cohanim* and the *Torah*-teachers; and he has to be put to death; but on the third day, he has to be raised to life."

[23] Then to everyone he said, "If anyone wants to come after me, let him say 'No' to himself, take up his execution-stake daily and keep following me. [24] For whoever tries to save his own life will destroy it, but whoever destroys his life on my account will save it. [25] What will it benefit a person if he gains the whole world but destroys or forfeits his own life? [26] For if someone is ashamed of me and of what I say, the Son of Man will be ashamed of him when he comes in his glory and that of the Father and of the holy angels. [27] I tell you the truth, there are some people standing here who will not experience death until they see the Kingdom of God."

[28] About a week after Yeshua said these things, he took Kefa, Yochanan and Ya'akov with him and went up to the hill country to pray. [29] As he was praying, the appearance of his face changed; and his clothing became gleaming white. [30] Suddenly there were two men talking with him — Moshe and Eliyahu! [31] They appeared in glorious splendor and spoke of his exodus, which he was soon to accomplish in Yerushalayim. [32] Kefa and those with him had been sound asleep; but on becoming fully awake, they saw his glory and the two men standing with him. [33] As the men were leaving Yeshua, Kefa said to him, not knowing what he was saying, "It's good that we're here, Rabbi! Let's put up three shelters — one for you, one for Moshe and one for Eliyahu." [34] As he spoke, a cloud came and enveloped them. They were frightened as they entered the cloud; [35] and a voice came out of the cloud, saying, "This is my Son, whom I have chosen. Listen to him!" [36] When the voice spoke, Yeshua was alone once more. They kept quiet — at that time they told no one anything of what they had seen.

[37] The next day, as they were coming down out of the hill country, a large crowd met him. [38] Suddenly a man in the crowd shouted, "Rabbi! Look at my son, I beg you, because he's my only child! [39] What happens is this: a spirit seizes him, and suddenly it lets out a shriek and throws him into convulsions with foaming at the mouth; and only with difficulty will it leave him. It's destroying him! [40] I asked your *talmidim* to drive the spirit out, but they couldn't." [41] "Perverted people, without any trust!" Yeshua answered, "How long do I have to be with you and put up with you? Bring your son here." [42] Even as the boy was coming, the demon dashed him to the ground and threw him into a fit. But Yeshua rebuked the unclean spirit, healed the boy and gave him back to his father. [43] All were struck with amazement at the greatness of God.

While they were all marvelling at everything Yeshua was doing, he said to his *talmidim*, ⁴⁴"Listen very carefully to what I'm going to say. The Son of Man is about to be betrayed into the hands of men." ⁴⁵ But they didn't understand what he meant by this. It had been concealed from them so that they would not grasp its meaning, and they were afraid to ask him about it.

⁴⁶ An argument arose among the *talmidim* as to which of them might be the greatest. ⁴⁷ But Yeshua, knowing the thoughts of their hearts, took a child, stood him beside himself, ⁴⁸ and said to them, "Whoever welcomes this child in my name welcomes me, and whoever welcomes me welcomes the One who sent me. In other words, the one who is least among you all — this is the one who is great." ⁴⁹ Yochanan responded, "Rabbi, we saw someone expelling demons in your name; and we stopped him because he doesn't follow you along with us." ⁵⁰ Yeshua said to him, "Don't stop such people, because whoever isn't against you is for you."

⁵¹ As the time approached for him to be taken up into heaven, he made his decision to set out for Yerushalayim. ⁵² He sent messengers ahead of him, who went and entered a village in Shomron to make preparations for him. ⁵³ However, the people there would not let him stay, because his destination was Yerushalayim. ⁵⁴ When the *talmidim* Ya'akov and Yochanan saw this, they said, "Sir, do you want us to call down **fire from heaven to destroy** them?"ˢ ⁵⁵ But he turned and rebuked them.* ⁵⁶ And they went on to another village.

⁵⁷ As they were traveling on the road, a man said to him, "I will follow you wherever you go." ⁵⁸ Yeshua answered him, "The foxes have holes, and the birds flying about have nests, but the Son of Man has no home of his own." ⁵⁹ To another he said, "Follow me!" but the man replied, "Sir, first let me go away and bury my father." ⁶⁰ Yeshua said, "Let the dead bury their own dead; you, go and proclaim the Kingdom of God!" ⁶¹ Yet another said, "I will follow you, sir, but first let me say good-by to the people at home." ⁶² To him Yeshua said, "No one who puts his hand to the plow and keeps looking back is fit to serve in the Kingdom of God."

10 ¹ After this, the Lord appointed seventy other *talmidim* and sent them on ahead in pairs to every town and place where he himself was about to go. ² He said to them, "To be sure, there is a large harvest. But there are few workers. Therefore, plead with the Lord of the Harvest that he speed workers out to gather in his harvest. ³ Get going now, but pay attention! I am sending you out like lambs among wolves. ⁴ Don't carry a money-belt or a pack, and don't stop to *shmoose* with people on the road.

---

* Some manuscripts have verses 9:55b-56a: ...and he said, "You don't know what Spirit you are of; ⁵⁶ for the Son of Man did not come to destroy people's lives, but to save."

ˢ 2 Kings 1:9-16

b'ra·**khah** — blessing
co·ha·**nim** — priest
E·li·**ya**·hu — Elijah
Ke·**fa** — Peter
Ma·shi·ach — Messiah
Mo·**she** — Moses
shmoose — talk comfortably
Shom·**ron** — Samaria
tal·mi·**dim** — disciples
*To·**rah**-teachers* — scribes
Ya·'a·kov — James
Ye·ru·sha·**la**·yim — Jerusalem
Ye·**shu**·a — Jesus
Yo·cha·**nan** — John
Yo·cha·**nan** the Immerser — John the Baptist

[5]"Whenever you enter a house, first say, 'Shalom!' to the household. [6]If a seeker of shalom is there, your 'Shalom!' will find its rest with him; and if there isn't, it will return to you. [7]Stay in that same house, eating and drinking what they offer, for a worker deserves his wages — don't move about from house to house.

[8]"Whenever you come into a town where they make you welcome, eat what is put in front of you. [9]Heal the sick there, and tell them, 'The Kingdom of God is near you.' [10]But whenever you enter a town and they don't make you welcome, go out into its streets and say, [11]'Even the dust of your town that sticks to our feet we wipe off as a sign against you! But understand this: the Kingdom of God is near!' [12]I tell you, it will be more tolerable on the Day of Judgment for S'dom than for that town.

[13]"Woe to you, Korazin! Woe to you, Beit-Tzaidah! For if the miracles done in you had been done in Tzor and Tzidon, they would long ago have put on sackcloth and ashes as evidence that they had changed their ways. [14]But at the Judgment it will be more bearable for Tzor and Tzidon than for you!

[15]"And you, K'far-Nachum, will you be exalted to heaven? No, you will be brought down to Sh'ol![t]

[16]"Whoever listens to you listens to me, also whoever rejects you rejects me, and whoever rejects me rejects the One who sent me."

[17]The seventy came back jubilant. "Lord," they said, "with your power, even the demons submit to us!" [18]Yeshua said to them, "I saw Satan fall like lightning from heaven. [19]Remember, I have given you authority; so you can trample down snakes and scorpions, indeed, all the Enemy's forces; and you will remain completely unharmed. [20]Nevertheless, don't be glad that the spirits submit to you; be glad that your names have been recorded in heaven."

[21]At that moment he was filled with joy by the Ruach HaKodesh and said, "Father, Lord of heaven and earth, I thank you because you concealed these things from the sophisticated and educated, yet revealed them to ordinary people. Yes, Father, I thank you that it pleased you to do this.

[22]"My Father has handed over everything to me. Indeed, no one fully knows who the Son is except the Father, and who the Father is except the Son and those to whom the Son wishes to reveal him." [23]Then, turning to the talmidim, he said, privately, "How blessed are the eyes that see what you are seeing! [24]Indeed, I tell you that many prophets and kings wanted to see the things you are seeing but did not see them, and to hear the things you are hearing but did not hear them."

[25]An expert in Torah stood up to try and trap him by asking, "Rabbi, what should I do to obtain eternal life?" [26]But Yeshua said to him, "What is written in the Torah? How do you read it?" [27]He answered, "You are to love Adonai your God with all your heart, with all your soul, with all your strength and with all your understanding; and your neighbor as yourself."[u] [28]"That's the right answer," Yeshua said. "Do this, and you will have life."

[29]But he, wanting to justify himself, said to Yeshua, "And who is my 'neighbor'?" [30]Taking up the question, Yeshua said: "A man was going down

---

t Isaiah 14:13, 15

u Deuteronomy 6:4, Leviticus 19:18

from Yerushalayim to Yericho when he was attacked by robbers. They stripped him naked and beat him up, then went off, leaving him half dead. ³¹ By coincidence, a *cohen* was going down on that road; but when he saw him, he passed by on the other side. ³² Likewise a *L'vi* who reached the place and saw him also passed by on the other side.

³³ "But a man from Shomron who was traveling came upon him; and when he saw him, he was moved with compassion. ³⁴ So he went up to him, put oil and wine on his wounds and bandaged them. Then he set him on his own donkey, brought him to an inn and took care of him. ³⁵ The next day, he took out two days' wages, gave them to the innkeeper and said, 'Look after him; and if you spend more than this, I'll pay you back when I return.' ³⁶ Of these three, which one seems to you to have become the 'neighbor' of the man who fell among robbers?" ³⁷ He answered, "The one who showed mercy toward him." Yeshua said to him, "You go and do as he did."

³⁸ On their way Yeshua and his *talmidim* came to a village where a woman named Marta welcomed him into her home. ³⁹ She had a sister called Miryam who also sat at the Lord's feet and heard what he had to say. ⁴⁰ But Marta was busy with all the work to be done; so, going up to him, she said, "Sir, don't you care that my sister has been leaving me to do all the work by myself?" ⁴¹ However, the Lord answered her, "Marta, Marta, you are fretting and worrying about so many things! ⁴² But there is only one thing that is essential. Miryam has chosen the right thing, and it won't be taken away from her."

11 ¹ One time Yeshua was in a certain place praying. As he finished, one of the *talmidim* said to him, "Sir, teach us to pray, just as Yochanan taught his *talmidim*." ² He said to them, "When you pray, say:

'Father,
May your name be kept holy.
May your Kingdom come.
³ Give us each day the food we need.
⁴ Forgive us our sins, for we too forgive
  everyone who has wronged us.
And do not lead us to hard testing.'"

⁵ He also said to them, "Suppose one of you has a friend; and you go to him in the middle of the night and say to him, 'Friend, lend me three loaves of bread, ⁶ because a friend of mine who has been travelling has just arrived at my house, and I have nothing for him to eat.' ⁷ Now the one inside may answer, 'Don't bother me! The door is already shut, my children are with me in bed — I can't get up to give you anything!' ⁸ But I tell you, even if he won't get up because the man is his

---

A·do·nai — the LORD, Jehovah
Beit-Tzai·**dah** — Bethsaida
co·hen — priest
K'far-Na·**chum** — Capernaum
Ko·ra·**zin** — Chorazin
L'vi — Levite
Mar·ta — Martha
Mir·**yam** — Miriam, Mary
Ru·ach-Ha·Ko·desh — Holy Spirit
Sa·**tan** — Satan, the Adversary
S'**dom** — Sodom
sha·lom — peace
Sha·lom! — Peace! (greeting)
Sh'ol — Sheol, Hades, hell
Shom·**ron** — Samaria
tal·mi·dim — disciples
To·rah — Teaching, "Law"; Pentateuch
Tzi·**don** — Sidon
Tzor — Tyre
Ye·ri·cho — Jericho
Ye·ru·sha·la·yim — Jerusalem
Ye·shu·a — Jesus
Yo·cha·**nan** — John

friend, yet because of the man's *chutzpah* he will get up and give him as much as he needs.

⁹"Moreover, I myself say to you: keep asking, and it will be given to you; keep seeking, and you will find; keep knocking, and the door will be opened to you. ¹⁰For everyone who goes on asking receives; and he who goes on seeking finds; and to him who continues knocking, the door will be opened.

¹¹"Is there any father here who, if his son asked him for a fish, would instead of a fish give him a snake? ¹²or if he asked for an egg would give him a scorpion? ¹³So if you, even though you are bad, know how to give your children gifts that are good, how much more will the Father keep giving the *Ruach HaKodesh* from heaven to those who keep asking him!"

¹⁴He was expelling a demon that was mute. When the demon had gone out, the man who had been mute spoke; and the people were astounded. ¹⁵But some of them said, "It is by Ba'al-zibbul, the ruler of the demons, that he expels the demons." ¹⁶And others, trying to trap him, demanded from him a sign from Heaven. ¹⁷But he, knowing what they were thinking, said to them, "Every kingdom divided against itself will be ruined, with one house collapsing on another. ¹⁸So if the Adversary too is divided against himself, how can his kingdom survive? I'm asking because you claim it is by Ba'al-zibbul that I drive out the demons. ¹⁹If I drive out demons by Ba'al-zibbul, by whom do your people drive them out? So, they will be your judges! ²⁰But if I drive out demons by **the finger of God**ᵛ, then the Kingdom of God has come upon you!

²¹"When a strong man who is fully equipped for battle guards his own house, his possessions are secure. ²²But when someone stronger attacks and defeats him, he carries off all the armor and weaponry on which the man was depending, and divides up the spoils. ²³Those who are not with me are against me, and those who do not gather with me are scattering.

²⁴"When an unclean spirit comes out of a person, it travels through dry country seeking rest. On finding none, it says, 'I will return to the house I left.' ²⁵When it arrives, it finds the house swept clean and put in order. ²⁶Then it goes and takes seven other spirits more evil than itself, and they come and live there — so that in the end the person is worse off than he was before."

²⁷As Yeshua was saying these things, a woman in the crowd raised her voice to call out, "How blessed is the mother that gave birth to you and nursed you from her breast!" ²⁸But he said, "Far more blessed are those who hear the word of God and obey it!"

²⁹As the people crowded around him, Yeshua went on to say, "This generation is a wicked generation! It asks for a sign, but no sign will be given to it — except the sign of Yonah. ³⁰For just as Yonah became a sign to the people of Nineveh, so will the Son of Man be for this generation. ³¹The Queen of the South will appear at the Judgment with the people of this generation and condemn them; for she came from the ends of the earth to hear the wisdom of Shlomo, and what is here now is greater than Shlomo. ³²The people of Nineveh will stand up at the Judgment with this generation and condemn it, for they turned to God from their sins when Yonah preached, and what is here now is greater than Yonah.

ᵛ Exodus 31:18

[33]"No one who has kindled a lamp hides it or places it under a bowl; rather, he puts it on a stand, so that those coming in may see its light. [34]The lamp of your body is the eye. When you have a 'good eye', [that is, when you are generous,] your whole body is full of light; but when you have an 'evil eye', [when you are stingy,] your body is full of darkness. [35]So take care that the light in you is not darkness! [36]If, then, your whole body is filled with light, with no part dark, it will be wholly lighted, as when a brightly lit lamp shines on you."

[37]As Yeshua spoke, a *Parush* asked him to eat dinner with him; so he went in and took his place at the table; [38]and the *Parush* was surprised that he didn't begin by doing *n'tilat yadayim* before the meal. [39]However, the Lord said to him, "Now then, you *P'rushim*, you clean the outside of the cup and plate; but inside, you are full of robbery and wickedness. [40]Fools! Didn't the One who made the outside make the inside too? [41]Rather, give as alms what is inside, and then everything will be clean for you!

[42]"But woe to you *P'rushim*! You pay your tithes of mint and rue and every garden herb, but you ignore justice and the love of God. You have an obligation to do these things — but without disregarding the others!

[43]"Woe to you *P'rushim*, because you love the best seat in the synagogues and being greeted deferentially in the marketplaces!

[44]"Woe to you, because you are like unmarked graves, which people walk over without knowing it."

[45]One of the experts in *Torah* answered him, "Rabbi, by saying these things you are insulting us also." [46]Yeshua said, "Woe to you *Torah* experts too! You load people down

with burdens they can hardly bear, and you won't lift a finger to help them!

[47]"Woe to you! You build tombs in memory of the prophets, but your fathers murdered them! [48]Thus you testify that you completely approve of what your fathers did — they did the killing, you do the building! [49]Therefore the Wisdom of God said, 'I will send them prophets and emissaries; they will kill some and persecute others;' [50]so that on this generation will fall the responsibility for all the prophets' blood that has been shed since the world was established, [51]from the blood of Hevel to the blood of Z'kharyah, who was killed between the altar and the Holy Place. Yes, I tell you, the responsibility for it will fall on this generation!

[52]"Woe to you *Torah* experts! For you have taken away the key of knowledge! Not only did you yourselves not go in, you also have stopped those who were trying to enter!"

[53]As Yeshua left that place, the *Torah*-teachers and the *P'rushim* began to oppose him bitterly and to provoke him to express his views on all sorts of subjects, [54]laying traps to catch him in something he might say.

Ba·**'al**·zib·**bul** — Beelzebul, Beelzebub (Satan)
chutz·pah — audacity
He·vel — Abel
Nin·e·**veh** — Nineveh
n'ti·lat-ya·da·yim — ritual handwashing
Pa·rush — Pharisee
P'ru·shim — Pharisees
Ru·ach-Ha-***Ko***·desh— Holy Spirit
Shlo·**mo** — Solomon
To·rah — Teaching, "Law"; Pentateuch
To·rah-teachers — scribes
Ye·**shu**·a — Jesus
Yo·**nah** — Jonah
Z'khar·**yah** — Zechariah

12 ¹Meanwhile, as a crowd in the tens of thousands gathered so closely as to trample each other down, Yeshua began to say to his *talmidim* first, "Guard yourselves from the *chametz* of the *P'rushim*, by which I mean their hypocrisy. ²There is nothing covered up that will not be uncovered, or hidden that will not become known. ³What you have spoken in the dark will be heard in the light, and what you have whispered behind closed doors will be proclaimed on the housetops.

⁴"My friends, I tell you: don't fear those who kill the body but then have nothing more they can do. ⁵I will show you whom to fear: fear him who after killing you has authority to throw you into Gey-Hinnom! Yes, I tell you, this is the one to fear! ⁶Aren't sparrows sold for next to nothing, five for two assarions? And not one of them has been forgotten by God. ⁷Why, every hair on your head has been counted! Don't be afraid, you are worth more than many sparrows.

⁸"Moreover, I tell you, whoever acknowledges me in the presence of others, the Son of Man will also acknowledge in the presence of God's angels. ⁹But whoever disowns me before others will be disowned before God's angels. ¹⁰Also, everyone who says something against the Son of Man will have it forgiven him; but whoever has blasphemed the *Ruach HaKodesh* will not be forgiven.

¹¹"When they bring you before the synagogues and the ruling powers and the authorities, don't worry about how you will defend yourself or what you will say; ¹²because when the time comes, the *Ruach HaKodesh* will teach you what you need to say."

¹³Someone in the crowd said to him, "Rabbi, tell my brother to share with me the property we inherited." ¹⁴But Yeshua answered him, "My friend, who appointed me judge or arbitrator over you?" ¹⁵Then to the people he said, "Be careful to guard against all forms of greed, because even if someone is rich, his life does not consist in what he owns." ¹⁶And he gave them this illustration: "There was a man whose land was very productive. ¹⁷He debated with himself, 'What should I do? I haven't enough room for all my crops.' ¹⁸Then he said, 'This is what I will do: I'll tear down my barns and build bigger ones, and I'll store all my wheat and other goods there. ¹⁹Then I'll say to myself, "You're a lucky man! You have a big supply of goods laid up that will last many years. Start taking it easy! Eat! Drink! Enjoy yourself!"' ²⁰But God said to him, 'You fool! This very night you will die! And the things you prepared — whose will they be?' ²¹That's how it is with anyone who stores up wealth for himself without being rich toward God."

²²To his *talmidim* Yeshua said, "Because of this I tell you, don't worry about your life — what you will eat or drink; or about your body — what you will wear. ²³For life is more than food, and the body is more than clothing. ²⁴Think about the ravens! They neither plant nor harvest, they have neither storerooms nor barns, yet God feeds them. You are worth much more than the birds! ²⁵Can any of you by worrying add an hour to his life? ²⁶If you can't do a little thing like that, why worry about the rest? ²⁷Think about the wild irises, and how they grow. They neither work nor spin thread; yet, I tell you, not even Shlomo in all his glory was clothed as beautifully as one of these. ²⁸If this is how God clothes grass, which is alive in the field today and thrown in the oven tomorrow, how much more will he clothe you! What little trust you have!

[29] "In other words, don't strive after what you will eat and what you will drink — don't be anxious. [30] For all the pagan nations in the world set their hearts on these things. Your Father knows that you need them too. [31] Rather, seek his Kingdom; and these things will be given to you as well. [32] Have no fear, little flock, for your Father has resolved to give you the Kingdom! [33] Sell what you own and do *tzedakah* — make for yourselves purses that don't wear out, riches in heaven that never fail, where no burglar comes near, where no moth destroys. [34] For where your wealth is, there your heart will be also.

[35] "Be dressed for action and have your lamps lit, [36] like people waiting for their master's return after a wedding feast; so that when he comes and knocks, they will open the door for him without delay. [37] Happy the slaves whom the master finds alert when he comes! Yes! I tell you he will put on his work clothes, seat them at the table, and come serve them himself! [38] Whether it is late at night or early in the morning, if this is how he finds them, those slaves are happy.

[39] "But notice this: no house-owner would let his house be broken into if he knew when the thief was coming. [40] You too, be ready! For the Son of Man will come when you are not expecting him."

[41] Kefa said, "Sir, are you telling this parable for our benefit only or for everyone's?" [42] The Lord replied, "*Nu*, who is the faithful and sensible manager whose master puts him in charge of the household staff to give them their share of food at the proper time? [43] It will go well with that servant if he is found doing his job when his master comes. [44] Yes, I tell you he will put him in charge of all he owns. [45] But if that servant says to himself, 'My master is taking his time coming,' and starts bullying the men- and women-servants, and eating and drinking, getting drunk, [46] then his master will come on a day when the servant isn't expecting him, at a time he doesn't know in advance; his master will cut him in two and put him with the disloyal. [47] Now the servant who knew what his master wanted but didn't prepare or act according to his will, will be whipped with many lashes; [48] however, the one who did what deserves a beating, but didn't know, will receive few lashes. From him who has been given much, much will be demanded — from someone to whom people entrust much, they ask still more.

[49] "I have come to set fire to the earth! And how I wish it were already kindled! [50] I have an immersion to undergo — how pressured I feel till it's over! [51] Do you think that I have come to bring peace in the Land? Not peace, I tell you, but division! [52] For from now on, a household of five will be divided, three against two, two against three.

[53] Father will be divided against son and **son against father,**

mother against daughter and **daughter against mother,**

mother-in-law against her daughter-in-law and **daughter-in-law against mother-in-law.**"[w]

---
w Micah 7:6
---

cha·metz — leaven
Gey-Hin·nom — Gehenna, hell
Ke·fa — Peter
nu — well? think about it
P'ru·shim — Pharisees
Ru·ach-Ha·Ko·desh — Holy Spirit
Shlo·mo — Solomon
tal·mi·dim — disciples
tze·da·kah — righteousness, charity
Ye·shu·a — Jesus
Yo·cha·nan — John

⁵⁴Then to the crowds Yeshua said, "When you see a cloudbank rising in the west, at once you say that a rainstorm is coming; ⁵⁵and when the wind is from the south, you say there will be a heat wave, and there is. ⁵⁶Hypocrites! You know how to interpret the appearance of the earth and the sky — how is it that you don't know how to interpret this present time? ⁵⁷Why don't you decide for yourselves what is the right course to follow? ⁵⁸If someone brings a lawsuit against you, take pains to settle with him first; otherwise he will take the matter to court, and the judge will turn you over to the bailiff, and the bailiff will throw you in jail. ⁵⁹I tell you, you won't get out of there till you have paid the last penny!"

13 ¹Just then, some people came to tell Yeshua about the men from the Galil whom Pilate had slaughtered just as they were slaughtering animals for sacrifice. ²His answer to them was, "Do you think that just because they died so horribly, these folks from the Galil were worse sinners than all the others from the Galil? ³No, I tell you. Rather, unless you turn to God from your sins, you will all die as they did! ⁴Or what about those eighteen people who died when the tower at Shiloach fell on them? Do you think they were worse offenders than all the other people living in Yerushalayim? ⁵No, I tell you. Rather, unless you turn from your sins, you will all die similarly."

⁶Then Yeshua gave this illustration: "A man had a fig tree planted in his vineyard, and he came looking for fruit but didn't find any. ⁷So he said to the man who took care of the vineyard, 'Here, I've come looking for fruit on this fig tree for three years now without finding any. Cut it down — why let it go on using up the soil?' ⁸But he answered,

'Sir, leave it alone one more year. I'll dig around it and put manure on it. ⁹If it bears fruit next year, well and good; if not, you will have it cut down then.'"

¹⁰Yeshua was teaching in one of the synagogues on *Shabbat*. ¹¹A woman came up who had a spirit which had crippled her for eighteen years; she was bent double and unable to stand erect at all. ¹²On seeing her, Yeshua called her and said to her, "Lady, you have been set free from your weakness!" ¹³He put his hands on her, and at once she stood upright and began to glorify God.

¹⁴But the president of the synagogue, indignant that Yeshua had healed on *Shabbat*, spoke up and said to the congregation, "There are six days in the week for working; so come during those days to be healed, not on *Shabbat*!" ¹⁵However, the Lord answered him, "You hypocrites! Each one of you on *Shabbat* — don't you unloose your ox or your donkey from the stall and lead him off to drink? ¹⁶This woman is a daughter of Avraham, and the Adversary kept her tied up for eighteen years! Shouldn't she be freed from this bondage on *Shabbat*?" ¹⁷By these words, Yeshua put to shame the people who opposed him; but the rest of the crowd were happy about all the wonderful things that were taking place through him.

¹⁸So he went on to say, "What is the Kingdom of God like? With what will we compare it? ¹⁹It is like a mustard seed that a man took and planted in his own garden, and it grew and became a tree, and the birds flying about nested in its branches."

²⁰Again he said, "With what will I compare the Kingdom of God? ²¹It is like yeast that a woman took and mixed with a bushel of flour, then waited until the whole batch of dough rose."

²² Yeshua continued traveling through town after town and village after village, teaching and making his way toward Yerushalayim. ²³ Someone asked him, "Are only a few people being saved?" ²⁴ He answered, "Struggle to get in through the narrow door, because — I'm telling you! — many will be demanding to get in and won't be able to, ²⁵ once the owner of the house has gotten up and shut the door. You will stand outside, knocking at the door and saying, 'Lord! Open up for us!' But he will answer, 'I don't know you or where you come from!' ²⁶ Then you will say, 'We ate and drank with you! You taught in our streets!' ²⁷ and he will tell you, 'I don't know where you're from. Get away from me, all you workers of wickedness!' ²⁸ You will cry and grind your teeth when you see Avraham, Yitzchak, Ya'akov and all the prophets inside the Kingdom of God, but yourselves thrown outside. ²⁹ Moreover, people will come from the east, the west, the north and the south to sit at table in the Kingdom of God. ³⁰ And notice that some who are last will be first, and some who are first will be last."

³¹ Just at that moment, some P'rushim came up and said to Yeshua, "Get out and go away from here, because Herod wants to kill you!" ³² He said to them, "Go, tell that fox, 'Pay attention: today and tomorrow I am driving out demons and healing people, and on the third day I reach my goal.' ³³ Nevertheless, I must keep travelling today, tomorrow and the next day; because it is unthinkable that a prophet should die anywhere but in Yerushalayim.

³⁴ "Yerushalayim! Yerushalayim! You kill the prophets! You stone those who are sent to you! How often I wanted to gather your children, just as a hen gathers her chickens under her wings, but you refused! ³⁵ Look! God is abandoning your house to you! I tell you, you will not see me again until you say, 'Blessed is he who comes in the name of Adonai!'"ˣ

14 ¹ One *Shabbat* Yeshua went to eat in the home of one of the leading *P'rushim*, and they were watching him closely. ² In front of him was a man whose body was swollen with fluid. ³ Yeshua spoke up and asked the *Torah* experts and *P'rushim*, "Does the *Torah* allow healing on *Shabbat* or not?" ⁴ But they said nothing. So, taking hold of him, he healed him and sent him away. ⁵ To them he said, "Which of you, if a son or an ox falls into a well, will hesitate to haul him out on *Shabbat*?" ⁶ And to these things they could give no answer.

⁷ When Yeshua noticed how the guests were choosing for themselves the best seats at the table, he told them this parable: ⁸ "When you are invited by someone to a wedding feast, don't sit down in the best seat; because if there is someone more important than you who has been invited, ⁹ the person who invited both of you might come and say to you, 'Give this man your place.' Then you will be humiliated as you go

---

x Psalm 118:26

A·do·nai — the LORD, Jehovah
Av·ra·ham — Abraham
the Ga·lil — Galilee
P'ru·shim — Pharisees
Shab·bat — the Sabbath
Shi·lo·ach — Siloam
To·rah — Teaching, "Law"; Pentateuch
Ya·'a·kov — Jacob
Ye·ru·sha·la·yim — Jerusalem
Ye·shu·a — Jesus
Yitz·chak — Isaac

to take the least important place. [10]Instead, when you are invited, go and sit in the least important place; so that when the one who invited you comes, he will say to you, 'Go on up to a better seat.' Then you will be honored in front of everyone sitting with you. [11]Because everyone who exalts himself will be humbled, but everyone who humbles himself will be exalted."

[12]Yeshua also said to the one who had invited him, "When you give a lunch or a dinner, don't invite your friends, brothers, relatives or rich neighbors; for they may well invite you in return, and that will be your repayment. [13]Instead, when you have a party, invite poor people, disfigured people, the crippled, the blind! [14]How blessed you will be that they have nothing with which to repay you! For you will be repaid at the resurrection of the righteous."

[15]On hearing this, one of the people at the table with Yeshua said to him, "How blessed are those who eat bread in the Kingdom of God!" [16]But he replied, "Once a man gave a banquet and invited many people. [17]When the time came for the banquet, he sent his slave to tell those who had been invited, 'Come! Everything is ready!' [18]But they responded with a chorus of excuses. The first said to him, 'I've just bought a field, and I have to go out and see it. Please accept my apologies.' [19]Another said, 'I've just bought five yoke of oxen, and I'm on my way to test them out. Please accept my apologies.' [20]Still another said, 'I have just gotten married, so I can't come.' [21]The slave came and reported these things to his master.

Then the owner of the house, in a rage, told his slave, 'Quick, go out into the streets and alleys of the city; and bring in the poor, the disfigured, the blind and the crippled!' [22]The slave said, 'Sir, what you ordered has been done, and there is still room.' [23]The master said to the slave, 'Go out to the country roads and boundary walls, and insistently persuade people to come in, so that my house will be full. [24]I tell you, not one of those who were invited will get a taste of my banquet!'"

[25]Large crowds were traveling along with Yeshua. Turning, he said to them, [26]"If anyone comes to me and does not hate his father, his mother, his wife, his children, his brothers and his sisters, yes, and his own life besides, he cannot be my *talmid*. [27]Whoever does not carry his own execution-stake and come after me cannot be my *talmid*.

[28]"Suppose one of you wants to build a tower. Don't you sit down and estimate the cost, to see if you have enough capital to complete it? [29]If you don't, then when you have laid the foundation but can't finish, all the onlookers start making fun of you [30]and say, 'This is the man who began to build, but couldn't finish!'

[31]"Or again, suppose one king is going out to wage war with another king. Doesn't he first sit down and consider whether he, with his ten thousand troops, has enough strength to meet the other one, who is coming against him with twenty thousand? [32]If he hasn't, then while the other is still far away, he sends a delegation to inquire about terms for peace.

[33]"So every one of you who doesn't renounce all that he has cannot be my *talmid*. [34]Salt is excellent. But if even the salt becomes tasteless, what can be used to season it? [35]It is fit for neither soil nor manure — people throw it out. Those who have ears that can hear, let them hear!"

15 [1] The tax-collectors and sinners kept gathering around to hear Yeshua, [2] and the *P'rushim* and *Torah*-teachers kept grumbling. "This fellow," they said, "welcomes sinners — he even eats with them!" [3] So he told them this parable: [4] "If one of you has a hundred sheep and loses one of them, doesn't he leave the other 99 in the desert and go after the lost one until he finds it? [5] When he does find it, he joyfully hoists it onto his shoulders; [6] and when he gets home, he calls his friends and neighbors together and says, 'Come, celebrate with me, because I have found my lost sheep!' [7] I tell you that in the same way, there will be more joy in heaven over one sinner who turns to God from his sins than over 99 righteous people who have no need to repent.

[8] "Another example: what woman, if she has ten drachmas and loses one of these valuable coins, won't light a lamp, sweep the house and search all over until she finds it? [9] And when she does find it, she calls her friends and neighbors together and says, 'Come, celebrate with me, because I have found the drachma I lost.' [10] In the same way, I tell you, there is joy among God's angels when one sinner repents."

[11] Again Yeshua said, "A man had two sons. [12] The younger of them said to his father, 'Father, give me the share of the estate that will be mine.' So the father divided the property between them. [13] As soon as he could convert his share into cash, the younger son left home and went off to a distant country, where he squandered his money in reckless living. [14] But after he had spent it all, a severe famine arose throughout that country, and he began to feel the pinch.

[15] "So he went and attached himself to one of the citizens of that country, who sent him into his fields to feed pigs. [16] He longed to fill his stomach with the carob pods the pigs were eating, but no one gave him any.

[17] "At last he came to his senses and said, 'Any number of my father's hired workers have food to spare; and here I am, starving to death! [18] I'm going to get up and go back to my father and say to him, "Father, I have sinned against Heaven and against you; [19] I am no longer worthy to be called your son; treat me like one of your hired workers."' [20] So he got up and started back to his father.

"But while he was still a long way off, his father saw him and was moved with pity. He ran and threw his arms around him and kissed him warmly. [21] His son said to him, 'Father, I have sinned against Heaven and against you; I am no longer worthy to be called your son — ' [22] but his father said to his slaves, 'Quick, bring out a robe, the best one, and put it on him; and put a ring on his finger and shoes on his feet; [23] and bring the calf that has been fattened up, and kill it; let's eat and have a celebration! [24] For this son of mine was dead, but now he's alive again! He was lost, but now he has been found!' And they began celebrating.

[25] "Now his older son was in the field. As he came close to the house, he heard music and dancing. [26] So he called one of the servants and asked, 'What's going on?' [27] The servant told him, 'Your brother has come back, and your father has slaughtered the calf that was fattened up, because he has gotten him back safe and sound.' [28] But the older

---

P'ru·shim — Pharisees
tal·mid — disciple
To·rah-teachers — scribes
Ye·shu·a — Jesus

101

son became angry and refused to go inside.

"So his father came out and pleaded with him. ²⁹'Look,' the son answered, 'I have worked for you all these years, and I have never disobeyed your orders. But you have never even given me a young goat, so that I could celebrate with my friends. ³⁰ Yet this son of yours comes, who squandered your property with prostitutes, and for him you slaughter the fattened calf!' ³¹'Son, you are always with me,' said the father, 'and everything I have is yours. ³² We had to celebrate and rejoice, because this brother of yours was dead but has come back to life — he was lost but has been found.'"

16 ¹Speaking to the *talmidim*, Yeshua said: "There was a wealthy man who employed a general manager. Charges were brought to him that his manager was squandering his resources. ²So he summoned him and asked him, 'What is this I hear about you? Turn in your accounts, for you can no longer be manager.'

³'"What am I to do?' said the manager to himself. 'My boss is firing me, I'm not strong enough to dig ditches, and I'm ashamed to go begging. ⁴ Aha! I know what I'll do — something that will make people welcome me into their homes after I've lost my job here!'

⁵"So, after making appointments with each of his employer's debtors, he said to the first, 'How much do you owe my boss?' ⁶'Eight hundred gallons of olive oil,' he replied. 'Take your note back,' he told him. 'Now, quickly! Sit down and write one for four hundred!' ⁷To the next he said, 'And you, how much do you owe?' 'A thousand bushels of wheat,' he replied. 'Take your note back and write one for eight hundred.'

⁸"And the employer of this dishonest manager applauded him for acting so shrewdly! For the worldly have more *sekhel* than those who have received the light — in dealing with their own kind of people!

⁹"Now what I say to you is this: use worldly wealth to make friends for yourselves, so that when it gives out, you may be welcomed into the eternal home. ¹⁰Someone who is trustworthy in a small matter is also trustworthy in large ones, and someone who is dishonest in a small matter is also dishonest in large ones. ¹¹So if you haven't been trustworthy in handling worldly wealth, who is going to trust you with the real thing? ¹²And if you haven't been trustworthy with what belongs to someone else, who will give you what ought to belong to you? ¹³No servant can be slave to two masters, for he will either hate the first and love the second, or scorn the second and be loyal to the first. You can't be a slave to both God and money."

¹⁴The *P'rushim* heard all this, and since they were money-lovers, they ridiculed him. ¹⁵He said to them, "You people make yourselves look righteous to others, but God knows your hearts; what people regard highly is an abomination before God! ¹⁶Up to the time of Yochanan there were the *Torah* and the Prophets. Since then the Good News of the Kingdom of God has been proclaimed, and everyone is pushing to get in. ¹⁷But it is easier for heaven and earth to pass away than for one stroke of a letter in the *Torah* to become void. ¹⁸Every man who divorces his wife and marries another woman commits adultery, and a man who marries a woman divorced by her husband commits adultery.

¹⁹"Once there was a rich man who used to dress in the most expensive clothing and spent his days in mag-

nificent luxury. ²⁰ At his gate had been laid a beggar named El'azar who was covered with sores. ²¹ He would have been glad to eat the scraps that fell from the rich man's table; but instead, even the dogs would come and lick his sores. ²² In time the beggar died and was carried away by the angels to Avraham's side; the rich man also died and was buried.

²³ "In Sh'ol, where he was in torment, the rich man looked up and saw Avraham far away with El'azar at his side. ²⁴ He called out, 'Father Avraham, take pity on me, and send El'azar just to dip the tip of his finger in water to cool my tongue, because I'm in agony in this fire!' ²⁵ However, Avraham said, 'Son, remember that when you were alive, you got the good things while he got the bad; but now he gets his consolation here, while you are the one in agony. ²⁶ Yet that isn't all: between you and us a deep rift has been established, so that those who would like to pass from here to you cannot, nor can anyone cross over from there to us.'

²⁷ "He answered, 'Then, father, I beg you to send him to my father's house, ²⁸ where I have five brothers, to warn them; so that they may be spared having to come to this place of torment too.' ²⁹ But Avraham said, 'They have Moshe and the Prophets; they should listen to them.' ³⁰ However, he said, 'No, father Avraham, they need more. If someone from the dead goes to them, they'll repent!' ³¹ But he replied, 'If they won't listen to Moshe and the Prophets, they won't be convinced even if someone rises from the dead!'"

17 ¹ Yeshua said to his *talmidim*, "It is impossible that snares will not be set. But woe to the person who sets them! ² It would be to his advantage that he have a millstone hung around

his neck and he be thrown into the sea, rather than that he ensnare one of these little ones. ³ Watch yourselves! If your brother sins, rebuke him; and if he repents, forgive him. ⁴ Also, if seven times in one day he sins against you, and seven times he comes to you and says, 'I repent,' you are to forgive him."
⁵ The emissaries said to the Lord, "Increase our trust." ⁶ The Lord replied, "If you had trust as tiny as a mustard seed, you could say to this fig tree, 'Be uprooted and replanted in the sea!' and it would obey you. ⁷ If one of you has a slave tending the sheep or plowing, when he comes back from the field, will you say to him, 'Come along now, sit down and eat'? ⁸ No, you'll say, 'Get my supper ready, dress for work, and serve me until I have finished eating and drinking; after that, you may eat and drink.' ⁹ Does he thank the slave because he did what he was told to do? No! ¹⁰ It's the same with you — when you have done everything you were told to do, you should be saying, 'We're just ordinary slaves, we have only done our duty.'"

¹¹ On his way to Yerushalayim, Yeshua passed along the border country between Shomron and the Galil. ¹² As he entered one of the villages, ten men with a skin disease met him. They stood at a distance ¹³ and called out, "Yeshua!

Av·ra·ham — Abraham
El·'a·zar — Lazarus
the Ga·lil — Galilee
Mo·she — Moses
P'ru·shim — Pharisees
se·khel — intelligence, common sense
Sh'ol — Sheol, Hades, hell
Shom·ron — Samaria
tal·mi·dim — disciples
To·rah — Teaching, "Law"; Pentateuch
Ye·ru·sha·la·yim — Jerusalem
Ye·shu·a — Jesus
Yo·cha·nan — John

Rabbi! Have pity on us!" ¹⁴On seeing them, he said, "Go and let the *cohanim* examine you!" And as they went, they were cleansed. ¹⁵One of them, as soon as he noticed that he had been healed, returned shouting praises to God, ¹⁶and fell on his face at Yeshua's feet to thank him. Now he was from Shomron. ¹⁷Yeshua said, "Weren't ten cleansed? Where are the other nine? ¹⁸Was no one found coming back to give glory to God except this foreigner?" ¹⁹And to the man from Shomron he said, "Get up, you may go; your trust has saved you."

²⁰The *P'rushim* asked Yeshua when the Kingdom of God would come. "The Kingdom of God," he answered, "does not come with visible signs; ²¹nor will people be able to say, 'Look! Here it is!' or, 'Over there!' Because, you see, the Kingdom of God is among you." ²²Then he said to his *talmidim*, "The time is coming when you will long to see even one of the days of the Son of Man, but you will not see it. ²³People will say to you, 'Look! Right here!' or, 'See! Over there!' Don't run off, don't follow them, ²⁴because the Son of Man in his day will be like lightning that flashes and lights up the sky from one horizon to the other. ²⁵But first he must endure horrible suffering and be rejected by this generation.

²⁶"Also, at the time of the Son of Man, it will be just as it was at the time of Noach. ²⁷People ate and drank, and men and women married, right up until the day Noach entered the ark; then the flood came and destroyed them all. ²⁸Likewise, as it was in the time of Lot— people ate and drank, bought and sold, planted and built; ²⁹but the day Lot left S'dom, fire and sulfur rained down from heaven and destroyed them all. ³⁰That is how it will be on the day the Son of Man is revealed. ³¹On that day,

if someone is on the roof with his belongings in his house, he must not go down to take them away. Similarly, if someone is in the field, he must not turn back — ³²remember Lot's wife! ³³Whoever aims at preserving his own life will lose it, but whoever loses his life will stay alive. ³⁴I tell you, on that night there will be two people in one bed — one will be taken and the other left behind. ³⁵There will be two women grinding grain together — one will be taken and the other left behind." ³⁶*

³⁷They asked him, "Where, Lord?" He answered, "Wherever there's a dead body, that's where the vultures gather."

18 ¹Then Yeshua told his *talmidim* a parable, in order to impress on them that they must always keep praying and not lose heart. ²"In a certain town, there was a judge who neither feared God nor respected other people. ³There was also in that town a widow who kept coming to him and saying, 'Give me a judgment against the man who is trying to ruin me.' ⁴For a long time he refused; but after awhile, he said to himself, 'I don't fear God, and I don't respect other people; ⁵but because this widow is such a *nudnik*, I will see to it that she gets justice — otherwise, she'll keep coming and pestering me till she wears me out!'"

⁶Then the Lord commented, "Notice what this corrupt judge says. ⁷Now won't God grant justice to his chosen people who cry out to him day and night? Is he delaying long over them? ⁸I tell you that he will judge in their favor, and quickly! But when the Son of Man comes, will he find this trust on the earth at all?"

⁹Also, to some who were relying on

---

* Some manuscripts have verse 36: Two men will be in a field — one will be taken and the other left behind.

their own righteousness and looking down on everyone else, he told this parable: [10]"Two men went up to the Temple to pray, one a *Parush* and the other a tax-collector. [11]The *Parush* stood and prayed to himself, 'O God! I thank thee that I am not like the rest of humanity — greedy, dishonest, immoral, or like this tax-collector! [12]I fast twice a week, I pay tithes on my entire income,...' [13]But the tax-collector, standing far off, would not even raise his eyes toward heaven, but beat his breast and said, 'God! Have mercy on me, sinner that I am!' [14]I tell you, this man went down to his home right with God rather than the other. For everyone who exalts himself will be humbled, but everyone who humbles himself will be exalted."

[15]People brought him babies to touch; but when the *talmidim* saw the people doing this, they rebuked them. [16]However, Yeshua called the children to him and said, "Let the children come to me and stop hindering them, because the Kingdom of God belongs to such as these. [17]Yes! I tell you that whoever does not receive the Kingdom of God like a little child will not enter it at all!"

[18]One of the leaders asked him, "Good rabbi, what should I do to obtain eternal life?" [19]Yeshua said to him, "Why are you calling me good? No one is good but God! [20]You know the *mitzvot* — 'Don't commit adultery, don't murder, don't steal, don't give false testimony, honor your father and mother,...'"[y] [21]He replied, "I have kept all these since I was a boy." [22]On hearing this Yeshua said to him, "There is one thing you still lack. Sell whatever you have, distribute the proceeds to the poor, and you will have riches in heaven. Then come, follow me!" [23]But when the man heard this, he became very sad, because he was very rich.

[24]Yeshua looked at him and said, "How hard it is for people with wealth to enter the Kingdom of God! [25]It's easier for a camel to pass through a needle's eye than for a rich man to enter the Kingdom of God!" [26]Those who heard this asked, "Then who can be saved?" [27]He said, "What is impossible humanly is possible with God."

[28]Kefa said, "Look, we have left our homes and followed you." [29]Yeshua answered them, "Yes! I tell you that everyone who has left house, wife, brothers, parents or children, for the sake of the kingdom of God, [30]will receive many times as much in the *'olam hazeh,* and in the *'olam haba* eternal life."

[31]Then, taking the Twelve, Yeshua said to them, "We are now going up to Yerushalayim, where everything written through the prophets about the Son of Man will come true. [32]For he will be handed over to the *Goyim* and be ridiculed, insulted and spat upon. [33]Then, after they have beaten him, they will kill him. But on the third day he will rise." [34]However, they under-

---

co·ha·nim — priests
Go·yim — Gentiles
Ke·fa — Peter
mitz·vot — commandments
No·ach — Noah
nud·nik — pest, bore
'o·lam ha·ba — the world/age to come
'o·lam ha·zeh — this world/age
Pa·rush — Pharisee
P'ru·shim — Pharisees
S'dom — Sodom
Shom·ron — Samaria
tal·mi·dim — disciples
Ye·ru·sha·la·yim — Jerusalem
Ye·shu·a — Jesus

---

[y] Exodus 20:12-13(12-16),
Deuteronomy 5:16-20

105

stood none of this; its meaning had been hidden from them, and they had no idea what he was talking about.

³⁵ As Yeshua approached Yericho, a blind man was sitting by the road, begging. ³⁶ When he heard the crowd going past, he asked what it was all about; ³⁷ and they told him, "Yeshua from Natzeret is passing by." ³⁸ He called out, "Yeshua! Son of David! Have pity on me!" ³⁹ Those in front scolded him in order to get him to shut up, but he shouted all the louder, "Son of David! Have pity on me!" ⁴⁰ Yeshua stopped and ordered the man to be brought to him. When he had come, Yeshua asked him, ⁴¹ "What do you want me to do for you?" The blind man said, "Lord, let me be able to see." ⁴² Yeshua said to him, "See again! Your trust has healed you!" ⁴³ Instantly he received his sight and began following him, glorifying God; and when all the people saw it, they too praised God.

19 ¹ Yeshua entered Yericho and was passing through, ² when a man named Zakkai appeared who was a chief tax-collector and a wealthy man. ³ He was trying to see who Yeshua was; but, being short, he couldn't, because of the crowd. ⁴ So he ran on ahead and climbed a fig tree in order to see him, for Yeshua was about to pass that way. ⁵ When he came to the place, he looked up and said to him, "Zakkai! Hurry! Come down, because I have to stay at your house today!" ⁶ He climbed down as fast as he could and welcomed Yeshua joyfully. ⁷ Everyone who saw it began muttering, "He has gone to be the house-guest of a sinner." ⁸ But Zakkai stood there and said to the Lord, "Here, Lord, I am giving half of all I own to the poor; and if I have cheated anyone, I will pay him back four times as much." ⁹ Yeshua said to him, "Today salvation has come to this house, inasmuch as this man too is a son of Avraham. ¹⁰ For the Son of Man came to seek and save what was lost."

¹¹ While they were listening to this, Yeshua went on to tell a parable, because he was near Yerushalayim, and the people supposed that the Kingdom of God was about to appear at any moment. ¹² Therefore he said, "A nobleman went to a country far away to have himself crowned king and then return. ¹³ Calling ten of his servants, he gave them ten *manim* [a *maneh* is about three months' wages] and said to them, 'Do business with this while I'm away.' ¹⁴ But his countrymen hated him, and they sent a delegation after him to say, 'We don't want this man to rule over us.'

¹⁵ "However, he returned, having been made king, and sent for the servants to whom he had given the money, to find out what each one had earned in his business dealings. ¹⁶ The first one came in and said, 'Sir, your *maneh* has earned ten more *manim*.' ¹⁷ 'Excellent!' he said to him. 'You are a good servant. Because you have been trustworthy in a small matter, I am putting you in charge of ten towns.' ¹⁸ The second one came and said, 'Sir, your *maneh* has earned five more *manim*;' ¹⁹ and to this one he said, 'You be in charge of five towns.'

²⁰ "Then another one came and said, 'Sir, here is your *maneh*. I kept it hidden in a piece of cloth, ²¹ because I was afraid of you — you take out what you didn't put in, and you harvest what you didn't plant.' ²² To him the master said, 'You wicked servant! I will judge you by your own words! So you knew, did you, that I was a severe man, taking out what I didn't put in and harvesting what I didn't plant? ²³ Then why didn't you put my money in the bank? Then, when I returned, I would have gotten it

back with interest!'²⁴To those standing by, he said, 'Take the *maneh* from him and give it to the one with ten *manim*.' ²⁵They said to him, 'Sir, he already has ten *manim*!'²⁶But the master answered, 'I tell you, everyone who has something will be given more; but from anyone who has nothing, even what he does have will be taken away. ²⁷However, as for these enemies of mine who did not want me to be their king, bring them here and execute them in my presence!'"

²⁸After saying this, Yeshua went on and began the ascent to Yerushalayim. ²⁹As he approached Beit-Pagey and Beit-Anyah, by the Mount of Olives, he sent two *talmidim*, ³⁰instructing them, "Go into the village ahead; on entering it, you will find a colt tied up that has never been ridden. Untie it and bring it here. ³¹If anyone asks why you are untying it, tell him, 'The Lord needs it.'" ³²Those who were sent went off and found it just as he had told them. ³³As they were untying the colt, its owners said to them, "Why are you untying the colt?" ³⁴and they said, "Because the Lord needs it." ³⁵They brought it to Yeshua; and, throwing their robes on the colt, they put Yeshua on it. ³⁶As he went along, people carpeted the road with their clothing; ³⁷and as he came near Yerushalayim, where the road descends from the Mount of Olives, the entire band of *talmidim* began to sing and praise God at the top of their voices for all the powerful works they had seen:

³⁸ "**Blessed is the King who is coming in the name of *Adonai*!**"ᶻ

"*Shalom* in heaven!"

and

"Glory in the highest places!"

---

z Psalm 118:26

³⁹Some of the *P'rushim* in the crowd said to him, "Rabbi! Reprimand your *talmidim*!" ⁴⁰But he answered them, "I tell you that if they keep quiet, the stones will shout!"

⁴¹When Yeshua had come closer and could see the city, he wept over it, ⁴²saying, "If you only knew today what is needed for *shalom*! But for now it is hidden from your sight. ⁴³For the days are coming upon you when your enemies will set up a barricade around you, encircle you, hem you in on every side, ⁴⁴and dash you to the ground, you and your children within your walls, leaving not one stone standing on another — and all because you did not recognize your opportunity when God offered it!"

⁴⁵Then Yeshua entered the Temple grounds and began driving out those doing business there, ⁴⁶saying to them, "The *Tanakh* says, '**My House is to be a house of prayer**,'ᵃ but you have made it into a **den of robbers!**"ᵇ

⁴⁷Every day he taught at the Temple. The head *cohanim*, the *Torah*-teachers

---

a Isaiah 56:7   b Jeremiah 7:11

=====

A·do·nai — the LORD, Jehovah
Av·ra·**ham** — Abraham
Beit-An·**yah** — Bethany
Beit-Pa·**gey** — Bethphage
co·ha·nim — priests
Da·**vid** — David
ma·neh (pl. *ma·nim*) — mina, pound
Na·tze·ret — Nazareth
P'ru·shim — Pharisees
sha·lom — peace
tal·mi·dim — disciples
Ta·nakh — Hebrew Scriptures, "Old Testament"
To·rah-teachers — scribes
Ye·ri·cho — Jericho
Ye·ru·sha·la·yim — Jerusalem
Ye·shu·a — Jesus
Zak·**kai** — Zacchaeus

and the leaders of the people tried to find a way of putting an end to him; ⁴⁸but they couldn't find any way of doing it, because all the people were hanging onto his every word.

20 ¹One day, as Yeshua was teaching the people at the Temple, making known the Good News, the head *cohanim* and the *Torah*-teachers, along with the elders, came up to him ²and said, "Tell us, what *s'mikhah* do you have that authorizes you to do these things? Who gave you this *s'mikhah*?" ³He answered, "I too will ask you a question. Tell me, ⁴the immersion of Yochanan — was it from Heaven or from a human source?" ⁵They discussed it among themselves, saying, "If we say, 'From Heaven,' he will say, 'Then why didn't you believe him?' ⁶But if we say, 'From a human source,' all the people will stone us, because they're convinced that Yochanan was a prophet." ⁷So they answered, "We don't know where it came from." ⁸Yeshua said to them, "Then I won't tell you by what *s'mikhah* I do these things."

⁹Next Yeshua told the people this parable: "A man planted a vineyard, rented it to tenant-farmers and went away for a long time. ¹⁰When the time came, he sent a servant to the tenants to receive his share of the crop from the vineyard; but the tenants beat him up and sent him away empty-handed. ¹¹He sent another servant; they beat him too, insulted him and sent him away empty-handed. ¹²He sent yet a third; this one they wounded and threw out.

¹³"Then the owner of the vineyard said, 'What am I to do? I will send my son, whom I love; maybe they will respect him.' ¹⁴But when the tenants saw him, they discussed it among themselves and said, 'This is the heir; let's kill him, so that the inheritance will be ours!' ¹⁵And they threw him out of the vineyard and killed him.

"Now what will the owner of the vineyard do to them? ¹⁶He will come and put an end to those tenants and give the vineyard to others!" When the people heard this, they said, "Heaven forbid!" ¹⁷But Yeshua looked searchingly at them and said, "Then what is this which is written in the *Tanakh*,

> 'The very rock which the builders rejected
> has become the cornerstone'?ᶜ

¹⁸Whoever falls on that stone will be broken in pieces; but if it falls on him, he will be crushed to powder!"

¹⁹The *Torah*-teachers and the head *cohanim* would have seized him at that very moment, because they knew that he had aimed this parable at them, but they were afraid of the people.

²⁰So they kept a close watch on the situation. They sent spies who hypocritically represented themselves as righteous, so that they might seize hold of something Yeshua said, as an excuse to hand him over to the jurisdiction and authority of the governor. ²¹They put to him this *sh'eilah*: "Rabbi, we know that you speak and teach straightforwardly, showing no partiality but really teaching what God's way is. ²²Does *Torah* permit us to pay taxes to the Roman Emperor or not?" ²³But he, spotting their craftiness, said to them, ²⁴"Show me a denarius! Whose name and picture does it have?" "The Emperor's," they replied. ²⁵"Then," he said to them, "give the Emperor what belongs to the Emperor. And give to God what belongs to God!" ²⁶They were unable to trap him by anything he

---

c Psalm 118:22

said publicly; indeed, amazed at his answer, they fell silent.

²⁷Some *Tz'dukim*, who say there is no resurrection, came to Yeshua ²⁸and put to him a *sh'eilah*: "Rabbi, Moshe wrote for us that **if a man dies leaving a wife but no children, his brother must take the wife and have children to preserve the man's family line.**ᵈ ²⁹Now there were seven brothers. The first took a wife and died childless, ³⁰also the second ³¹and third took her, and likewise all seven, but they all died without leaving children. ³²Lastly, the woman also died. ³³In the Resurrection, which one's wife will she be? For all seven were married to her."

³⁴Yeshua said to them, "In this age, men and women marry; ³⁵but those judged worthy of the age to come, and of resurrection from the dead, do not get married, ³⁶because they can no longer die. Being children of the Resurrection, they are like angels; indeed, they are children of God.

³⁷"But even Moshe showed that the dead are raised. In the passage about the bush, where he calls *Adonai* '**the God of Avraham, the God of Yitzchak and the God of Ya'akov.**'ᵉ ³⁸Now he is not God of the dead, but of the living — to him all are alive."

³⁹Some of the *Torah*-teachers answered, "Well spoken, Rabbi."⁴⁰For they no longer dared put to him a *sh'eilah*. ⁴¹But he said to them, "How is it that people say the Messiah is David's son?" ⁴²For David himself says in the book of Psalms,

⁴³ '***Adonai*** **said to my Lord,**
"Sit at my right hand
until I make your enemies your
footstool."'ᶠ

⁴⁴David thus calls him 'Lord'. So how can he be David's son?"

⁴⁵Within the hearing of all the people, Yeshua said to his *talmidim*, ⁴⁶"Watch out for the kind of *Torah*-teachers that like to walk around in robes and be greeted deferentially in the marketplaces, the kind that like to have the best seats in the synagogues and the places of honor at banquets, ⁴⁷the kind that swallow up widows' houses while making a show of *davvening* at great length. Their punishment will be all the worse!"

21 ¹Then Yeshua looked up, and as he watched the rich placing their gifts into the Temple offering-boxes, ²he also saw a poor widow put in two small coins. ³He said, "I tell you the truth, this poor widow has put in more than all the others. ⁴For they, out of their wealth, have contributed money they could easily spare; but she, out of her poverty, has given all she had to live on."

⁵As some people were remarking about the Temple, how beautiful its stonework and memorial decorations

---

A·do·nai — the LORD, Jehovah
Av·ra·ham — Abraham
co·ha·nim — priests
dav·ven·ing — praying
Da·vid — David
Mo·she — Moses
sh·'ei·lah — question
s'mi·khah — ordination
tal·mi·dim — disciples
Ta·nakh — Hebrew Scriptures, "Old Testament"
To·rah — Teaching, "Law"; Pentateuch
To·rah-teachers — scribes
Tz'du·kim — Sadducees
Ya·'a·kov — Jacob
Ye·shu·a — Jesus
Yitz·chak — Isaac
Yo·cha·nan — John

---

d Deuteronomy 25:5   *e* Exodus 3:6
f Psalm 110:1

were, he said, [6]"The time is coming when what you see here will be totally destroyed — not a single stone will be left standing!" [7] They asked him, "Rabbi, if this is so, when will these events take place? And what sign will show that they are about to happen?" [8] He answered, "Watch out! Don't be fooled! For many will come in my name, saying, 'I am he!' and, 'The time has come!' Don't go after them. [9] And when you hear of wars and revolutions, don't panic. For these things must happen first, but the end will not follow immediately."

[10] Then he told them, "Peoples will fight each other, nations will fight each other, [11] there will be great earthquakes, there will be epidemics and famines in various places, and there will be fearful sights and great signs from Heaven. [12] But before all this, they will arrest you and persecute you, handing you over to the synagogues and prisons; and you will be brought before kings and governors. This will all be on account of me, [13] but it will prove an opportunity for you to bear witness. [14] So make up your minds not to worry, rehearsing your defense beforehand; [15] for I myself will give you an eloquence and a wisdom that no adversary will be able to resist or refute. [16] You will be betrayed even by parents, brothers, relatives and friends; some of you they will have put to death; [17] and everyone will hate you because of me. [18] But not a hair of your head will be lost. [19] By standing firm you will save your lives.

[20] "However, when you see Yerushalayim surrounded by armies, then you are to understand that she is about to be destroyed. [21] Those in Y'hudah must escape to the hills, those inside the city must get out, and those in the country must not enter it. [22] For these are the days of vengeance, when everything that has been written in the *Tanakh* will come true. [23] What a terrible time it will be for pregnant women and nursing mothers! For there will be great distress in the Land and judgment on the people. [24] Some will fall by the edge of the sword, others will be carried into all the countries of the *Goyim*, and Yerushalayim will be trampled down by the *Goyim* until the age of the *Goyim* has run its course.

[25] "There will appear signs in the sun, moon and stars; and on earth, nations will be in anxiety and bewilderment at the sound and surge of the sea, [26] as people faint with fear at the prospect of what is overtaking the world; for **the powers in heaven will be shaken.**[g] [27] And then they will see **the Son of Man coming in a cloud** with tremendous power and glory.[h] [28] When these things start to happen, stand up and hold your heads high; because you are about to be liberated!"

[29] Then he told them a parable: "Look at the fig tree, indeed, all the trees. [30] As soon as they sprout leaves, you can see for yourselves that summer is near. [31] In the same way, when you see these things taking place, you are to know that the Kingdom of God is near! [32] Yes! I tell you that this people will certainly not pass away before it has all happened. [33] Heaven and earth will pass away, but my words will certainly not pass away.

[34] "But keep watch on yourselves, or your hearts will become dulled by carousing, drunkenness and the worries of everyday living, and that Day will be sprung upon you suddenly like a trap! [35] For it will close in on everyone, no matter where they live, throughout the whole world. [36] Stay alert, always pray-

---

g Haggai 2:6, 21   *h* Daniel 7:13-14

ing that you will have the strength to escape all the things that will happen and to stand in the presence of the Son of Man."

[37] Yeshua spent his days at the Temple, teaching; while at night he went out and stayed on the hill called the Mount of Olives. [38] All the people would rise with the dawn to come and hear him at the Temple courts. **22** [1] But the festival of *Matzah*, known as *Pesach*, was approaching; [2] and the head *cohanim* and the *Torah*-teachers began trying to find some way to get rid of Yeshua, because they were afraid of the people.

[3] At this point the Adversary went into Y'hudah from K'riot, who was one of the Twelve. [4] He approached the head *cohanim* and the Temple guard and discussed with them how he might turn Yeshua over to them. [5] They were pleased and offered to pay him money. [6] He agreed and began looking for a good opportunity to betray Yeshua without the people's knowledge.

[7] Then came the day of *matzah*, on which the Passover lamb had to be killed. [8] Yeshua sent Kefa and Yochanan, instructing them, "Go and prepare our *Seder*, so we can eat." [9] They asked him, "Where do you want us to prepare it?" [10] He told them, "As you're going into the city, a man carrying a jar of water will meet you. Follow him into the house he enters, [11] and say to its owner, 'The Rabbi says to you, "Where is the guest room, where I am to eat the *Pesach* meal with my *talmidim*?"' [12] He will show you a large room upstairs already furnished; make the preparations there." [13] They went and found things just as Yeshua had told them they would be, and they prepared for the *Seder*.

[14] When the time came, Yeshua and the emissaries reclined at the table, [15] and he said to them, "I have really wanted so much to celebrate this *Seder* with you before I die! [16] For I tell you, it is certain that I will not celebrate it again until it is given its full meaning in the Kingdom of God."

[17] Then, taking a cup of wine, he made the *b'rakhah* and said, "Take this and share it among yourselves. [18] For I tell you that from now on, I will not drink the 'fruit of the vine' until the Kingdom of God comes." [19] Also, taking a piece of *matzah*, he made the *b'rakhah*, broke it, gave it to them and said, "This is my body, which is being given for you; do this in memory of me." [20] He did the same with the cup after the meal, saying, "This cup is the New Covenant, ratified by my blood, which is being poured out for you.

[21] "But look! The person who is betraying me is here at the table with me! [22] The Son of Man is going to his death according to God's plan, but woe to that man by whom he is being betrayed!" [23] They began asking each other which of them could be about to do such a thing.

[24] An argument arose among them as to which of them should be considered the greatest. [25] But Yeshua said to them,

---

b'ra·khah — blessing
co·ha·nim — priests
Go·yim — Gentiles, nations, pagans
Ke·fa — Peter
ma·tzah — unleavened bread
Pe·sach — Passover
Se·der — Passover eve meal
tal·mi·dim — disciples
Ta·nakh — Hebrew Scriptures, "Old Testament"
To·rah-teachers — scribes
Ye·ru·sha·la·yim — Jerusalem
Ye·shu·a — Jesus
Y'hu·dah — Judea
Y'hu·dah from K'ri·ot— Judas Iscariot
Yo·cha·nan — John

"The kings of the *Goyim* lord it over them; and those in authority over them are given the title, 'Benefactor'. ²⁶ But not so with you! On the contrary, let the greater among you become like the younger, and one who rules like one who serves. ²⁷ For who is greater? The one reclining at the table? or the one who serves? It's the one reclining at the table, isn't it? But I myself am among you like one who serves.

²⁸ "You are the ones who have stayed with me throughout my trials. ²⁹ Just as my Father gave me the right to rule, so I give you an appointment, ³⁰ namely, to eat and drink at my table in my Kingdom and to sit on thrones judging the twelve tribes of Israel.

³¹ "Shim'on, Shim'on, listen! The Adversary demanded to have you people for himself, to sift you like wheat! ³² But I prayed for you, Shim'on, that your trust might not fail. And you, once you have turned back in repentance, strengthen your brothers!" ³³ Shim'on said to him, "Lord, I am prepared to go with you both to prison and to death!" ³⁴ Yeshua replied, "I tell you, Kefa, the rooster will not crow today until you have denied three times that you know me."

³⁵ He said to them, "When I sent you out without wallet, pack or shoes, were you ever short of anything?" "Not a thing," they answered. ³⁶ "But now," he said, if you have a wallet or a pack, take it; and if you don't have a sword, sell your robe to buy one. ³⁷ For I tell you this: the passage from the *Tanakh* that says, '**He was counted with transgressors,**'*ⁱ* has to be fulfilled in me; since what is happening to me has a purpose." ³⁸ They said, "Look, Lord, there are two swords right here!" "Enough!" he replied.

---

i Isaiah 53:12

³⁹ On leaving, Yeshua went as usual to the Mount of Olives; and the *talmidim* followed him. ⁴⁰ When he arrived, he said to them, "Pray that you won't be put to the test." ⁴¹ He went about a stone's throw away from them, kneeled down and prayed, ⁴² "Father, if you are willing, take this cup away from me; still, let not my will but yours be done." ⁴³ There appeared to him an angel from heaven giving him strength, ⁴⁴ and in great anguish he prayed more intensely, so that his sweat became like drops of blood falling to the ground. ⁴⁵ On rising from prayer and coming to the *talmidim*, he found them sleeping because of their grief. ⁴⁶ He said to them, "Why are you sleeping? Get up and pray that you won't be put to the test!"

⁴⁷ While he was still speaking, a crowd of people arrived, with the man called Y'hudah (one of the Twelve!) leading them. He came up to Yeshua to kiss him, ⁴⁸ but Yeshua said to him, "Y'hudah, are you betraying the Son of Man with a kiss?" ⁴⁹ When his followers saw what was going to happen, they said, "Lord, should we use our swords?" ⁵⁰ One of them struck at the slave of the *cohen hagadol* and cut off his right ear. ⁵¹ But Yeshua answered, "Just let me do this," and, touching the man's ear, he healed him.

⁵² Then Yeshua said to the head *cohanim*, the officers of the Temple guard and the elders who had come to seize him, "So you came out just as you would to the leader of a rebellion, with swords and clubs? ⁵³ Every day I was there with you in the Temple court, yet you didn't arrest me. But this is your hour — the hour when darkness rules."

⁵⁴ Having seized him, they led him away and brought him into the house of the *cohen hagadol*. Kefa followed at a distance; ⁵⁵ but when they had lit a fire

in the middle of the courtyard and sat down together, Kefa joined them. ⁵⁶ One of the servant girls saw him sitting in the light of the fire, stared at him and said, "This man also was with him." ⁵⁷ But he denied it: "Lady, I don't even know him." ⁵⁸ A little later, someone else saw him and said, "You're one of them too;" but Kefa said, "Man, I am not!" ⁵⁹ About an hour later, another man asserted emphatically, "There can be no doubt that this fellow was with him, because he too is from the Galil!" ⁶⁰ But Kefa said, "Man, I don't know what you're talking about!" And instantly, while he was still speaking, a rooster crowed. ⁶¹ The Lord turned and looked straight at Kefa; and Kefa remembered what the Lord had said, "Before the rooster crows today, you will deny me three times." ⁶² And he went outside and cried bitterly.

⁶³ Meanwhile, the men who were holding Yeshua made fun of him. They beat him, ⁶⁴ blindfolded him, and kept asking him, "Now, 'prophesy'! Who hit you that time?" ⁶⁵ And they said many other insulting things to him.

⁶⁶ At daybreak, the people's council of elders, including both head *cohanim* and *Torah*-teachers, met and led him off to their *Sanhedrin*, ⁶⁷ where they said, "If you are the *Mashiach*, tell us." He answered, "If I tell you, you won't believe me; ⁶⁸ and if I ask you, you won't answer. ⁶⁹ But from now on, the Son of Man will be **sitting at the right hand of** *HaG'vurah*," *ʲ* ⁷⁰ They all said, "Does this mean, then, that you are the Son of God?" And he answered them, "You say I am." ⁷¹ They said, "Why do we need additional testimony? We have heard it ourselves from his own mouth!"

23 ¹ With that, the whole *Sanhedrin* got up and brought Yeshua before Pilate, ²where they started accusing him. "We found this man subverting our nation, forbidding us to pay taxes to the Emperor and claiming that he himself is the Messiah — a king!" ³ Pilate asked him, "Are you the king of the Jews?" And he answered him, "The words are yours." ⁴ Pilate said to the head *cohanim* and the crowds, "I find no ground for a charge against this man." ⁵ But they persisted. "He is inciting the people with his teaching throughout all Y'hudah — he started in the Galil, and now he's here!" ⁶ On hearing this, Pilate asked if the man was from the Galil; ⁷ and when he learned that he was under Herod's jurisdiction, he sent him over to Herod, who at that time happened to be in Yerushalayim too.

⁸ Herod was delighted to see Yeshua, because he had heard about him and for a long time had been wanting to meet him; indeed, he hoped to see him perform some miracle. ⁹ He questioned him at great length, but Yeshua made no reply. ¹⁰ However, the head *cohanim* and the *Torah*-teachers stood there, vehemently pressing their case against him. ¹¹ Herod and his soldiers treated

---

co·ha·nim — priests
co·hen ha ga·dol — high priest
the Ga·lil — Galilee
Go·yim — Gentiles, nations, pagans
Ha·G'vu·rah — "the Power", i.e., God
Ke·fa — Peter
Ma·shi·ach — Messiah
San·hed·rin — Jewish religious court
Shim·'on — Simon
tal·mi·dim — disciples
Ta·nakh — Hebrew Scriptures, "Old Testament"
To·rah-teachers — scribes
Ye·shu·a — Jesus
Y'hu·dah — Judas

ʲ Psalm 110:1

Yeshua with contempt and made fun of him. Then, dressing him in an elegant robe, they sent him back to Pilate. [12] That day Herod and Pilate became friends with each other; previously they had been enemies.

[13] Pilate summoned the head *cohanim*, the leaders and the people, [14] and said to them, "You brought this man before me on a charge of subverting the people. I examined him in your presence and did not find the man guilty of the crime you are accusing him of. [15] And neither did Herod, because he sent him back to us. Clearly, he has not done anything that merits the death penalty. [16] Therefore, what I will do is have him flogged and release him." [17][*] [18] But with one voice they shouted, "Away with this man! Give us Bar-Abba!" [19] (He was a man who had been thrown in prison for causing a riot in the city and for murder.) [20] Pilate appealed to them again, because he wanted to release Yeshua. [21] But they yelled, "Put him to death on the stake! Put him to death on the stake!" [22] A third time he asked them, "But what has this man done wrong? I haven't found any reason to put him to death. So I'm going to have him flogged and set free." [23] But they went on yelling insistently, demanding that he be executed on the stake; and their shouting prevailed. [24] Pilate decided to grant their demand; [25] he released the man who had been thrown in prison for insurrection and murder, the one they had asked for; and Yeshua he surrendered to their will.

[26] As the Roman soldiers led Yeshua away, they grabbed hold of a man from Cyrene named Shim'on, who was on his way in from the country. They put the execution-stake on his back and made him carry it behind Yeshua. [27] Large numbers of people followed, including women crying and wailing over him. [28] Yeshua turned to them and said, "Daughters of Yerushalayim, don't cry for me; cry for yourselves and your children! [29] For the time is coming when people will say, 'The childless women are the lucky ones — those whose wombs have never borne a child, whose breasts have never nursed a baby!' [30] Then

They will begin to say to the mountains, 'Fall on us!' and to the hills, 'Cover us!'[k]

[31] For if they do these things when the wood is green, what is going to happen when it's dry?"

[32] Two other men, both criminals, were led out to be executed with him. [33] When they came to the place called The Skull, they nailed him to a stake; and they nailed the criminals to stakes, one on the right and one on the left. [34] Yeshua said, "Father, forgive them; they don't understand what they are doing."

They divided up his clothes by throwing dice.[l] [35] The people stood **watching**, and the rulers **sneered at** him.[m] "He saved others," they said, "so if he really is the Messiah, the one chosen by God, let him save himself!" [36] The soldiers too ridiculed him; they came up, offered him **vinegar**[n] [37] and said, "If you are the king of the Jews, save yourself!" [38] And there was a notice over him which read,

THIS IS
THE KING OF THE JEWS

---

* Some manuscripts have verse 17: For he was required to release one man to them at the festival.

k Hosea 10:8   *l* Psalm 22:19(18)
m Psalm 22:8(7)   *n* Psalm 69:22(21)

^{39} One of the criminals hanging there hurled insults at him. "Aren't you the Messiah? Save yourself and us!" ^{40} But the other one spoke up and rebuked the first, saying, "Have you no fear of God? You're getting the same punishment as he is. ^{41} Ours is only fair; we're getting what we deserve for what we did. But this man did nothing wrong." ^{42} Then he said, "Yeshua, remember me when you come as King." ^{43} Yeshua said to him, "Yes! I promise that you will be with me today in Gan-Eden."

^{44} It was now about noon, and darkness covered the whole Land until three o'clock in the afternoon; ^{45} the sun did not shine. Also the *parokhet* in the Temple was split down the middle. ^{46} Crying out with a loud voice, Yeshua said, "Father! **Into your hands I commit my spirit.**"^{o} With these words he gave up his spirit.

^{47} When the Roman officer saw what had happened, he began to praise God and said, "Surely this man was innocent!" ^{48} And when all the crowds that had gathered to watch the spectacle saw the things that had occurred, they returned home beating their breasts. ^{49} All his friends, including the women who had accompanied him from the Galil, had been standing at a distance; they saw it all.

^{50} There was a man named Yosef, a member of the *Sanhedrin*. He was a good man, a *tzaddik*; ^{51} and he had not been in agreement with either the *Sanhedrin's* motivation or their action. He came from the town of Ramatayim, a town of the Judeans; and he looked forward to the Kingdom of God. ^{52} This man approached Pilate and asked for Yeshua's body. ^{53} He took it down, wrapped it in a linen sheet, and placed it in a tomb cut into the rock, that had never been used.

^{54} It was Preparation Day, and a *Shabbat* was about to begin. ^{55} The women who had come with Yeshua from the Galil followed; they saw the tomb and how his body was placed in it. ^{56} Then they went back home to prepare spices and ointments.

On *Shabbat* the women rested, in obedience to the commandment; ^{1} but **24** on the first day of the week, while it was still very early, they took the spices they had prepared, went to the tomb, ^{2} and found the stone rolled away from the tomb! ^{3} On entering, they discovered that the body of the Lord Yeshua was gone! ^{4} They were standing there, not knowing what to think about it, when suddenly two men in dazzlingly bright clothing stood next to them. ^{5} Terror-stricken, they bowed down with their faces to the ground. The two men said to them, "Why are you looking for the living among the dead? ^{6} He is not here; he has been raised. Remember how he told you while he was still in the Galil, ^{7} 'The Son of Man must be delivered into the hands of sinful men and be executed on a stake as a criminal, then on the third day be raised again'?" ^{8} Then they remem-

---

o Psalm 31:6(5)

Bar-Ab·ba — Barabbas
co·ha·nim — priests
the Ga·lil — Galilee
Gan-E·den — Paradise
pa·ro·khet — curtain
Ra·ma·ta·yim — Arimathea
San·hed·rin — Jewish religious court
Shab·bat — the Sabbath
Shim·'on — Simon
To·rah-teachers — scribes
tzad·dik — righteous man
Ye·ru·sha·la·yim — Jerusalem
Ye·shu·a — Jesus
Y'hu·dah — Judea
Yo·sef — Joseph

bered his words; [9] and, returning from the tomb, they told everything to the Eleven and to all the rest. [10] The women who told the emissaries these things were Miryam of Magdala, Yochanah, Miryam the mother of Ya'akov, and the others in their circle.

[11] But the emissaries didn't believe them; in fact, they thought that what they said was utter nonsense! [12] However, Kefa got up and ran to the tomb. Stooping down, he saw only the burial cloths and went home wondering what had happened.

[13] That same day, two of them were going toward a village about seven miles from Yerushalayim called Amma'us, [14] and they were talking with each other about all the things that had happened. [15] As they talked and discussed, Yeshua himself came up and walked along with them, [16] but something kept them from recognizing him. [17] He asked them, "What are you talking about with each other as you walk along?" They stopped short, their faces downcast; [18] and one of them, named Cleopas, answered him, "Are you the only person staying in Yerushalayim that doesn't know the things that have been going on there the last few days?" [19] "What things?" he asked them. They said to him, "The things about Yeshua from Natzeret. He was a prophet and proved it by the things he did and said before God and all the people. [20] Our head *cohanim* and our leaders handed him over, so that he could be sentenced to death and executed on a stake as a criminal. [21] And we had hoped that he would be the one to liberate Israel! Besides all that, today is the third day since these things happened; [22] and this morning, some of the women astounded us. They were at the tomb early [23] and couldn't find his body, so they came back; but they also reported that they

had seen a vision of angels who say he's alive! [24] Some of our friends went to the tomb and found it exactly as the women had said, but they didn't see him."

[25] He said to them, "Foolish people! So unwilling to put your trust in everything the prophets spoke! [26] Didn't the Messiah have to die like this before entering his glory?" [27] Then, starting with Moshe and all the prophets, he explained to them the things that can be found throughout the *Tanakh* concerning himself.

[28] They approached the village where they were going. He made as if he were going on farther; [29] but they held him back, saying, "Stay with us, for it's almost evening, and it's getting dark." So he went in to stay with them. [30] As he was reclining with them at the table, he took the *matzah*, made the *b'rakhah*, broke it and handed it to them. [31] Then their eyes were opened, and they recognized him. But he became invisible to them. [32] They said to each other, "Didn't our hearts burn inside us as he spoke to us on the road, opening up the *Tanakh* to us?"

[33] They got up at once, returned to Yerushalayim and found the Eleven gathered together with their friends, [34] saying, "It's true! The Lord has risen! Shim'on saw him!" [35] Then the two told what had happened on the road and how he had become known to them in the breaking of the *matzah*.

[36] They were still talking about it when — there he was, standing among them! [37] Startled and terrified, they thought they were seeing a ghost. [38] But he said to them, "Why are you so upset? Why are these doubts welling up inside you? [39] Look at my hands and my feet — it is I, myself! Touch me and see — a ghost doesn't have flesh and bones, as you can see I do." [40] As he said this, he showed them his hands and feet.

116

[41]While they were still unable to believe it for joy and stood there dumbfounded, he said to them, "Have you something here to eat?" [42]They gave him a piece of broiled fish, [43]which he took and ate in their presence.

[44]Yeshua said to them, "This is what I meant when I was still with you and told you that everything written about me in the *Torah* of Moshe, the Prophets and the Psalms had to be fulfilled." [45]Then he opened their minds, so that they could understand the *Tanakh,* [46]telling them, "Here is what is says: the Messiah is to suffer and to rise from the dead on the third day; [47]and in his name repentance leading to forgiveness of sins is to be proclaimed to people from all nations, starting with Yerushalayim. [48]You are witnesses of these things. [49]Now I am sending forth upon you what my Father promised, so stay here in the city until you have been equipped with power from above."

[50]He led them out toward Beit-Anyah; then, raising his hands, he said a *b'rakhah* over them; [51]and as he was blessing them, he withdrew from them and was carried up into heaven. [52]They bowed in worship to him, then returned to Yerushalayim, overflowing with joy. [53]And they spend all their time in the Temple courts, praising God.

Am·ma·'us — Emmaus
Beit-An·yah — Bethany
b'ra·khah — blessing
Cle·o·pas — Cleopas
co·ha·nim — priests
the Ga·lil — Galilee
Ke·fa — Peter
ma·tzah — unleavened bread
Mir·yam — Miriam, Mary
Mir·yam of Mag·da·la — Mary Magdalene
Mo·she — Moses
Na·tze·ret — Nazareth
Shim·'on — Simon
Ta·nakh — Hebrew Scriptures, "Old Testament"
To·rah — Teaching, "Law"; Pentateuch
Ya·'a·kov — Jacob
Ye·ru·sha·la·yim — Jerusalem
Ye·shu·a — Jesus
Yo·cha·nah — Johanna
Yo·cha·nan — John

THE GOOD NEWS OF YESHUA THE MESSIAH, AS REPORTED BY

YOCHANAN (JOHN)

1 ¹ In the beginning was the Word,
and the Word was with God,

And the Word was God.
² He was with God in the beginning.

³ All things came to be through him,
and without him nothing made had
being.

⁴ In him was life,
and the life was the light of mankind.

⁵ The light shines in the darkness,
and the darkness has not suppressed
it.

⁶There was a man sent from God
whose name was Yochanan. ⁷He came
to be a testimony, to bear witness
concerning the light; so that through
him, everyone might put his trust in
God and be faithful to him. ⁸He himself
was not that light; no, he came to bear
witness concerning the light.

⁹ This was the true light,
which gives light to everyone entering
the world.

¹⁰ He was in the world — the world
came to be through him —
yet the world did not know him.

¹¹ He came to his own homeland,
yet his own people did not receive
him.

¹²But to as many as did receive him, to
those who put their trust in his person
and power, he gave the right to become
children of God, ¹³not because of
bloodline, physical impulse or human
intention, but because of God.

¹⁴ The Word became a human being
and lived with us,
and we saw his *Sh'khinah*,

The *Sh'khinah* of the Father's only
Son,
full of grace and truth.

¹⁵Yochanan witnessed concerning
him when he cried out, "This is the man
I was talking about when I said, 'The
one coming after me has come to rank
ahead of me, because he existed before
me.'"

¹⁶ We have all received from his fullness,
yes, grace upon grace.

¹⁷ For the *Torah* was given through
Moshe;
grace and truth came through Yeshua
the Messiah.

¹⁸No one has ever seen God; but the
only and unique Son, who is identical
with God and is at the Father's side —
he has made him known.

¹⁹Here is Yochanan's testimony:
when the Judeans sent *cohanim* and
L'viim from Yerushalayim to ask him,
"Who are you?" ²⁰he was very straight-
forward and stated clearly, "I am not
the Messiah." ²¹"Then who are you?"
they asked him. "Are you Eliyahu?"
"No, I am not," he said. "Are you 'the

prophet', the one we're expecting?" "No," he replied. ²²So they said to him, "Who are you? — so that we can give an answer to the people who sent us. What do you have to say about yourself?" ²³He answered in the words of Yesha'yahu the prophet, "I am

The voice of someone crying out: 'In the desert make the way of *Adonai* straight!'"ᵃ

²⁴Some of those who had been sent were *P'rushim*. ²⁵They asked him, "If you are neither the Messiah nor Eliyahu nor 'the prophet', then why are you immersing people?" ²⁶To them Yochanan replied, "I am immersing people in water, but among you is standing someone whom you don't know. ²⁷He is the one coming after me — I'm not good enough even to untie his sandal!" ²⁸All this took place in Beit-Anyah, east of the Yarden, where Yochanan was immersing.

²⁹The next day, Yochanan saw Yeshua coming toward him and said, "Look! God's lamb! The one who is taking away the sin of the world! ³⁰This is the man I was talking about when I said, 'After me is coming someone who has come to rank above me, because he existed before me.' ³¹I myself did not know who he was, but the reason I came immersing with water was so that he might be made known to Israel." ³²Then Yochanan gave this testimony: "I saw the Spirit coming down from heaven like a dove, and remaining on him. ³³I myself did not know who he was, but the one who sent me to immerse in water said to me, 'The one on whom you see the Spirit descending and remaining, this is the one who immerses in the *Ruach HaKodesh.*'

³⁴And I have seen and borne witness that this is the Son of God."

³⁵The next day, Yochanan was again standing with two of his *talmidim*. ³⁶On seeing Yeshua walking by, he said, "Look! God's lamb!" ³⁷His two *talmidim* heard him speaking, and they followed Yeshua. ³⁸Yeshua turned and saw them following him, and he asked them, "What are you looking for?" They said to him, "Rabbi!" (which means "Teacher!") "Where are you staying?" ³⁹He said to them, "Come and see." So they went and saw where he was staying, and remained with him the rest of the day — it was about four o'clock in the afternoon. ⁴⁰One of the two who had heard Yochanan and had followed Yeshua was Andrew the brother of Shim'on Kefa. ⁴¹The first thing he did was to find his brother Shim'on and tell him, "We've found the *Mashiach*!" (The word means "one who has been anointed".) ⁴²He took him to Yeshua. Looking at him, Yeshua said, "You are Shim'on Bar-Yochanan;

A·do·nai — the LORD, Jehovah
Beit-An·yah — Bethany
co·ha·nim — priests
E·li·ya·hu — Elijah
L'vi·im — Levites
Ma·shi·ach — Messiah
Mo·she — Moses
P'ru·shim — Pharisees
Ru·ach-Ha·Ko·desh — Holy Spirit
Shim·'on — Simon
Shim·'on Bar-Yo·cha·nan — Simon, son of John
Shim·'on Ke·fa — Simon Peter
Sh'khi·nah — God's manifest presence
tal·mi·dim — disciples
To·rah — Teaching, "Law"; Pentateuch
Yar·den — Jordan
Ye·ru·sha·la·yim — Jerusalem
Ye·sha'·ya·hu — Isaiah
Ye·shu·a — Jesus
Yo·cha·nan — John

ᵃ Isaiah 40:3

you will be known as Kefa." (The name means "rock".)

⁴³ The next day, having decided to leave for the Galil, Yeshua found Philip and said, "Follow me!" ⁴⁴ Philip was from Beit-Tzaidah, the town where Andrew and Kefa lived. ⁴⁵ Philip found Natan'el and told him, "We've found the one that Moshe wrote about in the *Torah*, also the Prophets — it's Yeshua Ben-Yosef from Natzeret!" ⁴⁶ Natan'el answered him, "Natzeret? Can anything good come from there?" "Come and see," Philip said to him. ⁴⁷ Yeshua saw Natan'el coming toward him and remarked about him, "Here's a true son of Israel — nothing false in him!" ⁴⁸ Natan'el said to him, "How do you know me?" Yeshua answered him, "Before Philip called you, when you were under the fig tree, I saw you." ⁴⁹ Natan'el said, "Rabbi, you are the Son of God! You are the King of Israel!" ⁵⁰ Yeshua answered him, "You believe all this just because I told you I saw you under the fig tree? You will see greater things than that!" ⁵¹ Then he said to him, "Yes indeed! I tell you that you will see **heaven** opened and **the angels of God going up and coming down**[b] on the Son of Man!"

2 ¹ Two days later, there was a wedding at Kanah in the Galil; and the mother of Yeshua was there. ² Yeshua too was invited to the wedding, along with his *talmidim*. ³ The wine ran out, and Yeshua's mother said to him, "They have no more wine." ⁴ Yeshua replied, "Mother, why should that concern me? — or you? My time hasn't come yet." ⁵ His mother said to the servants, "Do whatever he tells you." ⁶ Now six stone water-jars were standing there for the Jewish ceremonial washings, each with a capacity of twenty or thirty gallons. ⁷ Yeshua told them, "Fill the jars with water," and they filled them to the brim. ⁸ He said, "Now draw some out, and take it to the man in charge of the banquet;" and they took it. ⁹ The man in charge tasted the water; it had now turned into wine! He did not know where it had come from, but the servants who had drawn the water knew. So he called the bridegroom ¹⁰ and said to him, "Everyone else serves the good wine first and the poorer wine after people have drunk freely. But you have kept the good wine until now!" ¹¹ This, the first of Yeshua's miraculous signs, he did at Kanah in the Galil; he manifested his glory, and his *talmidim* came to trust in him. ¹² Afterwards, he, his mother and brothers, and his *talmidim* went down to K'far-Nachum and stayed there a few days.

¹³ It was almost time for the festival of *Pesach* in Y'hudah, so Yeshua went up to Yerushalayim. ¹⁴ In the Temple grounds he found those who were selling cattle, sheep and pigeons, and others who were sitting at tables exchanging money. ¹⁵ He made a whip from cords and drove them all out of the Temple grounds, the sheep and cattle as well. He knocked over the money-changers' tables, scattering their coins; ¹⁶ and to the pigeon-sellers he said, "Get these things out of here! How dare you turn my Father's house into a market?" ¹⁷ (His *talmidim* later recalled that the *Tanakh* says, **"Zeal for your house will devour me."**)[c] ¹⁸ So the Judeans confronted him by asking him, "What miraculous sign can you show us to prove you have the right to do all this?" ¹⁹ Yeshua answered them, "Destroy this temple, and in three days I will raise it up again." ²⁰ The Judeans said,

---

b Genesis 28:12

c Psalm 69:10(9)

"It took 46 years to build this Temple, and you're going to raise it in three days?" ²¹ But the "temple" he had spoken of was his body. ²² Therefore, when he was raised from the dead, his *talmidim* remembered that he had said this, and they trusted in the *Tanakh* and in what Yeshua had said.

²³ Now while Yeshua was in Yerushalayim at the *Pesach* festival, there were many people who "believed in his name" when they saw the miracles he performed. ²⁴ But he did not commit himself to them, for he knew what people are like — ²⁵ that is, he didn't need anyone to inform him about a person, because he knew what was in the person's heart.

3 ¹ There was a man among the *P'rushim*, named Nakdimon, who was a ruler of the Judeans. ² This man came to Yeshua by night and said to him, "Rabbi, we know it is from God that you have come as a teacher; for no one can do these miracles you perform unless God is with him." ³ "Yes, indeed," Yeshua answered him, "I tell you that unless a person is born again from above, he cannot see the Kingdom of God."

⁴ Nakdimon said to him, "How can a grown man be 'born'? Can he go back into his mother's womb and be born a second time?" ⁵ Yeshua answered, "Yes, indeed, I tell you that unless a person is born from water and the Spirit, he cannot enter the Kingdom of God. ⁶ What is born from the flesh is flesh, and what is born from the Spirit is spirit. ⁷ Stop being amazed at my telling you that you must be born again from above! ⁸ The wind blows where it wants to, and you hear its sound, but you don't know where it comes from or where it's going. That's how it is with everyone who has been born from the Spirit."

⁹ Nakdimon replied, "How can this happen?" ¹⁰ Yeshua answered him, "You hold the office of teacher in Israel, and you don't know this? ¹¹ Yes, indeed! I tell you that what we speak about, we know; and what we give evidence of, we have seen; but you people don't accept our evidence! ¹² If you people don't believe me when I tell you about the things of the world, how will you believe me when I tell you about the things of heaven? ¹³ No one has gone up into heaven; there is only the one who has come down from heaven, the Son of Man. ¹⁴ Just as Moshe lifted up the serpent in the desert, so must the Son of Man be lifted up; ¹⁵ so that everyone who trusts in him may have eternal life.

¹⁶ "For God so loved the world that he gave his only and unique Son, so that everyone who trusts in him may have eternal life, instead of being utterly destroyed. ¹⁷ For God did not send the Son into the world to judge the world, but rather so that through him, the world might be saved. ¹⁸ Those who trust in him are not judged; those who do not trust have been judged already,

---

Beit-Tzai·**dah** — Bethsaida
the Ga·**lil** — Galilee
Ka·**nah** — Cana
Ke·**fa** — Peter
K'far-Na·**chum** — Capernaum
Mo·**she** — Moses
Nak·di·**mon** — Nicodemus
Na·tan·**'el** — Nathanael
Na·**tze**·ret — Nazareth
Pe·sach — Passover
*P'ru·**shim*** — Pharisees
*tal·mi·**dim*** — disciples
*Ta·**nakh*** — Hebrew Scriptures, "Old Testament"
*To·**rah*** — Teaching, "Law"; Pentateuch
Ye·ru·sha·**la**·yim — Jerusalem
Ye·**shu**·a — Jesus
Ye·**shu**·a Ben-Yo·**sef** — Jesus, son of Joseph
Y'hu·**dah** — Judea

in that they have not trusted in the one who is God's only and unique Son.

¹⁹ "Now this is the judgment: the light has come into the world, but people loved the darkness rather than the light. Why? Because their actions were wicked. ²⁰ For everyone who does evil things hates the light and avoids it, so that his actions won't be exposed. ²¹ But everyone who does what is true comes to the light, so that all may see that his actions are accomplished through God."

²² After this, Yeshua and his *talmidim* went out into the countryside of Y'hudah, where he stayed awhile with them and immersed people. ²³ Yochanan too was immersing at Einayim, near Shalem, because there was plenty of water there; and people kept coming to be immersed. ²⁴ (This was before Yochanan's imprisonment.)

²⁵ A discussion arose between some of Yochanan's *talmidim* and a Judean about ceremonial washing; ²⁶ and they came to Yochanan and said to him, "Rabbi, you know the man who was with you on the other side of the Yarden, the one you spoke about? Well, here he is, immersing; and everyone is going to him!" ²⁷ Yochanan answered, "No one can receive anything unless it has been given to him from Heaven. ²⁸ You yourselves can confirm that I did not say I was the Messiah, but that I have been sent ahead of him. ²⁹ The bridegroom is the one who has the bride; but the bridegroom's friend, who stands and listens to him, is overjoyed at the sound of the bridegroom's voice. So this joy of mine is now complete. ³⁰ He must become more important, while I become less important.

³¹ "He who comes from above is above all. He who is from the earth is from the earth and talks from an earthly point of view; he who comes from heaven is above all. ³² He testifies about what he has actually seen and heard, yet no one accepts what he says! ³³ Whoever does accept what he says puts his seal on the fact that God is true, ³⁴ because the one whom God sent speaks God's words. For God does not give him the Spirit in limited degree — ³⁵ the Father loves the Son and has put everything in his hands. ³⁶ Whoever trusts in the Son has eternal life. But whoever disobeys the Son will not see that life but remains subject to God's wrath."

4 ¹ When Yeshua learned that the *P'rushim* had heard he was making and immersing more *talmidim* than Yochanan ² (although it was not Yeshua himself who immersed but his *talmidim*), ³ Yeshua left Y'hudah and set out again for the Galil. ⁴ This meant that he had to pass through Shomron.

⁵ He came to a town in Shomron called Sh'khem, near the field Ya'akov had given to his son Yosef. ⁶ Ya'akov's Well was there; so Yeshua, exhausted from his travel, sat down by the well; it was about noon. ⁷ A woman from Shomron came to draw some water; and Yeshua said to her, "Give me a drink of water." ⁸ (His *talmidim* had gone into town to buy food.) ⁹ The woman from Shomron said to him, "How is it that you, a Jew, ask for water from me, a woman of Shomron?" (For Jews don't associate with people from Shomron.) ¹⁰ Yeshua answered her, "If you knew God's gift, that is, who it is saying to you, 'Give me a drink of water,' then you would have asked him; and he would have given you living water."

¹¹ She said to him, "Sir, you don't have a bucket, and the well is deep; so where do you get this 'living water'? ¹² You aren't greater than our father

Ya'akov, are you? He gave us this well and drank from it, and so did his sons and his cattle." [13] Yeshua answered, "Everyone who drinks this water will get thirsty again, [14] but whoever drinks the water I will give him will never be thirsty again! On the contrary, the water I give him will become a spring of water inside him, welling up into eternal life!"

[15] "Sir, give me this water," the woman said to him, "so that I won't have to be thirsty and keep coming here to draw water." [16] He said to her, "Go, call your husband, and come back." [17] She answered, "I don't have a husband." Yeshua said to her, "You're right, you don't have a husband! [18] You've had five husbands in the past, and you're not married to the man you're living with now! You've spoken the truth!"

[19] "Sir, I can see that you are a prophet," the woman replied. [20] "Our fathers worshipped on this mountain, but you people say that the place where one has to worship is in Yerushalayim." [21] Yeshua said, "Lady, believe me, the time is coming when you will worship the Father neither on this mountain nor in Yerushalayim. [22] You people don't know what you are worshipping; we worship what we do know, because salvation comes from the Jews. [23] But the time is coming — indeed, it's here now — when the true worshippers will worship the Father spiritually and truly, for these are the kind of people the Father wants worshipping him. [24] God is spirit; and worshippers must worship him spiritually and truly."

[25] The woman replied, "I know that *Mashiach* is coming" (that is, "the one who has been anointed"). "When he comes, he will tell us everything." [26] Yeshua said to her, "I, the person speaking to you, am he."

[27] Just then, his *talmidim* arrived. They were amazed that he was talking with a woman; but none of them said, "What do you want?" or, "Why are you talking with her?" [28] So the woman left her water-jar, went back to the town and said to the people there, [29] "Come, see a man who told me everything I've ever done. Could it be that this is the Messiah?" [30] They left the town and began coming toward him.

[31] Meanwhile, the *talmidim* were urging Yeshua, "Rabbi, eat something." [32] But he answered, "I have food to eat that you don't know about." [33] At this, the *talmidim* asked one another, "Could someone have brought him food?" [34] Yeshua said to them, "My food is to do what the one who sent me wants and to bring his work to completion. [35] Don't you have a saying, 'Four more months and then the harvest'? Well, what I say to you is: open your eyes and look at the fields! They're already ripe for harvest! [36] The one who reaps receives his wages and gathers fruit for eternal life, so that the reaper and the sower may be glad together — [37] for in this matter, the proverb, 'One sows and another reaps,' holds true. [38] I sent you to reap what you haven't worked for. Others have done the hard labor, and you have benefitted from their work."

Ei·na·yim — Aenon, Enon
the Ga·lil — Galilee
Ma·shi·ach — Messiah
P'ru·shim — Pharisees
Sha·lem — Salim
Sh'khem — Sychar
Shom·ron — Samaria
tal·mi·dim — disciples
Ya·'a·kov — Jacob
Yar·den — Jordan
Ye·ru·sha·la·yim — Jerusalem
Ye·shu·a — Jesus
Y'hu·dah — Judea
Yo·cha·nan — John
Yo·sef — Joseph

³⁹ Many people from that town in Shomron put their trust in him because of the woman's testimony, "He told me all the things I did." ⁴⁰ So when these people from Shomron came to him, they asked him to stay with them. He stayed two days, ⁴¹ and many more came to trust because of what he said. ⁴² They said to the woman, "We no longer trust because of what you said, because we have heard for ourselves. We know indeed that this man really is the Savior of the world."

⁴³ After the two days, he went on from there toward the Galil. ⁴⁴ Now Yeshua himself said, "A prophet is not respected in his own country." ⁴⁵ But when he arrived in the Galil, the people there welcomed him, because they had seen all he had done at the festival in Yerushalayim; since they had been there too.

⁴⁶ He went again to Kanah in the Galil, where he had turned the water into wine. An officer in the royal service was there; his son was ill in K'far-Nachum. ⁴⁷ This man, on hearing that Yeshua had come from Y'hudah to the Galil, went and asked him to come down and heal his son, for he was at the point of death. ⁴⁸ Yeshua answered, "Unless you people see signs and miracles, you simply will not trust!" ⁴⁹ The officer said to him, "Sir, come down before my child dies." ⁵⁰ Yeshua replied, "You may go, your son is alive." The man believed what Yeshua said and left. ⁵¹ As he was going down, his servants met him with the news that his son was alive. ⁵² So he asked them at what time he had gotten better; and they said, "The fever left him yesterday at one o'clock in the afternoon." ⁵³ The father knew that that was the very hour when Yeshua had told him, "Your son is alive;" and he and all his household trusted. ⁵⁴ This was a second sign that Yeshua did; he

did it after he had come from Y'hudah into the Galil.

5 ¹ After this, there was a Judean festival; and Yeshua went up to Yerushalayim. ² In Yerushalayim, by the Sheep Gate, is a pool called in Aramaic, Beit-Zata, ³ in which lay a crowd of invalids — blind, lame, crippled. ⁴* ⁵ One man was there who had been ill for 38 years. ⁶ Yeshua, seeing this man and knowing that he had been there a long time, said to him, "Do you want to be healed?" ⁷ The sick man answered, "I have no one to put me in the pool when the water is disturbed; and while I'm trying to get there, someone goes in ahead of me." ⁸ Yeshua said to him, "Get up, pick up your mat and walk!" ⁹ Immediately the man was healed, and he picked up his mat and walked.

Now that day was *Shabbat*, ¹⁰ so the Judeans said to the man who had been healed, "It's *Shabbat*! It's against *Torah* for you to carry your mat!" ¹¹ But he answered them, "The man who healed me — he's the one who told me, 'Pick up your mat and walk.'" ¹² They asked him, "Who is the man who told you to pick it up and walk?" ¹³ But the man who had been healed didn't know who it was, because Yeshua had slipped away into the crowd.

¹⁴ Afterwards Yeshua found him in the Temple court and said to him, "See, you are well! Now stop sinning, or something worse may happen to you!" ¹⁵ The man went off and told the Judeans it was Yeshua who had healed

---

* Some manuscripts have verses 3b-4:..., waiting for the water to move; ⁴ for at certain times an angel of *Adonai* went down into the pool and disturbed the water, and whoever stepped into the water first after it was disturbed was healed of whatever disease he had.

him; 16 and on account of this, the Judeans began harassing Yeshua because he did these things on *Shabbat*.

17 But he answered them, "My Father has been working until now, and I too am working." 18 This answer made the Judeans all the more intent on killing him — not only was he breaking *Shabbat*; but also, by saying that God was his own Father, he was claiming equality with God. 19 Therefore, Yeshua said this to them: "Yes, indeed! I tell you that the Son cannot do anything on his own, but only what he sees the Father doing; whatever the Father does, the Son does too. 20 For the Father loves the Son and shows him everything he does; and he will show him even greater things than these, so that you will be amazed. 21 Just as the Father raises the dead and makes them alive, so too the Son makes alive anyone he wants. 22 The Father does not judge anyone but has entrusted all judgment to the Son, 23 so that all may honor the Son as they honor the Father. Whoever fails to honor the Son is not honoring the Father who sent him. 24 Yes, indeed! I tell you that whoever hears what I am saying and trusts the one who sent me has eternal life — that is, he will not come up for judgment but has already crossed over from death to life! 25 Yes, indeed! I tell you that there is coming a time — in fact, it's already here — when the dead will hear the voice of the Son of God, and those who listen will come to life. 26 For just as the Father has life in himself, so he has given the Son life to have in himself. 27 Also he has given him authority to execute judgment, because he is the Son of Man. 28 Don't be surprised at this; because the time is coming when all who are in the grave will hear his voice 29 and come out — those who have done good to a resurrection of life, and those who have done evil to a resurrection of judgment. 30 I can't do a thing on my own. As I hear, I judge; and my judgment is right; because I don't seek my own desire, but the desire of the one who sent me.

31 "If I testify on my own behalf, my testimony is not valid. 32 But there is someone else testifying on my behalf, and I know that the testimony he is making is valid — 33 you have sent to Yochanan, and he has testified to the truth. 34 Not that I collect human testimony; rather, I say these things so that you might be saved. 35 He was a lamp burning and shining, and for a little while you were willing to bask in his light.

36 "But I have a testimony that is greater than Yochanan's. For the things the Father has given me to do, the very things I am doing now, testify on my behalf that the Father has sent me.

37 "In addition, the Father who sent me has himself testified on my behalf. But you have never heard his voice or seen his shape; 38 moreover, his word does not stay in you, because you don't trust the one he sent. 39 You keep examining the *Tanakh* because you think that in it you have eternal life. Those very Scriptures bear witness to me,

---

A·do·nai — the LORD, Jehovah
Beit-Za·ta — Bethzatha
the Ga·lil — Galilee
Ka·nah — Cana
K'far-Na·chum — Capernaum
Shab·bat — the Sabbath
Shom·ron — Samaria
Ta·nakh — Hebrew Scriptures, "Old Testament"
To·rah — Teaching, "Law"; Pentateuch
Ye·ru·sha·la·yim — Jerusalem
Ye·shu·a — Jesus
Y'hu·dah — Judea
Yo·cha·nan — John

⁴⁰but you won't come to me in order to have life!

⁴¹"I don't collect praise from men, ⁴²but I do know you people — I know that you have no love for God in you! ⁴³I have come in my Father's name, and you don't accept me; if someone else comes in his own name, him you will accept. ⁴⁴How can you trust? You're busy collecting praise from each other, instead of seeking praise from God only.

⁴⁵"But don't think that it is I who will be your accuser before the Father. Do you know who will accuse you? Moshe, the very one you have counted on! ⁴⁶For if you really believed Moshe, you would believe me; because it was about me that he wrote. ⁴⁷But if you don't believe what he wrote, how are you going to believe what I say?"

6 ¹Some time later, Yeshua went over to the far side of Lake Kinneret (that is, Lake Tiberias), ²and a large crowd followed him, because they had seen the miracles he had performed on the sick. ³Yeshua went up into the hills and sat down there with his *talmidim*. ⁴Now the Judean festival of *Pesach* was coming up; ⁵so when Yeshua looked up and saw that a large crowd was approaching, he said to Philip, "Where will we be able to buy bread, so that these people can eat?" ⁶(Now Yeshua said this to test Philip, for Yeshua himself knew what he was about to do.) ⁷Philip answered, "Half a year's wages wouldn't buy enough bread for them — each one would get only a bite!" ⁸One of the *talmidim*, Andrew the brother of Shim'on Kefa, said to him, ⁹"There's a young fellow here who has five loaves of barley bread and two fish. But how far will they go. among so many?"

¹⁰Yeshua said, "Have the people sit down." There was a lot of grass there, so they sat down. The number of men was about five thousand. ¹¹Then Yeshua took the loaves of bread, and, after making a *b'rakhah*, gave to all who were sitting there, and likewise with the fish, as much as they wanted. ¹²After they had eaten their fill, he told his *talmidim*, "Gather the leftover pieces, so that nothing gets wasted." ¹³They gathered them and filled twelve baskets with the pieces from the five barley loaves left by those who had eaten.

¹⁴When the people saw the miracle he had performed, they said, "This has to be 'the prophet' who is supposed to come into the world." ¹⁵Yeshua knew that they were on the point of coming and seizing him, in order to make him king; so he went back to the hills again. This time he went by himself.

¹⁶When evening came, his *talmidim* went down to the lake, ¹⁷got into a boat and set out across the lake toward K'far-Nachum. By now it was dark, Yeshua had not yet joined them, ¹⁸and the sea was getting rough, because a strong wind was blowing. ¹⁹They had rowed three or four miles when they saw Yeshua approaching the boat, walking on the lake! They were terrified; ²⁰but he said to them, "Stop being afraid, it is I." ²¹Then they were willing to take him into the boat, and instantly the boat reached the land they were heading for.

²²The next day, the crowd which had stayed on the other side of the lake noticed that there had been only one boat there, and that Yeshua had not entered the boat with his *talmidim*, but that the *talmidim* had been alone when they sailed off. ²³Then other boats, from Tiberias, came ashore near the place where they had eaten the bread after the Lord had made the *b'rakhah*. ²⁴Accordingly, when the crowd saw that neither Yeshua nor his *talmidim*

were there, they themselves boarded the boats and made for K'far-Nachum in search of Yeshua. 25 When they found him on the other side of the lake, they asked him, "Rabbi, when did you get here?" 26 Yeshua answered, "Yes, indeed! I tell you, you're not looking for me because you saw miraculous signs, but because you ate the bread and had all you wanted! 27 Don't work for the food which passes away but for the food that stays on into eternal life, which the Son of Man will give you. For this is the one on whom God the Father has put his seal."

28 So they said to him, "What should we do in order to perform the works of God?" 29 Yeshua answered, "Here's what the work of God is: to trust in the one he sent!"

30 They said to him, "*Nu*, what miracle will you do for us, so that we may see it and trust you? What work can you perform? 31 Our fathers ate manna in the desert — as it says in the *Tanakh*, 'He gave them bread from heaven to eat.'*d* 32 Yeshua said to them, "Yes, indeed! I tell you it wasn't Moshe who gave you the bread from heaven. But my Father is giving you the genuine bread from heaven; 33 for God's bread is the one who comes down out of heaven and gives life to the world."

34 They said to him, "Sir, give us this bread from now on." 35 Yeshua answered, "I am the bread which is life! Whoever comes to me will never go hungry, and whoever trusts in me will never be thirsty. 36 I told you that you have seen but still don't trust. 37 Everyone the Father gives me will come to me, and whoever comes to me I will certainly not turn away. 38 For I have come down from heaven to do not my

own will but the will of the one who sent me. 39 And this is the will of the one who sent me: that I should not lose any of all those he has given me but should raise them up on the Last Day. 40 Yes, this is the will of my Father: that all who see the Son and trust in him should have eternal life, and that I should raise them up on the Last Day."

41 At this the Judeans began grumbling about him because he said, "I am the bread which has come down from heaven." 42 They said, "Isn't this Yeshua Ben-Yosef? We know his father and mother! How can he now say, 'I have come down from heaven'?" 43 Yeshua answered them, "Stop grumbling to each other! 44 No one can come to me unless the Father — the one who sent me — draws him. And I will raise him up on the Last Day. 45 It is written in the Prophets, 'They will all be taught by *Adonai.'e* Everyone who listens to the Father and learns from him comes to me. 46 Not that anyone has seen the Father except the one who is from God — he has seen the Father. 47 Yes, indeed! I tell you, whoever trusts has eternal life; 48 I am the bread which is life. 49 Your fathers ate the manna in the desert; they died. 50 But the bread that

e Isaiah 54:13

A·do·nai — the LORD, Jehovah
b'ra·khah — blessing
K'far-Na·chum — Capernaum
Lake Kin·ne·ret — the Sea of Galilee
Mo·she — Moses
nu — if so
Pe·sach — Passover
Shim·'on Ke·fa — Simon Peter
tal·mi·dim — disciples
Ta·nakh — Hebrew Scriptures, "Old Testament"
Ye·shu·a — Jesus
Ye·shua Ben-Yo·sef — Jesus, son of Joseph

d Psalm 78:24, Nehemiah 9:15

comes down from heaven is such that a person may eat it and not die. ⁵¹ I am the living bread that has come down from heaven; if anyone eats this bread, he will live forever. Furthermore, the bread that I will give is my own flesh; and I will give it for the life of the world."

⁵² At this, the Judeans disputed with one another, saying, "How can this man give us his flesh to eat?" ⁵³ Then Yeshua said to them, "Yes, indeed! I tell you that unless you eat the flesh of the Son of Man and drink his blood, you do not have life in yourselves. ⁵⁴ Whoever eats my flesh and drinks my blood has eternal life — that is, I will raise him up on the Last Day. ⁵⁵ For my flesh is true food, and my blood is true drink. ⁵⁶ Whoever eats my flesh and drinks my blood lives in me, and I live in him. ⁵⁷ Just as the living Father sent me, and I live through the Father, so also whoever eats me will live through me. ⁵⁸ So this is the bread that has come down from heaven — it is not like the bread the fathers ate; they're dead, but whoever eats this bread will live forever!" ⁵⁹ He said these things as he was teaching in a synagogue in K'far-Nachum.

⁶⁰ On hearing it, many of his *talmidim* said, "This is a hard word — who can bear to listen to it?" ⁶¹ But Yeshua, aware that his *talmidim* were grumbling about this, said to them, "This is a trap for you? ⁶² Suppose you were to see the Son of Man going back up to where he was before? ⁶³ It is the Spirit who gives life, the flesh is no help. The words I have spoken to you are Spirit and life, ⁶⁴ yet some among you do not trust." (For Yeshua knew from the outset which ones would not trust him, also which one would betray him.) ⁶⁵ "This," he said, "is why I told you that no one can come to me unless the Father has made it possible for him."

⁶⁶ From this time on, many of his *talmidim* turned back and no longer traveled around with him. ⁶⁷ So Yeshua said to the Twelve, "Don't you want to leave too?" ⁶⁸ Shim'on Kefa answered him, "Lord, to whom would we go? You have the word of eternal life. ⁶⁹ We have trusted, and we know that you are the Holy One of God." ⁷⁰ Yeshua answered them, "Didn't I choose you, the Twelve? Yet one of you is an adversary." ⁷¹ (He was speaking of Y'hudah Ben-Shim'on, from K'riot; for this man — one of the Twelve! — was soon to betray him.)

7 ¹ After this, Yeshua traveled around in the Galil, intentionally avoiding Y'hudah because the Judeans were out to kill him. ² But the festival of *Sukkot* in Y'hudah was near; ³ so his brothers said to him, "Leave here and go into Y'hudah, so that your *talmidim* can see the miracles you do; ⁴ for no one who wants to become known acts in secret. If you're doing these things, show yourself to the world!" ⁵ (His brothers spoke this way because they had not put their trust in him.) ⁶ Yeshua said to them, "My time has not yet come; but for you, any time is right. ⁷ The world can't hate you, but it does hate me, because I keep telling it how wicked its ways are. ⁸ You, go on up to the festival; as for me, I am not going up to this festival now, because the right time for me has not yet come." ⁹ Having said this, he stayed on in the Galil.

¹⁰ But after his brothers had gone up to the festival, he too went up, not publicly but in secret. ¹¹ At the festival, the Judeans were looking for him. "Where is he?" they asked. ¹² And among the crowds there was much whispering about him. Some said,

"He's a good man;" but others said, "No, he is deceiving the masses." ¹³ However, no one spoke about him openly, for fear of the Judeans.

¹⁴ Not until the festival was half over did Yeshua go up to the Temple courts and begin to teach. ¹⁵ The Judeans were surprised: "How does this man know so much without having studied?" they asked. ¹⁶ So Yeshua gave them an answer: "My teaching is not my own, it comes from the One who sent me. ¹⁷ If anyone wants to do his will, he will know whether my teaching is from God or I speak on my own. ¹⁸ A person who speaks on his own is trying to win praise for himself; but a person who tries to win praise for the one who sent him is honest, there is nothing false about him. ¹⁹ Didn't Moshe give you the *Torah*? Yet not one of you obeys the *Torah*! Why are you out to kill me?" ²⁰ "You have a demon!" the crowd answered. "Who's out to kill you?" ²¹ Yeshua answered them, "I did one thing; and because of this, all of you are amazed. ²² Moshe gave you *b'rit-milah* — not that it came from Moshe but from the Patriarchs — and you do a boy's *b'rit-milah* on *Shabbat*. ²³ If a boy is circumcised on *Shabbat* so that the *Torah* of Moshe will not be broken, why are you angry with me because I made a man's whole body well on *Shabbat*? ²⁴ Stop judging by surface appearances, and judge the right way!"

²⁵ Some of the Yerushalayim people said, "Isn't this the man they're out to kill? ²⁶ Yet here he is, speaking openly; and they don't say anything to him. It couldn't be, could it, that the authorities have actually concluded he's the Messiah? ²⁷ Surely not — we know where this man comes from; but when the Messiah comes, no one will know where he comes from." ²⁸ Whereupon Yeshua, continuing to teach in the Temple courts, cried out, "Indeed you do know me! And you know where I'm from! And I have not come on my own! The One who sent me is real. But him you don't know! ²⁹ I do know him, because I am with him, and he sent me!"

³⁰ At this, they tried to arrest him; but no one laid a hand on him; because his time had not yet come. ³¹ However, many in the crowd put their trust in him and said, "When the Messiah comes, will he do more miracles than this man has done?"

³² The *P'rushim* heard the crowd whispering these things about Yeshua; so the head *cohanim* and the *P'rushim* sent some of the Temple guards to arrest him. ³³ Yeshua said, "I will be with you only a little while longer; then I will go away to the One who sent me. ³⁴ You will look for me and not find me; indeed, where I am, you cannot come." ³⁵ The Judeans said to themselves, "Where is this man about to go, that we won't find him? Does he intend to go to the Greek Diaspora and teach the Greek-speaking Jews? ³⁶ And when he says, 'You will look for me and not find

---

b'rit-mi·lah — circumcision
co·ha·nim — priests
the Ga·lil — Galilee
K'far-Na·chum — Capernaum
Mo·she — Moses
P'ru·shim — Pharisees
Shab·bat — the Sabbath
Shim·'on Ke·fa — Simon Peter
Suk·kot — Tabernacles
tal·mi·dim — disciples
To·rah — Teaching, "Law"; Pentateuch
Ye·ru·sha·la·yim — Jerusalem
Ye·shu·a — Jesus
Y'hu·dah — Judea
Y'hu·dah Ben-Shim·'on, from K'ri·ot — Judas the son of Simon Iscariot

me; indeed, where I am, you cannot come' — what does he mean?"

³⁷Now on the last day of the festival *Hoshana Rabbah,* Yeshua stood and cried out, "If anyone is thirsty, let him keep coming to me and drinking! ³⁸Whoever puts his trust in me, as the Scripture says, rivers of living water will flow from his inmost being!" ³⁹(Now he said this about the Spirit, whom those who trusted in him were to receive later — the Spirit had not yet been given, because Yeshua had not yet been glorified.)

⁴⁰On hearing his words, some people in the crowd said, "Surely this man is 'the prophet';" ⁴¹others said, "This is the Messiah." But others said, "How can the Messiah come from the Galil? ⁴²Doesn't the *Tanakh* say that the Messiah is from **the seed of David**ᶠ and comes **from Beit-Lechem,**ᵍ the village where David lived?" ⁴³So the people were divided because of him. ⁴⁴Some wanted to arrest him, but no one laid a hand on him.

⁴⁵The guards came back to the head *cohanim* and the *P'rushim,* who asked them, "Why didn't you bring him in?" ⁴⁶The guards replied, "No one ever spoke the way this man speaks!" ⁴⁷"You mean you've been taken in as well?" the *P'rushim* retorted. ⁴⁸"Has any of the authorities trusted him? Or any of the *P'rushim?* No! ⁴⁹True, these *'am-ha'aretz* do, but they know nothing about the *Torah,* they are under a curse!"

⁵⁰Nakdimon, the man who had gone to Yeshua before and was one of them, said to them, ⁵¹"Our *Torah* doesn't condemn a man — does it? — until after hearing from him and finding out what he's doing."⁵²They replied, "You aren't from the Galil too, are you?

Study the *Tanakh,* and see for yourself that no prophet comes from the Galil!"

*⁵³Then they all left, each one to his **8** own home. ¹But Yeshua went to the Mount of Olives. ²At daybreak, he appeared again in the Temple Court, where all the people gathered around him, and he sat down to teach them. ³The *Torah*-teachers and the *P'rushim* brought in a woman who had been caught committing adultery and made her stand in the center of the group. ⁴Then they said to him, "Rabbi, this woman was caught in the very act of committing adultery. ⁵Now in our *Torah,* Moshe commanded that such a woman be stoned to death. What do you say about it?" ⁶They said this to trap him, so that they might have ground for bringing charges against him; but Yeshua bent down and began writing in the dust with his finger. ⁷When they kept questioning him, he straightened up and said to them, "The one of you who is without sin, let him be the first to throw a stone at her." ⁸Then he bent down and wrote in the dust again. ⁹On hearing this, they began to leave, one by one, the older ones first, until he was left alone, with the woman still there. ¹⁰Standing up, Yeshua said to her, "Where are they? Has no one condemned you?" ¹¹She said, "No one, sir." Yeshua said, "Neither do I condemn you. Now go, and don't sin any more."

¹²Yeshua spoke to them again: "I am the light of the world; whoever follows me will never walk in darkness but will have the light which gives life." ¹³So the

---

* Most scholars believe that 7:53-8:11, enclosed in brackets, is not from the pen of Yochanan. Many are of the opinion that it is a true story about Yeshua written by another of his disciples.

ᶠ 2 Samuel 7:12   ᵍ Micah 5:1(2)

P'rushim said to him, "Now you're testifying on your own behalf; your testimony is not valid." [14]Yeshua answered them, "Even if I do testify on my own behalf, my testimony is indeed valid; because I know where I came from and where I'm going; but you do not know where I came from or where I'm going. [15]You judge by merely human standards. As for me, I pass judgment on no one; [16]but if I were indeed to pass judgment, my judgment would be valid; because it is not I alone who judge, but I and the one who sent me. [17]And even in your *Torah* it is written that the testimony of two people is valid. [18]I myself testify on my own behalf, and so does the Father who sent me."

[19]They said to him, "Where is this 'father' of yours?" Yeshua answered, "You know neither me nor my Father; if you knew me, you would know my Father too." [20]He said these things when he was teaching in the Temple treasury room; yet no one arrested him, because his time had not yet come.

[21]Again he told them, "I am going away, and you will look for me, but you will die in your sin — where I am going, you cannot come." [22]The Judeans said, "Is he going to commit suicide? Is that what he means when he says, 'Where I am going, you cannot come'?" [23]Yeshua said to them, "You are from below, I am from above; you are of this world, I am not of this world. [24]This is why I said to you that you will die in your sins; for if you do not trust that I am who I say I am, you will die in your sins."

[25]At this, they said to him, "You? Who are you?" Yeshua answered, "Just what I've been telling you from the start. [26]There are many things I could say about you, and many judgments I could make. However, the one who sent me is true; so I say in the world only what I have heard from him." [27]They did not understand that he was talking to them about the Father. [28]So Yeshua said, "When you lift up the Son of Man, then you will know that I am who I say I am, and that of myself I do nothing, but say only what the Father has taught me. [29]Also, the One who sent me is still with me; he did not leave me to myself, because I always do what pleases him."

[30]Many people who heard him say these things trusted in him. [31]So Yeshua said to the Judeans who had trusted him, "If you obey what I say, then you are really my *talmidim*, [32]you will know the truth, and the truth will set you free." [33]They answered, "We are the seed of Avraham and have never been slaves to anyone; so what do you mean by saying, 'You will be set free'?" [34]Yeshua answered them, "Yes, indeed! I tell you that everyone who practices sin is a slave of sin. [35]Now a slave does not remain with a family forever, but a son does remain with it forever. [36]So if the Son frees you, you will really be free! [37]I know you are the seed of Avraham. Yet you are out to kill me,

---

'am-ha-'a-retz — ignorant masses

Av·ra·**ham** — Abraham

Beit·**Le**·chem — Bethlehem

co·ha·nim — priests

Da·**vid** — David

the Ga·**lil** — Galilee

Ho·sha·na Rab·bah — the greatest day

Mo·**she** — Moses

Nak·di·**mon** — Nicodemus

P'ru·shim — Pharisees

tal·mi·dim — disciples

Ta·nakh — Hebrew Scriptures, "Old Testament"

To·rah — Teaching, "Law"; Pentateuch

To·rah-teachers — scribes

Ye·**shu**·a — Jesus

because what I am saying makes no headway in you. ³⁸ I say what my Father has shown me; you do what your father has told you!"

³⁹ They answered him, "Our father is Avraham." Yeshua replied, "If you are children of Avraham, then do the things Avraham did! ⁴⁰ As it is, you are out to kill me, a man who has told you the truth which I heard from God. Avraham did nothing like that! ⁴¹ You are doing the things your father does." "We're not illegitimate children!" they said to him. "We have only one Father — God!" ⁴² Yeshua replied to them, "If God were your Father, you would love me; because I came out from God; and now I have arrived here. I did not come on my own; he sent me. ⁴³ Why don't you understand what I'm saying? Because you can't bear to listen to my message. ⁴⁴ You belong to your father, Satan, and you want to carry out your father's desires. From the start he was a murderer, and he has never stood by the truth, because there is no truth in him. When he tells a lie, he is speaking in character; because he is a liar — indeed, the inventor of the lie! ⁴⁵ But as for me, because I tell the truth you don't believe me. ⁴⁶ Which one of you can show me where I'm wrong? If I'm telling the truth, why don't you believe me? ⁴⁷ Whoever belongs to God listens to what God says; the reason you don't listen is that you don't belong to God."

⁴⁸ The Judeans answered him, "Aren't we right in saying you are from Shomron and have a demon?" ⁴⁹ Yeshua replied, "Me? I have no demon. I am honoring my Father. But you dishonor me. ⁵⁰ I am not seeking praise for myself. There is one who is seeking it, and he is the judge. ⁵¹ Yes, indeed! I tell you that whoever obeys my teaching will never see death."

⁵² The Judeans said to him, "Now we know for sure that you have a demon! Avraham died, and so did the prophets; yet you say, 'Whoever obeys my teaching will never taste death.' ⁵³ *Avraham avinu* died; you aren't greater than he, are you? And the prophets also died. Who do you think you are?" ⁵⁴ Yeshua answered, "If I praise myself, my praise counts for nothing. The one who is praising me is my Father, the very one about whom you keep saying, 'He is our God.' ⁵⁵ Now you have not known him, but I do know him; indeed, if I were to say that I don't know him, I would be a liar like you! But I do know him, and I obey his word. ⁵⁶ Avraham, your father, was glad that he would see my day; then he saw it and was overjoyed."

⁵⁷ "Why, you're not yet fifty years old," the Judeans replied, "and you have seen Avraham?" ⁵⁸ Yeshua said to them, "Yes, indeed! Before Avraham came into being, I AM!" ⁵⁹ At this, they picked up stones to throw at him; but Yeshua was hidden and left the Temple grounds.

9 ¹ As Yeshua passed along, he saw a man blind from birth. ² His *talmidim* asked him, "Rabbi, who sinned — this man or his parents — to cause him to be born blind?" ³ Yeshua answered, "His blindness is due neither to his sin nor to that of his parents; it happened so that God's power might be seen at work in him. ⁴ As long as it is day, we must keep doing the work of the One who sent me; the night is coming, when no one can work. ⁵ While I am in the world, I am the light of the world."

⁶ Having said this, he spit on the ground, made some mud with the saliva, put the mud on the man's eyes, ⁷ and said to him, "Go, wash off in the Pool of Shiloach!" (The name means "sent".) So he went and washed and came away seeing.

⁸His neighbors and those who previously had seen him begging said, "Isn't this the man who used to sit and beg?" ⁹Some said, "Yes, he's the one;" while others said, "No, but he looks like him." However, he himself said, "I'm the one." ¹⁰"How were your eyes opened?" they asked him. ¹¹He answered, "The man called Yeshua made mud, put it on my eyes, and told me, 'Go to Shiloach and wash!' So I went; and as soon as I had washed, I could see." ¹²They said to him, "Where is he?" and he replied, "I don't know."

¹³They took the man who had been blind to the *P'rushim*. ¹⁴Now the day on which Yeshua had made the mud and opened his eyes was *Shabbat*. ¹⁵So the *P'rushim* asked him again how he had become able to see; and he told them, "He put mud on my eyes, then I washed, and now I can see." ¹⁶At this, some of the *P'rushim* said, "This man is not from God, because he doesn't keep *Shabbat*." But others said, "How could a man who is a sinner do miracles like these?" And there was a split among them. ¹⁷So once more they spoke to the blind man: "Since you're the one whose eyes he opened, what do you say about him?" He replied: "He is a prophet."

¹⁸The Judeans, however, were unwilling to believe that he had formerly been blind, but now could see, until they had summoned the man's parents. ¹⁹They asked them, "Is this your son, who you say was born blind? How is it that now he can see?" ²⁰His parents answered, "We know that this is our son and that he was born blind; ²¹but how it is that he can see now, we don't know; nor do we know who opened his eyes. Ask him — he's old enough, he can speak for himself!" ²²The parents said this because they were afraid of the Judeans, for the Judeans had already agreed that anyone who acknowledged Yeshua as the Messiah would be banned from the synagogue. ²³This is why his parents said, "He's old enough, ask him."

²⁴So a second time they called the man who had been blind; and they said to him, "Swear to God that you will tell the truth! We know that this man is a sinner." ²⁵He answered, "Whether he's a sinner or not I don't know. One thing I do know: I was blind, now I see." ²⁶So they said to him, "What did he do to you? How did he open your eyes?" ²⁷"I already told you," he answered, "and you didn't listen. Why do you want to hear it again? Maybe you too want to become his *talmidim*?" ²⁸Then they railed at him. "You may be his *talmid*," they said, "but we are *talmidim* of Moshe! ²⁹We know that God has spoken to Moshe, but as for this fellow — we don't know where he's from!" ³⁰"What a strange thing," the man answered, "that you don't know where he's from — considering that he opened my eyes! ³¹We know that God doesn't listen to sinners; but if anyone fears God and does his will, God does listen to him. ³²In all history no one has ever heard of someone's opening the eyes of a man born blind. ³³If this man were not from God, he couldn't do a thing!" ³⁴"Why, you *mamzer*!" they retorted, "Are you lecturing us?" And they threw him out.

Av·ra·ham — Abraham
Av·ra·ham a·vi·nu — our father, Abraham
mam·zer — bastard, born in sin
Mo·she — Moses
P'ru·shim — Pharisees
Sa·tan — Satan
Shab·bat — the Sabbath
Shi·lo·ach — Siloam
Shom·ron — Samaria
tal·mid (pl. *tal·mi·dim*) — disciple
Ye·shu·a — Jesus

[35] Yeshua heard that they had thrown the man out. He found him and said, "Do you trust in the Son of Man?" [36] "Sir," he answered, "tell me who he is, so that I can trust in him." [37] Yeshua said to him, "You have seen him. In fact, he's the one speaking with you now." [38] "Lord, I trust!" he said, and he kneeled down in front of him.

[39] Yeshua said, "It is to judge that I came into this world, so that those who do not see might see, and those who do see might become blind." [40] Some of the *P'rushim* nearby heard this and said to him, "So we're blind too, are we?" [41] Yeshua answered them, "If you were blind, you would not be guilty of sin. But since you still say, 'We see,' your guilt remains.

10 [1] "Yes, indeed! I tell you, the person who doesn't enter the sheep-pen through the door, but climbs in some other way, is a thief and a robber. [2] But the one who goes in through the gate is the sheep's own shepherd. [3] This is the one the gate-keeper admits, and the sheep hear his voice. He calls his own sheep, each one by name, and leads them out. [4] After taking out all that are his own, he goes on ahead of them; and the sheep follow him because they recognize his voice. [5] They never follow a stranger but will run away from him, because strangers' voices are unfamiliar to them."

[6] Yeshua used this indirect manner of speaking with them, but they didn't understand what he was talking to them about. [7] So Yeshua said to them again, "Yes, indeed! I tell you that I am the gate for the sheep. [8] All those who have come before me have been thieves and robbers, but the sheep didn't listen to them. [9] I am the gate; if someone enters through me, he will be safe and will go in and out and find pasture. [10] The thief comes only in order to steal, kill and destroy; I have come so that they may have life, life in its fullest measure.

[11] "I am the good shepherd. The good shepherd lays down his life for the sheep. [12] The hired hand, since he isn't a shepherd and the sheep aren't his own, sees the wolf coming, abandons the sheep and runs away. Then the wolf drags them off and scatters them. [13] The hired worker behaves like this because that's all he is, a hired worker; so it doesn't matter to him what happens to the sheep. [14] I am the good shepherd; I know my own, and my own know me — [15] just as the Father knows me, and I know the Father — and I lay down my life on behalf of the sheep. [16] Also I have other sheep which are not from this pen; I need to bring them, and they will hear my voice; and there will be one flock, one shepherd.

[17] "This is why the Father loves me: because I lay down my life — in order to take it up again! [18] No one takes it away from me; on the contrary, I lay it down of my own free will. I have the power to lay it down, and I have the power to take it up again. This is what my Father commanded me to do."

[19] Again there was a split among the Judeans because of what he said. [20] Many of them said, "He has a demon!" and "He's *meshugga*! Why do you listen to him?" [21] Others said, "These are not the deeds of a man who is demonized — how can a demon open blind people's eyes?"

[22] Then came *Chanukkah* in Yerushalayim. It was winter, [23] and Yeshua was walking around inside the Temple area, in Shlomo's Colonnade. [24] So the Judeans surrounded him and said to him, "How much longer are you going to keep us in suspense? If you are the Messiah, tell us publicly!" [25] Yeshua answered them, "I have already told

you, and you don't trust me. The works I do in my Father's name testify on my behalf; ²⁶ but the reason you don't trust is that you are not included among my sheep. ²⁷ My sheep listen to my voice, I recognize them, they follow me, ²⁸ and I give them eternal life. They will absolutely never be destroyed, and no one will snatch them from my hands. ²⁹ My Father, who gave them to me, is greater than all; and no one can snatch from the Father's hands. ³⁰ I and the Father are one."

³¹ Once again the Judeans picked up rocks in order to stone him. ³² Yeshua answered them, "You have seen me do many good deeds that reflect the Father's power; for which one of these deeds are you stoning me?" ³³ The Judeans replied, "We are not stoning you for any good deed, but for blasphemy — because you, who are only a man, are making yourself out to be God [*Elohim*]." ³⁴ Yeshua answered them, "Isn't it written in your *Torah*, 'You people are *Elohim*'?"*ʰ* ³⁵ If he called '*Elohim*' the people to whom the word of *Elohim* was addressed (and the *Tanakh* cannot be broken), ³⁶ then are you telling the one whom the Father set apart as holy and sent into the world, 'You are committing blasphemy,' just because I said, 'I am a son of *Elohim*'?

³⁷ "If I am not doing deeds that reflect my Father's power, don't trust me. ³⁸ But if I am, then, even if you don't trust me, trust the deeds; so that you may understand once and for all that the Father is united with me, and I am united with the Father." ³⁹ One more time they tried to arrest him, but he slipped out of their hands.

⁴⁰ He went off again beyond the Yarden, where Yochanan had been immersing at first, and stayed there.

⁴¹ Many people came to him and said, "Yochanan performed no miracles, but everything Yochanan said about this man was true." ⁴² And many people there put their trust in him.

11 ¹ There was a man who had fallen sick. His name was El'azar, and he came from Beit-Anyah, the village where Miryam and her sister Marta lived. ² (This Miryam, whose brother El'azar had become sick, is the one who poured perfume on the Lord and wiped his feet with her hair.) ³ So the sisters sent a message to Yeshua, "Lord, the man you love is sick." ⁴ On hearing it, he said, "This sickness will not end in death. No, it is for God's glory, so that the Son of God may receive glory through it."

⁵ Yeshua loved Marta and her sister and El'azar; ⁶ so when he heard he was sick, first he stayed where he was two more days; ⁷ then, after this, he said to the *talmidim*, "Let's go back to Y'hudah." ⁸ The *talmidim* replied, "Rabbi! Just a short while ago the Judeans were out to stone you — and you want to go back there?" ⁹ Yeshua

---

Beit-An·**yah** — Bethany
Cha·nuk·kah — the Feast of Dedication
El·'a·**zar** — Lazarus
E·lo·him — God, gods
Mar·**ta** — Martha
me·shug·ga — crazy
Mir·**yam** — Miriam, Mary
P'ru·shim — Pharisees
Shlo·**mo** — Solomon
tal·mi·dim — disciples
Ta·nakh — Hebrew Scriptures, "Old Testament"
To·rah — Teaching, "Law"; Pentateuch
Yar·**den** — Jordan
Ye·ru·sha·la·yim — Jerusalem
Ye·shu·a — Jesus
Y'hu·**dah** — Judea
Yo·cha·nan — John

---

h Psalm 82:6

answered, "Aren't there twelve hours of daylight? If a person walks during daylight, he doesn't stumble; because he sees the light of this world. ¹⁰But if a person walks at night, he does stumble; because he has no light with him." ¹¹Yeshua said these things, and afterwards he said to the *talmidim*, "Our friend El'azar has gone to sleep; but I am going in order to wake him up." ¹²The *talmidim* said to him, "Lord, if he has gone to sleep, he will get better." ¹³Now Yeshua had used the phrase to speak about El'azar's death, but they thought he had been talking literally about sleep. ¹⁴So Yeshua told them in plain language, "El'azar has died. ¹⁵And for your sakes, I am glad that I wasn't there, so that you may come to trust. But let's go to him." ¹⁶Then T'oma (the name means "twin") said to his fellow *talmidim*, "Yes, we should go, so that we can die with him!"

¹⁷On arrival, Yeshua found that El'azar had already been in the tomb for four days. ¹⁸Now Beit-Anyah was about two miles from Yerushalayim, ¹⁹and many of the Judeans had come to Marta and Miryam in order to comfort them at the loss of their brother. ²⁰So when Marta heard that Yeshua was coming, she went out to meet him; but Miryam continued sitting *shiv'ah* in the house.

²¹Marta said to Yeshua, "Lord, if you had been here, my brother would not have died. ²²Even now I know that whatever you ask of God, God will give you." ²³Yeshua said to her, "Your brother will rise again." ²⁴Marta said, "I know that he will rise again at the Resurrection on the Last Day." ²⁵Yeshua said to her, "I AM the Resurrection and the Life! Whoever puts his trust in me will live, even if he dies; ²⁶and everyone living and trusting in me will never die. Do you believe this?"

²⁷She said to him, "Yes, Lord, I believe that you are the Messiah, the Son of God, the one coming into the world." ²⁸After saying this, she went off and secretly called Miryam, her sister: "The Rabbi is here and is calling for you." ²⁹When she heard this, she jumped up and went to him. ³⁰Yeshua had not yet come into the village but was still where Marta had met him; ³¹so when the Judeans who had been with Miryam in the house comforting her saw her get up quickly and go out, they followed her, thinking she was going to the tomb to mourn there.

³²When Miryam came to where Yeshua was and saw him, she fell at his feet and said to him, "Lord, if you had been here, my brother would not have died." ³³When Yeshua saw her crying, and also the Judeans who came with her crying, he was deeply moved and also troubled. ³⁴He said, "Where have you buried him?" They said, "Lord, come and see." ³⁵Yeshua cried; ³⁶so the Judeans there said, "See how he loved him!" ³⁷But some of them said, "He opened the blind man's eyes. Couldn't he have kept this one from dying?"

³⁸Yeshua, again deeply moved, came to the tomb. It was a cave, and a stone was lying in front of the entrance. ³⁹Yeshua said, "Take the stone away!" Marta, the sister of the dead man, said to Yeshua, "By now his body must smell, for it has been four days since he died!" ⁴⁰Yeshua said to her, "Didn't I tell you that if you keep trusting, you will see the glory of God?" ⁴¹So they removed the stone. Yeshua looked upward and said, "Father, I thank you that you have heard me. ⁴²I myself know that you always hear me, but I say this because of the crowd standing around, so that they may believe that you have sent me." ⁴³Having said this, he shouted, "El'azar! Come out!" ⁴⁴The

man who had been dead came out, his hands and feet wrapped in strips of linen and his face covered with a cloth. Yeshua said to them, "Unwrap him, and let him go!" 45 At this, many of the Judeans who had come to visit Miryam, and had seen what Yeshua had done, trusted in him.

46 But some of them went off to the P'rushim and told them what he had done. 47 So the head cohanim and the P'rushim called a meeting of the San-hedrin and said, "What are we going to do? — for this man is performing many miracles. 48 If we let him keep going on this way, everyone will trust in him, and the Romans will come and destroy both the Temple and the nation." 49 But one of them, Kayafa, who was cohen gadol that year, said to them, "You people don't know anything! 50 You don't see that it's better for you if one man dies on behalf of the people, so that the whole nation won't be de-stroyed." 51 Now he didn't speak this way on his own initiative; rather, since he was cohen gadol that year, he was prophesying that Yeshua was about to die on behalf of the nation, 52 and not for the nation alone, but so that he might gather into one the scattered children of God.

53 From that day on, they made plans to have him put to death. 54 Therefore Yeshua no longer walked around openly among the Judeans but went away from there into the region near the desert, to a town called Efrayim, and stayed there with his talmidim.

55 The Judean festival of Pesach was near, and many people went up from the country to Yerushalayim to perform the purification ceremony prior to Pesach. 56 They were looking for Yeshua, and as they stood in the Temple courts they said to each other, "What do you think? That he simply won't come to the festival?" 57 Moreover, the head cohanim and the P'rushim had given orders that anyone knowing Yeshua's whereabouts should inform them, so that they could have him arrested.

12 1 Six days before Pesach, Yeshua came to Beit-Anyah, where El'azar lived, the man Yeshua had raised from the dead; 2 so they gave a dinner there in his honor. Marta served the meal, and El'azar was among those at the table with him. 3 Miryam took a whole pint of pure oil of spikenard, which is very expensive, poured it on Yeshua's feet and wiped his feet with her hair, so that the house was filled with the fragrance of the perfume. 4 But one of the talmidim, Y'hudah from K'riot, the one who was about to betray him, said, 5 "This perfume is worth a year's wages! Why wasn't it sold and the money given to the poor?" 6 Now he said this not out of concern for the poor, but because he was a thief — he was in charge of the common purse and used to steal from it. 7 Yeshua said, "Leave her alone! She kept this for the day of my burial. 8 You always have the

Beit-An·**yah** — Bethany
co·ha·**nim** — priests
co·**hen** ga·**dol** — high priest
Ef·**ra**·yim — Ephraim
El·'a·**zar** — Lazarus
Ka·ya·**fa** — Caiaphas
Mar·ta — Martha
Mir·yam — Miriam, Mary
Pe·sach — Passover
P'ru·**shim** — Pharisees
San·hed·**rin** — Jewish religious court
sitting shiv·**'ah** — mourning
tal·mi·**dim** — disciples
T·**'o**·ma — Thomas
Ye·ru·sha·**la**·yim — Jerusalem
Ye·**shu**·a — Jesus
Y'hu·dah from K'ri·ot — Judas Iscariot

poor among you, but you will not always have me."

⁹A large crowd of Judeans learned that he was there; and they came not only because of Yeshua, but also so that they could see El'azar, whom he had raised from the dead. ¹⁰The head *cohanim* then decided to do away with El'azar too, ¹¹since it was because of him that large numbers of the Judeans were leaving their leaders and putting their trust in Yeshua.

¹²The next day, the large crowd that had come for the festival heard that Yeshua was on his way into Yerushalayim. ¹³They took palm branches and went out to meet him, shouting,

"Deliver us!"*ⁱ*

"Blessed is he who comes in the name of *Adonai*,*ʲ* **the King of Israel!"**

¹⁴After finding a donkey colt, Yeshua mounted it, just as the *Tanakh* says —

¹⁵ **"Daughter of Tziyon, don't be afraid!**
Look! Your King is coming,
sitting on a donkey's colt."*ᵏ*

¹⁶His *talmidim* did not understand this at first; but after Yeshua had been glorified, then they remembered that the *Tanakh* said this about him, and that they had done this for him. ¹⁷The group that had been with him when he called El'azar out of the tomb and raised him from the dead had been telling about it. ¹⁸It was because of this too that the crowd came out to meet him — they had heard that he had performed this miracle. ¹⁹The *P'rushim* said to each other, "Look, you're getting nowhere! Why, the whole world has gone after him!"

---

i Psalm 118:25 *j* Psalm 118:26
k Zechariah 9:9

²⁰Among those who went up to worship at the festival were some Greek-speaking Jews. ²¹They approached Philip, the one from Beit-Tzaidah in the Galil, with a request. "Sir," they said, "we would like to see Yeshua." ²²Philip came and told Andrew; then Andrew and Philip went and told Yeshua. ²³Yeshua gave them this answer: "The time has come for the Son of Man to be glorified. ²⁴Yes, indeed! I tell you that unless a grain of wheat that falls to the ground dies, it stays just a grain; but if it dies, it produces a big harvest. ²⁵He who loves his life loses it, but he who hates his life in this world will keep it safe right on into eternal life! ²⁶If someone is serving me, let him follow me; wherever I am, my servant will be there too. My Father will honor anyone who serves me.

²⁷"Now I am in turmoil. What can I say — 'Father, save me from this hour'? No, it was for this very reason that I have come to this hour. I will say this: ²⁸Father, glorify your name!" At this a *bat-kol* came out of heaven, "I have glorified it before, and I will glorify it again!" ²⁹The crowd standing there and hearing it said that it had thundered; others said, "An angel spoke to him." ³⁰Yeshua answered, "This *bat-kol* did not come for my sake but for yours. ³¹Now is the time for this world to be judged, now the ruler of this world will be expelled. ³²As for me, when I am lifted up from the earth, I will draw everyone to myself." ³³He said this to indicate what kind of death he would die.

³⁴The crowd answered, "We have learned from the *Torah* that the Messiah remains forever. How is it that you say the Son of Man has to be 'lifted up'? Who is this 'Son of Man'?" ³⁵Yeshua said to them, "The light will be with you only a little while longer.

Walk while you have the light, or the dark will overtake you; he who walks in the dark doesn't know where he's going. ³⁶While you have the light, put your trust in the light, so that you may become people of light." Yeshua said these things, then went off and kept himself hidden from them.

³⁷Even though he had performed so many miracles in their presence, they still did not put their trust in him, ³⁸in order that what Yesha'yahu the prophet had said might be fulfilled,

> **"*Adonai*, who has believed our report?**
> **To whom has the arm of *Adonai* been revealed?"ˡ**

³⁹The reason they could not believe was — as Yesha'yahu said elsewhere —

> ⁴⁰ **"He has blinded their eyes**
> **and hardened their hearts,**
> **so that they do not see with their eyes,**
> **understand with their hearts,**
> **and do *t'shuvah*,**
> **so that I could heal them."ᵐ**

⁴¹(Yesha'yahu said these things because he saw the *Sh'khinah* of Yeshua and spoke about him.) ⁴²Nevertheless, many of the leaders did trust in him; but because of the *P'rushim* they did not say so openly, out of fear of being banned from the synagogue; ⁴³for they loved praise from other people more than praise from God.

⁴⁴Yeshua declared publicly, "Those who put their trust in me are trusting not merely in me, but in the One who sent me. ⁴⁵Also those who see me see the One who sent me. ⁴⁶I have come as a light into the world, so that everyone who trusts in me might not remain in the dark. ⁴⁷If anyone hears what I am saying and does not observe it, I don't judge him; for I did not come to judge the world, but to save the world. ⁴⁸Those who reject me and don't accept what I say have a judge — the word which I have spoken will judge them on the Last Day. ⁴⁹For I have not spoken on my own initiative, but the Father who sent me has given me a command, namely, what to say and how to say it. ⁵⁰And I know that his command is eternal life. So what I say is simply what the Father has told me to say."

13 ¹It was just before the festival of *Pesach*, and Yeshua knew that the time had come for him to pass from this world to the Father. Having loved his own people in the world, he loved them to the end. ²They were at supper, and the Adversary had already put the desire to betray him into the heart of Y'hudah Ben-Shim'on from K'riot. ³Yeshua was aware that the Father had put everything in his power, and that he had come from God and was returning to God. ⁴So he rose from the table, removed his outer garments and

---

A·do·nai — the LORD, Jehovah
bat·kol — heavenly voice
Beit·**Za**·ta — Bethzatha
co·ha·nim — priests
El-'a·**zar** — Lazarus
the Ga·**lil** — Galilee
Pe·sach — Passover
P'ru·shim — Pharisees
Sh'khi·nah — glorious presence
tal·mi·dim — disciples
Ta·nakh — Hebrew Scriptures, "Old Testament"
To·rah — Teaching, "Law"; Pentateuch
To·rah-teachers — scribes
do *t'shu·vah* — repent, turn from sin to God
Tzi·**yon** — Zion
Ye·ru·sha·**la**·yim — Jerusalem
Ye·sha'·**ya**·hu — Isaiah
Ye·**shu**·a — Jesus
Y'hu·**dah** Ben-Shim·'**on**, from **K'ri·ot** — Judas the son of Simon Iscariot

---

l Isaiah 53:1   *m* Isaiah 6:10

wrapped a towel around his waist.
⁵Then he poured some water into a
basin and began to wash the feet of the
talmidim and wipe them off with the
towel wrapped around him.

⁶He came to Shim'on Kefa, who said
to him, "Lord! You are washing my
feet?" ⁷Yeshua answered him, "You
don't understand yet what I am doing,
but in time you will understand."
⁸"No!" said Kefa, "you will never wash
my feet!" Yeshua answered him, "If I
don't wash you, you have no share with
me." ⁹"Lord," Shim'on Kefa replied,
"not only my feet, but my hands and
head too!" ¹⁰Yeshua said to him, "A
man who has had a bath doesn't need
to wash, except his feet — his body is
already clean. And you people are
clean, but not all of you." ¹¹(He knew
who was betraying him; this is why he
said, "Not all of you are clean.")

¹²After he had washed their feet,
taken back his clothes and returned to
the table, he said to them, "Do you
understand what I have done to you?
¹³You call me 'Rabbi' and 'Lord,' and
you are right, because I am. ¹⁴Now if I,
the Lord and Rabbi, have washed your
feet, you also should wash each other's
feet. ¹⁵For I have set you an example,
so that you may do as I have done to
you. ¹⁶Yes, indeed! I tell you, a slave is
not greater than his master, nor is an
emissary greater than the one who sent
him. ¹⁷If you know these things, you
will be blessed if you do them.

¹⁸"I'm not talking to all of you — I
know which ones I have chosen. But
the words of the *Tanakh* must be
fulfilled that say, **'The one eating my
bread has turned against me.'**[n] ¹⁹I'm
telling you now, before it happens; so
that when it does happen, you may
believe that I AM who I say I am. ²⁰Yes,

indeed! I tell you that a person who
receives someone I send receives me,
and that anyone who receives me
receives the One who sent me.

²¹After saying this, Yeshua, in deep
anguish of spirit, declared, "Yes,
indeed! I tell you that one of you will
betray me.' ²²The *talmidim* stared at
one another, totally mystified — whom
could he mean? ²³One of his *talmidim*,
the one Yeshua particularly loved, was
reclining close beside him. ²⁴So Shim'on
Kefa motioned to him and said, "Ask
which one he's talking about." ²⁵Lean-
ing against Yeshua's chest, he asked
Yeshua, "Lord, who is it?" ²⁶Yeshua
answered, "It's the one to whom I give
this piece of *matzah* after I dip it in the
dish." So he dipped the piece of *matzah*
and gave it to Y'hudah Ben-Shim'on
from K'riot. ²⁷As soon as Y'hudah took
the piece of *matzah*, the Adversary
went into him. "What you are doing,
do quickly!" Yeshua said to him. ²⁸But
no one at the table understood why he
had said this to him. ²⁹Some thought
that since Y'hudah was in charge of the
common purse, Yeshua was telling him,
"Buy what we need for the festival," or
telling him to give something to the
poor. ³⁰As soon as he had taken the
piece of *matzah*, Y'hudah went out,
and it was night.

³¹After Y'hudah had left, Yeshua
said, "Now the Son of Man has been
glorified, and God has been glorified in
him. ³²If the Son has glorified God,
God will himself glorify the Son, and
will do so without delay. ³³Little children, I will be with you only a little
longer. You will look for me; and, as I
said to the Judeans, 'Where I am going,
you cannot come,' now I say it to you
as well.

³⁴"I am giving you a new command:
that you keep on loving each other. In
the same way that I have loved you,

---

n Psalm 41:10(9)

you are also to keep on loving each other. ³⁵Everyone will know that you are my *talmidim* by the fact that you have love for each other."

³⁶Shim'on Kefa said to him, "Lord, where are you going?" Yeshua answered, "Where I am going, you cannot follow me now; but you will follow later." ³⁷"Lord," Kefa said to him, "why can't I follow you now? I will lay down my life for you!" ³⁸Yeshua answered, "You will lay down your life for me? Yes, indeed! I tell you, before the rooster crows you will disown me three times. ¹Don't let yourselves **14** be disturbed. Trust in God and trust in me. ²In my Father's house are many places to live. If there weren't, I would have told you; because I am going there to prepare a place for you. ³Since I am going and preparing a place for you, I will return to take you with me; so that where I am, you may be also. ⁴Furthermore, you know where I'm going; and you know the way there."

⁵T'oma said to him, "Lord, we don't know where you're going, so how can we know the way?" ⁶Yeshua said, "I AM the Way — and the Truth and the Life; no one comes to the Father except through me. ⁷Because you have known me, you will also know my Father; from now on, you do know him — in fact, you have seen him."

⁸Philip said to him, "Lord, show us the Father, and it will be enough for us." ⁹Yeshua replied to him, "Have I been with you so long without your knowing me, Philip? Whoever has seen me has seen the Father; so how can you say, 'Show us the Father'? ¹⁰Don't you believe that I am united with the Father, and the Father united with me? What I am telling you, I am not saying on my own initiative; the Father living in me is doing his own works. ¹¹Trust me, that I am united with the Father, and the Father united with me. But if you can't, then trust because of the works themselves. ¹²"Yes, indeed! I tell you that whoever trusts in me will also do the works I do! Indeed, he will do greater ones, because I am going to the Father. ¹³In fact, whatever you ask for in my name, I will do; so that the Father may be glorified in the Son. ¹⁴If you ask for something in my name, I will do it.

¹⁵"If you love me, you will keep my commands; ¹⁶and I will ask the Father, and he will give you another comforting Counselor like me, the Spirit of Truth, to be with you forever. ¹⁷The world cannot receive him, because it neither sees nor knows him. You know him, because he is staying with you and will be united with you. ¹⁸I will not leave you orphans — I am coming to you. ¹⁹In just a little while, the world will no longer see me; but you will see me. Because I live, you too will live. ²⁰When that day comes, you will know that I am united with my Father, and you with me, and I with you. ²¹Whoever has my commands and keeps them is the one who loves me, and the one who loves me will be loved by my Father, and I will love him and reveal myself to him."

²²Y'hudah (not the one from K'riot) said to him, "What has happened,

---

Ke·**fa** — Peter
ma·tzah — unleavened bread
Shim·'on Ke·**fa** — Simon Peter
tal·mi·dim — disciples
Ta·nakh — Hebrew Scriptures, "Old Testament"
T·'o·ma — Thomas
Ye·**shu**·a — Jesus
Y'hu·**dah** (not the one from K'ri·ot) — Judas (not Iscariot)
Y'hu·**dah** Ben-Shim·'**on**, from K'ri·ot — Judas the son of Simon Iscariot

Lord, that you are about to reveal yourself to us and not to the world?" ²³ Yeshua answered him, "If someone loves me, he will keep my word; and my Father will love him, and we will come to him and make our home with him. ²⁴ Someone who doesn't love me doesn't keep my words — and the word you are hearing is not my own but that of the Father who sent me.

²⁵ "I have told you these things while I am still with you. ²⁶ But the Counselor, the *Ruach HaKodesh*, whom the Father will send in my name, will teach you everything; that is, he will remind you of everything I have said to you.

²⁷ "What I am leaving with you is *shalom* — I am giving you my *shalom*. I don't give the way the world gives. Don't let yourselves be upset or frightened. ²⁸ You heard me tell you, 'I am leaving, and I will come back to you.' If you loved me, you would have been glad that I am going to the Father; because the Father is greater than I. ²⁹ Also, I have said it to you now, before it happens; so that when it does happen, you will trust.

³⁰ "I won't be talking with you much longer, because the ruler of this world is coming. He has no claim on me; ³¹ rather, this is happening so that the world may know that I love the Father, and that I do as the Father has commanded me.

"Get up! Let's get going!"

15 ¹ "I am the real vine, and my Father is the gardener. ² Every branch which is part of me but fails to bear fruit, he cuts off; and every branch that does bear fruit, he prunes, so that it may bear more fruit. ³ Right now, because of the word which I have spoken to you, you are pruned. ⁴ Stay united with me, as I will with you — for just as the branch can't put

forth fruit by itself apart from the vine, so you can't bear fruit apart from me.

⁵ "I am the vine and you are the branches. Those who stay united with me, and I with them, are the ones who bear much fruit; because apart from me you can't do a thing. ⁶ Unless a person remains united with me, he is thrown away like a branch and dries up. Such branches are gathered and thrown into the fire, where they are burned up.

⁷ "If you remain united with me, and my words with you, then ask whatever you want, and it will happen for you. ⁸ This is how my Father is glorified — in your bearing much fruit; this is how you will prove to be my *talmidim*.

⁹ "Just as my Father has loved me, I too have loved you; so stay in my love. ¹⁰ If you keep my commands, you will stay in my love — just as I have kept my Father's commands and stay in his love. ¹¹ I have said this to you so that my joy may be in you, and your joy be complete.

¹² "This is my command: that you keep on loving each other just as I have loved you. ¹³ No one has greater love than a person who lays down his life for his friends. ¹⁴ You are my friends, if you do what I command you. ¹⁵ I no longer call you slaves, because a slave doesn't know what his master is about; but I have called you friends, because everything I have heard from my Father I have made known to you. ¹⁶ You did not choose me, I chose you; and I have commissioned you to go and bear fruit, fruit that will last; so that whatever you ask from the Father in my name he may give you. ¹⁷ This is what I command you: keep loving each other!

¹⁸ "If the world hates you, under-

stand that it hated me first. ¹⁹ If you belonged to the world, the world would have loved its own. But because you do not belong to the world — on the contrary, I have picked you out of the world — therefore the world hates you. ²⁰ Remember what I told you, 'A slave is not greater than his master.' If they persecuted me, they will persecute you too; if they kept my word, they will keep yours too. ²¹ But they will do all this to you on my account, because they don't know the One who sent me.

²² "If I had not come and spoken to them, they wouldn't be guilty of sin; but now, they have no excuse for their sin. ²³ Whoever hates me hates my Father also. ²⁴ If I had not done in their presence works which no one else ever did, they would not be guilty of sin; but now, they have seen them and have hated both me and my Father. ²⁵ But this has happened in order to fulfill the words in their *Torah* which read, '**They hated me for no reason at all.**'ᵒ

²⁶ "When the Counselor comes, whom I will send you from the Father — the Spirit of Truth, who keeps going out from the Father — he will testify on my behalf. ²⁷ And you testify too, because you have been with me from the outset.

16 ¹ "I have told you these things so that you won't be caught by surprise. ² They will ban you from the synagogue; in fact, the time will come when anyone who kills you will think he is serving God! ³ They will do these things because they have understood neither the Father nor me. ⁴ But I have told you this, so that when the time comes for it to happen, you will remember that I told you. I didn't tell you this at first, because I was with you. ⁵ But

now I am going to the One who sent me.

"Not one of you is asking me, 'Where are you going?' ⁶ Instead, because I have said these things to you, you are overcome with grief. ⁷ But I tell you the truth, it is to your advantage that I go away; for if I don't go away, the comforting Counselor will not come to you. However, if I do go, I will send him to you.

⁸ "When he comes, he will show that the world is wrong about sin, about righteousness and about judgment — ⁹ about sin, in that people don't put their trust in me; ¹⁰ about righteousness, in that I am going to the Father and you will no longer see me; ¹¹ about judgment, in that the ruler of this world has been judged.

¹² "I still have many things to tell you, but you can't bear them now. ¹³ However, when the Spirit of Truth comes, he will guide you into all the truth; for he will not speak on his own initiative but will say only what he hears. He will also announce to you the events of the future. ¹⁴ He will glorify me, because he will receive from what is mine and announce it to you. ¹⁵ Everything the Father has is mine; this is why I said that he receives from what is mine and will announce it to you.

¹⁶ "In a little while, you will see me no more; then, a little while later, you will see me." ¹⁷ At this, some of the *talmidim* said to one another, "What is this that he's telling us, 'In a little while, you won't see me; then, a little

---

ᵒ Psalms 35:19, 69:5(4)

Ru·ach Ha·Ko·desh — Holy Spirit
sha·lom — peace
tal·mi·dim — disciples
To·rah — Teaching, "Law"; Pentateuch; Hebrew Bible
Ye·shu·a — Jesus

while later, you will see me"? and, 'I am going to the Father"?" ¹⁸ They went on saying, "What is this 'little while'? We don't understand what he's talking about."

¹⁹ Yeshua knew that they wanted to ask him, so he said to them, "Are you asking each other what I meant by saying, 'In a little while, you won't see me; and then, a little while later, you will see me'? ²⁰ Yes, it's true. I tell you that you will sob and mourn, and the world will rejoice; you will grieve, but your grief will turn to joy. ²¹ When a woman is giving birth, she is in pain; because her time has come. But when the baby is born, she forgets her suffering out of joy that a child has come into the world. ²² So you do indeed feel grief now, but I am going to see you again. Then your hearts will be full of joy, and no one will take your joy away from you.

²³ "When that day comes, you won't ask anything of me! Yes, indeed! I tell you that whatever you ask from the Father, he will give you in my name. ²⁴ Till now you haven't asked for anything in my name. Keep asking, and you will receive, so that your joy may be complete.

²⁵ "I have said these these things to you with the help of illustrations; however, a time is coming when I will no longer speak indirectly but will talk about the Father in plain language. ²⁶ When that day comes, you will ask in my name. I am not telling you that I will pray to the Father on your behalf, ²⁷ for the Father himself loves you, because you have loved me and have believed that I came from God.

²⁸ "I came from the Father and have come into the world; again, I am leaving the world and returning to the Father."

²⁹ The *talmidim* said to him, "Look, you're talking plainly right now, you're not speaking indirectly at all. ³⁰ Now we know that you know everything, and that you don't need to have people put their questions into words. This makes us believe that you came from God."

³¹ Yeshua answered, "Now you do believe. ³² But a time is coming — indeed it has come already — when you will be scattered, each one looking out for himself; and you will leave me all alone. Yet I am not alone; because the Father is with me.

³³ "I have said these things to you so that, united with me, you may have *shalom*. In the world, you have *tsuris*. But be brave! I have conquered the world!"

17 ¹ After Yeshua had said these things, he looked up toward heaven and said, "Father, the time has come. Glorify your Son, so that the Son may glorify you — ² just as you gave him authority over all mankind, so that he might give eternal life to all those whom you have given him. ³ And eternal life is this: to know you, the one true God, and him whom you sent, Yeshua the Messiah.

⁴ "I glorified you on earth by finishing the work you gave me to do. ⁵ Now, Father, glorify me alongside yourself. Give me the same glory I had with you before the world existed.

⁶ "I made your name known to the people you gave me out of the world. They were yours, you gave them to me, and they have kept your word. ⁷ Now they know that everything you have given me is from you, ⁸ because the words you gave me I have given to them, and they have received them. They have really come to know that I came from you, and they have come to trust that you sent me.

[9] "I am praying for them. I am not praying for the world, but for those you have given to me, because they are yours. [10] Indeed, all I have is yours, and all you have is mine, and in them I have been glorified. [11] Now I am no longer in the world. They are in the world, but I am coming to you. Holy Father, guard them by the power of your name, which you have given to me, so that they may be one, just as we are. [12] When I was with them, I guarded them by the power of your name, which you have given to me; yes, I kept watch over them; and not one of them was destroyed (except the one meant for destruction, so that the *Tanakh* might be fulfilled). [13] But now, I am coming to you; and I say these things while I am still in the world so that they may have my joy made complete in themselves.

[14] "I have given them your word, and the world hated them, because they do not belong to the world — just as I myself do not belong to the world. [15] I don't ask you to take them out of the world, but to protect them from the Evil One. [16] They do not belong to the world, just as I do not belong to the world. [17] Set them apart for holiness by means of the truth — your word is truth. [18] Just as you sent me into the world, I have sent them into the world. [19] On their behalf I am setting myself apart for holiness, so that they too may be set apart for holiness by means of the truth.

[20] "I pray not only for these, but also for those who will trust in me because of their word, [21] that they may all be one. Just as you, Father, are united with me and I with you, I pray that they may be united with us, so that the world may believe that you sent me. [22] The glory which you have given to me, I have given to them; so that they may be one, just as we are one — [23] I united with them and you with me, so that they may be completely one, and the world thus realize that you sent me, and that you have loved them just as you have loved me.

[24] "Father, I want those you have given me to be with me where I am; so that they may see my glory, which you have given me because you loved me before the creation of the world. [25] Righteous Father, the world has not known you, but I have known you, and these people have known that you sent me. [26] I made your name known to them, and I will continue to make it known; so that the love with which you have loved me may be in them, and I myself may be united with them."

18 [1] After Yeshua had said all this, he went out with his *talmidim* across the stream that flows in winter through the Kidron Valley, to a spot where there was a grove of trees; and he and his *talmidim* went into it. [2] Now Y'hudah, who was betraying him, also knew the place; because Yeshua had often met there with his *talmidim*. [3] So Y'hudah went there, taking with him a detachment of Roman soldiers and some Temple guards provided by the head *cohanim* and the *P'rushim*; they carried weapons, lanterns and torches. [4] Yeshua, who knew everything that was going to happen to

---

co·ha·nim — priests
Kid·ron — Kedron, Cedron
P'ru·shim — Pharisees
sha·lom — peace
Ta·nakh — Hebrew Scriptures, "Old Testament"
tal·mi·dim — disciples
tsu·ris — troubles
Ye·shu·a — Jesus
Y'hu·dah — Judas

him, went out and asked them, "Whom do you want?" [5]"Yeshua from Natzeret," they answered. He said to them, "I AM." Also standing with them was Y'hudah, the one who was betraying him. [6]When he said, "I AM," they went backward from him and fell to the ground. [7]So he inquired of them once more, "Whom do you want?" and they said, "Yeshua from Natzeret." [8]"I told you, 'I AM,'" answered Yeshua, "so if I'm the one you want, let these others go." [9]This happened so that what he had said might be fulfilled, "I have not lost one of those you gave me."

[10]Then Shim'on Kefa, who had a sword, drew it and struck the slave of the *cohen hagadol*, cutting off his right ear; the slave's name was Melekh. [11]Yeshua said to Kefa, "Put your sword back in its scabbard! This is the cup the Father has given me; am I not to drink it?"

[12]So the detachment of Roman soldiers and their captain, together with the Temple Guard of the Judeans, arrested Yeshua, tied him up, [13]and took him first to Anan, the father-in-law of Kayafa, who was *cohen gadol* that fateful year. [14](It was Kayafa who had advised the Judeans that it would be good for one man to die on behalf of the people.) [15]Shim'on Kefa and another *talmid* followed Yeshua. The second *talmid* was known to the *cohen hagadol*, and he went with Yeshua into the courtyard of the *cohen hagadol*; [16]but Kefa stood outside by the gate. So the other *talmid*, the one known to the *cohen hagadol*, went back out and spoke to the woman on duty at the gate, then brought Kefa inside. [17]The woman at the gate said to Kefa, "Aren't you another of that man's *talmidim*?" He said, "No, I'm not."

[18]Now the slaves and guards had lit a fire because it was cold, and they were standing around it warming themselves; Kefa joined them and stood warming himself too.

[19]The *cohen hagadol* questioned Yeshua about his *talmidim* and about what he taught. [20]Yeshua answered, "I have spoken quite openly to everyone; I have always taught in a synagogue or in the Temple where all Jews meet together, and I have said nothing in secret; [21]so why are you questioning me? Question the ones who heard what I said to them; look, they know what I said." [22]At these words, one of the guards standing by slapped Yeshua in the face and said, "This is how you talk to the *cohen hagadol*?" [23]Yeshua answered him, "If I said something wrong, state publicly what was wrong; but if I was right, why are you hitting me?" [24]So Anan sent him, still tied up, to Kayafa the *cohen hagadol*.

[25]Meanwhile, Shim'on Kefa was standing and warming himself. They said to him, "Aren't you also one of his *talmidim*?" He denied it, saying, "No, I am not." [26]One of the slaves of the *cohen hagadol*, a relative of the man whose ear Kefa had cut off, said, "Didn't I see you with him in the grove of trees?" [27]So again Kefa denied it, and instantly a rooster crowed.

[28]They led Yeshua from Kayafa to the governor's headquarters. By now it was early morning. They did not enter the headquarters building because they didn't want to become ritually defiled and thus unable to eat the *Pesach* meal. [29]So Pilate went outside to them and said, "What charge are you bringing against this man?" [30]They answered, "If he hadn't done something wrong, we wouldn't

146

have brought him to you." ³¹Pilate said to them, "You take him and judge him according to your own law." The Judeans replied, "We don't have the legal power to put anyone to death." ³²This was so that what Yeshua had said, about how he was going to die, might be fulfilled.

³³So Pilate went back into the headquarters, called Yeshua and said to him, "Are you the king of the Jews?" ³⁴Yeshua answered, "Are you asking this on your own, or have other people told you about me?" ³⁵Pilate replied, "Am I a Jew? Your own nation and head *cohanim* have handed you over to me; what have you done?" ³⁶Yeshua answered, "My kingship does not derive its authority from this world's order of things. If it did, my men would have fought to keep me from being arrested by the Judeans. But my kingship does not come from here." ³⁷"So then," Pilate said to him, "you are a king, after all." Yeshua answered, "You say I am a king. The reason I have been born, the reason I have come into the world, is to bear witness to the truth. Every one who belongs to the truth listens to me." ³⁸Pilate asked him, "What is truth?"

Having said this, Pilate went outside again to the Judeans and told them, "I don't find any case against him. ³⁹However, you have a custom that at Passover I set one prisoner free. Do you want me to set free for you the 'king of the Jews'?" ⁴⁰But they yelled back, "No, not this man but Bar-Abba!" (Bar-Abba was a revolutionary.)

19 ¹Pilate then took Yeshua and had him flogged. ²The soldiers twisted thorn-branches into a crown and placed it on his head, put a purple robe on him, ³and went up to him,

saying over and over, "Hail, 'king of the Jews'!" and hitting him in the face.

⁴Pilate went outside once more and said to the crowd, "Look, I'm bringing him out to you to get you to understand that I find no case against him." ⁵So Yeshua came out, wearing the thorn-branch crown and the purple robe. Pilate said to them, "Look at the man!" ⁶When the head *cohanim* and the Temple guards saw him they shouted, "Put him to death on the stake! Put him to death on the stake!" Pilate said to them, "You take him out yourselves and put him to death on the stake, because I don't find any case against him." ⁷The Judeans answered him, "We have a law; according to that law, he ought to be put to death, because he made himself out to be the Son of God." ⁸On hearing this, Pilate became even more frightened.

⁹He went back into the headquarters and asked Yeshua, "Where are you from?" But Yeshua didn't answer. ¹⁰So Pilate said to him, "You refuse to speak to me? Don't you understand that it is in my power either to set you free or to have you executed on the stake?" ¹¹Yeshua answered, "You would have no power over me if it hadn't been given to you from above;

A·**nan** — Annas
Bar-Ab·ba — Barabbas
co·ha·nim — priests
co·hen (ha)·ga·dol — high priest
Ka·ya·**fa** — Caiaphas
Ke·**fa** — Peter
Me·lekh — Malchus
Na·**tze**·ret — Nazareth
Pe·sach — Passover
P'ru·shim — Pharisees
Shim·'on Ke·**fa** — Simon Peter
tal·mid (pl. *tal·mi·dim*) — disciple
Ye·**shu**·a — Jesus
Y'hu·dah — Judas

147

this is why the one who handed me over to you is guilty of a greater sin." [12]On hearing this, Pilate tried to find a way to set him free; but the Judeans shouted, "If you set this man free, it means you're not a 'Friend of the Emperor'! Everyone who claims to be a king is opposing the Emperor!" [13]When Pilate heard what they were saying, he brought Yeshua outside and sat down on the judge's seat in the place called The Pavement (in Aramaic, Gabta); [14]it was about noon on Preparation Day of *Pesach*. He said to the Judeans, "Here's your king!" [15]They shouted, "Take him away! Take him away! Put him to death on the stake!" Pilate said to them, "You want me to execute your king on a stake?" The head *cohanim* answered, "We have no king but the Emperor." [16]Then Pilate handed Yeshua over to them to have him put to death on the stake.

So they took charge of Yeshua. [17]Carrying the stake himself he went out to the place called Skull (in Aramaic, Gulgolta). [18]There they nailed him to the stake along with two others, one on either side, with Yeshua in the middle. [19]Pilate also had a notice written and posted on the stake; it read,

YESHUA FROM NATZERET THE KING OF THE JEWS

[20]Many of the Judeans read this notice, because the place where Yeshua was put on the stake was close to the city; and it had been written in Hebrew, in Latin and in Greek. [21]The Judeans' head *cohanim* therefore said to Pilate, "Don't write, 'The King of the Jews,' but 'He said, "I am King of the Jews."'" [22]Pilate answered, "What I have written, I have written."

[23]When the soldiers had nailed Yeshua to the stake, they took his clothes and divided them into four shares, a share for each soldier, with the under-robe left over. Now the under-robe was seamless, woven in one piece from top to bottom; [24]so they said to one another, "We shouldn't tear it in pieces; let's draw for it." This happened in order to fulfill the words from the *Tanakh*,

> "They divided my clothes among themselves
> and gambled for my robe."[p]

This is why the soldiers did these things.
[25]Nearby Yeshua's execution stake stood his mother, his mother's sister, Miryam the wife of Klofah, and Miryam from Magdala. [26]When Yeshua saw his mother and the *talmid* whom he loved standing there, he said to his mother, "Mother, this is your son." [27]Then he said to the *talmid*, "This is your mother." And from that time on, the *talmid* took her into his own home.

[28]After this, knowing that all things had accomplished their purpose, Yeshua, in order to fulfill the words of the *Tanakh*, said, "I'm thirsty." [29]A jar full of cheap sour wine was there; so they soaked a sponge in the wine, stuck it on the end of a hyssop branch and held it up to his mouth. [30]After Yeshua had taken the wine, he said, "It is accomplished!" And, letting his head droop, he delivered up his spirit.

[31]It was Preparation Day, and the Judeans did not want the bodies to remain on the stake on *Shabbat*, since it was an especially important *Shabbat*. So they asked Pilate to have the legs broken and the bodies removed. [32]The

---

p Psalm 22:19(18)

soldiers came and broke the legs of the first man who had been put on a stake beside Yeshua, then the legs of the other one; ³³ but when they got to Yeshua and saw that he was already dead, they didn't break his legs. ³⁴ However, one of the soldiers stabbed his side with a spear, and at once blood and water flowed out. ³⁵ The man who saw it has testified about it, and his testimony is true. And he knows that he tells the truth, so you too can trust. ³⁶ For these things happened in order to fulfill this passage of the *Tanakh*:

> "Not one of his bones will be broken."^q

³⁷ And again, another passage says,

> "They will look at him whom they have pierced."^r

³⁸ After this, Yosef of Ramatayim, who was a *talmid* of Yeshua, but a secret one out of fear of the Judeans, asked Pilate if he could have Yeshua's body. Pilate gave his consent, so Yosef came and took the body away. ³⁹ Also Nakdimon, who at first had gone to see Yeshua by night, came with some seventy pounds of spices — a mixture of myrrh and aloes. ⁴⁰ They took Yeshua's body and wrapped it up in linen sheets with the spices, in keeping with Judean burial practice. ⁴¹ In the vicinity of where he had been executed was a garden, and in the garden was a new tomb in which no one had ever been buried. ⁴² So, because it was Preparation Day for the Judeans, and because the tomb was close by, that is where they buried Yeshua.

20 ¹ Early on the first day of the week, while it was still dark, Miryam from Magdala went to the tomb and saw that the stone had been removed from the tomb. ² So she came running to Shim'on Kefa and the other *talmid*, the one Yeshua loved, and said to them, "They've taken the Lord out of the tomb, and we don't know where they've put him!"

³ Then Kefa and the other *talmid* started for the tomb. ⁴ They both ran, but the other *talmid* outran Kefa and reached the tomb first. ⁵ Stooping down, he saw the linen burial-sheets lying there but did not go in. ⁶ Then, following him, Shim'on Kefa arrived, entered the tomb and saw the burial-sheets lying there, ⁷ also the cloth that had been around his head, lying not with the sheets but in a separate place and still folded up. ⁸ Then the other *talmid*, who had arrived at the tomb first, also went in; he saw, and he trusted. ⁹ (They had not yet come to understand that the *Tanakh* teaches that the Messiah has to rise from the dead.)

---

co·ha·nim — priests
Gab·ta — elevated place(?)
Gul·gol·ta — Golgotha, Calvary
Ke·fa — Peter
Klo·fah — Clopas
Mir·yam — Miriam, Mary
Mir·yam from **Mag·da·la** — Mary Magdalene
Nak·di·mon — Nicodemus
Na·tze·ret — Nazareth
Pe·sach — Passover
Ra·ma·ta·yim — Arimathea
Shab·bat — the Sabbath
Shim·'on Ke·fa — Simon Peter
tal·mid — disciple
Ta·nakh — Hebrew Scriptures, "Old Testament"
Ye·shu·a — Jesus
Yo·sef — Joseph

---

q Psalm 34:21(20), Exodus 12:46, Numbers 9:12

r Zechariah 12:10

^{10}So the *talmidim* returned home, ^{11}but Miryam stood outside crying. As she cried, she bent down, peered into the tomb, ^{12}and saw two angels in white sitting where the body of Yeshua had been, one at the head and one at the feet. ^{13}"Why are you crying?" they asked her. "They took my Lord," she said to them, "and I don't know where they have put him."

^{14}As she said this, she turned around and saw Yeshua standing there, but she didn't know it was he. ^{15}Yeshua said to her, "Lady, why are you crying? Whom are you looking for?" Thinking he was the gardener, she said to him, "Sir, if you're the one who carried him away, just tell me where you put him; and I'll go and get him myself." ^{16}Yeshua said to her, "Miryam!" Turning, she cried out to him in Hebrew, "*Rabbani*!" (that is, "Teacher!") ^{17}"Stop holding onto me," Yeshua said to her, "because I haven't yet gone back to the Father. But go to my brothers, and tell them that I am going back to my Father and your Father, to my God and your God." ^{18}Miryam of Magdala went to the *talmidim* with the news that she had seen the Lord and that he had told her this.

^{19}In the evening that same day, the first day of the week, when the *talmidim* were gathered together behind locked doors out of fear of the Judeans, Yeshua came, stood in the middle and said, "*Shalom aleikhem*!" ^{20}Having greeted them, he showed them his hands and his side. The *talmidim* were overjoyed to see the Lord. ^{21}"*Shalom aleikhem*!" Yeshua repeated. "Just as the Father sent me, I myself am also sending you." ^{22}Having said this, he breathed on them and said to them, "Receive the *Ruach HaKodesh*! ^{23}If you forgive someone's sins, their sins are forgiven; if you hold them, they are held."

^{24}Now T'oma (the name means "twin"), one of the Twelve, was not with them when Yeshua came. ^{25}When the other *talmidim* told him, "We have seen the Lord," he replied, "Unless I see the nail marks in his hands, put my finger into the place where the nails were and put my hand into his side, I refuse to believe it."

^{26}A week later his *talmidim* were once more in the room, and this time T'oma was with them. Although the doors were locked, Yeshua came, stood among them and said, "*Shalom aleikhem*!" ^{27}Then he said to T'oma, "Put your finger here, look at my hands, take your hand and put it into my side. Don't be lacking in trust, but have trust!" ^{28}T'oma answered him, "My Lord and my God!" ^{29}Yeshua said to him, "Have you trusted because you have seen me? How blessed are those who do not see, but trust anyway!"

^{30}In the presence of the *talmidim* Yeshua performed many other miracles which have not been recorded in this book. ^{31}But these which have been recorded are here so that you may trust that Yeshua is the Messiah, the Son of God, and that by this trust you may have life because of who he is.

21 ^{1}After this, Yeshua appeared again to the *talmidim* at Lake Tiberias. Here is how it happened: ^{2}Shim'on Kefa and T'oma (his name means "twin") were together with Natan'el from Kanah in the Galil, the sons of Zavdai, and two other *talmidim*. ^{3}Shim'on Kefa said, "I'm going fishing." They said to him, "We're coming with you." They went and got into the boat, but that night they didn't catch anything. 4However, just as day was breaking, Yeshua stood on shore, but the *talmidim* didn't know it was he. 5He said to them, "You don't have any fish, do you?" "No," they answered him. 6He said to them, "Throw in your net to starboard and you will catch some." So they threw in their net, and there were so many fish in it that they couldn't haul it aboard. 7The *talmid* Yeshua loved said to Kefa, "It's the Lord!" On hearing it was the Lord, Shim'on Kefa threw on his coat, because he was stripped for work, and plunged into the lake; 8but the other *talmidim* followed in the boat, dragging the net full of fish; for they weren't far from shore, only about a hundred yards. 9When they stepped ashore, they saw a fire of burning coals with a fish on it, and some bread. 10Yeshua said to them, "Bring some of the fish you have just caught." 11Shim'on Kefa went up and dragged the net ashore. It was full of fish, 153 of them; but even with so many, the net wasn't torn. 12Yeshua said to them, "Come and have breakfast." None of the *talmidim* dared to ask him, "Who are you?" They knew it was the Lord. 13Yeshua came, took the bread and gave it to them, and did the same with the fish. 14This was now the third time Yeshua had appeared to the *talmidim* after being raised from the dead.

15After breakfast, Yeshua said to Shim'on Kefa, "Shim'on Bar-Yochanan, do you love me more than these?" He replied, "Yes, Lord, you know I'm your friend." He said to him, "Feed my lambs." 16A second time he said to him, "Shim'on Bar-Yochanan, do you love me?" He replied, "Yes, Lord, you know I'm your friend." He said to him, "Shepherd my sheep." 17The third time he said to him, "Shim'on Bar-Yochanan, are you my friend?" Shim'on was hurt that he questioned him a third time: "Are you my friend?" So he replied, "Lord, you know everything! You know I'm your friend!" Yeshua said to him, "Feed my sheep! 18Yes, indeed! I tell you, when you were younger, you put on your clothes and went where you wanted. But when you grow old, you will stretch out your hands, and someone else will dress you and carry you where you do not want to go." 19He said this to indicate the kind of death by which Kefa would bring glory to God. Then Yeshua said to him, "Follow me!"

20Kefa turned and saw the *talmid* Yeshua especially loved following behind, the one who had leaned against him at the supper and had asked, "Who is the one who is betraying you?" 21On seeing him, Kefa said to Yeshua, "Lord, what about him?" 22Yeshua said to him, "If I want him to stay on until I come, what is it to you? You, follow me!" 23Therefore the word spread among the brothers that

---

Ga·lil, the — Galilee

Ka·nah — Cana

Ke·fa — Peter

Mir·yam — Miriam, Mary

Mir·yam from Mag·da·la — Mary Magdalene

Na·tan·'el — Nathanael

Na·tze·ret — Nazareth

Rab·ba·ni — my great one, my teacher

Ru·ach-Ha·Ko·desh — Holy Spirit

Sha·lom a·lei·khem! — Peace be upon you(pl.)! (greeting)

Shim'on Bar-Yo·cha·nan — Simon, son of John

Shim·'on Ke·fa — Simon Peter

tal·mid (pl. *tal·mi·dim*) — disciple

Ta·nakh — Hebrew Scriptures, "Old Testament"

T·'o·ma — Thomas

Ye·shu·a — Jesus

Zav·dai — Zebedee

that *talmid* would not die. However, Yeshua didn't say he wouldn't die, but simply, "If I want him to stay on until I come, what is it to you?"

²⁴ This one is the *talmid* who is testifying about these things and who has recorded them.

And we know that his testimony is true.

²⁵ But there are also many other things Yeshua did; and if they were all to be recorded, I don't think the whole world could contain the books that would have to be written!

THE
ACTS

OF THE EMISSARIES OF YESHUA THE MESSIAH

1 ¹ Dear Theophilos:
In the first book, I wrote about everything Yeshua set out to do and teach, ² until the day when, after giving instructions through the *Ruach HaKodesh* to the emissaries whom he had chosen, he was taken up into heaven.

³ After his death he showed himself to them and gave many convincing proofs that he was alive. During a period of forty days they saw him, and he spoke with them about the Kingdom of God.

⁴ At one of these gatherings, he instructed them not to leave Yerushalayim but to wait for "what the Father promised, which you heard about from me. ⁵ For Yochanan used to immerse people in water; but in a few days, you will be immersed in the *Ruach HaKodesh*!"

⁶ When they were together, they asked him, "Lord, are you at this time going to restore self-rule to Israel?" ⁷ He answered, "You don't need to know the dates or the times; the Father has kept these under his own authority. ⁸ But you will receive power when the *Ruach HaKodesh* comes upon you; you will be my witnesses both in Yerushalayim and in all Y'hudah and Shomron, indeed to the ends of the earth!"

⁹ After saying this, he was taken up before their eyes; and a cloud hid him from their sight. ¹⁰ As they were staring into the sky after him, suddenly they saw two men dressed in white standing next to them. ¹¹ The men said, "You Galileans! Why are you standing, staring into space? This Yeshua, who has been taken away from you into heaven, will come back to you in just the same way as you saw him go into heaven."

¹² Then they returned the *Shabbat*-walk distance from the Mount of Olives to Yerushalayim. ¹³ After entering the city, they went to the upstairs room where they were staying. The names of the emissaries were Kefa, Ya'akov, Yochanan, Andrew, Philip, T'oma, Bar-Talmai, Mattityahu, Ya'akov Ben-Chalfai, Shim'on "the Zealot", and Y'hudah Ben-Ya'akov. ¹⁴ These all devoted themselves singlemindedly to

---

Bar-Tal·**mai** — Bartholomew
Ke·**fa** — Peter
Mat·tit·**ya**·hu — Matthew
Ru·ach-Ha·Ko·desh — Holy Spirit
Shab·bat — the Sabbath
Shim·**on** — Simon
Shom·**ron** — Samaria
tal·mid — disciple
T·**o**·ma — Thomas
Ya·**a·kov** — James
Ya·**a·kov** Ben-Chal·**fai** — James, the son of Alpheus
Ye·ru·sha·**la**·yim — Jerusalem
Ye·**shu**·a — Jesus
Y'hu·**dah** — Judea
Y'hu·**dah** Ben-Ya·**a·kov** — Judas, the son of James
Yo·cha·**nan** — John

prayer, along with some women, including Miryam (Yeshua's mother), and his brothers.

¹⁵During this period, when the group of believers numbered about 120, Kefa stood up and addressed his fellow-believers: ¹⁶"Brothers, the *Ruach HaKodesh* spoke in advance through David about Y'hudah, and these words of the *Tanakh* had to be fulfilled. He was guide for those who arrested Yeshua — ¹⁷he was one of us and had been assigned a part in our work." ¹⁸(With the money Y'hudah received for his evil deed, he bought a field; and there he fell to his death. His body swelled up and burst open, and all his insides spilled out. ¹⁹This became known to everyone in Yerushalayim, so they called that field *"Chakal-D'ma"*, which in their language means "Field of Blood".) ²⁰Now," said Kefa, "it is written in the book of Psalms,

**'Let his estate become desolate,
let there be no one to live in it;'**[a]

and

**'Let someone else take his place as
a supervisor.'**[b]

²¹Therefore, one of the men who have been with us continuously throughout the time the Lord Yeshua traveled around among us, ²²from the time Yochanan was immersing people until the day Yeshua was taken up from us — one of these must become a witness with us to his resurrection."

²³They nominated two men — Yosef Bar-Sabba, surnamed Justus, and Mattityahu. ²⁴Then they prayed, "Lord, you know everyone's heart. Show us which of these two you have chosen ²⁵to take over the work and the office of emissary that Y'hudah abandoned to

a Psalm 69:26(25)   b Psalm 109:8

go where he belongs." ²⁶Then they drew lots to decide between the two, and the lot fell to Mattityahu. So he was added to the eleven emissaries.

2 ¹The festival of *Shavu'ot* arrived, and the believers all gathered together in one place. ²Suddenly there came a sound from the sky like the roar of a violent wind, and it filled the whole house where they were sitting. ³Then they saw what looked like tongues of fire, which separated and came to rest on each one of them. ⁴They were all filled with the *Ruach HaKodesh* and began to talk in different languages, as the Spirit enabled them to speak.

⁵Now there were staying in Yerushalayim religious Jews from every nation under heaven. ⁶When they heard this sound, a crowd gathered; they were confused, because each one heard the believers speaking in his own language. ⁷Totally amazed, they asked, "How is this possible? Aren't all these people who are speaking from the Galil? ⁸How is it that we hear them speaking in our native languages? ⁹We are Parthians, Medes, Elamites; residents of Mesopotamia, Y'huda, Cappadocia, Pontus, Asia, ¹⁰Phrygia, Pamphylia, Egypt, the parts of Libya near Cyrene; visitors from Rome; ¹¹Jews by birth and proselytes; Jews from Crete and from Arabia . . . ! How is it that we hear them speaking in our own languages about the great things God has done? ¹²Amazed and confused, they all went on asking each other, "What can this mean?" ¹³But others made fun of them and said, "They've just had too much wine!"

¹⁴Then Kefa stood up with the Eleven and raised his voice to address them: "You Judeans, and all of you staying here in Yerushalayim! Let me tell you what this means! Listen carefully to me!

[15]"These people aren't drunk, as you suppose — it's only nine in the morning. [16]No, this is what was spoken about through the prophet Yo'el:

[17]'*Adonai* says:
"In the Last Days,
I will pour out from my Spirit upon everyone.
Your sons and daughters will prophesy,
your young men will see visions,
your old men will dream dreams.
[18] Even on my slaves, both men and women,
will I pour out from my Spirit in those days;
and they will prophesy.
[19] I will perform miracles in the sky above
and signs on the earth below —
blood, fire and thick smoke.
[20] The sun will become dark
and the moon blood
before the great and fearful Day of *Adonai* comes.
[21] And then, whoever calls on the name of *Adonai* will be saved.'"[c]

[22]"Men of Israel! Listen to this! Yeshua from Natzeret was a man demonstrated to you to have been from God by the powerful works, miracles and signs that God performed through him in your presence. You yourselves know this. [23]This man was arrested in accordance with God's predetermined plan and foreknowledge; and, through the agency of persons not bound by the *Torah*, you nailed him up on a stake and killed him!

[24]"But God has raised him up and freed him from the suffering of death; it was impossible that death could keep its hold on him. [25]For David says this about him:

'I saw *Adonai* always before me,
for he is at my right hand,
so that I will not be shaken.
[26] For this reason, my heart was glad;
and my tongue rejoiced;
and now my body too will live on in the certain hope
[27] that you will not abandon me to Sh'ol
or let your Holy One see decay.
[28] You have made known to me the ways of life;
you will fill me with joy by your presence.'[d]

[29]"Brothers, I know I can say to you frankly that the patriarch David died and was buried — his tomb is with us to this day. [30]Therefore, since he was a prophet and knew that God had sworn an oath to him that one of his descendants would sit on his throne, [31]he was speaking in advance about the resurrection of the Messiah, that it was he

---

d Psalm 16:8-11

===

A·do·nai — the LORD, Jehovah
Cha·kal-D'·ma — Akeldama, Aceldama
Da·**vid** — David
the Ga·**lil** — Galilee
Ke·**fa** — Peter
Mat·tit·**ya**·hu — Matthew
Mir·**yam** — Mary
Na·**tze**·ret — Nazareth
Ru·ach-Ha·Ko·desh — Holy Spirit
Sha·vu·'ot — Feast of Weeks, Pentecost
Sh'ol — Sheol, Hades, hell
Ta·nakh — Hebrew Scriptures, "Old Testament"
To·rah — Teaching, "Law"; Pentateuch
Ye·ru·sha·**la**·yim — Jerusalem
Ye·**shu**·a — Jesus
Y'hu·**dah** — Judas
Yo·cha·**nan** — John
Yo·'**el** — Joel
Yo·**sef** Bar-Sab·ba — Joseph Barsabbas

---

c Joel 3:1-5 (2:28-32)

who was not abandoned in Sh'ol and whose flesh did not see decay. ³²God raised up this Yeshua! And we are all witnesses of it!

³³"Moreover, he has been exalted to **the right hand** of God; has received from the Father what he promised, namely, the *Ruach HaKodesh*; and has poured out this gift, which you are both seeing and hearing. ³⁴For David did not ascend into heaven. But he says,

³⁵ '*Adonai* said to my Lord,
"Sit at my right hand
until I make your enemies a footstool
for your feet."'*ᵉ*

³⁶Therefore, let the whole house of Israel know beyond doubt that God has made him both Lord and Messiah — this Yeshua, whom you executed on a stake!"

³⁷On hearing this, they were stung in their hearts; and they said to Kefa and the other emissaries, "Brothers, what should we do?" ³⁸Kefa answered them, "Turn from sin, return to God, and each of you be immersed on the authority of Yeshua the Messiah into forgiveness of your sins, and you will receive the gift of the *Ruach HaKodesh*! ³⁹For the promise is for you, for your children, and for those far away — as many as *Adonai* our God may call!"

⁴⁰He pressed his case with many other arguments and kept pleading with them, "Save yourselves from this perverse generation!"

⁴¹So those who accepted what he said were immersed, and there were added to the group that day about three thousand people.

⁴²They continued faithfully in the teaching of the emissaries, in fellowship, in breaking bread and in the prayers. ⁴³Everyone was filled with

e Psalm 110:1

awe, and many miracles and signs took place through the emissaries. ⁴⁴All those trusting in Yeshua stayed together and had everything in common; ⁴⁵in fact, they sold their property and possessions and distributed the proceeds to all who were in need. ⁴⁶Continuing faithfully and with singleness of purpose to meet in the Temple courts daily, and breaking bread in their several homes, they shared their food in joy and simplicity of heart, ⁴⁷praising God and having the respect of all the people. And day after day the Lord kept adding to them those who were being saved.

3 ¹One afternoon at three o'clock, the hour of *minchah* prayers, as Kefa and Yochanan were going up to the Temple, ²a man crippled since birth was being carried in. Every day people used to put him at the Beautiful Gate of the Temple, so that he could beg from those going into the Temple court. ³When he saw Kefa and Yochanan about to enter, he asked them for some money. ⁴But they stared straight at him; and Kefa said, "Look at us!"⁵The crippled man fixed his attention on them, expecting to receive something from them. ⁶Kefa said, "I don't have silver, and I don't have gold; but what I do have I give to you: in the name of the Messiah, Yeshua of Natzeret, walk!" ⁷And taking hold of him by his right hand, Kefa pulled him up. Instantly his feet and ankles became strong; ⁸so that he sprang up, stood a moment, and began walking. Then he entered the Temple court with them, walking and leaping and praising God! ⁹Everyone saw him walking and praising God. ¹⁰They recognized him as the same man who had formerly sat begging at the Beautiful Gate of the Temple, and they were utterly amazed and confounded at what had happened to him. ¹¹While he clung to Kefa and Yochanan, all the people came running in astonishment toward them in Shlomo's Colonnade. [12] Seeing this, Kefa addressed the people: "Men of Israel! Why are you amazed at this? Or why do you stare at us as if we had made this man walk through some power or godliness of our own? [13] The **God of Avraham, Yitzchak and Ya'akov, the God of our fathers,**^f has glorified his servant Yeshua — the same Yeshua you handed over and disowned before Pilate, even after he had decided to release him. [14] You denied the holy and innocent one, and instead asked for the reprieve of a murderer! [15] You killed the author of life!

"But God has raised him from the dead! Of this we are witnesses. [16] And it is through putting trust in his name that his name has given strength to this man whom you see and know. Yes, it is the trust that comes through Yeshua which has given him this perfect healing in the presence of you all.

[17] "Now, brothers, I know that you did not understand the significance of what you were doing, neither did your leaders. [18] But this is how God fulfilled what he had announced in advance, when he spoke through all the prophets, namely, that his Messiah was to die. [19] "Therefore, repent and turn to God, so that your sins may be erased; [20] so that times of refreshing may come from the Lord's presence, and he may send the Messiah appointed in advance for you, that is, Yeshua. [21] He has to remain in heaven until the time comes for restoring everything, as God said long ago, when he spoke through the holy prophets. [22] For Moshe himself said, '**Adonai will raise up for you a prophet like me from among your**

___
f Exodus 3:6, 15

brothers. You are to listen to everything he tells you. [23] **Everyone who fails to listen to that prophet will be removed from the people and destroyed.'**^g [24] Indeed, all the prophets announced these days, starting with Shmu'el and continuing through all who followed.

[25] "You are the sons of the prophets; and you are included in the covenant which God made with our fathers when he said to Avraham, '**By your seed will all the families of the earth be blessed.'**^h [26] So it is to you first that God has sent his servant whom he has raised up, so that he might bless you by turning each one of you from your evil ways."

4 [1] Kefa and Yochanan were still speaking to the people when the *cohanim*, the captain in charge of the Temple police, and the *Tz'dukim* came upon them, [2] very annoyed that they were teaching the people the doctrine of resurrection from the dead and offering Yeshua as proof. [3] The Temple police arrested them; and since it was already evening, they put them in custody overnight. [4] However, many of

___
g Deuteronomy 18:15-16
h Genesis 22:18, 26:4

___
A·do·nai — the LORD, Jehovah
Av·ra·ham — Abraham
co·ha·nim — priests
Da·vid — David
Ke·fa — Peter
min·chah — afternoon sacrifice
Mo·she — Moses
Na·tze·ret — Nazareth
Ru·ach-Ha·Ko·desh — Holy Spirit
Shlo·mo — Solomon
Shmu·'el — Samuel
Sh'ol — Sheol, Hades, hell
Tz'du·kim — Sadducees
Ya·'a·kov — Jacob
Ye·shu·a — Jesus
Yitz·chak — Isaac
Yo·cha·nan — John

those who heard the message trusted; the number of men alone was about five thousand.

[5]The next day, the people's rulers, elders and *Torah*-teachers assembled in Yerushalayim, [6]along with Anan the *cohen hagadol,* Kayafa, Yochanan, Alexander and the other men from the family of the *cohen hagadol.* [7]They had the emissaries stand before them and asked, "By what power or in what name did you do this?"

[8]Then Kefa, filled with the *Ruach HaKodesh,* said to them, "Rulers and elders of the people! [9]If we are being examined today about a good deed done for a disabled person, if you want to know how he was restored to health, [10]then let it be known to you and to all the people of Israel that it is in the name of the Messiah, Yeshua from Natzeret, whom you had executed on a stake as a criminal but whom God has raised from the dead, that this man stands before you perfectly healed.

[11]"This Yeshua is the **stone rejected by** you builders which **has become the cornerstone.**[i] [12]There is salvation in no one else! For there is no other name under heaven given to mankind by whom we must be saved!"

[13]When they saw how bold Kefa and Yochanan were, even though they were untrained *'am-ha'aretz,* they were amazed; also they recognized them as having been with Yeshua. [14]Moreover, since they could see the man who had been healed standing right there beside them, there was nothing they could say to discredit the healing. [15]So they told them to step away from the *Sanhedrin* while they discussed the matter privately. [16]"What can we do with these men?" they asked each other. "Why, anyone in Yerushalayim can see that a

remarkable miracle has come about through them — we can't possible deny that. [17]But to prevent it from spreading any further among the people, let's warn them not to speak any more to anyone in this name."

[18]So they called them in again and ordered them under no circumstances to speak or teach in the name of Yeshua. [19]But Kefa and Yochanan answered, "You must judge whether it is right in the sight of God to listen to you rather than God. [20]As for us, we can't help talking about what we have actually seen and heard." [21]They threatened them some more but finally let them go — they couldn't punish them because of the people, for everyone was praising God over what had happened, [22]since the man who had been miraculously healed was more than forty years old.

[23]Upon being released, they went back to their friends and reported what the head *cohanim* and elders had said to them. [24]When they heard it, they raised their voices to God with singleness of heart. "Master," they prayed, "you **made heaven, earth, the sea and everything in them.**[j] [25]By the *Ruach HaKodesh,* through the mouth of our father David, your servant, you said,

> **'Why did the nations rage**
> **and the peoples devise useless**
> **plans?**
> 26 **The kings of the earth took their**
> **stand;**
> **and the rulers assembled together**
> **against** *Adonai*
> **and against his Messiah.'**[k]

[27]This has come true in this city, since Herod and Pontius Pilate, with *Goyim* and the peoples of Israel, all assembled against your holy servant

---

i Psalm 118:22   *j* Psalm 146:6   *k* Psalm 2:1-2

Yeshua, whom you made Messiah, ^{28}to do what your power and plan had already determined beforehand should happen.

^{29}"So now, Lord, take note of their threats; and enable your slaves to speak your message with boldness! ^{30}Stretch out your hand to heal and to do signs and miracles through the name of your holy servant Yeshua!"

^{31}While they were still praying, the place where they were gathered was shaken. They were all filled with the *Ruach HaKodesh,* and they spoke God's message with boldness.

^{32}All the many believers were one in heart and soul, and no one claimed any of his possessions for himself, but everyone shared everything he had. ^{33}With great power the emissaries continued testifying to the resurrection of the Lord Yeshua, and they were all held in high regard. ^{34}No one among them was poor, since those who owned lands or houses sold them and turned over the proceeds ^{35}to the emissaries to distribute to each according to his need. ^{36}Thus Yosef, whom the emissaries called Bar-Nabba (which means "the Exhorter"), a *L'vi* and a native of Cyprus, ^{37}sold a field which belonged to him and brought the money to the emissaries.

5 ^{1}But there was a man named Chananyah who, with his wife Shappirah, sold some property ^{2}and, with his wife's knowledge, witheld some of the proceeds for himself; although he did bring the rest to the emissaries. ^{3}Then Kefa said, "Why has the Adversary so filled your heart that you lie to the *Ruach HaKodesh* and keep back some of the money you received for the land? ^{4}Before you sold it, the property was yours; and after you sold it, the money was yours to use as you pleased. So what made you

decide to do such a thing! You have lied not to human beings but to God!"

^{5}On hearing these words, Chananyah fell down dead; and everyone who heard about it was terrified. ^{6}The young men got up, wrapped his body in a shroud, carried him out and buried him.

^{7}Some three hours later, his wife came in, unaware of what had happened. ^{8}Kefa challenged her: "Tell me, is it true that you sold the land for such-and-such a price?" "Yes," she answered, "that is what we were paid for it." ^{9}But Kefa came back at her, "Then why did you people plot to test the Spirit of the Lord? Listen! The men who buried your husband are at the door. They will carry you out too!" ^{10}Instantly she collapsed at his feet and died. The young men entered, found her there dead, carried her out and buried her beside her husband. ^{11}As a result of this, great fear came over the whole Messianic community, and indeed over everyone who heard about it.

A·do·nai — the LORD, Jehovah
'am·ha·'a·retz — ignorant masses
A·nan — Annas
Bar·Nab·ba — Barnabas
Cha·nan·yah — Ananias
co·ha·nim — priests
co·hen ha·ga·dol — high priest
Da·vid — David
Go·yim — Gentile, nations, pagans
Ka·ya·fa — Caiaphas
Ke·fa — Peter
L'vi — Levi
Na·tze·ret — Nazareth
Ru·ach Ha·Ko·desh — Holy Spirit
San·hed·rin — Jewish religious court
Shap·pi·rah — Sapphira
To·rah-teachers — scribes
Ye·ru·sha·la·yim — Jerusalem
Ye·shu·a — Jesus
Yo·cha·nan — John
Yo·sef — Joseph

[12] Meanwhile, through the emissaries many signs and miracles continued to be done among the people. United in mind and purpose, the believers met in Shlomo's Colonnade; [13] and no one else dared to join them. Nevertheless, the people continued to regard them highly; [14] and throngs of believers were added to the Lord, both men and women. [15] They went so far as to bring the sick into the streets and lay them on mattresses and stretchers, so that at least Kefa's shadow might fall on them as he passed by. [16] Crowds also gathered from the towns around Yerushalayim, bringing the sick and those afflicted with unclean spirits; and every one of them was healed.

[17] But the *cohen hagadol* and his associates, who were members of the party of the *Tz'dukim*, were filled with jealousy. [18] They arrested the emissaries and put them in the public jail. [19] But during the night, an angel of *Adonai* opened the doors of the prison, led them out and said, [20] "Go, stand in the Temple court and keep telling the people all about this new life!" [21] After hearing that, they entered the Temple area about dawn and began to teach.

Now the *cohen hagadol* and his associates came and called a meeting of the *Sanhedrin* (that is, of Israel's whole assembly of elders) and sent to the jail to have them brought. [22] But the officers who went did not find them in the prison. So they returned and reported, [23] "We found the jail securely locked and the guards standing at the doors; but when we opened it, we found no one inside!" [24] When the captain of the Temple police and the head *cohanim* heard these things, they were puzzled and wondered what would happen next.

[25] Then someone came and reported to them, "Listen! The men you ordered put in prison are standing in the Temple court, teaching the people!" [26] The captain and his officers went and brought them, but not with force; because they were afraid of being stoned by the people. [27] They conducted them to the *Sanhedrin*, where the *cohen hagadol* demanded of them, [28] "We gave you strict orders not to teach in this name! Look here! You have filled Yerushalayim with your teaching; moreover, you are determined to make us responsible for this man's death!"

[29] Kefa and the other emissaries answered, "We must obey God, not men. [30] **The God of our fathers**[l] raised up Yeshua, whereas you men killed him by having him **hanged on a stake.**[m] [31] God has exalted this man **at his right hand**[n] as Ruler and Savior, in order to enable Israel to do *t'shuvah* and have her sins forgiven. [32] We are witnesses to these things; so is the *Ruach HaKodesh*, whom God has given to those who obey him."

[33] On hearing this, the members of the *Sanhedrin* were infuriated and wanted to put the emissaries to death. [34] But one of the members of the *Sanhedrin* rose to his feet, a *Parush* named Gamli'el, a teacher of the *Torah* highly respected by all the people. He ordered the men put outside for a little while [35] and then addressed the court: "Men of Israel, take care what you do to these people. [36] Some time ago, there was a rebellion under Todah, who claimed to be somebody special; and a number of men, maybe four hundred, rallied behind him. But upon his being put to death, his whole following was broken up and came to nothing. [37] After this, Y'hudah HaG'lili led another uprising, back at the time of the enroll-

l Exodus 3:15   *m* Deuteronomy 21:22-23
n Psalm 110:1

ment for the Roman tax; and he got some people to defect to him. But he was killed, and all his followers were scattered. ³⁸So in the present case, my advice to you is not to interfere with these people, but to leave them alone. For if this idea or this movement has a human origin, it will collapse. ³⁹But if it is from God, you will not be able to stop them; you might even find yourselves fighting God!"

They heeded his advice. ⁴⁰After summoning the emissaries and flogging them, they commanded them not to speak in the name of Yeshua, and let them go. ⁴¹The emissaries left the *Sanhedrin* overjoyed at having been considered worthy of suffering disgrace on account of him. ⁴²And not for a single day, either in the Temple court or in private homes, did they stop teaching and proclaiming the Good News that Yeshua is the Messiah.

6 ¹Around this time, when the number of *talmidim* was growing, the Greek-speaking Jews began complaining against those who spoke Hebrew that their widows were being overlooked in the daily distribution. ²So the Twelve called a general meeting of the *talmidim* and said, "It isn't appropriate that we should neglect the Word of God in order to serve tables. ³Brothers, choose seven men from among yourselves who are known to be full of the Spirit and wisdom. We will appoint them to be in charge of this important matter, ⁴but we ourselves will give our full attention to praying and to serving the Word."

⁵What they said was agreeable to the whole gathering. They chose Stephen, a man full of faith and the *Ruach HaKodesh*, Philip, Prochoros, Nikanor, Timon, Parmenas and Nicholas, who was a proselyte from Antioch. ⁶They presented these men to the emissaries, who prayed and laid their hands on them.

⁷So the word of God continued to spread. The number of *talmidim* in Yerushalayim increased rapidly, and a large crowd of *cohanim* were becoming obedient to the faith.

⁸Now Stephen, full of grace and power, performed great miracles and signs among the people. ⁹But opposition arose from members of the Synagogue of the Freed Slaves (as it was called), composed of Cyrenians, Alexandrians and people from Cilicia and the province of Asia. They argued with Stephen, ¹⁰but they could not stand up against his wisdom or the Spirit by which he spoke.

¹¹So they secretly persuaded some men to allege, "We heard him speak blasphemously against Moshe and against God." ¹²They stirred up the people, as well as the elders and the *Torah*-teachers; so they came and arrested him and led him before the *Sanhedrin*. ¹³There they set up false witnesses who said, "This man never stops speaking against this holy place and against the *Torah*; ¹⁴for we have

---

A·do·*nai* — the LORD, Jehovah
co·ha·*nim* — priests
co·*hen* ha·ga·*dol* — high priest
Gam·li·'el — Gamaliel
Ke·**fa** — Peter
Mo·**she** — Moses
Pa·rush — Pharisee
Ru·ach-Ha·Ko·desh — Holy Spirit
San·hed·rin — Jewish religious court
Shlo·mo — Solomon
tal·mi·dim — disciples
To·**dah** — Theudas
To·rah — Teaching, "Law"; Pentateuch
do t'shu·**vah** — repent, turn from sin to God
Tz'du·kim — Sadducees
Ye·ru·sha·la·yim — Jerusalem
Ye·**shu**·a — Jesus
Y'hu·**dah** Ha·G'li·**li** — Judas the Galilean

heard him say that Yeshua from
Natzeret will destroy this place and will
change the customs Moshe handed
down to us."

15 Everyone sitting in the *Sanhedrin*
stared at Stephen and saw that his face
looked like the face of an angel.

7 1 The *cohen hagadol* asked, "Are
these accusations true?" 2 and
Stephen said:

"Brothers and fathers, listen to me!
The God of glory appeared to *Avraham avinu* in Mesopotamia before he
lived in Charan 3 **and said to him,
'Leave your land and your family, and
go into the land that I will show you.'**[o]
4 So he left the land of the Chaldeans
and lived in Charan. After his father
died, God made him move to this land
where you are living now. 5 He gave him
no inheritance in it, **not even space for
one foot;**[p] yet he promised to **give it to
him as a possession and to his descendants after him,**[q] even though at the
time he was childless. 6 What God said
to him was, **'Your descendants will be
aliens in a foreign land, where they will
be in slavery and oppressed for four
hundred years.** 7 But I will judge the
nation that enslaves them,' God said,
**'and afterwards they will leave and
worship me in this place.'**[r] 8 And he
gave him *b'rit-milah.* So he became the
father of Yitzchak and did his *b'rit-
milah* on the eighth day, and Yitzchak
became the father of Ya'akov, and
Ya'akov became the father of the
Twelve Patriarchs.

9 "Now the Patriarchs **grew jealous of
Yosef and sold him** into slavery **in
Egypt.** But *Adonai* was with him;[s] 10 he
rescued him from all his troubles and
**gave him favor and wisdom before
Pharaoh, king of Egypt, who appointed
him chief administrator over Egypt
and over all his household.** [t] 11 Now
there came a famine that caused much
suffering **throughout Egypt and
Cana'an**[u] 12 But when Ya'akov heard
that there was grain in Egypt, he sent
our fathers there the first time. 13 The
second time, Yosef **revealed his identity
to his brothers,**[v] and Yosef's family
became known to Pharaoh. 14 Yosef
then sent for his father Ya'akov and all
his relatives, 75 people. 15 And Ya'akov
went down to Egypt; there he died, as
did our other ancestors. 16 Their bodies
were removed to Sh'khem and buried
in the tomb Avraham had bought from
the family of Chamor in Sh'khem for a
certain sum of money.

17 "As the time drew near for the
fulfillment of the promise God had
made to Avraham, the number of our
people in Egypt **increased greatly,**
18 until **there arose another king over
Egypt who had no knowledge of
Yosef.**[w] 19 With cruel cunning this man
forced our fathers to put their newborn
babies outside their homes, so that they
would not survive.

20 "It was then that Moshe was born,
and he was beautiful in God's sight.
For three months he was reared in his
father's house; 21 and when he was put
out of his home, Pharaoh's daughter
took him and brought him up as her
own son. 22 So Moshe was trained in all
the wisdom of the Egyptians and
became both a powerful speaker and a
man of action.

23 "But when he was forty years old,
the thought came to him to visit his
brother Israelites. 24 On seeing one of
them being mistreated, he went to his

o Genesis 12:1 *p* Deuteronomy 2:5
q Genesis 12:7; 13:15; 15:4, 7, 18-21; 17:8; 24:7; 48:4 *r* Genesis 15:13-14, 16
s Genesis 37:11, 28; 39:1-3, 21, 23

t Genesis 41:37-44 *u* Genesis 41:54, 42:5
v Genesis 45:1 *w* Exodus 1:7-8

defense and took revenge by striking down the Egyptian. ²⁵ He supposed his brothers would understand that God was using him to rescue them, but they didn't understand. ²⁶ When he appeared the next day, as they were fighting, and tried to make peace between them by saying, 'Men, you are brothers! Why do you want to hurt each other?' ²⁷ the one who was mistreating his fellow pushed Moshe away and said, '**Who made you a ruler and judge over us?** ²⁸ **Do you want to kill me, the way you killed that Egyptian yesterday?'**^x ²⁹ On hearing this, Moshe fled the country and became an exile in the land of Midyan, where he had two sons.

³⁰ "After forty more years, an angel **appeared to him in the desert** near Mount Sinai **in the flames of a burning thorn bush.**^y ³¹ When Moshe saw this, he was amazed at the sight; and as he approached to get a better look, there came the voice of *Adonai*, ³²'**I am the God of your fathers, the God of Avraham, Yitzchak and Ya'akov.'** But Moshe trembled with fear and didn't dare to look. ³³ *Adonai* said to him, 'Take off your sandals, because the place where you are standing is holy ground. ³⁴ I have clearly seen how my people are being oppressed in Egypt, I have heard their cry, and I have come down to rescue them; and now I will send you to Egypt.'^z

³⁵ "This Moshe, whom they rejected, saying, '**Who made you a ruler and judge?'** is the very one whom God sent as both ruler and ransomer by means of the angel that appeared to him in the thorn bush. ³⁶ This man led them out, performing miracles and signs in Egypt, at the Red Sea and in the wilderness for forty years. ³⁷ This is the Moshe who

said to the people of Israel, '**God will raise up a prophet like me from among your brothers'**^a ³⁸ This is the man who was in the assembly in the wilderness, accompanied by the angel that had spoken to him at Mount Sinai and by our fathers, the man who was given living words to pass on to us.

³⁹ "But our fathers did not want to obey him. On the contrary, they rejected him and in their hearts turned to Egypt, ⁴⁰ saying to Aharon, '**Make us some gods to lead us; because this Moshe, who led us out of Egypt — we don't know what has become of him.'**^b ⁴¹ That was when they made an idol in the shape of a calf and offered a sacrifice to it and held a celebration in honor of what they had made with their own hands. ⁴² So God turned away from them and gave them over to worship the stars — as has been written in the book of the prophets,

---

^a Deuteronomy 18:15 ^b Exodus 32:1, 23

A·do·nai — the LORD, Jehovah
Ah·a·ron — Aaron
Av·ra·ham — Abraham
Av·ra·ham a·vi·nu — our father Abraham
b'rit-mi·lah — covenant of circumcision, circumcision ceremony
Ca·na·'an — Canaan
Cha·mor — Hamor, Emmor
Cha·ran — Haran, Charran
co·hen ha·ga·dol — high priest
Mid·yan — Midian, Madian
Mo·she — Moses
Na·tze·ret — Nazareth
San·hed·rin — Jewish religious court
Sh'khem — Shechem, Sychem
Si·nai — Sinai
To·rah — Teaching, "Law"; Pentateuch
To·rah-teachers — scribes
Ya·'a·kov — Jacob
Ye·shu·a — Jesus
Yitz·chak — Isaac
Yo·sef — Joseph

---

^x Exodus 2:14 ^y Exodus 3:1-2
^z Exodus 3:6-10

'People of Israel, it was not to me
that you offered slaughtered animals
and sacrifices for forty years in the
wilderness!
⁴³ No, you carried the tent of Molekh
and the star of your god Reifan,
the idols you made so that you
could worship them.
Therefore, I will send you into
exile beyond Babylon.'ᶜ

⁴⁴"Our fathers had the Tent of Witness in the wilderness. It had been
made just as God, who spoke to Moshe,
had ordered it made, according to the
pattern Moshe had seen. ⁴⁵Later on,
our fathers who had received it brought
it in with Y'hoshua when they took the
Land away from the nations that God
drove out before them.

"So it was until the days of David.
⁴⁶He enjoyed God's favor and asked if
he might provide a dwelling place for
the God of Ya'akov; ⁴⁷and Shlomo did
build him a house. ⁴⁸But HaElyon does
not live in places made by hand! As the
prophet says,

⁴⁹ '"Heaven is my throne," says
Adonai,
"and the earth is my footstool.
What kind of house could you
build for me?
What kind of place could you
devise for my rest?
⁵⁰ Didn't I myself make all these
things?"'ᵈ

⁵⁰"Stiffnecked people,ᵉ with
uncircumcised hearts and ears!ᶠ You
continually oppose the Ruach Ha-
Kodesh!ᵍ You do the same things your
fathers did! ⁵²Which of the prophets
did your fathers not persecute? They
killed those who told in advance about
the coming of the Tzaddik, and now
you have become his betrayers and
murderers! — ⁵³you!— who receive the
Torah as having been delivered by
angels — but do not keep it!"

⁵⁴On hearing these things, they were
cut to their hearts and ground their
teeth at him. ⁵⁵But he, full of the Ruach
HaKodesh, looked up to heaven and saw
God's Sh'khinah, with Yeshua standing
at the right hand of God.ʰ ⁵⁶"Look!" he
exclaimed, "I see heaven opened and the
Son of Man standing at the right hand
of God!"ʰ

⁵⁷At this, they began yelling at the
top of their voices, so that they wouldn't
have to hear him; and with one accord,
they rushed at him, ⁵⁸threw him outside
the city and began stoning him. And
the witnesses laid down their coats at
the feet of a young man named Sha'ul.

⁵⁹As they were stoning him, Stephen
called out to God, "Lord Yeshua!
Receive my spirit!" ⁶⁰Then he kneeled
down and shouted out, "Lord! Don't
hold this sin against them!" With that,
8 he died; ¹and Sha'ul gave his
approval to his murder.

Starting with that day, there arose
intense persecution against the Messianic community in Yerushalayim; all
but the emissaries were scattered
throughout the regions of Y'hudah and
Shomron. ²Some godly men buried
Stephen and mourned him deeply. ³But
Sha'ul set out to destroy the Messianic
community — entering house after
house, he dragged off both men and
women and handed them over to be
put in prison. ⁴However, those who
were scattered announced the Good
News of the Word wherever they went.

---

c   Amos 5:25-27
d   Isaiah 66:1-2   e   Exodus 32:9; 33:3,5
f   Leviticus 26:41; Jeremiah 6:10, 9:25(26)
g   Isaiah 63:10

h   Psalm 110:1

[5]Now Philip went down to a city in Shomron and was proclaiming the Messiah to them; [6]and the crowds were paying close attention to what Philip said, as they heard and saw the miraculous signs he was doing. [7]For many people were having unclean spirits driven out of them, shrieking; also many paralytics and crippled persons were being healed; [8]so that there was great joy in that city.

[9]But there was a man named Shim'on in the city who for some time had been practicing magic and astonishing the nation of Shomron, claiming to be somebody great. [10]Everyone gave heed to him, from the lowest to the highest, saying, "This man is the power of God called 'The Great Power'." [11]They followed him because for a considerable time he had amazed them with his magic.

[12]But when they came to believe Philip, as he announced the Good News concerning the Kingdom of God and the name of Yeshua the Messiah, they were immersed, both men and women. [13]Moreover, Shim'on himself came to believe; and after being immersed, he attached himself closely to Philip; and he was amazed as he saw the miraculous signs and great works of power that kept taking place.

[14]When the emissaries in Yerushalayim heard that Shomron had received the Word of God, they sent them Kefa and Yochanan, [15]who came down and prayed for them, that they might receive the Ruach HaKodesh. [16]For until then he had not come upon any of them; they had only been immersed into the name of the Lord Yeshua. [17]Then, as Kefa and Yochanan placed their hands on them, they received the Ruach HaKodesh.

[18]Shim'on saw that the Spirit was given when the emissaries placed their hands on them, and he offered them money [19]"Give this power to me, too," he said, "so that whoever I place my hands on will receive the Ruach HaKodesh." [20]But Kefa said to him, "Your silver go to ruin! — and you with it, for thinking the free gift of God can be bought! [21]You have no part at all in this matter; because in the eyes of God, your heart is crooked. [22]So repent of this wickedness of yours, and pray to the Lord. Perhaps you will yet be forgiven for holding such a thought in your heart. [23]For I see that you are extremely bitter and completely under the control of sin!" [24]Shim'on answered, "Pray to the Lord for me, so that none of the things you have spoken about will happen to me."

[25]Then, after giving a thorough witness and speaking the Word of the Lord, Kefa and Yochanan started back to Yerushalayim, announcing the Good News to many villages in Shomron.

[26]An angel of Adonai said to Philip, "Get up, and go southward on the road that goes down from Yerushalayim to

---

A·do·nai — the LORD, Jehovah
Da·**vid** — David
Ha·El·yon — the Most High, i.e., God
Ke·**fa** — Peter
Mo·lekh — Moloch
Rei·**fan** — Rephan, Remphan
Ru·ach Ha·Ko·desh — Holy Spirit
Sha·**'ul** — Saul (Paul)
Shim·**'on** — Simon
Shlo·**mo** — Solomon
Shom·**ron** — Samaria
*Sh'khi·**nah*** — God's manifest glory
*To·**rah*** — Teaching, "Law"; Pentateuch
the *Tzad·**dik*** — the Righteous One
Ya·'a·**kov** — Jacob
Ye·ru·sha·**la·**yim — Jerusalem
Ye·**shu·**a — Jesus
Y'ho·**shu·**a — Joshua, Jesus
Y'hu·**dah** — Judea
Yo·cha·**nan** — John

'Aza, the desert road.'" ²⁷ So he got up and went. On his way, he caught sight of an Ethiopian, a eunuch who was minister in charge of all the treasure of the Kandake, or queen, of Ethiopia. He had been to Yerushalayim to worship; ²⁸ and now, as he was returning home, he was sitting in his chariot, reading the prophet Yesha'yahu. ²⁹ The Spirit said to Philip, "Go over to this chariot, and stay close to it." ³⁰ As Philip ran up, he heard the Ethiopian reading from Yesha'yahu the prophet. "Do you understand what you're reading?" he asked. ³¹ "How can I," he said, "unless someone explains it to me?" And he invited Philip to climb up and sit with him.

³² Now the portion of the *Tanakh* that he was reading was this:

'He was like a sheep led to be slaughtered;

like a lamb silent before the shearer, he does not open his mouth.

³³ **He was humiliated and denied justice.**

Who will tell about his descendants, since his life has been taken from the earth?' *ⁱ*

³⁴ The eunuch said to Philip, "Here's my question to you — is the prophet talking about himself or someone else?" ³⁵ Then Philip started to speak — beginning with that passage, he went on to tell him the Good News about Yeshua.

³⁶ As they were going down the road, they came to some water; and the eunuch said, "Look! Here's some water! Is there any reason why I shouldn't be immersed?" ³⁷ * ³⁸ He

* Some manuscripts include verse 37: And Philip said, "If you believe with all your heart, you may." He answered, "I believe that Yeshua the Messiah is the Son of God."

ⁱ Isaiah 53:7-8

ordered the chariot to stop; then both Philip and the eunuch went down into the water, and Philip immersed him. ³⁹ When they came up out of the water, the Spirit of the Lord snatched Philip away. The eunuch saw no more of him, because he continued on his way — full of joy. ⁴⁰ But Philip showed up at Ashdod and continued proclaiming the Good News as he went through all the towns until he came to Caesarea.

9 ¹ Meanwhile, Sha'ul, still breathing murderous threats against the Lord's *talmidim*, went to the *cohen hagadol* ² and asked him for letters to the synagogues in Dammesek, authorizing him to arrest any people he might find, whether men or women, who belonged to "the Way", and bring them back to Yerushalayim.

³ He was on the road and nearing Dammesek, when suddenly a light from heaven flashed all around him. ⁴ Falling to the ground, he heard a voice saying to him, "Sha'ul! Sha'ul! Why do you keep persecuting me?" ⁵ "Sir, who are you?" he asked. "I am Yeshua, and you are persecuting me. ⁶ But get up, and go into the city, and you will be told what you have to do."

⁷ The men traveling with him stood speechless, hearing the voice but seeing no one. ⁸ They helped Sha'ul get up off the ground; but when he opened his eyes, he could see nothing. So, leading him by the hand, they brought him into Dammesek. ⁹ For three days he remained unable to see, and he neither ate nor drank.

¹⁰ There was a *talmid* in Dammesek, Chananyah by name; and in a vision the Lord said to him, "Chananyah!" He said, "Here I am, Lord." ¹¹ The Lord said to him, "Get up and go to Straight Street, to Y'hudah's house; and ask for a man from Tarsus named Sha'ul; for he is praying, ¹² and in a vision he has

seen a man named Chananyah coming in and placing his hands on him to restore his sight." [13]But Chananyah answered, "Lord, many have told me about this man, how much harm he has done to your people in Yerushalayim; [14]and here he has a warrant from the head *cohanim* to arrest everyone who calls on your name." [15]But the Lord said to him, "Go, because this man is my chosen instrument to carry my name to the *Goyim*, even to their kings, and to the sons of Israel as well. [16]For I myself will show him how much he will have to suffer on account of my name."

[17]So Chananyah left and went into the house. Placing his hands on him, he said, "Brother Sha'ul, the Lord — Yeshua, the one who appeared to you on the road as you were coming here — has sent me so that you may see again and be filled with the *Ruach HaKodesh*." [18]In that moment, something like scales fell away from Sha'ul's eyes; and he could see again. He got up and was immersed; [19]then he ate some food and regained his strength.

Sha'ul spent some days with the *talmidim* in Dammesek, [20]and immediately he began proclaiming in the synagogues that Yeshua is the Son of God. [21]All who heard him were amazed. They asked, "Isn't he the man who in Yerushalayim was trying to destroy the people who call on this name? In fact, isn't that why he came here, to arrest them and bring them back to the head *cohanim*?" [22]But Sha'ul was being filled with more and more power and was creating an uproar among the Jews living in Dammesek with his proofs that Yeshua is the Messiah.

[23]Quite some time later, the non-believing Jews gathered together and made plans to kill him; [24]but their plot became known to Sha'ul. They were watching the gates day and night in order to do away with him; [25]but under cover of night, his *talmidim* took him and let him down over the city wall, lowering him in a large basket.

[26]On reaching Yerushalayim, he tried to join the *talmidim*; but they were all afraid of him — they didn't believe he was a *talmid*. [27]However, Bar-Nabba got hold of him and took him to the emissaries. He told them how Sha'ul had seen the Lord while traveling, that the Lord had spoken to him, and how in Dammesek Sha'ul had spoken out boldly in the name of Yeshua. [28]So he remained with them and went all over Yerushalayim continuing to speak out boldly in the name of the Lord. [29]He talked and debated with the Greek-speaking Jews, but they began making attempts to kill him. [30]When the brothers learned of it, they brought him down to Caesarea and sent him away to Tarsus.

[31]Then the Messianic community throughout Y'hudah, the Galil and Shomron enjoyed peace and was built

---

A·do·nai — the LORD, Jehovah
Ash·dod — Azotus
'A·za — Gaza
Bar-Nab·ba — Barnabas
Cha·nan·yah — Ananias
co·ha·nim — priests
co·hen ha·ga·dol — high priest
Dam·me·sek — Damascus
the Ga·lil — Galilee
Go·yim — Gentiles, nations, pagans
Ke·fa — Peter
Ru·ach-Ha·Ko·desh — Holy Spirit
Sha·'ul — Saul (Paul)
Shom·ron — Samaria
tal·mid (pl. *tal·mi·dim*) — disciple
Ta·nakh — Hebrew Scriptures, "Old Testament"
Ye·ru·sha·la·yim — Jerusalem
Ye·sha'·ya·hu — Isaiah
Ye·shu·a — Jesus
Y'hu·dah — Judas, Judea

up. They lived in the fear of the Lord, with the counsel of the *Ruach Ha-Kodesh*; and their numbers kept multiplying.

³²As Kefa traveled around the countryside, he came down to the believers in Lud. ³³There he found a man named Aeneas who had lain bedridden for eight years, because he was paralyzed. ³⁴Kefa said to him, "Aeneas! Yeshua the Messiah is healing you! Get up, and make your bed!" ³⁵Everyone living in Lud and the Sharon saw him, and they turned to the Lord.

Now in Yafo there was a *talmidah* named Tavita ³⁶(which means "gazelle"); she was always doing *tzedakah* and other good deeds. ³⁷It happened that just at that time, she took sick and died. After washing her, they laid her in a room upstairs. ³⁸Lud is near Yafo, and the *talmidim* had heard that Kefa was there, so they sent two men to him and urged him, "Please come to us without delay." ³⁹Kefa got up and went with them.

When he arrived, they led him into the upstairs room. All the widows stood by him, sobbing and showing all the dresses and coats Tavita had made them while she was still with them. ⁴⁰But Kefa put them all outside, kneeled down and prayed. Then turning to the body, he said, "Tavita! Get up!" She opened her eyes; and on seeing Kefa, she sat up. ⁴¹He offered her his hand and helped her to her feet; then, calling the believers and the widows, he presented her to them alive. ⁴²This became known all over Yafo, and many people put their trust in the Lord. ⁴³Kefa stayed on in Yafo for some time with a man named Shim'on, a leather-tanner.

10 ¹There was a man in Caesarea named Cornelius, a Roman army officer in what was called the Italian Regiment. ²He was a devout man, a "God-fearer", as was his whole household; he gave generously to help the Jewish poor and prayed regularly to God. ³One afternoon around three o'clock he saw clearly in a vision an angel of God coming in and saying to him, "Cornelius!" ⁴Cornelius stared at the angel, terrified. "What is it, sir?" he asked. "Your prayers," replied the angel, "and your acts of charity have gone up into God's presence, so that he has you on his mind. ⁵Now send some men to Yafo to bring back a man named Shim'on, also called Kefa. ⁶He's staying with Shim'on the leather-tanner, who has a house by the sea." ⁷As the angel that had spoken to him went away, Cornelius called two of his household slaves and one of his military aides, who was a godly man; ⁸he explained everything to them and sent them to Yafo.

⁹The next day about noon, while they were still on their way and approaching the city, Kefa went up onto the roof of the house to pray. ¹⁰He began to feel hungry and wanted something to eat; but while they were preparing the meal, he fell into a trance ¹¹in which he saw heaven opened, and something that looked like a large sheet being lowered to the ground by its four corners. ¹²In it were all kinds of four-footed animals, crawling creatures and wild birds. ¹³Then a voice came to him, "Get up, Kefa, slaughter and eat!" ¹⁴But Kefa said, "No, sir! Absolutely not! I have never eaten food that was unclean or *treif*." ¹⁵The voice spoke to him a second time: "Stop treating as unclean what God has made clean." ¹⁶This happened three times, and then the sheet was immediately taken back up into heaven.

¹⁷Kefa was still puzzling over the meaning of the vision he had seen, when the men Cornelius had sent,

having inquired for Shim'on's house, stood at the gate [18]and called out to ask if the Shim'on known as Kefa was staying there. [19]While Kefa's mind was still on the vision, the Spirit said, "Three men are looking for you. [20]Get up, go downstairs, and have no misgivings about going with them, because I myself have sent them."

[21]So Kefa went down and said to the men, "You were looking for me? Here I am. What brings you here?" [22]They answered, "Cornelius. He's a Roman army officer, an upright man and a 'God-fearer', a man highly regarded by the whole Jewish nation; and he was told by a holy angel to have you come to his house and listen to what you have to say." [23]So Kefa invited them to be his guests.

The next day, he got up and went with them, accompanied by some of the brothers from Yafo; [24]and he arrived at Caesarea the day after that. Cornelius was expecting them — he had already called together his relatives and close friends. [25]As Kefa entered the house, Cornelius met him and fell prostrate at his feet. [26]But Kefa pulled him to his feet and said, "Stand up! I myself am just a man."

[27]As he talked with him, Kefa went inside and found many people gathered. [28]He said to them, "You are well aware that for a man who is a Jew to have close association with someone who belongs to another people, or to come and visit him, is something that just isn't done. But God has shown me not to call any person common or unclean; [29]so when I was summoned, I came without raising any questions. Tell me, then, why did you send for me?"

[30]Cornelius answered, "Three days ago around this time, I was at *minchah* prayers in my house, when suddenly a man in shining clothes stood in front of me [31]and said, 'God has heard your prayer and remembered your acts of charity. [32]Now send to Yafo and ask for Shim'on, known as Kefa; he is staying in the house of Shim'on, a leather-tanner, by the sea.' [33]So I sent for you immediately, and you have been kind enough to come. Now all of us are here in the presence of God to hear everything the Lord has ordered you to say."

[34]Then Kefa addressed them: "I now understand that God does not play favorites, [35]but that whoever fears him and does what is right is acceptable to him, no matter what people he belongs to.

[36]"Here is the message that he sent to the sons of Israel announcing *shalom* through Yeshua the Messiah, who is Lord of everything. [37]You know what has been going on throughout Y'hudah, starting from the Galil after the immersion that Yochanan proclaimed; [38]how God anointed Yeshua from Natzeret with the *Ruach HaKodesh* and with power; how Yeshua went about doing good and healing all the people

---

the Ga·**lil** — Galilee
Ke·**fa** — Peter
Lud — Lydda
min·chah — afternoon Temple sacrifice
Na·tze·ret — Nazareth
Rei·**fan** — Rephan, Remphan
Ru·ach Ha·Ko·desh — Holy Spirit
sha·lom — peace
the Sha·**ron** — Sharon (coastal plain)
Shim·**'on** — Simon
Shom·**ron** — Samaria
tal·mi·dah — female disciple
tal·mi·dim — disciples
Ta·vi·ta — Tabitha, Dorcas
treif — torn, not *kosher* (i.e., not permitted by the Jewish dietary laws)
tze·da·kah — righteousness, charity
Ya·**fo** — Jaffa, Joppa
Ye·ru·sha·**la**·yim — Jerusalem
Ye·**shu**·a — Jesus
Y'hu·**dah** — Judea
Yo·cha·**nan** — John

oppressed by the Adversary, because God was with him.

³⁹ "As for us, we are witnesses of everything he did, both in the Judean countryside and in Yerushalayim. They did away with him by **hanging him on a stake;**ʲ ⁴⁰ but God raised him up on the third day and let him be seen, ⁴¹ not by all the people, but by witnesses God had previously chosen, that is, by us, who ate and drank with him after he had risen again from the dead.

⁴² "Then he commanded us to proclaim and attest to the Jewish people that this man has been appointed by God to judge the living and the dead. ⁴³ All the prophets bear witness to him, that everyone who puts his trust in him receives forgiveness of sins through his name."

⁴⁴ Kefa was still saying these things when the *Ruach HaKodesh* fell on all who were hearing the message. ⁴⁵ All the believers from the Circumcision faction who had accompanied Kefa were amazed that the gift of the *Ruach HaKodesh* was also being poured out on the *Goyim*, ⁴⁶ for they heard them speaking in tongues and praising God. Kefa's response was, ⁴⁷ "Is anyone prepared to prohibit these people from being immersed in water? After all, they have received the *Ruach HaKodesh*, just as we did." ⁴⁸ And he ordered that they be immersed in the name of Yeshua the Messiah. Then they asked Kefa to stay on with them for a few days.

11 ¹ The emissaries and the brothers throughout Y'hudah heard that the *Goyim* had received the word of God; ² but when Kefa went up to Yerushalayim, the members of the Circumcision faction criticized him, ³ saying, "You went into the homes of uncir-

---

ʲ Deuteronomy 21:23

cumcised men and even ate with them!"

⁴ In reply, Kefa began explaining in detail what had actually happened: ⁵ "I was in the city of Yafo, praying; and in a trance I had a vision. I saw something like a large sheet being lowered by its four corners from heaven, and it came down to me. ⁶ I looked inside and saw four-footed animals, beasts of prey, crawling creatures and wild birds. ⁷ Then I heard a voice telling me, 'Get up, Kefa, slaughter and eat!' ⁸ I said, 'No, sir! Absolutely not! Nothing unclean or *treif* has ever entered my mouth!' ⁹ But the voice spoke again from heaven: 'Stop treating as unclean what God has made clean.' ¹⁰ This happened three times, and then everything was pulled back up into heaven.

¹¹ "At that very moment, three men who had been sent to me from Caesarea arrived at the house where I was staying; ¹² and the Spirit told me to have no misgivings about going back with them. These six brothers also came with me, and we went into the man's house. ¹³ He told us how he had seen the angel standing in his house and saying, 'Send to Yafo and bring back Shim'on, known as Kefa. ¹⁴ He has a message for you which will enable you and your whole household to be saved.'

¹⁵ "But I had hardly begun speaking when the *Ruach HaKodesh* fell on them, just as on us at the beginning! ¹⁶ And I remembered that the Lord had said, 'Yochanan used to immerse people in water, but you will be immersed in the *Ruach HaKodesh*.' ¹⁷ Therefore, if God gave them the same gift as he gave us after we had come to put our trust in the Lord Yeshua the Messiah, who was I to stand in God's way?"

¹⁸ On hearing these things, they stopped objecting and began to praise God, saying, "This means that God has

enabled the *Goyim* as well to do *t'shuvah* and have life!"

[19] Now those who had been scattered because of the persecution which had arisen over Stephen went as far as Phoenicia, Cyprus and Antioch; they spoke God's word, but only to Jews. [20] However, some of these, men from Cyprus and Cyrene, when they arrived at Antioch, began speaking to the Greeks too, proclaiming the Good News of the Lord Yeshua. [21] The hand of the Lord was with them, and a great number of people trusted and turned to the Lord.

[22] News of this reached the ears of the Messianic community in Yerushalayim, and they sent Bar-Nabba to Antioch. [23] On arriving and seeing for himself the grace of God at work, he was glad; and he encouraged them all to remain true to the Lord with their whole hearts; [24] for he was a good man, full of the *Ruach HaKodesh* and trust.

[25] Then Bar-Nabba went off to Tarsus to look for Sha'ul; [26] and when he found him, he brought him to Antioch. They met with the congregation there for a whole year and taught a sizeable crowd. Also it was in Antioch that the *talmidim* for the first time were called "Messianic".

[27] During this time, some prophets came down from Yerushalayim to Antioch; [28] and one of them named Agav stood up and through the Spirit predicted that there was going to be a severe famine throughout the Roman Empire. (It took place while Claudius was Emperor.) [29] So the *talmidim* decided to provide relief to the brothers living in Y'hudah, each according to his means; [30] and they did it, sending their contribution to the elders in the care of Bar-Nabba and Sha'ul.

12 [1] It was around this time that King Herod began arresting and persecuting certain members of the Messianic community; [2] and he had Ya'akov, Yochanan's brother, put to death by the sword. [3] When Herod saw how much this pleased the Judeans, he went on to arrest Kefa as well. It was during the Days of *Matzah*, [4] so when Herod seized him, he threw him in prison, handing him over to be guarded by four squads of four soldiers each, with the intention of bringing him to public trial after *Pesach*. [5] So Kefa was being held under watch in prison, but intense prayer was being made to God on his behalf by the Messianic community.

[6] The night before Herod was going to bring him to trial, Kefa was sleeping between two soldiers. He was bound with two chains; and guards were at the door, keeping watch over the prison. [7] Suddenly an angel of *Adonai* stood there, and a light shone in the cell. He tapped Kefa's side and woke him. "Hurry! Get up!" he said; and the chains fell off his hands. [8] The angel said to him, "Put on your clothes and

---

A·do·nai — the LORD, Jehovah
A·gav — Agabus
Bar-Nab·ba — Barnabas
the Ga·lil — Galilee
Go·yim — Gentiles, nations, pagans
Ke·fa — Peter
ma·tzah — unleavened bread
Na·tze·ret — Nazareth
Pe·sach — Passover
Ru·ach-Ha·Ko·desh — Holy Spirit
Sha·'ul — Saul (Paul)
Shim·'on — Simon
tal·mi·dim — disciples
treif — torn, not *kosher* (i.e., not permitted by the Jewish dietary laws)
do t'shu·vah — repent, turn from sin to God
Ya·'a·kov — James
Ya·fo — Jaffa, Joppa
Ye·ru·sha·la·yim — Jerusalem
Ye·shu·a — Jesus
Y'hu·dah — Judea
Yo·cha·nan — John

sandals," and he did. "Throw on your robe," he said, "and follow me!" ⁹Going out, Kefa followed him but did not realize that what was happening through the angel was real — he thought he was seeing a vision. ¹⁰Having passed a first guard and a second, they arrived at the iron gate leading to the city. This opened to them by itself, and they made their exit. They went down the length of one street, and suddenly the angel left him. ¹¹Then Kefa came to himself and said, "Now I know for sure that the Lord sent his angel to rescue me from Herod's power and from everything the Judean people were hoping for."

¹²Realizing what had happened, he went to the house of Miryam the mother of Yochanan (surnamed Mark), where many people had gathered to pray. ¹³He knocked at the outside door, and a servant named Rhoda came to answer. ¹⁴She recognized Kefa's voice and was so happy that she ran back in without opening the door, and announced that Kefa was standing outside. ¹⁵"You're out of your mind!" they said to her. But she insisted it was true. So they said, "It is his angel." ¹⁶Meanwhile, Kefa kept knocking; and when they opened the door and saw him, they were amazed. ¹⁷Motioning to them with his hand to be quiet, he told them how the Lord had brought him out of the prison and said, "Tell all this to Ya'akov and the brothers." Then he left and went elsewhere.

¹⁸When daylight came, there was no small commotion among the soldiers over what had become of Kefa. ¹⁹Herod had a thorough search made for him, but they failed to find him, so he cross-examined the guards and ordered them put to death. Then Herod went down from Y'hudah to Caesarea and spent some time there.

²⁰Now Herod was very angry with the people of Tzor and Tzidon, so they joined together and sought an audience with him. After securing the support of Blastus, the king's chief personal servant, they asked for peace; because they depended on the king's lands for their food supply. ²¹A day was set, and Herod in his royal robes sat on the throne and made a speech to them. ²²The mob cried out, "This is the voice of a god, not a man!" ²³At once, because Herod did not give the glory to God, an angel of *Adonai* struck him down. He was eaten away by worms and died.

²⁴But the word of the Lord went on growing and being multiplied.

²⁵Bar-Nabba and Sha'ul, having completed their errand, returned from Yerushalayim, bringing with them Yochanan, surnamed Mark.

13 ¹In the Antioch congregation were prophets and teachers — Bar-Nabba, Shim'on (known as "the Black"), Lucius (from Cyrene), Menachem (who had been brought up with Herod the governor) and Sha'ul. ²One time when they were worshipping the Lord and fasting, the *Ruach HaKodesh* said to them, "Set aside for me Bar-Nabba and Sha'ul for the work to which I have called them." ³After fasting and praying, they placed their hands on them and sent them off.

⁴So these two, after they had been sent out by the *Ruach HaKodesh*, went down to Seleucia and from there sailed to Cyprus. ⁵After landing in Salamis, they began proclaiming the word of God in the synagogues, with Yochanan (Mark) as an assistant; ⁶and thus they made their way throughout the whole island.

They ended up in Paphos, where they found a Jewish sorcerer and pseudo-prophet named Bar-Yeshua.

[7] He had attached himself to the governor, Sergius Paulus, who was an intelligent man. Now the governor had called for Bar-Nabba and Sha'ul and was anxious to hear the message about God; [8] but the sorcerer Elymas (for that is how his name is translated) opposed them, doing his best to turn the governor away from the faith. [9] Then Sha'ul, also known as Paul, filled with the *Ruach HaKodesh*, stared straight at him and said, [10]"You son of Satan, full of fraud and evil! You enemy of everything good! Won't you ever stop **making crooked the straight paths of the Lord?**[k] [11]So now, look! The hand of the Lord is upon you; and for a while you will be blind, unable to see the sun." Immediately mist and darkness came over Elymas; and he groped about, trying to find someone to lead him by the hand. [12]Then, on seeing what had happened, the governor trusted, astounded by the teaching about the Lord.

[13] Having set sail from Paphos, Sha'ul and his companions arrived at Perga in Pamphylia. There Yochanan left them and returned to Yerushalayim, [14]but the others went on from Perga to Pisidian Antioch, and on *Shabbat* they went into the synagogue and sat down. [15]After the reading from the *Torah* and from the Prophets, the synagogue leaders sent them a message, "Brothers, if any of you has a word of exhortation for the people, speak!" [16]So Sha'ul stood, motioned with his hand, and said:

"Fellow Israelites and God-fearers, listen! [17]The God of this people Israel chose our fathers. He made the people great during the time when they were living as aliens in Egypt and **with a stretched-out arm he led them out of that land.**[l] [18]For some **forty years**[m] he took care of them in the desert, [19]and after he had destroyed **seven nations**[n] in the land of Cana'an he gave their land to his people as an inheritance. [20]All this took about 450 years. After that, **he gave them judges,**[o] down to the prophet Shmuel. [21]Then they asked for a king, and God gave them Sha'ul Ben-Kish, a man from the tribe of Binyamin. After forty years, [22]God removed him and raised up David as king for them, making his approval known with these words, '**I found David** Ben-Yishai to be **a man after** my **own heart**; he will do everything I want.'[p]

[23]"In keeping with his promise, God has brought to Israel from this man's descendants a deliverer, Yeshua. [24]Now before the coming of Yeshua, Yochanan

---

[k] Proverbs 10:9

[l] Exodus 6:6, 12:51
[m] Exodus 16:35, Numbers 14:34
[n] Deuteronomy 7:1 [o] Judges 2:16
[p] Psalm 89:21(20), 1 Samuel 13:14

A·do·nai — the LORD, Jehovah
Bar-Nab·ba — Barnabas
Bar-Ye·shu·a — Barjesus
Bin·ya·min — Benjamin
Ca·na·'an — Canaan
Da·vid Ben-Yi·shai — David, the son of Jesse
Ke·fa — Peter
Me·na·chem — Manaen
Mir·yam — Miriam, Mary
Ru·ach-Ha·Ko·desh — Holy Spirit
Sa·tan — Satan
Shab·bat — the Sabbath
Sha·'ul — Saul (Paul)
Sha·'ul Ben-Kish — Saul, the son of Kish
Shim·'on — Simon
Shmu·el — Samuel
To·rah — Teaching, "Law"; Pentateuch
Tzi·don — Sidon
Tzor — Tyre
Ya·'a·kov — James
Ye·ru·sha·la·yim — Jerusalem
Y'hu·dah — Judea
Yo·cha·nan — John

proclaimed to all the people of Israel an immersion in connection with turning to God from sin. [25]But as Yochanan was ending his work, he said, 'What do you suppose I am? Well — I'm not! But after me is coming someone, the sandals of whose feet I am unworthy to untie.'

[26]"Brothers! — sons of Avraham and those among you who are 'God-fearers'! It is to us that the message of this deliverance has been sent! [27]For the people living in Yerushalayim and their leaders did not recognize who Yeshua was or understand the message of the Prophets read every *Shabbat*, so they fulfilled that message by condemning him. [28]They could not find any legitimate ground for a death sentence; nevertheless they asked Pilate to have him executed; [29]and when they had carried out all the things written about him, he was taken down from the stake[q] and placed in a tomb. [30]"But God raised him from the dead! [31]He appeared for many days to those who had come up with him from the Galil to Yerushalayim; and they are now his witnesses to the people.

[32]"As for us, we are bringing you the Good News that what God promised to the fathers, [33]he has fulfilled for us the children in raising up Yeshua, as indeed it is written in the second Psalm,

'You are my Son;
today I have become your Father.'[r]

[34]And as for his raising him up from the dead, to return to decay no more, he said,

'I will give the holy and trust-worthy things of David to you.'[s]

[35]This is explained elsewhere:

'You will not let your Holy One see decay.'[t]

[36]For David did indeed serve God's purposes in his own generation; but after that, he died, was buried with his fathers and did **see decay.** [37]However, the one God raised up did not **see decay.**

[38]"Therefore, brothers, let it be known to you that through this man is proclaimed forgiveness of sins! [39]That is, God clears everyone who puts his trust in this man, even in regard to all the things concerning which you could not be cleared by the *Torah* of Moshe.

[40]"Watch out, then, so that this word found in the Prophets may not happen to you:

[41]'You Mockers! Look, and marvel, and die!
For in your own time, I am doing a work
that you simply will not believe, even if someone explains it to you!'"[u]

[42]As they left, the people invited Sha'ul and Bar-Nabba to tell them more about these matters the following *Shabbat*. [43]When the synagogue meeting broke up, many of the born Jews and devout proselytes followed Sha'ul and Bar-Nabba, who spoke with them and urged them to keep holding fast to the love and kindness of God.

[44]The next *Shabbat*, nearly the whole city gathered together to hear the message about the Lord; [45]but when the Jews who had not believed saw the crowds, they were filled with jealousy and spoke up against what Sha'ul was saying and insulted him. [46]However, Sha'ul and Bar-Nabba answered boldly: "It was necessary that God's word be spoken first to you. But since

---

q Deuteronomy 21:23   r Psalm 2:7
s Isaiah 55:3

t Psalm 16:10   u Habakkuk 1:5

you are rejecting it and are judging yourselves unworthy of eternal life — why, we're turning to the *Goyim!* ⁴⁷For that is what *Adonai* has ordered us to do:

'I have set you as a light for the *Goyim*,
to be for deliverance to the ends of the earth.'" *ᵛ*

⁴⁸The Gentiles were very happy to hear this. They honored the message about the Lord, and as many as had been appointed to eternal life came to trust. ⁴⁹And the message about the Lord was carried throughout the whole region. ⁵⁰But the unbelieving Jews stirred up the women "God-fearers" of high social standing and the leading men of the city, and they organized persecution against Sha'ul and Bar-Nabba and expelled them from their district. ⁵¹However, Sha'ul and Bar-Nabba shook off the dust of their feet against them and went on to Iconium; ⁵²and the *talmidim* were filled with joy and with the *Ruach HaKodesh.*

14 ¹In Iconium the same thing happened — they went into the synagogue and spoke in such a way that a large number of both Jews and Greeks came to trust. ²But the Jews who would not be persuaded stirred up the Gentiles and poisoned their minds against the brothers. ³Therefore, Sha'ul and Bar-Nabba remained for a long time, speaking boldly about the Lord, who bore witness to the message about his love and kindness by enabling them to perform signs and miracles. ⁴However, the people of the city were divided — some sided with the unbelieving Jews, others with the emissaries. ⁵Eventually the unbelievers, both

Jews and Gentiles, together with their leaders, made a move to mistreat the emissaries, even to stone them; ⁶but they learned of it and escaped to Lystra and Derbe, towns in Lycaonia, and to the surrounding country, ⁷where they continued proclaiming the Good News.

⁸There was a man living in Lystra who could not use his feet — crippled from birth, he had never walked. ⁹This man listened to Sha'ul speaking. Sha'ul, looking at him intently and seeing that he had faith to be healed, ¹⁰said with a loud voice, "Stand up on your feet!" He jumped up and began to walk. ¹¹When the crowds saw what Sha'ul had done, they began to shout in the Lycaonian language, "The gods have come down to us in the form of men!" ¹²They began calling Bar-Nabba "Zeus" and Sha'ul "Hermes", since he did most of the talking; ¹³and the priest of Zeus, whose temple was just outside the city, brought bulls and wreaths to the city gates, intending to offer a sacrifice to them with the people.

¹⁴When the emissaries Bar-Nabba and Sha'ul heard of it, they tore their clothes and ran into the crowd, shouting ¹⁵"Men! Why are you doing this?

---

v Isaiah 49:6

A·do·**nai** — the LORD, Jehovah
Av·ra·**ham** — Abraham
Bar-**Nab**·ba — Barnabas
Da·**vid** — David
the Ga·**lil** — Galilee
go·yim — Gentiles, nations, pagans
Mo·**she** — Moses
Ru·ach Ha·Ko·desh — Holy Spirit
Shab·bat — the Sabbath
Sha·**'ul** — Saul (Paul)
tal·mi·dim — disciples
To·rah — Teaching, "Law"; Pentateuch
Ye·ru·sha·**la**·yim — Jerusalem
Ye·**shu**·a — Jesus
Yo·cha·**nan** — John

We're just men, human like you! We are announcing Good News to you — turn from these worthless things to the living **God who made heaven and earth and the sea and everything in them!**[w] ¹⁶ In times past, he allowed all peoples to walk in their own ways; ¹⁷ yet he did not leave himself without evidence of his nature; because he does good things, giving you rains from heaven and crops in their seasons, filling you with food and your hearts with happiness!" ¹⁸ Even saying this barely kept the crowds from sacrificing to them.

¹⁹ Then some unbelieving Jews came from Antioch and Iconium. They won over the crowds, stoned Sha'ul and dragged him outside the city, thinking he was dead. ²⁰ But as the *talmidim* gathered around him, he got up and went back into the town. The next day, he left with Bar-Nabba for Derbe.

²¹ After proclaiming the Good News in that city and making many people into *talmidim*, they returned to Lystra, Iconium and Antioch, ²² strengthening the *talmidim*, encouraging them to remain true to the faith, and reminding them that it is through many hardships that we must enter the Kingdom of God. ²³ After appointing elders for them in every congregation, Sha'ul and Bar-Nabba, with prayer and fasting, committed them to the Lord in whom they had put their trust.

²⁴ Passing through Pisidia, they came to Pamphylia. ²⁵ After speaking the message in Perga, they came down to Attalia; and from there, they sailed back to Antioch, ²⁶ the place where they had been handed over to the care of God for the work which they had now completed.

²⁷ When they arrived, they gathered the Messianic community together and reported what God had done through them, that he had opened a door of faith to the Gentiles. ²⁸ And they stayed for some time there with the *talmidim*.

15 ¹ But some men came down from Y'hudah to Antioch and began teaching the brothers, "You can't be saved unless you undergo *b'rit-milah* in the manner prescribed by Moshe." ² This brought them into no small measure of discord and dispute with Sha'ul and Bar-Nabba. So the congregation assigned Sha'ul, Bar-Nabba and some of themselves to go and put this *sh'eilah* before the emissaries and the elders up in Yerushalayim.

³ After being sent off by the congregation, they made their way through Phoenicia and Shomron, recounting in detail how the Gentiles had turned to God; and this news brought great joy to all the brothers.

⁴ On arrival in Yerushalayim, they were welcomed by the Messianic community, including the emissaries and the elders; and they reported what God had done through them. ⁵ But some of those who had come to trust were from the party of the *P'rushim*; and they stood up and said, "It is necessary to circumcise them and direct them to observe the *Torah* of Moshe."

⁶ The emissaries and the elders met to look into this matter. ⁷ After lengthy debate, Kefa got up and said to them, "Brothers, you yourselves know that a good while back, God chose me from among you to be the one by whose mouth the *Goyim* should hear the message of the Good News and come to trust. ⁸ And God, who knows the heart, bore them witness by giving the *Ruach HaKodesh* to them, just as he did to us; ⁹ that is, he made no distinction between us and them, but cleansed their heart by trust. ¹⁰ So why are you putting God to the test now by placing

w Psalm 146:6

a yoke on the neck of the *talmidim* which neither our fathers nor we have had the strength to bear? [11] No, it is through the love and kindness of the Lord Yeshua that we trust and are delivered — and it's the same with them."

[12] Then the whole assembly kept still as they listened to Bar-Nabba and Sha'ul tell what signs and miracles God had done through them among the Gentiles. [13] Ya'akov broke the silence to reply. "Brothers," he said, "hear what I have to say. [14] Shim'on has told in detail what God did when he first began to show his concern for taking from among the *Goyim* a people to bear his name. [15] And the words of the Prophets are in complete harmony with this — for it is written,

[16] '"After this, I will return;
and I will rebuild the fallen tent of David.
I will rebuild its ruins,
I will restore it,
[17] so that the rest of mankind may seek the Lord,
that is, all the *Goyim* who have been called by my name,"
[18] says *Adonai*, who is doing these things.'[x]

All this has been known for ages.

[19] "Therefore, my opinion is that we should not put obstacles in the way of the *Goyim* who are turning to God. [20] Instead, we should write them a letter telling them to abstain from things polluted by idols, from fornication, from what is strangled and from blood. [21] For from the earliest times, Moshe has had in every city those who proclaim him, with his words being read in the synagogues every *Shabbat*."

[22] Then the emissaries and the elders, together with the whole Messianic community, decided to select men from among themselves to send to Antioch with Sha'ul and Bar-Nabba. They sent Y'hudah, called Bar-Sabba, and Sila, both leading men among the brothers, [23] with the following letter:

From: The emissaries and the elders, your brothers

To: The brothers from among the Gentiles throughout Antioch, Syria and Cilicia:

Greetings!

[24] We have heard that some people went out from among us without our authorization, and that they have upset you with their talk, unsettling your minds. [25] So we have decided unanimously to select men and send them to you with our dear friends Bar-Nabba and Sha'ul, [26] who have dedicated their lives to upholding the

---

A·do·nai — the LORD, Jehovah
Bar-Nab·ba — Barnabas
Bar-Sab·ba — Barsabbas
b'rit-mi·lah — circumcision
Da·vid — David
Go·yim — Gentiles, nations, pagans
Ke·fa — Peter
Mo·she — Moses
P'ru·shim — Pharisees
Ru·ach-Ha·Ko·desh — Holy Spirit
Shab·bat — the Sabbath
Sha·'ul — Saul (Paul)
sh'ei·lah — question
Shim·'on — Simon
Shom·ron — Samaria
Si·la — Silas
tal·mi·dim — disciples
To·rah — Teaching, "Law"; Pentateuch
Ya·'a·kov — James
Ye·ru·sha·la·yim — Jerusalem
Ye·shu·a — Jesus
Y'hu·dah — Judea, Judas

---

x Amos 9:11-12

name of our Lord, Yeshua the Messiah. ²⁷So we have sent Y'hudah and Sila, and they will confirm in person what we are writing.

²⁸For it seemed good to the *Ruach HaKodesh* and to us not to lay any heavier burden on you than the following requirements: ²⁹to abstain from what has been sacrificed to idols, from blood, from things strangled, and from fornication. If you keep yourselves from these, you will be doing the right thing.

Shalom!

³⁰The messengers were sent off and went to Antioch, where they gathered the group together and delivered the letter. ³¹After reading it, the people were delighted by its encouragement. ³²Y'hudah and Sila, who were also prophets, said much to encourage and strengthen the brothers. ³³After they had spent some time there, they were sent off with a greeting of "*Shalom!*" from the brothers to those who had sent them. ³⁴* ³⁵But Sha'ul and Bar-Nabba stayed in Antioch, where they and many others taught and proclaimed the Good News of the message about the Lord.

³⁶After some time, Sha'ul said to Bar-Nabba, "Let's go back and visit the brothers in all the towns where we proclaimed the message about the Lord, and see how they're doing." ³⁷Now Bar-Nabba wanted to take with them Yochanan, the one called Mark. ³⁸But Sha'ul thought it would be unwise to take this man with them, since he had gone off and left them in Pamphylia to do the work by themselves. ³⁹There was such sharp disagreement over this that they separated from each other,

---

* Some manuscripts include verse 34: But it seemed good to Sila to stay there.

with Bar-Nabba taking Mark and sailing off to Cyprus.

⁴⁰However, Sha'ul chose Sila and left, after the brothers had committed him to the love and kindness of the Lord. ⁴¹He went through Syria and Cilicia, strengthening the congregations.

16 ¹Sha'ul came down to Derbe and went on to Lystra, where there lived a *talmid* named Timothy. He was the son of a Jewish woman who had come to trust, and a Greek father. ²All the brothers in Lystra and Iconium spoke well of Timothy. ³Sha'ul wanted Timothy to accompany him; so he took him and did a *b'rit-milah*, because of the Jews living in those areas; for they all knew that his father had been a Greek.

⁴As they went on through the towns, they delivered to the people the decisions reached by the emissaries and the elders in Yerushalayim for them to observe. ⁵Accordingly, the congregations were strengthened in the faith and increased in number day by day.

⁶They traveled through the region of Phrygia and Galatia, because they had been prevented by the *Ruach Ha-Kodesh* from speaking the message in the province of Asia. ⁷When they came to the frontier of Mysia, they tried to go into Bithynia; but the Spirit of Yeshua would not let them. ⁸So, after passing by Mysia, they came down to Troas.

⁹There a vision appeared to Sha'ul at night. A man from Macedonia was standing and begging him, "Come over to Macedonia and help us!" ¹⁰As soon as he had seen the vision, we lost no time getting ready to leave for Macedonia; for we concluded that God had called us to proclaim the Good News to them.

¹¹Sailing from Troas, we made a straight run to Samothrace; the next day we went to Neapolis; ¹²and from

there, we went on to Philippi, a Roman colony and the leading city of that part of Macedonia. We spent a few days in this city; [13] then on *Shabbat*, we went outside the gate to the riverside, where we understood a *minyan* met. We sat down and began speaking to the women who had gathered there. [14] One of those listening was a woman from the city of Thyatira named Lydia, a dealer in fine purple cloth. She was already a "God-fearer", and the Lord opened up her heart to respond to what Sha'ul was saying. [15] After she and the members of her household had been immersed, she gave us this invitation: "If you consider me to be faithful to the Lord, come and stay in my house." And she insisted till we went.

[16] Once, when we were going to the place where the *minyan* gathered, we were met by a slave girl who had in her a snake-spirit that enabled her to predict the future. She earned a lot of money for her owners by telling fortunes. [17] This girl followed behind Sha'ul and the rest of us and kept screaming, "These men are servants of God *HaElyon*! They're telling you how to be saved!" [18] She kept this up day after day, until Sha'ul, greatly disturbed, turned and said to the spirit, "In the name of Yeshua the Messiah, I order you to come out of her!" And the spirit did come out, at that very moment.

[19] But when her owners saw that what had come out was any further prospect of profit for them, they seized Sha'ul and Sila and dragged them to the market square to face the authorities. [20] Bringing them to the judges, they said, "These men are causing a lot of trouble in our city, since they are Jews. [21] What they are doing is advocating customs that are against the law for us to accept or practice, since we are

Romans." [22] The mob joined in the attack against them, and the judges tore their clothes off them and ordered that they be flogged. [23] After giving them a severe beating, they threw them in prison, charging the jailer to guard them securely. [24] Upon receiving such an order, he threw them into the inner cell and clamped their feet securely between heavy blocks of wood.

[25] Around midnight, Sha'ul and Sila were praying and singing hymns to God, while the other prisoners listened attentively. [26] Suddenly there was a violent earthquake which shook the prison to its foundations. All the doors flew open and everyone's chains came loose. [27] The jailer awoke, and when he saw the doors open he drew his sword and was about to kill himself, for he assumed that the prisoners had escaped. [28] But Sha'ul shouted, "Don't harm yourself! We're all here!"

[29] Calling for lights, the jailer ran in, began to tremble and fell down in front of Sha'ul and Sila. [30] Then, leading them outside, he said, "Men, what must I do to be saved?" [31] They said, "Trust in the Lord Yeshua, and you will be saved — you and your household!" [32] Whereupon they told him and every-

---

Bar-Nab·ba — Barnabas
Bar-Sab·ba — Barsabbas
b'rit-mi·lah — ritual circumcision
Ha·El·yon — the Most High, i.e., God
min·yan — quorum of ten or more men gathered for Jewish worship
Ru·ach-Ha·Ko·desh — Holy Spirit
Shab·bat — the Sabbath
Sha·lom! — Peace! (greeting)
Sha·'ul — Saul (Paul)
Si·la — Silas
tal·mid — disciple
Ye·ru·sha·la·yim — Jerusalem
Ye·shu·a — Jesus
Y'hu·dah — Judas; Judea
Yo·cha·nan — John

one in his household the message about the Lord.

³³ Then, even at that late hour of the night, the jailer took them and washed off their wounds; and without delay, he and all his people were immersed. ³⁴ After that, he brought them up to his house and set food in front of them; and he and his entire household celebrated their having come to trust in God. ³⁵ The next morning, the judges sent police officers with the order, "Release those men." ³⁶ The jailer told Sha'ul, "The judges have sent word to release both of you. So come out, and go on your way in peace." ³⁷ But Sha'ul said to the officers, "After flogging us in public when we hadn't been convicted of any crime and are Roman citizens, they threw us in prison. Now they want to get rid of us secretly? Oh, no! Let them come and escort us out themselves!"

³⁸ The officers reported these words to the judges, who became frightened when they heard that Sha'ul and Sila were Roman citizens. ³⁹ They came and apologized to them; then, after escorting them out, requested them to leave the city. ⁴⁰ From the prison they went to Lydia's house, and after seeing and encouraging the brothers they departed.

17 ¹ After passing through Amphipolis and Apollonia, Sha'ul and Sila came to Thessalonica, where there was a synagogue. ² According to his usual practice, Sha'ul went in; and on three *Shabbatot* he gave them *drashot* from the *Tanakh*, ³ explaining and proving that the Messiah had to suffer and rise again from the dead, and that "this Yeshua whom I am proclaiming to you is the Messiah." ⁴ Some of the Jews were persuaded and threw in their lot with Sha'ul and Sila, as did a great many of the Greek men who were

"God-fearers", and not a few of the leading women.

⁵ But the unbelieving Jews grew jealous; so they got together some vicious men from the riffraff hanging around in the market square, collected a crowd and started a riot in the city. They attacked Jason's house, hoping to bring Sha'ul and Sila out to the mob. ⁶ But when they didn't find them, they dragged Jason and some other brothers before the city authorities and shouted, "These men who have turned the whole world upside down have come here too! ⁷ And Jason has let them stay in his home! All of them are defying the decrees of the Emperor; because they assert that there is another king, Yeshua!" ⁸ Their words threw the crowd and the authorities into a turmoil, ⁹ so that only after Jason and the others had posted bond did they let them go. ¹⁰ But as soon as night fell, the brothers sent Sha'ul and Sila off to Berea.

As soon as they arrived, they went to the synagogue. ¹¹ Now the people here were of nobler character than the ones in Thessalonica; they eagerly welcomed the message, checking the *Tanakh* every day to see if the things Sha'ul was saying were true. ¹² Many of them came to trust, as did a number of prominent Greek women and not a few Greek men.

¹³ But when the unbelieving Jews of Thessalonica learned that the word of God had been proclaimed by Sha'ul in Berea as well, they went there too to make trouble and agitate the crowds. ¹⁴ The brothers sent Sha'ul away at once to go down to the seacoast, while Sila and Timothy stayed behind. ¹⁵ Sha'ul's escort went with him as far as Athens, then left with instructions for Sila and Timothy to come as quickly as they could.

¹⁶ While Sha'ul was waiting for them

in Athens, his spirit within him was disturbed at the sight of the city full of idols. ¹⁷ So he began holding discussions in the synagogue with the Jews and the "God-fearers", and in the market square every day with the people who happened to be there. ¹⁸ Also a group of Epicurean and Stoic philosophers started meeting with him. Some asked, "What is this babbler trying to say?" Others, because he proclaimed the Good News about Yeshua and the resurrection, said, "He sounds like a propagandist for foreign gods." ¹⁹ They took and brought him before the High Council, saying, "May we know what this new teaching is that you are presenting? ²⁰ Some of the things we are hearing from you strike us as strange, and we would like to know what they mean." ²¹ (All the Athenians and the foreigners living there used to spend their spare time talking or hearing about the latest intellectual fads.)

²² Sha'ul stood up in the Council meeting and said, "Men of Athens: I see how very religious you are in every way! ²³ For as I was walking around, looking at your shrines, I even found an altar which had been inscribed, 'To An Unknown God.' So, the one whom you are already worshipping in ignorance — this is the one I proclaim to you.

²⁴ "The God who made the universe and everything in it, and who is Lord of heaven and earth, does not live in man-made temples; ²⁵ nor is he served by human hands, as if he lacked something; since it is he himself who gives life and breath and everything to everyone.

²⁶ "From one man he made every nation living on the entire surface of the earth, and he fixed the limits of their territories and the periods when they would flourish. ²⁷ God did this so that people would look for him and perhaps reach out and find him — although in fact, he is not far from each one of us, ²⁸ 'for in him we live and move and exist.' Indeed, as some of the poets among you have said, 'We are actually his children.' ²⁹ So, since we are children of God, we shouldn't suppose that God's essence resembles gold, silver or stone shaped by human technique and imagination.

³⁰ "In the past, God overlooked such ignorance; but now he is commanding all people everywhere to turn to him from their sins. ³¹ For he has set a Day when he will judge the inhabited world, and do it justly, by means of a man whom he has designated. And he has given public proof of it by resurrecting this man from the dead."

³² At the mention of a resurrection of dead people, some began to scoff; while others said, "We want to hear you again on this subject." ³³ So Sha'ul left the meeting. ³⁴ But some men stayed with him and came to trust, including the High Council member Dionysius; there was also a woman named Damaris; and others came to trust along with them.

18 ¹ After this, Sha'ul left Athens and went to Corinth, ² where he met a Jewish man named Aquila, originally from Pontus but having recently come with his wife Priscilla from Italy, because Claudius had issued a decree expelling all the Jews from Rome. Sha'ul went to see them; ³ and

---

dra·shot — teachings, sermons
Shab·bat·tot — Sabbaths
Sha·'ul — Saul (Paul)
Si·la — Silas
Ta·nakh — Hebrew Scriptures, "Old Testament"
Ye·shu·a — Jesus

because he had the same trade as they, making tents, he stayed on with them; and they worked together.

⁴Sha'ul also began carrying on discussions every *Shabbat* in the synagogue, where he tried to convince both Jews and Greeks. ⁵But after Sila and Timothy arrived from Macedonia, Sha'ul felt pressed by the urgency of the message and testified in depth to the Jews that Yeshua is the Messiah. ⁶However when they set themselves against him and began hurling insults, he shook out his clothes and said to them, "Your blood be on your own heads! For my part, I am clean; from now on, I will go to the *Goyim!*"

⁷So he left them and went into the home of a "God-fearer" named Titius Justus, whose house was right next door to the synagogue. ⁸Crispus, the president of the synagogue, came to trust in the Lord, along with his whole household; also many of the Corinthians who heard trusted and were immersed.

⁹One night, in a vision, the Lord said to Sha'ul, "Don't be afraid, but speak right up, and don't stop, ¹⁰because I am with you. No one will succeed in harming you, for I have many people in this city." ¹¹So Sha'ul stayed there for a year and a half, teaching them the word of God.

¹²But when Gallio became the Roman governor of Achaia, the unbelieving Jews made a concerted attack on Sha'ul and took him to court, ¹³saying, "This man is trying to persuade people to worship God in ways that violate the *Torah.*" ¹⁴Sha'ul was just about to open his mouth, when Gallio said to the Jews, "Listen, you Jews, if this were a case of inflicted injury or a serious crime, I could reasonably be expected to hear you out patiently. ¹⁵But since it involves questions about words and names and your own law, then you must deal with it yourselves. I flatly refuse to judge such matters." ¹⁶And he had them ejected from the court. ¹⁷They all grabbed Sosthenes, the president of the synagogue, and gave him a beating in full view of the bench; but Gallio showed no concern whatever.

¹⁸Sha'ul remained for some time, then said good-bye to the brothers and sailed off to Syria, after having his hair cut short in Cenchrea, because he had taken a vow; with him were Priscilla and Aquila.

¹⁹They came to Ephesus, and he left them there; but he himself went into the synagogue and held dialogue with the Jews. ²⁰When they asked him to stay with them longer, he declined; ²¹however, in his farewell he said, "God willing, I will come back to you." Then he set sail from Ephesus.

²²After landing at Caesarea, he went up to Yerushalayim and greeted the Messianic community. Then he came down to Antioch, ²³spent some time there, and afterwards set out and passed systematically through the region of Galatia and Phrygia, strengthening all the *talmidim.*

²⁴Meanwhile, a Jewish man named Apollos, a native of Alexandria, came to Ephesus. He was an eloquent speaker with a thorough knowledge of the *Tanakh.* ²⁵This man had been informed about the Way of the Lord, and with great spiritual fervor he spoke and taught accurately the facts about Yeshua, but he knew only the immersion of Yochanan. ²⁶He began to speak out boldly in the synagogue; but when Priscilla and Aquila heard him, they took him aside and explained to him the Way of God in fuller detail. ²⁷When he made plans to cross over into Achaia, the brothers encouraged him and wrote the *talmidim* there to wel-

come him. On arrival, he greatly helped those who through grace had come to trust; ²⁸for he powerfully and conclusively refuted the unbelieving Jews in public, demonstrating by the *Tanakh* that Yeshua is the Messiah.

19 ¹While Apollos was in Corinth, Sha'ul completed his travels through the inland country and arrived at Ephesus, where he found a few *talmidim*. ²He asked them, "Did you receive the *Ruach HaKodesh* when you came to trust?" "No," they said to him, "we have never even heard that there is such a thing as the *Ruach HaKodesh*." ³"In that case," he said, "into what were you immersed?" "The immersion of Yochanan," they answered. ⁴Sha'ul said, "Yochanan practiced an immersion in connection with turning from sin to God; but he told the people to put their trust in the one who would come after him, that is, in Yeshua." ⁵On hearing this, they were immersed into the name of the Lord Yeshua; ⁶and when Sha'ul placed his hands on them, the *Ruach HaKodesh* came upon them; so that they began speaking in tongues and prophesying. ⁷In all, there were about twelve of these men.

⁸Sha'ul went into the synagogue; and for three months he spoke out boldly, engaging in dialogue and trying to persuade people about the Kingdom of God. ⁹But some began hardening themselves and refusing to listen; and when these started defaming the Way before the whole synagogue, Sha'ul withdrew, took the *talmidim* with him, and commenced holding daily dialogues in Tyrannus's *yeshivah*. ¹⁰This went on for two years; so that everyone, both Jews and Greeks, living in the province of Asia heard the message about the Lord.

¹¹God did extraordinary miracles through Sha'ul. ¹²For instance, handkerchiefs and aprons that had touched him were brought to sick people; they would recover from their ailments; and the evil spirits would leave them.

¹³Then some of the Jewish exorcists who traveled from place to place tried to make use of the name of the Lord Yeshua in connection with people who had evil spirits. They would say, "I exorcise you by the Yeshua that Sha'ul is proclaiming!" ¹⁴One time, seven sons of a Jewish *cohen gadol* named Skeva were doing this; ¹⁵and the evil spirit answered them. It said, "Yeshua I know. And Sha'ul I recognize. But you? Who are you?" ¹⁶Then the man with the evil spirit fell upon them, overpowered them and gave them such a beating that they ran from the house, naked and bleeding.

¹⁷When all this became known to the residents of Ephesus, fear fell on all of them, Jews and Greeks alike; and the name of the Lord Yeshua came to be held in high regard. ¹⁸Many of those who had earlier made professions of faith now came and admitted publicly their evil deeds; ¹⁹and a considerable number of those who had engaged in occult practices threw their scrolls in a pile and burned them in public. When they calculated the value of the scrolls, it came to fifty thousand drachmas. ²⁰Thus the message about the Lord

---

co·hen ga·dol — high priest
Go·yim — Gentiles, nations, pagans
Ru·ach-Ha·Ko·desh — Holy Spirit
Shab·bat — the Sabbath
Sha·'ul — Saul (Paul)
Si·la — Silas
tal·mi·dim — disciples
Ta·nakh — Hebrew Scriptures, "Old Testament"
To·rah — Teaching, "Law"; Pentateuch
Ye·ru·sha·la·yim — Jerusalem
ye·shi·vah — school for learning *Torah*
Yo·cha·nan — John

continued in a powerful way to grow in influence.

²¹ Some time later, Sha'ul decided by the Spirit to pass through Macedonia and Achaia and then go to Yerushalayim. "After I have been there," he said, "I must visit Rome." ²² So he dispatched two of his helpers, Timothy and Erastus, to Macedonia; but he himself remained in the province of Asia for awhile.

²³ It was at this time that a major furore arose concerning the Way. ²⁴ There was a silversmith named Demetrius who manufactured from silver, objects connected with the worship of the goddess Artemis; and he provided no small amount of work for the craftsmen. ²⁵ He called a meeting of them and of those engaged in similar trades, and said, "Men, you understand that this line of business provides us our living. ²⁶ And you can see and hear for yourselves that not only here in Ephesus, but in practically the whole province of Asia, this Sha'ul has convinced and turned away a considerable crowd by saying that man-made gods aren't gods at all. ²⁷ Now the danger is not only that the reputation of our trade will suffer, but that the temple of the great goddess Artemis will come to be taken lightly. It could end up with the goddess herself, who is worshipped throughout the province of Asia and indeed throughout the whole world, being ignominiously brought down from her divine majesty!"

²⁸ Hearing this, they were filled with rage and began bellowing, "Great is Artemis of the Ephesians!" ²⁹ Soon the whole city was in an uproar. As one man, the mob rushed into the theater, dragging along Gaius and Aristarchus, Sha'ul's traveling companions from Macedonia. ³⁰ Sha'ul himself wanted to appear before the crowd, but the talmidim wouldn't let him. ³¹ Even some of the officials of the province, friends of his, sent a message begging him not to risk entering the theater. ³² Meanwhile, some were shouting one thing and others something else, because the assembly was in complete confusion, and the great majority didn't even know why they were there. ³³ Some of the crowd explained the situation to Alexander, whom the Jews had pushed to the front. So Alexander motioned for silence, hoping to make a defense speech to the people. ³⁴ But as soon as they recognized that he was a Jew, they began bellowing in unison, "Great is Artemis of the Ephesians!" and they kept it up for about two hours.

³⁵ At last, the city clerk was able to quiet the crowd. "Men of Ephesus!" he said, "Is there anyone who doesn't know that the city of Ephesus is the guardian of the temple of the great Artemis, and of the sacred stone which fell from the sky? ³⁶ Since this is beyond dispute, you had better calm down and not do anything rash. ³⁷ For you have brought these men here who have neither robbed the temple nor insulted your goddess. ³⁸ So if Demetrius and his fellow craftsmen have a complaint against anyone, the courts are open and the judges are there — let them bring charges and countercharges. ³⁹ But if there is something more you want, it will have to be settled in a lawful assembly. ⁴⁰ For we are in danger of being accused of rioting on account of what has happened today. There is no justification for it; and if we are asked, we will be unable to give any reasonable explanation for this disorderly gathering." ⁴¹ And with these words, he dismissed the assembly.

20 ¹ After the furore died down, Sha'ul sent for the talmidim and encouraged them, then took his leave and set out on his way to Macedonia. [2]He went through that area, and, after saying much to encourage them, passed on to Greece, [3]where he spent three months. As he was preparing to set sail for Syria, he discovered a plot against him by the unbelieving Jews; so he changed his mind and decided to return by way of Macedonia. [4]Sopater from Berea, the son of Pyrrhus, accompanied him; as did Aristarchus and Secundus from Thessalonica, Gaius from Derbe, Timothy, and Tychicus and Trophimus from the province of Asia. [5]These men went on and waited for us in Troas, [6]while we sailed from Philippi after the Days of *Matzah*. Five days later, we met them in Troas, where we spent a week.

[7]On *Motza'ei-Shabbat,* when we were gathered to break bread, Sha'ul addressed them. Since he was going to leave the next day, he kept talking until midnight. [8]Now there were many oil lamps burning in the upstairs room where we were meeting, [9]and there was a young fellow named Eutychus sitting on the window-sill. As Shau'l's *drash* went on and on, Eutychus grew sleepier and sleepier; until finally he went sound asleep and fell from the third storey to the ground. When they picked him up, he was dead. [10]But Sha'ul went down, threw himself onto him, put his arms around him and said, "Don't be upset, he's alive!" [11]Then he went back upstairs, broke the bread and ate. He continued talking with them till daylight, then left. [12]So, greatly relieved, they brought the boy home alive.

[13]We went on ahead to the ship and set sail for Assos, where we were planning to take Sha'ul aboard — he had arranged this because he wanted to go there by land. [14]After he met us at Assos, we took him aboard and went on to Mitylene. [15]The next day, we sailed from there and arrived off Chios; the following day, we crossed over to Samos; and the day after that, we reached Miletus. [16]For Sha'ul had decided to bypass Ephesus on his voyage, in order to avoid losing time in the province of Asia, because he was hurrying to get to Yerushalayim, if possible in time to celebrate *Shavu'ot.*

[17]But he did send from Miletus to Ephesus, summoning the elders of the Messianic community. [18]When they arrived, he said to them, "You yourselves know how, from the first day I set foot in the province of Asia, I was with you the whole time, [19]serving the Lord with much humility and with tears, in spite of the tests I had to undergo because of the plots of the unbelieving Jews. [20]You know that I held back nothing that could be helpful to you, and that I taught you both in public and from house to house, [21]declaring with utmost seriousness the same message to Jews and Greeks alike: turn from your sin to God; and put your trust in our Lord, Yeshua the Messiah.

[22]"And now, compelled by the Spirit, I am going to Yerushalayim. I don't know what will happen to me there, [23]other than that in every city the *Ruach HaKodesh* keeps warning me that imprisonment and persecution await me. [24]But I consider my own life of no importance to me whatsoever, as

---

drash — teaching, sermon
ma·tzah — unleavened bread
Mo·tza·'ei-Shab·bat — Saturday night
Ru·ach Ha·Ko·desh — Holy Spirit
Sha·'ul — Saul (Paul)
Sha·vu·'ot — the feast of Weeks, Pentecost
tal·mi·dim — disciples
Ye·ru·sha·la·yim — Jerusalem
Ye·shu·a — Jesus

long as I can finish the course ahead of me, the task I received from the Lord Yeshua — to declare in depth the Good News of God's love and kindness.

²⁵ "Now, listen! I know that none of you people among whom I have gone about proclaiming the Kingdom will ever see me again. ²⁶ Therefore, I testify on this day that I am innocent of the blood of all. ²⁷ For I did not shrink from proclaiming to you the whole plan of God.

²⁸ "Watch out for yourselves, and for all the flock in which the *Ruach HaKodesh* has placed you as leaders, to shepherd God's Messianic community, which he won for himself at the cost of his own Son's blood. ²⁹ I know that after I leave, savage wolves will come in among you; and they won't spare the flock. ³⁰ Even from among your own number, men will arise and teach perversions of the truth, in order to drag away the *talmidim* after themselves. ³¹ So stay alert! Remember that for three years, night and day, with tears in my eyes, I never stopped warning you!

³² "And now I entrust you to the care of the Lord and to the message of his love and kindness, for it can build you up and give you an inheritance among all those who have been set apart for God.

³³ "I have not wanted for myself anyone's silver or gold or clothing. ³⁴ You yourselves know that these hands of mine have provided not only for my own needs, but for the needs of my co-workers as well. ³⁵ In everything I have given you an example of how, by working hard like this, you must help the weak, remembering the words of the Lord Yeshua himself, 'There is more happiness in giving than in receiving.'"

³⁶ When he had finished speaking,

Sha'ul kneeled down with them all and prayed. ³⁷ They were all in tears as they threw their arms around his neck and kissed him farewell. ³⁸ What saddened them the most was his remark that they would never see him again. Then they accompanied him to the ship.

21 ¹ After we had torn ourselves away from the Ephesian elders, we set sail and made a straight run to Cos. The next day we went to Rhodes, and from there to Patara. ² On finding a ship that was crossing over to Phoenicia, we embarked and set sail. ³ After sighting Cyprus, we passed it on the left, sailed to Syria and landed at Tzor, because that was where the ship was unloading its cargo. ⁴ Having searched out the *talmidim* there, we remained for a week. Guided by the Spirit, they told Sha'ul not to go up to Yerushalayim; ⁵ but when the week was over, we left to continue our journey. All of them, with their wives and children, accompanied us until we were outside the town. Kneeling on the beach and praying, ⁶ we said good-bye to each other. Then we boarded the ship, and they returned home.

⁷ When the voyage from Tzor was over, we arrived at Ptolemais. There we greeted the brothers and stayed with them overnight. ⁸ The following day, we left and came to Caesarea, where we went to the home of Philip the proclaimer of the Good News, one of the Seven, and stayed with him. ⁹ He had four unmarried daughters with the gift of prophecy.

¹⁰ While we were staying there, a prophet named Agav came down from Y'hudah ¹¹ to visit us. He took Sha'ul's belt, tied up his own hands and feet and said, "Here is what the *Ruach HaKodesh* says: the man who owns this belt — the Judeans in Yerushalayim will tie him up just like this and hand

him over to the *Goyim.*' [12]When we heard this, both we and the people there begged him not to go up to Yerushalayim; [13]but Sha'ul answered, "What are you doing, crying and trying to weaken my resolve? I am prepared not only to be tied up, but even to die in Yerushalayim for the name of the Lord Yeshua." [14]And when he would not be convinced, we said, "May the Lord's will be done," and kept quiet.

[15]So at the end of our stay, we packed and went up to Yerushalayim; [16]and with us went some of the *talmidim* from Caesarea. They brought us to the home of the man with whom we were to stay, Mnason from Cyprus, who had been a *talmid* since the early days.

[17]In Yerushalayim, the brothers received us warmly. [18]The next day Sha'ul and the rest of us went in to Ya'akov, and all the elders were present. [19]After greeting them, Sha'ul described in detail each of the things God had done among the Gentiles through his efforts.

[20]On hearing it, they praised God; but they also said to him, "You see, brother, how many tens of thousands of believers there are among the Judeans, and they are all zealots for the *Torah.* [21]Now what they have been told about you is that you are teaching all the Jews living among the *Goyim* to apostatize from Moshe, telling them not to have a *b'rit-milah* for their sons and not to follow the traditions.

[22]"What, then, is to be done? They will certainly hear that you have come. [23]So do what we tell you. We have four men who are under a vow. [24]Take them with you, be purified with them, and pay the expenses connected with having their heads shaved. Then everyone will know that there is nothing to these rumors which they have heard about you; but that, on the contrary, you

yourself stay in line and keep the *Torah.*

[25]"However, in regard to the *Goyim* who have come to trust in Yeshua, we all joined in writing them a letter with our decision that they should abstain from what had been sacrificed to idols, from blood, from what is strangled and from fornication."

[26]The next day Sha'ul took the men, purified himself along with them and entered the Temple to give notice of when the period of purification would be finished and the offering would have to be made for each of them. [27]The seven days were almost up when some unbelieving Jews from the province of Asia saw him in the Temple, stirred up all the crowd and grabbed him. [28]"Men of Israel, help!" they shouted. "This is the man who goes everywhere teaching everyone things against the people, against the *Torah* and against this place! And now he has even brought some *Goyim* into the Temple and defiled this holy place!" [29](They had previously seen Trophimus from Ephesus in the city with him and assumed that Sha'ul had brought him into the Temple.)

[30]The whole city was aroused, and

A·**gav** — Agabus
b'rit-mi·lah — circumcision
Go·yim — Gentiles, nations, pagans
Mo·**she** — Moses
Ru·ach-Ha·Ko·desh — Holy Spirit
Sha·'**ul** — Saul (Paul)
tal·mid (pl. *tal·mi·dim*) — disciple
Ta·nakh — Hebrew Scriptures, "Old Testament"
To·rah — Teaching, "Law"; Pentateuch
Tzor — Tyre
Ya·'a·kov — James
Ye·ru·sha·la·yim — Jerusalem
Ye·shu·a — Jesus
Y'hu·dah — Judea

people came running from all over. They seized Sha'ul and dragged him out of the Temple, and at once the gates were shut. ^{31}But while they were attempting to kill him, word reached the commander of the Roman battalion that all Yerushalayim was in turmoil. ^{32}Immediately he took officers and soldiers and charged down upon them. As soon as they saw the commander, they quit beating Sha'ul.

^{33}Then the commander came up, arrested him and ordered him to be tied up with two chains. He asked who he was and what he had done. ^{34}Everyone in the crowd shouted something different; so, since he couldn't find out what had happened because of the uproar, he ordered him brought to the barracks. ^{35}When Sha'ul got to the steps, he actually had to be carried by the soldiers, because the mob was so wild — ^{36}the crowd kept following and screaming, "Kill him!"

^{37}As Sha'ul was about to be brought into the barracks, he said to the commander, "Is it all right if I say something to you?" The commander said, "You know Greek! ^{38}Say, aren't you that Egyptian who tried to start a revolution a while back, and led four thousand armed terrorists out into the desert?" ^{39}Sha'ul said, "I am a Jew from Tarsus in Cilicia, a citizen of an important city; and I ask your permission to let me speak to the people."

^{40}Having received permission, Sha'ul stood on the steps and motioned with his hand to the people. When they finally became still, he addressed them in Hebrew:

22 ^{1}"Brothers and fathers! Listen to me as I make my defense before you now!" ^{2}When they heard him speaking to them in Hebrew, they settled down more; so he continued: ^{3}"I am a Jew, born in Tarsus of Cilicia, but brought up in this city and trained at the feet of Gamli'el in every detail of the *Torah* of our forefathers. I was a zealot for God, as all of you are today. ^{4}I persecuted to death the followers of this Way, arresting both men and women and throwing them in prison. ^{5}The *cohen hagadol* and the whole *Sanhedrin* can also testify to this. Indeed, after receiving letters from them to their colleagues in Dammesek, I was on my way there in order to arrest the ones in that city too and bring them back to Yerushalayim for punishment.

^{6}"As I was traveling and approaching Dammesek, around noon, suddenly a brilliant light from heaven flashed all around me! ^{7}I fell to the ground and heard a voice saying to me, 'Sha'ul! Sha'ul! Why do you keep persecuting me?' ^{8}I answered, 'Sir, who are you?' 'I am Yeshua from Natzeret,' he said to me, 'and you are persecuting me!' ^{9}Those who were with me did see the light, but they didn't hear the voice of the one who was speaking to me. ^{10}I said, 'What should I do, Lord?' And the Lord said to me, 'Get up, and go into Dammesek, and there you will be told about everything that has been laid out for you to do.' ^{11}I had been blinded by the brightness of the light, so my companions led me by the hand into Dammesek.

^{12}"A man named Chananyah, an observant follower of the *Torah* who was highly regarded by the entire Jewish community there, ^{13}came to me, stood by me and said, 'Brother Sha'ul, see again!' And at that very moment, I recovered my sight and saw him. ^{14}He said, '**The God of our fathers**^{y} determined in advance that you should know his will, see the *Tzaddik* and hear his voice; ^{15}because you will be a

---

^{y} Exodus 3:15

witness for him to everyone of what you have seen and heard. ¹⁶ So now, what are you waiting for? Get up, immerse yourself and have your sins washed away as you call on his name.'

¹⁷ "After I had returned to Yerushalayim, it happened that as I was praying in the Temple, I went into a trance, ¹⁸ and I saw Yeshua. 'Hurry!' he said to me, 'Get out of Yerushalayim immediately, because they will not accept what you have to say about me.' ¹⁹ I said, 'Lord, they know themselves that in every synagogue I used to imprison and flog those who trusted in you; ²⁰ also that when the blood of your witness Stephen was being shed, I was standing there too, in full agreement; I was even looking after the clothes of the ones who were killing him!' ²¹ But he said, 'Get going! For I am going to send you far away — to the *Goyim!*'"

²² They had been listening to him up to this point; but now they shouted at the top of their lungs, "Rid the earth of such a man! He's not fit to live!" ²³ They were screaming, waving their clothes and throwing dust into the air; ²⁴ so the commander ordered him brought into the barracks and directed that he be interrogated and whipped, in order to find out why they were yelling at him like this.

²⁵ But as they were stretching him out with thongs to be flogged, Sha'ul said to the captain standing by, "Is it legal for you to whip a man who is a Roman citizen and hasn't even had a trial?" ²⁶ When the captain heard that, he went and reported it to the commander, "Do you realize what you're doing? This man is a Roman citizen!" ²⁷ The commander came and said to Sha'ul, "Tell me, are you a Roman citizen?" "Yes," he said. ²⁸ The commander replied, "I bought this citizenship for a sizeable sum of money." "But I was born to it,"

Sha'ul said. ²⁹ At once the men who had been about to interrogate him drew back from him; and the commander was afraid too, because he realized that he had put this man who was a Roman citizen in chains.

³⁰ However, the next day, since he wanted to know the specific charge the Judeans were bringing against him, he released him and ordered the head *cohanim* and the whole *Sanhedrin* to meet. Then he brought Sha'ul down and put him in front of them.

23 ¹ Sha'ul looked straight at them and said, "Brothers, I have been discharging my obligations to God with a perfectly clear conscience, right up until today." ² But the *cohen hagadol*, Chananyah, ordered those standing near him to strike him on the mouth. ³ Then Sha'ul said to him, "God will strike you, you whitewashed wall! Will you sit there judging me according to the *Torah*, yet in violation of the *Torah* order me to be struck?" ⁴ The men nearby said, "This is the *cohen hagadol* of God that you're insulting!" ⁵ Sha'ul said, "I didn't know, brothers, that he was the *cohen hagadol*; for it says in the *Torah*, **'You are not to speak disparagingly of a ruler of your people.'**ᶻ

⁶ But knowing that one part of the

---

z Exodus 22:27(28)

Cha·nan·**yah** — Ananias
co·hen ha·ga·dol — high priest
Dam·me·sek — Damascus
Gam·li·'el — Gamaliel
Go·yim — Gentiles, nations, pagans
Na·tze·ret — Nazareth
San·hed·rin — Jewish religious court
Sha·'ul — Saul (Paul)
To·rah — Teaching, "Law"; Pentateuch
Tzad·dik — Righteous One
Ye·ru·sha·la·yim — Jerusalem
Ye·shu·a — Jesus

Sanhedrin consisted of *Tz'dukim* and the other of *P'rushim*, Sha'ul shouted, "Brothers, I myself am a *Parush* and the son of *P'rushim*; and it is concerning the hope of the resurrection of the dead that I am being tried!" 7 When he said this, an argument arose between the *P'rushim* and the *Tz'dukim*, and the crowd was divided. 8 For the *Tz'dukim* deny the resurrection and the existence of angels and spirits; whereas the *P'rushim* acknowledge both. 9 So there was a great uproar, with some of the *Torah*-teachers who were on the side of the *P'rushim* standing up and joining in — "We don't find anything wrong with this man; and if a spirit or an angel spoke to him, what of it?" 10 The dispute became so violent that the commander, fearing that Sha'ul would be torn apart by them, ordered the soldiers to go down, take him by force and bring him back into the barracks.

11 The following night, the Lord stood by him and said, "Take courage! For just as you have borne a faithful witness to me in Yerushalayim, so now you must bear witness in Rome."

12 The next day, some of the Judeans formed a conspiracy. They took an oath, saying they would neither eat nor drink until they had killed Sha'ul; 13 more than forty were involved in this plot. 14 They went to the head *cohanim* and the elders and said, "We have bound ourselves by an oath to taste no food until we have killed Sha'ul. 15 What you are to do is make it appear to the commander that you and the *Sanhedrin* want to get more accurate information about Sha'ul's case, so that he will bring him down to you; while we, for our part, are prepared to kill him before he ever gets here."

16 But the son of Sha'ul's sister got wind of the planned ambush, and he went into the barracks and told Sha'ul. 17 Sha'ul called one of the officers and said, "Take this man up to the commander; he has something to tell him." 18 So he took him and brought him to the commander and said, "The prisoner Sha'ul called me and asked me to bring this young man to you, because he has something to tell you." 19 The commander took him by the hand, led him aside privately and asked, "What is it you have to tell me?" 20 He said, "The Judeans have agreed to ask you tomorrow to bring Sha'ul down to the *Sanhedrin* on the pretext that they want to investigate his case more thoroughly. 21 But don't let yourself be talked into it, because more than forty men are lying in wait for him. They have taken an oath neither to eat nor to drink until they kill him; and they are ready now, only waiting for you to give your consent to their request."

22 The commander let the young man go, cautioning him, "Don't tell anyone that you have reported this to me." 23 Then he summoned two of the captains and said, "Get two hundred infantry soldiers ready to leave for Caesarea at nine o'clock tonight, and seventy mounted cavalry and two hundred spearmen; 24 also provide replacements for Sha'ul's horse when it gets tired; and bring him through safely to Felix the governor." 25 And the commander wrote the following letter:

26 From: Claudius Lysias

To: His Excellency, Governor Felix: Greetings!

27 This man was seized by the Judeans and was about to be killed by them, when I came on the scene with my troops and rescued him. After learning that he was a Roman citizen, 28 I wanted to understand exactly what

they were charging him with; so I brought him down to their "*Sanhedrin*".

²⁹ I found that he was charged in connection with questions of their "*Torah*", but that there was no charge deserving death or prison.

³⁰ But when I was informed of a plot against the man, I immediately sent him to you and also ordered his accusers to state their case against him before you.

³¹ So the soldiers, following their orders, took Sha'ul during the night and brought him to Antipatris, ³² then returned to the barracks after leaving the cavalry to go on with him. ³³ The cavalry took him to Caesarea, delivered the letter to the governor, and handed Sha'ul over to him. ³⁴ The governor read the letter and asked what province he was from. On learning he was from Cilicia, ³⁵ he said, "I will give you a full hearing after your accusers have also arrived," and ordered him to be kept under guard in Herod's headquarters.

24 ¹ After five days, the *cohen hagadol* Chananyah came down with some elders and a lawyer named Tertullus, and they presented their case against Sha'ul to the governor. ² Sha'ul was called, and Tertullus began to make the charges: "Felix, Your Excellency, it is because of you that we enjoy unbroken peace, and it is your foresight that has brought to this nation ³ so many reforms in so many areas. It is with the utmost gratitude that we receive this. ⁴ But, in order not to take up too much of your time, I beg your indulgence to give us a brief hearing.

⁵ "We have found this man a pest. He is an agitator among all the Jews throughout the world and a ringleader of the sect of the *Natzratim*. ⁶ He even

tried to profane the Temple, but we arrested him. ⁷* ⁸ By questioning this man yourself, you will be able to learn all about the things of which we are accusing him." ⁹ The Judeans also joined in the accusation and alleged that these were the facts.

¹⁰ When the governor motioned for Sha'ul to speak, he replied, "I know that you have been judge over this nation for a number of years, so I am glad to make my defense. ¹¹ As you can verify for yourself, it has not been more than twelve days since I went up to worship in Yerushalayim; ¹² and neither in the Temple nor in the synagogues nor anywhere else in the city did they find me either arguing with anyone or collecting a crowd. ¹³ Nor can they give any proof of the things of which they are accusing me.

¹⁴ "But this I do admit to you: I worship the **God of our fathers**[a] in accordance with the Way (which they call a sect). I continue to believe everything that accords with the *Torah* and everything written in the Prophets.

---

* Some manuscripts include verses 6b-8a: We wanted to try him under our own law, ⁷ but Lysias the commander intervened. He took him out of our hands by force ⁸ and ordered his accusers to appear before you.

[a] Exodus 3:15

Cha·nan·yah — Ananias
co·ha·nim — priests
co·hen ha·ga·dol — high priest
Natz·ra·tim — Nazarenes, followers of the Man from Nazareth
Pa·rush (pl. *P'ru·shim*) — Pharisee
San·hed·rin — Jewish religious court
Sha·'ul — Saul (Paul)
To·rah — Teaching, "Law"; Pentateuch
To·rah-teachers — scribes
Tz'du·kim — Sadducees
Ye·ru·sha·la·yim — Jerusalem

¹⁵And I continue to have a hope in God — which they too accept — that there will be a resurrection of both the righteous and the unrighteous. ¹⁶Indeed, it is because of this that I make a point of always having a clear conscience in the sight of both God and man.

¹⁷"After an absence of several years, I came to Yerushalayim to bring a charitable gift to my nation and to offer sacrifices. ¹⁸It was in connection with the latter that they found me in the Temple. I had been ceremonially purified, I was not with a crowd, and I was not causing a disturbance. ¹⁹But some Jews from the province of Asia — they ought to be here before you to make a charge if they have anything against me! ²⁰Or else, let these men themselves say what crime they found me guilty of when I stood in front of the *Sanhedrin,* ²¹other than this one thing which I shouted out when I was standing among them: 'I am on trial before you today because I believe in the resurrection of the dead!'"

²²But Felix, who had rather detailed knowledge of things connected with the Way, put them off, saying, "When Lysias the commander comes down, I will decide your case." ²³He ordered the captain to keep Sha'ul in custody, but to let him have considerable liberty and not prevent any of his friends from taking care of his needs.

²⁴After some days, Felix came with his wife Drusilla, who was Jewish. He sent for Sha'ul and listened to him as he spoke about trusting in the Messiah Yeshua. ²⁵But when Sha'ul began to discuss righteousness, self-control and the coming Judgment, Felix became frightened and said, "For the time being, go away! I will send for you when I get a chance." ²⁶At the same time, he hoped that Sha'ul would offer him a bribe; so he sent for him rather often and kept talking with him.

²⁷After two years, Felix was succeeded by Porcius Festus; but because Felix wanted to grant the Judeans a favor, he left Sha'ul still a prisoner.

25 ¹Three days after Festus had entered the province, he went up from Caesarea to Yerushalayim. ²There the head *cohanim* and the Judean leaders informed him of the case against Sha'ul, and they asked him ³to do them the favor of having the man sent to Yerushalayim. (They had plotted to have him ambushed and killed *en route*.) ⁴Festus replied that Sha'ul was being kept under guard in Caesarea, and that he was about to go there shortly himself. ⁵"So," he said, "let competent men among you come down with me and press charges against the man, if he has done something wrong."

⁶After staying with them at most eight or ten days, Festus went down to Caesarea; and on the following day, he took his seat in court and ordered Sha'ul to be brought in. ⁷When he arrived, the Judeans who had come down from Yerushalayim stood around him, bringing many serious charges against him which they could not prove. ⁸In reply, Sha'ul said, "I have committed no offense — not against the *Torah* to which the Jews hold, not against the Temple, and not against the Emperor."

⁹But Festus, wanting to do the Judeans a favor, asked Sha'ul, "Would you be willing to go up to Yerushalayim and be tried before me there on these charges?" ¹⁰Sha'ul replied, "I am standing right now in the court of the Emperor, and this is where I should be tried. I have done no wrong to the Judeans, as you very well know. ¹¹If I am a wrongdoer, if I have done some-

thing for which I deserve to die, then I am ready to die. But if there is nothing to these charges which they are bringing against me, no one can give me to them just to grant a favor! I appeal to the Emperor!" [12] Then Festus, after talking with his advisers, answered, "You have appealed to the Emperor; you will go to the Emperor!"

[13] After some days, King Agrippa and Bernice arrived at Caesarea to pay their respects to Festus. [14] Since they were staying on there for some time, Festus had the opportunity to acquaint the king with Sha'ul's situation. "There is a man here," he said, "who was left behind in custody by Felix. [15] When I was in Yerushalayim, the head *cohanim* and the elders of the Judeans informed me about him and asked me to pronounce judgment against him. [16] My answer to them was that it is not the custom with Romans to give up an accused man just to grant a favor, before he has met his accusers face to face and had the opportunity to defend himself against the charge. [17] So when they arrived here with me, I did not delay, but took my seat in court the next day and ordered the man brought in.

[18] "When the accusers stood up, instead of charging him with some serious crime as I had expected, [19] they disputed with him about certain points of their own religion, and particularly about somebody called Yeshua, who had died, but who Sha'ul claimed was alive. [20] Being at a loss as to how to investigate such questions, I asked him if he would be willing to go to Yerushalayim and be tried on these matters there. [21] But since Sha'ul appealed to be kept in custody and have his case decided by His Imperial Majesty, I ordered him held until I could send him to the Emperor."

[22] Agrippa said to Festus, "I myself have been wanting to hear the man." "Tomorrow," he replied, "you will hear him."

[23] So the next day, Agrippa and Bernice came with much pageantry; they entered the audience room accompanied by military commanders and the prominent men of the city. Then, at the command of Festus, Sha'ul was brought in. [24] Festus said, "King Agrippa and all of you here with us, do you see this man? The whole Judean community has complained to me about him both in Yerushalayim and here, crying that he shouldn't be allowed to remain alive. [25] But I discovered that he had done nothing that deserves a death sentence. Now when he himself appealed to the Emperor, I decided to send him. [26] However, I have nothing specific to write to His Majesty about him. This is why I have brought him before all of you, and especially before you, King Agrippa — so that after we have examined him, I might have something to write. [27] It seems irrational to me to send a prisoner without also indicating what the charges against him are."

26 [1] Agrippa said to Sha'ul, "You have permission to speak on your own behalf." Then Sha'ul motioned with his hand and began his defense:

[2] "King Agrippa, I consider myself fortunate that it is before you today that I am defending myself against all the charges made against me by Jews, [3] because you are so well informed

---

co · ha · nim — priests
San · hed · rin — Jewish religious court
Sha · 'ul — Saul (Paul)
To · rah — Teaching, "Law"; Pentateuch
Ye · ru · sha · la · yim — Jerusalem
Ye · shu · a — Jesus

about all the Jewish customs and controversies. Therefore, I beg you to listen to me patiently.

4 "So then! All Jews know how I lived my life from my youth on, both in my own country and in Yerushalayim. 5 They have known me for a long time; and if they are willing, they can testify that I have followed the strictest party in our religion — that is, I have lived as a *Parush*. 6 How ironic it is that I stand on trial here because of my hope in the promise made to our fathers! 7 It is the fulfillment of this very promise that our twelve tribes hope to attain, as they resolutely carry on their acts of worship night and day; yet it is in connection with this hope, Your Majesty, that I am being accused by Jews! 8 Why do you people consider it incredible that God raises the dead?

9 "I used to think it was my duty to do all I could to combat the name of Yeshua from Natzeret; 10 and in Yerushalayim I did so. After receiving authority from the head *cohanim*, I myself threw many of God's people in prison; when they were put to death, I cast my vote against them. 11 Often I went from one synagogue to another, punishing them and trying to make them blaspheme; and in my wild fury against them, I even went so far as to persecute them in cities outside the country.

12 "On one such occasion, I was traveling to Dammesek with the full authority and power of the head *cohanim*. 13 I was on the road, and it was noon, Your Majesty, when I saw a light from heaven, brighter than the sun, shining around me and my traveling companions. 14 We all fell to the ground; and then I heard a voice saying to me, in Hebrew, 'Sha'ul! Sha'ul! Why do you keep persecuting me? It's hard on you to be kicking against the ox-

goads!' 15 I said, 'Who are you, sir?' and the Lord answered, 'I am Yeshua, and you are persecuting me! 16 But get up, and stand on your feet! I have appeared to you to appoint you to serve and bear witness to what you have already seen of me, and to what you will see when I appear to you in the future. 17 I will deliver you from the People and from the *Goyim*. I am sending you 18 to open their eyes; so that they will turn from darkness to light, from the power of the Adversary to God, and thus receive forgiveness of sins and a place among those who have been separated for holiness by putting their trust in me.'

19 "So, King Agrippa, I did not disobey the vision from heaven! 20 On the contrary, I announced first in Dammesek, then in Yerushalayim and throughout Y'hudah, and also to the *Goyim*, that they should turn from their sins to God and then do deeds consistent with that repentance. 21 It was because of these things that Jews seized me in the Temple and tried to kill me. 22 However, I have had God's help; so to this day, I stand testifying to both small and great, saying nothing but what both the prophets and Moshe said would happen — 23 that the Messiah would die, and that he, as the first to rise from the dead, would proclaim light to both the People and the *Goyim*."

24 But just as he reached this point in his defence, Festus shouted at the top of his voice, "Sha'ul, you're out of your mind! So much learning is driving you crazy!"

25 But Sha'ul said, "No, I am not 'crazy', Festus, Your Excellency; on the contrary, I am speaking words of truth and sanity. 26 For the king understands these matters, so to him I express myself freely, because I am sure that none of these things have been hidden

from him. After all, they didn't happen in some back alley. ²⁷ King Agrippa, do you believe the prophets? I know you believe!"

²⁸ Agrippa said to Sha'ul, "In this short time, you're trying to convince me to become Messianic?" ²⁹ Sha'ul replied, "Whether it takes a short time or a long time, I wish to God that not only you, but also everyone hearing me today, might become just like me — except for these chains!"

³⁰ Then the king got up, and with him the governor and Bernice and the others sitting with them. ³¹ After they had left, they said to one another, "This man is doing nothing that deserves either death or prison." ³² And Agrippa said to Festus, "If he hadn't appealed to the Emperor, he could have been released."

27 ¹ Once it had been decided that we should set sail for Italy, they handed Sha'ul and some other prisoners over to an officer of the Emperor's Regiment named Julius. ² We embarked in a ship from Adramyttium which was about to sail to the ports along the coast of the province of Asia, and put out to sea, accompanied by Aristarchus, a Macedonian from Thessalonica. ³ The next day, we landed at Tzidon; and Julius considerately allowed Sha'ul to go visit his friends and receive what he needed. ⁴ Putting to sea from there, we sailed close to the sheltered side of Cyprus because the winds were against us, ⁵ then across the open sea along the coasts of Cilicia and Pamphylia; and so we reached Myra in Lycia.

⁶ There the Roman officer found an Alexandrian vessel sailing to Italy and put us aboard. ⁷ For a number of days we made little headway, and we arrived off Cnidus only with difficulty. The wind would not let us continue any

farther along the direct route; so we ran down along the sheltered side of Crete from Cape Salmone; ⁸ and, continuing to struggle on, hugging the coast, we reached a place called Pleasant Harbor, near the town of Lasea.

⁹ Since much time had been lost, and continuing the voyage was risky, because it was already past *Yom-Kippur*, Sha'ul advised them, ¹⁰ "Men, I can see that our voyage is going to be a catastrophe, not only with huge losses to the cargo and the ship but with loss of our lives as well." ¹¹ However, the officer paid more attention to the pilot and the ship's owner than to what Sha'ul said. ¹² Moreover, since the harbor was not well suited to sitting out the winter, the majority reached the decision to sail on from there in the hope of reaching Phoenix, another harbor in Crete, and wintering there, where it is protected from the southwest and northwest winds.

¹³ When a gentle southerly breeze began to blow, they thought that they had their goal within grasp; so they raised the anchor and started coasting by Crete close to shore. ¹⁴ But before long there struck us from land a full gale from the northeast, the kind they call an Evrakilon. ¹⁵ The ship was caught up and unable to face the wind, so we gave way to it and were driven along.

---

co·ha·nim — priests
Dam·me·sek — Damascus
Go·yim — Gentiles, nations, pagans
Na·tze·ret — Nazareth
Pa·rush (pl. *P'ru·shim*) — Pharisee
Sha·'ul — Saul (Paul)
Tzi·don — Sidon
Ye·ru·sha·la·yim — Jerusalem
Ye·shu·a — Jesus
Y'hu·dah — Judea
Yom-Kip·pur — Day of Atonement

¹⁶ As we passed into the lee of a small island called Cauda, we managed with strenuous effort to get control of the lifeboat. ¹⁷ They hoisted it aboard, then fastened cables tightly around the ship itself to reinforce it. Fearing they might run aground on the Syrtis sandbars, they lowered the masts and sails and thus continued drifting. ¹⁸ But because we were fighting such heavy weather, the next day they began to jettison nonessentials; ¹⁹ and the third day, they threw the ship's sailing equipment overboard with their own hands. ²⁰ For many days neither the sun nor the stars appeared, while the storm continued to rage, until gradually all hope of survival vanished.

²¹ It was then, when they had gone a long time without eating, that Sha'ul stood up in front of them and said, "You should have listened to me and not set out from Crete; if you had, you would have escaped this disastrous loss. ²² But now, my advice to you is to take heart; because not one of you will lose his life — only the ship will be lost. ²³ For this very night, there stood next to me an angel of the God to whom I belong and whom I serve. ²⁴ He said, 'Don't be afraid, Sha'ul! You have to stand before the Emperor. Look! God has granted you all those who are sailing with you.' ²⁵ So, men, take heart! For I trust God and believe that what I have been told will come true. ²⁶ Nevertheless, we have to run aground on some island."

²⁷ It was the fourteenth night, and we were still being driven about in the Adriatic Sea, when around midnight the sailors sensed that we were nearing land. ²⁸ So they dropped a plumbline and found the water one hundred and twenty feet deep. A little farther on, they took another sounding and found it ninety feet. ²⁹ Fearing we might run on the rocks, they let out four anchors from the stern and prayed for daylight to come.

³⁰ At this point, the crew made an attempt to abandon ship — they lowered the lifeboat into the sea, pretending that they were about to let out some anchors from the bow. ³¹ Sha'ul said to the officer and the soldiers, "Unless these men remain aboard the ship, you yourselves cannot be saved." ³² Then the soldiers cut the ropes holding the lifeboat and let it go.

³³ Just before daybreak, Sha'ul urged them all to eat, saying, "Today is the fourteenth day you have been in suspense, going hungry, eating nothing. ³⁴ Therefore I advise you to take some food; you need it for your own survival. For not one of you will lose so much as a hair from his head." ³⁵ When he had said this, he took bread, said the *b'rakhah* to God in front of everyone, broke it and began to eat. ³⁶ With courage restored, they all ate some food themselves. ³⁷ Altogether there were 276 of us on board the ship. ³⁸ After they had eaten all they wanted, they lightened the ship by dumping the grain into the sea.

³⁹ When day broke, they didn't recognize the land; but they noticed a bay with a sand beach, where they decided to run the ship aground if they could. ⁴⁰ So they cut away the anchors and left them in the sea; at the same time, they loosened the ropes that held the rudders out of the water. Then they hoisted the foresail to the wind and headed for the beach. ⁴¹ But they encountered a place where two currents meet, and ran the vessel aground on the sandbar there. The bow stuck and would not move, while the pounding of the surf began to break up the stern.

⁴² At this point the soldiers' thought was to kill the prisoners, so that none of

them would swim off and escape. ⁴³ But the officer, wanting to save Sha'ul, kept them from carrying out their plan. He ordered those who could swim to throw themselves overboard first and head for shore, ⁴⁴ and the rest to use planks or whatever they could find from the ship. Thus it was that everyone reached land safely.

28 ¹ After our escape, we learned that the island was called Malta. ² Its people showed extraordinary kindness — it was cold and it had started to rain, so they lit a bonfire and welcomed us all. ³ Sha'ul had gathered a bundle of sticks and was adding them to the fire, when a poisonous snake, driven out by the heat, fastened itself to his hand. ⁴ The islanders saw the creature hanging from Sha'ul's hand and said to one another, "This man must be a murderer. Even though he escaped the sea, justice has not allowed him to live." ⁵ But he shook the snake off into the fire and suffered no harm. ⁶ They waited, expecting him to swell up or suddenly fall down dead; but after waiting a long time and seeing that nothing amiss was happening to him, they reversed their opinion and said he was a god.

⁷ Nearby were lands belonging to the governor of the island, whose name was Publius. He received us in a friendly manner and put us up for three days. ⁸ Now it so happened that Publius' father was lying in bed, sick with fever attacks and dysentery. Sha'ul went in to him, prayed, placed his hands on him and healed him. ⁹ After this happened, the rest of those on the island who had ailments came and were healed. ¹⁰ They heaped honors on us; and when the time came for us to sail, they provided the supplies we needed.

¹¹ After three months, we sailed away on a ship from Alexandria called "Twin Gods", which had passed the winter at the island. ¹² We landed at Syracuse and stayed three days. ¹³ From there, we arrived at Rhegium by tacking; but after one day, a south wind sprang up; so we made it to Puteoli the second day. ¹⁴ There we found brothers who invited us to spend a week with them. And so we went on toward Rome.

¹⁵ The brothers there had heard about us and came as far as Appian Market and Three Inns to meet us. When Sha'ul saw them, he thanked God and took courage. ¹⁶ And when we arrived at Rome, the officer allowed Sha'ul to stay by himself, though guarded by a soldier.

¹⁷ After three days Sha'ul called a meeting of the local Jewish leaders. When they had gathered, he said to them: "Brothers, although I have done nothing against either our people or the traditions of our fathers, I was made a prisoner in Yerushalayim and handed over to the Romans. ¹⁸ They examined me and were ready to release me, because I had done nothing to justify a death sentence. ¹⁹ But when the Judeans objected, I was forced to appeal to the Emperor — not that I had any charge to make against my own people. ²⁰ This is why I have asked to see you and speak with you, for it is because of the hope of Israel that I have this chain around me."

²¹ They said to him, "We have not received any letters about you from Y'hudah, and none of the brothers who have come from there has reported or said anything bad about you. ²² But we do think it would be appropriate to hear your views from you, yourself; for all we know about this sect is that

---

b'ra·khah — blessing
Sha·'ul — Saul (Paul)
Ye·ru·sha·la·yim — Jerusalem
Y'hu·dah — Judea

people everywhere are speaking against it."

²³So they arranged a day with him and came to his quarters in large numbers. From morning until evening he explained the matter to them, giving a thorough witness about the Kingdom of God and making use of both the *Torah* of Moshe and the Prophets to persuade them about Yeshua. ²⁴Some were convinced by what he said, ²⁵while others refused to believe.

So they left, disagreeing among themselves, after Sha'ul had made one final statement: "The *Ruach HaKodesh* spoke well in saying to your fathers through Yesha'yahu the prophet,

²⁶**"Go to this people and say,
"You will keep on hearing, but never understand,
and you will keep on seeing but never perceive,
²⁷because the heart of this people has grown thick —**

**with their ears they barely hear,
and their eyes they have closed,
for fear that they should see with their eyes,
hear with their ears,
understand with their heart,
and do *t'shuvah*,
so that I could heal them.'"**[b]

²⁸Therefore, let it be known to you that this salvation of God has been sent to the *Goyim*, and they will listen!"²⁹*

³⁰Sha'ul remained two whole years in a place he rented for himself; and he continued receiving all who came to see him, ³¹openly and without hindrance proclaiming the Kingdom of God and teaching about the Lord Yeshua the Messiah.

---

* Some manuscripts include verse 29: After he had said this, the Jews left, arguing vehemently among themselves.

b Isaiah 6:9-10

THE LETTER FROM YESHUA'S EMISSARY, SHA'UL (PAUL) TO THE MESSIANIC COMMUNITY IN ROME:

ROMANS

1 [1]From: Sha'ul, a slave of the Messiah Yeshua, an emissary because I was called and set apart for the Good News of God.

[2]God promised this Good News in advance through his prophets in the Tanakh. [3]It concerns his Son — he is descended from David physically; [4]he was powerfully demonstrated to be Son of God spiritually, set apart by his having been resurrected from the dead; he is Yeshua the Messiah, our Lord.

[5]Through him we received grace and were given the work of being an emissary on his behalf promoting trust-grounded obedience among all the Gentiles, [6]including you, who have been called by Yeshua the Messiah.

[7]To: All those in Rome whom God loves, who have been called, who have been set apart for him:

Grace to you and *shalom* from God our Father and the Lord Yeshua the Messiah.

[8]First, I thank my God through Yeshua the Messiah for all of you, because the report of your trust is spreading throughout the whole world. [9]For God, whom I serve in my spirit by spreading the Good News about his Son, is my witness that I regularly remember you [10]in my prayers; and I always pray that somehow, now or in the future, I might, by God's will, succeed in coming to visit you. [11]For I long to see you, so that I might share with you some spiritual gift that can make you stronger — [12]or, to put it another way, so that by my being with you, we might, through the faith we share, encourage one another. [13]Brothers, I want you to know that although I have been prevented from visiting you until now, I have often planned to do so, in order that I might have some fruit among you, just as I have among the other Gentiles. [14]I owe a debt to both civilized Greeks and uncivilized people, to both the educated and the ignorant; [15]therefore I am eager to proclaim the Good News also to you who live in Rome.

[16]For I am not ashamed of the Good News, since it is God's powerful means of bringing salvation to everyone who keeps on trusting, to the Jew especially,

---

Da·**vid** — David
Go·**yim** — Gentiles, nations, pagans
Mo·**she** — Moses
Ru·ach Ha·Ko·desh — Holy Spirit
sha·lom — peace
Sha·**'ul** — Saul (Paul)
Ta·nakh — Hebrew Scriptures, "Old Testament"
To·rah — Teaching, "Law"; Pentateuch
do *t'shu·vah* — repent, turn from sin to God
Ye·ru·sha·**la**·yim — Jerusalem
Ye·sha'·**ya**·hu — Isaiah
Ye·**shu**·a — Jesus

but equally to the Gentile. ^{17} For in it is revealed how God makes people righteous in his sight; and from beginning to end it is through trust — as the *Tanakh* puts it, **"But the person who is righteous will live his life by trust."**^{a}

^{18} What is revealed is God's anger from heaven against all the godlessness and wickedness of people who in their wickedness keep suppressing the truth; ^{19} because what is known about God is plain to them, since God has made it plain to them. ^{20} For ever since the creation of the universe his invisible qualities — both his eternal power and his divine nature — have been clearly seen, because they can be understood from what he has made. Therefore, they have no excuse; ^{21} because, although they know who God is, they do not glorify him as God or thank him. On the contrary, they have become futile in their thinking; and their undiscerning hearts have become darkened. ^{22} Claiming to be wise, they have become fools! ^{23} In fact, they have exchanged the glory of the immortal God for mere images, like a mortal human being, or like birds, animals or reptiles!

^{24} This is why God has given them up to the vileness of their hearts' lusts, to the shameful misuse of each other's bodies. ^{25} They have exchanged the truth of God for falsehood, by worshipping and serving created things, rather than the Creator — praised be he for ever. *Amen.* ^{26} This is why God has given them up to degrading passions; so that their women exchange natural sexual relations for unnatural; ^{27} and likewise the men, giving up natural relations with the opposite sex, burn with passion for one another, men committing shameful acts with other

men and receiving in their own persons the penalty appropriate to their perversion. ^{28} In other words, since they have not considered God worth knowing, God has given them up to worthless ways of thinking; so that they do improper things. ^{29} They are filled with every kind of wickedness, evil, greed and vice; stuffed with jealousy, murder, quarrelling, dishonesty and ill-will; they are gossips, ^{30} slanderers, haters of God; they are insolent, arrogant and boastful; they plan evil schemes; they disobey their parents; ^{31} they are brainless, faithless, heartless and ruthless. ^{32} They know well enough God's righteous decree that people who do such things deserve to die; yet not only do they keep doing them, but they applaud others who do the same.

2 ^{1} Therefore you have no excuse, whoever you are, passing judgment; for when you judge someone else, you are passing judgment against yourself; since you who are judging do the same things he does. ^{2} We know that God's judgment lands impartially on those who do such things; ^{3} do you think that you, a mere man passing judgment on others who do such things, yet doing them yourself, will escape the judgment of God? ^{4} Or perhaps you despise the riches of his kindness, forbearance and patience; because you don't realize that God's kindness is intended to lead you to turn from your sins. ^{5} But by your stubbornness, by your unrepentant heart, you are storing up anger for yourself on the Day of Anger, when God's righteous judgment will be revealed; ^{6} for he **will pay back each one according to his deeds.**^{b} ^{7} To those who seek glory, honor and immortality by perseverance in doing good, he will pay back eternal life. ^{8} But

---

a Habakkuk 2:4

b Psalm 62:13(12), Proverbs 24:12

to those who are self-seeking, who disobey the truth and obey evil, he will pay back wrath and anger.

⁹ Yes, he will pay back misery and anguish to every human being who does evil, to the Jew first, then to the Gentile; ¹⁰ but glory and honor and *shalom* to everyone who keeps doing what is good, to the Jew first, then to the Gentile. ¹¹ For God does not show favoritism. ¹² All who have sinned outside the framework of *Torah* will die outside the framework of *Torah*; and all who have sinned within the framework of *Torah* will be judged by *Torah*. ¹³ For it is not merely the hearers of *Torah* whom God considers righteous; rather, it is the doers of what *Torah* says who will be made righteous in God's sight. ¹⁴ For whenever Gentiles, who have no *Torah*, do naturally what the *Torah* requires, then these, even though they don't have *Torah*, for themselves are *Torah*! ¹⁵ For their lives show that the conduct the *Torah* dictates is **written in their hearts.**ᶜ Their consciences also bear witness to this, for their conflicting thoughts sometimes accuse them and sometimes defend them ¹⁶ on a day when God passes judgment on people's inmost secrets. (According to the Good News as I proclaim it, he does this through the Messiah Yeshua.)

¹⁷ But if you call yourself a Jew and rest on *Torah* and boast about God ¹⁸ and know his will and give your approval to what is right, because you have been instructed from the *Torah*; ¹⁹ and if you have persuaded yourself that you are a guide to the blind, a light in the darkness, ²⁰ an instructor for the spiritually unaware and a teacher of children, since in the *Torah* you have the embodiment of knowledge and truth; ²¹ then, you who teach others, don't you teach yourself? Preaching, **"Thou shalt not steal,"**ᵈ do you steal? ²² Saying, **"Thou shalt not commit adultery,"**ᵉ do you commit adultery? Detesting idols, do you commit idolatrous acts? ²³ You who take such pride in *Torah*, do you, by disobeying the *Torah*, dishonor God? — ²⁴ as it says in the *Tanakh*, **"For it is because of you that God's name is blasphemed by the Goyim."**ᶠ ²⁵ For circumcision is indeed of value if you do what *Torah* says. But if you are a transgressor of *Torah*, your circumcision has become uncircumcision! ²⁶ Therefore, if an uncircumcised man keeps the righteous requirements of the *Torah*, won't his uncircumcision be counted as circumcision? ²⁷ Indeed, the man who is physically uncircumcised but obeys the *Torah* will stand as a judgment on you who have had a *b'rit-milah* and have *Torah* written out but violate it! ²⁸ For the real Jew is not merely Jewish outwardly: true circumcision is not only external and physical. ²⁹ On the contrary, the real Jew is one inwardly; and true circumcision is of the heart, spiritual not literal; so that his praise comes not from other people but from God.

3 ¹ Then what advantage has the Jew? What is the value of being circumcised? ² Much in every way! In the first place, the Jews were entrusted

---

ᶜ Jeremiah 31:32(33)

ᵈ Exodus 20:13(15), Deuteronomy 5:19
ᵉ Exodus 20:13(14), Deuteronomy 5:18
ᶠ Isaiah 52:5, Ezekiel 36:20

A · **men** — So be it
b'rit-mi · **lah** — circumcision
Go · yim — Gentiles, nations, pagans
sha · lom — peace
Ta · nakh — Hebrew Scriptures, "Old Testament"
To · rah — Teaching, "Law"; Pentateuch
Ye · shu · a — Jesus

with the very words of God. [3] If some of them were unfaithful, so what? Does their faithlessness cancel God's faithfulness? [4] Heaven forbid! God would be true even if everyone were a liar! — as the *Tanakh* says,

> "so that you, God, may be proved right in your words
> and win the verdict when you are put on trial."[g]

[5] Now if our unrighteousness highlights God's righteousness, what should we say? That God is unrighteous to inflict his anger on us? (I am speaking here the way people commonly do.) [6] Heaven forbid! Else, how could God judge the world? [7] "But," you say, "if, through my lie, God's truth is enhanced and brings him greater glory, why am I still judged merely for being a sinner?" [8] Indeed! Why not say (as some people slander us by claiming we do say), "Let us do evil, so that good may come of it"? Against them the judgment is a just one!

[9] So are we Jews better off? Not entirely; for I have already made the charge that all people, Jews and Gentiles alike, are controlled by sin. [10] As the *Tanakh* puts it,

> "There is no one righteous, not even one! —
> No one understands,
> [11] no one seeks God,
> [12] all have turned away
> and at the same time become useless;
> there is no one who shows kindness, not a single one![h]

[13] "Their throats are open graves, they use their tongues to deceive.[i]
Vipers' venom is under their lips.[j]

[14] Their mouths are full of curses and bitterness.[k]

[15] "Their feet rush to shed blood,
[16] in their ways are ruin and misery,
[17] and the way of *shalom* they do not know.[l]

[18] "There is no fear of God before their eyes."[m]

[19] Moreover, we know that whatever the *Torah* says, it says to those living within the framework of the *Torah*; in order that every mouth may be stopped and the whole world be shown to deserve God's adverse judgment. [20] For in his sight no one alive will be considered righteous[n] on the ground of legalistic observance of *Torah* commands, because what *Torah* really does is show people how sinful they are.

[21] But now, quite apart from *Torah*, God's way of making people righteous in his sight has been made clear — although the *Torah* and the Prophets give their witness to it as well — [22] and it is a righteousness that comes from God, through the faithfulness of Yeshua the Messiah, to all who continue trusting. For it makes no difference whether one is a Jew or a Gentile, [23] since all have sinned and come short of earning God's praise. [24] By God's grace, without earning it, all are granted the status of being considered righteous before him, through the act redeeming us from our enslavement to sin that was accomplished by the Messiah Yeshua. [25] God put Yeshua forward as the *kapparah* for sin through his faithfulness in respect to his bloody sacrificial death. This vindicated God's righteousness; because, in his forbearance, he

---

g Psalm 51:6(4)   h Psalm 14:1-3, 53:1-3
i Psalm 5:10(9)   j Psalm 140:4(3)

k Psalm 10:7
l Isaiah 59:7-8, Proverbs 1:16
m Psalm 36:2(1)   n Psalm 143:2

had passed over, [with neither punishment nor remission,] the sins people had committed in the past; 26 and it vindicates his righteousness in the present age by showing that he is righteous himself and is also the one who makes people righteous on the ground of Yeshua's faithfulness.

27 So what room is left for boasting? None at all! What kind of *Torah* excludes it? One that has to do with legalistic observance of rules? No, rather, a *Torah* that has to do with trusting. 28 Therefore, we hold the view that a person comes to be considered righteous by God on the ground of trusting, which has nothing to do with legalistic observance of *Torah* commands.

29 Or is God the God of the Jews only? Isn't he also the God of the Gentiles? Yes, he is indeed the God of the Gentiles; 30 because, as you will admit, **God is one.**[o] Therefore, he will consider righteous the circumcised on the ground of trusting and the uncircumcised through that same trusting. 31 Does it follow that we abolish *Torah* by this trusting? Heaven forbid! On the contrary, we confirm *Torah*.

4 1 Then what should we say Avraham, our forefather, obtained by his own efforts? 2 For if Avraham came to be considered righteous by God because of legalistic observances, then he has something to boast about. But this is not how it is before God! 3 For what does the *Tanakh* say? **"Avraham put his trust in God, and it was credited to his account as righteousness."**[p] 4 Now the account of someone who is working is credited not on the ground of grace but on the ground of what is owed him. 5 However, in the case of one who is not working but rather is trusting in him who makes ungodly people righteous, his trust is credited to him as righteousness.

6 In the same way, the blessing which David pronounces is on those whom God credits with righteousness apart from legalistic observances:

> 7 **"Blessed are those whose transgressions are forgiven,**
> **whose sins are covered over;**
> 8 **Blessed is the man whose sin *Adonai* will not reckon against his account."**[q]

9 Now is this blessing for the circumcised only? Or is it also for the uncircumcised? For we say that Avraham's **trust was credited to his account as righteousness;** 10 but what state was he in when it was so credited — circumcision or uncircumcision? Not in circumcision, but in uncircumcision! 11 In fact, he received circumcision as a sign, as a seal of the righteousness he had been credited with on the ground of the trust he had had while he was still uncircumcised. This happened so that he could be the father of every uncircumcised person who trusts and thus has righteousness credited to him, 12 and at the same time be the father of every circumcised person who not only has had a *b'rit-milah*, but also follows in the footsteps of the trust which

o Deuteronomy 6:4 *p* Genesis 15:6

q Psalm 32:1-2

A·do·nai — the LORD, Jehovah
Av·ra·**ham** — Abraham
b'rit-mi·lah — circumcision
Da·**vid** — David
kap·pa·rah — atonement, propitiation
sha·lom — peace
Ta·nakh — Hebrew Scriptures, "Old Testament"
To·rah — Teaching, "Law"; Pentateuch
Ye·**shu**·a — Jesus

Avraham avinu had when he was still uncircumcised.

¹³ For the promise to Avraham and his **seed**ʳ that he would inherit the world did not come through legalism but through the righteousness that trust produces. ¹⁴ For if the heirs are produced by legalism, then trust is pointless and the promise worthless. ¹⁵ For what law brings is punishment. But where there is no law, there is also no violation.

¹⁶ The reason the promise is based on trusting is so that it may come as God's free gift, a promise that can be relied on by all the **seed**, not only those who live within the framework of the *Torah*, but also those with the kind of trust Avraham had — *Avraham avinu* for all of us. ¹⁷ This accords with the *Tanakh*, where it says, **"I have appointed you to be a father to many nations."**ˢ Avraham is our father in God's sight because he trusted God as the one who gives life to the dead and calls nonexistent things into existence. ¹⁸ For he was past hope, yet in hope he trusted that he would indeed become **a father to many nations,** in keeping with what he had been told, **"So many will your seed be."**ᵗ ¹⁹ His trust did not waver when he considered his own body — which was as good as dead, since he was about a hundred years old — or when he considered that Sarah's womb was dead too. ²⁰ He did not by lack of trust decide against God's promises. On the contrary, by trust he was given power as he gave glory to God, ²¹ for he was fully convinced that what God had promised he could also accomplish. ²² This is why **it was credited to his account as righteousness.**ᵘ

²³ But the words, **"it was credited to his account …,"** were not written for him only. ²⁴ They were written also for us, who will certainly have our account credited too, because we have trusted in him who raised Yeshua our Lord from the dead — ²⁵ Yeshua, who was delivered over to death because of our offences and raised to life in order to make us righteous.

5 ¹ So, since we have come to be considered righteous by God because of our trust, let us continue to have *shalom* with God through our Lord, Yeshua the Messiah. ² Also through him and on the ground of our trust, we have gained access to this grace in which we stand; so let us boast about the hope of experiencing God's glory. ³ But not only that, let us also boast in our troubles; because we know that trouble produces endurance, ⁴ endurance produces character, and character produces hope; ⁵ and this hope does not let us down, because God's love for us has already been poured out in our hearts through the *Ruach HaKodesh* who has been given to us.

⁶ For while we were still helpless, at the right time, the Messiah died on behalf of ungodly people. ⁷ Now it is a rare event when someone gives up his life even for the sake of somebody righteous, although possibly for a truly good person one might have the courage to die. ⁸ But God demonstrates his own love for us in that the Messiah died on our behalf while we were still sinners. ⁹ Therefore, since we have now come to be considered righteous by means of his bloody sacrificial death, how much more will we be delivered through him from the anger of God's judgment! ¹⁰ For if we were reconciled with God through his Son's death when we were enemies, how much more will we be delivered by his life, now that we are reconciled! ¹¹ And not only will we

---

r Genesis 15:3, 5   s Genesis 17:5
t Genesis 15:5   u Genesis 15:6

be delivered in the future, but we are boasting about God right now, because he has acted through our Lord Yeshua the Messiah, through whom we have already received that reconciliation.

[12] Here is how it works: it was through one individual that sin entered the world, and through sin, death; and in this way death passed through to the whole human race, inasmuch as everyone sinned. [13] Sin was indeed present in the world before *Torah* was given, but sin is not counted as such when there is no *Torah*. [14] Nevertheless death ruled from Adam until Moshe, even over those whose sinning was not exactly like Adam's violation of a direct command. In this, Adam prefigured the one who was to come.

[15] But the free gift is not like the offence. For if, because of one man's offence, many died, then how much more has God's grace, that is, the gracious gift of one man, Yeshua the Messiah, overflowed to many! [16] No, the free gift is not like what resulted from one man's sinning; for from one sinner came judgment that brought condemnation; but the free gift came after many offences and brought acquittal. [17] For if, because of the offence of one man, death ruled through that one man; how much more will those receiving the overflowing grace, that is, the gift of being considered righteous, rule in life through the one man Yeshua the Messiah!

[18] In other words, just as it was through one offence that all people came under condemnation, so also it is through one righteous act that all people come to be considered righteous. [19] For just as through the disobedience of the one man, many were made sinners, so also through the obedience of the other man, many will be made righteous. [20] And the *Torah* came into the picture so that the offence would proliferate; but where sin proliferated, grace proliferated even more. [21] All this happened so that just as sin ruled by means of death, so also grace might rule through causing people to be considered righteous, so that they might have eternal life, through Yeshua the Messiah, our Lord.

6 [1] So then, are we to say, "Let's keep on sinning, so that there can be more grace"? [2] Heaven forbid! How can we, who have died to sin, still live in it? [3] Don't you know that those of us who have been immersed into the Messiah Yeshua have been immersed into his death? [4] Through immersion into his death we were buried with him; so that just as, through the glory of the Father, the Messiah was raised from the dead, likewise we too might live a new life. [5] For if we have been united with him in a death like his, we will also be united with him in a resurrection like his. [6] We know that our old self was put to death on the execution-stake with him, so that the entire body of our sinful propensities might be destroyed, and we might no longer be enslaved to sin. [7] For someone who has died has been cleared from sin. [8] Now since we died with the Messiah, we trust that we will also live with him. [9] We know that the Messiah has been raised from the dead, never to die again; death has no

---

A·dam — Adam
Av·ra·ham — Abraham
Av·ra·ham a·vi·nu — Abraham, our father
b'rit-mi·lah — circumcision
Mo·she — Moses
Ru·ach-Ha·Ko·desh — Holy Spirit
Sa·rah — Sarah
sha·lom — peace
Ta·nakh — Hebrew Scriptures, "Old Testament"
To·rah — Teaching, "Law"; Pentateuch
Ye·shu·a — Jesus

authority over him. ¹⁰ For his death was a unique event that need not be repeated; but his life, he keeps on living for God. ¹¹ In the same way, consider yourselves to be dead to sin but alive for God, by your union with the Messiah Yeshua.

¹² Therefore, do not let sin rule in your mortal bodies, so that it makes you obey its desires; ¹³ and do not offer any part of yourselves to sin as an instrument for wickedness. On the contrary, offer yourselves to God as people alive from the dead, and your various parts to God as instruments for righteousness. ¹⁴ For sin will not have authority over you; because you are not under legalism but under grace.

¹⁵ Therefore, what conclusion should we reach? "Let's go on sinning, because we're not under legalism but under grace"? Heaven forbid! ¹⁶ Don't you know that if you present yourselves to someone as obedient slaves, then, of the one whom you are obeying, you are slaves — whether of sin, which leads to death, or of obedience, which leads to being made righteous? ¹⁷ By God's grace, you, who were once slaves to sin, obeyed from your heart the pattern of teaching to which you were exposed; ¹⁸ and after you had been set free from sin, you became enslaved to righteousness. ¹⁹ (I am using popular language because your human nature is so weak.) For just as you used to offer your various parts as slaves to impurity and lawlessness, which led to more lawlessness; so now offer your various parts as slaves to righteousness, which leads to being made holy, set apart for God. ²⁰ For when you were slaves of sin, you were free in relationship to righteousness; ²¹ but what benefit did you derive from the things of which you are now ashamed? The end result of those things was death. ²² However, now, freed from sin and enslaved to God, you do get the benefit — it consists in being made holy, set apart for God, and its end result is eternal life. ²³ For what one earns from sin is death; but eternal life is what one receives as a free gift from God, in union with the Messiah Yeshua, our Lord.

7 ¹ Surely you know, brothers — for I am speaking to those who understand *Torah* — that the *Torah* has authority over a person only so long as he lives? ² For example, a married woman is bound by *Torah* to her husband while he is alive; but if the husband dies, she is released from the part of the *Torah* that deals with husbands. ³ Therefore, while the husband is alive, she will be called an adulteress if she marries another man; but if the husband dies, she is free from that part of the *Torah*; so that if she marries another man, she is not an adulteress.

⁴ Thus, my brothers, you have been made dead with regard to the *Torah* through the Messiah's body, so that you may belong to someone else, namely, the one who has been raised from the dead, in order for us to bear fruit for God. ⁵ For when we were living according to our old nature, the passions connected with sins worked through the *Torah* in our various parts, with the result that we bore fruit for death. ⁶ But now we have been released from this aspect of the *Torah*, because we have died to that which had us in its clutches, so that we are serving in the new way provided by the Spirit and not in the old way of outwardly following the letter of the law.

⁷ Therefore, what are we to say? That the *Torah* is sinful? Heaven forbid! Rather, the function of the *Torah* was that without it, I would not have known what sin is. For example, I would not have become conscious of

what greed is if the *Torah* had not said, **"Thou shalt not covet."**[v] ⁸But sin, seizing the opportunity afforded by the commandment, worked in me all kinds of evil desires — for apart from *Torah*, sin is dead. ⁹I was once alive, outside the framework of *Torah*. But when the commandment really encountered me, sin sprang to life, ¹⁰and I died. The commandment that was intended to bring me life was found to be bringing me death! ¹¹For sin, seizing the opportunity afforded by the commandment, deceived me; and through the commandment, sin killed me. ¹²So the *Torah* is holy; that is, the commandment is holy, just and good.

¹³Then did something good become for me the source of death? Heaven forbid! Rather, it was sin working death in me through something good, so that sin might be clearly exposed as sin, so that sin through the commandment might come to be experienced as sinful beyond measure. ¹⁴For we know that the *Torah* is of the Spirit; but as for me, I am bound to the old nature, sold to sin as a slave. ¹⁵I don't understand my own behavior — I don't do what I want to do; instead, I do the very thing I hate! ¹⁶Now if I am doing what I don't want to do, I am agreeing that the *Torah* is good. ¹⁷But now it is no longer "the real me" doing it, but the sin housed inside me. ¹⁸For I know that there is nothing good housed inside me — that is, inside my old nature. I can want what is good, but I can't do it! ¹⁹For I don't do the good I want; instead, the evil that I don't want is what I do! ²⁰But if I am doing what "the real me" doesn't want, it is no longer "the real me" doing it but the sin housed inside me. ²¹So I find it to be the rule, a kind of perverse "*torah*", that

although I want to do what is good, evil is right there with me! ²²For in my inner self I completely agree with God's *Torah*; ²³but in my various parts, I see a different "*torah*", one that battles with the *Torah* in my mind and makes me a prisoner of sin's "*torah*", which is operating in my various parts. ²⁴What a miserable creature I am! Who will rescue me from this body bound for death? ²⁵Thanks be to God, he will! — through Yeshua the Messiah, our Lord!

To sum up: with my mind, I am a slave of God's *Torah*; but with my old nature, I am a slave of sin's "*torah*".

8 ¹Therefore, there is no longer any condemnation awaiting those who are in union with the Messiah Yeshua. ²Why? Because the *Torah* of the Spirit, which produces this life in union with Messiah Yeshua, has set me free from the "*torah*" of sin and death. ³For what the *Torah* could not do by itself, because it lacked the power to make the old nature cooperate, God did by sending his own Son as a human being with a nature like our own sinful one. God did this in order to deal with sin, and in so doing he executed the punishment against sin in human nature, ⁴so that the just requirement of the *Torah* might be fulfilled in us who do not run our lives according to what our old nature wants but according to what the Spirit wants. ⁵For those who identify with their old nature set their minds on the things of the old nature, but those who identify with the Spirit set their minds on the things of the Spirit. ⁶Having one's mind controlled by the old nature is death, but having

---

[v] Exodus 20:14(17), Deuteronomy 5:21

to·rah — law, principle
To·rah — Teaching, "Law"; Pentateuch
Ye·shu·a — Jesus

one's mind controlled by the Spirit is life and *shalom*. [7]For the mind controlled by the old nature is hostile to God, because it does not submit itself to God's *Torah* — indeed, it cannot. [8]Thus, those who identify with their old nature cannot please God.

[9]But you, you do not identify with your old nature but with the Spirit — provided the Spirit of God is living inside you, for anyone who doesn't have the Spirit of the Messiah doesn't belong to him. [10]However, if the Messiah is in you, then, on the one hand, the body is dead because of sin; but, on the other hand, the Spirit is giving life because God considers you righteous. [11]And if the Spirit of the One who raised Yeshua from the dead is living in you, then the One who raised the Messiah Yeshua from the dead will also give life to your mortal bodies through his Spirit living in you.

[12]So then, brothers, we don't owe a thing to our old nature that would require us to live according to our old nature. [13]For if you live according to your old nature, you will certainly die; but if, by the Spirit, you keep putting to death the practices of the body, you will live.

[14]All who are led by God's Spirit are God's sons. [15]For you did not receive a spirit of slavery to bring you back again into fear; on the contrary, you received the Spirit, who makes us sons and by whose power we cry out, "*Abba!*" (that is, "Dear Father!"). [16]The Spirit himself bears witness with our own spirits that we are children of God; [17]and if we are children, then we are also heirs, heirs of God and joint-heirs with the Messiah — provided we are suffering with him in order also to be glorified with him.

[18]I don't think the sufferings we are going through now are even worth comparing with the glory that will be revealed to us in the future. [19]The creation waits eagerly for the sons of God to be revealed; [20]for the creation was made subject to frustration — not willingly, but because of the one who subjected it. But it was given a reliable hope [21]that it too would be set free from its bondage to decay and would enjoy the freedom accompanying the glory that God's children will have. [22]We know that until now, the whole creation has been groaning as with the pains of childbirth; [23]and not only it, but we ourselves, who have the first-fruits of the Spirit, groan inwardly as we continue waiting eagerly to be made sons — that is, to have our whole bodies redeemed and set free. [24]It was in this hope that we were saved. But if we see what we hope for, it isn't hope — after all, who hopes for what he already sees? [25]But if we continue hoping for something we don't see, then we still wait eagerly for it, with perseverance.

[26]Similarly, the Spirit helps us in our weakness; for we don't know how to pray the way we should. But the Spirit himself pleads on our behalf with groanings too deep for words; [27]and the one who searches hearts knows exactly what the Spirit is thinking, because his pleadings for God's people accord with God's will. [28]Furthermore, we know that God causes everything to work together for the good of those who love God and are called in accordance with his purpose; [29]because those whom he knew in advance, he also determined in advance would be conformed to the pattern of his Son, so that he might be the firstborn among many brothers; [30]and those whom he thus determined in advance, he also called; and those whom he called, he also caused to be considered righteous; and those whom he caused to be considered righteous,

he also glorified!

[31] What, then, are we to say to these things? If God is for us, who can be against us? [32] He who did not spare even his own Son, but gave him up on behalf of us all — is it possible that, having given us his Son, he would not give us everything else too? [33] So who will bring a charge against God's chosen people? Certainly not God — he is the one who causes them to be considered righteous! [34] Who punishes them? Certainly not the Messiah Yeshua, who died and — more than that — has been raised, is at the right hand of God and is actually pleading on our behalf! [35] Who will separate us from the love of the Messiah? Trouble? Hardship? Persecution? Hunger? Poverty? Danger? War? [36] As the *Tanakh* puts it,

> **"For your sake we are being put to death all day long,**
>
> **we are considered sheep to be slaughtered."**[w]

[37] No, in all these things we are super-conquerors, through the one who has loved us. [38] For I am convinced that neither death nor life, neither angels nor other heavenly rulers, neither what exists nor what is coming, [39] neither powers above nor powers below, nor any other created thing will be able to separate us from the love of God which comes to us through the Messiah Yeshua, our Lord.

9 [1] I am speaking the truth — as one who belongs to the Messiah, I do not lie; and also bearing witness is my conscience, governed by the *Ruach HaKodesh*: [2] my grief is so great, the pain in my heart so constant, [3] that I could wish myself actually under God's curse and separated from the Messiah, if it would help my brothers, my own

flesh and blood, [4] the people of Israel! They were made God's children, the *Sh'khinah* has been with them, the covenants are theirs, likewise the giving of the *Torah*, the Temple service and the promises; [5] the Patriarchs are theirs; and from them, as far as his physical descent is concerned, came the Messiah, who is over all. Praised be *Adonai* for ever! *Amen.*

[6] But the present condition of Israel does not mean that the Word of God has failed.

For not everyone from Israel is truly part of Israel; [7] indeed, not all the descendants are **seed of Avraham**[x]; rather, **"What is to be called your 'seed' will be in Yitzchak."**[y] [8] In other words, it is not the physical children who are children of God, but the children the promise refers to who are considered seed. [9] For this is what the promise said: **"At the time set, I will come; and Sarah will have a son."**[z] [10] And even more to the point is the case of Rivkah; for both her children were conceived in a single act with Yitzchak, our father; [11] and before they were born, before they had done anything at all, either good or bad (so that God's plan might remain a

---

x 2 Chronicles 20:7, Psalm 105:6
y Genesis 21:12   z Genesis 18:14

Ab·ba — dear Father, "Dad"
A·do·nai — the LORD, Jehovah
A·men — So be it
Av·ra·ham — Abraham
Riv·kah — Rebecca
Ru·ach-Ha·Ko·desh — Holy Spirit
Sa·rah — Sarah
sha·lom — peace
Sh'khi·nah — the manifest glorious presence of God
Ta·nakh — Hebrew Scriptures, "Old Testament"
To·rah — Teaching, "Law"; Pentateuch
Ye·shu·a — Jesus
Yitz·chak — Isaac

---

w Psalm 44:23(22)

matter of his sovereign choice, [12]not dependent on what they did, but on God, who does the calling), it was said to her, **"The older will serve the younger."**[a] [13]This accords with where it is written, **"Ya'akov I loved, but Esav I hated."**[b]

[14]So are we to say, "It is unjust for God to do this"? Heaven forbid! [15]For to Moshe he says, **"I will have mercy on whom I have mercy, and I will pity whom I pity."**[c] [16]Thus it doesn't depend on human desires or efforts, but on God, who has mercy. [17]For the *Tanakh* says to Pharaoh, **"It is for this very reason that I raised you up, so that in connection with you I might demonstrate my power, so that my name might be known throughout the world."**[d] [18]So then, he has mercy on whom he wants, and he hardens whom he wants.

[19]But you will say to me, "Then why does he still find fault with us? After all, who resists his will?" [20]Who are you, a mere human being, to talk back to God? **Will what is formed say to him who formed it, "Why did you make me this way?"**[e] [21]Or has the potter no right to make from a given lump of clay this pot for honorable use and that one for dishonorable? [22]Now what if God, even through he was quite willing to demonstrate his anger and make known his power, patiently put up with people who deserved punishment and were ripe for destruction? [23]What if he did this in order to make known the riches of his glory to those who are the objects of his mercy, whom he prepared in advance for glory — [24]that is, to us, whom he called not only from among the Jews but also from among the

Gentiles? [25]As indeed he says in Hoshea,

> **"Those who were not my people I will call my people;**
> her who was not loved I will call loved;
> [26]and in the very place where they were told, 'You are not my people,'
> there they will be called sons of the living God!"**[f]

[27]But Yesha'yahu, referring to Israel, cries out,

> **"Even if the number of people in Israel is as large**
> as the number of grains of sand by the sea,
> only a remnant will be saved.
> [28]For *Adonai* will fulfill his word on the earth
> with certainty and without delay."**[g]

[29]Also, as Yesha'yahu said earlier,

> **"If *Adonai-Tzva'ot* had not left us a seed,**
> we would have become like S'dom,
> we would have resembled 'Amora."**[h]

[30]So, what are we to say? This: that Gentiles, even though they were not striving for righteousness, have obtained righteousness, but it is a righteousness grounded in trusting! [31]However, Israel, even though they kept pursuing a *Torah* that offers righteousness, did not reach what the *Torah* offers. [32]Why? Because they did not pursue righteousness as being grounded in trusting but as if it were grounded in doing legalistic works. They stumbled over the **stone that**

---

a Genesis 25:23 *b* Malachi 1:2-3
c Exodus 33:19 *d* Exodus 9:16
e Isaiah 29:16, 45:9
f Hosea 2:25(23), 2:1(1:10)
g Isaiah 10:22-23
h Isaiah 1:9

makes people stumble.*i* ³³As the *Tanakh* puts it,

"Look, I am laying in Tziyon
a stone that will make people
stumble,
a rock that will trip them up.
But he who rests his trust on it
will not be humiliated."*j*

10 ¹Brothers, my heart's deepest desire and my prayer to God for Israel is for their salvation; ²for I can testify to their zeal for God. But it is not based on correct understanding; ³for, since they are unaware of God's way of making people righteous and instead seek to set up their own, they have not submitted themselves to God's way of making people righteous. ⁴For the goal at which the *Torah* aims is the Messiah, who offers righteousness to everyone who trusts. ⁵For Moshe writes about the righteousness grounded in the *Torah* that **the person who does these things will attain life through them.***k* ⁶Moreover, the righteousness grounded in trusting says:

"Do not say in your heart, 'Who will ascend to heaven?'" —

that is, to bring the Messiah down —

⁷or,

"'Who will descend into Sh'ol?'" —

that is, to bring the Messiah up from the dead. ⁸What, then, does it say?

"The word is near you, in your mouth and in your heart"*l* —

that is, the word about trust which we proclaim, namely, ⁹that if you acknowledge publicly with your mouth that Yeshua is Lord and trust in your heart that God raised him from the dead, you

will be delivered. ¹⁰For with the heart one goes on trusting and thus continues toward righteousness, while with the mouth one keeps on making public acknowledgement and thus continues toward deliverance. ¹¹For the passage quoted says that *everyone* who **rests his trust on** him **will not be humiliated.***m* ¹²That means that there is no difference between Jew and Gentile — *Adonai* is the same for everyone, rich toward everyone who calls on him, ¹³since ***everyone* who calls on the name of *Adonai* will be delivered.***n*

¹⁴But how can they call on someone if they haven't trusted in him? And how can they trust in someone if they haven't heard about him? And how can they hear about someone if no one is proclaiming him? ¹⁵And how can people proclaim him unless God sends them? — as the *Tanakh* puts it,

"How beautiful are the feet of those announcing good news about good things!"*o*

¹⁶The problem is that they haven't all

---

m Isaiah 28:16   *n* Joel 3:5(2:32)
o Isaiah 52:7

A·do·nai — the LORD, Jehovah
A·do·nai-Tzva·'ot — the Lord (Jehovah) of
  Hosts (heaven's armies)
'A·mo·ra — Gomorrah
E·sav — Esau
Ho·she·a — Hosea
Mo·she — Moses
S'dom — Sodom
Sh·'ol — Sheol, Hades, the world of the dead
Ta·nakh — Hebrew Scriptures, "Old Testa-
  ment"
To·rah — Teaching, "Law"; Pentateuch
Tzi·yon — Zion
Ya·'a·kov — Jacob
Ye·sha'·ya·hu — Isaiah
Ye·shu·a — Jesus

---

i Isaiah 8:14   *j* Isaiah 28:16
k Leviticus 18:5   *l* Deuteronomy 30:11-14

paid attention to the Good News and obeyed it. For Yesha'yahu says,

> **"*Adonai*, who has trusted what he has heard from us?"**[p]

¹⁷So trust comes from what is heard, and what is heard comes through a word proclaimed about the Messiah. ¹⁸"But, I say, isn't it rather that they didn't hear?" No, they did hear —

> **"Their voice has gone out throughout the whole world**
> **and their words to the ends of the earth."**[q]

¹⁹"But, I say, isn't it rather that Israel didn't understand?"

> **"I will provoke** you **to jealousy over a non-nation,**
> **over a nation void of understanding I will make** you **angry."**[r]

²⁰Moreover, Yesha'yahu boldly says,

> **"I was found by those who were not looking for me,**
> **I became known to those who did not ask for me;"**[s]

²¹but to Israel he says,

> **"All day long I held out my hands to a people who kept disobeying and contradicting."**[t]

11 ¹"In that case, I say, isn't it that God has repudiated his people?" Heaven forbid! For I myself am a son of Israel, from the **seed of Avraham**[u], of the tribe of Binyamin. ²**God has not repudiated his people**[v], whom he chose

in advance. Or don't you know what the *Tanakh* says about Eliyahu? He pleads with God against Israel, ³"*Adonai*, they have killed your prophets and torn down your altars, and I'm the only one left, and now they want to kill me too!"**[w]** ⁴But what is God's answer to him? **"I have kept for myself seven thousand men who have not knelt down to Ba'al."**[x] ⁵It's the same way in the present age: there is a remnant, chosen by grace. ⁶(Now if it is by grace, it is accordingly not based on legalistic works; if it were otherwise, grace would no longer be grace.) ⁷What follows is that Israel has not attained the goal for which she is striving. The ones chosen have obtained it, but the rest have been made stonelike, ⁸just as the *Tanakh* says,

> **"God has given them a spirit of dullness —**
> **eyes that do not see**
> **and ears that do not hear,**
> **right down to the present day."**[y]

⁹And David says,

> **"Let their dining table become for them**
> **a snare** and a trap, **a pitfall and a punishment.**
> ¹⁰ **Let their eyes be darkened, so that they can't see,**
> **with their backs bent continually."**[z]

¹¹"In that case, I say, isn't it that they have stumbled with the result that they have permanently fallen away?" Heaven forbid! Quite the contrary, it is by means of their stumbling that the deliverance has come to the Gentiles, in order to **provoke them to jealousy.**[a]

---

p Isaiah 53:1   q Psalm 19:5(4)
r Deuteronomy 32:21
s Isaiah 65:1   t Isaiah 65:2
u 2 Chronicles 20:7, Psalm 105:6
v 1 Samuel 12:22, Psalm 94:14

w 1 Kings 19:10, 14   x 1 Kings 19:18
y Deuteronomy 29:4, Isaiah 29:10
z Psalm 69:23-24(22-23)
a Deuteronomy 32:21

12 Moreover, if their stumbling is bringing riches to the world — that is, if Israel's being placed temporarily in a condition less favored than that of the Gentiles is bringing riches to the latter — how much greater riches will Israel in its fullness bring them!

13 However, to those of you who are Gentiles I say this: since I myself am an emissary sent to the Gentiles, I make known the importance of my work 14 in the hope that somehow I may **provoke** some of my own people **to jealousy** and save some of them! 15 For if their casting Yeshua aside means reconciliation for the world, what will their accepting him mean? It will be life from the dead!

16 Now if the *challah* offered as first-fruits is holy, so is the whole loaf. And if the root is holy, so are the branches. 17 But if some of the branches were broken off, and you — a wild olive — were grafted in among them and have become equal sharers in the rich root of the olive tree, 18 then don't boast as if you were better than the branches! However, if you do boast, remember that you are not supporting the root, the root is supporting you. 19 So you will say, "Branches were broken off so that I might be grafted in." 20 True, but so what? They were broken off because of their lack of trust. However, you keep your place only because of your trust. So don't be arrogant; on the contrary, be terrified! 21 For if God did not spare the natural branches, he certainly won't spare you! 22 So take a good look at God's kindness and his severity: on the one hand, severity toward those who fell off; but, on the other hand, God's kindness toward you — provided you maintain yourself in that kindness! Otherwise, you too will be cut off! 23 Moreover, the others, if they do not persist in their lack of trust, will be grafted in; because God is

able to graft them back in. 24 For if you were cut out of what is by nature a wild olive tree and grafted, contrary to nature, into a cultivated olive tree, how much more will these natural branches be grafted back into their own olive tree!

25 For, brothers, I want you to understand this truth which God formerly concealed but has now revealed, so that you won't imagine you know more than you actually do. It is that stoniness, to a degree, has come upon Israel, until the Gentile world enters in its fullness; 26 and that it is in this way that all Israel will be saved. As the *Tanakh* says,

"**Out of Tziyon will come the Redeemer;**
  he will turn away ungodliness from Ya'akov
27 **and this will be my covenant with them, ...**
  when I take away their sins."*b*

28 With respect to the Good News they are hated for your sake. But with respect to being chosen they are loved for the Patriarchs' sake, 29 for God's free gifts and his calling are irrevocable. 30 Just as you yourselves were dis-

---

b Isaiah 59:20-21, 27:9

A·do·nai — the LORD, Jehovah
Av·ra·ham — Abraham
Ba·'al — Baal
Bin·ya·min — Benjamin
chal·lah — loaf or cake set aside for the *cohanim* in the Temple
Da·vid — David
E·li·ya·hu — Elijah
Ta·nakh — Hebrew Scriptures, "Old Testament"
Tzi·yon — Zion
Ya·'a·kov — Jacob
Ye·sha'·ya·hu — Isaiah

obedient to God before but have received mercy now because of Israel's disobedience; ³¹so also Israel has been disobedient now, so that by your showing them the same mercy that God has shown you, they too may now receive God's mercy. ³²For God has shut up all mankind together in disobedience, in order that he might show mercy to all.

³³ O the depth of the riches
   and the wisdom and knowledge of
      God!
   How inscrutable are his judgments!
   How unsearchable are his ways!

³⁴ For, **Who has known the mind of the
      Lord?**
   Who has been his counselor?ᶜ

³⁵ Or, **Who has given him anything
      and made him pay it back?**ᵈ

³⁶ For from him and through him
   and to him are all things.
   To him be the glory forever!
   Amen.

12 ¹I exhort you, therefore, brothers, in view of God's mercies, to offer yourselves as a sacrifice, living and set apart for God. This will please him; it is the logical "Temple worship" for you. ²In other words, do not let yourselves be conformed to the standards of the *'olam hazeh.* Instead, keep letting yourselves be transformed by the renewing of your minds; so that you will know what God wants and will agree that what he wants is good, satisfying and able to succeed. ³For I am telling every single one of you, through the grace that has been given to me, not to have exaggerated ideas about your own importance. Instead, develop a sober estimate of yourself

based on the standard which God has given to each of you, namely, trust. ⁴For just as there are many parts that compose one body, but the parts don't all have the same function; ⁵so there are many of us, and in union with the Messiah we comprise one body, with each of us belonging to the others. ⁶But we have gifts that differ and which are meant to be used according to the grace that has been given to us. If your gift is prophecy, use it to the extent of your trust; ⁷if it is serving, use it to serve; if you are a teacher, use your gift in teaching; ⁸if you are a counselor, use your gift to comfort and exhort; if you are someone who gives, do it simply and generously; if you are in a position of leadership, lead with diligence and zeal; if you are one who does acts of mercy, do them cheerfully.

⁹Don't let love be a mere outward show. Recoil from what is evil, and cling to what is good. ¹⁰Love each other devotedly and with brotherly love; and set examples for each other in showing respect. ¹¹Don't be lazy when hard work is needed, but serve the Lord with spiritual fervor. ¹²Rejoice in your hope, be patient in your troubles, and continue steadfastly in prayer. ¹³Share what you have with God's people, and practice hospitality.

¹⁴Bless those who persecute you — bless them, don't curse them! ¹⁵Rejoice with those who rejoice, and weep with those who weep. ¹⁶Be sensitive to each other's needs — don't think yourselves better than others, but make humble people your friends. Don't be conceited. ¹⁷Repay no one evil for evil, but try to do what everyone regards as good. ¹⁸If possible, and to the extent that it depends on you, live in peace with all people. ¹⁹Never seek revenge, my friends; instead, leave that to God's anger; for in the *Tanakh* it is written,

ᶜ Isaiah 40:13   ᵈ Job 41:3

"*Adonai* says, 'Vengeance is my responsibility; I will repay.'"[e]

[20] On the contrary,

"If your enemy is hungry, feed him;
if he is thirsty, give him something to drink.
For by doing this, you will heap fiery coals of shame on his head."[f]

[21] Do not be conquered by evil, but conquer evil with good.

13 [1] Everyone is to obey the governing authorities. For there is no authority that is not from God, and the existing authorities have been placed where they are by God. [2] Therefore, whoever resists the authorities is resisting what God has instituted; and those who resist will bring judgment on themselves. [3] For rulers are no terror to good conduct, but to bad. Would you like to be unafraid of the person in authority? Then simply do what is good, and you will win his approval; [4] for he is God's servant, there for your benefit. But if you do what is wrong, be afraid! Because it is not for nothing that he holds the power of the sword; for he is God's servant, there as an avenger to punish wrongdoers. [5] Another reason to obey, besides fear of punishment, is for the sake of conscience. [6] This is also why you pay taxes; for the authorities are God's public officials, constantly attending to these duties. [7] Pay everyone what he is owed: if you owe the tax-collector, pay your taxes; if you owe the revenue-collector, pay revenue; if you owe someone respect, pay him respect; if you owe someone honor, pay him honor. [8] Don't owe anyone anything — except to love one another; for whoever loves his fellow human being

has fulfilled *Torah*. [9] For the commandments, "Don't commit adultery," "Don't murder," "Don't steal," "Don't covet,"[g] and any others are summed up in this one rule: "Love your neighbor as yourself."[h] [10] Love does not do harm to a neighbor; therefore love is the fullness of *Torah*.

[11] Besides all this, you know at what point of history we stand; so it is high time for you to rouse yourselves from sleep; for the final deliverance is nearer than when we first came to trust. [12] The night is almost over, the day is almost here. So let us put aside the deeds of darkness and arm ourselves with the weapons of light. [13] Let us live properly, as people do in the daytime — not partying and getting drunk, not engaging in sexual immorality and other excesses, not quarrelling and being jealous. [14] Instead, clothe yourselves with the Lord Yeshua the Messiah; and don't waste your time thinking about how to provide for the sinful desires of your old nature.

14 [1] Now as for a person whose trust is weak, welcome him — but not to get into arguments over opinions. [2] One person has the trust that will allow him to eat anything, while another whose trust is weak eats only vegetables. [3] The one who eats anything must not look down on the one who abstains; and the abstainer must not pass judgment on the one

---

g Exodus 20:13-14(13-17), Deuteronomy 5:17-18

h Leviticus 19:18

A·do·nai — the LORD, Jehovah

A·men — So be it

'o·lam ha·zeh — this world

Ta·nakh — Hebrew Scriptures, "Old Testament"

To·rah — Teaching, "Law"; Pentateuch

---

e Deuteronomy 32:25   *f* Proverbs 25:21-22

who eats anything, because God has accepted him — ⁴who are you to pass judgment on someone else's servant? It is before his own master that he will stand or fall; and the fact is that he will stand, because the Lord is able to make him stand.

⁵One person considers some days more holy than others, while someone else regards them as being all alike. What is important is for each to be fully convinced in his own mind. ⁶He who observes a day as special does so to honor the Lord. Also he who eats anything, eats to honor the Lord, since he gives thanks to God; likewise the abstainer abstains to honor the Lord, and he too gives thanks to God. ⁷For none of us lives only in relation to himself, and none of us dies only in relation to himself; ⁸for if we live, we live in relation to the Lord; and if we die, we die in relation to the Lord. So whether we live or die, we belong to the Lord — ⁹indeed, it was for this very reason that the Messiah died and came back to life, so that he might be Lord of both the dead and the living. ¹⁰You then, why do you pass judgment on your brother? Or why do you look down on your brother? For all of us will stand before God's judgment seat; ¹¹since it is written in the *Tanakh*,

> "As I live, says *Adonai*, every knee will bend before me,
> and every tongue will publicly acknowledge God."ⁱ

¹²So then, every one of us will have to give an account of himself to God.

¹³Therefore, let's stop passing judgment on each other! Instead, make this one judgment — not to put a stumbling-block or a snare in a brother's way. ¹⁴I know — that is, I have been persuaded

by the Lord Yeshua the Messiah — that nothing is unclean in itself. But if a person considers something unclean, then for him it is unclean; ¹⁵and if your brother is being upset by the food you eat, your life is no longer one of love. Do not, by your eating habits, destroy someone for whom the Messiah died! ¹⁶Do not let what you know to be good, be spoken of as bad; ¹⁷for the Kingdom of God is not eating and drinking, but righteousness, *shalom* and joy in the *Ruach HaKodesh*. ¹⁸Anyone who serves the Messiah in this fashion both pleases God and wins the approval of other people.

¹⁹So then, let us pursue the things that make for *shalom* and mutual upbuilding. ²⁰Don't tear down God's work for the sake of food. True enough, all things are clean; but it is wrong for anybody by his eating to cause someone to fall away. ²¹What is good is not to eat meat or drink wine or do anything that causes your brother to stumble. ²²The belief you hold about such things, keep between yourself and God. Happy the person who is free of self-condemnation when he approves of something! ²³But the doubter comes under condemnation if he eats, because his action is not based on trust. And anything not based on trust is a sin.

15 ¹So we who are strong have a duty to bear the weaknesses of those who are not strong, rather than please ourselves. ²Each of us should please his neighbor and act for his good, thus building him up. ³For even the Messiah did not please himself; rather, as the *Tanakh* says, 'The insults of those insulting you fell on me.'ʲ ⁴For everything written in the past was written to teach us, so that with the encouragement of the *Tanakh* we might

---

ⁱ Isaiah 45:23

ʲ Psalm 69:10(9)

patiently hold on to our hope. ⁵And may God, the source of encouragement and patience, give you the same attitude among yourselves as the Messiah Yeshua had, ⁶so that with one accord and with one voice you may glorify the God and Father of our Lord Yeshua the Messiah.

⁷So welcome each other, just as the Messiah has welcomed you into God's glory. ⁸For I say that the Messiah became a servant of the Jewish people in order to show God's truthfulness by making good his promises to the Patriarchs, ⁹and in order to show his mercy by causing the Gentiles to glorify God — as it is written in the *Tanakh*,

> "Because of this I will acknowledge
>   you among the Gentiles
> and sing praise to your name.'ᵏ

¹⁰And again it says,

> "Gentiles, rejoice with his people."ˡ

¹¹And again,

> "Praise *Adonai*, all Gentiles!
> Let all peoples praise him!"ᵐ

¹²And again, Yesha'yahu says,

> "The root of Yishai will come,
> he who arises to rule Gentiles;
> Gentiles will put their hope in
>   him."ⁿ

¹³May God, the source of hope, fill you completely with joy and *shalom* as you continue trusting, so that by the power of the *Ruach HaKodesh* you may overflow with hope.

¹⁴Now I myself am convinced, my brothers, that you are full of goodness, filled with knowledge and well able to counsel each other. ¹⁵But on some

points I have written you quite boldly by way of reminding you about them, because of the grace God has given me ¹⁶to be a servant of the Messiah Yeshua for the Gentiles, with the priestly duty of presenting the Good News of God, so that the Gentiles may be an acceptable offering, made holy by the *Ruach HaKodesh*.

¹⁷In union with the Messiah Yeshua, then, I have reason to be proud of my service to God; ¹⁸for I will not dare speak of anything except what the Messiah has accomplished through me to bring the Gentiles to obedience by my words and deeds, ¹⁹through the power of signs and miracles, through the power of the Spirit of God. So from Yerushalayim all the way to Illyricum I have fully proclaimed the Good News of the Messiah. ²⁰I have always made it my ambition to proclaim the Good News where the Messiah was not yet known, so that I would not be building on someone else's foundation, ²¹but rather, as the *Tanakh* puts it,

> "Those who have not been told
>   about him will see,
> and those who have not heard will
>   understand."ᵒ

²²This is also why I have so often been prevented from visiting you. ²³But now, since there is no longer a place in these regions that needs me, and since I have wanted for many years to come to you,

---

o Isaiah 52:15

A·do·nai — the LORD, Jehovah
Ru·ach-Ha·Ko·desh — Holy Spirit
sha·lom — peace
Ta·nakh — Hebrew Scriptures, "Old Testament"
Ye·ru·sha·la·yim — Jerusalem
Ye·sha'·ya·hu — Isaiah
Ye·shu·a — Jesus
Yi·shai — Jesse

---

k 2 Samuel 22:50, Psalm 18:50(49)
l Deuteronomy 32:43
m Psalm 117:1   *n* Isaiah 11:10

²⁴ I hope to see you as I pass through on my way to Spain, and to have you help me travel there after I have enjoyed your company awhile. ²⁵ But now I am going to Yerushalayim with aid for God's people there. ²⁶ For Macedonia and Achaia thought it would be good to make some contribution to the poor among God's people in Yerushalayim. ²⁷ They were pleased to do it, but the fact is that they owe it to them. For if the Gentiles have shared with the Jews in spiritual matters, then the Gentiles clearly have a duty to help the Jews in material matters. ²⁸ So when I have finished this task and made certain that they have received this fruit, I will leave for Spain and visit you on my way there; ²⁹ and I know that when I come to you, it will be with the full measure of the Messiah's blessings. ³⁰ And now I urge you, brothers, by our Lord Yeshua the Messiah and by the love of the Spirit, to join me in my struggle by praying to God on my behalf ³¹ that I will be rescued from the unbelievers in Y'hudah, and that my service for Yerushalayim will be acceptable to God's people there. ³² Then, if it is God's will, I will come to you with joy and have a time of rest among you. ³³ Now may the God of *shalom* be with you all. *Amen.*

16 ¹ I am introducing to you our sister Phoebe, *shammash* of the congregation at Cenchrea, ² so that you may welcome her in the Lord, as God's people should, and give her whatever assistance she may need from you; for she has been a big help to many people — including myself. ³ Give my greetings to Priscilla and Aquila, my fellow workers for the Messiah Yeshua. ⁴ They risked their necks to save my life; not only I thank them, but also all the Messianic communities among the Gentiles. ⁵ And give my greetings to the congregation that meets in their house.

Give my greetings to my dear friend Epaenetus, who was the first person in the province of Asia to put his trust in the Messiah. ⁶ Give my greetings to Miryam, who has worked very hard for you. ⁷ Greetings to Andronicus and Junia, relatives of mine who were in prison with me. They are well known among the emissaries; also they came to trust in the Messiah before I did. ⁸ Greetings to Ampliatus, my dear friend in the Lord. ⁹ Greetings to Urbanus, our fellow-worker for the Messiah, and to my dear friend Stachys. ¹⁰ Greetings to Appeles, whose trust in the Messiah has been tested and proved.

Greet those in the household of Aristobulus. ¹¹ Greet my relative, Herodion. ¹² Greet Tryphaena and Tryphosa, women who are working hard for the Lord.

Greet my dear friend Persis, another woman who has done a lot of hard work for the Lord. ¹³ Greet Rufus, chosen by the Lord, and his mother, who has been a mother to me too. ¹⁴ Greet Asyncritus, Phlegon, Hermes, Patrobas, Hermas and the brothers who are with them. ¹⁵ Greet Philologus, Julia, Nereus and his sister, and Olympas, and all of God's people who are with them. ¹⁶ Greet one another with a holy kiss. All the Messiah's congregations send their greetings to you.

¹⁷ I urge you, brothers, to watch out for those who cause divisions and put snares alongside the teaching in which you have been trained — keep away from them. ¹⁸ For men like these are not

serving our Lord the Messiah but their own belly; by smooth talk and flattery they deceive the innocent. ¹⁹ For everyone has heard about your obedience; therefore I rejoice over you. However, I want you to be wise concerning good, but innocent concerning evil. ²⁰ And God, the source of *shalom*, will soon crush the Adversary under your feet.

The grace of our Lord Yeshua be with you.

²¹ Timothy, my fellow-worker, sends greetings to you; so do Lucius, Jason and Sosipater, my relatives.

²² I, Tertius, the one writing down this letter, greet you in the Lord.

²³ My host Gaius, in whose home the whole congregation meets, greets you. Erastus the city treasurer and brother Quartus greet you. ²⁴ *

---

* Some manuscripts have verse 24: The grace of our Lord Yeshua the Messiah be with you all. *Amen.*

²⁵ Now to God, who can strengthen you, according to my Good News,
in harmony with the revelation of the secret truth
which is the proclamation of Yeshua the Messiah,
kept hidden in silence for ages and ages,
²⁶ but manifested now through prophetic writings,
in keeping with the command of God the Eternal,
and communicated to all the Gentiles to promote in them trust-grounded obedience —
²⁷ to the only wise God, through Yeshua the Messiah,
be the glory forever and ever!
Amen.

A · men — So be it
Mir · **yam** — Miriam, Mary
sha · lom — peace
sham · mash — servant, attendant, deacon
Y'hu · **dah** — Judea
Ye · **shu** · a — Jesus
Ye · ru · sha · **la** · yim — Jerusalem

1 CORINTHIANS

1 [1] From: Sha'ul, called by God's will to be an emissary of the Messiah Yeshua; and from brother Sosthenes

[2] To: God's Messianic community in Corinth, consisting of those who have been set apart by Yeshua the Messiah and called to be God's holy people — along with everyone everywhere who calls on the name of our Lord Yeshua the Messiah, their Lord as well as ours:

[3] Grace to you and *shalom* from God our Father and the Lord Yeshua the Messiah.

[4] I thank my God always for you because of God's love and kindness given to you through the Messiah Yeshua, [5] in that you have been enriched by him in so many ways, particularly in power of speech and depth of knowledge. [6] Indeed, the testimony about the Messiah has become firmly established in you; [7] so that you are not lacking any spiritual gift and are eagerly awaiting the revealing of our Lord Yeshua the Messiah. [8] He will enable you to hold out until the end and thus be blameless on the Day of our Lord Yeshua the Messiah — [9] God is trustworthy: it was he who called you into fellowship with his Son, Yeshua the Messiah, our Lord.

[10] Nevertheless, brothers, I call on you in the name of our Lord Yeshua the Messiah to agree, all of you, in what you say, and not to let yourselves remain split into factions but be restored to having a common mind and a common purpose. [11] For some of Chloe's people have made it known to me, my brothers, that there are quarrels among you. [12] I say this because one of you says, "I follow Sha'ul;" another says, "I follow Apollos;" another, "I follow Kefa;" while still another says, "I follow the Messiah!" [13] Has the Messiah been split in pieces? Was it Sha'ul who was put to death on a stake for you? Were you immersed into the name of Sha'ul? [14] I thank God that I didn't immerse any of you except Crispus and Gaius — [15] otherwise someone might say that you were indeed immersed into my name. [16] (Oh yes, I did also immerse Stephanas and his household; beyond that, I can't remember whether I immersed anyone else.)

[17] For the Messiah did not send me to immerse but to proclaim the Good News — and to do it without relying on "wisdom" that consists of mere rhetoric, so as not to rob the Messiah's execution-stake of its power. [18] For the message about the execution-stake is nonsense to those in the process of being destroyed, but to us in the process of being saved it is the power of God. [19] Indeed, the *Tanakh* says,

> **"I will destroy the wisdom of the wise**
> **and frustrate the intelligence of the intelligent."**[a]

---

[a] Isaiah 29:14

²⁰ Where does that leave the philosopher, the *Torah*-teacher, or any of today's thinkers? Hasn't God made this world's wisdom look pretty foolish? ²¹ For God's wisdom ordained that the world, using its own wisdom, would not come to know him. Therefore God decided to use the "nonsense" of what we proclaim as his means of saving those who come to trust in it. ²² Precisely because Jews ask for signs and Greeks try to find wisdom, ²³ we go on proclaiming a Messiah executed on a stake as a criminal! To Jews this is an obstacle, and to Greeks it is nonsense; ²⁴ but to those who are called, both Jews and Greeks, this same Messiah is God's power and God's wisdom! ²⁵ For God's "nonsense" is wiser than humanity's "wisdom".

And God's "weakness" is stronger than humanity's "strength". ²⁶ Just look at yourselves, brothers; look at those whom God has called! Not many of you are wise by the world's standards, not many wield power or boast noble birth. ²⁷ But God chose what the world considers nonsense in order to shame the wise; God chose what the world considers weak in order to shame the strong; ²⁸ and God chose what the world looks down on as common or regards as nothing in order to bring to nothing what the world considers important; ²⁹ so that no one should boast before God. ³⁰ It is his doing that you are united with the Messiah Yeshua. He has become wisdom for us from God, and righteousness and holiness and redemption as well! ³¹ Therefore — as the *Tanakh* says — **"Let anyone who wants to boast, boast about *Adonai*."**[b]

2 ¹ As for me, brothers, when I arrived among you, it was not with surpassing eloquence or wisdom that I came announcing to you the previously concealed truth about God; ² for I had decided that while I was with you I would forget everything except Yeshua the Messiah, and even him only as someone who had been executed on a stake as a criminal. ³ Also I myself was with you as somebody weak, nervous and shaking all over from fear; ⁴ and neither the delivery nor the content of my message relied on compelling words of "wisdom" but on a demonstration of the power of the Spirit, ⁵ so that your trust might not rest on human wisdom but on God's power.

⁶ Yet there is a wisdom that we are speaking to those who are mature enough for it. But it is not the wisdom of this world or of this world's leaders, who are in the process of passing away. ⁷ On the contrary, we are communicating a secret wisdom from God which has been hidden until now but which, before history began, God had decreed would bring us glory. ⁸ Not one of this world's leaders has understood it; because if they had, they would not have executed the Lord from whom this glory flows. ⁹ But, as the *Tanakh* says,

> **"No eye has seen,**
> **no ear has heard**
> **and no one's heart has imagined**
> **all the things God has prepared for**
> **those who love him."**[c]

---

c   Isaiah 64:3(4), 52:15

================

A·do·nai — the LORD, Jehovah
Ke·fa — Peter
sha·lom — peace
Sha·'ul — Saul (Paul)
Ta·nakh — Hebrew Scriptures, "Old Testament"
To·rah-teacher — scribe
Ye·shu·a — Jesus

---

b   Jeremiah 9:23(24)

¹⁰ It is to us, however, that God has revealed these things. How? Through the Spirit. For the Spirit probes all things, even the profoundest depths of God. ¹¹ For who knows the inner workings of a person except the person's own spirit inside him? So too no one knows the inner workings of God except God's Spirit. ¹² Now we have not received the spirit of the world but the Spirit of God, so that we might understand the things God has so freely given us. ¹³ These are the things we are talking about when we avoid the manner of speaking that human wisdom would dictate and instead use a manner of speaking taught by the Spirit, by which we explain things of the Spirit to people who have the Spirit. ¹⁴ Now the natural man does not receive the things from the Spirit of God — to him they are nonsense! Moreover, he is unable to grasp them, because they are evaluated through the Spirit. ¹⁵ But the person who has the Spirit can evaluate everything, while no one is in a position to evaluate him.

¹⁶ **For who has known the mind of Adonai?**
Who will counsel him? *d*

But we have the mind of the Messiah!

3 ¹ As for me, brothers, I couldn't talk to you as spiritual people but as worldly people, as babies, so far as experience with the Messiah is concerned. ² I gave you milk, not solid food, because you were not yet ready for it. But you aren't ready for it now either! ³ For you are still worldly! Isn't it obvious from all the jealousy and quarrelling among you that you are worldly and living by merely human standards? ⁴ For when one says, "I follow Sha'ul" and another, "I follow

Apollos," aren't you being merely human? ⁵ After all, what is Apollos? What is Sha'ul? Only servants through whom you came to trust. Indeed, it was the Lord who brought you to trust through one of us or through another. ⁶ I planted the seed, and Apollos watered it, but it was God who made it grow. ⁷ So neither the planter nor the waterer is anything, only God who makes things grow — ⁸ planter and waterer are the same.

However, each will be rewarded according to his work. ⁹ For we are God's co-workers; you are God's field, God's building. ¹⁰ Using the grace God gave me, I laid a foundation, like a skilled master-builder; and another man is building on it. But let each one be careful how he builds. ¹¹ For no one can lay any foundation other than the one already laid, which is Yeshua the Messiah. ¹² Some will use gold, silver or precious stones in building on this foundation; while others will use wood, grass or straw. ¹³ But each one's work will be shown for what it is; the Day will disclose it, because it will be revealed by fire — the fire will test the quality of each one's work. ¹⁴ If the work someone has built on the foundation survives, he will receive a reward; ¹⁵ if it is burned up, he will have to bear the loss: he will still escape with his life, but it will be like escaping through a fire.

¹⁶ Don't you know that you people are God's temple and that God's Spirit lives in you? ¹⁷ So if anyone destroys God's temple, God will destroy him. For God's temple is holy, and you yourselves are that temple.

¹⁸ Let no one fool himself. If someone among you thinks he is wise (by this world's standards), let him become "foolish" so that he may become really wise. ¹⁹ For the wisdom of this world is

---

d Isaiah 40:13

nonsense, as far as God is concerned; inasmuch as the *Tanakh* says, "**He traps the wise in their own cleverness,**"[e] [20] and again, "***Adonai* knows that the thoughts of the wise are worthless.**"[f] [21] So let no one boast about human beings, for all things are yours — [22] whether Sha'ul or Apollos or Kefa or the world or life or death or the present or the future: they all belong to you, [23] and you belong to the Messiah, and the Messiah belongs to God.

4 [1] So, you should regard us as the Messiah's servants, as trustees of God's secret truths. [2] Now the one thing that is asked of a trustee is that he be found trustworthy. [3] And it matters very little to me how I am evaluated by you or by any human court; in fact, I don't even evaluate myself. [4] I am not aware of anything against me, but this does not make me innocent. The one who is evaluating me is the Lord. [5] So don't pronounce judgment prematurely, before the Lord comes; for he will bring to light what is now hidden in darkness; he will expose the motives of people's hearts; and then each will receive from God whatever praise he deserves.

[6] Now in what I have said here, brothers, I have used myself and Apollos as examples to teach you not to go beyond what the *Tanakh* says, proudly taking the side of one leader against another. [7] After all, what makes you so special? What do you have that you didn't receive as a gift? And if in fact it was a gift, why do you boast as if it weren't? [8] You are glutted already? You are rich already? You have become kings, even though we are not? Well, I wish you really were kings, so that we might share the kingship with you! [9] For I think God has been placing us emissaries on display at the tail of the parade, like men condemned to die in the public arena: we have become a spectacle before the whole universe, angels as well as men. [10] For the Messiah's sake we are fools, but united with the Messiah you are wise! We are weak, but you are strong; you are honored, but we are dishonored. [11] Till this very moment we go hungry and thirsty, we are dressed in rags, we are treated roughly, we wander from place to place, [12] we exhaust ourselves working with our own hands for our living. When we are cursed, we keep on blessing; when we are persecuted, we go on putting up with it; [13] when we are slandered, we continue making our appeal. We are the world's garbage, the scum of the earth — yes, to this moment!

[14] I am not writing you this to make you feel ashamed, but, as my dear children, to confront you and get you to change. [15] For even if you have ten thousand trainers in connection with the Messiah, you do not have many fathers; for in connection with the Messiah Yeshua it was I who became your father by means of the Good News. [16] Therefore I urge you to imitate me. [17] This is why I have sent you Timothy, my beloved and trustworthy child in the Lord. He will remind you of the way of life I follow in union with the Messiah Yeshua and teach everywhere in every congregation.

[18] When I didn't come to visit you, some of you became arrogant. [19] But I am coming to you soon, if the Lord wills; and I will take cognizance not of

---

A·do·nai — the LORD, Jehovah
Ke·fa — Peter
Sha·'ul — Saul (Paul)
Ta·nakh — Hebrew Scriptures, "Old Testament"
Ye·shu·a — Jesus

---

e Job 5:13   f Psalm 94:11

the talk of these arrogant people but of their power. ²⁰ For the Kingdom of God is not a matter of words but of power. ²¹ Which do you prefer — should I come to you with a stick? or with love in a spirit of gentleness?

5 ¹ It is actually being reported that there is sexual sin among you, and it is sexual sin of a kind that is condemned even by pagans — a man is living with his stepmother! ² And you stay proud? Shouldn't you rather have felt some sadness that would have led you to remove from your company the man who has done this thing? ³ For I myself, even though I am absent physically, am with you spiritually; and I have already judged the man who has done this as if I were present. ⁴ In the name of the Lord Yeshua, when you are assembled, with me present spiritually and the power of our Lord Yeshua among us, ⁵ hand over such a person to the Adversary for his old nature to be destroyed, so that his spirit may be saved in the Day of the Lord.

⁶ Your boasting is not good. Don't you know the saying, "It takes only a little *chametz* to leaven a whole batch of dough?" ⁷ Get rid of the old *chametz*, so that you can be a new batch of dough, because in reality you are unleavened. For our *Pesach* lamb, the Messiah, has been sacrificed. ⁸ So let us celebrate the *Seder* not with leftover *chametz*, the *chametz* of wickedness and evil, but with the *matzah* of purity and truth.

⁹ In my earlier letter I wrote you not to associate with people who engage in sexual immorality. ¹⁰ I didn't mean the sexually immoral people outside your community, or the greedy, or the thieves or the idol-worshippers — for then you would have to leave the world altogether! ¹¹ No, what I wrote you was not to associate with anyone who is sup-

posedly a brother but who also engages in sexual immorality, is greedy, worships idols, is abusive, gets drunk or steals. With such a person you shouldn't even eat! ¹² For what business is it of mine to judge outsiders? Isn't it those who are part of the community that you should be judging? ¹³ God will judge those who are outside. Just **expel the evildoer from among yourselves.**[g]

6 ¹ How dare one of you with a complaint against another go to court before pagan judges and not before God's people? ² Don't you know that God's people are going to judge the universe? If you are going to judge the universe, are you incompetent to judge these minor matters? ³ Don't you know that we will judge angels, not to mention affairs of everyday life? ⁴ So if you require judgments about matters of everyday life, why do you put them in front of men who have no standing in the Messianic community? ⁵ I say, shame on you! Can it be that there isn't one person among you wise enough to be able to settle a dispute between brothers? ⁶ Instead, a brother brings a lawsuit against another brother, and that before unbelievers!

⁷ Actually, if you are bringing lawsuits against each other, it is already a defeat for you. Why not rather be wronged? Why not rather be cheated? ⁸ Instead, you yourselves wrong and cheat; and you do it to your own brothers! ⁹ Don't you know that unrighteous people will have no share in the Kingdom of God? Don't delude yourselves — people who engage in sex before marriage, who worship idols, who engage in sex after marriage with someone other than their spouse, who

g Deuteronomy 13:6; 17:7, 12; 19:19; 21:21; 22:21, 24; 24:7

engage in active or passive homo-
sexuality, [10] who steal, who are greedy,
who get drunk, who assail people with
contemptuous language, who rob —
none of them will share in the Kingdom
of God. [11] Some of you used to do these
things. But you have cleansed yourselves, you have been set apart for God,
you have come to be counted righteous
through the power of the Lord Yeshua
the Messiah and the Spirit of our God.
[12] You say, "For me, everything is
permitted"? Maybe, but not everything
is helpful. "For me, everything is permitted"? Maybe, but as far as I am
concerned, I am not going to let anything gain control over me. [13] "Food is
meant for the stomach and the stomach
for food"? Maybe, but God will put an
end to both of them. Anyhow, the body
is not meant for sexual immorality but
for the Lord, and the Lord is for the
body. [14] God raised up the Lord, and he
will raise us up too by his power.

[15] Don't you know that your bodies
are parts of the Messiah? So, am I to
take parts of the Messiah and make
them parts of a prostitute? Heaven
forbid! [16] Don't you know that a man
who joins himself to a prostitute
becomes physically one with her? For
the *Tanakh* says, **"The two will become
one flesh;"** [h] [17] but the person who is
joined to the Lord is one spirit. [18] Run
from sexual immorality! Every other
sin a person commits is outside the
body, but the fornicator sins against his
own body. [19] Or don't you know that
your body is a temple for the *Ruach
HaKodesh* who lives inside you, whom
you received from God? The fact is,
you don't belong to yourselves; [20] for
you were bought at a price. So use your
bodies to glorify God.

7 [1] Now to deal with the questions
you wrote about: "Is it good for a
man to keep away from women?"
[2] Well, because of the danger of sexual
immorality, let each man have his own
wife and each woman her own husband. [3] The husband should give his
wife what she is entitled to in the
marriage relationship, and the wife
should do the same for her husband.
[4] The wife is not in charge of her own
body, but her husband is; likewise, the
husband is not in charge of his own
body, but his wife is. [5] Do not deprive
each other, except for a limited time, by
mutual agreement, and then only so as
to have extra time for prayer; but
afterwards, come together again. Otherwise, because of your lack of self-
control, you may succumb to the
Adversary's temptation. [6] I am giving
you this as a suggestion, not as a
command. [7] Actually, I wish everyone
were like me; but each has his own gift
from God, one this, another that.

[8] Now to the single people and the
widows I say that it is fine if they
remain unmarried like me; [9] but if they
can't exercise self-control, they should
get married; because it is better to be
married than to keep burning with
sexual desire.

[10] To those who are married I have a
command, and it is not from me but
from the Lord: a woman is not to
separate herself from her husband [11] But
if she does separate herself, she is to
remain single or be reconciled with her

---

[h] Genesis 2:24

cha·metz — yeast, leaven
ma·tzah — unleavened bread
Pe·sach — Passover
Ru·ach-Ha·Ko·desh — Holy Spirit
Se·der — Passover eve meal
Ta·nakh — Hebrew Scriptures, "Old Testa-
ment"
Ye·shu·a — Jesus

husband. Also, a husband is not to leave his wife.

[12] To the rest I say — I, not the Lord: if any brother has a wife who is not a believer, and she is satisfied to go on living with him, he should not leave her. [13] Also, if any woman has an unbelieving husband who is satisfied to go on living with her, she is not to leave him. [14] For the unbelieving husband has been set aside for God by the wife, and the unbelieving wife has been set aside for God by the brother — otherwise your children would be "unclean", but as it is, they are set aside for God. [15] But if the unbelieving spouse separates himself, let him be separated. In circumstances like these, the brother or sister is not enslaved — God has called you to a life of peace. [16] For how do you know, wife, whether you will save your husband? Or how do you know, husband, whether you will save your wife?

[17] Only let each person live the life the Lord has assigned him and live it in the condition he was in when God called him. This is the rule I lay down in all the congregations. [18] Was someone already circumcised when he was called? Then he should not try to remove the marks of his circumcision. Was someone uncircumcised when he was called? He shouldn't undergo *b'rit-milah*. [19] Being circumcised means nothing, and being uncircumcised means nothing; what does mean something is keeping God's commandments. [20] Each person should remain in the condition he was in when he was called.

[21] Were you a slave when you were called? Well, don't let it bother you; although if you can gain your freedom, take advantage of the opportunity. [22] For a person who was a slave when he was called is the Lord's freedman; likewise, someone who was a free man when he was called is a slave of the Messiah. [23] You were bought at a price, so do not become slaves of other human beings. [24] Brothers, let each one remain with God in the condition in which he was called.

[25] Now the question about the unmarried: I do not have a command from the Lord, but I offer an opinion as one who by the Lord's mercy is worthy to be trusted. [26] I suppose that in a time of stress like the present it is good for a person to stay as he is. [27] That means that if a man has a wife, he should not seek to be free of her; and if he is unmarried, he should not look for a wife. [28] But if you marry you do not sin, and if a girl marries she does not sin. It is just that those who get married will have the normal problems of married life, and I would rather spare you. [29] What I am saying, brothers, is that there is not much time left: from now on a man with a wife should live as if he had none — [30] and those who are sad should live as if they weren't, those who are happy as if they weren't, [31] and those who deal in worldly affairs as if not engrossed in them — because the present scheme of things in this world won't last much longer. [32] What I want is for you to be free of concern. An unmarried man concerns himself with the Lord's affairs, [33] with how to please the Lord; but the married man concerns himself with the world's affairs, with how to please his wife; [34] and he finds himself split. Likewise the woman who is no longer married or the girl who has never been married concerns herself with the Lord's affairs, with how to be holy both physically and spiritually; but the married woman concerns herself with the world's affairs, with how to please her husband. [35] I am telling you this for your own benefit, not to put restrictions on you — I am simply concerned that you live in a

proper manner and serve the Lord with undivided devotion.

^{36} Now if a man thinks he is behaving dishonorably by treating his fiancee this way, and if there is strong sexual desire, so that marriage is what ought to happen; then let him do what he wants — he is not sinning: let them get married. ^{37} But if a man has firmly made up his mind, being under no compulsion but having complete control over his will, if he has decided within himself to keep his fiancee a virgin, he will be doing well. ^{38} So the man who marries his fiancee will do well, and the man who doesn't marry will do better.

^{39} A wife is bound to her husband as long as he lives, but if the husband dies she is free to marry anyone she wishes, provided he is a believer in the Lord. ^{40} However, in my opinion, she will be happier if she remains unmarried, and in saying this I think I have God's Spirit.

8 ^{1} Now about food sacrificed to idols: we know that, as you say, "We all have knowledge." Yes, that is so, but "knowledge" puffs a person up with pride; whereas love builds up. ^{2} The person who thinks he "knows" something doesn't yet know in the way he ought to know. ^{3} However, if someone loves God, God knows him.

^{4} So, as for eating food sacrificed to idols, we "know" that, as you say, "An idol has no real existence in the world, and there is only one God." ^{5} For even if there are so-called "gods", either in heaven or on earth — as in fact there are "gods" and "lords" galore — ^{6} yet for us there is one God, the Father, from whom all things come and for whom we exist; and one Lord, Yeshua the Messiah, through whom were created all things and through whom we have our being.

^{7} But not everyone has this knowl-edge. Moreover, some people are still so accustomed to idols that when they eat food which has been sacrificed to them, they think of it as really affected by the idol; and their consciences, being weak, are thus defiled. ^{8} Now food will not improve our relationship with God — it will be neither poorer if we abstain nor richer if we eat. ^{9} However, watch out that your mastery of the situation does not become a stumblingblock to the weak. ^{10} You have this "knowledge"; but suppose someone with a weak conscience sees you sitting, eating a meal in the temple of an idol. Won't he be built up wrongly to eat this food which has been sacrificed to idols? ^{11} Thus by your "knowledge" this weak person is destroyed, this brother for whom the Messiah died; ^{12} and so, when you sin against the brothers by wounding their conscience when it is weak, you are sinning against the Messiah!

^{13} To sum up, if food will be a snare for my brother, I will never eat meat again, lest I cause my brother to sin.

9 ^{1} Am I not a free man? Am I not an emissary of the Messiah? Haven't I seen Yeshua our Lord? And aren't you yourselves the result of my work for the Lord? ^{2} Even if to others I am not an emissary, at least I am to you; for you are living proof that I am the Lord's emissary. ^{3} That is my defense when people put me under examination.

^{4} Don't we have the right to be given food and drink? ^{5} Don't we have the right to take along with us a believing wife, as do the other emissaries, also the Lord's brothers and Kefa? ^{6} Or are

---

b'rit-mi·lah — covenantal circumcision
Ke·**fa** — Peter
Ye·**shu**·a — Jesus

Bar-Nabba and I the only ones required to go on working for our living? ⁷ Did you ever hear of a soldier paying his own expenses? or of a farmer planting a vineyard without eating its grapes? Who shepherds a flock without drinking some of the milk? ⁸ What I am saying is not based merely on human authority, because the *Torah* says the same thing — ⁹ for in the *Torah* of Moshe it is written, **"You are not to put a muzzle on an ox when it is treading out the grain."***ⁱ* If God is concerned about cattle, ¹⁰ all the more does he say this for our sakes. Yes, it was written for us, meaning that he who plows and he who threshes should work expecting to get a share of the crop. ¹¹ If we have sown spiritual seed among you, is it too much if we reap a material harvest from you? ¹² If others are sharing in this right to be supported by you, don't we have a greater claim to it?

But we don't make use of this right. Rather, we put up with all kinds of things so as not to impede in any way the Good News about the Messiah. ¹³ Don't you know that those who work in the Temple get their food from the Temple, and those who serve at the altar get a share of the sacrifices offered there? ¹⁴ In the same way, the Lord directed that those who proclaim the Good News should get their living from the Good News.

¹⁵ But I have not made use of any of these rights. Nor am I writing now to secure them for myself, for I would rather die than be deprived of my ground for boasting! ¹⁶ For I can't boast merely because I proclaim the Good News — this I do from inner compulsion: woe is me if I don't proclaim the Good News! ¹⁷ For if I do this willingly, I have a reward; but if I do it unwillingly, I still do it, simply because I've been entrusted with a job. ¹⁸ So then, what is my reward? Just this: that in proclaiming the Good News I can make it available free of charge, without making use of the rights to which it entitles me.

¹⁹ For although I am a free man, not bound to do anyone's bidding, I have made myself a slave to all in order to win as many people as possible. ²⁰ That is, with Jews, what I did was put myself in the position of a Jew, in order to win Jews. With people in subjection to a legalistic perversion of the *Torah*, I put myself in the position of someone under such legalism, in order to win those under this legalism, even though I myself am not in subjection to a legalistic perversion of the *Torah*. ²¹ With those who live outside the framework of *Torah*, I put myself in the position of someone outside the *Torah* in order to win those outside the *Torah* — although I myself am not outside the framework of God's *Torah* but within the framework of *Torah* as upheld by the Messiah. ²² With the "weak" I became "weak", in order to win the "weak". With all kinds of people I have become all kinds of things, so that in all kinds of circumstances I might save at least some of them.

²³ But I do it all because of the rewards promised by the Good News, so that I may share in them along with the others who come to trust. ²⁴ Don't you know that in a race all the runners compete, but only one wins the prize? So then, run to win! ²⁵ Now every athlete in training submits himself to strict discipline, and he does it just to win a laurel wreath that will soon wither away. But we do it to win a crown that will last forever. ²⁶ Accordingly, I don't run aimlessly but straight for the finish line; I don't shadow-box

---

ⁱ Deuteronomy 25:4

but try to make every punch count. ²⁷I treat my body hard and make it my slave so that, after proclaiming the Good News to others, I myself will not be disqualified.

10 ¹For, brothers, I don't want you to miss the significance of what happened to our fathers. All of them were guided by the pillar of cloud, and they all passed through the sea, ²and in connection with the cloud and with the sea they all immersed themselves into Moshe, ³also they all ate the same food from the Spirit, ⁴and they all drank the same drink from the Spirit — for they drank from a Spirit-sent Rock which followed them, and that Rock was the Messiah. ⁵Yet with the majority of them God was not pleased, so their bodies were strewn across the desert.

⁶Now these things took place as prefigurative historical events, warning us not to set our hearts on evil things as they did. ⁷Don't be idolaters, as some of them were — as the *Tanakh* puts it, **"The people sat down to eat and drink, then got up to indulge in revelry."**ʲ ⁸And let us not engage in sexual immorality, as some of them did, with the consequence that 23,000 died in a single day. ⁹And let us not put the Messiah to the test, as some of them did, and were destroyed by snakes. ¹⁰And don't grumble, as some of them did, and were destroyed by the Destroying Angel.

¹¹These things happened to them as prefigurative historical events, and they were written down as a warning to us who are living in the *acharit-hayamim*. ¹²Therefore, let anyone who thinks he is standing up be careful not to fall! ¹³No temptation has seized you beyond what people normally experience, and God can be trusted not to allow you to be tempted beyond what you can bear. On the contrary, along with the temptation he will also provide the way out, so that you will be able to endure.

¹⁴Therefore, my dear friends, run from idolatry! ¹⁵I speak to you as sensible people; judge for yourselves what I am saying. ¹⁶The "cup of blessing" over which we make the *b'rakhah* — isn't it a sharing in the bloody sacrificial death of the Messiah? The bread we break, isn't it a sharing in the body of the Messiah? ¹⁷Because there is one loaf of bread, we who are many constitute one body, since we all partake of the one loaf of bread. ¹⁸Look at physical Israel: don't those who eat the sacrifices participate in the altar? ¹⁹So, what am I saying? That food sacrificed to idols has any significance in itself? or that an idol has significance in itself? ²⁰No, what I am saying is that the things which pagans sacrifice, they sacrifice not to God but to demons; and I don't want you to become sharers of the demons! ²¹You can't drink both a cup of the Lord and a cup of demons, you can't partake in both a meal of the Lord and a meal of demons. ²²Or are we trying to make the Lord jealous? We aren't stronger than he is, are we?

²³"Everything is permitted," you say? Maybe, but not everything is helpful. "Everything is permitted?" Maybe, but not everything is edifying. ²⁴No one should be looking out for his own interests, but for those of his fellow.

---

a·cha·rit-ha·ya·mim — the end of days, the last times
Bar-Nab·ba — Barnabas
b'ra·khah — blessing
Mo·she — Moses
Ta·nakh — Hebrew Scriptures, "Old Testament"
To·rah — Teaching, "Law"; Pentateuch
To·rah-teacher — scribe

ʲ Exodus 32:6

²⁵Eat whatever is sold in the meat market without raising questions of conscience, ²⁶for **the earth and everything in it belong to the Lord.**[k] ²⁷If some unbeliever invites you to a meal, and you want to go, eat whatever is put in front of you without raising questions of conscience. ²⁸But if someone says to you, "This meat was offered as a sacrifice," then don't eat it, out of consideration for the person who pointed it out and also for conscience's sake — ²⁹however, I don't mean your conscience but that of the other person. You say, "Why should my freedom be determined by someone else's conscience? ³⁰If I participate with thankfulness, why am I criticized over something for which I myself bless God?" ³¹Well, whatever you do, whether it's eating or drinking or anything else, do it all so as to bring glory to God. ³²Do not be an obstacle to anyone — not to Jews, not to Gentiles, and not to God's Messianic Community. ³³Just as I try to please everyone in everything I do, not looking out for my own interests but for those of the many, so that they may be saved;

11 ¹try to imitate me, even as I myself try to imitate the Messiah.

²Now I praise you because you have remembered everything I told you and observe the traditions just the way I passed them on to you. ³But I want you to understand that the head of every man is the Messiah, and the head of a wife is her husband, and the head of the Messiah is God. ⁴Every man who prays or prophesies wearing something down over his head brings shame to his head, ⁵but every woman who prays or prophesies with her head unveiled brings shame to her head — there is no difference between her and a woman who has had her head shaved. ⁶For if a woman is not veiled, let her also have her hair cut short; but if it is shameful for a woman to wear her hair cut short or to have her head shaved, then let her be veiled. ⁷For a man indeed should not have his head veiled, because he is the image and glory of God, and the woman is the glory of man. ⁸For man was not made from woman, but woman from man; ⁹and indeed man was not created for the sake of the woman but woman for the sake of the man. ¹⁰The reason a woman should show by veiling her head that she is under authority has to do with the angels. ¹¹Nevertheless, in union with the Lord neither is woman independent of man nor is man independent of woman; ¹²for as the woman was made from the man, so also the man is now born through the woman. But everything is from God. ¹³Decide for yourselves: is it appropriate for a woman to pray to God when she is unveiled? ¹⁴Doesn't the nature of things itself teach you that a man who wears his hair long degrades himself? ¹⁵But a woman who wears her hair long enhances her appearance, because her hair has been given to her as a covering. ¹⁶However, if anyone wants to argue about it, the fact remains that we have no such custom, nor do the Messianic communities of God.

¹⁷But in giving you this next instruction I do not praise you, because when you meet together it does more harm than good! ¹⁸For, in the first place, I hear that when you gather together as a congregation you divide up into cliques; and to a degree I believe it ¹⁹(granted that there must be some divisions among you in order to show who are the ones in the right). ²⁰Thus, when you gather together, it is not to eat a meal of the Lord; ²¹because as you eat your meal, each one goes ahead on his own; so that one stays hungry while

---

k Psalm 24:1, 50:12, 89:13(12)

another is already drunk! ^{22}Don't you have homes to eat and drink in? Or are you trying to show your contempt for God's Messianic community and embarrass those who are poor? What am I supposed to say to you? Am I supposed to praise you? Well, for this I don't praise you!

^{23}For what I received from the Lord is just what I passed on to you — that the Lord Yeshua, on the night he was betrayed, took bread; ^{24}and after he had made the *b'rakhah* he broke it and said, "This is my body, which is for you. Do this as a memorial to me;" ^{25}likewise also the cup after the meal, saying, "This cup is the New Covenant effected by my blood; do this, as often as you drink it, as a memorial to me." ^{26}For as often as you eat this bread and drink the cup, you proclaim the death of the Lord, until he comes.

^{27}Therefore, whoever eats the Lord's bread or drinks the Lord's cup in an unworthy manner will be guilty of desecrating the body and blood of the Lord! ^{28}So let a person examine himself first, and then he may eat of the bread and drink from the cup; ^{29}for a person who eats and drinks without recognizing the body eats and drinks judgment upon himself. ^{30}This is why many among you are weak and sick, and some have died! ^{31}If we would examine ourselves, we would not come under judgment. ^{32}But when we are judged by the Lord, we are being disciplined, so that we will not be condemned along with the world.

^{33}So then, my brothers, when you gather together to eat, wait for one another. ^{34}If someone is hungry, he should eat at home, so that when you meet together it will not result in judgment.

As for the other matters, I will instruct you about them when I come.

12 ^{1}But, brothers, I do not want you to go on being ignorant about the things of the Spirit. ^{2}You know that when you were pagans, no matter how you felt you were being led, you were being led astray to idols, which can't speak at all. ^{3}Therefore, I want to make it clear to you that no one speaking by the Spirit of God ever says, "Yeshua is cursed!" and no one can say, "Yeshua is Lord," except by the *Ruach HaKodesh.*

^{4}Now there are different kinds of gifts, but the same Spirit gives them. ^{5}Also there are different ways of serving, but it is the same Lord being served. ^{6}And there are different modes of working, but it is the same God working them all in everyone. ^{7}Moreover, to each person is given the particular manifestation of the Spirit that will be for the common good. ^{8}To one, through the Spirit, is given a word of wisdom; to another, a word of knowledge, in accordance with the same Spirit; ^{9}to another, faith, by the same Spirit; and to another, gifts of healing, by the one Spirit; ^{10}to another, the working of miracles; to another, prophecy; to another the ability to judge between spirits; to another, the ability to speak in different kinds of tongues; and to yet another, the ability to interpret tongues. ^{11}One and the same Spirit is at work in all these things, distributing to each person as he chooses. ^{12}For just as the body is one but has many parts; and all the parts of the body, though many, constitute one body; so it is with the Messiah. ^{13}For it was by one Spirit that we were all immersed into one body, whether Jews

b'ra·khah — blessing
Ru·ach-Ha·Ko·desh — Holy Spirit
Ye·shu·a — Jesus

or Gentiles, slaves or free; and we were all given the one Spirit to drink.
¹⁴ For indeed the body is not one part but many. ¹⁵ If the foot says, "I'm not a hand, so I'm not part of the body," that doesn't make it stop being part of the body. ¹⁶ And if the ear says, "I'm not an eye, so I'm not part of the body," that doesn't make it stop being part of the body. ¹⁷ If the whole body were an eye, how could it hear? If it were all hearing, how could it smell? ¹⁸ But as it is, God arranged each of the parts in the body exactly as he wanted them. ¹⁹ Now if they were all just one part, where would the body be? ²⁰ But as it is, there are indeed many parts, yet just one body. ²¹ So the eye cannot say to the hand, "I don't need you;" or the head to the feet, "I don't need you." ²² On the contrary, the parts of the body that seem to be less important turn out to be all the more necessary; ²³ and upon body parts which we consider less dignified we bestow greater dignity; and the parts that aren't attractive are the ones we make as attractive as we can, ²⁴ while our attractive parts have no need for such treatment. Indeed, God has put the body together in such a way that he gives greater dignity to the parts that lack it, ²⁵ so that there will be no disagreements within the body, but rather all the parts will be equally concerned for all the others. ²⁶ Thus if one part suffers, all the parts suffer with it; and if one part is honored, all the parts share its happiness.

²⁷ Now you together constitute the body of the Messiah, and individually you are parts of it. ²⁸ And God has placed in the Messianic Community first, emissaries; second, prophets; third, teachers; then those who work miracles; then those with gifts of healing; those with ability to help; those skilled in administration; and

those who speak in various tongues. ²⁹ Not all are emissaries, are they? Not all are prophets, are they? or teachers? or miracle-workers? ³⁰ Not all have gifts of healing, not all speak in tongues, not all interpret, do they? ³¹ Eagerly seek the better gifts.

But now I will show you the best way of all.

13 ¹ I may speak in the tongues
of men, even angels;
but if I lack love,
I have become merely
blaring brass
or a cymbal clanging.

² I may have the gift
of prophecy,
I may fathom all mysteries,
know all things,
have all faith —
enough to move mountains;
but if I lack love,
I am nothing.

³ I may give away
everything that I own,
I may even hand over
my body to be burned;
but if I lack love,
I gain nothing.

⁴ Love is patient and kind,
not jealous, not boastful,
⁵ not proud, rude or selfish,
not easily angered,
and it keeps no record
of wrongs.
⁶ Love does not gloat
over other people's sins
but takes its delight
in the truth.
⁷ Love always bears up,
always trusts,
always hopes,
always endures.

[8] Love never ends;
    but prophecies will pass,
tongues will cease,
    knowledge will pass.
[9] For our knowledge is partial,
    and our prophecy partial;
[10] but when the perfect comes,
    the partial will pass.

[11] When I was a child,
    I spoke like a child,
thought like a child,
    argued like a child;
now that I
    have become a man,
I have finished
    with childish ways.

[12] For now we see
    obscurely in a mirror,
but then it will be
    face to face.
Now I know partly;
    then I will know fully,
just as God
    has fully known me.

[13] But for now,
    three things last —
trust, hope,
    love;
and the greatest of these
    is love.

14 [1] Pursue love!

However, keep on eagerly seeking the things of the Spirit; and especially seek to be able to prophesy. [2] For someone speaking in a tongue is not speaking to people but to God, because no one can understand, since he is uttering mysteries in the power of the Spirit. [3] But someone prophesying is speaking to people, edifying, encouraging and comforting them. [4] A person speaking in a tongue does edify himself, but a person prophesying edifies the congregation. [5] I wish you would all speak in tongues, but even more I wish

you would all prophesy. The person who prophesies is greater than the person who speaks in tongues, unless someone gives an interpretation, so that the congregation can be edified.

[6] Brothers, suppose I come to you now speaking in tongues. How can I be of benefit to you unless I bring you some revelation or knowledge or prophecy or teaching? [7] Even with lifeless musical instruments, such as a flute or a harp, how will anyone recognize the melody if one note can't be distinguished from another? [8] And if the bugle gives an unclear sound, who will get ready for battle? [9] It's the same with you: how will anyone know what you are saying unless you use your tongue to produce intelligible speech? You will be talking to the air! [10] There are undoubtedly all kinds of sounds in the world, and none is altogether meaningless; [11] but if I don't know what a person's sounds mean, I will be a foreigner to the speaker and the speaker will be a foreigner to me. [12] Likewise with you: since you eagerly seek the things of the Spirit, seek especially what will help in edifying the congregation.

[13] Therefore someone who speaks in a tongue should pray for the power to interpret. [14] For if I pray in a tongue, my spirit does pray, but my mind is unproductive. [15] So, what about it? I will pray with my spirit, but I will also pray with my mind; I will sing with my spirit, but I will also sing with my mind. [16] Otherwise, if you are giving thanks with your spirit, how will someone who has not yet received much instruction be able to say, "*Amen,*" when you have finished giving thanks, since he doesn't know what you are saying? [17] For undoubt-

---

A · men — So be it

edly you are giving thanks very nicely, but the other person is not being edified. [18] I thank God that I speak in tongues more than all of you, [19] but in a congregation meeting I would rather say five words with my mind in order to instruct others than ten thousand words in a tongue!

[20] Brothers, don't be children in your thinking. In evil, be like infants; but in your thinking, be grown-up. [21] In the *Torah* it is written,

> "By other tongues,
> by the lips of foreigners
> I will speak to this people.
> But even then they will not listen
> to me," says *Adonai*.[1]

[22] Thus tongues are a sign not for believers but for unbelievers, while prophecy is not for unbelievers but for believers. [23] So if the whole congregation comes together with everybody speaking in tongues, and uninstructed people or unbelievers come in, won't they say you're crazy? [24] But if you all prophesy, and some unbeliever or uninstructed person enters, he is convicted of sin by all, he is brought under judgment by all, [25] and the secrets of his heart are laid bare; so he falls on his face and worships God, saying, "God is really here among you!"

[26] What is our conclusion, brothers? Whenever you come together, let everyone be ready with a psalm or a teaching or a revelation, or ready to use his gift of tongues or give an interpretation; but let everything be for edification. [27] If the gift of tongues is exercised, let it be by two or at most three, and each in turn; and let someone interpret. [28] And if there is no one present who can interpret, let the people who speak in tongues keep silent when the congrega-

tion meets — they can speak to themselves and to God. [29] Let two or three prophets speak, while the others weigh what is said. [30] And if something is revealed to a prophet who is sitting down, let the first one be silent. [31] For you can all prophesy one by one, with the result that all will learn something and all will be encouraged. [32] Also, the prophets' spirits are under the prophets' control; [33] for God is not a God of unruliness but of *shalom*.

As in all the congregations of God's people, [34] let the wives remain silent when the congregation meets; they are certainly not permitted to speak out. Rather, let them remain subordinate, as also the *Torah* says; [35] and if there is something they want to know, let them ask their own husbands at home; for it is shameful for a woman to speak out in a congregational meeting.

[36] Did the word of God originate with you? Or are you the only people it has reached? [37] If anyone thinks he is a prophet or is endowed with the Spirit, let him acknowledge that what I am writing you is a command of the Lord. [38] But if someone doesn't recognize this, then let him remain unrecognized.

[39] So, my brothers, eagerly seek to prophesy; and do not forbid speaking in tongues; [40] but let all things be done in a proper and orderly way.

15 [1] Now, brothers, I must remind you of the Good News which I proclaimed to you, and which you received, and on which you have taken your stand, [2] and by which you are being saved — provided you keep holding fast to the message I proclaimed to you. For if you don't, your trust will have been in vain. [3] For among the first things I passed on to you was what I also received, namely this: the Messiah died for our sins, in accordance with what the *Tanakh* says;

---

[1] Isaiah 28:11

234

⁴and he was buried; and he was raised on the third day, in accordance with what the *Tanakh* says; ⁵and he was seen by Kefa, then by the Twelve; ⁶and afterwards he was seen by more than five hundred brothers at one time, the majority of whom are still alive, though some have died. ⁷Later he was seen by Ya'akov, then by all the emissaries; ⁸and last of all he was seen by me, even though I was born at the wrong time. ⁹For I am the least of all the emissaries, unfit to be called an emissary, because I persecuted the Messianic Community of God. ¹⁰But by God's grace I am what I am, and his grace towards me was not in vain; on the contrary, I have worked harder than all of them, although it was not I but the grace of God with me. ¹¹Anyhow, whether I or they, this is what we proclaim, and this is what you believed.

¹²But if it has been proclaimed that the Messiah has been raised from the dead, how is it that some of you are saying there is no such thing as a resurrection of the dead? ¹³If there is no resurrection of the dead, then the Messiah has not been raised; ¹⁴and if the Messiah has not been raised, then what we have proclaimed is in vain; also your trust is in vain; ¹⁵furthermore, we are shown up as false witnesses for God in having testified that God raised up the Messiah, whom he did not raise if it is true that the dead are not raised. ¹⁶For if the dead are not raised, then the Messiah has not been raised either; ¹⁷and if the Messiah has not been raised, your trust is useless, and you are still in your sins. ¹⁸Also, if this is the case, those who died in union with the Messiah are lost. ¹⁹If it is only for this life that we have put our hope in the Messiah, we are more pitiable than anyone.

²⁰But the fact is that the Messiah *has*

been raised from the dead, the firstfruits of those who have died. ²¹For since death came through a man, also the resurrection of the dead has come through a man. ²²For just as in connection with Adam all die, so in connection with the Messiah all will be made alive. ²³But each in his own order: the Messiah is the firstfruits; then those who belong to the Messiah, at the time of his coming; ²⁴then the culmination, when he hands over the Kingdom to God the Father, after having put an end to every rulership, yes, to every authority and power. ²⁵For he has to rule until he puts all his enemies under his feet. ²⁶The last enemy to be done away with will be death, ²⁷for "He put everything in subjection under his feet."*ᵐ*. But when it says that "everything" has been subjected, obviously the word does not include God, who is himself the one subjecting everything to the Messiah. ²⁸Now when everything has been subjected to the Son, then he will subject himself to God, who subjected everything to him; so that God may be everything in everyone.

²⁹Were it otherwise, what would the people accomplish who are immersed on behalf of the dead? If the dead are not actually raised, why are people immersed for them? ³⁰For that matter, we ourselves — why do we keep facing danger hour by hour? ³¹Brothers, by the right to be proud which the Messiah

---

m Psalm 8:7(6)

A·**dam** — Adam
A·do·nai — the LORD, Jehovah
Ke·**fa** — Peter
sha·lom — peace
Ta·nakh — Hebrew Scriptures, "Old Testament"
To·rah — Teaching, "Law"; Pentateuch
Ya·'a·kov — Jacob

Yeshua our Lord gives me, I solemnly tell you that I die every day. [32] If my fighting with "wild beasts" in Ephesus was done merely on a human basis, what do I gain by it? If dead people are not raised, we might as well live by the saying, **"Let's eat and drink, for tomorrow we die!"**[n] [33] Don't be fooled. "Bad company ruins good character." [34] Come to your senses! Live righteously and stop sinning! There are some people who lack knowledge of God — I say this to your shame.

[35] But someone will ask, "In what manner are the dead raised? What sort of body do they have?" [36] Stupid! When you sow a seed, it doesn't come alive unless it first dies. [37] Also, what you sow is not the body that will be, but a bare seed of, say, wheat or something else; [38] but God gives it the body he intended for it; and to each kind of seed he gives its own body. [39] Not all living matter is the same living matter; on the contrary, there is one kind for human beings, another kind of living matter for animals, another for birds and another for fish. [40] Further, there are heavenly bodies and earthly bodies; but the beauty of heavenly bodies is one thing, while the beauty of earthly bodies is something else. [41] The sun has one kind of beauty, the moon another, the stars yet another; indeed, each star has its own individual kind of beauty.

[42] So it is with the resurrection of the dead. When the body is "sown", it decays; when it is raised, it cannot decay. [43] When sown, it is without dignity; when raised, it will be beautiful. When sown, it is weak; when raised, it will be strong. [44] When sown, it is an ordinary human body; when raised, it will be a body controlled by the Spirit. If there is an ordinary human body,

there is also a body controlled by the Spirit. [45] In fact, the *Tanakh* says so: Adam, the first man, **became a living human being;**[o] but the last "Adam" has become a life-giving Spirit. [46] Note, however, that the body from the Spirit did not come first, but the ordinary human one; the one from the Spirit comes afterwards. [47] The first man is from the earth, made of dust; the second man is from heaven. [48] People born of dust are like the man of dust, and people born from heaven are like the man from heaven; [49] and just as we have borne the image of the man of dust, so also we will bear the image of the man from heaven.

[50] Let me say this, brothers: flesh and blood cannot share in the Kingdom of God, nor can something that decays share in what does not decay. [51] Look, I will tell you a secret — not all of us will die! But we will all be changed! [52] It will take but a moment, the blink of an eye, at the final *shofar*. For the *shofar* will sound, and the dead will be raised to live forever, and we too will be changed. [53] For this material which can decay must be clothed with imperishability, this which is mortal must be clothed with immortality. [54] When what decays puts on imperishability and what is mortal puts on immortality, then this passage in the *Tanakh* will be fulfilled:

"Death is swallowed up in victory.[p]

[55] **"Death, where is your victory?
Death, where is your sting?"**[q]

[56] The sting of death is sin; and sin draws its power from the *Torah*; [57] but thanks be to God, who gives us the victory through our Lord Yeshua the Messiah!

[58] So, my dear brothers, stand firm and unmovable, always doing the

---

n Isaiah 22:13, 56:12

o Genesis 2:7 p Isaiah 25:8 q Hosea 13:14

Lord's work as vigorously as you can, knowing that united with the Lord your efforts are not in vain.

16 ¹Now, in regard to the collection being made for God's people: you are to do the same as I directed the congregations in Galatia to do. ²Every week, on *Motza'ei-Shabbat*, each of you should set some money aside, according to his resources, and save it up; so that when I come I won't have to do fundraising. ³And when I arrive, I will give letters of introduction to the people you have approved, and I will send them to carry your gift to Yerushalayim. ⁴If it seems appropriate that I go too, they will go along with me.

⁵I will visit you after I have gone through Macedonia, for I am intending to pass through Macedonia, ⁶and I may stay with you or even spend the winter, so that you may help me continue my travels wherever I may go. ⁷For I don't want to see you now, when I am only passing through; because I am hoping to spend some time with you, if the Lord allows it. ⁸But I will remain in Ephesus until *Shavu'ot*, ⁹because a great and important door has opened for my work, and there are many people opposing me.

¹⁰If Timothy comes, see that he has nothing to be afraid of while he is with you; for he is doing the Lord's work, just as I am. ¹¹So let no one treat him with disrespect. Help him on his way in peace, so that he will return to me, for the brothers and I are expecting him.

¹²As for brother Apollos, I strongly urged him to go and visit you along with the other brothers; and although it was not at all his desire to come at this time, he will come when he has the opportunity.

¹³Stay alert, stand firm in the faith, behave like a *mentsh*, grow strong. ¹⁴Let everything you do be done in love.

¹⁵Now, brothers, you know that the household of Stephanas were the first people in Achaia to put their trust in the Messiah, and they have devoted themselves to serving God's people. ¹⁶I urge you to submit yourselves to people like these and to everyone who works and toils with them. ¹⁷I am glad that Stephanas and Fortunatus and Achaicus are here, because they have helped make up for your not being here. ¹⁸They have refreshed my spirit, just as they have yours. I want you to show appreciation for people like these.

¹⁹The congregations in the province of Asia send greetings to you. Aquila and Priscilla greet you in union with the Lord, as does the congregation that meets in their house. ²⁰All the brothers send you their greetings. Greet one another with a holy kiss.

²¹*Now, I, Sha'ul, greet you in my own handwriting:*

²²*If anyone does not love the Lord, a curse on him! Marana, ta! [Our Lord, come!]*

²³*May the grace of the Lord Yeshua be with you.*

²⁴*My love is with you all, in union with the Messiah Yeshua.*

A·**dam** — Adam
Ma·ra·na, ta! — our Lord, come!
mentsh — a real person, energetic, moral and compassionate
Mo·tza· 'ei-Shab·bat — Saturday night
Sha·'ul — Saul (Paul)
Sha·vu·'ot — Feast of Weeks, Pentecost
sho·far — ram's horn
Ta·nakh — Hebrew Scriptures, "Old Testament"
To·rah — Teaching, "Law"; Pentateuch
Ye·ru·sha·la·yim — Jerusalem

2 CORINTHIANS

1 [1] From: Sha'ul, by God's will an emissary of the Messiah Yeshua, and brother Timothy

To: God's Messianic community in Corinth, along with all God's people throughout Achaia:

[2] Grace to you and *shalom* from God our Father and the Lord Yeshua the Messiah.

[3] Praised be God, Father of our Lord Yeshua the Messiah, compassionate Father, God of all encouragement and comfort; [4] who encourages us in all our trials, so that we can encourage others in whatever trials they may be undergoing with the encouragement we ourselves have received from God. [5] For just as the Messiah's sufferings overflow into us, so through the Messiah our encouragement also overflows. [6] So if we undergo trials, it is for your encouragement and deliverance; and if we are encouraged, that should encourage you when you have to endure sufferings like those we are experiencing. [7] Moreover, our hope for you remains staunch, because we know that as you share in the sufferings, you will also share in the encouragement.

[8] For, brothers, we want you to know about the trials we have undergone in the province of Asia. The burden laid on us was so far beyond what we could bear that we even despaired of living through it. [9] In our hearts we felt we were under sentence of death. However,

this was to get us to rely not on ourselves but on God, who raises the dead! [10] He rescued us from such deadly peril, and he will rescue us again! The one in whom we have placed our hope will indeed continue to rescue us. [11] And you must add your help by praying for us; for the more people there are praying, the more people there will be to give thanks when their prayer for us is answered.

[12] For we take pride in this: that our conscience assures us that in our dealings with the world, and especially with you, we have conducted ourselves with frankness and godly pureness of motive — not by worldly wisdom but by God-given grace. [13] There are no hidden meanings in our letters other than what you can read and understand; and my hope is that you will understand fully, [14] as indeed you have already understood us in part; so that on the Day of our Lord Yeshua you can be as proud of us as we are of you.

[15] So sure was I of this that I had planned to come and see you, so that you might have the benefit of a second visit. [16] I wanted to visit you on my way to Macedonia, visit you again on my way back from Macedonia, and then have you send me on my way to Y'hudah.

[17] Did I make these plans lightly? Or do I make plans the way a worldly man does, ready to say, "Yes, yes," and "No, no," in the same breath? [18] As surely as

God is trustworthy, we don't say "Yes" when we mean "No". ^{19}For the Son of God, the Messiah Yeshua, who was proclaimed among you through us — that is, through me and Sila and Timothy — was not a yes-and-no man; on the contrary, with him it is always "Yes!" ^{20}For however many promises God has made, they all find their "Yes" in connection with him; that is why it is through him that we say the "*Amen*" when we give glory to God. ^{21}Moreover, it is God who sets both us and you in firm union with the Messiah; he has anointed us, ^{22}put his seal on us, and given us his Spirit in our hearts as a guarantee for the future.

^{23}I call God to witness — he knows what my life is like — that the reason I held back from coming to Corinth was out of consideration for you! ^{24}We are not trying to dictate how you must live out your trust in the Messiah, for in your trust you are standing firm. Rather, we are working with you for your own happiness.

2 ^{1}So I made up my mind that I would not pay you another painful visit. ^{2}For if I cause you pain, who is left to make me happy except the people I have pained? ^{3}Indeed, this is why I wrote as I did — so that when I came, I would not have to be pained by those who ought to be making me happy; for I had enough confidence in all of you to believe that unless I could be happy, none of you could be happy either. ^{4}I wrote to you with a greatly distressed and anguished heart, and with many tears, not in order to cause you pain, but to get you to realize how very much I love you.

^{5}Now if someone has been a cause of pain, it is not I whom he has pained, but, in some measure — I don't want to overstate it — all of you. ^{6}For such a person the punishment already imposed on him by the majority is sufficient, ^{7}so that now you should do the opposite — forgive him, encourage him, comfort him. Otherwise such a person might be swallowed up in overwhelming depression. ^{8}So I urge you to show that you really do love him. ^{9}The reason I wrote you was to see if you would pass the test, to see if you would fully obey me. ^{10}Anyone you forgive, I forgive too. For indeed, whatever I have forgiven, if there has been anything to forgive, has been for your sake in the presence of the Messiah ^{11}so that we will not be taken advantage of by the Adversary — for we are quite aware of his schemes!

^{12}Now when I went to Troas to proclaim the Good News of the Messiah, since a door had been opened for me by the Lord, ^{13}I could not rest, because I failed to find my brother Titus. So I left the people there and went on to Macedonia.

^{14}But thanks be to God, who in the Messiah constantly leads us in a triumphal procession and through us spreads everywhere the fragrance of what it means to know him! ^{15}For to God we are the aroma of the Messiah, both among those being saved and among those being lost; ^{16}to the latter, we are the smell of death leading only to more death; but to the former, we are the sweet smell of life leading to more life. Who is equal to such a task? ^{17}For we are not like a lot of folks who go about huckstering God's message for a fee; on the contrary, we speak out of a sincere heart, as people sent by God,

---

A · men — So be it
sha · lom — peace
Sha · 'ul — Saul (Paul)
Si · la — Silas
Ye · shu · a — Jesus
Y'hu · dah — Judea

standing in God's presence, living in union with the Messiah.

3 ¹Are we starting to recommend ourselves again? Or do we, like some, need letters of recommendation either to you or from you? ²You yourselves are our letter of recommendation, written on our hearts, known and read by everyone. ³You make it clear that you are a letter from the Messiah placed in our care, written not with ink but by the Spirit of the living God, not on stone tablets but on human hearts.

⁴Such is the confidence we have through the Messiah toward God. ⁵It is not that we are competent in ourselves to count anything as having come from us; on the contrary, our competence is from God. ⁶He has even made us competent to be workers serving a New Covenant, the essence of which is not a written text but the Spirit. For the written text brings death, but the Spirit gives life.

⁷Now if that which worked death, by means of a written text engraved on stone tablets, came with glory — such glory that the people of Israel could not stand to look at Moshe's face because of its brightness, even though that brightness was already fading away — ⁸won't the working of the Spirit be accompanied by even greater glory? ⁹For if there was glory in what worked to declare people guilty, how much more must the glory abound in what works to declare people innocent! ¹⁰In fact, by comparison with this greater glory, what was made glorious before has no glory now. ¹¹For if there was glory in what faded away, how much more glory must there be in what lasts.

¹²Therefore, with a hope like this, we are very open — ¹³unlike Moshe, who put a veil over his face, so that the people of Israel would not see the fading brightness come to an end.

¹⁴What is more, their minds were made stonelike; for to this day the same veil remains over them when they read the Old Covenant; it has not been unveiled, because only by the Messiah is the veil taken away. ¹⁵Yes, till today, whenever Moshe is read, a veil lies over their heart. ¹⁶"But," says the *Torah*, **"whenever someone turns to *Adonai*, the veil is taken away."**[a] ¹⁷Now, "*Adonai*" in this text means the Spirit. And where the Spirit of *Adonai* is, there is freedom. ¹⁸So all of us, with faces unveiled, see as in a mirror the glory of the Lord; and we are being changed into his very image, from one degree of glory to the next, by *Adonai* the Spirit.

4 ¹God has shown us such mercy that we do not lose courage as we do the work he has given us. ²Indeed, we refuse to make use of shameful underhanded methods, employing deception or distorting God's message. On the contrary, by making very clear what the truth is, we commend ourselves to everyone's conscience in the sight of God. ³So if indeed our Good News is veiled, it is veiled only to those in the process of being lost. ⁴They do not come to trust because the god of the *'olam hazeh* has blinded their minds, in order to prevent them from seeing the light shining from the Good News about the glory of the Messiah, who is the image of God. ⁵For what we are proclaiming is not ourselves, but the Messiah Yeshua as Lord, with ourselves as slaves for you because of Yeshua. ⁶For it is the God who once said, "Let light shine out of darkness," who has made his light shine in our hearts, the light of the knowledge of God's glory shining in the face of the Messiah Yeshua.

---

a Exodus 34:34

[7]But we have this treasure in clay jars, so that it will be evident that such overwhelming power comes from God and not from us. [8]We have all kinds of troubles, but we are not crushed; we are perplexed, yet not in despair; [9]persecuted, yet not abandoned; knocked down, yet not destroyed. [10]We always carry in our bodies the dying of Yeshua, so that the life of Yeshua may be manifested in our bodies too. [11]For we who are alive are always being handed over to death for Yeshua's sake, so that Yeshua's life also might be manifested in our mortal bodies. [12]Thus death is at work in us but life in you.

[13]The *Tanakh* says, **"I trusted, therefore I spoke."**[b] Since we have that same Spirit who enables us to trust, we also trust and therefore speak; [14]because we know that he who raised the Lord Yeshua will also raise us with Yeshua and bring us along with you into his presence. [15]All this is for your sakes, so that as grace flows out to more and more people, it may cause thanksgiving to overflow and bring glory to God.

[16]This is why we do not lose courage. Though our outer self is heading for decay, our inner self is being renewed daily. [17]For our light and transient troubles are achieving for us an everlasting glory whose weight is beyond description. [18]We concentrate not on what is seen but on what is not seen, since things seen are temporary, but things not seen are eternal.

5 [1]We know that when the tent which houses us here on earth is torn down, we have a permanent building from God, a building not made by human hands, to house us in heaven. [2]For in this tent, our earthly body, we groan with desire to have around us the home from heaven that will be ours.

[3]With this around us we will not be found naked. [4]Yes, while we are in this body, we groan with the sense of being oppressed: it is not so much that we want to take something off, but rather to put something on over it; so that what must die may be swallowed up by the Life. [5]Moreover, it is God who has prepared us for this very thing, and as a pledge he has given us his Spirit.

[6]So we are always confident — we know that so long as we are at home in the body, we are away from our home with the Lord; [7]for we live by trust, not by what we see. [8]We are confident, then, and would much prefer to leave our home in the body and come to our home with the Lord.

[9]Therefore, whether at home or away from home, we try our utmost to please him; [10]for we must all appear before the Messiah's court of judgment, where everyone will receive the good or bad consequences of what he did while he was in the body.

[11]So it is with the fear of the Lord before us that we try to persuade people. Moreover, God knows us as we really are; and I hope that in your consciences you too know us as we really are. [12]We are not recommending ourselves to you again but giving you a reason to be proud of us, so that you will be able to answer those who boast about a person's appearance rather than his inner qualities. [13]If we are insane, it is for God's sake; and if we are sane, it is for your sake. [14]For the Messiah's love has hold of us, because

---

[b] Psalm 116:10

A·do·nai — the LORD, Jehovah

Mo·she — Moses

'o·lam ha·zeh — this world

Ta·nakh — Hebrew Scriptures, "Old Testament"

To·rah — Teaching, "Law"; Pentateuch

Ye·shu·a — Jesus

we are convinced that one man died on behalf of all mankind (which implies that all mankind was already dead), [15] and that he died on behalf of all in order that those who live should not live any longer for themselves but for the one who on their behalf died and was raised. [16] So from now on, we do not look at anyone from a worldly viewpoint. Even if we once regarded the Messiah from a worldly viewpoint, we do so no longer. [17] Therefore, if anyone is united with the Messiah, he is a new creation — the old has passed; look, what has come is fresh and new! [18] And it is all from God, who through the Messiah has reconciled us to himself and has given us the work of that reconciliation, [19] which is that God in the Messiah was reconciling mankind to himself, not counting their sins against them, and entrusting to us the message of reconciliation. [20] Therefore we are ambassadors of the Messiah; in effect, God is making his appeal through us. What we do is appeal on behalf of the Messiah, "Be reconciled to God! [21] God made this sinless man be a sin offering on our behalf, so that in union with him we might fully share in God's righteousness."

6 [1] As God's fellow-workers we also urge you not to receive his grace and then do nothing with it. [2] For he says,

> "At the acceptable time I heard you;
> in the day of salvation I helped you."[c]

[3] We try not to put obstacles in anyone's path, so that no one can find fault with the work we do. [4] On the contrary, we try to commend ourselves in every way as workers for God by continually enduring troubles, hardships, calamities, [5] beatings, imprisonments, riots, overwork, lack of sleep and food. [6] We commend ourselves by our purity, knowledge, patience and kindness; by the *Ruach HaKodesh*; by genuineness of love [7] and truthfulness of speech; and by God's power. We commend ourselves through our use of righteous weapons, whether for pressing our cause or defending it; [8] through being honored and dishonored, praised and blamed, considered deceptive and sincere, [9] unknown and famous. And we commend ourselves as God's workers headed for death, yet look! we're alive! as punished, yet not killed; [10] as having reason to be sad, yet always filled with joy; as poor, yet making many people rich; as having nothing, yet having everything!

[11] Dear friends in Corinth! We have spoken frankly to you, we have opened our hearts wide. [12] Any constraint you feel has not been imposed by us, but by your own inner selves. [13] So, just to be "fair" (I am using the language of children), open wide your hearts too.

[14] Do not yoke yourselves together in a team with unbelievers. For how can righteousness and lawlessness be partners? What fellowship does light have with darkness? [15] What harmony can there be between the Messiah and B'liya'al? What does a believer have in common with an unbeliever? [16] What agreement can there be between the temple of God and idols? For we are the temple of the living God — as God said,

> "I will house myself in them,...
> and I will walk among you.
> I will be their God,
> and they will be my people."[d]

---

c Isaiah 49:8

d Leviticus 26:12; Exodus 6:7; Jeremiah 31:32(33), 32:38; Ezekiel 37:27

[17] Therefore *Adonai* says,

> "'Go out from their midst;
> separate yourselves;
> don't even touch what is unclean.[e]
> Then I myself will receive you.[f]
> [18] In fact, I will be your Father,
> and you will be my sons and
> daughters,'
> says *Adonai-Tzva'ot.*"[g]

7 [1] Therefore, my dear friends, since we have these promises, let us purify ourselves from everything that can defile either body or spirit, and strive to be completely holy, out of reverence for God.

[2] Make room for us in your hearts — we haven't wronged anyone, we haven't corrupted anyone, we haven't exploited anyone. [3] I am not saying this to put blame on you, for I have already said that you have a place in our hearts, whether we live together or die together; [4] that I am very confident in you; that I am very proud of you; that you have filled me with encouragement; and that in spite of all our troubles, I am overflowing with joy.

[5] For indeed when we came into Macedonia, our bodies had no rest. On the contrary, we faced all kinds of troubles — altercations without, apprehensions within. [6] But God, who encourages the downhearted, encouraged us with the arrival of Titus! [7] However, it was not only his arrival which encouraged us, but also how encouraged he was about you, as he told us how you long to see me, how distressed you are over my situation, how zealous you are in my defense — this news made me even happier!

[8] If I caused you pain by my letter, I do not regret it. Even if I did regret it

before — for I do see that that letter did distress you, though only for a short time — [9] now I rejoice not because you were pained, but because the pain led you to turn back to God. For you handled the pain in God's way, so that you were not harmed by us at all. [10] Pain handled in God's way produces a turning from sin to God which leads to salvation, and there is nothing to regret in that! But pain handled in the world's way produces only death. [11] For just look at what handling the pain God's way produced in you! What earnest diligence, what eagerness to clear yourselves, what indignation, what fear, what longing, what zeal, what readiness to put things right! In everything you have proved yourselves blameless in the matter. [12] So even though I wrote to you, it was not for the sake of either the one who did the wrong or the one wronged, but so that before God you could see for yourselves how deep is your devotion to us. [13] This is the reason we have been encouraged.

Besides our own encouragement, we had the even greater joy of seeing how happy Titus was, because all of you set his mind at rest. [14] For I had boasted somewhat about you to him, and now I have not been made to look foolish. On the contrary, just as everything we have said to you is true, so too our boasting in front of Titus has proved true. [15] And his affection for you is all the greater as he remembers how ready you were to obey and how you received him with reverence and respect. [16] I am glad that I can have such complete confidence in you.

---

[e] Isaiah 52:11   [f] Ezekiel 20:41, 34
[g] 2 Samuel 7:14, 8; Isaiah 43:6

A·do·nai — the LORD, Jehovah
A·do·nai-Tzva·'ot — the LORD (Jehovah) of Hosts (heaven's armies)
B'li·ya·'al — Belial
Ru·ach-Ha·Ko·desh — Holy Spirit

8 [1] Now, brothers, we must tell you about the grace God has given the congregations in Macedonia. [2] Despite severe trials, and even though they are desperately poor, their joy has overflowed in a wealth of generosity. [3] I tell you they have not merely given according to their means, but of their own free will they have given beyond their means. [4] They begged and pleaded with us for the privilege of sharing in this service for God's people. [5] Also, they didn't do this in the way we had expected, but first they gave themselves to the Lord, which means, by God's will, to us.

[6] All this has led us to urge Titus to bring this same gracious gift to completion among you, since he has already made a beginning of it. [7] Just as you excel in everything — in faith, in speech, in knowledge, in diligence of every kind, and in your love for us — see that you excel in this gift too. [8] I am not issuing an order; rather, I am testing the genuineness of your love against the diligence of others. [9] For you know how generous our Lord Yeshua the Messiah was — for your sakes he impoverished himself, even though he was rich, so that he might make you rich by means of his poverty. [10] As I say, in regard to this matter I am only giving an opinion. A year ago you were not only the first to take action but the first to want to do so. Now it would be to your advantage [11] to finish what you started, so that your eagerness in wanting to commence the project may be matched by your eagerness to complete it, as you contribute from what you have. [12] For if the eagerness to give is there, the acceptability of the gift will be measured by what you have, not by what you don't have. [13] It is not that relief for others should cause trouble for you, but that there should

be a kind of reciprocity: [14] at present your abundance can help those in need; so that when you are in need, their abundance can help you — thus there is reciprocity. [15] It is as the *Tanakh* says,

> "He who gathered much had nothing extra,
> and he who gathered little had nothing lacking."[h]

[16] Now I thank God for making Titus as devoted to you as we are; [17] for he not only responded to our urging, but, being so devoted, he is coming to you on his own initiative. [18] And with him we are sending the brother whose work for the Good News is praised in all the congregations; [19] not only that, he has also been appointed by the congregations to travel with us, so that the way we administer this charitable work will bring honor to the Lord and show our eagerness to help. [20] Our aim in this is to show that our conduct in dealing with these substantial sums is above reproach; [21] for **we take pains to do what is right** not only **in the sight of God** but **also** in the sight of **other people.**[i] [22] With these two we are sending another brother of ours, one whose diligence we have tested many times in many ways, but who is now all the more diligent because of his great confidence in you. [23] As for Titus, he is my partner who works with me on your behalf; and the other brothers with him are emissaries of the congregations and bring honor to the Messiah. [24] So the love you show these men will justify our pride in you to them, and through them to the congregations that sent them.

9 [1] There is really no need for me to write you about this offering for God's people — [2] I know how eager you

---

h Exodus 16:18   *i* Proverbs 3:4 (Septuagint)

are, and I boast about you to the Macedonians. I tell them, "Achaia has been ready since last year," and it was your zeal that stirred up most of them. ³But now I am sending the brothers so that our boast about you in this regard will not prove hollow, so that you will be ready, as I said you would be. ⁴For if some Macedonians were to come with me and find you unprepared, we would be humiliated at having been so confident — to say nothing of how you would feel. ⁵So I thought it necessary to urge these brothers to go on to you ahead of me and prepare your promised gift in plenty of time; this way it will be ready when I come and will be a genuine gift, not something extracted by pressure.

⁶Here's the point: he who plants sparingly also harvests sparingly. ⁷Each should give according to what he has decided in his heart, not grudgingly or under compulsion, for **God loves a cheerful giver.**ʲ ⁸Moreover, God has the power to provide you with every gracious gift in abundance, so that always in every way you will have all you need yourselves and be able to provide abundantly for every good cause — ⁹as the *Tanakh* says,

> **"He gave generously to the poor;**
> **his *tzedakah* lasts forever."**ᵏ

¹⁰He who provides both seed for the planter and bread for food will supply and multiply your seed and increase the harvest of your *tzedakah*. ¹¹You will be enriched in every way, so that you can be generous in everything. And through us your generosity will cause people to thank God, ¹²because rendering this holy service not only provides for the needs of God's people, but it also overflows in the many thanks people will be giving to God. ¹³In offering this service you prove to these people that you glorify God by actually doing what your acknowledgement of the Good News of the Messiah requires, namely, sharing generously with them and with everyone. ¹⁴And in their prayers for you they will feel a strong affection for you because of how gracious God has been to you. ¹⁵Thanks be to God for his indescribable gift!

10 ¹Now it is I myself, Sha'ul, making an appeal to you with the meekness and forbearance that come from the Messiah, I who am considered timid when face-to-face with you but intimidating from a distance. ²But I beg you not to force me to be intimidating when I am with you, as I expect to be toward some who regard us as living in a worldly way. ³For although we do live in the world, we do not wage war in a worldly way; ⁴because the weapons we use to wage war are not worldly. On the contrary, they have God's power for demolishing strongholds. We demolish arguments ⁵and every arrogance that raises itself up against the knowledge of God; we take every thought captive and make it obey the Messiah. ⁶And when you have become completely obedient, then we will be ready to punish every act of disobedience.

⁷You are looking at the surface of things. If anyone is convinced that he belongs to the Messiah, he should remind himself that we belong to the Messiah as much as he does. ⁸For even if I boast a little too much about the authority the Lord has given us —

ʲ Proverbs 22:8 (Septuagint)
ᵏ Psalm 112:9

Sha·'ul — Saul (Paul)
Ta·nakh — Hebrew Scriptures, "Old Testament"
tze·da·kah — righteousness, charitable giving

authority to build you up, not tear you down — I am not ashamed. ⁹ My object is not to seem as if I were trying to frighten you with these letters. ¹⁰ Someone says, "His letters are weighty and powerful, but when he appears in person he is weak, and as a speaker he is nothing." ¹¹ Such a person should realize that what we say in our letters when absent, we will do when present.

¹² We don't dare class or compare ourselves with some of the people who advertise themselves. In measuring themselves against each other and comparing themselves with each other, they are simply stupid. ¹³ We will not boast about what lies outside the area of work which God has given us; rather, we will boast within our assigned area, and that area does reach as far as you. ¹⁴ We are not overextending our boasting as if we had not reached as far as you; for we did come all the way to you with the Good News of the Messiah. ¹⁵ We do not boast about the area in which others labor; but our hope is that as your trust grows, we will be magnified in your midst in relation to our own area of work, so that we can go on to do even more, ¹⁶ namely, to proclaim the Good News in regions beyond you. Our hope is not to boast about the work already done by someone else.

¹⁷ So, **let anyone who wants to boast, boast about _Adonai_;** *ᴵ* ¹⁸ because it is not the one who recommends himself who is worthy of approval, but the one whom the Lord recommends.

11 ¹ I would like you to bear with me in a little foolishness — please do bear with me! ² For I am jealous for you with God's kind of jealousy; since I promised to present you as a pure virgin in marriage to your one husband, the Messiah; ³ and I fear that somehow your minds may be seduced away from simple and pure devotion to the Messiah, just as Chavah was deceived by the serpent and his craftiness. ⁴ For if someone comes and tells you about some other Yeshua than the one we told you about, or if you receive a spirit different from the one you received or accept some so-called "good news" different from the Good News you already accepted, you bear with him well enough! ⁵ For I don't consider myself in any way inferior to these "super-emissaries". ⁶ I may not be a skilled speaker, but I do have the knowledge; anyhow, we have made this clear to you in every way and in every circumstance.

⁷ Or did I sin in humbling myself so that you could be exalted, in proclaiming God's Good News to you free of charge? ⁸ I robbed other congregations by accepting support from them in order to serve you. ⁹ And when I was with you and had needs, I did not burden anyone: my needs were met by the brothers who came from Macedonia. In nothing have I been a burden to you, nor will I be. ¹⁰ The truthfulness of the Messiah is in me, so that this boast concerning me is not going to be silenced anywhere in Achaia. ¹¹ Why won't I ever accept your support? Is it that I don't love you? God knows I do! ¹² No, I do it — and will go on doing it — in order to cut the ground from under those who want an excuse to boast that they work the same way we do. ¹³ The fact is that such men are pseudo-emissaries: they tell lies about their work and masquerade as emissaries of the Messiah. ¹⁴ There is nothing surprising in that, for the Adversary himself masquerades as an angel of light; ¹⁵ so it's no great thing if his workers masquerade as servants of

---

ᴵ Jeremiah 9:23(24)

246

righteousness. They will meet the end their deeds deserve.

¹⁶ I repeat: don't let anyone think I am a fool. But even if you do, at least receive me as a fool; so that I too may do a little boasting! ¹⁷ What I am saying is not in accordance with the Lord; rather, this conceited boasting is spoken as a fool would speak. ¹⁸ Since many people boast in a worldly way, I too will boast this way. ¹⁹ For since you yourselves are so wise, you gladly put up with fools! ²⁰ You put up with it if someone makes slaves of you, exploits you, takes you in, puffs himself up, slaps you in the face. ²¹ To my shame, I must admit that we have been too "weak" to do such things!

But if anyone dares to boast about something — I'm talking like a fool! — I am just as daring. ²² Are they Hebrews? So am I. Are they Israelites? So am I. Are they descendants of Avraham? So am I. ²³ Are they servants of the Messiah? (I'm talking like a madman!) I'm a better one! I've worked much harder, been imprisoned more often, suffered more beatings, been near death over and over. ²⁴ Five times I received "forty lashes less one" from the Jews. ²⁵ Three times I was beaten with rods. Once I was stoned. Three times I was shipwrecked. I spent a night and a day in the open sea. ²⁶ In my many travels I have been exposed to danger from rivers, danger from robbers, danger from my own people, danger from Gentiles, danger in the city, danger in the desert, danger at sea, danger from false brothers. ²⁷ I have toiled and endured hardship, often not had enough sleep, been hungry and thirsty, frequently gone without food, been cold and naked. ²⁸ And besides these external matters, there is the daily pressure of my anxious concern for all the congregations. ²⁹ Who is weak with-

out my sharing his weakness? Who falls into sin without my burning inside?

³⁰ If I must boast, I will boast about things that show how weak I am. ³¹ God the Father of the Lord Yeshua — blessed be he forever — knows that I am not lying! ³² When I was in Dammesek, the governor under King Aretas had the city of Dammesek guarded in order to arrest me; ³³ but I was lowered in a basket through an opening in the wall and escaped his clutches.

12 ¹ I have to boast. There is nothing to be gained by it, but I will go on to visions and revelations of the Lord. ² I know a man in union with the Messiah who fourteen years ago was snatched up to the third heaven; whether he was in the body or outside the body I don't know, God knows. ³ And I know that such a man — whether in the body or apart from the body I don't know, God knows — ⁴ was snatched into Gan-Eden and heard things that cannot be put into words, things unlawful for a human being to utter. ⁵ About such a man I will boast; but about myself I will not boast, except in regard to my weaknesses. ⁶ If I did want to boast, I would not be foolish; because I would be speaking the truth. But, because of the extraordinary greatness of the revelations, I refrain, so that no one will think more of me than what my words or deeds may warrant. ⁷ Therefore, to keep me from becoming overly proud, I was given a thorn in my flesh, a messenger from the Adversary to pound away at me, so that I wouldn't grow conceited.

A·do·nai — the LORD, Jehovah
Av·ra·ham — Abraham
Cha·vah — Eve
Dam·me·sek — Damascus
Gan-E·den — Paradise
Ye·shu·a — Jesus

⁸ Three times I begged the Lord to take this thing away from me; ⁹ but he told me, "My grace is enough for you, for my power is brought to perfection in weakness." Therefore, I am very happy to boast about my weaknesses, in order that the Messiah's power will rest upon me. ¹⁰ Yes, I am well pleased with weaknesses, insults, hardships, persecutions and difficulties endured on behalf of the Messiah; for it is when I am weak that I am strong.

¹¹ I have behaved like a fool, but you forced me to do it — you who should have been commending me. For I am in no way inferior to the "super-emissaries", even if I am nothing. ¹² The things that prove I am an emissary — signs, wonders and miracles — were done in your presence, despite what I had to endure. ¹³ Is there any way in which you have been behind any of the other congregations, other than in my not having been a burden to you? For this unfairness, please forgive me!

¹⁴ Look, I am ready this third time to come and visit you; and I will not be a burden to you; for it is not what you own that I want, but you! Children are not supposed to save up for their parents, but parents for their children. ¹⁵ And as for me, I will most gladly spend everything I have and be spent myself too for your sakes. If I love you more, am I to be loved less?

¹⁶ Let it be granted, then, that I was not a burden to you; but, crafty fellow that I am, I took you with trickery! ¹⁷ Was it perhaps through someone I sent you ¹⁸ that I took advantage of you? I urged Titus to go and sent the brother with him; Titus didn't take advantage of you, did he? Didn't we live by the same Spirit and show you the same path?

¹⁹ Perhaps you think that all this time we have been defending ourselves before you. No, we have been speaking in the sight of God, as those united with the Messiah should; and, my dear friends, it is all for your upbuilding. ²⁰ For I am afraid of coming and finding you not the way I want you to be, and also of not being found the way you want me to be. I am afraid of finding quarreling and jealousy, anger and rivalry, slander and gossip, arrogance and disorder. ²¹ I am afraid that when I come again, my God may humiliate me in your presence, and that I will be grieved over many of those who sinned in the past and have not repented of the impurity, fornication and debauchery that they have engaged in.

13 ¹ This will be the third time that I have come to visit you. **Any charge must be established by the testimony of two or three witnesses.**[m] ² To those who sinned in the past and to the rest I say beforehand while absent the same thing I said when I was with you the second time: if I come again I will not spare you — ³ since you are looking for proof of the Messiah speaking in me. He is not weak in dealing with you, but he is powerful among you. ⁴ For although he was executed on a stake in weakness, now he lives by God's power. And we too are weak in union with him, but in dealing with you we will live with him by God's power.

⁵ Examine yourselves to see whether you are living the life of trust. Test yourselves. Don't you realize that Yeshua the Messiah is in you? — unless you fail to pass the test. ⁶ But I hope you will realize that we are not failures. ⁷ And we pray to God that you will do nothing wrong. We are not concerned with our appearing successful, but with your doing what is right, even if we appear to be failures. ⁸ For we cannot

m Deuteronomy 19:15

act against the truth, only for it. ⁹ So we rejoice whenever we are weak and you are strong; indeed, what we pray for is that you become perfect. ¹⁰ I write these things while away from you, so that when I am with you I will not have to use my authority to deal sharply with you, for the Lord gave it to me for building up and not for tearing down.

¹¹ And now, brothers, *shalom*! Put yourselves in order, pay attention to my advice, be of one mind, live in *shalom* — and the God of love and *shalom* will be with you.

¹² Greet one another with a holy kiss. ¹³ All God's people send greetings to you.

¹⁴ The grace of the Lord Yeshua the Messiah,
the love of God
and the fellowship of the *Ruach HaKodesh*
be with you all.

Ru·ach-Ha·Ko·desh — Holy Spirit
sha·lom — peace
Ye·shu·a — Jesus

249

THE LETTER FROM YESHUA'S EMISSARY, SHA'UL (PAUL) TO THE MESSIANIC COMMUNITIES IN GALATIA:

GALATIANS

1 ¹From: Sha'ul, an emissary — I received my commission not from human beings or through human mediation but through Yeshua the Messiah and God the Father, who raised him from the dead — also from all the brothers with me

²To: The Messianic communities in Galatia:

³Grace and *shalom* to you from God our Father and from the Lord Yeshua the Messiah, ⁴who gave himself for our sins, so that he might deliver us from the present evil world-system, in obedience to the will of God, our Father. ⁵To him be the glory forever and ever! *Amen.*

⁶I am astounded that you are so quick to remove yourselves from me, the one who called you by the Messiah's grace, and turn to some other supposedly "Good News", ⁷which is not good news at all! What is really happening is that certain people are pestering you and trying to pervert the genuine Good News of the Messiah. ⁸But even if we — or, for that matter, an angel from heaven! — were to announce to you some so-called "Good News" contrary to the Good News we did announce to you, let him be under a curse forever! ⁹We said it before, and I say it again: if anyone announces "Good News" contrary to what you received, let him be under a curse forever!

¹⁰Now does that sound as if I were trying to win human approval? No! I want God's approval! Or that I'm trying to cater to people? If I were still doing that, I would not be a servant of the Messiah.

¹¹Furthermore, let me make clear to you, brothers, that the Good News as I proclaim it is not a human product; ¹²because neither did I receive it from someone else nor was I taught it — it came through a direct revelation from Yeshua the Messiah. ¹³For you have heard about my former way of life in traditional Judaism — how I did my best to persecute God's Messianic Community and destroy it; ¹⁴and how, since I was more of a zealot for the traditions handed down by my forefathers than most Jews my age, I advanced in traditional Judaism more rapidly than they did.

¹⁵But when God, who picked me out before I was born and called me by his grace, chose ¹⁶to reveal his Son to me, so that I might announce him to the Gentiles, I did not consult anyone; ¹⁷and I did not go up to Yerushalayim to see those who were emissaries before me. Instead, I immediately went off to Arabia and afterwards returned to Dammesek. ¹⁸Not until three years later did I go up to Yerushalayim to make Kefa's acquaintance, and I stayed with him for two weeks, ¹⁹but I did not see any of the other emissaries except Ya'akov the Lord's brother. ²⁰(Concern-

ing these matters I am writing you about, I declare before God that I am not lying!) ²¹Next I went to Syria and Cilicia; ²²but in Y'hudah, the Messianic congregations didn't even know what I looked like — ²³they were only hearing the report, "The one who used to persecute us now preaches the Good News of the faith he was formerly out to destroy;" ²⁴and they praised God for me.

2 ¹Then after fourteen years I again went up to Yerushalayim, this time with Bar-Nabba; and I took with me Titus. ²I went up in obedience to a revelation, and I explained to them the Good News as I proclaim it among the Gentiles — but privately, to the acknowledged leaders. I did this out of concern that my current or previous work might have been in vain.

³But they didn't force my Gentile companion Titus to undergo *b'rit-milah*. ⁴Indeed, the question came up only because some men who pretended to be brothers had been sneaked in — they came in surreptitiously to spy out the freedom we have in the Messiah Yeshua, so that they might enslave us. ⁵Not even for a minute did we give in to them so that the truth of the Good News might be preserved for you.

⁶Moreover, those who were the acknowledged leaders — what they were makes no difference to me; God does not judge by outward appearances — these leaders added nothing to me. ⁷On the contrary, they saw that I had been entrusted with the Good News for the Uncircumcised, just as Kefa had been for the Circumcised; ⁸since the One working in Kefa to make him an emissary to the Circumcised had worked in me to make me an emissary to the Gentiles. ⁹So, having perceived what grace had been given to me, Ya'akov, Kefa and Yochanan, the acknowledged pillars of the commu-

nity, extended to me and Bar-Nabba the right hand of fellowship; so that we might go to the Gentiles, and they to the Circumcised. ¹⁰Their only request was that we should remember the poor — which very thing I have spared no pains to do.

¹¹Furthermore, when Kefa came to Antioch, I opposed him publicly, because he was clearly in the wrong. ¹²For prior to the arrival of certain people from the community headed by Ya'akov, he had been eating with the Gentile believers; but when they came, he withdrew and separated himself, because he was afraid of the faction who favored circumcising Gentile believers. ¹³And the other Jewish believers became hypocrites along with him, so that even Bar-Nabba was led astray by their hypocrisy. ¹⁴But when I saw that they were not walking a straight path, keeping in line with the truth of the Good News, I said to Kefa, right in front of everyone, "If you, who are a Jew, live like a *Goy* and not like a Jew, why are you forcing the *Goyim* to live like Jews? ¹⁵We are Jews by birth, not so-called '*Goyishe* sinners'; ¹⁶even so, we have come to realize that a person is not declared righteous by God on the ground of his legalistic

---

A·**men** — So be it
b'rit·mi·**lah** — covenantal circumcision
Bar·**Nab**·ba — Barnabas
Dam·**me**·sek — Damascus
Goy (pl. *Go·yim*) — Gentile
Goy·i·she — Gentile (adjective)
Ke·**fa** — Peter
sha·lom — peace
Sha·'**ul** — Saul (Paul)
To·rah — Teaching, "Law"; Pentateuch
Ya·'a·**kov** — James
Ye·ru·sha·**la**·yim — Jerusalem
Ye·**shu**·a — Jesus
Y'hu·**dah** — Judea
Yo·cha·**nan** — John

observance of *Torah* commands, but through the Messiah Yeshua's trusting faithfulness. Therefore, we too have put our trust in Messiah Yeshua and become faithful to him, in order that we might be declared righteous on the ground of the Messiah's trusting faithfulness and not on the ground of our legalistic observance of *Torah* commands. For on the ground of legalistic observance of *Torah* commands, **no one will be declared righteous."**[a]

[17] But if, in seeking to be declared righteous by God through our union with the Messiah, we ourselves are indeed found to be sinners, then is the Messiah an aider and abetter of sin? Heaven forbid! [18] Indeed, if I build up again the legalistic bondage which I destroyed, I really do make myself a transgressor. [19] For it was through letting the *Torah* speak for itself that I died to its traditional legalistic misinterpretation, so that I might live in direct relationship with God. [20] When the Messiah was executed on the stake as a criminal, I was too; so that my proud ego no longer lives. But the Messiah lives in me, and the life I now live in my body I live by the same trusting faithfulness that the Son of God had, who loved me and gave himself up for me. [21] I do not reject God's gracious gift; for if the way in which one attains righteousness is through legalism, then the Messiah's death was pointless.

3 [1] You stupid Galatians! Who has put you under a spell? Before your very eyes Yeshua the Messiah was clearly portrayed as having been put to death as a criminal! [2] I want to know from you just this one thing: did you receive the Spirit by legalistic observance of *Torah* commands or by trusting in what you heard and being faith-

ful to it? [3] Are you that stupid? Having begun with the Spirit's power, do you think you can reach the goal under your own power? [4] Have you suffered so much for nothing? If that's the way you think, your suffering certainly will have been for nothing! [5] What about God, who supplies you with the Spirit and works miracles among you — does he do it because of your legalistic observance of *Torah* commands or because you trust in what you heard and are faithful to it?

[6] It was the same with Avraham: **"He trusted in God and was faithful to him, and that was credited to his account as righteousness."**[b] [7] Be assured, then, that it is those who live by trusting and being faithful who are really children of Avraham. [8] Also the *Tanakh*, foreseeing that God would consider the Gentiles righteous when they live by trusting and being faithful, told the Good News to Avraham in advance by saying, **"In connection with you, all the *Goyim* will be blessed."**[c] [9] So then, those who rely on trusting and being faithful are blessed along with Avraham, who trusted and was faithful.

[10] For everyone who depends on legalistic observance of *Torah* commands lives under a curse, since it is written, **"Cursed is everyone who does not keep on doing everything written in the Scroll of the *Torah*."**[d] [11] Now it is evident that no one comes to be declared righteous by God through legalism, since **"The person who is righteous will attain life by trusting and being faithful."**[e] [12] Furthermore, legalism is not based on trusting and being faithful, but on a misuse of the text that says, **"Anyone who does these things**

---

a Psalm 143:2

b Genesis 15:6   *c* Genesis 12:3
d Deuteronomy 27:26   *e* Habakkuk 2:4

will attain life through them."*f* ¹³The Messiah redeemed us from the curse pronounced in the *Torah* by becoming cursed on our behalf; for the *Tanakh* says, **"Everyone who hangs from a stake comes under a curse."**ᵍ ¹⁴Yeshua the Messiah did this so that in union with him the Gentiles might receive the blessing announced to Avraham, so that through trusting and being faithful, we might receive what was promised, namely, the Spirit.

¹⁵Brothers, let me make an analogy from everyday life: when someone swears an oath, no one else can set it aside or add to it. ¹⁶Now the promises were made to Avraham and to his **seed.** It doesn't say, "and to seeds," as if to many; on the contrary, it speaks of one — **"and to your seed"**ʰ — and this "one" is the Messiah. ¹⁷Here is what I am saying: the legal part of the *Torah*, which came into being 430 years later, does not nullify an oath sworn by God, so as to abolish the promise. ¹⁸For if the inheritance comes from the legal part of the *Torah*, it no longer comes from a promise. But God gave it to Avraham through a promise.

¹⁹So then, why the legal part of the *Torah*? It was added in order to create transgressions, until the coming of the **seed** about whom the promise had been made. Moreover, it was handed down through angels and a mediator. ²⁰Now a mediator implies more than one, but God is one.

²¹Does this mean that the legal part of the *Torah* stands in opposition to God's promises? Heaven forbid! For if the legal part of the *Torah* which God gave had had in itself the power to give life, then righteousness really would have come by legalistically following

such a *Torah.* ²²But instead, the *Tanakh* shuts up everything under sin; so that what had been promised might be given, on the ground of Yeshua the Messiah's trusting faithfulness, to those who continue trustingly faithful.

²³Now before the time for this trusting faithfulness came, we were imprisoned in subjection to the system which results from perverting the *Torah* into legalism, kept under guard until this yet-to-come trusting faithfulness would be revealed. ²⁴Accordingly, the *Torah* functioned as a custodian until the Messiah came, so that we might be declared righteous on the ground of trusting and being faithful. ²⁵But now that the time for this trusting faithfulness has come, we are no longer under a custodian.

²⁶For in union with the Messiah, you are all children of God through this trusting faithfulness; ²⁷because as many of you as were immersed into the Messiah have clothed yourselves with the Messiah, in whom ²⁸there is neither Jew nor Gentile, neither slave nor freeman, neither male nor female; for in union with the Messiah Yeshua, you are all one. ²⁹Also, if you belong to the Messiah, you are **seed** of Avraham and heirs according to the promise.

4 ¹What I am saying is that as long as the heir is a minor he is no different from a slave, even though he is the legal owner of the estate; ²rather, he is subject to guardians and caretakers until the time previously set by his father. ³So it is with us — when we

---

f Leviticus 18:5 *g* Deuteronomy 21:22-23
h Genesis 12:7, 13:15, 17:7, 24:7

Av·ra·**ham** — Abraham
Go·yim — Gentiles, nations, pagans
Ta·nakh — Hebrew Scriptures, "Old Testament"
To·rah — Teaching, "Law"; Pentateuch
Ye·shu·a — Jesus

were "children" we were slaves to the elemental spirits of the universe; [4]but when the appointed time arrived, God sent forth his Son. He was born from a woman, born into a culture in which legalistic perversion of the *Torah* was the norm, [5]so that he might redeem those in subjection to this legalism and thus enable us to be made God's sons. [6]Now because you are sons, God has sent forth into our hearts the Spirit of his Son, the Spirit who cries out, "*Abba!*" (that is, "Dear Father!"). [7]So through God you are no longer a slave but a son, and if you are a son you are also an heir.

[8]In the past, when you did not know God, you served as slaves beings which in reality are non-gods. [9]But now you do know God, and, more than that, you are known by God. So how is it that you turn back again to those weak and miserable elemental spirits? Do you want to enslave yourselves to them once more? [10]You observe special days, months, seasons and years! [11]I fear for you that my work among you has been wasted!

[12]Brothers, I beg of you: put yourselves in my place — after all, I put myself in your place. It isn't that you have done me any wrong — [13]you know that it was because I was ill that I proclaimed the Good News to you at first; [14]and even though my physical condition must have tempted you to treat me with scorn, you did not display any sign of disdain or disgust. No, you welcomed me as if I had been an angel of God, as if I had been the Messiah Yeshua himself! [15]So what has become of the joy you felt? For I bear you witness that had it been possible, you would have gouged out your eyes and given them to me. [16]Have I now become your enemy because I tell you the truth? [17]True, these teachers are zealous

for you, but their motives are not good. They want to separate you from us so that you will become zealous for them. [18]To be zealous is good, provided always that the cause is good. Indeed, whether I am present with you or not, [19]my dear children, I am suffering the pains of giving birth to you all over again — and this will go on until the Messiah takes shape in you. [20]I wish I could be present with you now and change my tone of voice. I don't know what to do with you.

[21]Tell me, you who want to be in subjection to the system that results from perverting the *Torah* into legalism, don't you hear what the *Torah* itself says? [22]It says that Avraham had two sons, one by the slave woman and one by the free woman. [23]The one by the slave woman was born according to the limited capabilities of human beings, but the one by the free woman was born through the miracle-working power of God fulfilling his promise. [24]Now, to make a *midrash* on these things: the two women are two covenants. One is from Mount Sinai and bears children for slavery — this is Hagar. [25]Hagar is Mount Sinai in Arabia; she corresponds to the present Yerushalayim, for she serves as a slave along with her children. [26]But the Yerushalayim above is free, and she is our mother; [27]for the *Tanakh* says,

> "Rejoice, you barren woman who does not bear children!
> Break forth and shout, you who are not in labor!
> For the deserted wife will have more children
> than the one whose husband is with her!"[i]

[28]You, brothers, like Yitzchak, are chil-

---

i Isaiah 54:1

dren referred to in a promise of God.
²⁹ But just as then the one born according to limited human capability persecuted the one born through the Spirit's supernatural power, so it is now. ³⁰ Nevertheless, what does the *Tanakh* say? **"Get rid of the slave woman and her son, for by no means will the son of the slave woman inherit along with the son of the free woman!"**ʲ ³¹ So, brothers, we are children not of the slave woman, but of the free woman.

5 ¹ What the Messiah has freed us for is freedom! Therefore, stand firm, and don't let yourselves be tied up again to a yoke of slavery. ² Mark my words — I, Sha'ul, tell you that if you undergo *b'rit-milah* the Messiah will be of no advantage to you at all! ³ Again, I warn you: any man who undergoes *b'rit-milah* is obligated to observe the entire *Torah*! ⁴ You who are trying to be declared righteous by God through legalism have severed yourselves from the Messiah! You have fallen away from God's grace! ⁵ For it is by the power of the Spirit, who works in us because we trust and are faithful, that we confidently expect our hope of attaining righteousness to be fulfilled. ⁶ When we are united with the Messiah Yeshua, neither being circumcised nor being uncircumcised matters; what matters is trusting faithfulness expressing itself through love.

⁷ You were running the race well; who has stopped you from following the truth? ⁸ Whatever means of persuasion he used was not from the One who calls you. ⁹ "It takes only a little *chametz* to leaven the whole batch of dough." ¹⁰ I am confident that since you are united with the Lord, you will take no other view; and I am confident that the one who has been disturbing you, whoever

he may be, will have to bear his punishment.

¹¹ And as for me, brothers, if I am still preaching that circumcision is necessary, why am I still being persecuted? If that were the case, my preaching about the execution-stake would cause no offense whatever. ¹² I wish the people who are bothering you would go the whole way and castrate themselves!

¹³ For, brothers, you were called to be free. Only do not let that freedom become an excuse for allowing your old nature to have its way. Instead, serve one another in love. ¹⁴ For the whole of the *Torah* is summed up in this one sentence: **"Love your neighbor as yourself;"**ᵏ ¹⁵ but if you go on snapping at each other and tearing each other to pieces, watch out, or you will be destroyed by each other!

¹⁶ What I am saying is this: run your lives by the Spirit. Then you will not do what your old nature wants. ¹⁷ For the old nature wants what is contrary to the Spirit, and the Spirit wants what is contrary to the old nature. These oppose each other, so that you find yourselves unable to carry out your good intentions. ¹⁸ But if you are led by the Spirit, then you are not in subjec-

---

k Leviticus 19:18

Ab·ba — dear Father, "Dad"
Av·ra·ham — Abraham
b'rit-mi·lah — covenantal circumcision
cha·metz — yeast, leaven
Ha·gar — Hagar
mid·rash — allegorical or homiletical interpretation loosely based on a text
Sha·'ul — Saul (Paul)
Si·nai — Sinai
Ta·nakh — Hebrew Scriptures, "Old Testament"
To·rah — Teaching, "Law"; Pentateuch
Ye·ru·sha·la·yim — Jerusalem
Ye·shu·a — Jesus
Yitz·chak — Isaac

---

j Genesis 21:10

tion to the system that results from perverting the *Torah* into legalism.

^{19} And it is perfectly evident what the old nature does. It expresses itself in sexual immorality, impurity and indecency; ^{20} in idol-worship and misuse of drugs in connection with the occult; in feuding, fighting, becoming jealous and getting angry; in selfish ambition, factionalism, intrigue ^{21} and envy; in drunkenness, orgies and things like these. I warn you now as I have warned you before: those who do such things will have no share in the Kingdom of God!

^{22} But the fruit of the Spirit is love, joy, peace, patience, kindness, goodness, faithfulness, ^{23} humility, self control. Nothing in the *Torah* stands against such things.

^{24} Moreover, those who belong to the Messiah Yeshua have put their old nature to death on the stake, along with its passions and desires. ^{25} Since it is through the Spirit that we have Life, let it also be through the Spirit that we order our lives day by day.

^{26} Let us not become conceited, provoking and envying each other.

6 ^{1} Brothers, suppose someone is caught doing something wrong. You who have the Spirit should set him right, but in a spirit of humility, keeping an eye on yourselves so that you won't be tempted too. ^{2} Bear one another's burdens — in this way you will be fullfilling the *Torah*'s true meaning, which the Messiah upholds. ^{3} For if anyone thinks he is something when he is really nothing, he is fooling himself. ^{4} So let each of you scrutinize his own actions. Then if you do find something to boast about, at least the boasting will be based on what you have actually done and not merely on a judgment that you are better than someone else; ^{5} for each person will carry his own load. ^{6} But whoever is being instructed

in the Word should share all the good things he has with his instructor. ^{7} Don't delude yourselves: no one makes a fool of God! A person reaps what he sows. ^{8} Those who keep sowing in the field of their old nature, in order to meet its demands, will eventually reap ruin; but those who keep sowing in the field of the Spirit will reap from the Spirit everlasting life. ^{9} So let us not grow weary of doing what is good; for if we don't give up, we will in due time reap the harvest. ^{10} Therefore, as the opportunity arises, let us do what is good to everyone, and especially to the family of those who are trustingly faithful.

^{11} *Look at the large letters I use as I close in my own handwriting.*

^{12} *It is those who want to look good outwardly who are trying to get you to be circumcised. The only reason they are doing it is to escape persecution for preaching about the Messiah's execution-stake.* ^{13} *For even those who are getting circumcised don't observe the Torah. On the contrary, they want you to get circumcised so that they can boast of having gained your adherence.* ^{14} *But as for me, Heaven forbid that I should boast about anything except the execution-stake of our Lord Yeshua the Messiah! Through him, as far as I am concerned,* the world has been put to death on the stake; and through him, as far as the world is concerned, I have been put to death on the stake.

[15] For neither being circumcised nor being uncircumcised matters; what matters is being a new creation. [16] And as many as order their lives by this rule, shalom upon them and mercy, and upon the Israel of God!

[17] From now on, I don't want anyone to give me any more tsuris, because I have scars on my body to prove that I belong to Yeshua!

[18] The grace of our Lord Yeshua the Messiah be with your spirit, brothers. Amen.

A·men — So be it
sha·lom — peace
To·rah — Teaching, "Law"; Pentateuch
tsur·is — troubles
Ye·shu·a — Jesus

THE LETTER FROM YESHUA'S EMISSARY, SHA'UL (PAUL) TO THE MESSIANIC COMMUNITY IN EPHESUS:

EPHESIANS

1 ¹From: Sha'ul, by God's will an emissary of the Messiah Yeshua

To: God's people living in Ephesus, that is, those who are trusting in the Messiah Yeshua:

²Grace to you and *shalom* from God our Father and the Lord Yeshua the Messiah.

³Praised be *Adonai*, Father of our Lord Yeshua the Messiah, who in the Messiah has blessed us with every spiritual blessing in heaven. ⁴In the Messiah he chose us in love before the creation of the universe to be holy and without defect in his presence. ⁵He determined in advance that through Yeshua the Messiah we would be his sons — in keeping with his pleasure and purpose — ⁶so that we would bring him praise commensurate with the glory of the grace he gave us through the Beloved One.

⁷In union with him, through the shedding of his blood, we are set free — our sins are forgiven; this accords with the wealth of the grace ⁸he has lavished on us. In all his wisdom and insight ⁹he has made known to us his secret plan, which by his own will he designed beforehand in connection with the Messiah ¹⁰and will put into effect when the time is ripe — his plan to place everything in heaven and on earth under the Messiah's headship.

¹¹Also in union with him we were given an inheritance, we who were picked in advance according to the purpose of the One who effects everything in keeping with the decision of his will, ¹²so that we who earlier had put our hope in the Messiah would bring him praise commensurate with his glory.

¹³Furthermore, you who heard the message of the truth, the Good News offering you deliverance, and put your trust in the Messiah were sealed by him with the promised *Ruach HaKodesh*, ¹⁴who guarantees our inheritance until we come into possession of it and thus bring him praise commensurate with his glory.

¹⁵For this reason, ever since I heard about your trust in the Lord Yeshua and your love for all God's people, ¹⁶I have not stopped giving thanks for you. In my prayers I keep asking ¹⁷the God of our Lord Yeshua the Messiah, the glorious Father, to give you a spirit of wisdom and revelation, so that you will have full knowledge of him. ¹⁸I pray that he will give light to the eyes of your hearts, so that you will understand the hope to which he has called you, what rich glories there are in the inheritance he has promised his people, ¹⁹and how surpassingly great is his power working in us who trust him. It works with the same mighty strength he used ²⁰when he worked in the Messiah to raise him from the dead and seat him at his right hand in heaven, ²¹far above every ruler, authority,

power, dominion or any other name that can be named either in the *'olam hazeh* or in the *'olam haba.* ²²Also, he has **put all things under his feet**[a] and made him head over everything for the Messianic Community, ²³which is his body, the full expression of him who fills all creation.

2 ¹You used to be dead because of your sins and acts of disobedience. ²You walked in the ways of the *'olam hazeh* and obeyed the Ruler of the Powers of the Air, who is still at work among the disobedient. ³Indeed, we all once lived this way — we followed the passions of our old nature and obeyed the wishes of our old nature and our own thoughts. In our natural condition we were headed for God's wrath, just like everyone else.

⁴But God is so rich in mercy and loves us with such intense love ⁵that, even when we were dead because of our acts of disobedience, he brought us to life along with the Messiah — it is by grace that you have been delivered. ⁶That is, God raised us up with the Messiah Yeshua and seated us with him in heaven, ⁷in order to exhibit in the ages to come how infinitely rich is his grace, how great is his kindness toward us who are united with the Messiah Yeshua. ⁸For you have been delivered by grace through trusting, and even this is not your accomplishment but God's gift. ⁹You were not delivered by your own actions; therefore no one should boast. ¹⁰For we are of God's making, created in union with the Messiah Yeshua for a life of good actions already prepared by God for us to do.

¹¹Therefore, remember your former state: you Gentiles by birth — called the Uncircumcised by those who,

merely because of an operation on their flesh, are called the Circumcised — ¹²at that time had no Messiah. You were estranged from the national life of Israel. You were foreigners to the covenants embodying God's promise. You were in this world without hope and without God.

¹³But now, you who were once far off have been brought near through the shedding of the Messiah's blood. ¹⁴For he himself is our *shalom* — he has made us both one and has broken down the *m'chitzah* which divided us ¹⁵by destroying in his own body the enmity occasioned by the *Torah*, with its commands set forth in the form of ordinances. He did this in order to create in union with himself from the two groups a single new humanity and thus make *shalom*, ¹⁶and in order to reconcile to God both in a single body by being executed on a stake as a criminal and thus killing in himself that enmity.

¹⁷Also, when he came, **he announced as Good News *shalom* to you far off and *shalom* to those nearby,**[b] ¹⁸news that through him we both have access in one Spirit to the Father.

¹⁹So then, you are no longer foreigners and strangers. On the contrary, you are fellow-citizens with God's people and members of God's family. ²⁰You have built on the foundation of the emissaries and the prophets, with

---

a Psalm 8:7(6)

b Isaiah 57:19

A·do·nai — the LORD, Jehovah
m'chi·tzah — dividing wall
'o·lam ha·ba — the world/age to come
'o·lam ha·zeh — this world/age
Ru·ach-Ha·Ko·desh — Holy Spirit
sha·lom — peace
Sha·'ul — Saul (Paul)
To·rah — Teaching, "Law"; Pentateuch
Ye·shu·a — Jesus

the cornerstone being Yeshua the Messiah himself. ²¹ In union with him, the whole building is held together, and it is growing into a holy temple in union with the Lord. ²² Yes, in union with him, you yourselves are being built together into a spiritual dwelling-place for God!

3 ¹ It is a consequence of this that I, Sha'ul, am a prisoner of the Messiah Yeshua on behalf of you Gentiles. ² I assume that you have heard of the work God in his grace has given me to do for your benefit, ³ and that it was by a revelation that this secret plan was made known to me. I have already written about it briefly, ⁴ and if you read what I have written, you will grasp how I understand this secret plan concerning the Messiah. ⁵ In past generations it was not made known to mankind as the Spirit is now revealing it to his emissaries and prophets, ⁶ that in union with the Messiah and through the Good News the Gentiles were to be joint heirs, a joint body and joint sharers with the Jews in what God has promised. ⁷ I became a servant of this Good News by God's gracious gift, which he gave me through the operation of his power. ⁸ To me, the least important of all God's holy people, was given this privilege of announcing to the Gentiles the Good News of the Messiah's unfathomable riches, ⁹ and of letting everyone see how this secret plan is going to work out. This plan, kept hidden for ages by God, the Creator of everything, ¹⁰ is for the rulers and authorities in heaven to learn, through the existence of the Messianic Community, how many-sided God's wisdom is. ¹¹ This accords with God's age-old purpose, accomplished in the Messiah Yeshua, our Lord. ¹² In union with him, through his faithfulness, we have boldness and confidence when we approach God. ¹³ So I ask you not to be

discouraged by the troubles I endure on your behalf — it is all for your glory.

¹⁴ For this reason, I fall on my knees before the Father, ¹⁵ from whom every fatherland in heaven and on earth receives its name. ¹⁶ I pray that from the treasures of his glory he will empower you with inner strength by his Spirit, ¹⁷ so that the Messiah may live in your hearts through your trusting. Also I pray that you will be rooted and founded in love, ¹⁸ so that you, with all God's people, will be given strength to grasp the breadth, length, height and depth of the Messiah's love, ¹⁹ yes, to know it, even though it is beyond all knowing, so that you will be filled with all the fullness of God.

²⁰ Now to him who by his power working in us is able to do far beyond anything we can ask or imagine, ²¹ to him be glory in the Messianic Community and in the Messiah Yeshua from generation to generation forever. *Amen.*

4 ¹ Therefore I, the prisoner united with the Lord, beg you to lead a life worthy of the calling to which you have been called.

² Always be humble, gentle and patient, bearing with one another in love, ³ and making every effort to preserve the unity the Spirit gives through the binding power of *shalom.* ⁴ There is one body and one Spirit, just as when you were called you were called to one hope. ⁵ And there is one Lord, one trust, one immersion, ⁶ and one God, the Father of all, who rules over all, works through all and is in all.

⁷ Each one of us, however, has been given grace to be measured by the Messiah's bounty. ⁸ This is why it says,

> **"After he went up into the heights,**
> **he led captivity captive**
> **and he gave gifts to mankind."**ᶜ

ᶜ Psalm 68:19(18)

⁹Now this phrase, **"he went up"**, what can it mean if not that he first went down into the lower parts, that is, the earth? ¹⁰The one who went down is himself the one who also **went up**, far above all of heaven, in order to fill all things. ¹¹Furthermore, **he gave** some people as emissaries, some as prophets, some as proclaimers of the Good News, and some as shepherds and teachers. ¹²Their task is to equip God's people for the work of service that builds the body of the Messiah, ¹³until we all arrive at the unity implied by trusting and knowing the Son of God, at full manhood, at the standard of maturity set by the Messiah's perfection.

¹⁴We will then no longer be infants tossed about by the waves and blown along by every wind of teaching, at the mercy of people clever in devising ways to deceive. ¹⁵Instead, speaking the truth in love, we will in every respect grow up into him who is the head, the Messiah. ¹⁶Under his control, the whole body is being fitted and held together by the support of every joint, with each part working to fulfill its function; this is how the body grows and builds itself up in love.

¹⁷Therefore I say this — indeed, in union with the Lord I insist on it: do not live any longer as the pagans live, with their sterile ways of thinking. ¹⁸Their intelligence has been shrouded in darkness, and they are estranged from the life of God, because of the ignorance in them, which in turn comes from resisting God's will. ¹⁹They have lost all feeling, so they have abandoned themselves to sensuality, practicing any kind of impurity and always greedy for more. ²⁰But this is not the lesson you learned from the Messiah! ²¹If you really listened to him and were instructed about him, then you learned that since what is in Yeshua is truth, ²²then,

so far as your former way of life is concerned, you must strip off your old nature, because your old nature is thoroughly rotted by its deceptive desires; ²³and you must let your spirits and minds keep being renewed, ²⁴and clothe yourselves with the new nature created to be godly, which expresses itself in the righteousness and holiness that flow from the truth.

²⁵Therefore, stripping off falsehood, **let everyone speak truth with his neighbor,**ᵈ because we are intimately related to each other as parts of a body. ²⁶**Be angry, but don't sin**ᵉ — don't let the sun go down before you have dealt with the cause of your anger; ²⁷otherwise you leave room for the Adversary.

²⁸The thief must stop stealing; instead, he should make an honest living by his own efforts. This way he will be able to share with those in need.

²⁹Let no harmful language come from your mouth, only good words that are helpful in meeting the need, words that will benefit those who hear them. ³⁰Don't cause grief to God's *Ruach HaKodesh*, for he has stamped you as his property until the day of final redemption. ³¹Get rid of all bitterness, rage, anger, violent assertiveness and slander, along with all spitefulness. ³²Instead, be kind to each other, tenderhearted; and forgive each other, just as in the Messiah God has also forgiven you.

5 ¹So imitate God, as his dear children; ²and live a life of love, just as also the Messiah loved us, indeed, on our behalf gave himself up as an offer-

---

d Zechariah 8:16   *e* Psalm 4:5(4)

A·**men** — So be it
Ru·ach-Ha·Ko·desh — Holy Spirit
sha·lom — peace
Sha·'ul — Saul (Paul)
Ye·shu·a — Jesus

ing, as a slaughtered sacrifice to God with a pleasing fragrance. ³Among you there should not even be mentioned sexual immorality, or any kind of impurity, or greed; these are utterly inappropriate for God's holy people. ⁴Also out of place are obscenity and stupid talk or coarse language; instead, you should be giving thanks. ⁵For of this you can be sure: every sexually immoral, impure or greedy person — that is, every idol-worshipper — has no share in the Kingdom of the Messiah and of God. ⁶Let no one deceive you with empty talk; for it is because of these things that God's judgment is coming on those who disobey him. ⁷So don't become partners with them!

⁸For you used to be darkness; but now, united with the Lord, you are light. Live like children of light, ⁹for the fruit of the light is in every kind of goodness, righteousness and truth — ¹⁰try to determine what will please the Lord. ¹¹Have nothing to do with the deeds produced by darkness, but instead expose them, ¹²for it is shameful even to speak of the things these people do in secret. ¹³But everything exposed to the light is revealed clearly for what it is, ¹⁴since anything revealed is a light. This is why it says,

"Get up, sleeper! Arise from the dead,
and the Messiah will shine on you!"

¹⁵Therefore, pay careful attention to how you conduct your life — live wisely, not unwisely. ¹⁶Use your time well, for these are evil days. ¹⁷So don't be foolish, but try to understand what the will of the Lord is.

¹⁸Don't get drunk with wine, because it makes you lose control. Instead, keep on being filled with the Spirit — ¹⁹sing psalms, hymns and spiritual songs to each other; sing to the Lord and make music in your heart to him; ²⁰always give thanks for everything to God the Father in the name of our Lord Yeshua the Messiah.

²¹Submit to one another in fear of the Messiah. ²²Wives should submit to their husbands as they do to the Lord; ²³because the husband is head of the wife, just as the Messiah, as head of the Messianic Community, is himself the one who keeps the body safe. ²⁴Just as the Messianic Community submits to the Messiah, so also wives should submit to their husbands in everything.

²⁵As for husbands, love your wives, just as the Messiah loved the Messianic Community, indeed, gave himself up on its behalf, ²⁶in order to set it apart for God, making it clean through immersion in the *mikveh*, so to speak, ²⁷in order to present the Messianic Community to himself as a bride to be proud of, without a spot, wrinkle or any such thing, but holy and without defect. ²⁸This is how husbands ought to love their wives — like their own bodies; for the man who loves his wife is loving himself. ²⁹Why, no one ever hated his own flesh! On the contrary, he feeds it well and takes care of it, just as the Messiah does the Messianic Community, ³⁰because we are parts of his Body. ³¹**"Therefore a man will leave his father and mother and remain with his wife, and the two will become one."**[f] ³²There is profound truth hidden here, which I say concerns the Messiah and the Messianic Community. ³³However, the text also applies to each of you individually: let each man love his wife as he does himself, and see that the wife respects her husband.

6 ¹Children, what you should do in union with the Lord is obey your parents, for this is right. ²**"Honor your**

f Genesis 2:24

father and mother" — this is the first Commandment that embodies a promise — ³ "so that it may go well with you, and you may live long in the Land."^g

⁴ Fathers, don't irritate your children and make them resentful; instead, raise them with the Lord's kind of discipline and guidance.

⁵ Slaves, obey your human masters with the same fear, trembling and single-heartedness with which you obey the Messiah. ⁶ Don't obey just to win their favor, serving only when they are watching you; but serve as slaves of the Messiah, doing what God wants with all your heart. ⁷ Work willingly as slaves, as people do who are serving not merely human beings but the Lord. ⁸ Remember that whoever does good work, whether he be a slave or a free man, will be rewarded by the Lord.

⁹ And masters, treat your slaves the same way. Don't threaten them. Remember that in heaven both you and they have the same Master, and he has no favorites.

¹⁰ Finally, grow powerful in union with the Lord, in union with his mighty strength! ¹¹ Use all the armor and weaponry that God provides, so that you will be able to stand against the deceptive tactics of the Adversary. ¹² For we are not struggling against human beings, but against the rulers, authorities and cosmic powers governing this darkness, against the spiritual forces of evil in the heavenly realm. ¹³ So take up every piece of war equipment God provides; so that when the evil day comes, you will be able to resist; and when the battle is won, you will still be standing. ¹⁴ Therefore, stand! Have the belt of **truth buckled around** your **waist,**^h put on **righteousness for a breastplate,**ⁱ ¹⁵ and wear on your **feet the readiness that comes from the Good News of** **shalom.**^j ¹⁶ Always carry the shield of trust, with which you will be able to extinguish all the flaming arrows of the Evil One. ¹⁷ And take **the helmet of deliverance;**^k along with the sword given by the Spirit, that is, the Word of God; ¹⁸ as you pray at all times, with all kinds of prayers and requests, in the Spirit, vigilantly and persistently, for all God's people.

¹⁹ And pray for me, too, that whenever I open my mouth, the words will be given to me to be bold in making known the secret of the Good News, ²⁰ for which I am an ambassador in chains. Pray that I may speak boldly, the way I should.

²¹ Now, so that you may also be informed about how I am and what I am doing, Tychicus, the dear brother and a faithful worker for the Lord, will tell you everything. ²² This is the very reason I have sent him to you, so that you may know how we are getting along and so that he may comfort and encourage you.

²³ *Shalom* to the brothers. May God the Father and the Lord Yeshua the Messiah give you love and trust. ²⁴ Grace be to all who love our Lord Yeshua the Messiah with undying love.

g Exodus 20:12, Deuteronomy 5:16

h Isaiah 11:5   i Isaiah 59:17
j Isaiah 52:7   k Isaiah 59:17

mik · veh — ritual purification pool
sha · lom — peace
Ye · shu · a — Jesus

PHILIPPIANS

1 [1] From: Sha'ul and Timothy, slaves of the Messiah Yeshua

To: All God's people united with the Messiah Yeshua and living in Philippi, along with the congregation leaders and *shammashim*:

[2] Grace to you and *shalom* from God our Father and the Lord Yeshua the Messiah.

[3] I thank my God every time I think of you. [4] Whenever I pray for all of you I always pray with joy, [5] because you have shared in proclaiming the Good News from the very first day until now. [6] And I am sure of this: that the One who began a good work among you will keep it growing until it is completed on the Day of the Messiah Yeshua. [7] It is right for me to think this way about you all, because I have you on my heart; for whether I am in chains or defending and establishing the Good News, you are all sharing with me in this privileged work. [8] God can testify how I long for all of you with the deep affection of the Messiah Yeshua.

[9] And this is my prayer: that your love may more and more overflow in fullness of knowledge and depth of discernment, [10] so that you will be able to determine what is best and thus be pure and without blame for the Day of the Messiah, [11] filled with the fruit of righteousness that comes through Yeshua the Messiah — to the glory and praise of God.

[12] Now, brothers, I want you to know that what has happened to me has helped in advancing the Good News. [13] It has become clear to the whole palace and to everyone else that it is because of the Messiah that I am in chains. [14] Also, my being in prison has given most of the brothers in the Lord confidence, so that they have become much more bold in speaking the word of God fearlessly. [15] True, some are proclaiming the Messiah out of jealousy and rivalry, but others are doing it in goodwill. [16] The latter act from love, aware that I am put where I am for defending the Good News; [17] while the former announce the Messiah out of selfish ambition, with impure motives, supposing they can stir up trouble for me in prison. [18] But so what? All that matters is that in every way, whether honestly or in pretense, the Messiah is being proclaimed; and in that I rejoice.

Yes, and I will continue to rejoice, [19] for I know that **this will work out for my deliverance**,[a] because of your prayers and the support I get from the Spirit of Yeshua the Messiah. [20] It all accords with my earnest expectation and hope that I will have nothing to be ashamed of; but rather, now, as always, the Messiah will be honored by my body, whether it is alive or dead. [21] For to me, life is the Messiah, and death is

---

a   Job 13:16

gain. ²²But if by living on in the body I can do fruitful work, then I don't know which to choose. ²³I am caught in a dilemma: my desire is to go off and be with the Messiah — that is better by far — ²⁴but because of you, the greater need is to stay on in the body. ²⁵Yes, I am convinced of this; so I know I will stay on with you in order to help you progress in the faith and have joy in it. ²⁶Then, through my being with you again, you will have even greater reason for boasting about the Messiah Yeshua.

²⁷Only conduct your lives in a way worthy of the Good News of the Messiah; so that whether I come and see you or I hear about you from a distance, you stand firm, united in spirit, fighting with one accord for the faith of the Good News, ²⁸not frightened by anything the opposition does. This will be for them an indication that they are headed for destruction and you for deliverance. And this is from God; ²⁹because for the Messiah's sake it has been granted to you not only to trust in him but also to suffer on his behalf, ³⁰to fight the same battles you once saw me fight and now hear that I am still fighting.

2 ¹Therefore, if you have any encouragement for me from your being in union with the Messiah, any comfort flowing from love, any fellowship with me in the Spirit, or any compassion and sympathy, ²then complete my joy by having a common purpose and a common love, by being one in heart and mind. ³Do nothing out of rivalry or vanity; but, in humility, regard each other as better than yourselves — ⁴look out for each other's interests and not just for your own.

⁵Let your attitude toward one another be governed by your being in union with the Messiah Yeshua:

⁶ Though he was in the form of God,
    he did not regard equality with God
    something to be possessed by force.
⁷ On the contrary, he emptied himself,
    in that he took the form of a slave
    by becoming like human beings are.
And when he appeared as a human being,
⁸   he humbled himself still more
    by becoming obedient even to death —
death on a stake as a criminal!

⁹   Therefore God raised him to the highest place
    and gave him the name above every name;
¹⁰ that in honor of the name given Yeshua,
    every knee will bow —
    in heaven, on earth and under the earth
¹¹ **and every tongue will acknowledge**[b]
    that Yeshua the Messiah is *Adonai* —
    to the glory of God the Father.

¹²So, my dear friends, just as you have always obeyed when I was with you, it is even more important that you obey now when I am away from you: keep working out your deliverance **with fear and trembling,**[c] ¹³for God is the one working among you both the willing and the working for what pleases him. ¹⁴Do everything without *kvetching* or arguing, ¹⁵so that you may be blameless and pure children of God, without defect in the midst of **a**

---

b Isaiah 45:23   c Psalm 2:11

==========

A·do·nai — the LORD, Jehovah
kvetch·ing — complaining
sha·lom — peace
sham·ma·shim — those serving the congregation, deacons
Sha·'ul — Saul (Paul)
Ye·shu·a — Jesus

twisted and perverted generation,[d] among whom you shine like stars in the sky, ¹⁶ as you hold on to the Word of Life. If you do this, I will be able to boast, when the Day of the Messiah comes, that I did not run or toil for nothing. ¹⁷ Indeed, even if my lifeblood is poured out as a drink offering over the sacrifice and service of your faith, I will still be glad and rejoice with you all. ¹⁸ Likewise, you too should be glad and rejoice with me.

¹⁹ But I hope in the Lord Yeshua to send Timothy to you shortly, so that I too may be cheered by knowing how you are doing. ²⁰ I have no one who compares with him, who will care so sincerely for your welfare — ²¹ people all put their own interests ahead of the Messiah Yeshua's. ²² But you know his character, that like a child with his father he slaved with me to advance the Good News. ²³ So I hope to send him just as soon as I see how things will go with me, ²⁴ and I am confident in the Lord that before long I myself will come too.

²⁵ Also I considered it necessary to send you Epaphroditus, my brother, fellow-worker and fellow-soldier, the emissary whom you sent to take care of my needs; ²⁶ since he has been longing for you all and has been distressed because you heard he was ill. ²⁷ Indeed he was ill, close to death; but God had mercy on him — and not only on him, but also on me — otherwise I would have had sorrow piled on sorrow. ²⁸ Therefore, I am all the more eager to send him, so that you may rejoice when you see him again; and I, for my part, may be less sad. ²⁹ So give him a joyful welcome in the Lord; honor such people. ³⁰ For he risked his life and nearly died working for the Messiah, in order to give me the help you were not in a position to give.

3 ¹ In conclusion, my brothers: rejoice in union with the Lord.

It is no trouble for me to repeat what I have written you before, and for you it will be a safeguard: ² beware of the dogs, those evildoers, the Mutilated! ³ For it is we who are the Circumcised, we who worship by the Spirit of God and make our boast in the Messiah Yeshua! We do not put confidence in human qualifications, ⁴ even though I certainly have grounds for putting confidence in such things. If anyone else thinks he has grounds for putting confidence in human qualifications, I have better grounds:

⁵
- *b'rit-milah* on the eighth day,
- an Israelite by birth,
- from the tribe of Binyamin,
- a Hebrew-speaker, with Hebrew-speaking parents,
- in regard to the *Torah*, a *Parush*,

⁶
- in regard to zeal, a persecutor of the Messianic Community,
- in regard to the righteousness demanded by legalism, blameless.

⁷ But the things that used to be advantages for me, I have, because of the Messiah, come to consider a disadvantage. ⁸ Not only that, but I consider everything a disadvantage in comparison with the supreme value of knowing the Messiah Yeshua as my Lord. It was because of him that I gave up everything and regard it all as garbage, in order to gain the Messiah ⁹ and be found in union with him, not having any righteousness of my own based on legalism, but having that righteousness which comes through the Messiah's faithfulness, the righteousness from God based on trust. ¹⁰ Yes, I gave it all up in order to know him, that is, to know the power of his resurrec-

---

[d] Deuteronomy 32:5

tion and the fellowship of his sufferings as I am being conformed to his death, ¹¹so that somehow I might arrive at being resurrected from the dead. ¹²It is not that I have already obtained it or already reached the goal — no, I keep pursuing it in the hope of taking hold of that for which the Messiah Yeshua took hold of me. ¹³Brothers, I, for my part, do not think of myself as having yet gotten hold of it; but one thing I do: forgetting what is behind me and straining forward toward what lies ahead, ¹⁴I keep pursuing the goal in order to win the prize offered by God's upward calling in the Messiah Yeshua. ¹⁵Therefore, as many of us as are mature, let us keep paying attention to this; and if you are differently minded about anything, God will also reveal this to you. ¹⁶Only let our conduct fit the level we have already reached.

¹⁷Brothers, join in imitating me, and pay attention to those who live according to the pattern we have set for you. ¹⁸For many — I have told you about them often before, and even now I say it with tears — live as enemies of the Messiah's execution-stake. ¹⁹They are headed for destruction! Their god is the belly; they are proud of what they ought to be ashamed of, since they are concerned about the things of the world. ²⁰But we are citizens of heaven, and it is from there that we expect a Deliverer, the Lord Yeshua the Messiah. ²¹He will change the bodies we have in this humble state and make them like his glorious body, using the power which enables him to bring everything under his control.

4 ¹So, my brothers, whom I love and long for, my joy and my crown, my dear friends, keep standing firm in union with the Lord.

²I beg Evodia and I beg Syntyche to agree with each other in union with the Lord. ³I also request you, loyal Syzygus, to help these women; for they have worked hard proclaiming the Good News with me, along with Clement and the rest of my fellow-workers whose names are in the Book of Life.

⁴Rejoice in union with the Lord always! I will say it again: rejoice! ⁵Let everyone see how reasonable and gentle you are. The Lord is near! ⁶Don't worry about anything; on the contrary, make your requests known to God by prayer and petition, with thanksgiving. ⁷Then God's *shalom*, passing all understanding, will keep your hearts and minds safe in union with the Messiah Yeshua. ⁸In conclusion, brothers, focus your thoughts on what is true, noble, righteous, pure, lovable or admirable, on some virtue or on something praiseworthy. ⁹Keep doing what you have learned and received from me, what you have heard and seen me doing; then the God who gives *shalom* will be with you.

¹⁰In union with the Lord I greatly rejoice that now, after this long time, you have let your concern for me express itself again. Of course, you were concerned for me all along, but you had no opportunity to express it. ¹¹Not that I am saying this to call attention to any need of mine; since, as far as I am concerned, I have learned to be content regardless of circumstances. ¹²I know what it is to be in want, and I know what it is to have more than enough — in everything and in every

---

Bin·ya·*min* — Benjamin
b'rit-mi·lah — circumcision
Pa·rush — Pharisee
sha·lom — peace
To·rah — Teaching, "Law"; Pentateuch
Ye·shu·a — Jesus

way I have learned the secret of being full and being hungry, of having abundance and being in need. [13] I can do all things through him who gives me power.

[14] Nevertheless, it was good of you to share in my trouble. [15] And you Philippians yourselves know that in the early days of my work spreading the Good News, when I left Macedonia, not a single congregation shared with me in the matter of giving and receiving — only you. [16] Indeed, in Thessalonica when I needed it, you sent me aid twice. [17] I am not seeking the gift; rather, I am looking for what will increase the credit balance of your account. [18] I have been more than paid in full: I have been filled, since I have received from Epaphroditus the gifts you sent — they are **a fragrant aroma,**[e] an acceptable sacrifice, one that pleases God well. [19] Moreover, my God will fill every need of yours according to his glorious wealth, in union with the Messiah Yeshua. [20] And to God our Father be the glory forever and ever. *Amen.*

[21] Greet each of God's people in the Messiah Yeshua. The brothers with me send their greetings to you. [22] All God's people send greetings, but especially those in the Emperor's household.

[23] The grace of the Lord Yeshua the Messiah be with your spirit.

---

e Genesis 8:21, Exodus 29:18

COLOSSIANS

1 ¹From: Sha'ul, by God's will an emissary of the Messiah Yeshua, and brother Timothy

²To: God's people in Colosse, faithful brothers in the Messiah:

Grace to you and *shalom* from God our Father.

³Whenever we pray, we always give thanks for you to God, the Father of our Lord Yeshua the Messiah. ⁴For we have heard of your trust in the Messiah Yeshua and of the love you have for all God's people. ⁵Both spring from the confident hope that you will receive what is stored up for you in heaven. You heard of this earlier in the message about the truth. This Good News ⁶has made its presence felt among you, just as it is also **being fruitful and multiplying**ᵃ throughout the world in the same way as it has among you since the day you heard and understood the grace of God as it really is. ⁷You learned it from Epaphras, our dear fellow-slave and a faithful worker for the Messiah on your behalf; ⁸and he has told us about the love which the Spirit has given you.

⁹Therefore, from the day we heard of it, we have not stopped praying for you, asking God to fill you with the knowledge of his will in all the wisdom and understanding which the Spirit gives; ¹⁰so that you may live lives worthy of the Lord and entirely pleasing to him, **being fruitful** in every good work **and multiplying** in the full knowledge of God. ¹¹We pray that you will be continually strengthened with all the power that comes from his glorious might; so that you will be able to persevere and be patient in any situation, joyfully ¹²giving thanks to the Father for having made you fit to share in the inheritance of his people in the light. ¹³He has rescued us from the domain of darkness and transferred us into the Kingdom of his dear Son.

¹⁴It is through his Son that we have redemption — that is, our sins have been forgiven. ¹⁵He is the visible image of the invisible God. He is supreme over all creation, ¹⁶because in connection with him were created all things — in heaven and on earth, visible and invisible, whether thrones, lordships, rulers or authorities — they have all been created through him and for him. ¹⁷He existed before all things, and he holds everything together.

¹⁸Also he is head of the Body, the Messianic Community — he is the beginning, the firstborn from the dead, so that he might hold first place in everything. ¹⁹For it pleased God to

---

ᵃ Genesis 1:28

A·**men** — So be it
sha·lom — peace
Sha·'**ul** — Saul (Paul)
Ye·**shu**·a — Jesus

have his full being live in his Son ²⁰ and through his Son to reconcile to himself all things, whether on earth or in heaven, making peace through him, through having his Son shed his blood by being executed on a stake.

²¹ In other words, you, who at one time were separated from God and had a hostile attitude towards him because of your wicked deeds, ²² he has now reconciled in the Son's physical body through his death; in order to present you holy and without defect or reproach before himself — ²³ provided, of course, that you continue in your trusting, grounded and steady, and don't let yourselves be moved away from the hope offered in the Good News you heard.

This is the Good News that has been proclaimed in all creation under heaven; and I, Sha'ul, have become a servant of it. ²⁴ I rejoice in my present sufferings on your behalf! Yes, I am completing in my own flesh what has been lacking of the Messiah's afflictions, on behalf of his Body, the Messianic Community. ²⁵ I became a servant of the Good News because God gave me this work to do for your benefit. The work is to make fully known the message from God, ²⁶ the secret hidden for generations, for ages, but now made clear to the people he has set apart for himself. ²⁷ To them God wanted to make known how great among the Gentiles is the glorious richness of this secret. And the secret is this: the Messiah is united with you people! In that rests your hope of glory! ²⁸ We, for our part, proclaim him; we warn, confront and teach everyone in all wisdom; so that we may present everyone as having reached the goal, united with the Messiah. ²⁹ It is for this that I toil, striving with all the energy that he stirs up in me so mightily.

2 ¹ For I want you to know how hard I work for you, for those in Laodicea, and for the rest of those who have not met me personally. ² My purpose is that they may be encouraged, that they may be joined together in love, and that they may have all the riches derived from being assured of understanding and fully knowing God's secret truth, which is — the Messiah! ³ It is in him that all the treasures of wisdom and knowledge are hidden.

⁴ I say this so that no one will fool you with plausible but specious arguments. ⁵ For although I am away from you physically, I am with you in spirit, rejoicing as I see the disciplined and resolute firmness of your trust in the Messiah. ⁶ Therefore, just as you received the Messiah Yeshua as Lord, keep living your life united with him. ⁷ Remain deeply rooted in him; continue being built up in him and confirmed in your trust, the way you were taught, so that you overflow in thanksgiving.

⁸ Watch out, so that no one will take you captive by means of philosophy and empty deceit, following human tradition which accords with the elemental spirits of the world but does not accord with the Messiah. ⁹ For in him, bodily, lives the fullness of all that God is. ¹⁰ And it is in union with him that you have been made full — he is the head of every rule and authority.

¹¹ Also it was in union with him that you were circumcised with a circumcision not done by human hands, but accomplished by stripping away the old nature's control over the body. In this circumcision done by the Messiah, ¹² you were buried along with him by being immersed; and in union with him, you were also raised up along with him by God's faithfulness that worked when he raised Yeshua from the dead.

[13] You were dead because of your sins, that is, because of your "foreskin", your old nature. But God made you alive along with the Messiah by forgiving you all your sins. [14] He wiped away the bill of charges against us. Because of the regulations, it stood as a testimony against us; but he removed it by nailing it to the execution-stake. [15] Stripping the rulers and authorities of their power, he made a public spectacle of them, triumphing over them by means of the stake.

[16] So don't let anyone pass judgment on you in connection with eating and drinking, or in regard to a Jewish festival or *Rosh-Chodesh* or *Shabbat*. [17] These are a shadow of things that are coming, but the body is of the Messiah. [18] Don't let anyone deny you the prize by insisting that you engage in self-mortification or angel-worship. Such people are always going on about some vision they have had, and they vainly puff themselves up by their worldly outlook. [19] They fail to hold to the Head, from whom the whole Body, receiving supply and being held together by its joints and ligaments, grows as God makes it grow. [20] If, along with the Messiah, you died to the elemental spirits of the world, then why, as if you still belonged to the world, are you letting yourselves be bothered by its rules? — [21] "Don't touch this!" "Don't eat that!" "Don't handle the other!" [22] Such prohibitions are concerned with things meant to perish by being used [not by being avoided!], and they are based on **man-made rules and teachings.**[b] [23] They do indeed have the outward appearance of wisdom, with their self-imposed religious observances, false humility and asceticism; but they have no value at all in

restraining people from indulging their old nature.

3 [1] So if you were raised along with the Messiah, then seek the things above, where the Messiah is **sitting at the right hand** of God.[c] [2] Focus your minds on the things above, not on things here on earth. [3] For you have died, and your life is hidden with the Messiah in God. [4] When the Messiah, who is our life, appears, then you too will appear with him in glory!

[5] Therefore, put to death the earthly parts of your nature — sexual immorality, impurity, lust, evil desires and greed (which is a form of idolatry); [6] for it is because of these things that God's anger is coming on those who disobey him. [7] True enough, you used to practice these things in the life you once lived; [8] but now, put them all away — anger, exasperation, meanness, slander and obscene talk. [9] Never lie to one another; because you have stripped away the old self, with its ways, [10] and have put on the new self, which is continually being renewed in fuller and fuller knowledge, closer and closer to the image of its Creator. [11] The new self allows no room for discriminating between Gentile and Jew, circumcised and uncircumcised, foreigner, savage, slave, free man; on the contrary, in all, the Messiah is everything.

[12] Therefore, as God's chosen people, holy and dearly loved, clothe yourselves with feelings of compassion and with kindness, humility, gentleness and patience. [13] Bear with one another; if anyone has a complaint against someone else, forgive him. Indeed, just as

---

b Isaiah 29:13

c Psalm 110:1

Rosh-Cho·desh — beginning of the month
Shab·bat — the Sabbath
Sha·'ul — Saul (Paul)
Ye·shu·a — Jesus

the Lord has forgiven you, so you must forgive.

[14] Above all these, clothe yourselves with love, which binds everything together perfectly; [15] and let the *shalom* which comes from the Messiah be your heart's decision-maker, for this is why you were called to be part of a single Body.

And be thankful — [16] let the Word of the Messiah, in all its richness, live in you, as you teach and counsel each other in all wisdom, and as you sing psalms, hymns and spiritual songs with gratitude to God in your hearts. [17] That is, everything you do or say, do in the name of the Lord Yeshua, giving thanks through him to God the Father.

[18] Wives, subject yourselves to your husbands, as is appropriate in the Lord.

[19] Husbands, love your wives and don't treat them harshly.

[20] Children, obey your parents in everything; for this pleases the Lord.

[21] Fathers, don't irritate your children and make them resentful, or they will become discouraged.

[22] Slaves, obey your human masters in everything, not serving only when they are watching you, to win their favor, but singleheartedly, fearing the Lord. [23] Whatever work you do, put yourself into it, as those who are serving not merely other people, but the Lord. [24] Remember that as your reward, you will receive the inheritance from the Lord. You are slaving for the Lord, for the Messiah. [25] Don't worry — whoever is doing wrong will be paid in kind for his wrong, and there is no favoritism shown.

4 [1] Masters, treat your slaves justly and fairly. Remember that you too have a Master in heaven.

[2] Keep persisting in prayer, staying alert in it and being thankful. [3] Include prayer for us, too, that God may open a door for us to proclaim the message about the secret of the Messiah — for that is why I am in prison. [4] And pray that I may speak, as I should, in a way that makes the message clear.

[5] Behave wisely toward outsiders, making full use of every opportunity — [6] let your conversation always be gracious and interesting, so that you will know how to respond to any particular individual.

[7] Our dear brother Tychicus, who is a faithful worker and fellow-slave in the Lord, will give you all the news about me. [8] I have sent him to you for this very reason — so that you might know how we are, and so that he might encourage you. [9] I have sent him with Onesimus, the dear and faithful brother, who is one of you; they will tell you everything that has happened here.

[10] Aristarchus, my fellow prisoner, sends greetings, as does Mark, Bar-Nabba's cousin, concerning whom you have received instructions — if he comes to you, welcome him. [11] Yeshua, the one called Justus, also sends greetings. These three are among the Circumcised; and among my fellow-workers for the Kingdom of God, only they have turned out to be a comfort to me.

[12] Epaphras sends greetings; he is one of you, a slave of the Messiah Yeshua who always agonizes in his prayer on your behalf, praying that you may stand firm, mature and fully confident, as you devote yourselves completely to God's will. [13] For I can testify to him that he works hard for you and for those in Laodicea and Hierapolis.

[14] Our dear friend Luke, the doctor, and Demas send you greetings.

[15] Give my greetings to the brothers in Laodicea, also to Nympha and the congregation that meets in her home.

[16] After this letter has been read to you, have it read also in the congregation of the Laodiceans; and you, in turn, are to read the letter that will come from Laodicea. [17] And tell Archippus, "See that you complete the task you were given in the Lord."

[18] This greeting I, Sha'ul, write with my own hand.

Remember my imprisonment! Grace be with you!

Bar-Nab·ba — Barnabas
sha·lom — peace
Sha·'ul — Saul (Paul)
Ye·shu·a — Jesus

1 THESSALONIANS

1 ¹From: Sha'ul, Sila and Timothy

To: The Messianic community of the Thessalonians, united with God the Father and the Lord Yeshua the Messiah:

Grace to you and *shalom*.

²We always thank God for all of you, regularly mentioning you in our prayers, ³calling to mind before God our Father what our Lord Yeshua the Messiah has brought about in you — how your trust produces action, your love hard work, and your hope perseverance. ⁴We know, brothers, that God has loved and chosen you; ⁵that the Good News we brought did not become for you a matter only of words, but also one of power, the *Ruach HaKodesh* and total conviction — just as you know how we lived for your sakes when we were with you. ⁶You, indeed, became imitators of us and of the Lord; so that even though you were going through severe troubles, you received the Word with joy from the *Ruach HaKodesh*.

⁷Thus you became a pattern for all the believers in Macedonia and Achaia; ⁸for the Lord's message sounded forth from you not only in Macedonia and Achaia, but everywhere your trust toward God became known. The result is that we don't need to say anything; ⁹since they themselves keep telling us about the welcome we received from you and how you turned to God from idols, to serve the true God, the one who is alive, ¹⁰and to wait for his Son Yeshua, whom he raised from the dead, to appear from heaven and rescue us from the impending fury of God's judgment.

2 ¹You yourselves know, brothers, that our visit to you was not fruitless. ²On the contrary, although we had already suffered and been outraged in Philippi, as you know, we had the courage, united with our God, to tell you the Good News even under great pressure. ³For the appeal we make does not flow from error or from impure motives, neither do we try to trick people. ⁴Instead, since God has tested us and found us fit to be entrusted with Good News, this is how we speak: not to win favor with people but with God, who tests our hearts. ⁵For, as you know, never did we employ flattering talk, nor did we put on a false front to mask greed — God is witness. ⁶Nor did we seek human praise — either from you or from others. ⁷As emissaries of the Messiah, we could have made our weight felt; but instead, we were gentle when we were with you, like a mother feeding and caring for her children. ⁸We were so devoted to you that we were glad to share with you not only God's Good News but also our own lives, because you had become very dear to us. ⁹For you remember, brothers, our toil and hardship, how we worked night and day not to put a burden on any of you while we were proclaiming God's Good News to you. ¹⁰ You are witnesses, and so is God, of how holy, righteous and blameless our behavior was in the sight of you believers; ¹¹ for you know that we treated each one of you the way a father treats his children — we encouraged you and comforted you ¹² and appealed to you to lead lives worthy of God, who calls you into his Kingdom and glory.

¹³ Another reason we regularly thank God is that when you heard the Word of God from us, you received it not merely as a human word, but as it truly is, God's Word, which is at work in you believers. ¹⁴ For, brothers, you came to be imitators of God's congregations in Y'hudah that are united with the Messiah Yeshua — you suffered the same things from your countrymen as they did from the Judeans who ¹⁵ both killed the Lord Yeshua and the prophets, and chased us out too. They are displeasing God and opposing all mankind ¹⁶ by trying to keep us from speaking to the Gentiles, so that they may be delivered. Their object seems to be always to make their sins as bad as possible! But God's fury will catch up with them in the end.

¹⁷ And as for us, brothers, when we were deprived of your company for a short time — in person, but not in thought — we missed you and tried hard to come and see you. ¹⁸ We wanted so much to come to you — I, Sha'ul, tried more than once — but the Adversary stopped us. ¹⁹ For when our Lord Yeshua returns, what will be our hope, our joy, our crown to boast about? Won't it be you? ²⁰ Yes, you are our glory and our joy!

3 ¹ So, when we could no longer stand it, we agreed to be left in Athens alone ² and sent Timothy, our brother and God's fellow worker for the Good News of the Messiah, to make you solid and encourage you in your trust; ³ so that none of you would let these persecutions unsettle him. For you yourselves know that these are bound to come to us; ⁴ even when we were with you, we kept telling you in advance that we were about to be persecuted; and indeed it has happened, as you know. ⁵ That is the reason why, after I could stand it no longer, I sent to find out about your trust. I was afraid that somehow the Tempter had tempted you, and our hard work had been wasted.

⁶ But now Timothy has come to us from you, bringing good news about your trust and love, and telling us that you remember us well and are always longing to see us, just as we long to see you. ⁷ Because of this, brothers, in spite of all our trouble and distress, we were comforted over you — because of your trust; ⁸ so that now we are alive; since you continue to stand fast, united with the Lord.

⁹ Indeed, how can we thank God enough for you or express to our God all the joy we feel because of you? ¹⁰ Night and day we pray as hard as we can that we will be able to see you face to face and supply whatever short-comings there may be in your trust. ¹¹ May God our Father and our Lord Yeshua direct our way to you.

¹² And as for you, may the Lord make you increase and overflow in love toward each other, indeed, toward everyone, just as we do toward you;

Ru·ach-Ha·Ko·desh — Holy Spirit
sha·lom — peace
Sha·'ul — Saul (Paul)
Si·la — Silas
Ye·shu·a — Jesus
Y'hu·dah — Judea

¹³ so that he may give you the inner strength to be blameless, by reason of your holiness, when you stand before God our Father at the coming of our Lord Yeshua with all his angels.

4 ¹ Therefore, brothers, just as you learned from us how you had to live in order to please God, and just as you are living this way now, we ask you — indeed, united with the Lord Yeshua, we urge you — to keep doing so more and more. ² For you know what instructions we gave you on the authority of the Lord Yeshua. ³ What God wants is that you be holy, that you keep away from sexual immorality, ⁴ that each of you know how to manage his sexual impulses in a holy and honorable manner, ⁵ without giving in to lustful desires, like the pagans who don't know God. ⁶ No one should wrong his brother in this matter or take advantage of him, because the Lord punishes all who do such things — as we have explained to you before at length. ⁷ For God did not call us to live an unclean life but a holy one. ⁸ Therefore, whoever rejects this teaching is rejecting not a man but God, indeed, the One who gives you the *Ruach HaKodesh*, which is his.

⁹ Concerning love for the brothers we do not need to write you, for you yourselves have been taught by God to love each other; ¹⁰ and you do love all the brothers throughout Macedonia. But we urge you, brothers, to do it even more.

¹¹ Also, make it your ambition to live quietly, to mind your own business and to earn your living by your own efforts — just as we told you. ¹² Then your daily life will gain the respect of outsiders, and you will not be dependent on anyone.

¹³ Now, brothers, we want you to know the truth about those who have died; otherwise, you might become sad the way other people do who have nothing to hope for. ¹⁴ For since we believe that Yeshua died and rose again, we also believe that in the same way God, through Yeshua, will take with him those who have died. ¹⁵ When we say this, we base it on the Lord's own word: we who remain alive when the Lord comes will certainly not take precedence over those who have died. ¹⁶ For the Lord himself will come down from heaven with a rousing cry, with a call from one of the ruling angels, and with God's *shofar*; those who died united with the Messiah will be the first to rise; ¹⁷ then we who are left still alive will be caught up with them in the clouds to meet the Lord in the air; and thus we will always be with the Lord. ¹⁸ So encourage each other with these words.

5 ¹ But you have no need to have anything written to you, brothers, about the times and dates when this will happen; ² because you yourselves well know that the Day of the Lord will come like a thief in the night. ³ When people are saying, "Everything is so peaceful and secure," then destruction will suddenly come upon them, the way labor pains come upon a pregnant woman, and there is no way they will escape.

⁴ But you, brothers, are not in the dark, so that the Day should take you by surprise like a thief; ⁵ for you are all people who belong to the light, who belong to the day. We don't belong to the night or to darkness, ⁶ so let's not be asleep, like the rest are; on the contrary, let us stay alert and sober. ⁷ People who sleep, sleep at night; and people who get drunk, get drunk at night. ⁸ But since we belong to the day, let us stay sober, **putting on** trust and love **as a breastplate and the hope of being**

delivered as a helmet.[a] [9] For God has not intended that we should experience his fury, but that we should gain deliverance through our Lord Yeshua the Messiah, [10] who died on our behalf so that whether we are alive or dead, we may live along with him. [11] Therefore, encourage each other, and build each other up — just as you are doing.

[12] We ask you, brothers, to respect those who are working hard among you, those who are guiding you in the Lord and confronting you in order to help you change. [13] Treat them with the highest regard and love because of the work they are doing. Live at peace among yourselves; [14] but we urge you, brothers, to confront those who are lazy, your aim being to help them change, to encourage the timid, to assist the weak, and to be patient with everyone.

[15] See that no one repays evil for evil; on the contrary, always try to do good to each other, indeed, to everyone.

[16] Always be joyful. [17] Pray regularly. [18] In everything give thanks, for this is what God wants from you who are united with the Messiah Yeshua.

[19] Don't quench the Spirit, [20] don't despise inspired messages. [21] But do test everything — hold onto what is good, [22] but keep away from every form of evil.

[23] May the God of *shalom* make you completely holy — may your entire spirit, soul and body be kept blameless for the coming of our Lord Yeshua the Messiah. [24] The one calling you is faithful, and he will do it.

[25] Brothers, keep praying for us.

[26] Greet all the brothers with a holy kiss.

[27] I charge you in the Lord to have this letter read to all the brothers.

[28] The grace of our Lord Yeshua the Messiah be with you.

---

[a] Isaiah 59:17

Ru·ach-Ha· Ko·desh — Holy Spirit
sha· lom — peace
sho· far — ram's horn
Ye·shu·a — Jesus

2 THESSALONIANS

1 ¹From: Sha'ul, Sila and Timothy

To: The Messianic community of the Thessalonians, united with God our Father and the Lord Yeshua the Messiah:

²Grace to you and *shalom* from God the Father and the Lord Yeshua the Messiah.

³We have to keep thanking God for you always, brothers, as is appropriate; because your trust continues to grow greater, and the love you each have for one another continues to increase. ⁴Therefore, we boast about you in the congregations of God because of your perseverance and trust in all the persecutions and troubles you are going through. ⁵This is clear evidence that God's judgment is just; and as a result, you will be counted worthy of the Kingdom of God for which you are suffering. ⁶For it is justice for God to pay back trouble to those who are troubling you, ⁷and to give rest along with us to you who are being troubled, when the Lord Yeshua is revealed from heaven with his mighty angels **⁸in a fiery flame. Then he will punish those who don't know God,**[a] that is, those who don't listen to the Good News of our Lord Yeshua and obey it. ⁹They will suffer the just penalty of eternal destruction, **far away from the face of the Lord and the glory of his might.**[b]

¹⁰On that Day, when he comes to be glorified by his holy people and admired by all who have trusted, you will be among them, because you trusted our witness to you. ¹¹With this in view, we always pray for you that our God may make you worthy of his calling and may fulfill by his power every good purpose of yours and every action stemming from your trust. ¹²In this way, the name of our Lord Yeshua will be glorified in you, and you in him, in accordance with the grace of our God and the Lord Yeshua the Messiah.

2 ¹But in connection with the coming of our Lord Yeshua the Messiah and our gathering together to meet him, we ask you, brothers, ²not to be easily shaken in your thinking or anxious because of a spirit or a spoken message or a letter supposedly from us claiming that the Day of the Lord has already come. ³Don't let anyone deceive you in any way.

For the Day will not come until after the Apostasy has come and the man who separates himself from *Torah* has been revealed, the one destined for doom. ⁴He will oppose himself to **everything** that people call a **god** or make an object of worship; **he will put himself above** them all, so that he will sit in the Temple **of God** and proclaim that he himself is **God.**[c]

---

[a] Isaiah 66:15, Jeremiah 10:25, Psalm 79:6

[b] Isaiah 2:10, 19, 21   [c] Ezekiel 28:2

⁵Don't you remember that when I was still with you, I used to tell you these things? ⁶And now you know what is restraining, so that he may be revealed in his own time. ⁷For already this separating from *Torah* is at work secretly, but it will be secretly only until he who is restraining is out of the way. ⁸Then the one who embodies separation from *Torah* will be revealed, the one whom the Lord Yeshua **will slay with the breath of his mouth**^*d* and destroy by the glory of his coming.

⁹When this man who avoids *Torah* comes, the Adversary will give him the power to work all kinds of false miracles, signs and wonders. ¹⁰He will enable him to deceive, in all kinds of wicked ways, those who are headed for destruction because they would not receive the love of the truth that could have saved them. ¹¹This is why God is causing them to go astray, so that they will believe the Lie. ¹²The result will be that all who have not believed the truth, but have taken their pleasure in wickedness, will be condemned.

¹³But we have to keep thanking God for you always, brothers whom the Lord loves, because God chose you as firstfruits for deliverance by giving you the holiness that has its origin in the Spirit and the faithfulness that has its origin in the truth. ¹⁴He called you to this through our Good News, so that you could have the glory of our Lord Yeshua the Messiah.

¹⁵Therefore, brothers, stand firm; and hold to the traditions you were taught by us, whether we spoke them or wrote them in a letter. ¹⁶And may our Lord Yeshua the Messiah himself and God our Father, who has loved us and by his grace given us eternal comfort and a good hope, ¹⁷comfort your

hearts and strengthen you in every good word and deed.

3 ¹Finally, brothers, pray for us that the Lord's message may spread rapidly and receive honor, just as it did with you; ²and that we may be rescued from wicked and evil people, for not everyone has trust. ³But the Lord is worthy of trust; he will make you firm and guard you from the Evil One. ⁴Yes, united with the Lord we are confident about you, that you are doing the things we are telling you to do, and that you will keep on doing them. ⁵May the Lord direct your hearts into God's love and the perseverance which the Messiah gives.

⁶Now, in the name of the Lord Yeshua the Messiah we command you, brothers, to stay away from any brother who is leading a life of idleness, a life not in keeping with the tradition you received from us. ⁷For you yourselves know how you must imitate us, that we were not idle when we were among you. ⁸We did not accept anyone's food without paying; on the contrary, we labored and toiled, day and night, working so as not to be a burden to any of you. ⁹It was not that we hadn't the right to be supported, but so that we could make ourselves an example to imitate. ¹⁰For even when we were with you, we gave you this command: if someone won't work, he shouldn't eat! ¹¹We hear that some of you are leading a life of idleness — not busy working, just busybodies! ¹²We command such people — and in union with the Lord Yeshua the Messiah we urge them — to settle down, get to work, and earn their

---

sha·lom — peace
Sha·'ul — Saul (Paul)
Si·la — Silas
To·rah — Teaching, "Law"; Pentateuch
Ye·shu·a — Jesus

---

d Isaiah 11:4, Job 4:9

own living. 13 And you brothers who are doing what is good, don't slack off! 14 Furthermore, if anyone does not obey what we are saying in this letter, take note of him and have nothing to do with him, so that he will be ashamed. 15 But don't consider him an enemy; on the contrary, confront him as a brother and try to help him change.

16 Now may the Lord of *shalom* himself give you *shalom* always in all ways. The Lord be with all of you.

17 The greeting in my own handwriting: From Sha'ul. This is the mark of genuineness in every letter, this is what my handwriting looks like.

18 The grace of our Lord Yeshua the Messiah be with you all.

1 TIMOTHY

1 ¹From: Sha'ul, an emissary of the Messiah Yeshua by command of God our deliverer and the Messiah Yeshua our hope

²To: Timothy, a true son because of your trust:

Grace, mercy and *shalom* from God the Father and the Messiah Yeshua our Lord.

³As I counseled you when I was leaving for Macedonia, stay on in Ephesus, so that you may order certain people who are teaching a different doctrine to stop. ⁴Have them stop devoting their attention to myths and never-ending genealogies; these divert people to speculating instead of doing God's work, which requires trust. ⁵The purpose of this order is to promote love from a clean heart, from a good conscience and from sincere trust. ⁶Some, by aiming amiss, have wandered off into fruitless discussion. ⁷They want to be teachers of *Torah*, but they understand neither their own words nor the matters about which they make such emphatic pronouncements. ⁸We know that the *Torah* is good, provided one uses it in the way the *Torah* itself intends. ⁹We are aware that *Torah* is not for a person who is righteous, but for those who are heedless of *Torah* and rebellious, ungodly and sinful, wicked and worldly, for people who kill their fathers and mothers, for murderers, ¹⁰the sexually immoral — both hetero-

sexual and homosexual — slave-dealers, liars, perjurers, and anyone who acts contrary to the sound teaching ¹¹that accords with the Good News of the glorious and blessed God.

This Good News was entrusted to me; ¹²and I thank the one who has given me strength, the Messiah Yeshua, our Lord, that he considered me trustworthy enough to put me in his service, ¹³even though I used to be a man who blasphemed and persecuted and was arrogant! But I received mercy because I had acted in unbelief, not understanding what I was doing. ¹⁴Our Lord's grace overflowed to me with trust and love that come through the Messiah Yeshua. ¹⁵So here is a statement you can trust, one that fully deserves to be accepted: the Messiah came into the world to save sinners, and I'm the number one sinner! ¹⁶But this is precisely why I received mercy — so that in me, as the number one sinner, Yeshua the Messiah might demonstrate how very patient he is, as an example to those who would later come to trust in him and thereby have eternal life. ¹⁷So to the King — eternal, imperishable and invisible, the only God there is — let there be honor and glory for ever and ever! *Amen.*

A·men — So be it.
sha·lom — peace
Sha·'ul — Saul (Paul)
To·rah — Teaching, "Law"; Pentateuch
Ye·shu·a — Jesus

¹⁸This charge, son Timothy, I put to you, in keeping with the prophecies already made about you, so that by these prophecies you may fight the good fight, ¹⁹armed with trust and a good conscience. By rejecting conscience, some have made shipwreck of their trust; ²⁰among them are Hymenaeus and Alexander. I have turned them over to the Adversary, so that they will learn not to insult God.

2 ¹First of all, then, I counsel that petitions, prayers, intercessions and thanksgivings be made for all human beings, ²including kings and all in positions of prominence; so that we may lead quiet and peaceful lives, being godly and upright in everything. ³This is what God, our deliverer, regards as good; this is what meets his approval.

⁴He wants all humanity to be delivered and come to full knowledge of the truth. ⁵For **God is one;**[a] and there is but one Mediator between God and humanity, Yeshua the Messiah, himself human, ⁶who gave himself as a ransom on behalf of all, thus providing testimony to God's purpose at just the right time. ⁷This is why I myself was appointed a proclaimer, even an emissary — I am telling the truth, not lying! — a trustworthy and truthful teacher of the *Goyim.*

⁸Therefore, it is my wish that when the men pray, no matter where, they should lift up hands that are holy — they should not become angry or get into arguments.

⁹Likewise, the women, when they pray, should be dressed modestly and sensibly in respectable attire, not with elaborate hairstyles and gold jewelry, or pearls, or expensive clothes. ¹⁰Rather, they should adorn themselves with what is appropriate for women

who claim to be worshipping God, namely, good deeds.

¹¹Let a woman learn in peace, fully submitted; ¹²but I do not permit a woman to teach a man or exercise authority over him; rather, she is to remain at peace. ¹³For Adam was formed first, then Chavah. ¹⁴Also it was not Adam who was deceived, but the woman who, on being deceived, became involved in the transgression. ¹⁵Nevertheless, the woman will be delivered through childbearing, provided that she continues trusting, loving and living a holy life with modesty.

3 ¹Here is a statement you can trust: anyone aspiring to be a congregation leader is seeking worthwhile work. ²A congregation leader must be above reproach, he must be faithful to his wife, temperate, self-controlled, orderly, hospitable and able to teach. ³He must not drink excessively or get into fights; rather, he must be kind and gentle. He must not be a lover of money. ⁴He must manage his own household well, having children who obey him with all proper respect; ⁵for if a man can't manage his own household, how will he be able to care for God's Messianic community? ⁶He must not be a new believer, because he might become puffed up with pride and thus fall under the same judgment as did the Adversary. ⁷Furthermore, he must be well regarded by outsiders, so that he won't fall into disgrace and into the Adversary's trap.

⁸Likewise, the *shammashim* must be of good character, people whose word can be trusted. They must not give themselves to excessive drinking or be greedy for dishonest gain. ⁹They must possess the formerly hidden truth of the faith with a clean conscience. ¹⁰And first, let them be tested; then, if they prove themselves blameless, let them

---

a Deuteronomy 6:4

be appointed *shammashim*. ¹¹ Similarly, the wives must be of good character, not gossips, but temperate, faithful in everything. ¹² Let the *shammashim* each be faithful to his wife, managing his children and household well. ¹³ For those who serve well as *shammashim* gain good standing for themselves and much boldness in the trust that comes through Yeshua the Messiah.

¹⁴ I hope to visit you soon; but I am writing these things ¹⁵ so that if I am delayed, you may know how one should behave in the household of God, which is the Messianic Community of the living God, the pillar and support of the truth. ¹⁶ Great beyond all question is the formerly hidden truth underlying our faith:

He was manifested physically
and proved righteous spiritually,

seen by angels
and proclaimed among the nations,

trusted throughout the world
and raised up in glory to heaven.

4 ¹ The Spirit expressly states that in the *acharit-hayamim* some people will apostatize from the faith by paying attention to deceiving spirits and things taught by demons. ² Such teachings come from the hypocrisy of liars whose own consciences have been burned, as if with a red-hot branding iron. ³ They forbid marriage and require abstinence from foods which God created to be eaten with thanksgiving by those who have come to trust and to know the truth. ⁴ For everything created by God is good, and nothing received with thanksgiving needs to be rejected, ⁵ because the word of God and prayer make it holy.

⁶ If you present all this to the brothers, you will be serving the Messiah Yeshua well; it will show that you have

digested the words of the faith and of the good teaching which you have followed. ⁷ But refuse godless *bubbe-meises*, and exercise yourself in godliness. ⁸ For although physical exercise does have some value, godliness is valuable for everything, since it holds promise both for the present life and for the life to come. ⁹ Here is a statement you can trust, one that fully deserves to be accepted ¹⁰ (indeed, it is for this that we toil and strive): we have our hope set on a living God who is the deliverer of all humanity, especially of those who trust.

¹¹ Command these things and teach them. ¹² Don't let anyone look down on you because of your youth; on the contrary, set the believers an example in your speech, behavior, love, trust and purity. ¹³ Until I come, pay attention to the public reading of the Scriptures. ¹⁴ Do not neglect your gift, which you were given through a prophecy when the body of elders gave you *s'mikhah*. ¹⁵ Be diligent about this work, throw yourself into it, so that your progress may be clear to everyone. ¹⁶ Pay attention to yourself and to the teaching, continue in it, for by so doing you will deliver both yourself and those who hear you.

5 ¹ Do not rebuke an older man sharply, but appeal to him as you would to a father; treat younger men like brothers, ² older women like

---

a·cha·rit-ha·ya·mim — End Times
A·**dam** — Adam
bub·*be-mei·ses* — old wives' tales, foolish stories
Cha·**vah** — Eve
Go·yim — Gentiles, nations, pagans
sham·ma·shim — those serving the congregation, deacons
s'mi·khah — ordination, laying on of hands
Ye·shu·a — Jesus

mothers and younger women like sisters, with absolute purity.

³ Show respect to widows who are really in need. ⁴ But if a widow has children or grandchildren, first let them learn to do their religious duty to their own family and thus repay some of the debt they owe their forebears, for this is what is acceptable in the sight of God. ⁵ Now the widow who is really in need, the one who has been left all alone, has set her hope on God and continues in petitions and prayers night and day. ⁶ But the one who is self-indulgent is already dead, even though she lives. ⁷ And instruct them about this, so that they will not be open to blame. ⁸ Moreover, anyone who does not provide for his own people, especially for his family, has disowned the faith and is worse than an unbeliever.

⁹ Let a widow be enrolled on the list of widows only if she is more than sixty years old, was faithful to her husband, ¹⁰ and is known for her good deeds — as one who has reared her children well, showed hospitality, washed the feet of God's people, helped those in trouble, and engaged in all kinds of good work. ¹¹ But refuse to enroll younger widows, for when they begin to feel natural passions that alienate them from the Messiah, they want to get married. ¹² This brings them under condemnation for having set aside the trust they had at first. ¹³ Besides that, they learn to be idle, going around from house to house; and not only idle, but gossips and busybodies, saying things they shouldn't. ¹⁴ Therefore, I would rather the young widows get married, have children and take charge of their homes, so as to give the opposition no occasion for slandering us. ¹⁵ For already some have turned astray to follow the Adversary.

¹⁶ If any believing woman has relatives who are widows, she should provide relief for them — the congregation shouldn't be burdened, so that it may help the widows who are really in need.

¹⁷ The leaders who lead well should be considered worthy of double honor, especially those working hard at communicating the Word and at teaching. ¹⁸ For the *Tanakh* says, **"You are not to muzzle an ox when it is treading out the grain,"**[b] in other words, "The worker deserves his wages." ¹⁹ Never listen to any accusation against a leader unless it is supported **by two or three witnesses.**[c] ²⁰ Rebuke before the whole assembly those leaders who continue sinning, as a warning to the others. ²¹ Before God, the Messiah Yeshua and the chosen angels, I solemnly charge you to observe these instructions, not pre-judging and not doing anything out of favoritism. ²² Do not be hasty in granting *s'mikhah* to anyone, and do not share in other people's sins — keep yourself pure.

²³ Stop drinking water; instead, use a little wine for the sake of your digestion and because of your frequent illnesses.

²⁴ The sins of some people are obvious and go ahead of them to judgment, but the sins of others follow afterwards. ²⁵ Likewise, good deeds are obvious; and even when they are not, they can't stay hidden.

6 ¹ Those who are under the yoke of slavery should regard their masters as worthy of full respect, so that the name of God and the teaching will not be brought into disrepute. ² And those who have believing masters are not to show them less respect on the ground that they are brothers; on the contrary, they should serve all the more diligently,

---

b Deuteronomy 25:4

c Deuteronomy 17:6, 19:15

since those benefitting from their service are believers whom they love.

Teach and exhort people about these things. ³If anyone teaches differently and does not agree to the sound precepts of our Lord Yeshua the Messiah and to the doctrine that is in keeping with godliness, ⁴he is swollen with conceit and understands nothing. Instead, he has a morbid desire for controversies and word-battles, out of which come jealousy, dissension, insults, evil suspicions, ⁵and constant wrangling among people whose minds no longer function properly and who have been deprived of the truth, so that they imagine that religion is a road to riches. ⁶Now true religion does bring great riches, but only to those who are content with what they have. ⁷For we have brought nothing into the world; and we can take nothing out of it; ⁸so if we have food and clothing, we will be satisfied with these. ⁹Furthermore, those whose goal is to be rich fall into temptation; they get trapped in many foolish and hurtful ambitions which plunge them into ruin and destruction. ¹⁰For the love of money is a root of all the evils; because of this craving, some people have wandered away from the faith and pierced themselves to the heart with many pains.

¹¹But you, as a man of God, flee from these things; and pursue righteousness, godliness, faithfulness, love, steadfastness, gentleness. ¹²Fight the good fight of the faith, take hold of the eternal life to which you were called when you testified so well to your faith before many witnesses. ¹³I charge you before God, who gives life to all things, and before the Messiah Yeshua, who in his witness to Pontius Pilate gave the same good testimony, ¹⁴to obey your commission spotlessly and irreproachably until our Lord Yeshua the Messiah appears. ¹⁵His appearing will be brought about in its own time by the blessed and sole Sovereign, who is King of kings and Lord of lords, ¹⁶who alone is immortal, who dwells in unapproachable light that no human being has ever seen or can see — to him be honor and eternal power. *Amen.*

¹⁷As for those who do have riches in this present world, charge them not to be proud and not to let their hopes rest on the uncertainties of riches but to rest their hopes on God, who richly provides us with all things for our enjoyment. ¹⁸Charge them to do good, to be rich in good deeds, to be generous and ready to share. ¹⁹In this way they will treasure up for themselves a good foundation for the future, so that they may lay hold of the real life.

²⁰Oh, Timothy! Keep safe what has been entrusted to you. Turn away from the ungodly babblings and the argumentative opposition of what is falsely called "knowledge". ²¹For many who promise this "knowledge" have missed the mark, as far as the faith is concerned. Grace be with you.

A·men — So be it
s'mi·khah — ordination, laying on of hands
Ta·nakh — Hebrew Scriptures, "Old Testament"
Ye·shu·a — Jesus

2 TIMOTHY

1 ¹From: Sha'ul, an emissary of the Messiah Yeshua by God's will, which holds forth a promise of life through being united with Messiah Yeshua

²To: Timothy, my dear son:

Grace, mercy and *shalom* from God the Father and the Messiah Yeshua, our Lord.

³I give thanks to God, whom, like my forbears, I worship with a clean conscience, as I regularly remember you in my prayers night and day. ⁴I am reminded of your tears, and I long to see you, so that I might be filled with joy. ⁵I recall your sincere trust, the same trust that your grandmother Lois and your mother Eunice had first; and I am convinced that you too now have this trust.

⁶For this reason, I am reminding you to fan the flame of God's gift, which you received through *s'mikhah* from me. ⁷For God gave us a Spirit who produces not timidity, but power, love and self-discipline. ⁸So don't be ashamed of bearing testimony to our Lord or to me, his prisoner. On the contrary, accept your share in suffering disgrace for the sake of the Good News. God will give you the strength for it, ⁹since he delivered us and called us to a life of holiness as his people. It was not because of our deeds, but because of his own purpose and the grace which he gave to us who are united with the Messiah Yeshua. He did this before the beginning of time, ¹⁰but made it public only now through the appearing of our Deliverer, the Messiah Yeshua, who abolished death and, through the Good News, revealed life and immortality.

¹¹It was for this Good News that I was appointed a proclaimer, emissary and teacher of the *Goyim;* ¹²and this is why I suffer as I do. But I am not ashamed, because I know in whom I have put my trust, and I am persuaded that he can keep safe until that Day what he has entrusted to me. ¹³Follow the pattern of the sound teachings you have heard from me, with trust and the love which is yours in the Messiah Yeshua. ¹⁴Keep safe the great treasure that has been entrusted to you, with the help of the *Ruach HaKodesh* who lives in us.

¹⁵You know that everyone in the province of Asia turned away from me, including Phygelus and Ermogenes. ¹⁶May the Lord show mercy to the household of Onesiphorus, because he was often a comfort to me and was not ashamed of my being in prison. ¹⁷On the contrary, when he came to Rome, he diligently searched for me and found me. ¹⁸May the Lord grant it to him to find mercy from *Adonai* on that Day. And you know very well how much he helped me in Ephesus.

2 ¹So then, you, my son, be empowered by the grace that comes from the Messiah Yeshua. ²And the things you heard from me, which were supported by many witnesses, these things commit to faithful people, such as will be competent to teach others also. ³Accept your share in suffering disgrace as a good soldier of the Messiah Yeshua. ⁴No soldier on duty gets involved with civilian affairs, since he has to please his commanding officer. ⁵Also an athlete can't win a contest unless he competes according to the rules. ⁶The farmer who has done the hard work should be the first to receive a share of the harvest. ⁷Think about what I am saying, for the Lord will enable you to understand everything.

⁸Remember Yeshua the Messiah, who was raised from the dead, who was a descendant of David. This is the Good News I proclaim, ⁹and for which I am suffering to the point of being bound in chains — but the Word of God is not bound in chains! ¹⁰Why do I persevere through it all? For the sake of those who have been chosen, so that they too may obtain the deliverance that comes through the Messiah Yeshua, with eternal glory. ¹¹Here is a statement you can trust:

If we have died with him,
we will also live with him.

¹² If we persevere,
we will also rule with him.

If we disown him,
he will also disown us.

¹³ If we are faithless,
he remains faithful,
for he cannot disown himself.

¹⁴Keep reminding people of this, and charge them solemnly before the Lord not to engage in word-battles. They accomplish nothing useful and are a catastrophe for the hearers! ¹⁵Do all you can to present yourself to God as someone worthy of his approval, as a worker with no need to be ashamed, because he deals straightforwardly with the Word of the Truth. ¹⁶But keep away from godless babbling, for those who engage in it will only become more ungodly, ¹⁷and their teaching will eat away at people like gangrene. Hymenaeus and Philetus are among these; ¹⁸they have missed the mark, as far as the truth is concerned, by saying that our resurrection has already taken place; and they are overturning some people's faith. ¹⁹Nevertheless, God's firm foundation stands, stamped with these words: **"The Lord knows his own,"**ᵃ and, **"Let everyone who claims he belongs to the Lord stand apart from wrongdoing."**ᵇ

²⁰In a large house there are dishes and pots not only of gold and silver, but also of wood and clay. That is, some are meant for honorable use and some for dishonorable. ²¹If a person keeps himself free of defilement by the latter, he will be a vessel set aside for honorable use by the master of the house and ready for every kind of good work. ²²So, flee the passions of youth; and, along with those who call on the Lord from a pure heart, pursue righteousness, faithfulness, love and peace. ²³But stay away from stupid and ignorant controversies — you know that they lead to fights, ²⁴and a slave of the Lord shouldn't fight. On the contrary, he

---

a Numbers 16:5, Nahum 1:7

b Numbers 16:26

A·do·nai — the LORD, Jehovah
Da·vid —David
Go·yim — Gentiles, nations, pagans
Ru·ach-Ha·Ko·desh — Holy Spirit
sha·lom — peace
Sha·'ul — Saul (Paul)
s'mi·khah — ordination, laying on of hands
Ye·shu·a — Jesus

should be kind to everyone, a good teacher, and not resentful when mistreated. ²⁵ Also he should be gentle as he corrects his opponents. For God may perhaps grant them the opportunity to turn from their sins, acquire full knowledge of the truth, ²⁶ come to their senses and escape the trap of the Adversary, after having been captured alive by him to do his will.

3 ¹ Moreover, understand this: in the *acharit-hayamim* will come trying times. ² People will be self-loving, money-loving, proud, arrogant, insulting, disobedient to parents, ungrateful, unholy, ³ heartless, unappeasable, slanderous, uncontrolled, brutal, hateful of good, ⁴ traitorous, headstrong, swollen with conceit, loving pleasure rather than God, ⁵ as they retain the outer form of religion but deny its power.

Stay away from these people! ⁶ For some of them worm their way into homes and get control of weak-willed women who are heaped with sins and swayed by various impulses, ⁷ who are always learning but never able to come to full knowledge of the truth. ⁸ In the same way as Jannes and Jambres opposed Moshe, so also these people oppose the truth. They are people with corrupted minds, whose trust cannot pass the test. ⁹ However, they won't get very far; because everyone will see how stupid they are, just as happened with those two.

¹⁰ But you, you have closely followed my teaching, conduct, purpose in life, trust, steadfastness, love and perseverance — ¹¹ as well as the persecutions and sufferings that came my way in Antioch, Iconium and Lystra. What persecutions I endured! Yet the Lord rescued me from all of them. ¹² And indeed, all who want to live a godly life united with the Messiah Yeshua will be persecuted, ¹³ while evil people and impostors will go from bad to worse, deceiving others and being deceived themselves.

¹⁴ But you, continue in what you have learned and have become convinced of, recalling the people from whom you learned it; ¹⁵ and recalling too how from childhood you have known the Holy Scriptures, which can give you the wisdom that leads to deliverance through trusting in Yeshua the Messiah. ¹⁶ All Scripture is God-breathed and is valuable for teaching the truth, convicting of sin, correcting faults and training in right living; ¹⁷ thus anyone who belongs to God may be fully equipped for every good work.

4 ¹ I solemnly charge you before God and the Messiah Yeshua, who will judge the living and the dead when he appears and establishes his Kingdom: ² proclaim the Word! Be on hand with it whether the time seems right or not. Convict, censure and exhort with unfailing patience and with teaching.

³ For the time is coming when people will not have patience for sound teaching, but will cater to their passions and gather around themselves teachers who say whatever their ears itch to hear. ⁴ Yes, they will stop listening to the truth, but will turn aside to follow myths.

⁵ But you, remain steady in every situation, endure suffering, do the work that a proclaimer of the Good News should, and do everything your service to God requires.

⁶ For as for me, I am already being poured out on the altar; yes, the time for my departure has arrived. ⁷ I have fought the good fight, I have finished the race, I have kept the faith. ⁸ All that awaits me now is the crown of righteousness which the Lord, "the Righteous Judge", will award to me on that

Day — and not only to me, but also to all who have longed for him to appear.

⁹ Do your best to come to me soon. ¹⁰ For Demas, because he has fallen in love with this present world, has deserted me and gone off to Thessalonica; Crescens has gone to Galatia; Titus has gone to Dalmatia — ¹¹ only Luke is with me. Take Mark, and bring him with you, because he is a very useful helper in my work. ¹² But Tychicus I have sent to Ephesus. ¹³ When you come, bring the coat which I left with Carpus in Troas, also the scrolls and especially the parchments. ¹⁴ Alexander the metalworker did me a great deal of harm; the Lord will **render to him according to his works;**[c] ¹⁵ and you should guard against him, because he bitterly opposed everything we said.

¹⁶ The first time I had to present my defense, no one stood by me; everyone deserted me — may it not be counted

against them. ¹⁷ But the Lord stood by me and gave me power to proclaim the full message for all the *Goyim* to hear, and I was **rescued from the lion's mouth.**[d] ¹⁸ The Lord will rescue me from every evil attack and bring me safely into his heavenly Kingdom. To him be the glory forever and ever. *Amen.*

¹⁹ Greet Priscilla and Aquila and the household of Onesiphorus. ²⁰ Erastus has remained in Corinth, and Trophimus I left ill at Miletus. ²¹ Do your best to come before winter. Eubulus sends greetings to you, as do Pudens, Linus, Claudia and all the brothers.

²² The Lord be with your spirit. Grace be with you.

---

[c] 2 Samuel 3:39; Psalms 28:4, 62:13(12); Proverbs 24:12

[d] Psalm 22:22(21); Daniel 6:21, 23

---

a·cha·rit-ha·ya·mim — Last Days
A·men — So be it
Go·yim — Gentiles, nations, pagans
Mo·she — Moses
Ye·shu·a — Jesus

THE LETTER FROM YESHUA'S EMISSARY, SHA'UL (PAUL) TO

TITUS

1 ¹ From: Sha'ul, God's slave and an emissary of Yeshua the Messiah, sent to promote among God's chosen people the trust and knowledge of truth which lead to godliness ² and which are based on the certain hope of eternal life. God, who does not lie, promised that life before the beginning of time ³ but made public this word of his in its own season through a proclamation with which I have been entrusted by order of God, our Deliverer.

⁴ To: Titus, a true son in the faith we share:

Grace and *shalom* from God the Father and from the Messiah Yeshua, our Deliverer.

⁵ The reason I left you in Crete was so that you might attend to the matters still not in order and appoint congregation leaders in each city — those were my instructions. ⁶ A leader must be blameless, husband to one wife, with believing children who do not have a reputation for being wild or rebellious. ⁷ For an overseer, as someone entrusted with God's affairs, must be blameless — he must not be self-willed or quick-tempered, he must not drink excessively, get into fights or be greedy for dishonest gain. ⁸ On the contrary, he must be hospitable, devoted to good, sober-mindedness, uprightness, holiness and self-control. ⁹ He must hold firmly to the trustworthy Message that agrees with the doctrine; so that by his sound teaching he will be able to exhort and encourage, and also to refute those who speak against it.

¹⁰ For there are many, especially from the Circumcision faction, who are rebellious, who delude people's minds with their worthless and misleading talk. ¹¹ They must be silenced; because they are upsetting entire households by teaching what they have no business teaching, and doing it for the sake of dishonest gain. ¹² Even one of the Cretans' own prophets has said, "Cretans are always liars, evil brutes, lazy gluttons" — ¹³ and it's true! For this reason, you must be severe when you rebuke those who have followed this false teaching, so that they will come to be sound in their trust ¹⁴ and no longer pay attention to Judaistic myths or to the commands of people who reject the truth.

¹⁵ To all who are themselves pure, everything is pure. But to those who are defiled and without trust, nothing is pure — even their minds and consciences have been defiled. ¹⁶ They claim to know God, but with their actions they deny him. They are detestable and disobedient; they have proved themselves unfit to do anything good.

2 ¹ But you, explain what kind of behavior goes along with sound teaching. ² Tell the older men to be serious, sensible, self-controlled and sound in their trust, love and perseverance.

³Likewise, tell the older women to behave the way people leading a holy life should. They shouldn't be slanderers or slaves to excessive drinking. They should teach what is good, ⁴thus training the younger women to love their husbands and children, ⁵to be self-controlled and pure, to take good care of their homes and submit to their husbands. In this way, God's message will not be brought into disgrace.

⁶Similarly, urge the young men to be self-controlled, ⁷and in everything set them an example yourself by doing what is good. When you are teaching, have integrity and be serious; ⁸let everything you say be so wholesome that an opponent will be put to shame because he will have nothing bad to say about us.

⁹Tell slaves to submit to their masters in everything, to give satisfaction without talking back ¹⁰or pilfering. On the contrary, they should demonstrate complete faithfulness always, so that in every way they will make the teaching about God our Deliverer more attractive.

¹¹For God's grace, which brings deliverance, has appeared to all people. ¹²It teaches us to renounce godlessness and worldly pleasures, and to live self-controlled, upright and godly lives now, in this age; ¹³while continuing to expect the blessed fulfillment of our certain hope, which is the appearing of the *Sh'khinah* of our great God and the appearing of our Deliverer, Yeshua the Messiah. ¹³He gave himself up on our behalf in order to free us from all violation of *Torah* and purify for himself a people who would be his own, eager to do good.

¹⁵These are the things you should say. Encourage and rebuke with full authority; don't let anyone look down on you.

3 ¹Remind people to submit to the government and its officials, to obey them, to be ready to do any honorable kind of work, ²to slander no one, to avoid quarrelling, to be friendly, and to behave gently towards everyone.

³For at one time, we too were foolish and disobedient, deceived and enslaved by a variety of passions and pleasures. We spent our lives in evil and envy; people hated us, and we hated each other. ⁴But when the kindness and love for mankind of God our Deliverer was revealed, ⁵he delivered us. It was not on the ground of any righteous deeds we had done, but on the ground of his own mercy. He did it by means of the *mikveh* of rebirth and the renewal brought about by the *Ruach HaKodesh*, ⁶whom he poured out on us generously through Yeshua the Messiah, our Deliverer. ⁷He did it so that by his grace we might come to be considered righteous by God and become heirs, with the certain hope of eternal life. ⁸You can trust what I have just said, and I want you to speak with confidence about these things, so that those who have put their trust in God may apply themselves to doing good deeds. These are both good in themselves and valuable to the community.

⁹But avoid stupid controversies, genealogies, quarrels and fights about the *Torah*; because they are worthless and futile. ¹⁰Warn a divisive person once, then a second time; and after that, have nothing more to do with

---

mik·veh — ritual immersion pool
Ru·ach-Ha·Ko·desh — Holy Spirit of God
sha·lom — peace
Sha·'ul — Saul (Paul)
Sh'khi·nah — the glorious manifest presence of God
To·rah — Teaching, "Law"; Pentateuch
Ye·shu·a — Jesus

him. [11] You may be sure that such a person has been perverted and is sinning; he stands self-condemned.

[12] When I send Artemas or Tychicus to you, do your best to come to me in Nicopolis, for I have decided to spend the winter there. [13] Do your best to help Zenas the *Torah* expert and Apollos with their arrangements for travelling, so that they will lack nothing. [14] And have our people learn to apply themselves to doing good deeds that meet genuine needs, so that they will not be unproductive.

[15] All who are with me send you greetings. Give our greetings to our friends in the faith.

Grace be with you all.

THE LETTER FROM YESHUA'S EMISSARY, SHA'UL (PAUL)
TO
PHILEMON

¹From: Sha'ul, a prisoner for the sake of the Messiah Yeshua, and brother Timothy

To: Our dear fellow-worker Philemon, ²along with sister Apphia, our fellow-soldier Archippus and the congregation that gathers in your home:

³Grace and *shalom* to you from God our Father and the Lord Yeshua the Messiah.

⁴I thank my God every time I mention you in my prayers, Philemon, ⁵for I am hearing about your love and commitment to the Lord Yeshua and to all God's people. ⁶I pray that the fellowship based on your commitment will produce full understanding of every good thing that is ours in union with the Messiah. ⁷For your love has given me much joy and encouragement. Brother, you have refreshed the hearts of God's people.

⁸Therefore, I would not hesitate, in union with the Messiah, to direct you to do the thing you ought to do. ⁹But since I, Sha'ul, am the kind of person I am, an old man and now for the Messiah Yeshua's sake a prisoner besides, I prefer to appeal to you on the basis of love. ¹⁰My request to you concerns my son, of whom I became the father while here in prison, Onesimus. ¹¹His name means "useful", and although he was once useless to you, he has now become most useful — not only to you but also to me; ¹²so that in

returning him to you I am sending a part of my very heart. ¹³I would dearly have loved to keep him with me, in order for him to serve me in your place while I am in prison because of the Good News. ¹⁴But I didn't want to do anything without your consent, so that the good you do for me may be voluntary and not forced.

¹⁵Perhaps the reason he was separated from you for a brief period was so that you could have him back forever, ¹⁶no longer as a slave but as more than a slave, as a dear brother. And that he is, especially to me. But how much dearer he must be to you, both humanly and in union with the Lord!

¹⁷So if you are in fellowship with me, receive him as you would me. ¹⁸And if he has wronged you in any way or owes you anything, charge it to me.

¹⁹ *I, Sha'ul, write with my own hand: I will repay it.*

(I won't mention, of course, that you owe me your very life.) ²⁰Yes, brother, please do me this favor in the Lord; refresh my heart in the Messiah.

²¹Trusting that you will respond positively, I write knowing that you will

---

sha·lom — peace
Sha·'ul — Saul (Paul)
To·rah — Teaching, "Law"; Pentateuch
Ye·shu·a — Jesus

indeed do more than I am asking.

²²One more thing: please get a room ready for me. For I hope that through the prayers of you all, God will give me a chance to visit you.

²³Epaphras, my fellow-prisoner for the sake of the Messiah Yeshua, sends greetings to you, ²⁴as do Mark, Aristarchus, Demas and Luke, my fellow-workers.

²⁵The grace of the Lord Yeshua the Messiah be with your spirit.

MESSIANIC JEWS (HEBREWS)

1 ¹In days gone by, God spoke in many and varied ways to the Fathers through the prophets. ²But now, in the *acharit-hayamim*, he has spoken to us through his Son, to whom he has given ownership of everything and through whom he created the universe. ³This Son is the radiance of the *Sh'khinah*, the very expression of God's essence, upholding all that exists by his powerful word; and after he had, through himself, made purification for sins, he **sat down at the right hand of** *HaG'dulah BaM'romim.*'*ᵃ*

⁴So he has become much better than angels, and the name God has given him is superior to theirs. ⁵For to which of the angels did God ever say,

> "You are my Son;
> today I have become your
> Father"?*ᵇ*

Also, God never said of any angel,

> "I will be his Father
> and he will be my Son."*ᶜ*

⁶And again, when God brings his First-born into the world, he says,

> "Let all God's angels worship
> him."*ᵈ*

⁷Indeed, when speaking of angels, he says,

> "... who makes his angels winds
> and his servants fiery flames;"*ᵉ*

⁸but to the Son, he says,

> "Your throne, O God, will last
> forever and ever;
> you rule your Kingdom with a
> scepter of equity;
> ⁹ you have loved righteousness and
> hated wickedness.
> Therefore, O God, your God has
> anointed you
> with the oil of joy in preference to
> your companions;"*ᶠ*

¹⁰and,

> "In the beginning, Lord, you laid
> the foundations of the earth;
> heaven is the work of your hands.
> ¹¹ They will vanish, but you will
> remain;
> like clothing, they will all grow
> old;
> ¹² and you will fold them up like a
> coat.
> Yes, they will be changed like
> clothing,
> but you remain the same,
> your years will never end."*ᵍ*

---

a Psalm 110:1   *b* Psalm 2:7
c 2 Samuel 7:14, 1 Chronicles 17:13
d Psalm 97:7

e Psalm 104:4   *f* Psalm 45:7-8(6-7)
g Psalm 102:26-28(25-27)

===

a·cha·rit-ha·ya·mim — End Times
Ha·G'du·lah Ba·M'ro·mim—the Power Above
Sh'khi·nah — God's manifest glory
Ye·shu·a — Jesus

¹³ Moreover, to which of the angels has he ever said,

> "Sit at my right hand
> until I make your enemies a footstool for your feet"?*h*

¹⁴ Aren't they all merely spirits who serve, sent out to help those whom God will deliver?

2 ¹ Therefore, we must pay much more careful heed to the things we have heard, so that we will not drift away. ² For if the word God spoke through angels became binding, so that every violation and act of disobedience received its just deserts in full measure, ³ then how will we escape if we ignore such a great deliverance? This deliverance, which was first declared by the Lord, was confirmed to us by those who heard him; ⁴ while God also bore witness to it with various signs, wonders and miracles, and with gifts of the *Ruach HaKodesh* which he distributed as he chose.

⁵ For it was not to angels that God subjected the *'olam haba* — which is what we are talking about. ⁶ And there is a place where someone has given this solemn testimony:

> "What is mere man, that you concern yourself with him?
> or the son of man, that you watch over him with such care?
> ⁷ You made him a little lower than the angels,
> you crowned him with glory and honor,
> ⁸ you put everything in subjection under his feet."*i*

In subjecting **everything** to him, he left nothing unsubjected to him. However, at present, we don't see **everything** subjected to him — at least, not yet.

⁹ But we do see Yeshua — who indeed **was made** for **a little** while **lower than the angels** — now **crowned with glory and honor** because he suffered death, so that by God's grace he might taste death for all humanity. ¹⁰ For in bringing many sons to glory, it was only fitting that God, the Creator and Preserver of everything, should bring the Initiator of their deliverance to the goal through sufferings. ¹¹ For both Yeshua, who sets people apart for God, and the ones being set apart have a common origin — this is why he is not ashamed to call them **brothers** ¹² when he says,

> "I will proclaim your name to my brothers;
> in the midst of the congregation I will sing your praise."*j*

¹³ Also,

> "I will put my trust in him,..."*k*

and then it goes on,

> "Here I am, along with the children God has given me."*l*

¹⁴ Therefore, since the **children** share a common physical nature as human beings, he became like them and shared that same human nature; so that by his death he might render ineffective the one who had power over death (that is, the Adversary) ¹⁵ and thus set free those who had been in bondage all their lives because of their fear of death.

¹⁶ Indeed it is obvious that he does not take hold of angels to help them; on the contrary,

> "He takes hold of the seed of Avraham."*m*

---

h Psalm 110:1   *i* Psalm 8:5-7(4-6)

j Psalm 22:23(22)
k Isaiah 8:17 (Septuagint)
l Isaiah 8:18   *m* Isaiah 41:8-9

[17] This is why he had to become like his brothers in every respect — so that he might become a merciful and faithful *cohen gadol* in the service of God, making a *kapparah* for the sins of the people. [18] For since he himself suffered death when he was put to the test, he is able to help those who are being tested now.

3 [1] Therefore, brothers whom God has set apart, who share in the call from heaven, think carefully about Yeshua, whom we acknowledge publicly as God's emissary and as *cohen gadol*. [2] He was **faithful** to God, who appointed him; just as

> "Moshe was faithful in all God's house."[n]

[3] But Yeshua deserves more honor than Moshe, just as the builder of the **house** deserves more honor than the **house**. [4] For every **house** is built by someone, but the one who built everything is God. [5] Also, **Moshe was faithful** *in* all God's house, as a **servant** giving witness to things God would divulge later. [6] But the Messiah, as Son, **was faithful** *over* **God's house**. And we are that **house** of his, provided we hold firmly to the courage and confidence inspired by what we hope for.

[7] Therefore, as the *Ruach HaKodesh* says,

> "Today, if you hear God's voice,
> [8] don't harden your hearts, as you did in the Bitter Quarrel
> on that day in the Wilderness when you put God to the test.
> [9] Yes, your fathers put me to the test;
> they challenged me, and they saw my work for forty years!

> [10] Therefore, I was disgusted with that generation —
> I said, 'Their hearts are always going astray,
> they have not understood how I do things;'
> [11] and in my anger, I swore that they would not enter my rest."[o]

[12] Watch out, brothers, so that there will not be in any one of you an evil heart lacking trust, which could lead you to apostatize from the living God! [13] Instead, keep exhorting each other every day, as long as it is called **Today**, so that none of you will become **hardened** by the deceit of sin. [14] For we have become sharers in the Messiah, provided, however, that we hold firmly to the conviction we began with, right through until the goal is reached.

[15] Now where it says,

> "Today, if you hear God's voice, don't harden your hearts, as you did in the Bitter Quarrel,"[p]

[16] who were the people who, after they **heard**, quarreled so **bitterly**? All those whom Moshe brought out of Egypt. [17] And with whom was God **disgusted for forty years**? Those who sinned — yes, they fell dead in the **Wilderness!** [18] And to whom was it that he **swore that they would not enter** his **rest**? Those who were disobedient. [19] So we see that they were unable to **enter** because of lack of trust.

---

o Psalm 95:7-11   *p* Psalm 95:7-8

====

Av·ra·ham — Abraham
co·hen ga·dol — high priest
kap·pa·rah — atonement, propitiation
Mo·she — Moses
'o·lam ha·ba — the world/age to come
Ru·ach·Ha·Ko·desh — Holy Spirit
Ye·shu·a — Jesus

---

n Numbers 12:7

4 ¹Therefore, let us be terrified of the possibility that, even though the promise of **entering** his **rest** remains, any one of you might be judged to have fallen short of it; ²for Good News has also been proclaimed to us, just as it was to them. But the message they heard didn't do them any good, because those who **heard** it did not combine it with trust. ³For it is we who have trusted who **enter** the **rest.**

It is just as he said,

> "And in my anger, I swore
> that they would not enter my
> rest."*q*

He swore this even though his **works** have been in existence since the founding of the universe. ⁴For there is a place where it is said, concerning the seventh day,

> "And God rested on the seventh
> day from all his works."*r*

⁵And once more, our present text says,

> "They will not enter my rest."*s*

⁶Therefore, since it still remains for some to **enter** it, and those who received the Good News earlier did **not enter,** ⁷he again fixes a certain day, "**Today**," saying through David, so long afterwards, in the text already given,

> "Today, if you hear God's voice,
> don't harden your hearts."*t*

⁸For if Y'hoshua had given them rest, God would not have spoken later of another "day".

⁹So there remains a *Shabbat*-keeping for God's people. ¹⁰For the one who has **entered** God's **rest** has also **rested from his** own **works,** as God did from his. ¹¹Therefore, let us do our best to

enter that **rest;** so that no one will fall short because of the same kind of disobedience.

¹²See, the Word of God is alive! It is at work and is sharper than any double-edged sword — it cuts right through to where soul meets spirit and joints meet marrow, and it is quick to judge the inner reflections and attitudes of the heart. ¹³Before God, nothing created is hidden, but all things are naked and open to the eyes of him to whom we must render an account.

¹⁴Therefore, since we have a great *cohen gadol* who has passed through to the highest heaven, Yeshua, the Son of God, let us hold firmly to what we acknowledge as true. ¹⁵For we do not have a *cohen gadol* unable to empathize with our weaknesses; since in every respect he was tempted just as we are, the only difference being that he did not sin. ¹⁶Therefore, let us confidently approach the throne from which God gives grace, so that we may receive mercy and find grace in our time of need.

5 ¹For every *cohen gadol* taken from among men is appointed to act on people's behalf with regard to things concerning God, to offer gifts and sacrifices for sins. ²He can deal gently with the ignorant and with those who go astray, since he too is subject to weakness. ³Also, because of this weakness, he has to offer sacrifices for his own sins, as well as those of the people. ⁴And no one takes this honor upon himself; rather, he is called by God, just as Aharon was.

⁵So neither did the Messiah glorify himself to become *cohen gadol*; rather, it was the One who said to him,

> "You are my Son;
> today I have become your
> Father."*u*

---

q Psalm 95:11   *r* Genesis 2:2
s Psalm 95:11   *t* Psalm 95:7-8

---

u Psalm 2:7

⁶ Also, as he says in another place,

"You are a *cohen* forever,
to be compared with Malki-
Tzedek."ᵛ

⁷ During Yeshua's life on earth, he offered up prayers and petitions, crying aloud and shedding tears, to the One who had the power to deliver him from death; and he was heard because of his godliness. ⁸ Even though he was the Son, he learned obedience through his sufferings. ⁹ And after he had been brought to the goal, he became the source of eternal deliverance to all who obey him, ¹⁰ since he had been proclaimed by God as a *cohen gadol* to be compared with Malki-Tzedek.

¹¹ We have much to say about this subject, but it is hard to explain, because you have become sluggish in understanding. ¹² For although by this time you ought to be teachers, you need someone to teach you the very first principles of God's Word all over again! You need milk, not solid food! ¹³ Anyone who has to drink milk is still a baby, without experience in applying the Word about righteousness. ¹⁴ But solid food is for the mature, for those whose faculties have been trained by continuous exercise to distinguish good from evil.

6 ¹ Therefore, leaving behind the initial lessons about the Messiah, let us go on to maturity, not laying again the foundation of turning from works that lead to death, trusting God, ² and instruction about washings, *s'mikhah*, the resurrection of the dead and eternal punishment. ³ And, God willing, this is what we will do.

⁴ For when people have once been enlightened, tasted the heavenly gift, become sharers in the *Ruach Ha-Kodesh*, ⁵ and tasted the goodness of God's Word and the powers of the *'olam haba* — ⁶ and then have fallen away — it is impossible to renew them so that they turn from their sin, as long as for themselves they keep executing the Son of God on the stake all over again and keep holding him up to public contempt. ⁷ For the land that soaks up frequent rains and then brings forth a crop useful to its owners receives a blessing from God; ⁸ but if **it keeps producing thorns and thistles,** it fails the test and is close to being **cursed;**ʷ in the end, it will be burned.

⁹ Now even though we speak this way, dear friends, we are confident that you have the better things that come with being delivered. ¹⁰ For God is not so unfair as to forget your work and the love you showed for him in your past service to his people — and in your present service too. ¹¹ However, we want each one of you to keep showing the same diligence right up to the end, when your hope will be realized; ¹² so that you will not become sluggish, but will be imitators of those who by their trust and patience are receiving what has been promised.

¹³ For when God made his promise to Avraham, he swore an oath to do what he had promised; and since there was no one greater than himself for him to

---

ʷ Genesis 3:17-18

A·ha·**ron** — Aaron
Av·ra·**ham** — Abraham
co·**hen** — priest
co·**hen** ga·**dol** — high priest
Da·**vid** — David
Mal·ki-**Tze**·dek — Melchizedek
'o·**lam** ha·**ba** — the world/age to come
Ru·ach-Ha·**Ko**·desh — Holy Spirit
Shab·**bat** — the Sabbath
s'mi·**khah** — ordination, laying on of hands
Ye·**shu**·a — Jesus
Y'ho·**shu**·a — Joshua

ᵛ Psalm 110:4

swear by, **he swore by himself**ˣ ¹⁴and said,

**"I will certainly bless you,
and I will certainly give you many
descendants;"**ʸ

¹⁵and so, after waiting patiently, Avraham saw the promise fulfilled. ¹⁶Now people swear oaths by someone greater than themselves, and confirmation by an oath puts an end to all dispute. ¹⁷Therefore, when God wanted to demonstrate still more convincingly the unchangeable character of his intentions to those who were to receive what he had promised, he added an oath to the promise; ¹⁸so that through two unchangeable things, in neither of which God could lie, we, who have fled to take a firm hold on the hope set before us, would be strongly encouraged. ¹⁹We have this hope as a sure and safe anchor for ourselves, a hope that goes right on through to what is inside the *parokhet*, ²⁰where a forerunner has entered on our behalf, namely, Yeshua, who has become **a *cohen* gadol forever, to be compared with Malki-Tzedek.**ᶻ

7 ¹This **Malki-Tzedek, king of Shalem, a *cohen* of God *HaElyon*, met Avraham on his way back from the slaughter of the kings and blessed him;** ²also Avraham **gave him a tenth of everything.**ᵃ

Now first of all, by translation of his name, he is "king of righteousness;" and then he is also **king of Shalem**, which means "king of peace."

³There is no record of his father, mother, ancestry, birth or death; rather, like the Son of God, he continues as a *cohen* for all time.

⁴Just think how great he was! Even the Patriarch Avraham **gave him a tenth** of the choicest spoils. ⁵Now the descendants of L'vi who became *cohanim* have a commandment in the *Torah* to take a tenth of the income of the people, that is, from their own brothers, despite the fact that they too are descended from Avraham. ⁶But Malki-Tzedek, even though he was not descended from L'vi, took a tenth from Avraham.

Also, he blessed Avraham, the man who received God's promises; ⁷and it is beyond all dispute that the one who blesses has higher status than the one who receives the blessing.

⁸Moreover, in the case of the *cohanim*, the tenth is received by men who die; while in the case of Malki-Tzedek, it is received by someone who is testified to be still alive.

⁹One might go even further and say that L'vi, who himself receives tenths, paid a tenth through Avraham; ¹⁰inasmuch as he was still in his ancestor Avraham's body when Malki-Tzedek met him.

¹¹Therefore, if it had been possible to reach the goal through the system of *cohanim* derived from L'vi (since in connection with it, the people were given the *Torah*), what need would there have been for another, different kind of *cohen*, the one spoken of as **to be compared with Malki-Tzedek** and not to be compared with Aharon? ¹²For if the system of *cohanim* is transformed, there must of necessity occur a transformation of *Torah*. ¹³The one about whom these things are said belongs to another tribe, from which no one has ever served at the altar; ¹⁴for everyone knows that our Lord arose out of Y'hudah, and that Moshe said nothing about this tribe when he spoke about *cohanim*.

---

x Genesis 22:16   *y* Genesis 22:17
z Psalm 110:4   *a* Genesis 14:17-20

¹⁵ It becomes even clearer if a "different kind of *cohen*," one like Malki-Tzedek, arises, ¹⁶ one who became a *cohen* not by virtue of a rule in the *Torah* concerning physical descent, but by virtue of the power of an indestructible life. ¹⁷ For it is stated,

> "You are a *cohen* FOREVER,
> to be compared with Malki-Tzedek."*ᵇ*

¹⁸ Thus, on the one hand, the earlier rule is set aside because of its weakness and inefficacy ¹⁹ (for the *Torah* did not bring anything to the goal); and, on the other hand, a hope of something better is introduced, through which we are drawing near to God.

²⁰ What is more, God swore an oath. For no oath was sworn in connection with those who become *cohanim* now; ²¹ but Yeshua became a *cohen* by the oath which God swore when he said to him,

> "*Adonai* has sworn and will not change his mind,
> 'You are a *cohen* forever.'"*ᶜ*

²² Also this shows how much better is the covenant of which Yeshua has become guarantor.

²³ Moreover, the present *cohanim* are many in number, because they are prevented by death from continuing in office. ²⁴ But because he lives forever, his position as *cohen* does not pass on to someone else; ²⁵ and consequently, he is totally able to deliver those who approach God through him; since he is alive forever and thus forever able to intercede on their behalf.

²⁶ This is the kind of *cohen gadol* that meets our need — holy, without evil, without stain, set apart from sinners and raised higher than the heavens;

²⁷ one who does not have the daily necessity, like the other *cohanim g'dolim*, of offering up sacrifices first for their own sins and only then for those of the people; because he offered one sacrifice, once and for all, by offering up himself. ²⁸ For the *Torah* appoints as *cohanim g'dolim* men who have weakness; but the text which speaks about the swearing of the oath, a text written later than the *Torah*, appoints a Son who has been brought to the goal forever.

8 ¹ Here is the whole point of what we have been saying: we do have just such a *cohen gadol* as has been described. And he does **sit at the right hand of** *HaG'dulah* in heaven.*ᵈ* ² There he serves in the Holy Place, that is, in the true Tent of Meeting, the one erected not by human beings but by *Adonai*.

³ For every *cohen gadol* is appointed to offer both gifts and sacrifices; so this *cohen gadol* too has to have something he can offer. ⁴ Now if he were on earth, he wouldn't be a *cohen* at all, since there already are *cohanim* offering the

---

d Psalm 110:1

A·do·nai — the LORD, Jehovah
A·ha·ron — Aaron
Av·ra·ham — Abraham
co·hen (pl. *co·ha·nim*) — priest
co·hen ga·dol (pl. *co·ha·nam g'do·lim*) — high priest
Ha·El·yon — the Most High
Ha·G'du·lah — the Majesty (i.e., God)
L'vi — Levi
Mal·ki-Tze·dek — Melchizedek
Mo·she — Moses
pa·ro·khet — curtain separating the Holiest Place from the rest of the Temple
Sha·lem — Salem (Jerusalem)
To·rah — Teaching, "Law"; Pentateuch
Ye·shu·a — Jesus
Y'hu·dah — Judah

---

b Psalm 110:4   *c* Psalm 110:4

gifts required by the *Torah*. ⁵But what they are serving is only a copy and shadow of the heavenly original; for when Moshe was about to erect the Tent, God warned him, "See to it that you make everything according to the pattern you were shown on the mountain."*e*

⁶But now the work Yeshua has been given to do is far superior to theirs, just as the covenant he mediates is better. For this covenant has been given as *Torah* on the basis of better promises. ⁷Indeed, if the first covenant had not given ground for faultfinding, there would have been no need for a second one. ⁸For God does find fault with the people when he says,

"'See! The days are coming,'
    says *Adonai*,
'when I will establish
    over the house of Israel
and over the house of Y'hudah
    a new covenant.

⁹ "'It will not be like the covenant
    which I made with their fathers
on the day when I took them by
    their hand
    and led them forth out of the
        land of Egypt;
because they, for their part, did not
    remain faithful to my cove-
    nant;
    so I, for my part, stopped
        concerning myself with them,'
    says *Adonai*.

¹⁰ "'For this is the covenant which I
    will make
    with the house of Israel after
        those days,' says *Adonai*:
'I will put my *Torah* in their minds
    and write it on their hearts;
I will be their God,
    and they will be my people;

¹¹ "'None of them will teach his
    fellow-citizen
    or his brother, saying, "Know
        Adonai!"
For all will know me,
    from the least of them to the
        greatest,
¹² because I will be merciful toward
    their wickednesses
    and remember their sins no
        more.'"*f*

¹³By using the term, "new", he has made the first covenant "old"; and something being made old, something in the process of aging, is on its way to vanishing altogether.

9 ¹Now the first covenant had both regulations for worship and a Holy Place here on earth. ²A tent was set up, the outer one, which was called the Holy Place; in it were the *menorah*, the table and the Bread of the Presence. ³Behind the second *parokhet* was a tent called the Holiest Place, ⁴which had the golden altar for burning incense and the Ark of the Covenant, entirely covered with gold. In the Ark were the gold jar containing the manna, Aharon's rod that sprouted and the stone Tablets of the Covenant; ⁵and above it were the *k'ruvim* representing the *Sh'khinah*, casting their shadow on the lid of the Ark — but now is not the time to discuss these things in detail.

⁶With things so arranged, the *cohanim* go into the outer tent all the time to discharge their duties; ⁷but only the *cohen hagadol* enters the inner one; and he goes in only once a year, and he must always bring blood, which he offers both for himself and for the sins committed in ignorance by the people. ⁸By this arrangement, the *Ruach HaKodesh* showed that so long as the first Tent had standing, the way into the

---

e Exodus 25:40

f Jeremiah 31:30-33(31-34)

Holiest Place was still closed. 9 This symbolizes the present age and indicates that the conscience of the person performing the service cannot be brought to the goal by the gifts and sacrifices he offers. 10 For they involve only food and drink and various ceremonial washings — regulations concerning the outward life, imposed until the time for God to reshape the whole structure.

11 But when the Messiah appeared as *cohen gadol* of the good things that are happening already, then, through the greater and more perfect Tent which is not man-made (that is, it is not of this created world), 12 he entered the Holiest Place once and for all.

And he entered not by means of the blood of goats and calves, but by means of his own blood, thus setting people free forever. 13 For if sprinkling ceremonially unclean persons with the blood of goats and bulls and the ashes of a heifer restores their outward purity; 14 then how much more the blood of the Messiah, who, through the eternal Spirit, offered himself to God as a sacrifice without blemish, will purify our conscience from works that lead to death, so that we can serve the living God!

15 It is because of this death that he is mediator of a **new covenant** [or **will**]. *g* Because a death has occurred which sets people free from the transgressions committed under the first covenant, those who have been called may receive the promised eternal inheritance. 16 For where there is a will, there must necessarily be produced evidence of its maker's death, 17 since a will goes into effect only upon death; it never has force while its maker is still alive.

18 This is why the first covenant too

g Jeremiah 31:30(31)

was inaugurated with blood. 19 After Moshe had proclaimed every command of the *Torah* to all the people, he took the blood of the calves with some water and used scarlet wool and hyssop to sprinkle both the scroll itself and all the people; 20 and he said, **"This is the blood of the covenant which God has ordained for you."** *h* 21 Likewise, he sprinkled with the blood both the Tent and all the things used in its ceremonies. 22 In fact, according to the *Torah*, almost everything is purified with blood; indeed, without the shedding of blood there is no forgiveness of sins.

23 Now this is how the copies of the heavenly things had to be purified, but the heavenly things themselves require better sacrifices than these. 24 For the Messiah has entered a Holiest Place which is not man-made and merely a copy of the true one, but into heaven itself, in order to appear now on our behalf in the very presence of God.

25 Further, he did not enter heaven to offer himself over and over again, like the *cohen hagadol* who enters the Holiest Place year after year with blood that is not his own; 26 for then he would have had to suffer death many times —

h Exodus 24:8

A·do·nai — the LORD, Jehovah
A·ha·ron — Aaron
co·hen (pl. *co·ha·nim*) — priest
co·hen (ha)ga·dol — (the) high priest
k'ru·vim — cherubim
me·no·rah — lampstand
Mo·she — Moses
pa·ro·khet — curtain separating the Holiest Place from the rest of the Temple
Ru·ach-Ha·Ko·desh — Holy Spirit
Sh'khi·nah — the manifest glorious presence of God
To·rah — Teaching, "Law"; Pentateuch
Ye·shu·a — Jesus
Y'hu·dah — Judah

from the founding of the universe on. But as it is, he has appeared once at the end of the ages in order to do away with sin through the sacrifice of himself. ²⁷ Just as human beings have to die once, but after this comes judgment; ²⁸ so also the Messiah, having been offered once to **bear the sins of many,** *[i]* will appear a second time, not to deal with sin, but to deliver those who are eagerly waiting for him.

10 ¹ For the *Torah* has in it a shadow of the good things to come, but not the actual manifestation of the originals. Therefore, it can never, by means of the same sacrifices repeated endlessly year after year, bring to the goal those who approach the Holy Place to offer them. ² Otherwise, wouldn't the offering of those sacrifices have ceased? For if the people performing the service had been cleansed once and for all, they would no longer have sins on their conscience. ³ No, it is quite the contrary — in these sacrifices is a reminder of sins, year after year. ⁴ For it is impossible that the blood of bulls and goats should take away sins. ⁵ This is why, on coming into the world, he says,

"It has not been your will to have
an animal sacrifice and a meal
offering;
rather, you have prepared for me a
body.
⁶ No, you have not been pleased
with burnt offerings and sin
offerings.
⁷ Then I said, 'Look!
In the scroll of the book it is
written about me.
I have come to do your will.'" *[j]*

⁸ In saying first, "**You** neither willed nor were **pleased with animal sacrifices,**

meal offerings, burnt offerings and sin offerings," things which are offered in accordance with the *Torah*; ⁹ and then, **"Look, I have come to do your will;"** he takes away the first system in order to set up the second. ¹⁰ It is in connection with this **will** that we have been separated for God and made holy, once and for all, through the **offering** of Yeshua the Messiah's **body.**

¹¹ Now every *cohen* stands every day doing his service, offering over and over the same sacrifices, which can never take away sins. ¹² But this one, after he had offered for all time a single sacrifice for sins, **sat down at the right hand** of God, ¹³ from then on to wait **until** his **enemies** be made **a footstool for** his **feet.** *[k]* ¹⁴ For by a single offering he has brought to the goal for all time those who are being set apart for God and made holy.

¹⁵ And the *Ruach HaKodesh* too bears witness to us; for after saying,

¹⁶ "'This is the covenant which I will
make
with them after those days,' says
Adonai:
'I will put my *Torah* on their
hearts,
and write it on their minds,'" *[l]*

¹⁷ he then adds,

"'And their sins and their wicked-
nesses
I will remember no more.'" *[m]*

¹⁸ Now where there is forgiveness for these, an offering for sins is no longer needed.

¹⁹ So, brothers, we have confidence to use the way into the Holiest Place opened by the blood of Yeshua. ²⁰ He inaugurated it for us as a new and living

---

i Isaiah 53:12 *j* Psalm 40:7-9(6-8)

k Psalm 110:1 *l* Jeremiah 31:32(33)
m Jeremiah 31:33(34)

way through the *parokhet*, by means of his flesh. [21] We also have a great *cohen* over God's household. [22] Therefore, let us approach the Holiest Place with a sincere heart, in the full assurance that comes from trusting — with our hearts **sprinkled clean** from a bad conscience and our bodies washed with **pure water.**[n] [23] Let us continue holding fast to the hope we acknowledge, without wavering; for the One who made the promise is trustworthy. [24] And let us keep paying attention to one another, in order to spur each other on to love and good deeds, [25] not neglecting our own congregational meetings, as some have made a practice of doing, but, rather, encouraging each other.

And let us do this all the more as you see the Day approaching. [26] For if we deliberately continue to sin after receiving the knowledge of the truth, there no longer remains a sacrifice for sins, [27] but only the terrifying prospect of Judgment, of **raging fire that will consume the enemies.**[o]

[28] Someone who disregards the *Torah* of Moshe is **put to death** without mercy **on the word of two or three witnesses.**[p] [29] Think how much worse will be the punishment deserved by someone who has trampled underfoot the Son of God; who has treated as something common the **blood of the covenant**[q] which made him holy; and who has insulted the Spirit, giver of God's grace!

[30] For the One we know is the One who said,

> **"Vengeance is my responsibility;**
> **I will repay,"**

and then said,

> **"*Adonai* will judge his people."**[r]

[31] It is a terrifying thing to fall into the hands of the living God!

[32] But remember the earlier days, when, after you had received the light, you endured a hard struggle with sufferings. [33] Sometimes you were publicly disgraced and persecuted, while at other times you stood loyally by those who were treated this way. [34] For you shared the sufferings of those who had been put in prison. Also when your possessions were seized, you accepted it gladly; since you knew that what you possessed was better and would last forever.

[35] So don't throw away that courage of yours, which carries with it such a great reward. [36] For you need to hold out; so that, by having done what God wills, you may receive what he has promised. [37] For

> **"There is so, so little time!**
> **The One coming will indeed come,**
> **he will not delay.**
> [38] **But the person who is righteous**
> **will live his life by trusting,**
> **and if he shrinks back, I will not be**
> **pleased with him."**[s]

[39] However, we are not the kind who **shrink back** and are destroyed; on the contrary, we keep **trusting** and thus preserve our lives!

---

s   Habakkuk 2:3-4

===

A·do·nai — the LORD, Jehovah
co·hen — priest
co·hen ha·ga·dol — high priest
Mo·she — Moses
pa·ro·khet — curtain separating the Holiest Place from the rest of the Temple
Ru·ach-Ha·Ko·desh — Holy Spirit
Sh'khi·nah — the manifest glorious presence of God
To·rah — Teaching, "Law"; Pentateuch
Ye·shu·a — Jesus

---

n   Ezekiel 36:25   *o*   Isaiah 26:11
p   Deuteronomy 17:6, 19:15
q   Exodus 24:8   *r*   Deuteronomy 32:35-36

11 [1]**Trusting**[t] is being confident of what we hope for, convinced about things we do not see. [2]It was for this that Scripture attested the merit of the people of old.

[3]By **trusting,** we understand that the universe was created through a spoken word of God, so that what is seen did not come into being out of existing phenomena.

[4]By **trusting,** Hevel offered a greater sacrifice than Kayin; because of this, he was attested as righteous, with God giving him this testimony on the ground of his gifts. Through having **trusted,** he still continues to speak, even though he is dead.

[5]By **trusting,** Chanoch was taken away from this life without seeing death — **"He was not to be found, because God took him away"** — for he has been attested as having been, prior to being taken away, **well pleasing to God.**[u] [6]And without **trusting,** it is impossible to be **well pleasing to God,** because whoever approaches him must **trust** that he does exist and that he becomes a Rewarder to those who seek him out.

[7]By **trusting,** Noach, after receiving divine warning about things as yet unseen, was filled with holy fear and built an ark to save his household. Through this **trusting,** he put the world under condemnation and received the righteousness that comes from trusting.

[8]By **trusting,** Avraham obeyed, after being called to **go out**[v] to a place which God would give him as a possession; indeed, he **went out** without knowing where he was going. [9]By **trusting,** he lived as a temporary resident in the Land of the promise, as if it were not his, staying in tents with Yitzchak and Ya'akov, who were to receive what was promised along with him. [10]For he was looking forward to the city with permanent foundations, of which the architect and builder is God.

[11]By **trusting,** he received potency to father a child, even when he was past the age for it, as was Sarah herself; because he regarded the One who had made the promise as **trust**worthy. [12]Therefore this one man, who was virtually dead, fathered descendants

> **as numerous as the stars in the sky,**
> **and as countless as the grains of sand on the seashore.**[w]

[13]All these people kept on **trusting** until they died, without receiving what had been promised. They had only seen it and welcomed it from a distance, while acknowledging that they were **aliens and temporary residents on the earth.**[x] [14]For people who speak this way make it clear that they are looking for a fatherland. [15]Now if they were to keep recalling the one they left, they would have an opportunity to return; [16]but as it is, they aspire to a better fatherland, a heavenly one. This is why God is not ashamed to be called *their* God, for he has prepared for them a city.

[17]By **trusting,** Avraham, when he was put to the test, offered up Yitzchak as a sacrifice. Yes, he offered up his only son, he who had received the promises, [18]to whom it had been said, **"What is called your 'seed' will be in Yitzchak."**[y] [19]For he had concluded that God could even raise people from the dead! And, figuratively speaking, he did so receive him.

t Habakkuk 2:4 *u* Genesis 5:24
v Genesis 12:1

w Genesis 15:5-6, 22:17, 32:13(12); Exodus 32:13; Deuteronomy 1:10, 10:22
x 1 Chronicles 29:15 *y* Genesis 21:12

[20]By **trusting,** Yitzchak in his blessings over Ya'akov and Esav made reference to events yet to come.

[21]By **trusting,** Ya'akov, when he was dying, blessed each of Yosef's sons, **leaning on his walking-stick as he bowed in prayer.**[z]

[22]By **trusting,** Yosef, near the end of his life, remembered about the Exodus of the people of Israel and gave instructions about what to do with his bones.

[23]By **trusting,** the parents of Moshe **hid him for three months** after he was born, **because they saw that he was a beautiful child,**[a] and they weren't afraid of the king's decree.

[24]By **trusting,** Moshe, **after he had grown up,**[b] refused to be called the son of Pharaoh's daughter. [25]He chose being mistreated along with God's people rather than enjoying the passing pleasures of sin. [26]He had come to regard abuse suffered on behalf of the Messiah as greater riches than the treasures of Egypt, for he kept his eyes fixed on the reward.

[27]By **trusting,** he left Egypt, not fearing the king's anger; he persevered as one who sees the unseen.

[28]By **trusting,** he obeyed the requirements for the *Pesach,* including the smearing of the blood, so that the Destroyer of the firstborn would not touch the firstborn of Israel.

[29]By **trusting,** they walked through the Red Sea as through dry land; when the Egyptians tried to do it, the sea swallowed them up.

[30]By **trusting,** the walls of Yericho fell down — after the people had marched around them for seven days.

[31]By **trusting,** Rachav the prostitute welcomed the spies and therefore did not die along with those who were disobedient.

[32]What more shoud I say? There isn't time to tell about Gid'on, Barak, Shimshon, Yiftach, David, Shmu'el and the prophets; [33]who, through **trusting,** conquered kingdoms, worked righteousness, received what was promised, **shut the mouths of lions,**[c] [34]quenched the power of fire, escaped the edge of the sword, had their weakness turned to strength, grew mighty in battle and routed foreign armies. [35]Women received back their dead resurrected; other people were stretched on the rack and beaten to death, refusing to be ransomed, so that they would gain a better resurrection. [36]Others underwent the trials of being mocked and whipped, then chained and imprisoned. [37]They were stoned, sawed in two, murdered by the sword; they went about clothed in sheepskins and goatskins, destitute, persecuted, mistreated, [38]wandering about in deserts and mountains, living in caves and holes in the ground! The

---

c Daniel 6:23

===

Av·ra·**ham** — Abraham
Ba·**rak** — Barak
Cha·**noch** — Enoch
Da·**vid** — David
E·**sav** — Esau
Gid·**'on** — Gideon
He·vel — Abel
Ka·yin — Cain
Mo·**she** — Moses
No·ach — Noah
Pe·sach — Passover
Ra·**chav** — Rahab
Sa·**rah** — Sarah
Shim·**shon** — Samson
Shmu·**'el** — Samuel
Ya·'a·**kov** — Jacob
Ye·ri·**cho** — Jericho
Yif·**tach** — Jephthah
Yitz·**chak** — Isaac
Yo·**sef** — Joseph

---

z Genesis 47:31 (Septuagint)
a Exodus 2:2   *b* Exodus 2:11

world was not worthy of them! [39] All of these had their merit attested because of their **trusting.** Nevertheless, they did not receive what had been promised, [40] because God had planned something better that would involve us, so that only with us would they be brought to the goal.

12 [1] So then, since we are surrounded by such a great cloud of witnesses, let us, too, put aside every impediment — that is, the sin which easily hampers our forward movement — and keep running with endurance in the contest set before us, [2] looking away to the Initiator and Completer of that **trusting,**[d] Yeshua — who, in exchange for obtaining the joy set before him, endured execution on a stake as a criminal, scorning the shame, and has sat down **at the right hand of** the throne of God.[e] [3] Yes, think about him who endured such hostility against himself from sinners, so that you won't grow tired or **become despondent.** [4] You have not yet resisted to the point of shedding blood in the contest against sin.

[5] Also you have forgotten the counsel which speaks with you as sons:

> **"My son, don't despise the discipline of _Adonai_**
> **or become despondent when he corrects you.**
> [6] **For _Adonai_ disciplines those he loves**
> **and whips everyone he accepts as a son."**[f]

[7] Regard your endurance as **discipline;** God is dealing with you as **sons.** For what son goes undisciplined by his father? [8] All legitimate sons undergo **discipline;** so if you don't, you're a _mamzer_ and not a son!

[9] Furthermore, we had physical fathers who disciplined us, and we respected them; how much more should we submit to our spiritual Father and live! [10] For they disciplined us only for a short time and only as best they could; but he disciplines us in a way that provides genuine benefit to us and enables us to share in his holiness.

[11] Now, all **discipline,** while it is happening, does indeed seem painful, not enjoyable; but for those who have been trained by it, it later produces its peaceful fruit, which is righteousness. [12] So,

> **strengthen your drooping arms,**
> **and steady your tottering knees;**[g]

[13] and

> **make a level path for your feet;**[h]

so that what has been injured will not get wrenched out of joint but rather will be healed.

[14] Keep pursuing _shalom_ with everyone and the holiness without which no one will see the Lord. [15] See to it that no one misses out on God's grace, that no **root of bitterness**[i] springing up causes trouble and thus contaminates many, [16] and that no one is sexually immoral, or godless like Esav, who in exchange for a single meal gave up his rights as the firstborn. [17] For you know that afterwards, when he wanted to obtain his father's blessing, he was rejected; indeed, even though he sought it with tears, his change of heart was to no avail.

[18] For you have not come to a tangible mountain, to an ignited fire, to darkness, to murk, to a whirlwind, [19] to the

---

_d_ Habakkuk 2:4   _e_ Psalm 110:1
_f_ Proverbs 3:11-12

_g_ Isaiah 35:3   _h_ Proverbs 4:26
_i_ Deuteronomy 29:17

sound of a *shofar*, and to a voice whose words made the hearers beg that no further message be given to them — ²⁰for they couldn't bear what was being commanded them, **"If even a beast touches the mountain, it is to be stoned to death;"**[j] ²¹ and so terrifying was the sight that Moshe said, **"I am quaking with dread."**[k]

²² On the contrary, you have come to Mount Tziyon, that is, the city of the living God, heavenly Yerushalayim; to myriads of angels in festive assembly; ²³ to a community of the firstborn whose names have been recorded in heaven; to a Judge who is God of everyone; to spirits of righteous people who have been brought to the goal; ²⁴ to the mediator of a new covenant, Yeshua; and to the sprinkled blood that speaks better things than that of Hevel.

²⁵ See that you don't reject the One speaking! For if those did not escape who rejected him when he gave divine warning on earth, think how much less we will escape if we turn away from him when he warns from heaven. ²⁶ Even then, his voice shook the earth; but now, he has made this promise:

> **"One more time I will shake not only the earth, but heaven too!"**[l]

²⁷ And this phrase, **"one more time"**, makes clear that the things shaken are removed, since they are created things, so that the things not **shaken** may remain. ²⁸ Therefore, since we have received an unshakeable Kingdom, let us have grace, through which we may offer service that will please God, with reverence and fear. ²⁹ For indeed,

> **"Our God is a consuming fire!"**[m]

13 ¹ Let brotherly friendship continue; ²but don't forget to be friendly to outsiders; for in so doing, some people, without knowing it, have entertained angels. ³ Remember those in prison and being mistreated, as if you were in prison with them and undergoing their torture yourselves.

⁴ Marriage is honorable in every respect; and, in particular, sex within marriage is pure. But God will indeed punish fornicators and adulterers.

⁵ Keep your lives free from the love of money; and be satisfied with what you have; for God himself has said, **"I will never fail you or abandon you."**[n] ⁶ Therefore, we say with confidence,

> **"*Adonai* is my helper; I will not be afraid —**
> **what can a human being do to me?"**[o]

⁷ Remember your leaders, those who spoke God's message to you. Reflect on the results of their way of life, and imitate their trust — ⁸ Yeshua the Messiah is the same yesterday, today and forever.

⁹ Do not be carried away by various strange teachings; for what is good is for the heart to be strengthened by grace, not by foods. People who have made these the focus of their lives have not benefitted thereby.

---

n Deuteronomy 31:6   o Psalm 118:6

A·do·nai — the LORD, Jehovah
E·sav — Esau
He·vel — Abel
mam·zer — illegitimate child
Mo·she — Moses
sha·lom — peace
sho·far — ram's horn
Tzi·yon — Zion
Ye·ru·sha·la·yim — Jerusalem
Ye·shu·a — Jesus

---

j Exodus 19:12-13   k Deuteronomy 9:19
l Haggai 2:6
m Deuteronomy 4:24, 9:3; Isaiah 33:14

[10] We have an altar from which those who serve in the Tent are not permitted to eat. [11] For the *cohen hagadol* brings the blood of animals into the Holiest Place as a sin offering, but their bodies are **burned outside the camp.**[p] [12] So too Yeshua suffered death outside the gate, in order to make the people holy through his own blood. [13] Therefore, let us go out to him who is **outside the camp** and share his disgrace. [14] For we have no permanent city here; on the contrary, we seek the one to come. [15] Through him, therefore, **let us offer God a sacrifice of praise** continually.[q] For this is the natural product of lips that acknowledge his name.

[16] But don't forget doing good and sharing with others, for with such **sacrifice**s God is well pleased.

[17] Obey your leaders and submit to them, for they keep watch over your lives, as people who will have to render an account. So make it a task of joy for

them, not one of groaning; for that is of no advantage to you.

[18] Keep praying for us, for we are certain that we have a clear conscience and want to conduct ourselves properly in everything we do. [19] And all the more I beg you to do this, so that I may be restored to you that much sooner.

[20] The God of *shalom* brought up from the dead the great Shepherd of the sheep, our Lord Yeshua, by the blood of an eternal covenant. [21] May that God equip you with every good thing you need to do his will; and may he do in us whatever pleases him, through Yeshua the Messiah. To him be the glory forever and ever. *Amen.*

[22] Now I urge you, brothers, to bear with my message of exhortation; for I have written you only briefly.

[23] Know that our brother Timothy has been released. If he comes soon enough, I will bring him with me when I come to see you.

[24] Greet all your leaders and all God's people. The people from Italy send greetings to you.

[25] Grace be with you all.

---

p Leviticus 16:27

q Leviticus 7:12, 22:9; Psalms 50:14, 23; 107:22; 116:17; 2 Chronicles 29:31

THE LETTER FROM
YA'AKOV (JAMES)

1 ¹From: Ya'akov, a slave of God and of the Lord Yeshua the Messiah

To: The Twelve Tribes in the Diaspora:

Shalom!

²Regard it all as joy, my brothers, when you face various kinds of temptations; ³for you know that the testing of your trust produces perseverance. ⁴But let perseverance do its complete work; so that you may be complete and whole, lacking in nothing. ⁵Now if any of you lacks wisdom, let him ask God, who gives to all generously and without reproach; and it will be given to him. ⁶But let him ask in trust, doubting nothing; for the doubter is like a wave in the sea being tossed and driven by the wind. ⁷Indeed that person should not think that he will receive anything from the Lord, ⁸because he is double-minded, unstable in all his ways.

⁹Let the brother in humble circumstances boast about his high position. ¹⁰But let the rich brother boast about his being humbled; since, like a wildflower, he will pass away. ¹¹For just as the sun rises with the *sharav* and dries up the plant, so that its flower falls off and its beauty is destroyed, so too the rich person going about his business will wither away.

¹²How blessed is the man who perseveres through temptation! For after he has passed the test, he will receive as his crown the Life which God has promised to those who love him. ¹³No one being tempted should say, "I am being tempted by God." For God cannot be tempted by evil, and God himself tempts no one. ¹⁴Rather, each person is being tempted whenever he is being dragged off and enticed by the bait of his own desire. ¹⁵Then, having conceived, the desire gives birth to sin; and when sin is fully grown, it gives birth to death.

¹⁶Don't delude yourselves, my dear brothers — ¹⁷every good act of giving and every perfect gift is from above, coming down from the Father who made the heavenly lights; with him there is neither variation nor darkness caused by turning. ¹⁸Having made his decision, he gave birth to us through a Word that can be relied upon, in order that we should be a kind of firstfruits of all that he created. ¹⁹Therefore, my dear brothers, let every person be quick to listen but slow to speak, slow to get angry; ²⁰for a man's anger does not accomplish God's righteousness!

²¹So rid yourselves of all vulgarity and obvious evil, and receive meekly the Word implanted in you that can

---

A·men — So be it
co·hen ha·ga·dol — high priest
Sha·lom! — Peace! (a greeting)
sha·rav — hot, dry wind from the deserts east of Israel
Ya·'a·kov — James
Ye·shu·a — Jesus

311

save your lives. ²²Don't deceive yourselves by only hearing what the Word says, but do it! ²³For whoever hears the Word but doesn't do what it says is like someone who looks at his face in a mirror, ²⁴who looks at himself, goes away and immediately forgets what he looks like. ²⁵But if a person looks closely into the perfect *Torah*, which gives freedom, and continues, becoming not a forgetful hearer but a doer of the work it requires, then he will be blessed in what he does.

²⁶Anyone who thinks he is religiously observant but does not control his tongue is deceiving himself, and his observance counts for nothing. ²⁷The religious observance that God the Father considers pure and faultless is this: to care for orphans and widows in their distress and to keep oneself from being contaminated by the world.

2 ¹My brothers, practice the faith of our Lord Yeshua, the glorious Messiah, without showing favoritism. ²Suppose a man comes into your synagogue wearing gold rings and fancy clothes, and also a poor man comes in dressed in rags. ³If you show more respect to the man wearing the fancy clothes and say to him, "Have this good seat here," while to the poor man you say, "You, stand over there," or, "Sit down on the floor by my feet," ⁴then aren't you creating distinctions among yourselves, and haven't you made yourselves into judges with evil motives?

⁵Listen, my dear brothers, hasn't God chosen the poor of the world to be rich in faith and to receive the Kingdom which he promised to those who love him? ⁶But you despise the poor! Aren't the rich the ones who oppress you and drag you into court? ⁷Aren't they the ones who insult the good name of Him to whom you belong? ⁸If you truly attain the goal of Kingdom *Torah*, in conformity with the passage that says, **"Love your neighbor as yourself,"**[a] you are doing well. ⁹But if you show favoritism, your actions constitute sin, since you are convicted under the *Torah* as transgressors.

¹⁰For a person who keeps the whole *Torah*, yet stumbles at one point, has become guilty of breaking them all. ¹¹For the One who said, **"Don't commit adultery,"**[b] also said, **"Don't murder."**[c] Now, if you don't commit adultery but do murder, you have become a transgressor of the *Torah*.

¹²Keep speaking and acting like people who will be judged by a *Torah* which gives freedom. ¹³For judgment will be without mercy toward one who doesn't show mercy; but mercy wins out over judgment.

¹⁴What good is it, my brothers, if someone claims to have faith but has no actions to prove it? Is such "faith" able to save him? ¹⁵Suppose a brother or sister is without clothes and daily food, ¹⁶and someone says to him, "*Shalom!* Keep warm and eat hearty!" without giving him what he needs, what good does it do? ¹⁷Thus, faith by itself, unaccompanied by actions, is dead.

¹⁸But someone will say that you have faith and I have actions. Show me this faith of yours without the actions, and I will show you my faith *by* my actions! ¹⁹You believe that **"God is one"**?[d] Good for you! The demons believe it too — the thought makes them shudder with fear! ²⁰But, foolish fellow, do you want to be shown that such "faith" apart from actions is barren?

²¹Wasn't *Avraham avinu* declared

---

a Leviticus 19:18

b Exodus 20:13(14), Deuteronomy 5:18

c Exodus 20:13, Deuteronomy 5:17

d Deuteronomy 6:4

righteous because of actions when he offered up his son Yitzchak on the altar? ²²You see that his faith worked with his actions; by the actions the faith was made complete; ²³and the passage of the *Tanakh* was fulfilled which says, **"Avraham had faith in God, and it was credited to his account as righteousness."**ᵉ He was even called **God's friend.**ᶠ ²⁴You see that a person is declared righteous because of actions and not because of faith alone.

²⁵Likewise, wasn't Rachav the prostitute also declared righteous because of actions when she welcomed the messengers and sent them out by another route? ²⁶Indeed, just as the body without a spirit is dead, so too faith without actions is dead.

3 ¹Not many of you should become teachers, my brothers, since you know that we will be judged more severely. ²For we all stumble in many ways; if someone does not stumble in what he says, he is a mature man who can bridle his whole body. ³If we put a bit into a horse's mouth to make it obey us, we control its whole body as well. ⁴And think of a ship — although it is huge and is driven by strong winds, yet the pilot can steer it wherever he wants with just a small rudder. ⁵So too the tongue is a tiny part of the body, yet it boasts great things. See how a little fire sets a whole forest ablaze! ⁶Yes, the tongue is a fire, a world of wickedness. The tongue is so placed in our body that it defiles every part of it, setting ablaze the whole of our life; and it is set on fire by Gey-Hinnom itself. ⁷For people have tamed and continue to tame all kinds of animals, birds, reptiles and sea creatures; ⁸but the tongue no one can tame — it is an unstable and

evil thing, full of death-dealing poison! ⁹With it we bless *Adonai*, the Father; and with it we curse people, who were made **in the image of God.**ᵍ ¹⁰Out of the same mouth come blessing and cursing! Brothers, it isn't right for things to be this way. ¹¹A spring doesn't send both fresh and bitter water from the same opening, does it? ¹²Can a fig tree yield olives, my brothers? or a grapevine, figs? Neither does salt water produce fresh.

¹³Who among you is wise and understanding? Let him demonstrate it by his good way of life, by actions done in the humility that grows out of wisdom. ¹⁴But if you harbor in your hearts bitter jealousy and selfish ambition, don't boast and attack the truth with lies! ¹⁵This wisdom is not the kind that comes down from above; on the contrary, it is worldly, unspiritual, demonic. ¹⁶For where there are jealousy and selfish ambition, there will be disharmony and every foul practice. ¹⁷But the wisdom from above is, first of all, pure, then peaceful, kind, open to reason, full of mercy and good fruits, without partiality and without hypocrisy. ¹⁸And peacemakers who sow seed in peace raise a harvest of righteousness.

4 ¹What is causing all the quarrels and fights among you? Isn't it your desires battling inside you? ²You

---

ᵍ Genesis 1:26-27

---

*A·do·**nai*** — the LORD, Jehovah
Av·ra·**ham** — Abraham
*Av·ra·**ham** a·vi·nu* — our father, Abraham
Gey-Hin·**nom** — Gehenna, hell
Ra·**chav** — Rahab
*Sha·**lom!*** — Peace! (a greeting)
*Ta·**nakh*** — Hebrew Scriptures, "Old Testament"
*To·**rah*** — Teaching, "Law"; Pentateuch
Ye·**shu**·a — Jesus
Yitz·**chak** — Isaac

ᵉ Genesis 15:6
ᶠ Isaiah 41:8, 2 Chronicles 20:7

desire things and don't have them. You kill, and you are jealous, and you still can't get them. So you fight and quarrel. The reason you don't have is that you don't pray! ³Or you pray and don't receive, because you pray with the wrong motive, that of wanting to indulge your own desires.

⁴You unfaithful wives! Don't you know that loving the world is hating God? Whoever chooses to be the world's friend makes himself God's enemy! ⁵Or do you suppose the Scripture speaks in vain when it says that there is a spirit in us which longs to envy? ⁶But the grace he gives is greater, which is why it says,

**"God opposes the arrogant,
but to the humble he gives grace."**[h]

⁷Therefore, submit to God. Moreover, take a stand against the Adversary, and he will flee from you. ⁸Come close to God, and he will come close to you. Clean your hands, sinners; and purify your hearts, you double-minded people! ⁹Wail, mourn, sob! Let your laughter be turned into mourning and your joy into gloom! ¹⁰Humble yourselves before the Lord, and he will lift you up.

¹¹Brothers, stop speaking against each other! Whoever speaks against a brother or judges a brother is speaking against *Torah* and judging *Torah*. And if you judge *Torah*, you are not a doer of what *Torah* says, but a judge. ¹²There is but one Giver of *Torah*; he is also the Judge, with the power to deliver and to destroy. Who do you think you are, judging your fellow human being?

¹³Now listen, you who say, "Today or tomorrow we will go to such-and-such a city, stay there a year trading and make a profit"! ¹⁴You don't even know

if you will be alive tomorrow! For all you are is a mist that appears for a little while and then disappears. ¹⁵Instead, you ought to say, "If *Adonai* wants it to happen, we will live" to do this or that. ¹⁶But as it is, in your arrogance you boast. All such boasting is evil. ¹⁷So then, anyone who knows the right thing to do and fails to do it is committing a sin.

5 ¹Next, a word for the rich: weep and wail over the hardships coming upon you! ²Your riches have rotted, and your clothes have become motheaten; ³your gold and silver have corroded, and their corrosion will be evidence against you and will eat up your flesh like fire! This is the *acharit-hayamim*, and you have been storing up wealth! ⁴Listen! The wages you have fraudulently withheld from the workers who mowed your fields are calling out against you, and the outcries of those who harvested have reached the ears of *Adonai Tzva'ot*. ⁵You have led a life of luxury and self-indulgence here on earth — in a time of slaughter, you have gone on eating to your heart's content. ⁶You have condemned, you have murdered the innocent; they have not withstood you.

⁷So, brothers, be patient until the Lord returns. See how the farmer waits for the precious "fruit of the earth" — he is patient over it until it receives **the fall and spring rains.**[i] ⁸You too, be patient; keep up your courage; for the Lord's return is near. ⁹Don't grumble against one another, brothers, so that you won't come under condemnation — look! the Judge is standing at the door! ¹⁰As an example of suffering mistreatment and being patient, brothers, take the prophets who spoke in the

---

h Proverbs 3:34

i Deuteronomy 11:14, Jeremish 5:24,
   Joel 2:23

name of *Adonai.* ¹¹ Look, we regard those who persevered as blessed. You have heard of the perseverance of Iyov, and you know what the purpose of *Adonai* was, that **Adonai is very compassionate and merciful.**ʲ

¹² Above all, brothers, stop swearing oaths — not "By heaven," not "By the earth," and not by any other formula; rather, let your "Yes" be simply "Yes" and your "No" simply "No," so that you won't fall under condemnation. ¹³ Is someone among you in trouble? He should pray. Is someone feeling good? He should sing songs of praise. ¹⁴ Is someone among you ill? He should call for the elders of the congregation. They will pray for him and rub olive oil on him in the name of the Lord. ¹⁵ The prayer offered with trust will heal the one who is ill — the Lord will restore his health; and if he has committed sins, he will be forgiven. ¹⁶ Therefore, openly acknowledge your sins to one another, and pray for each other, so that you may be healed. The prayer of a righteous person is powerful and effective. ¹⁷ Eliyahu was only a human being like us; yet he prayed fervently that it might not rain, and no rain fell on the Land for three years and six months. ¹⁸ Then he prayed again, and heaven gave rain, and the Land produced its crops.

¹⁹ My brothers, if one of you wanders from the truth, and someone causes him to return, ²⁰ you should know that whoever turns a sinner from his wandering path will save him from death and **cover many sins.**ᵏ

---

k Proverbs 10:12

a·cha·rit-ha·ya·mim — "end of the days", Last Times

A·do·nai — the LORD, Jehovah

A·do·nai-Tzva'·ot — the LORD (Jehovah) of Hosts (heaven's armies)

E·li·ya·hu — Elijah

I·yov — Job

Ta·nakh — Hebrew Scriptures, "Old Testament"

To·rah — Teaching, "Law"; Pentateuch

---

j Exodus 34:6; Psalms 103:8, 111:4

1 KEFA (1 PETER)

1 [1] From: Kefa, an emissary of Yeshua the Messiah

To: God's chosen people, living as aliens in the Diaspora — in Pontus, Galatia, Cappadocia, the province of Asia, and Bythinia — [2] chosen according to the foreknowledge of God the Father and set apart by the Spirit for obeying Yeshua the Messiah and for sprinkling with his blood:

Grace and *shalom* be yours in full measure.

[3] Praised be God, Father of our Lord Yeshua the Messiah, who, in keeping with his great mercy, has caused us, through the resurrection of Yeshua the Messiah from the dead, to be born again to a living hope, [4] to an inheritance that cannot decay, spoil or fade, kept safe for you in heaven. [5] Meanwhile, through trusting, you are being protected by God's power for a deliverance ready to be revealed at the Last Time. [6] Rejoice in this, even though for a little while you may have to experience grief in various trials. [7] Even gold is tested for genuineness by fire. The purpose of these trials is so that your trust's genuineness, which is far more valuable than perishable gold, will be judged worthy of praise, glory and honor at the revealing of Yeshua the Messiah.

[8] Without having seen him, you love him. Without seeing him now, but trusting in him, you continue to be full of joy that is glorious beyond words. [9] And you are receiving what your trust is aiming at, namely, your deliverance.

[10] The prophets, who prophesied about this gift of deliverance that was meant for you, pondered and inquired diligently about it. [11] They were trying to find out the time and circumstances to which the Spirit of the Messiah in them was referring in predicting the Messiah's sufferings and the glorious things to follow. [12] It was revealed to them that their service when they spoke about these things was not for their own benefit, but for yours. And these same things have now been proclaimed to you by those who communicated the Good News to you through the *Ruach HaKodesh* sent from heaven. Even angels long to look into these things!

[13] Therefore, get your minds ready for work, keep yourselves under control, and fix your hopes fully on the gift you will receive when Yeshua the Messiah is revealed. [14] As people who obey God, do not let yourselves be shaped by the evil desires you used to have when you were still ignorant. [15] On the contrary, following the Holy One who called you, become holy yourselves in your entire way of life; [16] since the *Tanakh* says,

"You are to be holy because I am holy."[a]

---

a Leviticus 11:44, 45; 19:2; 20:7

^{17} Also, if you are addressing as Father the one who judges impartially according to each person's actions, you should live out your temporary stay on earth in fear. ^{18} You should be aware that the ransom paid to free you from the worthless way of life which your fathers passed on to you did not consist of anything perishable like silver or gold; ^{19} on the contrary, it was the costly bloody sacrificial death of the Messiah, as of a lamb without defect or spot. ^{20} God knew him before the founding of the universe, but revealed him in the *acharit-hayamim* for your sakes. ^{21} Through him you trust in God, who raised him from the dead and gave him glory; so that your trust and hope are in God.

^{22} Now that you have purified yourselves by obeying the truth, so that you have a sincere love for your brothers, love each other deeply, with all your heart. ^{23} You have been born again not from some seed that will decay, but from one that cannot decay, through the living Word of God that lasts forever. ^{24} For

> all humanity is like grass,
> all its glory is like a wildflower —
> the grass withers, and the flower falls off;
> ^{25} but the Word of *Adonai* lasts forever.^{b}

Moreover, this **"Word"** is the Good News which has been proclaimed to you.

2 ^{1} Therefore, rid yourselves of all malice, of all deceit, hypocrisy and envy, and of all the ways there are of speaking against people; ^{2} and be like newborn babies, thirsty for the pure milk of the Word; so that by it, you may grow up into deliverance. ^{3} For you have **tasted** that *Adonai* is good.^{c}

^{4} As you come to him, the living **stone**, rejected by people but **chosen** by God and **precious** to him, ^{5} you yourselves, as living **stones**, are being built into a spiritual house to be *cohanim* set apart for God to offer spiritual sacrifices acceptable to him through Yeshua the Messiah. ^{6} This is why the *Tanakh* says,

> **"Look! I am laying in Tziyon a stone,**
> **a chosen and precious cornerstone;**
> **and whoever rests his trust on it**
> **will certainly not be humiliated."**^{d}

^{7} Now to you who keep **trusting**, he is **precious**. But to those who are not trusting,

> **"The very stone that the builders rejected**
> **has become the cornerstone;"**^{e}

^{8} also he is

> **a stone that will make people stumble,**
> **a rock over which they will trip.**^{f}

They are **stumbling** at the Word, disobeying it — as had been planned. ^{9} But you are a **chosen people,**^{g} the King's *cohanim*,^{h} a holy nation,^{i} a

---

b Isaiah 40:6-8 c Psalm 34:9(8)

d Isaiah 28:16 e Psalm 118:22
f Isaiah 8:14
g Isaiah 43:20; Deuteronomy 7:6, 10:15
h Exodus 19:6, Isaiah 61:6
i Exodus 19:6

a·cha·rit-ha·ya·mim — End Times
A·do·nai — the LORD, Jehovah
co·ha·nim — priests
Ke·**fa** — Peter
Ru·ach-Ha·Ko·desh — Holy Spirit
sha·lom — peace
Ta·nakh — Hebrew Scriptures, "Old Testament"
Tzi·yon — Zion
Ye·shu·a — Jesus

people for God to possess!*ʲ* Why? In order for you to declare the praises of the One who called you out of darkness into his wonderful light. ¹⁰Once you were **not a people,** but now you are **God's people;** before, you **had not received mercy,** but now you **have received mercy.**ᵏ

¹¹Dear friends, I urge you as **aliens and temporary residents**ˡ not to give in to the desires of your old nature, which keep warring against you; ¹²but to live such good lives among the pagans that even though they now speak against you as evildoers, they will, as a result of seeing your good actions, give glory to God on the Day of his coming. ¹³For the sake of the Lord, submit yourselves to every human authority — whether to the emperor as being supreme, ¹⁴or to governors as being sent by him to punish wrongdoers and praise those who do what is good. ¹⁵For it is God's will that your doing good should silence the ignorant talk of foolish people. ¹⁶Submit as people who are free, but not letting your freedom serve as an excuse for evil; rather, submit as God's slaves. ¹⁷Be respectful of all — keep loving the brotherhood, fearing God and honoring the emperor.

¹⁸Household servants, submit yourselves to your masters, showing them full respect — and not only those who are kind and considerate, but also those who are harsh. ¹⁹For it is a grace when someone, because he is mindful of God, bears up under the pain of undeserved punishment. ²⁰For what credit is there in bearing up under a beating you deserve for doing something wrong? But if you bear up under punishment, even though you have done what is right, God looks on it with favor. ²¹Indeed, this is what you were called to; because the Messiah too suffered, on your behalf, leaving an example so that you should follow in his steps.

²²"He committed no sin,
   nor was any deceit found on his lips."ᵐ

²³When he was insulted, he didn't retaliate with insults; when he suffered, he didn't threaten, but handed them over to him who judges justly. ²⁴**He** himself **bore our sins**ⁿ in his body on the **stake,**ᵒ so that we might die to sins and live for righteousness — **by his wounds you were healed.**ᵖ ²⁵For you used to be **like sheep gone astray,** but now **you have turned to**ᵠ the Shepherd, who watches over you.

3 ¹In the same way, wives, submit to your husbands; so that even if some of them do not believe the Word, they will be won over by your conduct, without your saying anything, ²as they see your respectful and pure behavior. ³Your beauty should not consist in externals such as fancy hairstyles, gold jewelry or what you wear; ⁴rather, let it be the inner character of your heart, with the imperishable quality of a gentle and quiet spirit. In God's sight this is of great value. ⁵This is how the holy women of the past who put their hope in God used to adorn themselves and submit to their husbands, ⁶the way Sarah obeyed Avraham, honoring him as her lord. You are her daughters if you do what is right and do not succumb to fear.

⁷You husbands, likewise, conduct

---

j Isaiah 43:21, Exodus 19:5
k Hosea 2:25(23)
l Genesis 23:4, 47:9; Psalm 39:13(12); 1 Chronicles 29:15

m Isaiah 53:9   *n* Isaiah 53:4, 12
o Deuteronomy 21:22-23
p Isaiah 53:5   *q* Isaiah 53:6

your married lives with understanding. Although your wife may be weaker physically, you should respect her as a fellow-heir of the gift of Life. If you don't, your prayers will be blocked.

⁸Finally, all of you, be one in mind and feeling; love as brothers; and be compassionate and humble-minded, ⁹not repaying evil with evil or insult with insult, but, on the contrary, with blessing. For it is to this that you have been called, so that you may receive a blessing. ¹⁰For

> "Whoever wants to love life
>   and see good days
> must keep his tongue from evil
>   and his lips from speaking
>   deceit,
> ¹¹ turn from evil
>   and do good,
> seek peace
>   and chase after it.
> ¹² For *Adonai* keeps his eyes on the
>   righteous,
> and his ears are open to their
>   prayers;
> but the face of *Adonai* is against
>   those who do evil things."*ʳ*

¹³For who will hurt you if you become zealots for what is good? ¹⁴But even if you do suffer for being righteous, you are blessed! Moreover, **don't fear what they fear or be disturbed,** ¹⁵but **treat** the Messiah **as holy, as Lord** in your hearts;*ˢ* while remaining always ready to give a reasoned answer to anyone who asks you to explain the hope you have in you — yet with humility and fear, ¹⁶keeping your conscience clear, so that when you are spoken against, those who abuse the good behavior flowing from your union with the Messiah may be put to shame. ¹⁷For if God has in fact willed that you

should suffer, it is better that you suffer for doing what is good than for doing what is evil.

¹⁸For the Messiah himself died for sins, once and for all, a righteous person on behalf of unrighteous people, so that he might bring you to God. He was put to death in the flesh but brought to life by the Spirit; ¹⁹and in this form he went and made a proclamation to the imprisoned spirits, ²⁰to those who were disobedient long ago, in the days of Noach, when God waited patiently during the building of the ark, in which a few people — to be specific, eight — were delivered by means of water. ²¹This also prefigures what delivers us now, the water of immersion, which is not the removal of dirt from the body, but one's pledge to keep a good conscience toward God, through the resurrection of Yeshua the Messiah. ²²He has gone into heaven and is **at the right hand of** God,*ᵗ* with angels, authorities and powers subject to him.

4 ¹Therefore, since the Messiah suffered physically, you too are to arm yourselves with the same attitude. For whoever has suffered physically is finished with sin, ²with the result that he lives the rest of his earthly life no longer controlled by human desires, but by God's will. ³For you have spent enough time already living the way the pagans want you to live — in debauchery, lust, drunkenness, orgies, wild parties and forbidden idol-worship. ⁴They think it strange that you don't plunge with them into the same flood

---

ᵗ Psalm 110:1

A·do·nai — the LORD, Jehovah
Av·ra·ham — Abraham
No·ach — Noah
Sa·rah — Sarah
Ye·shu·a — Jesus

ʳ Psalm 34:13-17(12-16)   *ˢ* Isaiah 8:12-13

of dissoluteness, and so they heap insults on you. ⁵But they will have to give an account to him who stands ready to judge the living and the dead. ⁶This is why he was proclaimed to those who have died; it was so that, although physically they would receive the judgment common to all humanity, they might live by the Spirit in the way that God has provided.

⁷The accomplishing of the goal of all things is close at hand. Therefore, keep alert and self-controlled, so that you can pray. ⁸More than anything, keep loving each other actively; because **love covers many sins.**ᵘ ⁹Welcome one another into your homes without grumbling. ¹⁰As each one has received some spiritual gift, he should use it to serve others, like good managers of God's many-sided grace — ¹¹if someone speaks, let him speak God's words; if someone serves, let him do so out of strength that God supplies; so that in everything God may be glorified through Yeshua the Messiah — to him be glory and power forever and ever. *Amen.*

¹²Dear friends, don't regard as strange the fiery ordeal occurring among you to test you, as if something extraordinary were happening to you. ¹³Rather, to the extent that you share the fellowship of the Messiah's sufferings, rejoice; so that you will rejoice even more when his *Sh'khinah* is revealed. ¹⁴If you are being insulted because you bear the name of the Messiah, how blessed you are! For the Spirit of the *Sh'khinah*, that is, the Spirit of God, is resting on you! ¹⁵Let none of you suffer for being a murderer or a thief or an evildoer or a meddler in other people's affairs. ¹⁶But if anyone suffers for being Messianic, let him not be ashamed; but let him bring glory to God by the way he bears this name. ¹⁷For the time has come for the judgment to begin. It begins with the household of God; and if it starts with us, what will the outcome be for those who are disobeying God's Good News? —

¹⁸ **"If the righteous is barely delivered,**

where will the ungodly and sinful end up?"ᵛ

¹⁹So let those who are suffering according to God's will entrust themselves to a faithful Creator by continuing to do what is good.

5 ¹Therefore, I urge the congregation leaders among you, as a fellow-leader and witness to the Messiah's sufferings, as well as a sharer in the glory to be revealed: ²shepherd the flock of God that is in your care, exercising oversight not out of constraint, but willingly, as God wants; and not out of a desire for dishonest gain, but with enthusiasm; ³also not as *macher*s domineering over those in your care, but as people who become examples to the flock. ⁴Then, when the Chief Shepherd appears, you will receive glory as your unfading crown.

⁵Likewise, you who are less experienced, submit to leaders. Further, all of you should clothe yourselves in humility toward one another, because

God opposes the arrogant,
but to the humble he gives grace.ʷ

⁶Therefore, humble yourselves under the mighty hand of God, so that at the right time he may lift you up. ⁷Throw all your anxieties upon him, because he cares about you.

⁸Stay sober, stay alert! Your enemy, the Adversary, stalks about like a

---

u Proverbs 10:12

v Proverbs 11:31   *w* Proverbs 3:34

roaring lion looking for someone to devour. ⁹Stand against him, firm in your trust, knowing that your brothers throughout the world are going through the same kinds of suffering. ¹⁰You will have to suffer only a little while; after that, God, who is full of grace, the one who called you to his eternal glory in union with the Messiah, will himself restore, establish and strengthen you and make you firm. ¹¹To him be the power forever and ever. *Amen.*

¹²Through Sila, whom I regard as a faithful brother, I have written you briefly, encouraging you and giving my witness that this is God's true grace. Stand firm in it!

¹³Your sister congregation in Babylon, chosen along with you, sends greetings to you, as does my son Mark. ¹⁴Greet each other with a kiss of love.

"*Shalom aleikhem!*" to all who belong to the Messiah.

A·men — So be it

ma·cher — self-important activist, "big wheel"

Sha·lom a·lei·khem! — Peace be upon you(pl.)! (greeting)

Sh'khi·nah — the manifest glorious presence of God

Si·la — Silas

Ye·shu·a — Jesus

2 KEFA (2 PETER)

1 ¹ From: Shim'on Kefa, a slave and emissary of Yeshua the Messiah

To: Those who, through the righteousness of our God and of our Deliverer Yeshua the Messiah, have been given the same kind of trust as ours:

² May grace and *shalom* be yours in full measure, as you come to a full knowledge of God and Yeshua our Lord.

³ God's power has given us everything we need for life and godliness, through our knowing the One who called us to his own glory and goodness. ⁴ By these he has given us valuable and superlatively great promises, so that through them you might come to share in God's nature and escape the corruption which evil desires have brought into the world.

⁵ For this very reason, try your hardest to furnish your faith with goodness, goodness with knowledge, ⁶ knowledge with self-control, self-control with perseverance, perseverance with godliness, ⁷ godliness with brotherly affection, and brotherly affection with love. ⁸ For if you have these qualities in abundance, they keep you from being barren and unfruitful in the knowledge of our Lord Yeshua the Messiah. ⁹ Indeed, whoever lacks them is blind, so shortsighted that he forgets that his past sins have been washed away. ¹⁰ Therefore, brothers, try even harder to make your being called and chosen a certainty. For if you keep doing this, you will never stumble. ¹¹ Thus you will be generously supplied with everything you need to enter the eternal Kingdom of our Lord and Deliverer, Yeshua the Messiah.

¹² For this reason, I will always remind you about these things, even though you know them and are firmly established in the truth you already have. ¹³ And I consider it right to keep stirring you up with reminders, as long as I am in the tent of this body. ¹⁴ I know that I will soon lay aside this tent of mine, as our Lord Yeshua the Messiah has made clear to me. ¹⁵ And I will do my best to see that after my exodus, you will be able to remember these things at all times.

¹⁶ For when we made known to you the power and the coming of our Lord Yeshua the Messiah, we did not rely on cunningly contrived myths. On the contrary, we saw his majesty with our own eyes. ¹⁷ For we were there when he received honor and glory from God the Father; and the voice came to him from the grandeur of the *Sh'khinah*, saying, "This is my son, whom I love; I am well pleased with him!" ¹⁸ We heard this voice come out of heaven when we were with him on the holy mountain.

¹⁹ Yes, we have the prophetic Word made very certain. You will do well to pay attention to it as to a light shining

in a dark, murky place, until the Day dawns and the Morning Star rises in your hearts. ²⁰ First of all, understand this: no prophecy of Scripture is to be interpreted by an individual on his own; ²¹ for never has a prophecy come as a result of human willing — on the contrary, people moved by the *Ruach HaKodesh* spoke a message from God.

2 ¹ But among the people there were also false prophets, just as there will be false teachers among you. Under false pretenses they will introduce destructive heresies, even denying the Master who bought them, and thus bring on themselves swift destruction. ² Many will follow their debaucheries; and because of them, the true Way will be maligned. ³ In their greed they will exploit you with fabricated stories.

Their punishment, decreed long ago, is not idle; their destruction is not asleep! ⁴ For God did not spare the angels who sinned; on the contrary, he put them in gloomy dungeons lower than Sh'ol to be held for judgment. ⁵ And he did not spare the ancient world; on the contrary, he preserved Noach, a herald of righteousness, with seven others, and brought the Flood upon a world of ungodly people. ⁶ And he condemned the cities of S'dom and 'Amora, reducing them to ashes and ruin, as a warning to those in the future who would live ungodly lives; ⁷ but he rescued Lot, a righteous man who was distressed by the debauchery of those unprincipled people; ⁸ for the wicked deeds which that righteous man saw and heard, as he lived among them, tormented his righteous heart day after day. ⁹ So the Lord knows how to rescue the godly from trials and how to hold the wicked until the Day of Judgment while continuing to punish them, ¹⁰ especially those who follow their old

natures in lust for filth and who despise authority.

Presumptuous and self-willed, these false teachers do not tremble at insulting angelic beings; ¹¹ whereas angels, though stronger and more powerful, do not bring before the Lord an insulting charge against them. ¹² But these people, acting without thinking, like animals without reason, born to be captured and destroyed, insult things about which they know nothing. When they are destroyed, their destruction will be total — ¹³ they will be paid back harm as wages for the harm they are doing.

Their idea of pleasure is carousing in broad daylight; they are spots and defects revelling in their deceptions as they share meals with you — ¹⁴ for they have eyes always on the lookout for a woman who will commit adultery, eyes that never stop sinning; and they have a heart that has exercised itself in greed; so that they seduce unstable people. What a cursed brood!

¹⁵ These people have left the straight way and wandered off to follow the way of Bil'am Ben-B'or, who loved the wages of doing harm ¹⁶ but was rebuked for his sin — a dumb beast of burden spoke out with a human voice and restrained the prophet's insanity! ¹⁷ Waterless springs they are, mists driven by a gust of wind; for them has been reserved the blackest darkness.

'A·mo·**ra** — Gomorrah
Bil·'**am** Ben-B'**or** — Balaam, the son of Beor
No·ach — Noah
Ru·ach-Ha·Ko·desh — Holy Spirit
S'**dom** — Sodom
sha·lom — peace
Shim·'on Ke·**fa** — Simon Peter
Sh'khi·nah — the manifest glorious presence of God
Sh'ol Sheol, Hades, hell
Ye·shu·a — Jesus

¹⁸ Mouthing grandiosities of nothingness, they play on the desires of the old nature, in order to seduce with debaucheries people who have just begun to escape from those whose way of life is wrong. ¹⁹ They promise them freedom, but they themselves are slaves of corruption; for a person is slave to whatever has defeated him. ²⁰ Indeed, if they have once escaped the pollutions of the world through knowing our Lord and Deliverer, Yeshua the Messiah, and then have again become entangled and defeated by them, their latter condition has become worse than their former. ²¹ It would have been better for them not to have known the Way of righteousness than, fully knowing, to turn from the holy command delivered to them. ²² What has happened to them accords with the true proverb, **"A dog returns to its own vomit."**[a] Yes, "The pig washed itself, only to wallow in the mud!"

3 ¹ Dear friends, I am writing you now this second letter; and in both letters I am trying to arouse you to wholesome thinking by means of reminders; ² so that you will keep in mind the predictions of the holy prophets and the command given by the Lord and Deliverer through your emissaries.

³ First, understand this: during the Last Days, scoffers will come, following their own desires ⁴ and asking, "Where is this promised 'coming' of his? For our fathers have died, and everything goes on just as it has since the beginning of creation." ⁵ But, wanting so much to be right about this, they overlook the fact that it was by God's Word that long ago there were heavens, and there was land which arose out of water and existed between the waters, ⁶ and that by means of these things the world of that time was flooded with water and destroyed. ⁷ It is by that same Word that the present heavens and earth, having been preserved, are being kept for fire until the Day of Judgment, when ungodly people will be destroyed.

⁸ Moreover, dear friends, do not ignore this: with the Lord, one day is like a thousand years and **a thousand years like one day.**[b] ⁹ The Lord is not slow in keeping his promise, as some people think of slowness; on the contrary, he is patient with you; for it is not his purpose that anyone should be destroyed, but that everyone should turn from his sins. ¹⁰ However, the Day of the Lord will come "like a thief." On that Day the heavens will disappear with a roar, the elements will melt and disintegrate, and the earth and everything in it will be burned up.

¹¹ Since everything is going to be destroyed like this, what kind of people should you be? You should lead holy and godly lives, ¹² as you wait for the Day of God and work to hasten its coming. That Day will bring on the destruction of the heavens by fire, and the elements will melt from the heat; ¹³ but we, following along with his promise, wait for **new heavens and a new earth,**[c] in which righteousness will be at home. ¹⁴ Therefore, dear friends, as you look for these things, do everything you can to be found by him without spot or defect and at peace. ¹⁵ And think of our Lord's patience as deliverance, just as our dear brother Sha'ul also wrote you, following the wisdom God gave him. ¹⁶ Indeed, he speaks about these things in all his letters. They contain some things that are hard to understand, things which

---

a Proverbs 26:11

b Psalm 90:4   *c* Isaiah 65:17, 66:22

the uninstructed and unstable distort, to their own destruction, as they do the other Scriptures.

[17] But you, dear friends, since you know this in advance, guard yourselves; so that you will not be led away by the errors of the wicked and fall from your own secure position. [18] And keep grow-ing in grace and knowledge of our Lord and Deliverer, Yeshua the Messiah. To him be the glory, both now and forever! *Amen.*

A · *men* — So be it
Sha·'ul — Saul (Paul)
Ye·shu·a — Jesus

1 YOCHANAN (1 JOHN)

1 ¹ The Word, which gives life!
He existed from the beginning.
We have heard him,
we have seen him with our eyes,
we have contemplated him,
we have touched him with
our hands!

² The life appeared,
and we have seen it.
We are testifying to it,
and announcing it to you—
eternal life!

He was with the Father,
and he appeared to us.
³ What we have seen and heard,
we are proclaiming to you;
so that you too
may have fellowship with us.
Our fellowship
is with the Father
and with his Son,
Yeshua the Messiah.

⁴ We are writing these things
so that our joy may be
complete

⁵ And this is the message which we have heard from him and proclaim to you: God is light, and there is no darkness in him — none! ⁶ If we claim to have fellowship with him while we are walking in the darkness, we are lying and not living out the truth. ⁷ But if we are walking in the light, as he is in the light, then we have fellowship with each other, and the blood of his Son Yeshua purifies us from all sin.

⁸ If we claim not to have sin, we are deceiving ourselves, and the truth is not in us. ⁹ If we acknowledge our sins, then, since he is trustworthy and just, he will forgive them and purify us from all wrongdoing.

¹⁰ If we claim we have not been sinning, we are making him out to be a liar, and his Word is not in us.

2 ¹ My children, I am writing you these things so that you won't sin. But if anyone does sin, we have Yeshua the Messiah, the *Tzaddik*, who pleads our cause with the Father. ² Also, he is the *kapparah* for our sins — and not only for ours, but also for those of the whole world.

³ The way we can be sure we know him is if we are obeying his commands. ⁴ Anyone who says, "I know him," but doesn't obey his commands is a liar — the truth is not in him. ⁵ But if someone does what he says, then truly love for God has been brought to its goal in him. This is how we are sure that we are united with him. ⁶ A person who claims to be continuing in union with him ought to conduct his life the way he did.

⁷ Dear friends, I am not writing you a new command. On the contrary, it is an old command, which you have had from the beginning; the old command is the message which you have heard before. ⁸ Yet I am writing you a new command, and its truth is seen both in

him and in you, because the darkness is passing away and the true light is already shining. ⁹Anyone who claims to be in this light while hating his brother is still in the dark. ¹⁰The person who keeps loving his brother remains in the light, and there is nothing in him that could make him trip. ¹¹But the person who hates his brother is in the dark — yes, he is walking in the dark, and he doesn't know where he is going, because the darkness has blinded his eyes.

¹² You children, I am writing you
because your sins have been forgiven
for his sake.

¹³ You fathers, I am writing you
because you have known him who
has existed from the beginning.

You young people, I am writing you
because you have overcome the Evil
One.

¹⁴ You children, I have written you
because you have known the Father.

You fathers, I have written you
because you have known him who
has existed from the beginning.

You young people, I have written you
because you are strong —
the Word of God remains in you,
and you have overcome the Evil One.

¹⁵Do not love the world or the things of the world. If someone loves the world, then love for the Father is not in him; ¹⁶because all the things of the world — the desires of the old nature, the desires of the eyes, and the pretensions of life — are not from the Father but from the world. ¹⁷And the world is passing away, along with its desires. But whoever does God's will remains forever.

¹⁸Children, this is the Last Hour. You have heard that an Anti-Messiah is coming; and in fact, many anti-Messiahs have arisen now — which is how we know that this is the Last Hour. ¹⁹They went out from us, but they weren't part of us; for had they been part of us, they would have remained with us.

²⁰But you have received the Messiah's anointing from *HaKadosh*, and you know all this. ²¹It is not because you don't know the truth that I have written to you, but because you do know it, and because no lie has its origin in the truth. ²²Who is a liar at all, if not the person who denies that Yeshua is the Messiah? Such a person is an anti-Messiah — he is denying the Father and the Son. ²³Everyone who denies the Son is also without the Father, but the person who acknowledges the Son has the Father as well. ²⁴Let what you heard from the beginning remain in you. If what you heard from the beginning remains in you, you will also remain in union with both the Son and the Father. ²⁵And this is what he has promised us: eternal life.

²⁶I have written you these things about the people who are trying to deceive you. ²⁷As for you, the Messianic anointing you received from the Father remains in you, so that you have no need for anyone to teach you. On the contrary, as his Messianic anointing continues to teach you about all things, and is true, not a counterfeit, so, just as he taught you, remain united with him.

²⁸And now, children, remain united with him; so that when he appears, we may have confidence and not shrink back from him in shame at his coming. ²⁹If you know that he is righteous, you

Ha·Ka·dosh — the Holy One
kap·pa·rah — atonement
Tzad·dik — Righteous One
Ye·shu·a — Jesus

should also know that he is the Father of everyone who does what is right.

3 ¹See what love the Father has lavished on us in letting us be called God's children! For that is what we are. The reason the world does not know us is that it has not known him. ²Dear friends, we are God's children now; and it has not yet been made clear what we will become. We do know that when he appears, we will be like him; because we will see him as he really is.

³And everyone who has this hope in him continues purifying himself, since God is pure. ⁴Everyone who keeps sinning is violating *Torah* — indeed, sin is violation of *Torah*. ⁵You know that he appeared in order to take away sins, and that there is no sin in him. ⁶So no one who remains united with him continues sinning; everyone who does continue sinning has neither seen him nor known him.

⁷Children, don't let anyone deceive you — it is the person that keeps on doing what is right who is righteous, just as God is righteous. ⁸The person who keeps on sinning is from the Adversary, because from the very beginning the Adversary has kept on sinning. It was for this very reason that the son of God appeared, to destroy these doings of the Adversary. ⁹No one who has God as his Father keeps on sinning, because the seed planted by God remains in him. That is, he cannot continue sinning, because he has God as his Father. ¹⁰Here is how one can distinguish clearly between God's children and those of the Adversary: everyone who does not continue doing what is right is not from God.

Likewise, anyone who fails to keep loving his brother is not from God. ¹¹For this is the message which you have heard from the beginning: that we should love each other ¹²and not be like Kayin, who was from the Evil One and murdered his own brother. Why did he murder him? Because his own actions were evil, and his brother's were righteous. ¹³Don't be amazed, brothers, if the world hates you. ¹⁴We, for our part, know that we have passed from death to life because we keep loving the brothers. The person who fails to keep on loving is still under the power of death. ¹⁵Everyone who hates his brother is a murderer, and you know that no murderer has eternal life in him.

¹⁶The way that we have come to know love is through his having laid down his life for us. And we ought to lay down our lives for the brothers! ¹⁷If someone has worldly possessions and sees his brother in need, yet closes his heart against him, how can he be loving God? ¹⁸Children, let us not love with words and talk, but with actions and in reality!

¹⁹Here is how we will know that we are from the truth and will set our hearts at rest in his presence: ²⁰if our hearts know something against us, God is greater than our hearts, and he knows everything. ²¹Dear friends, if our hearts know nothing against us, we have confidence in approaching God; ²²then, whatever we ask for, we receive from him; because we are obeying his commands and doing the things that please him.

²³This is his command: that we are to trust in the person and power of his Son Yeshua the Messiah and to keep loving one another, just as he commanded us. ²⁴Those who obey his commands remain united with him and he with them.

Here is how we know that he remains united with us: by the Spirit whom he

4 gave us. ¹Dear friends, don't trust every spirit. On the contrary, test the spirits to see whether they are from God; because many false prophets have gone out into the world. ²Here is how you recognize the Spirit of God: every spirit which acknowledges that Yeshua the Messiah came as a human being is from God, ³and every spirit which does not acknowledge Yeshua is not from God — in fact, this is the spirit of the Anti-Messiah. You have heard that he is coming. Well, he's here now, in the world already!

⁴You, children, are from God and have overcome the false prophets, because he who is in you is greater than he who is in the world. ⁵They are from the world; therefore, they speak from the world's viewpoint; and the world listens to them. ⁶We are from God. Whoever knows God listens to us; whoever is not from God doesn't listen to us. This is how we distinguish the Spirit of truth from the spirit of error.

⁷Beloved friends, let us love one another; because love is from God; and everyone who loves has God as his Father and knows God. ⁸Those who do not love, do not know God; because God is love. ⁹Here is how God showed his love among us: God sent his only Son into the world, so that through him we might have life. ¹⁰Here is what love is: not that we have loved God, but that he loved us and sent his Son to be the *kapparah* for our sins.

¹¹Beloved friends, if this is how God loved us, we likewise ought to love one another. ¹²No one has ever seen God; if we love one another, God remains united with us, and our love for him has been brought to its goal in us. ¹³Here is how we know that we remain united with him and he with us: he has given to us from his own Spirit. ¹⁴Moreover, we have seen and we testify that the Father has sent his Son as Deliverer of the world. ¹⁵If someone acknowledges that Yeshua is the Son of God, God remains united with him, and he with God.

¹⁶Also we have come to know and trust the love that God has for us. God is love; and those who remain in this love remain united with God, and God remains united with them.

¹⁷Here is how love has been brought to maturity with us: as the Messiah is, so are we in the world. This gives us confidence for the Day of Judgment. ¹⁸There is no fear in love. On the contrary, love that has achieved its goal gets rid of fear, because fear has to do with punishment; the person who keeps fearing has not been brought to maturity in regard to love.

¹⁹We ourselves love now because he loved us first. ²⁰If anyone says, "I love God," and hates his brother, he is a liar. For if a person does not love his brother, whom he has seen, then he cannot love God, whom he has not seen. ²¹Yes, this is the command we have from him: whoever loves God must love his brother too.

5 ¹Everyone who believes that Yeshua is the Messiah has God as his father, and everyone who loves a father loves his offspring too. ²Here is how we know that we love God's children: when we love God, we also do what he commands. ³For loving God means obeying his commands. Moreover, his commands are not burdensome, ⁴because everything which has God as its Father overcomes the world. And this is what victoriously overcomes the world: our trust. ⁵Who does overcome the world if not the person who believes that Yeshua is the Son of God?

⁶He is the one who came by means of water and blood, Yeshua the Messiah —

---

kap·pa·rah — atonement, propitiation
Ka·yin — Cain
To·rah — Teaching, "Law"; Pentateuch
Ye·shu·a — Jesus

not with water only, but with the water and the blood. And the Spirit bears witness, because the Spirit is the truth. ⁷There are three witnesses — ⁸the Spirit, the water and the blood — and these three are in agreement. ⁹If we accept human witness, God's witness is stronger, because it is the witness which God has given about his Son. ¹⁰Those who keep trusting in the Son of God have this witness in them. Those who do not keep trusting God have made him out to be a liar, because they have not trusted in the witness which God has given about his Son. ¹¹And this is the witness: God has given us eternal life, and this life is in his Son. ¹²Those who have the Son have the life; those who do not have the Son of God do not have the life. ¹³I have written you these things so that you may know that you have eternal life — you who keep trusting in the person and power of the Son of God.

¹⁴This is the confidence we have in his presence: if we ask anything that accords with his will, he hears us. ¹⁵And if we know that he hears us — whatever we ask — then we know that we have what we have asked from him.

¹⁶If anyone sees his brother committing a sin that does not lead to death, he will ask; and God will give him life for those whose sinning does not lead to death. There is sin that does lead to death; I am not saying he should pray about that. ¹⁷All wrongdoing is sin, but there is sin that does not lead to death.

¹⁸We know that everyone who has God as his Father does not go on sinning; on the contrary, the Son born of God protects him, and the Evil One does not touch him.

¹⁹We know that we are from God, and that the whole world lies in the power of the Evil One.

²⁰And we know that the Son of God has come and has given us discernment, so that we may know who is genuine; moreover, we are united with the One who is genuine, united with his Son Yeshua the Messiah. He is the genuine God and eternal life.

²¹Children, guard yourselves against false gods!

2 YOCHANAN (2 JOHN)

¹ From: The Elder

To: The chosen lady and her children, whom I love in truth — and not only I but also all who have come to know the truth — ²because of the Truth which remains united with us and will be with us forever:

³Grace, mercy and *shalom* will be with us from God the Father and from Yeshua the Messiah, the Son of the Father, in truth and love.

⁴I was very happy when I found some of your children living in truth, just as the Father commanded us. ⁵And now, dear lady, I am requesting that we love one another — not as if this were a new command I am writing you, for it is the one which we have had from the beginning. ⁶Moreover, love is this: that we should live according to his commands. This is the command, as you people have heard from the beginning; live by it!

⁷For many deceivers have gone out into the world, people who do not acknowledge Yeshua the Messiah's coming as a human being. Such a person is a deceiver and an anti-Messiah. ⁸Watch yourselves, so that you won't lose what you have worked for, but will receive your full reward. ⁹Everyone who goes ahead and does not remain true to what the Messiah has taught does not have God. Those who remain true to his teaching have both the Father and the Son. ¹⁰If someone comes to you and does not bring this teaching, don't welcome him into your home. Don't even say, "*Shalom!*" to him; ¹¹for the person who says, "*Shalom!*" to him shares in his evil deeds.

¹²Although I have much to write you people, I would rather not use paper and ink. Instead, I hope to come and see you and to talk with you face to face, so that our joy may be complete.

¹³The children of your chosen sister send you their greetings.

Sha·lom! — Peace! (a greeting)
Ye·shu·a — Jesus

3 YOCHANAN (3 JOHN)

¹From: The Elder

To: Dear Gaius, whom I love in truth:

²Dear friend, I am praying that everything prosper with you and that you be in good health, as I know you are prospering spiritually. ³For I was so happy when some brothers came and testified how faithful you are to the truth, as you continue living in the truth. ⁴Nothing gives me greater joy than hearing that my children are living in the truth.

⁵Dear friend, you are faithful in all the work you are doing for the brothers, even when they are strangers to you. ⁶They have testified to your love in front of the congregation. You will be doing well if you send them on their way in a manner worthy of God, ⁷since it was for the sake of *HaShem* that they went out without accepting anything from the *Goyim*. ⁸It is we, therefore, who should support such people; so that we may share in their work for the truth.

⁹I wrote something to the congregation; but Diotrephes, who likes to be the *macher* among them, doesn't recognize our authority. ¹⁰So if I come, I will bring up everything he is doing, including his spiteful and groundless gossip about us. And as if that weren't enough for him, he refuses to recognize the brothers' authority either; moreover, he stops those who want to do so and tries to drive them out of the congregation!

¹¹Dear friend, don't imitate the bad, but the good. Those who do what is good are from God; those who do what is bad are not from God.

¹²Everyone speaks well of Demetrius, and so does the truth itself. We vouch for him, and you know that our testimony is true.

¹³I have much to write you, but I don't want to write with pen and ink; ¹⁴however, I am hoping to see you very soon, and we will speak face to face.

¹⁵*Shalom* to you. Your friends send you their greetings. Greet each of our friends by name.

Y'HUDAH (JUDE)

¹From: Y'hudah, a slave of Yeshua the Messiah and a brother of Ya'akov

To: Those who have been called, who are loved by God the Father and kept for Yeshua the Messiah:

²May mercy, love and *shalom* be yours in full measure.

³Dear friends, I was busily at work writing to you about the salvation we share, when I found it necessary to write, urging you to keep contending earnestly for the faith which was once and for all passed on to God's people. ⁴For certain individuals, the ones written about long ago as being meant for this condemnation, have wormed their way in — ungodly people who pervert God's grace into a license for debauchery and disown our only Master and Lord, Yeshua the Messiah.

⁵Since you already know all this, my purpose is only to remind you that *Adonai*, who once delivered the people from Egypt, later destroyed those who did not trust. ⁶And the angels that did not keep within their original authority, but abandoned their proper sphere, he has kept in darkness, bound with everlasting chains for the Judgment of the Great Day. ⁷And S'dom, 'Amora and the surrounding cities, following a pattern like theirs, committing sexual sins and perversions, lie exposed as a warning of the everlasting fire awaiting those who must undergo punishment.

⁸Likewise, these people, with their visions, defile their own flesh, despise godly authority and insult angelic beings. ⁹When Mikha'el, one of the ruling angels, took issue with the Adversary, arguing over the body of Moshe, he did not dare bring against him an insulting charge, but said, "May *Adonai* rebuke you." ¹⁰However, these people insult anything they don't understand; and what they do understand naturally, without thinking, like animals — by these things they are destroyed!

¹¹Woe to them, in that they have walked the road of Kayin, they have given themselves over for money to the error of Bil'am, they have been destroyed in the rebellion of Korach.

A·dam — Adam
A·do·nai — the LORD, Jehovah
'A·mo·ra — Gomorrah
Bil·'am — Balaam
Cha·noch — Enoch
Go·yim — Gentiles, nations, pagans
Ha·Shem — "the Name" (i.e., God)
Ka·yin — Cain
Ko·rach — Korah
ma·cher — self-important activist, "big wheel", "operator"
Mi·kha·'el — Michael
Mo·she — Moses
S'dom — Sodom
Sha·lom! — Peace! (a greeting)
Ya·'a·kov — James
Ye·shu·a — Jesus
Y'hu·dah — Jude

¹²These men are filthy spots at your festive gatherings meant to foster love; they share your meals without a qualm, while caring only for themselves. They are waterless clouds carried along by the winds; trees without fruit even in autumn, and doubly dead because they have been uprooted; ¹³savage sea-waves heaving forth their shameful deeds like foam; wandering stars for whom the blackest darkness has been reserved forever.

¹⁴Moreover, Chanoch, in the seventh generation starting with Adam, also prophesied about these men, saying, "Look! *Adonai* came with his myriads of holy ones ¹⁵to execute judgment against everyone, that is, to convict all the godless for their godless deeds which they have done in such a godless way, and for all the harsh words these godless sinners have spoken against him."

¹⁶These people are grumblers and complainers, they follow their evil passions, their mouths speak grandiosities, and they flatter others to gain advantage.

¹⁷But you, dear friends, keep in mind the words spoken in advance by the emissaries of our Lord Yeshua the Messiah. ¹⁸They told you, "During the *acharit-hayamim* there will be scoffers following their own godless passions." ¹⁹These are the people who cause divisions. They are controlled by their impulses, because they don't have the Spirit.

²⁰But you, dear friends, build yourselves up in your most holy faith, and pray in union with the *Ruach Ha-Kodesh*. ²¹Thus keep yourselves in God's love, as you wait for our Lord Yeshua the Messiah to give you the mercy that leads to eternal life.

²²Rebuke some who are disputing; ²³save others, snatching them out of the fire; and to yet others, show mercy, but with fear, hating even the clothes stained by their vices.

²⁴Now,

to the one who can keep you from falling
and set you without defect and full of joy
in the presence of his *Sh'khinah* —
²⁵to God alone, our Deliverer,
through Yeshua the Messiah, our Lord —
be glory, majesty, power and authority
before all time, now and forever.

Amen.

THE

REVELATION

OF YESHUA THE MESSIAH TO YOCHANAN (JOHN)

1 ¹This is the revelation which God gave to Yeshua the Messiah, so that he could show his servants what must happen very soon. He communicated it by sending his angel to his servant Yochanan, ²who bore witness to the Word of God and to the testimony of Yeshua the Messiah, as much as he saw. ³Blessed are the reader and hearers of the words of this prophecy, provided they obey the things written in it! For the time is near!

⁴From: Yochanan

To: The seven Messianic communities in the province of Asia:

Grace and *shalom* to you from the One who is, who was and who is coming; from the sevenfold Spirit before his throne; ⁵and from Yeshua the Messiah, the faithful witness, the firstborn from the dead and the ruler of the earth's kings.

To him, the one who loves us, who has freed us from our sins at the cost of his blood, ⁶who has caused us to be a kingdom, that is, *cohanim* for God, his Father — to him be the glory and the rulership forever and ever. *Amen.*

⁷ **Look! He is coming with the clouds!**[a]
Every eye will see him,
including those who **pierced him;**
and **all the tribes of the Land will**
mourn him.[b]

Yes! *Amen!*

⁸ "I am the 'A' and the 'Z'," says *Adonai*,
God of heaven's armies,
the One who is, who was and who is coming.

⁹I, Yochanan, am a brother of yours and a fellow-sharer in the suffering, kingship and perseverance that come from being united with Yeshua. I had been exiled to the island called Patmos for having proclaimed the message of God and borne witness to Yeshua. ¹⁰I came to be, in the Spirit, on the Day of the Lord; and I heard behind me a loud voice, like a trumpet, ¹¹saying, "Write down what you see on a scroll, and send it to the seven Messianic communities — Ephesus, Smyrna, Pergamum, Thyatira, Sardis, Philadelphia and Laodicea!" ¹²I turned around to see who was speaking to me; and when I had turned, I saw seven gold *menorah*s; ¹³and among the *menorah*s

a·cha·rit-ha·ya·mim — Last Times
A·do·nai — the LORD, Jehovah
A·men — So be it
Cha·noch — Enoch
co·ha·nim — priests
me·no·rah — lampstand
Ru·ach-Ha·Ko·desh — Holy Spirit
sha·lom — peace, Peace! (a greeting)
Sh'khi·nah — the glorious manifest presence of God
Ye·shu·a — Jesus
Yo·cha·nan — John

---

a Daniel 7:13   *b* Zechariah 12:10, 12, 14

was someone like a Son of Man,*c* wearing a robe down to his feet and a gold band around his chest. ¹⁴His head and hair were as white as snow-white wool, his eyes like a fiery flame, ¹⁵his feet like burnished brass refined in a furnace, and his voice like the sound of rushing waters.*d* ¹⁶In his right hand he held seven stars, out of his mouth went a sharp double-edged sword, and his face was like the sun shining in full strength.

¹⁷When I saw him, I fell down at his feet like a dead man. He placed his right hand upon me and said, "Don't be afraid! I am the First and the Last, ¹⁸the Living One. I was dead, but look! — I am alive forever and ever! And I hold the keys to Death and Sh'ol. ¹⁹So write down what you see, both what is now, and what will happen afterwards. ²⁰Here is the secret meaning of the seven stars you saw in my right hand, and of the seven gold *menorah*s: the seven stars are the angels of the seven Messianic communities, and the seven *menorah*s are the seven Messianic communities.

2 ¹"To the angel of the Messianic community in Ephesus, write: 'Here is the message from the one who holds the seven stars in his right hand and walks among the seven gold *menorah*s: ²"I know what you have been doing, how hard you have worked, how you have persevered, and how you can't stand wicked people; so you tested those who call themselves emissaries but aren't — and you found them to be liars. ³You are persevering, and you have suffered for my sake without growing weary. ⁴But I have this against you: you have lost the love you had at first. ⁵Therefore, remember

where you were before you fell, and turn from this sin, and do what you used to do before. Otherwise, I will come to you and remove your *menorah* from its place — if you don't turn from your sin! ⁶But you have this in your favor: you hate what the Nicolaitans do — I hate it too. ⁷Those who have ears, let them hear what the Spirit is saying to the Messianic communities. To him winning the victory I will give the right to eat from the Tree of Life which is in God's *Gan-Eden*.'"

⁸"To the angel of the Messianic community in Smyrna, write: 'Here is the message from the First and the Last, who died and came alive again: ⁹"I know how you are suffering and how poor you are (though in fact you are rich!), and I know the insults of those who call themselves Jews but aren't — on the contrary, they are a synagogue of the Adversary. ¹⁰Don't be afraid of what you are about to suffer. Look, the Adversary is going to have some of you thrown in prison, in order to put you to the test; and you will face an ordeal for ten days. Remain faithful, even to the point of death; and I will give you life as your crown. ¹¹Those who have ears, let them hear what the Spirit is saying to the Messianic communities. He who wins the victory will not be hurt at all by the second death.'"

¹²"To the angel of the Messianic community in Pergamum, write: 'Here is the message from the one who has the sharp double-edged sword: ¹³"I know where you are living, there where the Adversary's throne is. Yet you are holding onto my name. You did not deny trusting me even at the time when my faithful witness Antipas was put to death in your town, there where the Adversary lives. ¹⁴Nevertheless, I have a few things against you: you have some people who hold to the teaching

---

c Daniel 7:13

d Daniel 10:5-6; Ezekiel 1:24, 43:2

of Bil'am, who taught Balak to set a trap for the people of Israel, so that they would eat food that had been sacrificed to idols and commit sexual sin. [15] Likewise, you too have people who hold to the teaching of the Nicolaitans. [16] Therefore, turn from these sins. Otherwise, I will come to you very soon and make war against them with the sword of my mouth. [17] Those who have ears, let them hear what the Spirit is saying to the Messianic communities. To him winning the victory I will give some of the hidden manna. I will also give him a white stone, on which is written a new name that nobody knows except the one receiving it.'"

[18] "To the angel of the Messianic community in Thyatira, write: 'Here is the message from the Son of God, whose eyes are like a fiery flame and whose feet are like burnished brass: [19] "I know what you are doing, your love, trust, service and perseverance. And I know that you are doing more now than before. [20] But I have this against you: you continue to tolerate that Izevel woman, the one who claims to be a prophet, but is teaching and deceiving my servants to commit sexual sin and eat food that has been sacrificed to idols. [21] I gave her time to turn from her sin, but she doesn't want to repent of her immorality. [22] So I am throwing her into a sickbed; and those who commit adultery with her I am throwing into great trouble, unless they turn from the sins connected with what she does; [23] and I will strike her children dead! Then all the Messianic communities will know that I am the one who searches minds and hearts, and that I will give to each of you what your deeds deserve. [24] But to the rest of you in Thyatira, to those who do not hold this teaching, who have not learned

what some people call the 'deep things' of the Adversary, I say this: I am not loading you up with another burden; [25] only hold fast to what you have until I come. [26] To him who wins the victory and does what I want until the goal is reached,

I will give him authority over the nations;
[27] he will rule them with a staff of iron and dash them to pieces like pottery,[e]

[28] just as I have received authority from my Father. I will also give him the morning star. [29] Those who have ears, let them hear what the Spirit is saying to the Messianic communities.'"

3 [1] "To the angel of the Messianic community in Sardis, write: 'Here is the message from the one who has the sevenfold Spirit of God and the seven stars: "I know what you are doing — you have a reputation for being alive, but in fact you are dead! [2] Wake up, and strengthen what remains, before it dies too! For I have found what you are doing incomplete in the sight of my God. [3] So remember what you received and heard, and obey it, and turn from your sin! For if you don't wake up, I will come like a thief; and you don't know at what moment I will come upon you. [4] Nevertheless, you do have a few people in Sardis who have not soiled their clothes; and they will walk with me, clothed in white, because they are worthy. [5] He who wins the victory will, like them, be dressed in

---

[e] Psalm 2:8-9

===

Ba·lak — Balak
Bil·'am — Balaam
Gan-E·den — Paradise
I·ze·vel — Jezebel
me·no·rah — lampstand
Sh'ol — Sheol, Hades, hell

white clothing; and I will not blot his name out of the Book of Life; in fact, I will acknowledge him individually before my Father and before his angels. ⁶Those who have ears, let them hear what the Spirit is saying to the Messianic communities."'

⁷"To the angel of the Messianic community in Philadelphia, write: 'Here is the message of *HaKadosh*, the True One, the one who has **the key of David, who, if he opens something, no one else can shut it, and if he closes something, no one else can open it:**ᶠ ⁸"I know what you are doing. Look, I have put in front of you an open door, and no one can shut it. I know that you have but little power, yet you have obeyed my message and have not disowned me. ⁹Here, I will give you some from the synagogue of the Adversary, those who call themselves Jews but aren't — on the contrary, they are lying — see, I will cause them to come and prostrate themselves at your feet, and they will know that I have loved you. ¹⁰Because you did obey my message about persevering, I will keep you from the time of trial coming upon the whole world to put the people living on earth to the test. ¹¹I am coming soon; hold on to what you have, so that no one will take away your crown. ¹²I will make him who wins the victory a pillar in the Temple of my God, and he will never leave it. Also I will write on him the name of my God and the name of my God's city, the new Yerushalayim coming down out of heaven from my God, and my own new name. ¹³Those who have ears, let them hear what the Spirit is saying to the Messianic communities."'

¹⁴"To the angel of the Messianic community in Laodicea, write: 'Here is the message from the *Amen*, the faithful and true witness, the Ruler of God's creation: ¹⁵"I know what you are doing: you are neither cold nor hot. How I wish you were either one or the other! ¹⁶So, because you are lukewarm, neither cold nor hot, I will vomit you out of my mouth! ¹⁷For you keep saying, '**I am rich, I have gotten rich**ᵍ, I don't need a thing!' You don't know that you are the one who is wretched, pitiable, poor, blind and naked! ¹⁸My advice to you is to buy from me gold refined by fire, so that you may be rich; and white clothing, so that you may be dressed and not have to be ashamed of your nakedness; and eyesalve to rub on your eyes, so that you may see. ¹⁹As for me, I rebuke and discipline everyone I love; so exert yourselves, and turn from your sins! ²⁰Here, I'm standing at the door, knocking. If someone hears my voice and opens the door, I will come in to him and eat with him, and he will eat with me. ²¹I will let him who wins the victory sit with me on my throne, just as I myself also won the victory and sat down with my Father on his throne. ²²Those who have ears, let them hear what the Spirit is saying to the Messianic communities."'"

4 ¹After these things, I looked; and there before me was a door standing open in heaven; and the voice like a trumpet which I had heard speaking with me before said, "Come up here, and I will show you what must happen after these things." ²Instantly I was in the Spirit, and there before me in heaven stood a throne, and on the throne someone was sitting. ³The one sitting there gleamed like diamonds and rubies, and a rainbow shining like emerald encircled the throne.

⁴Surrounding the throne were 24 other thrones, and on the thrones sat 24

ᶠ Isaiah 22:22

ᵍ Hosea 12:9

elders dressed in white clothing and wearing gold crowns on their heads. ⁵From the throne came forth lightnings and voices and thunderings; and before the throne were seven flaming torches, which are the sevenfold Spirit of God. ⁶In front of the throne was what looked like a sea of glass, clear as crystal.

In the center, around the throne, were four living beings covered with eyes in front and behind. ⁷**The first** living being was like **a lion, the second** living being was like **an ox, the third** living being had **a face** that looked **human, and the fourth** living being was like a flying **eagle.**^h ⁸**Each** of the four living beings **had six wings**^i and was covered with eyes inside and out; and day and night they never stop saying,

> "Holy, holy, holy is *Adonai,* God of heaven's armies,^j
>
> the One who was, who is and who is coming!"

⁹And whenever the living beings give glory, honor and thanks to the One sitting on the throne, to the One who lives forever and ever, ¹⁰the 24 elders fall down before the One sitting on the throne, who lives forever and ever, and worship him. They throw their crowns in front of the throne and say,

¹¹ "You are worthy, *Adonai Eloheynu,*
> to have glory, honor and power,
> because you created all things —
> yes, because of your will they were created
> and came into being!"

5 ¹Then I saw in the right hand of the One sitting on the throne a scroll with writing on both sides and sealed with seven seals; ²and I saw a mighty angel proclaiming in a loud voice, "Who is worthy to open the scroll and break its seals?" ³But no one in heaven, on earth or under the earth was able to open the scroll or look inside it. ⁴I cried and cried, because no one was found worthy to open the scroll or look inside it. ⁵One of the elders said to me, "Don't cry. Look, the Lion of the tribe of Y'hudah, the Root of David, has won the right to open the scroll and its seven seals."

⁶Then I saw standing there with the throne and the four living beings, in the circle of the elders, a Lamb that appeared to have been slaughtered. He had seven horns and seven eyes, which are the sevenfold Spirit of God sent out into all the earth. ⁷He came and took the scroll out of the right hand of the One sitting on the throne. ⁸When he took the scroll, the four living beings and the 24 elders fell down in front of the Lamb. Each one held a harp and gold bowls filled with pieces of incense, which are the prayers of God's people; ⁹and they sang a new song,

> "You are worthy to take the scroll
> and break its seals;
> because you were slaughtered;
> at the cost of blood you ransomed for God
> persons from every tribe, language, people and nation.
> ¹⁰ You made them into a kingdom for God to rule,
> *cohanim* to serve him;
> and they will rule over the earth."

---

^h Ezekiel 1:5-10   ^i Isaiah 6:2

^j Isaiah 6:3; Amos 3:13, 4:13

A·men — So be it

A·do·nai — the LORD, Jehovah

A·do·nai E·lo·hey·nu — the LORD (Jehovah), our God

co·ha·nim — priests

Da·vid — David

Ha·Ka·dosh — the Holy One

Y'hu·dah — Judah

11 Then I looked, and I heard the sound of a vast number of angels — thousands and thousands, millions and millions! They were all around the throne, the living beings and the elders; 12 and they shouted out,

> "Worthy is the slaughtered Lamb
> to receive power, riches, wisdom,
> strength, honor, glory and praise!"

13 And I heard every creature in heaven, on earth, under the earth and on the sea — yes, everything in them — saying,

> "To the One sitting on the throne
> and to the Lamb
> belong praise, honor, glory and
>   power
> forever and ever!"

14 The four living beings said, "*Amen!*" and the elders fell down and worshipped.

6 1 Next I watched as the Lamb broke the first of the seven seals, and I heard one of the four living beings say in a thundering voice, "Go!" 2 I looked, and there in front of me was a white horse; its rider had a bow and was given a crown; and he rode off as a conqueror to conquer.

3 When he broke the second seal, I heard the second living being say, "Go!" 4 Another horse went out, a red one; and its rider was given the power to take peace away from the earth and make people slaughter each other. He was given a great sword.

5 When he broke the third seal, I heard the third living being say, "Go!" I looked, and there in front of me was a black horse, and its rider held in his hand a pair of scales. 6 Then I heard what sounded like a voice from among the four living beings say, "Two pounds of wheat for a day's wages! Six pounds of barley for the same price! But don't damage the oil or the wine!"

7 When he broke the fourth seal, I heard the voice of the fourth living being say, "Go!" 8 I looked, and there in front of me was a pallid, sickly-looking horse. Its rider's name was Death, and Sh'ol followed behind him. They were given authority to kill one-quarter of the world by war, by famine, by plagues and with the wild animals of the earth.

9 When the Lamb broke the fifth seal, I saw underneath the altar the souls of those who had been put to death for proclaiming the Word of God, that is, for bearing witness. 10 They cried out in a loud voice, "Sovereign Ruler, *Ha-Kadosh*, the True One, how long will it be before you judge the people living on earth and avenge our blood?" 11 Each of them was given a white robe; and they were told to wait a little longer, until the full number of their fellow-servants should be reached, of their brothers who would be killed, just as they had been.

12 Then I watched as he broke the sixth seal, and there was a great earthquake, the sun turned black as sackcloth worn in mourning, and the full moon became blood-red. 13 The stars fell from heaven to earth just as a fig tree drops its figs when shaken by a strong wind. 14 The sky receded like a scroll being rolled up, and every mountain and island was moved from its place. 15 Then the earth's kings, the rulers, the generals, the rich and the mighty — indeed, everyone, slave and free — hid himself in caves and among the rocks in the mountains, 16 **and said to the mountains and rocks, "Fall on us, and hide us**[k] from the face of the One sitting on the throne and from the fury of the Lamb! 17 For the Great Day of their fury has come, and who can stand?"

---

k Hosea 10:8

7 [1]After this, I saw four angels standing at the four corners of the earth, holding back the four winds of the earth, so that no wind would blow on the land, on the sea or on any tree. [2]I saw another angel coming up from the east with a seal from the living God, and he shouted to the four angels who had been given power to harm the land and the sea, [3]"Do not harm the land or the sea or the trees until we have sealed the servants of our God on their foreheads!" [4]I heard how many were sealed — 144,000 from every tribe of the people of Israel:

[5] From the tribe of Y'hudah, 12,000 were sealed;
  from the tribe of Re'uven, 12,000;
  from the tribe of Gad, 12,000;
[6] from the tribe of Asher, 12,000;
  from the tribe of Naftali, 12,000;
  from the tribe of M'nasheh, 12,000;
[7] from the tribe of Shim'on, 12,000;
  from the tribe of L'vi, 12,000;
  from the tribe of Yissakhar, 12,000;
[8] from the tribe of Z'vulun, 12,000;
  from the tribe of Yosef, 12,000;
  from the tribe of Binyamin, 12,000.

[9]After this, I looked; and there before me was a huge crowd, too large for anyone to count, from every nation, tribe, people and language. Thery were standing in front of the throne and in front of the Lamb, dressed in white robes and holding palm branches in their hands; [10]and they shouted,

"Victory to our God,
  who sits on the throne,
  and to the Lamb!"

[11]All the angels stood around the throne, the elders and the four living beings; they fell face down before the throne and worshipped God, saying,

[12]"Amen!

"Praise and glory,
  wisdom and thanks,
  honor and power and strength
  belong to our God
  forever and ever!
  Amen!"

[13]Then one of the elders asked me, "These people dressed in white robes — who are they, and where are they from?" [14]"Sir," I answered, "you know." Then he told me, "These are the people who have come out of the Great Persecution. They have washed their robes and made them white with the blood of the Lamb. [15]That is why they are before God's throne.

"Day and night they serve him
  in his Temple;
  and the One who sits on the throne
  will put his *Sh'khinah* upon them.

[16] **"They will never again be hungry,**
  they will never again be thirsty,
  the sun will not beat down on
    them,
  nor will any burning heat[l]

[17] **"For the Lamb at the center of the**
    throne

---

l Isaiah 49:10

===

A·**men** — So be it
A·**sher** — Asher, Aser
Bin·ya·**min** — Benjamin
Gad — Gad
*Ha·Ka·**dosh*** — the Holy One
L'**vi** — Levi
M'na·**sheh** — Manasseh, Manasses
Naf·ta·**li** — Naphtali, Nephthalim
Re·'u·**ven** — Reuben
Shim·'**on** — Simeon
*Sh'khi·**nah*** — the glorious manifest presence of God
Sh'**ol** — Shcol, Hades, hell
Y'hu·**dah** — Judah
Yis·sa·**khar** — Issachar
Yo·**sef** — Joseph
Z'vu·**lun** — Zebulun, Zabulon

will shepherd them, will lead them to springs of living water;[m]
and God will wipe every tear from their eyes."[n]

8 [1]When the Lamb broke the seventh seal, there was silence in heaven for what seemed like half an hour. [2]Then I saw the seven angels who stand before God, and they were given seven *shofar*s. [3]Another angel came and stood at the altar with a gold incense-bowl, and he was given a large quantity of incense to add to the prayers of all God's people on the gold altar in front of the throne. [4]The smoke of the incense went up with the prayers of God's people from the hand of the angel before God. [5]Then the angel took the incense-bowl, filled it with fire from the altar and threw it down onto the earth; and there followed peals of thunder, voices, flashes of lightning and an earthquake.

[6]Now the seven angels with the seven *shofar*s prepared to sound them.

[7]The first one sounded his *shofar*; and there came hail and fire mingled with blood, and it was thrown down upon the earth. A third of the earth was burned up, a third of the trees were burned up, and all green grass was burned up.

[8]The second angel sounded his *shofar*, and what looked like an enormous blazing mountain was hurled into the sea. A third of the sea turned to blood, [9]a third of the living creatures in the sea died, and a third of the ships were destroyed.

[10]The third angel sounded his *shofar*; and a great star, blazing like a torch, fell from the sky onto a third of the rivers and onto the springs of water. [11]The name of the star was "Bitterness", and a third of the water became bitter, and many people died from the water that had been turned bitter.

[12]The fourth angel sounded his *shofar*; and a third of the sun was struck, also a third of the moon and a third of the stars; so that a third of them were darkened, the day had a third less light, and the night likewise.

[13]Then I looked, and I heard a lone eagle give a loud cry, as it flew in midheaven, "Woe! Woe! Woe to the people living on earth, because of the remaining blasts from the three angels who have yet to sound their *shofar*s!"

9 [1]The fifth angel sounded his *shofar*; and I saw a star that had fallen out of heaven onto the earth, and he was given the key to the shaft leading down to the Abyss. [2]He opened the shaft of the Abyss, and there went up smoke from the shaft like the smoke of a huge furnace; the sun was darkened, and the sky too, by the smoke from the shaft. [3]Then out of the smoke onto the earth came locusts, and they were given power like the power scorpions have on earth. [4]They were instructed not to harm the grass on the earth, any green plant or any tree, but only the people who did not have the seal of God on their foreheads. [5]The locusts were not allowed to kill them, only to inflict pain on them for five months; and the pain they caused was like the pain of a scorpion sting. [6]In those days people will seek death but will not find it; they will long to die, but death will elude them.

[7]Now these locusts looked like horses outfitted for battle. On their heads were what looked like crowns of gold, and their faces were like human faces. [8]They had hair like women's hair, and their teeth were like those of lions. [9]Their chests were like iron breast-

---

m Isaiah 49:10, Jeremiah 2:13, Ezekiel 34:23, Psalm 23:1-2

n Isaiah 25:8

plates, and the sound their wings made
was like the roar of many horses and
chariots rushing into battle. 10 They had
tails like those of scorpions, with stings;
and in their tails was their power to
hurt people for five months. 11 They had
as king over them the angel of the
Abyss, whose name in Hebrew is
"*Abaddon*" and in our language,
"Destroyer".
12 The first woe has passed, but there
are still two woes to come.
13 The sixth angel sounded his *shofar*;
and I heard a voice from the four horns
of the gold altar before God, 14 saying to
the sixth angel, the one with the *shofar*,
"Release the four angels that are bound
at the great river Euphrates!" 15 And
they were released. These four angels
had been kept ready for this moment,
for this day and month and year, to kill
a third of mankind; 16 and the number
of cavalry soldiers was two hundred
million! — I heard the number.
17 Here is how the horses looked in
the vision: the riders had breastplates
that were fire-red, iris-blue and sulfur-
yellow; the horses' heads were like
lions' heads; and from their mouths
issued fire, smoke and sulfur. 18 It was
these three plagues that killed a third of
mankind — the fire, smoke and sulfur
issuing from the horses' mouths. 19 For
the power of the horses was in their
mouths — and also in their tails, for
their tails were like snakes with heads,
and with them they could cause injury.
20 The rest of mankind, those who
were not killed by these plagues, even
then did not turn from what they had
made with their own hands — they did
not stop worshipping demons and **idols
made of gold, silver, bronze, stone and
wood, which cannot see or hear or
walk.**[o] 21 Nor did they turn from their
murdering, their misuse of drugs in
connection with the occult, their sexual
immorality or their stealing.

10 1 Then I saw another mighty
angel coming down from
heaven. He was dressed in a cloud, with
a rainbow over his head; his face was
like the sun, his legs like columns of
fire; 2 and he had a little scroll lying
open in his hand. He planted his right
foot on the sea and his left foot on the
land, 3 and shouted in a voice as loud as
the roar of a lion; and when he shouted,
seven thunderclaps sounded with voices
that spoke. 4 When the seven thunders
spoke, I was about to write; but I heard
a voice from heaven say,

"Seal up the things the seven thunders
said,
do not write them down!"

5 Then the angel I saw standing on
the sea and on the land **lifted his right
hand toward heaven** 6 and swore by the
One who lives forever and ever,[p] **who
created heaven and what is in it, earth
and what is in it, and the sea and what is
in it:**[q] "There will be no more delay; 7 on
the contrary, in the days of the sound
from the seventh angel when he sounds
his *shofar*, the hidden plan of God will
be brought to completion, the Good
News as he proclaimed it to his servants
the prophets."
8 Next the voice which I had heard
from heaven spoke to me again and
said, "Go, take the scroll lying open in
the hand of the angel standing on the
sea and on the land!" 9 So I went over to
the angel and asked him to give me the

---

o Psalms 115:4-7, 135:15-17; Daniel 5:23

p Deuteronomy 32:40, Daniel 12:7

q Nehemiah 9:6; see also Exodus 20:11, Psalm 146:6

A·bad·don — destruction, loss, hell
sho·far — ram's horn

little scroll; and he said to me, "Take it and eat it. It will turn your stomach bitter, but in your mouth it will be sweet as honey." ¹⁰ I took the little scroll from the angel's hand and ate it; and in my mouth it was sweet as honey; but after I had swallowed it, my stomach turned bitter. ¹¹ Then I was told, "You must prophesy again about many peoples, nations, languages and kings."

11 ¹ I was given a measuring rod like a stick and told, "Get up, and measure the Temple of God and the altar, and count how many people are worshipping there! ² But the court outside the Temple, leave that out; don't measure it; because it has been given to the *Goyim*, and they will trample over the holy city for 42 months.

³ "Also I will give power to my two witnesses; and they will prophesy for 1260 days, dressed in sackcloth." ⁴ These are the two olive trees and the two *menorah*s standing before the Lord of the earth. ⁵ If anyone tries to do them harm, fire comes out of their mouth and consumes their enemies — yes, if anyone tries to harm them, that is how he must die. ⁶ They have the authority to shut up the sky, so that no rain falls during the period of their prophesying; also they have the authority to turn the waters into blood and to strike the earth with every kind of plague as often as they want.

⁷ When they finish their witnessing, the beast coming up out of the Abyss will fight against them, overcome them and kill them; ⁸ and their dead bodies will lie in the main street of the great city whose name, to reflect its spiritual condition, is "S'dom" and "Egypt" — the city where their Lord was executed on a stake. ⁹ Some from the nations, tribes, languages and peoples see their bodies for three-and-a-half days and

do not permit the corpses to be placed in a tomb. ¹⁰ The people living in the Land rejoice over them, they celebrate and send each other gifts, because these two prophets tormented them so.

¹¹ But after the three-and-a-half days a breath of life from God entered them, they stood up on their feet, and great fear fell on those who saw them. ¹² Then the two heard a loud voice from heaven saying to them, "Come up here!" And they went up into heaven in a cloud, while their enemies watched them. ¹³ In that hour there was a great earthquake, and a tenth of the city collapsed. Seven thousand people were killed in the earthquake, and the rest were awestruck and gave glory to the God of heaven.

¹⁴ The second woe has passed; see, the third woe is coming quickly.

¹⁵ The seventh angel sounded his *shofar*; and there were loud voices in heaven, saying,

> "The kingdom of the world
> has become the Kingdom
> of our Lord and his Messiah,
> and he will rule forever and ever!"

¹⁶ The 24 elders sitting on their thrones in God's presence fell on their faces and worshipped God, ¹⁷ saying,

> "We thank you, **Adonai,**
> **God of heaven's armies,**[r]
> the One who is and was,
> that you have taken your power
> and have begun to rule.

¹⁸ **"The *Goyim* raged.**[s]
> But now your rage has come,
> the time for the dead to be judged,
> the time for rewarding your ser-
>   vants the prophets
> and your holy people,
> those who stand in awe of your
>   name,

---

[r] Amos 3:13, 4:13   [s] Psalm 2:1

both small and great.
It is also the time for destroying
those who destroy the earth.''

[19] Then the Temple of God in heaven
was opened, and the Ark of the
Covenant was seen in his Temple; and
there were flashes of lightning, voices,
peals of thunder, an earthquake and
violent hail.

12 [1] Now a great sign was seen in
heaven — a woman clothed with
the sun, under her feet the moon, and
on her head a crown of twelve stars.
[2] She was pregnant and about to give
birth, and she screamed in the agony of
labor.

[3] Another sign was seen in heaven —
there was a great red dragon with seven
heads and ten horns, and on his heads
were seven royal crowns. [4] Its tail swept
a third of the stars out of heaven and
threw them down to the earth. It stood
in front of the woman about to give
birth; so that it might devour the child
the moment it was born.

[5] She gave birth to a son, a male
child, the one who will rule **all the
nations with a staff of iron.**[t] But her
child was snatched up to God and his
throne; [6] and she fled into the desert,
where she has a place prepared by God
so that she can be taken care of for 1260
days.

[7] Next there was a battle in heaven —
Mikha'el and his angels fought against
the dragon, and the dragon and his
angels fought back. [8] But it was not
strong enough to win, so that there was
no longer any place for them in heaven.
[9] The great dragon was thrown out, that
ancient serpent, also known as the
Devil and Satan [the Adversary], the
deceiver of the whole world. He was
hurled down to the earth, and his
angels were hurled down with him.

[t] Psalm 2:9

[10] Then I heard a loud voice in heaven
saying,

"Now have come God's victory,
power and kingship,
and the authority of his Messiah;
because the Accuser of our brothers,
who accuses them day and night
before God,
has been thrown out!

[11] "They defeated him because of the
Lamb's blood
and because of the message of
their witness.
Even when facing death
they did not cling to life.

[12] "Therefore, rejoice,
heaven and you who live there!
But woe to you, land and sea,
for the Adversary has come down
to you,
and he is very angry,
because he knows that his time
is short!''

[13] When the dragon saw that he had
been hurled down to the earth, he went
in pursuit of the woman who had given
birth to the male child. [14] But the
woman was given the two wings of the
great eagle, so that she could fly to her
place in the desert, where she is taken
care of for **a season and two seasons
and half a season,**[u] away from the
serpent's presence. [15] The serpent
spewed water like a river out of its
mouth after the woman, in order to

[u] Daniel 7:25, 12:7

A·do·nai — the LORD, Jehovah
Go·yim — Gentiles, nations, pagans
me·no·rah — lampstand
Mi·kha·'el — Michael
Sa·tan — Satan, the Adversary
S'dom — Sodom
sho·far — ram's horn

345

sweep her away in the flood; ¹⁶but the land came to her rescue — it opened its mouth and swallowed up the river which the dragon had spewed out of its mouth. ¹⁷The dragon was infuriated over the woman and went off to fight the rest of her children, those who obey God's commands and bear witness to Yeshua.

¹⁸Then the dragon stood on the seashore; **13** ¹and I saw a beast come up out of the sea, with ten horns and seven heads. On its horns were ten royal crowns and on its heads blasphemous names. ²The beast which I saw was like a leopard, but with feet like those of a bear and a mouth like the mouth of a lion. To it the dragon gave its power, its throne and great authority. ³One of the heads of the beast appeared to have received a fatal wound, but its fatal wound was healed, and the whole earth followed after the beast in amazement. ⁴They worshipped the dragon, because he had given his authority to the beast; and they worshipped the beast, saying,

"Who is like the beast?
Who can fight against it?"

⁵It was given a mouth speaking arrogant blasphemies; and it was given authority to act for 42 months. ⁶So it opened its mouth in blasphemies against God to insult his name and his *Sh'khinah*, and those living in heaven; ⁷it was allowed to make war on God's holy people and to defeat them; and it was given authority over every tribe, people, language and nation. ⁸Everyone living on earth will worship it except those whose names are written in the Book of Life belonging to the Lamb slaughtered before the world was founded. ⁹Those who have ears, let them hear!

¹⁰ **"If anyone is meant for captivity, into captivity he goes!**

**If anyone is to be killed with the sword,
with the sword he is to be killed!"**ᵛ

This is when God's holy people must persevere and trust!

¹¹Then I saw another beast coming up out of the earth. It had two horns like those of a lamb, but it spoke like a dragon. ¹²It exercises all the authority of the first beast in its presence; and it makes the earth and its inhabitants worship the first beast, the one whose fatal wound had been healed. ¹³It performs great miracles, even causing fire to come down from heaven onto the earth as people watch. ¹⁴It deceives the people living on earth by the miracles it is allowed to perform in the presence of the beast, and it tells them to make an image honoring the beast that was struck by the sword but came alive again. ¹⁵It was allowed to put breath into the image of the beast, so that the image of the beast could even speak; and it was allowed to cause anyone who would not worship the image of the beast to be put to death. ¹⁶Also it forces everyone — great and small, rich and poor, free and slave — to receive a mark on his right hand or on his forehead ¹⁷preventing anyone from buying or selling unless he has the mark, that is, the name of the beast or the number of its name. ¹⁸This is where wisdom is needed; those who understand should count the number of the beast, for it is the number of a person, and its number is 666.

14 ¹Then I looked, and there was the Lamb standing on Mount Tziyon; and with him were 144,000 who had his name and his Father's

---

ᵛ Jeremiah 15:2, 43:11

346

name written on their foreheads. [2]I heard a sound from heaven like the sound of rushing waters and like the sound of pealing thunder; the sound I heard was also like that of harpists playing on their harps. [3]They were singing a new song before the throne and before the four living beings and the elders, and no one could learn the song except the 144,000 who have been ransomed from the world. [4]These are the ones who have not defiled themselves with women, for they are virgins; they follow the Lamb wherever he goes; they have been ransomed from among humanity as firstfruits for God and the Lamb; [5]on their lips no lie was found — they are without defect.

[6]Then I saw another angel flying in mid-heaven with everlasting Good News to proclaim to those living on the earth — to every nation, tribe, language and people. [7]In a loud voice he said,

"Fear God, give him glory,
for the hour has come when he will pass judgment!
Worship the One who made heaven and earth,
the sea and the springs of water!"

[8]Another angel, a second one, followed, saying,

"She has fallen! She has fallen! Babylon the Great!"[w]
She made all the nations drink the wine
of God's fury caused by her whoring!"

[9]Another angel, a third one, followed them and said in a loud voice, "If anyone worships the beast and its image and receives the mark on his forehead or on his hand, [10]he will indeed drink the wine of God's fury

poured undiluted into the cup of his rage. He will be tormented by fire and sulfur before the holy angels and before the Lamb, [11]and the smoke from their tormenting goes up forever and ever. They have no rest, day or night, those who worship the beast and its image and those who receive the mark of its name." [12]This is when perseverance is needed on the part of God's people, those who observe his commands and exercise Yeshua's faithfulness.

[13]Next I heard a voice from heaven saying, "Write: 'How blessed are the dead who die united with the Lord, from now on!' 'Yes,' says the Spirit, 'now they may rest from their efforts, for the things they have accomplished follow along with them.'"

[14]Then I looked, and there before me was a white cloud. Sitting on the cloud was someone **like a Son of Man**[x] with a gold crown on his head and a sharp sickle in his hand. [15]Another angel came out of the Temple and shouted to the one sitting on the cloud, "Start using your sickle to reap, because the time to reap has come — the earth's harvest is ripe!" [16]The one sitting on the cloud swung his sickle over the earth, and the earth was harvested.

[17]Another angel came out of the Temple in heaven, and he too had a sharp sickle. [18]Then out from the altar went yet another angel, who was in charge of the fire; and he called in a loud voice to the one with the sharp sickle, "Use your sharp sickle, and gather the clusters of grapes from the earth's vine, because they are ripe!" [19]The angel swung his sickle down onto

---

x Daniel 7:13

Sh'khi·nah — the glorious manifest presence of God
Tzi·yon — Zion
Ye·shu·a — Jesus

---

w Isaiah 21:9

the earth, gathered the earth's grapes and threw them into the great winepress of God's fury. [20] The winepress was trodden outside the city, and blood flowed from the winepress as high as the horses' bridles for two hundred miles!

15 [1] Then I saw another sign in heaven, a great and wonderful one — seven angels with the seven plagues that are the final ones; because with them, God's fury is finished. [2] I saw what looked like a sea of glass mixed with fire. Those defeating the beast, its image and the number of its name were standing by the sea of glass, holding harps which God had given them. [3] They were singing the song of Moshe, the servant of God, and the song of the Lamb:

> "Great and wonderful are the things you have done,
> **Adonai, God of heaven's armies!**[y]

> "Just and true are your ways,
> king of the nations!

[4] "*Adonai*, who will not fear and glorify your name?
> because you alone are holy.

> "All nations will come and worship before you,
> for your righteous deeds have been revealed."

[5] After this I looked, and the sanctuary (that is, the Tent of Witness in heaven) was opened, [6] and out of the sanctuary came the seven angels with the seven plagues. They were dressed in clean bright linen and had gold belts around their chests. [7] One of the four living beings gave to the seven angels seven gold bowls filled with the fury of God, who lives forever and ever. [8] Then the sanctuary was filled with smoke from God's *Sh'khinah*, that is, from his power; and no one could enter the sanctuary until the seven plagues of the seven angels had accomplished their purpose.

16 [1] I heard a loud voice from the sanctuary say to the seven angels, "Go, and pour out on the earth the seven bowls of God's fury!"

[2] So the first one went and poured his bowl onto the earth, and disgusting and painful sores appeared on all the people who had the mark of the beast and worshipped its image.

[3] The second one poured out his bowl into the sea, and it became like the blood of a dead person, and every living thing in the sea died.

[4] The third one poured out his bowl into the rivers and springs of water, and they turned to blood. [5] Then I heard the angel of the waters say,

> "O *HaKadosh*, the One who is and was,
> you are just in these judgments of yours.
[6] They poured out the blood of your people and your prophets,
> so you have made them drink blood. They deserve it!"

[7] Then I heard the altar say,

> "Yes, *Adonai*, **God of heaven's armies,**[z]
> your judgments are true and just!"

[8] The fourth one poured out his bowl on the sun, and it was permitted to burn people with fire. [9] People were burned by the intense heat; yet they cursed the name of God, who had the authority over these plagues, instead of turning from their sins to give him glory.

[10] The fifth one poured out his bowl on the throne of the beast, and its

---

y Amos 3:13, 4:13

z Amos 3:13, 4:13

kingdom grew dark. People gnawed on their tongues from the pain, [11] yet they cursed the God of heaven because of their pains and sores, and did not turn from their sinful deeds.

[12] The sixth one poured out his bowl on the great river Euphrates, and its water dried up, in order to prepare the way for the kings from the east. [13] And I saw three unclean spirits that looked like frogs; they came from the mouth of the dragon, from the mouth of the beast and from the mouth of the false prophet. [14] They are miracle-working demonic spirits which go out to the kings of the whole inhabited world to assemble them for the War of the Great Day of *Adonai-Tzva'ot*. [15] ("Look! I am coming like a thief! How blessed are those who stay alert and keep their clothes clean, so that they won't be walking naked and be publicly put to shame!") [16] And they gathered the kings to the place which in Hebrew is called Har Megiddo.

[17] The seventh one poured out his bowl on the air, and a loud voice came out of the Temple from the throne, saying, "It is done!" [18] There were flashes of lightning, voices and peals of thunder; and there was a massive earthquake, such as has never occurred since mankind has been on earth, so violent was the earthquake. [19] The great city was split into three parts, the cities of the nations fell, and God remembered Babylon the Great and made her drink the wine from the cup of his raging fury. [20] Every island fled, and no mountains were to be found. [21] And huge seventy-pound hailstones fell on people from the sky. But the people cursed God for the plague of hail, that it was such a terrible plague.

17 [1] Then came one of the angels with the seven bowls; and he said to me, "Come, I will show you the judgment of the great whore who is sitting by many waters. [2] The kings of the earth went whoring with her, and the people living on earth have become drunk from the wine of her whoring." [3] He carried me off in the Spirit to a desert, and I saw a woman sitting on a scarlet beast filled with blasphemous names and having seven heads and ten horns. [4] The woman was dressed in purple and scarlet and glittered with gold, precious stones and pearls. In her hand was a gold cup filled with the obscene and filthy things produced by her whoring. [5] On her forehead was written a name with a hidden meaning,

BABYLON THE GREAT
MOTHER OF WHORES AND OF
THE EARTH'S OBSCENITIES

[6] I saw the woman drunk from the blood of God's people, that is, from the blood of the people who testify about Yeshua.

On seeing her, I was altogether astounded. [7] Then the angel said to me, "Why are you astounded? I will tell you the hidden meaning of the woman and of the beast with seven heads and ten horns that was carrying her. [8] The beast you saw once was, now is not, and will come up from the Abyss; but it is on its way to destruction. The people living on earth whose names have not been written in the Book of Life since the founding of the world will be astounded

---

A·do·nai — the LORD, Jehovah

A·do·nai-Tzva·'ot — the LORD (Jehovah) of Hosts (heaven's armies)

Ha·Ka·dosh — the Holy One

Har-Me·gid·do — the hill of Megiddo, Armageddon

Mo·she — Moses

Sh'khi·nah — the glorious manifest presence of God

Ye·shu·a — Jesus

to see the beast that once was, now is not, but is to appear. ^{9}This calls for a mind with wisdom: the seven heads are seven hills on which the woman is sitting; also they are seven kings — ^{10}five have fallen, one is living now and the other is yet to come; and when he does come, he must remain only a little while. ^{11}The beast which once was and now is not is an eighth king; it comes from the seven and is on its way to destruction. ^{12}The ten horns you saw are ten kings who have not yet begun to rule, but they receive power as kings for one hour, along with the beast. ^{13}They have one mind, and they hand over their power and authority to the beast. ^{14}They will go to war against the Lamb, but the Lamb will defeat them, because he is Lord of lords and King of kings, and those who are called, chosen and faithful will overcome along with him."

^{15}Then he said to me, "The waters that you saw, where the whore is sitting, are peoples, crowds, nations and languages. ^{16}As for the ten horns that you saw and the beast, they will hate the whore, bring her to ruin, leave her naked, eat her flesh and consume her with fire. ^{17}For God put it in their hearts to do what will fulfill his purpose, that is, to be of one mind and give their kingdom to the beast until God's words have accomplished their intent. ^{18}And the woman you saw is the great city that rules over the kings of the earth."

18 ^{1}After these things, I saw another angel coming down from heaven. He had great authority, the earth was lit up by his splendor. ^{2}He cried out in a strong voice,

> **"She has fallen! She has fallen!**
> **Babylon the Great!**^{a}

---

a Isaiah 21:9

> She has become a home for demons,
> a prison for every unclean spirit,
> a prison for every unclean, hated bird.

^{3} "For all the nations have drunk of the wine
> of God's fury caused by her whoring —
> yes, the kings of the earth went whoring with her,
> and from her unrestrained love of luxury
> the world's businessmen have grown rich."

^{4}Then I heard another voice out of heaven say:

> "My people, come out of her! —
> so that you will not share in her sins,
> so that you will not be infected by her plagues,
> ^{5} for her sins are a sticky mass piled up to heaven,
> and God has remembered her crimes.

^{6} "Render to her as she rendered to others!
> Pay her back double for what she has done!
> Use the cup in which she has brewed
> to brew her a double-sized drink!

^{7} "Give her as much torment and sorrow
> as the glory and luxury she gave herself!
> For in her heart she says, 'I sit a queen —
> I am not a widow, I will never see sorrow.'

^{8} "Therefore, her plagues will come in a single day —

death, sorrow and famine;
and she will be burned with fire,
because *Adonai*, God, her Judge,
is mighty"

⁹The kings of the earth who went whoring with her and shared her luxury will sob and wail over her when they see the smoke as she burns. ¹⁰Standing at a distance, for fear of her torment, they will say,

"Oh no! The great city!
Babylon, the mighty city!
In a single hour
your judgment has come!"

¹¹The world's businessmen weep and mourn over her, because no one is buying their merchandise any more — ¹²stocks of gold and silver, gems and pearls, fine linen and purple, silk and scarlet, all rare woods, all ivory goods, all kinds of things made of scented wood, brass, iron and marble; ¹³cinnamon, cardamom, incense, myrrh, frankincense, wine, oil, flour, grain, cattle, sheep, horses, chariots — and bodies — and people's souls.

¹⁴ The fruits you lusted for with all your heart have gone!
All the luxury and flashiness have been destroyed, never to return!

¹⁵The sellers of these things, who got rich from her, will stand at a distance, for fear of her torment, weeping and mourning, ¹⁶and saying,

"Oh no! The great city used to wear fine linen, purple and scarlet!
She glittered with gold, precious stones and pearls!
¹⁷ Such great wealth —
in a single hour, ruined!"

All the ship masters, passengers, sailors and everyone making his living from the sea stood at a distance ¹⁸and cried out when they saw the smoke as she burned, "What city was like the great city?" ¹⁹And they threw dust on their heads as they wept and mourned, saying,

"Oh no! The great city!
The abundance of her wealth
made all the ship owners rich!
In a single hour she is ruined!"

²⁰ Rejoice over her, heaven!
Rejoice, people of God, emissaries and prophets!
For in judging her, God has vindicated you.

²¹Then a mighty angel picked up a boulder the size of a great millstone, and hurled it into the sea, saying,

"With violence like this
will the great city Babylon
be hurled down,
never to be found again!

²² "The sound of harpists and musicians,
flute-players and trumpeters
will never again be heard in you.

"No worker of any trade will ever again be found in you,
the sound of a mill will never again be heard in you,
²³ the light of a lamp will never again shine in you,
the voice of bridegroom and bride will never again be heard in you.

"For your businessmen were the most powerful on earth,
all the nations were deceived by your magic spell.

²⁴ "In her was found the blood of prophets and of God's people,
indeed, of all who have ever been slaughtered on earth!"

A·do·nai — the LORD, Jehovah

19 [1] After these things, I heard what sounded like the roar of a huge crowd in heaven, shouting,

"*Halleluyah*!
The victory, the glory, the power of our God!
[2] For his judgments are true and just.
He has judged the great whore who corrupted the earth with her whoring.
He has taken vengeance on her who has the blood of his servants on her hands."

[3] And a second time they said,

"*Halleluyah*!
Her smoke goes up forever and ever!"

[4] The 24 elders and the four living beings fell down and worshipped God, sitting on the throne, and said,

"*Amen*!
Halleluyah!"

[5] And a voice went out from the throne, saying,

"Praise our God,
all you his servants,
you who fear him,
small and great!"

[6] Then I heard what sounded like the roar of a huge crowd, like the sound of rushing waters, like loud peals of thunder, saying,

"*Halleluyah*!
Adonai, **God of heaven's armies,**[b]
has begun his reign!

[7] "Let us rejoice and be glad!
Let us give him the glory!
For the time has come for the wedding of the Lamb,

and his Bride has prepared herself —
[8] fine linen, bright and clean has been given her to wear."

("Fine linen" means the righteous deeds of God's people.)
[9] And the angel said to me, "Write: 'How blessed are those who have been invited to the wedding feast of the Lamb!'" Then he added, "These are God's very words." [10] I fell at his feet to worship him; but he said, "Don't do that! I'm only a fellow-servant with you and your brothers who have the testimony of Yeshua. Worship God! For the testimony of Yeshua is the Spirit of prophecy."

[11] Then I saw heaven opened, and there before me was a white horse. Sitting on it was the one called Faithful and True, and it is in righteousness that he passes judgment and goes to battle. [12] His eyes were like a fiery flame, and on his head were many royal crowns. And he had a name written which no one knew but himself. [13] He was wearing a robe that had been soaked in blood, and the name by which he is called is, "THE WORD OF GOD". [14] The armies of heaven, clothed in fine linen, white and pure, were following him on white horses. [15] And out of his mouth comes a sharp sword with which to strike down nations — **"He will rule them with a staff of iron."**[c] It is he who treads the winepress from which flows the wine of the furious rage of *Adonai*, God of heaven's armies. [16] And on his robe and on his thigh he has a name written: "KING OF KINGS AND LORD OF LORDS".

[17] Then I saw an angel standing in the sun, and he cried out in a loud voice to all the birds that fly about in midheaven, "Come, gather together for the

---

[b] Amos 3:13, 4:13

[c] Psalm 2:9

great feast God is giving, ^{18}to eat the flesh of kings, the flesh of generals, the flesh of important men, the flesh of horses and their riders and the flesh of all kinds of people, free and slave, small and great!" ^{19}I saw the beast and the kings of the earth and their armies gathered together to do battle with the rider of the horse and his army. ^{20}But the beast was taken captive, and with it the false prophet who, in its presence, had done the miracles which he had used to deceive those who had received the mark of the beast and those who had worshipped his image. The beast and the false prophet were both thrown alive into the lake of fire that burns with sulfur. ^{21}The rest were killed with the sword that goes out of the mouth of the rider on the horse, and all the birds gorged themselves on their flesh.

20 ^{1}Then I saw an angel coming down from heaven, who had the key to the Abyss and a great chain in his hand. ^{2}He seized the dragon, that ancient serpent, who is the Devil and Satan [the Adversary], and chained him up for a thousand years. ^{3}He threw him into the Abyss, locked it and sealed it over him; so that he could not deceive the nations any more until the thousand years were over. After that, he has to be set free for a little while.

^{4}Then I saw thrones, and those seated on them received authority to judge. And I saw the souls of those who had been beheaded for testifying about Yeshua and proclaiming the Word of God, also those who had not worshipped the beast or its image and had not received the mark on their foreheads and on their hands. They came to life and ruled with the Messiah for a thousand years. ^{5}(The rest of the dead did not come to life until the thousand years were over.) This is the first resurrection. ^{6}Blessed and holy is anyone who has a part in the first resurrection; over him the second death has no power. On the contrary, they will be *cohanim* of God and of the Messiah, and they will rule with him for the thousand years.

^{7}When the thousand years are over, the Adversary will be set free from his prison ^{8}and will go out to deceive the nations in the four quarters of the earth, **Gog and Magog,**^{d} to gather them for the battle. Their number is countless as the sand on the seashore; ^{9}and they came up over the breadth of the Land and surrounded the camp of God's people and the city he loves. But fire came down from heaven and consumed them. ^{10}The Adversary who had deceived them was hurled into the lake of fire and sulfur, where the beast and the false prophet were; and they will be tormented day and night forever and ever.

^{11}Then I saw a great white throne and the One sitting on it. Earth and heaven fled from his presence, and no place was found for them. ^{12}And I saw the dead, both great and small, standing in front of the throne. Books were opened; and another book was opened, the Book of Life; and the dead were judged from what was written in the books, according to what they had done. ^{13}The sea gave up the dead in it; and Death and Sh'ol gave up the dead

---

d Ezekiel 38:2

===

$A \cdot do \cdot nai$ — the LORD, Jehovah
$A \cdot men$ — So be it
$co \cdot ha \cdot nim$ — priests
Gog — Gog
$Hal \cdot le \cdot lu \cdot yah!$ — Hallelujah!, Praise the LORD (Yah)!
$Ma \cdot gog$ — Magog
$Sa \cdot tan$ — Satan
Sh'ol — Sheol, Hades, hell
$Ye \cdot shu \cdot a$ — Jesus

in them; and they were judged, each according to what he had done. ¹⁴Then Death and Sh'ol were hurled into the lake of fire. This is the second death — the lake of fire. ¹⁵Anyone whose name was not found written in the Book of Life was hurled into the lake of fire.

21 ¹Then I saw **a new heaven and a new earth,**ᵉ for the old heaven and the old earth had passed away, and the sea was no longer there. ²Also I saw the holy city, New Yerushalayim, coming down out of heaven from God, prepared like a bride beautifully dressed for her husband. ³I heard a loud voice from the throne say, "See! God's *Sh'khinah* is with mankind, **and he will live with them. They will be his peoples, and he himself, God-with-them, will be their God.**ᶠ ⁴He will wipe away every tear from their eyes. There will no longer be any death; and there will no longer be any mourning, crying or pain; because the old order has passed away."

⁵Then the One sitting on the throne said, "Look! I am making everything new!" Also he said, "Write, 'These words are true and trustworthy!'" ⁶And he said to me "It is done! I am the 'A' and the 'Z', the Beginning and the End. To anyone who is thirsty I myself will give water free of charge from the Fountain of Life. ⁷He who wins the victory will receive these things, and I will be his God, and he will be my son. ⁸But as for the cowardly, the untrustworthy, the vile, the murderers, the sexually immoral, those who misuse drugs in connection with the occult, idol-worshippers, and all liars — their destiny is the lake burning with fire and sulphur, the second death."

⁹One of the seven angels having the seven bowls full of the seven last plagues approached me and said, "Come! I will show you the Bride, the Wife of the Lamb." ¹⁰He carried me off in the Spirit to the top of a great, high mountain and showed me the holy city, Yerushalayim, coming down out of heaven from God. ¹¹It had the *Sh'khinah* of God, so that its brilliance was like that of a priceless jewel, like a crystal-clear diamond. ¹²It had a great, high wall with twelve gates; at the gates were twelve angels; and inscribed on the gates were the names of the twelve tribes of Israel. ¹³There were three gates to the east, three gates to the north, three gates to the south and three gates to the west. ¹⁴The wall of the city was built on twelve foundation-stones, and on these were the twelve names of the twelve emissaries of the Lamb.

¹⁵The angel speaking with me had a gold measuring-rod with which to measure the city, its gates and its wall. ¹⁶The city is laid out in a square, its length equal to its width. With his rod he measured the city at 1500 miles, with length, width and height the same. ¹⁷He measured its wall at 216 feet by human standards of measurement, which the angel was using. ¹⁸The wall was made of diamond and the city of pure gold resembling pure glass. ¹⁹The foundations of the city wall were decorated with all kinds of precious stones — the first foundation stone was diamond, the second sapphire, the third chalcedony, the fourth emerald, ²⁰the fifth sardonyx, the sixth carnelian, the seventh chrysolite, the eighth beryl, the ninth topaz, the tenth chrysoprase, the eleventh turquoise and the twelfth amethyst. ²¹The twelve gates were twelve pearls, with each gate made of a single pearl. The city's main street was pure gold, transparent as glass.

---

e Isaiah 65:17, 66:22
f Leviticus 26:11-12; Isaiah 7:14, 8:8, 10; Jeremiah 31:33(34); Ezekiel 37:27; 2 Chronicles 6:18

²²I saw no Temple in the city, for *Adonai,* God of heaven's armies, is its Temple, as is the Lamb. ²³The city has no need for the sun or the moon to shine on it, because God's *Sh'khinah* gives it light, and its lamp is the Lamb. ²⁴The nations will walk by its light, and the kings of the earth will bring their splendor into it. ²⁵Its gates will never close, they will stay open all day because night will not exist there, ²⁶and the honor and splendor of the nations will be brought into it. ²⁷Nothing impure may enter it, nor anyone who does shameful things or lies; the only ones who may enter are those whose names are written in the Lamb's Book of Life.

22 ¹Then the angel showed me the river of the water of life, sparkling like crystal, flowing from the throne of God and of the Lamb. ²Between the main street and the river was the Tree of Life producing twelve kinds of fruit, a different kind every month; and the leaves of the tree were for healing the nations — ³no longer will there be any curses. The throne of God and of the Lamb will be in the city, and his servants will worship him; ⁴they will see his face, and his name will be on their foreheads; ⁵Night will no longer exist, so they will need neither the light of a lamp nor the light of the sun, because *Adonai,* God, will shine upon them. And they will reign as kings forever and ever.

⁶Then he said to me, "These words are true and trustworthy: *Adonai,* God of the spirits of the prophets, sent his angel to show his servants the things that must happen soon."

⁷"Look! I am coming very soon! Blessed is the person who obeys the words of the prophecy written in this book!"

⁸Then I, Yochanan, the one hearing and seeing these things, when I heard and saw them, I fell down to worship at the feet of the angel showing them to me. ⁹But he said to me, "Don't do that! I am only a fellow-servant with you and your brothers, the prophets and the people who obey the words in this book. Worship God!"

¹⁰Then he said to me, "Don't **seal up the words of the prophecy in this book,**ᵍ because the time of their fulfillment is near.

¹¹ "Whoever keeps acting wickedly,
    let him go on acting wickedly;
whoever is filthy, let him go on
    being made filthy.
"Also, whoever is righteous, let
    him go on doing what is right-
    eous,
and whoever is holy, let him go on
    being made holy."

¹²"Pay attention!" says Yeshua, "I am coming soon, and my rewards are with me to give to each person according to what he has done. ¹³I am the 'A' and the 'Z', the First and the Last, the Beginning and the End." ¹⁴How blessed are those who wash their robes, so that they have the right to eat from the Tree of Life and go through the gates into the city! ¹⁵Outside are the homosexuals, those who misuse drugs in connection with the occult, the sexually immoral, murderers, idol-worshippers, and everyone who loves and practices falsehood. ¹⁶"I,

---

ᵍ Daniel 12:4

A·do·nai — the LORD, Jehovah
Sh'khi·nah — the glorious manifest presence of God
Sh'ol — Sheol, Hades, hell
Ye·ru·sha·la·yim — Jerusalem
Ye·shu·a — Jesus
Yo·cha·nan — John

Yeshua, have sent my angel to give you this testimony for the Messianic communities. I am the Root and Offspring of David, the bright Morning Star. [17] The Spirit and the Bride say, 'Come!' Let anyone who hears say, 'Come!' And let anyone who is thirsty come — let anyone who wishes, take the water of life free of charge."

[18] I warn everyone hearing the words of the prophecy in this book that if anyone adds to them, God will add to him the plagues written in this book. [19] And if anyone takes anything away from the words in the book of this prophecy, God will take away his share in the Tree of Life and the holy city, as described in this book.

[20] "The one who is testifying to these things says, 'Yes, I am coming soon!'"

Amen! Come, Lord Yeshua!

[21] May the grace of the Lord Yeshua be with all!

A·men — So be it
Da·vid — David
Ye·shu·a — Jesus

PRONOUNCING EXPLANATORY GLOSSARY

Format

Names of persons and places are printed in ordinary type, other terms in *italics*. All terms are Hebrew except where [A] indicates Aramaic, [Y] Yiddish, and [O] some other language. Usual English renderings are shown in parentheses. The definition or explanation follows a dash. At the end of each entry is given the book, chapter and verse where the term appears (see abbreviation below); a "+" means it appears in at least one subsequent verse; "f." or "ff." means it appears only in the verse or verses immediately following.

Pronunciation

Dots separate syllables unless hyphens or apostrophes do the job already. Accented syllables are printed in **boldface**. Vowels are pronounced as italicized in the following words: f*a*ther, *ai*sle, b*e*d, n*eigh*, wh*ey*, *i*nvest (usually not accented) or mar*i*ne (usually accented), *o*bey, r*u*le. As for consonants, *"ch"* is pronounced as in Johann Sebastian Ba*ch*, and so is *"kh"*; *"g"* is always hard (*g*ive); other consonants are more or less as in English. The guttural stop *aleph* is represented by an apostrophe(') before a vowel (example: Natan'el, pronounced Na·tan·'el and not Na·ta·nel). The stronger guttural stop *'ayin* (closer to the hard "g" sound) is represented by a reverse apostrophe (') before or after a vowel. The pronunciation shown for Hebrew and Aramaic is that used in Israel; Ashkenazic (German and eastern European) pronunciations common in English-speaking countries often shift *"a"* sounds towards *"o"*, turn some *"t's"* to *"s's"*, and accent the next-to-last syllable where the Israelis accent the last, e.g., **Shab**·*bos* instead of Shab·**bat**.

Abbreviations of Books in The *Jewish New Testament*

Ac	Acts	Ro	Romans
1C	1 Corinthians	Rv	Revelation
2C	2 Corinthians	1Th	1 Thessalonians
Co	Colossians	2Th	2 Thessalonians
Ep	Ephesians	1Ti	1 Timothy
Ga	Galatians	2Ti	2 Timothy
1K	1 Kefa (1 Peter)	Ti	Titus
2K	2 Kefa (2 Peter)	1Y	1 Yochanan (1 John)
Lk	Luke	2Y	2 Yochanan (2 John)
MJ	Messianic Jews (Hebrews)	3Y	3 Yochanan (3 John)
Mk	Mark	Ya	Ya'akov (James)
Mt	Mattityahu (Matthew)	Yd	Y'hudah (Jude)
Pm	Philemon	Yn	Yochanan (John)
Pp	Philippians		

A·bad·don — The king and/or angel of the Bottomless Pit (Abyss). From the Hebrew root *a-b-d*, "lose, destroy". The Greek translation of the name is *Apollyon*, which means "Destroyer". Rv 9:11.

Ab·ba [A] — An affectionate way to say "father", hence, "Dear father", "Dad", or even "Daddy". Though originally Aramaic the word was incorporated into ancient Hebrew. Israeli children call their fathers, *"Abba"*. Mk 14:36+.

a·cha·rit-ha·ya·mim — Literally, "the end of the days". The End Times or "latter days", when the *'olam hazeh* is coming to a close and the *'olam haba* is about to begin. 1C 10:11+.

A·chaz (Ahaz) — King of Y'hudah, father of Hezekiah; in Messianic genealogy. Mt. 1:9.

A·dam — the first man; the word means "man" generically; from Hebrew root *a-d-m,* "red", from which also comes the word *adamah*, "earth". Lk 3:38+.

Ad·di — in Messianic genealogy. Lk 3:28.

Ad·min — in Messianic genealogy. Lk 3:33.

A·do·nai — literally, "my Lord", but used in Judaism in lieu of the tetragrammaton (the Hebrew name of God consisting of the four letters, *yud-heh-vav-heh*), which is usually rendered in English as *"Y-H-V-H"*, "Yahweh", "Jehovah" or "the LORD". Mt 1:20+.

A·do·nai E·lo·hey·nu — LORD *(Y-H-V-H)*, our God (see *elohim*). Mk 12:29.

A·do·nai-Tzva·'ot (the Lord of Sabaoth) — LORD *(Y-H-V-H)* of (heaven's) armies, LORD of Hosts. Ro 9:29+.

A·gav (Agabus) — a New Testament prophet. Ac 11:28, 21:10.

A·ha·ron (Aaron) — Moshe's brother; traditionally the first *cohen gadol*. Lk 1:5+.

am-ha·'a·retz — literally, "people of the Land", that is, ordinary, unlearned people; used pejoratively in the first century: "boors". May be used as a singular noun to describe an individual: "He's just an *am-ha'aretz.*" Yn 7:49, Ac 4:13.

A·men — "It is true," "So be it," "May it become true." Spoken after a prayer or statement to indicate agreement. (1) Most translators take Yeshua's *"Amen"* as referring forward to what he was about to say: "Truly, I say to you,..." But there is no other instance of *"Amen"* pointing forward in early Jewish literature, and the context does not require it. Yeshua uses *"Amen"* to refer back, either seriously or ironically, to what he or someone else has said, or to what has just happened. Mt 5:18+. (2) Occasionally the term indicates to the congregation to say *"Amen"* at the end of a prayer. Mt 6:13+.

Am·ma·'us (Emmaus) — town of uncertain location about seven miles from Jerusalem. Lk 24:13.

Am·mi·na·dav (Amminadab) — in Messianic genealogy. Mt 1:4, Lk 3:33.

A·mon — in Messianic genealogy. Mt 1:10.

'A·mo·ra (Gomorrah, Gomorrha) — wicked city near the Dead Sea destroyed by God in the days of Avraham and Lot (Genesis 19), therefore a symbol of unrepentance. Mt 10:15+.

A·motz (Amos) — in Messianic genealogy, Lk 3:25.

A·nan (Annas) — *cohen gadol* when Yochanan and Yeshua were young, later a behind-the-scenes power. Lk 3:2+.

Ar·ni — in Messianic genealogy. Some versions have Ram (Aram). Lk 3:33.

Ar·pach·shad (Arphaxad) — in Messianic genealogy. Lk 3:36.

A·sa — Judean king; in Messianic genealogy. Mt 1:7.

Ash·dod (Azotus) — one of the five Philistine cities, located on Mediterranean coast of Israel, 20 miles south of modern Tel Aviv. Ac 8:40.

A·sher (Aser) — one of the twelve tribes of Israel. Lk 2:36, Rv 7:6.

Av·i·chud (Abiud) — in Messianic genealogy. Mt 1:13.

a·vi·nu — our father. Lk 1:73+.

A·vi·yah (Abijah, Abia) — (1) king of Y'hudah and ancestor of King David; in Messianic genealogy. Mt. 1:7. (2) one of the 24 divisions of the priesthood. Lk 1:5.

Av·ra·ham (Abraham) — First of the three Patriarchs of the Jewish people. Mt 1:1+.

Av·ra·ham a·vi·nu — Abraham, our father. Lk 1:73+.

Av·ya·tar (Abiathar) — cohen gadol at the time of King David. Mk 2:26.

'A·za (Gaza) — Philip took "the road that goes down from Yerushalayim to 'Aza, the desert road." 'Aza, some 40 miles south of modern Tel Aviv, was the southernmost of the five Philistine cities. A modern "'Aza Road" heads from downtown Yerushalayim towards Gaza and the Negev desert for a mile or so before it gets another name. Ac 8:26.

A·zur (Azor) — in Messianic genealogy. Mt 1:13.

Ba·'al (Baal) — the chief male god of the Phoenicians and Canaanites. The word means "lord", "master", and by extension, "husband". Ro 11:4.

Ba·'al-Zib·bul (Beelzevul) or Ba·'al-Z'vuv (Beelzebub); the manuscripts differ — derogatory names for the Adversary (Satan; see Mt 4:1). The latter is the name of a Philistine god (2 Kings 1:2) and means "lord of the flies". The former means "lord of heaven, lord of a high abode", hence "prince"; but it also suggests a word play on zevel, "rubbish, excrement". Mt 10:25+.

Ba·lak (Balac) — king of Moab who hired Bil'am to curse Israel (Numbers 22-24). Rv 2:14.

bar [A] — son. "Bar-" before a name means "son of" or "descendant of"; by extension it can also mean "having the properties of". Compare ben. Mt 10:3+.

Bar-Ab·ba (Barabbas) [A] — criminal released by Pontius Pilate instead of Yeshua the Messiah. The Aramaic name means "son of father". Mt 27:16+.

Bar-Nab·ba (Barnabas) [A] — talmid who worked with Sha'ul of Tarsus. In the New Testament the name is said to mean "the Exhorter"; it may be related to the Hebrew word navi, "prophet". Ac 4:36+.

Bar-Sab·ba (Barsabbas; the name may possibly be Bar-Shabbat, "son of Shabbat") [A] — surname of two figures. (1) The twelfth emissary, replacing Y'hudah from K'riot. Ac 1:23. (2) Disciple sent with Sila to Antioch bearing a letter from the emissaries. Ac 15:22.

Bar-Tal·mai (Bartholomew) [A] — one of the twelve emissaries. The name may mean "son of ptolemy", that is, son of an Egyptian ruler. Mt 10:3+.

Bar-Ti·mai (Bartimaeus) [A] — blind beggar whom Yeshua healed (see Timai). Mk 10:46.

Bar-Ye·shu·a (Barjesus) [A] — false prophet also called Elymas. Ac 13:6.

Bar-Yo·cha·**nan** (Barjona, son of John) [A] — Shim'on Kefa (Peter) is identified as Shim'on, son of Yochanan. Mt 16:17, Yn 21:15-17.

Ba·**rak** — D'vorah's general who defeated the Canaanite general, Sisera (Judges 4-5). MJ 11:32.

bat — daughter. "Bat-" before a name means "daughter of". Lk 2:36.

bat-kol — a voice from heaven; literally, "daughter of a voice". Mt 3:17, Yn 12:28.

Beit-An·**yah** (Bethany) — the name means "house of poverty". (1) Village east of Yerushalayim, on the Mount of Olives. Mt 21:17+. (2) Village on east bank of Yarden River. Yn 1:28.

Beit-Le·chem (Bethlehem) — birthplace of Yeshua and of King David; literally, "house of bread". Mt 2:1+.

Beit-Pa·**gey** (Bethphage) — village east of Jerusalem, on the Mount of Olives, near Beit-Anyah. Mt 21:1+.

Beit-Tzai·**dah** (Bethsaida) — literally, "house of nets". Native town of Andrew, Kefa and Philip on the west side of Lake Kinneret. Mt 11:21+.

Beit-Za·ta (Bethzatha); some manuscripts have Beit-Chasda (Bethesda) [A] — location of pool where Yeshua healed a man ill for 38 years. Beit-Zata may mean "house of olives"; Beit Chasda means "house of mercy". Yn 5:2.

ben — son. "Ben-" before a name means "son of" or "descendant of"; by extension it can also mean "having the properties of". Compare *bar*. Mt 4:21+.

Ben-Ha M'vo·rakh — Son of the Blessed, i.e., Son of God. Mk 14:61.

Be·rekh·**yah** (Berachiah, Barachiah, Barachias) — ancestor of the prophet Z'kharyah. Mt 23:35.

Bil·'**am** Ben-B·'**or** (Balaam son of Beor (Bosor)) — Midianite prophet hired by King Balak of Moab to curse Israel. Although he obeyed God and not Balak in blessing Israel, he led Israel astray into idol worship, including both sexual sin and eating sacrifices offered to idols (Numbers 22-25, 31; Psalm 106). 2 Kefa 2:15+.

Bin·ya·**min** (Benjamin) — one of the twelve tribes of Israel. The name means "son of (the) right (hand)". Ac 13:21+.

B'li·ya·'al (Belial) — another name for Satan, the Adversary. The Hebrew means "witout profit, worthless". 2C 6:15.

B'nei-Re·gesh — Greek *Boanergês* transliterates either this phrase, which means "sons of rage, sons of tumult", or Hebrew B'nei-Ro·gez, "sons of anger". Both fit the translation supplied by the text itself, "Thunderers". Yeshua gave this name to Zavdai's sons, probably because of their fiery zeal (Mk 9:38, Lk 9:5). Mk 3:17.

Bo·'az (Boaz, Boöz) — the great-grandfather of King David, in Messianic genealogy. Mt 1:5, Lk 3:32.

b'ra·khah, pl. *b'ra·khot* — blessing, benediction. The word comes from *berekh* ("knee") and shows the connection between worship and kneeling. To "make a *b'rakhah*" is to say a blessing, to bless. Mt 9:8+.

b'rit — covenant, contract. The major biblical covenants are those God made through Noach (Genesis 9), Avraham (Genesis 17), Moshe (Exodus 19-24), David (2 Samuel 7) and Yeshua (Jeremiah 31, Mt 26:28+). The first is with all mankind, the next three relate primarily to the Jewish people, and the last, though made with the Jewish people, brings all mankind into relationship with all the covenants.

B'rit Cha·da·shah — New Covenant, New Testament. The term is used in the Introduction but not in the text of the *Jewish New Testament.* (However, the New Covenant is mentioned at Mt 26:28, Mk 14:24, Lk 22:20, 1 C 11:25, Ga 4:25, and throughout MJ 7:22-10:31, as well as in the *Tanakh* at Jeremiah 31:30-34).

b'rit-mi·lah — literally, "covenant of circumcision" (see Genesis 17). The term can mean either the act or the ceremony of covenantal circumcision, which is normally performed on the eighth day of a male Jew's life and required of any male Gentile who converts to Judaism. Lk 1:59+.

bub·be-mei·ses [Y] — "old wives' tales"; literally, "grandmothers' stories". 1Ti 4:7.

Ca·na·'an (Canaan, Chanaan) — ancient name for the Land of Israel used at Mt 15:22 to identify the origin of the Gentile woman who approached Yeshua in the region of Tzor and Tzidon, and twice in an historical setting (Ac 7:11, 13:18); in the latter Sha'ul points out that God gave Cana'an to the people of Israel as an inheritance. See more at *Eretz-Israel.*

Cha·kal-D'ma (Akeldama, Aceldama) [A] — "which in their language means 'Field of Blood'." Ac 1:19.

Chal·fai (Alphaeus, Alpheus) — father of Ya'akov Ben-Chalfai, who was one of Yeshua's twelve *talmidim.* Mt 10:3+.

chal·lah — loaf or cake. The modern popular meaning is the special bread eaten on *Shabbat.* But in Romans 11:16 it refers to the share of the dough set aside for the *cohanim* in accordance with Numbers 15:20 (where the word appears) and *Mishna* tractate *Challah.*

cha·metz — leavened dough, either cooked or not. The term is also used loosely to refer to the yeast or other leavening agent itself. Mt 16:6+.

Cha·mor (Hamor, Emmor) — Owner of a field in Sh'khem. Ac 7:16.

Cha·nah Bat-P'nu·'el (Anna the daughter of Phanuel) — aged prophet who spoke about Yeshua. Lk 2:36.

Cha·nan·yah (Ananias) — (1) Believer who lied to the Holy Spirit. Ac 5:1+. (2) Messianic Jew in Damascus who prayed for Sha'ul to receive his sight. Ac 9:10+. (3) *Cohen gadol* at the time of Sha'ul's trial. Ac 23:2+.

Cha·noch (Enoch) — seventh in descent from Adam in Messianic genealogy. According to Genesis 5:24 he did not die, at least not in the usual way, but "walked with God, and he was not, for God took him." Lk 3:37+.

Cha·nuk·kah — the Feast of Dedication, honoring Temple rededication by the Maccabees (164 B.C.E.) after its profanation under Seleucid king Antiochus IV. Yn 10:22.

Cha·ran (Haran, Charran) — city in the Fertile Crescent (near the border between modern Syria and Turkey) where *Avraham avinu* stopped for many years before continuing on to Cana'an. Ac 7:2ff.

Cha·vah (Eve) — the first woman. 2C 11:3, 1Ti 2:13.

Ches·li (Esli) — in Messianic genealogy. Lk 3:25.

Chetz·ron (Hezron, Esrom) — ancestor of Avraham, in genealogy of Yeshua. Mt 1:3, Lk 3:33.

Chiz·ki·ya·hu (Hezekiah, Ezekias) — king of Judah, in Messianic genealogy. Mt 1:9-10.

chutz·pah — boldness, audacity, insolence, nerve, gall, or a combination thereof, weighted according to the situational need. Lk 11:8.

co·hen, pl. *co·ha·nim* — priest (in the Temple or Tabernacle). Mt 2:4+.

co·hen ga·dol, pl. *co·ha·nim g'do·lim* — high priest. *Co·hen ha·ga·dol* means "the high priest". Mt 26:3+.

Dal·ma·**nu**·ta (Dalmanutha) — place of uncertain location along west shore of Lake Kinneret; perhaps identical with or near Magdala. Mk 8:10.

Dam·**me**·sek (Damascus) — ancient city, now capital of modern Syria. Ac 9:2+.

Da·ni·**'el** — *Tanakh* prophet. Mt 24:15.

Da·**vid** — king of Israel and ancestor of Yeshua the Messiah. Mt 1:1+.

*dav·ven·*ing [Y] — praying. Mt 23:14+.

de·na·ri·us [O] — a Roman coin, the standard daily wage for a common laborer. Mt 20:2+.

Di·a·spo·ra, the [O] — the Dispersion, i.e., the scattering of the Jewish people in exile (Hebrew *galut*) to the far corners of the earth which began during the reign of the Judean kings but was hastened by the Assyrian conquest (732 B.C.E.), the Babylonian conquest (586 B.C.E.), the destruction of the Temple (70 C.E.) and the Bar-Kokhva Rebellion (132-135 C.E.). It continues to this day, but reversal started in the 19th century as Jews began returning to *Eretz-Israel*. Today 3.7 million Jews live in Israel and about 9 million in the Diaspora. Ya 1:1+.

drash, pl. *dra·shot* — homily, sermon, teaching, Bible study. Ac 17:2.

E·**fra**·yim (Ephraim) — one of the two sons of Yosef the son of the Patriarch Ya'akov, hence a half-tribe (see M'nasheh); in the New Testament Efrayim is mentioned only as a town northeast of Yerushalayim. Yn 11:54.

Ei·**na**·yim (Aenon, Ainon, Enon) — place "near Shalem" where Yochanan immersed; the name means "springs". It may be near Beit-Sh'an in the north, near Sh'khem in Samaria, or northeast of Yerushalayim. Yn 3:23.

El·**'a**·**zar** (Eleazar, Lazarus) — (1) Ancestor of Yeshua. Mt 1:15. (2) Beggar outside rich man's home in story told by Yeshua. Lk 16:20ff. (3) Brother of Marta and Miryam #6; Yeshua raised him from the dead. Yn 11:1ff.

E·**li** (Heli) — in Messianic genealogy; father or grandfather of Yosef #3, or father of Miryam #2, depending on interpretation. Lk 3:23

E·li! E·li! L'mah sh'vak·ta·ni? [A] — "which means, 'My God! My God! Why have you deserted me?'" Mt 27:46.

El·**'i**·**chud** (Eliud) — in Messianic genealogy. Mt 1:14-15.

Eli·**'ez**·er — in Messianic genealogy. Lk 3:29.

E·li·**sha** (Eliseus) — *Tanakh* prophet and miracle-worker, Eliyahu's disciple. Lk 4:27.

E·li·**she**·va (Elisabeth, Elizabeth) — mother of Yochanan the Immerser. Lk 1:5+.

E·li·**ya**·hu (Elijah, Elias) — *Tanakh* prophet and miracle-worker who did not die but was taken up into heaven. Malachi 3:23(4:5) says he will herald "the great and terrible day of *Adonai.*" Therefore Jewish tradition regards him as the forerunner of the Messiah. Mt 11:14+.

El·ma·**dan** (Elmadam, Elmodam) — in Messianic genealogy. Lk 3:28.

E·lo·hi! E·lo·hi! L'mah sh'vak·ta·ni? [A] — "which means, 'My God! My God! Why have you deserted me?'"

E·lo·him — God, gods. Yeshua uses both meanings in his word-play at Yn 10:33-36.

El·ya·kim (Eliakim) — two persons in Messianic genealogy. The name means "God will raise up." Mt 1:13, Lk 3:30.

E·nosh (Enos) — grandson of Adam, in Messianic genealogy. Lk 3:38.

Er — in Messianic genealogy. Lk 3:28.

E·retz-Is·ra·el — the Land of Israel. In the New Testament this territory is called *Eretz-Israel*, Israel, Cana'an (see glossary entries), and, most often, simply "the Land". See Introduction, page xxiii. Mt 2:20-21.

E·sav (Esau) — brother of *Ya'akov avinu.* Ro 9:13+.

E·ver (Eber) — ancestor of Avraham, in Messianic genealogy. Lk 3:35.

E·ver-Ha·Yar·den — a part of *Eretz-Israel* on the east bank of the Jordan river in what is now the country of Jordan. Mt 4:25.

Gab·ta [A] — "the place called the Pavement." Yn 19:13.

Gad — one of the twelve tribes of Israel. Rv 7:5.

Ga·lil, the (Galilee) — the Galil is the portion of *Eretz-Israel* west of Lake Kinneret and north of the Yizre'el (Jezreel) Valley. Mt 2:22+.

Ga·lil-of-the *Go·yim* (Galilee of the nations) — the portion of *Eretz-Israel* east of the Galil and of Lake Kinneret in what is now the country of Jordan. Its name describes the fact that it was inhabited largely by non-Jews. Mt 4:15.

Gam·li·'el (Gamaliel) — a major figure in non-Messianic Judaism, the first to be given the title *Rabban* ("our great one"). Of him the *Mishna* says, "When *Rabban* Gamli'el the Elder died, the glory of the *Torah* ceased, and purity and modesty died." (*Sotah* 9:15) He was Sha'ul's teacher, and he warned the *Sanhedrin* not to act rashly against the Messianic Jews. Ac 5:34-39, 22:3.

Gan-E·den (Paradise) — literally, "Garden of Eden"; in Judaism the term also refers to Paradise. Lk 23:43.

Gat-Sh'ma·nim (Gethsemane) — garden where Yeshua prayed and was apprehended by the Temple police. The term is odd, meaning, literally, "wine-press of oils". Since it is located on the flank of the Mount of Olives, it is presumed that the garden was an olive orchard with an olive-oil press. Mt 26:36+.

Gav·ri·'el (Gabriel) — Angel sent in the *Tanakh* to Dani'el and in the New Testament to Z'kharyah #2 and Miryam #2. Lk 1:19, 26.

get — rabbinic term for a "writing of divorcement", as spoken of in Deuteronomy 24:1-4. Mt 5:31+.

Gey-Hin·nom (Gehenna) — literally, "valley of Hinnom", located south of (the Old City of) Yerushalayim, where the city's rubbish was burned; hence, metaphorically, because of the fires, hell. Mt 5:22+.

Gid·'on (Gideon, Gedeon) — a judge of Israel (Judges 6-8). MJ 11:32.

Gi·no·sar (Gennesaret) — town on northwest coast of Lake Kinneret. Mt 14:34+.

Gog — chief prince of Meshech and Tubal, from land of Magog, leads final battle against God (Ezekiel 38-39). Rv 20:8.

Goy, pl. *Go·yim* — The Greek word *ethnos* is rendered variously in the *Jewish New Testament* as "Gentile", "nation", "pagan", "non-Jew", and *"Goy"*; other versions sometimes render it "heathen". As used among English-speaking Jews *Goyim* means "Non-Jews", i.e., those outside "our group"; as with all words employed in this way, it can have a positive, a neutral or a negative connotation, depending on the speaker and the situation. In the *Jewish New Testament*, to avoid suggesting exclusivist overtones when the text does not intend them, the word is used rather rarely to translate *ethnos* and then only when God is speaking or when a Jew is addressing other Jews. Mt 5:47+.

Goy·i·she [Y] — Gentile (adjective). Ga 2:15.

Gul·gol·ta (Golgotha, Calvary) [A] — "which means 'place of a skull,'" the place where Yeshua was executed on a stake. Archeologists are in general agreement that the traditional site of Gulgolta, in the Church of the Holy Sepulchre within the Old City of Yerushalayim, is the correct one. Mt 27:33+.

Ha·El·yon — "the Most High", "the Highest", i.e., God. Mk 5:7+.

Ha·gar (Agar) — Sarah's handmaiden (Genesis 16, 21). Ga 4:24f.

Ha·G'du·lah — "the Greatness", "the Majesty", i.e., *Y-H-V-H*. MJ 8:1.

Ha·G'du·lah Ba·M'ro·mim — "the Greatness on High", a euphemism for *Y-H-V-H*. MJ 1:3.

Ha·G'vu·rah — "the Power", a euphemism for *Y-H-V-H*. Mt 26:64.

Ha·Ka·dosh — "the Holy One", a euphemism for *Y-H-V-H*. 1Y 2:20.

Hal·lel — literally, "praise". The "Egyptian" *Hallel* consists of Psalms 113-118; the "Great" *Hallel* is Psalm 136. Both are recited as part of the *Seder* service. Mt 26:30+.

Hal·le·lu·yah! (Hallelujah!) — a command in the plural, "Praise *Yah!*" (*Yah* is a name of God; see Psalm 68:5(4)). Sometimes rendered: "Praise the LORD!" Rv 19:1ff.

Ha·M'vo·rakh — "the Blessed One", a

euphemism for *Y-H-V-H*. Mk 14:61.

Har-Me·gid·do (Armageddon) — the "hill of Megiddo", an ancient town with more than twenty archeological layers covering the period from nearly 6000 years ago until the fourth century B.C.E. It was chosen again and again as the site for a city because of its strategic location guarding a pass on the *Via Maris* (the "Way of the Sea") joining Egypt and Assyria and overlooking the Valley of Yizre'el (Jezreel, Esdraelon), apparently the site of the final eschatological battle. However, Greek *armageddon* could be rendering Har Migdo ("hill of his glory"), in which case it refers to Mount Tziyon in Yerushalayim. Rv 16:9.

Ha·Shem — "the Name", i.e., *Y-H-V-H*, hence a euphemism for God. 3Y 7.

He·vel (Abel) — Adam and Eve's second son, killed by Kayin (Genesis 4). Mt 23:35+.

Hip·pa·tach! (Ephphatha!) — "Be opened!" Mk 7:34.

Ho·sha·na Rab·bah — literally, the "great hosanna", the "great save-us-please". It refers to the last day, "the great day", of the week-long *Sukkot* festival, when, in Temple times, water was brought from the Pool of Shiloach for a brilliant ceremony. The day is still noted in modern Judaism. Yn 7:37.

Ho·she·a (Hosea, Osee) — one of the twelve "minor prophets" in the *Tanakh*. Ro 9:25.

Im·ma·nu·'el (Immanuel, Emmanuel) — Name to be given to the child of the *'almah* (young woman, virgin) in Isaiah 7:14 and applied by Mattityahu to Yeshua. The name means "God with us" or "God is with us." Mt 1:23.

Is·ra·el — (1) The descendants of the

Patriarch Ya'akov, who is himself called Israel (Genesis 32:10), i.e., the Jewish people. Mt 2:6+. (2) The Land of Israel. Mt 2:20-21, 10:23; Lk 4:25, 27. (3) Those within Israel who remain faithful to God. Ro 9:6, and perhaps implied at 1C 10:18 and/or Ga 6:16. (4) All Jewish and Gentile believers in God and his Messiah Yeshua. Perhaps implied at Ga 6:16 and/or Ep 2:12-13.

I·yov (Job) — the world's best-known sufferer, who learned from his sufferings. Ya 5:11.

I·ze·vel (Jezebel) — wife of King Ahab of Israel, encouraged idolatry. Rv 2:20.

Ka·nah (Cana) — town in the Galil where Yeshua did two miracles. Home of Yeshua's *talmid* Natan'el. Possibly identical with the Arab town of Kana-el-Jelil ("Jelil" is the Arabic form of "Galil"), about five miles north of Tzippori (Sepphoris), near Natzeret. Yn 2:1+.

kap·pa·rah — atonement, expiation, propitiation; more loosely: forgiveness, pardon. Ro 3:23; MJ 2:17; 1Y 2:2, 3:10.

Ka·ya·fa (Caiaphas) — *cohen gadol* at the time of Yeshua. Mt 26:3+.

Ka·yin (Cain) — Adam and Eve's first son, who killed Hevel (Genesis 4). MJ 11:4+.

Ke·fa (Cephas, Peter) — name given by Yeshua to Shim'on Bar-Yochanan; it means "rock" in Aramaic, as does the Greek equivalent, *petros*. Mt 4:18+.

Kei·nan (Cainan) — great-grandson of Adam; in Messianic genealogy. Lk 3:37.

K'far-Na·chum (Capernaum) — town on northwest shore of Lake Kinneret where Yeshua did much of his ministry. The name means "village of Nahum". Mt 4:13+.

Kid·ron (Cedron) — valley east of the Old City of Yerushalayim, separating it from the Mount of Olives. Yn 18:1.

Kin·ne·ret, Lake — modern Israel's name for the Sea of Galilee. The name or a variant is found seven times in the *Tanakh*, first at Numbers 34:11, where it is rendered in most English versions as "Chinnereth". Mt 4:18+.

Kish — father of Israel's first king, Sha'ul. Ac 13:20.

Klo·fah (Clopas, Cleopas, Cleophas) — Yeshua's uncle-by-marriage Yn 19:25.

Ko·rach (Korah, Core) — Levite who led rebellion against Moshe in the desert; God punished Korach by having the earth swallow him alive (Numbers 16, 26). Yd 11.

Ko·ra·zin (Chorazin) — city on the shore of Lake Kinneret two miles north of K'far-Nachum. Mt 11:21+.

kor·ban (corban) — sacrifice, i.e., an animal sacrifice, but Mark explains the term as meaning "a gift to God". Mk 7:11.

Ko·sam (Cosam) — in Messianic genealogy. Lk 3:28.

K'ri·ot — town about twenty miles south of Yerushalayim. Home of Judas Iscariot (Y'hudah from K'riot; see glossary entry). Mt 10:4+.

k'ru·vim (cherubim, cherubims) — Heavenly creatures (angels) who guarded the way to the Tree of Life in Gan-Eden (Genesis 3:24), were described by Ezekiel as having four faces and four wings (Ez 10:20-21), and were ridden by God (Psalm 18:11(10)); compare the "living beings" of Rv 4:6ff. The term also refers to the gold-overlaid wooden images of same, constructed in obedience to God's command, which overshadowed the Ark of the

Covenant in the Tabernacle and in the Temple MJ 9:5.

Ku·za (Chuza) [A] — Herod's finance minister. The name means "little jug". Lk 8:3.

kvetch·ing [Y] — complaining, fretting, whining. Pp 2:14.

Le·mekh (Lamech) — father of Noach; in Messianic genealogy. Lk 3:36.

Lot — Avraham's nephew, saved from God's destruction of S'dom. Lk 17:28+.

Lud (Lod, Lydda) — town in the plain northwest of Yerushalayim and east of what is now Tel Aviv and Yafo, near Ben-Gurion International Airport. Ac 9:32ff.

L'vi (Levite), pl. *L'vi'im* — Temple worker. The *Torah* prescribes that the descendents of L'vi would be priests and Levites. Lk 10:32+.

L'vi (Levi) — (1) Third son of the Patriarch Ya'akov. MJ 7:5+. (2) The tribe of Israel descended from him. Rv. 7:7. (3-4) Two ancestors of Yeshua. Lk 3:24, 29. (5) A disciple of Yeshua also known as Mattityahu. Mk 2:14+.

L'vi ben-Chal**fai** — Levi, the son of Alpheus; same as L'vi #5 above. Mk 2:14+.

Ma·chat (Maath) — in Messianic genealogy. Lk 3:26.

ma·cher [Y] — literally, "doer, maker". Someone zealous and active in a group, a "big wheel", but often with overtones of self-importance, hence a person who "throws his weight around," has "connections", is an "operator" or "fixer". 1K 5:3.

Ma·ga·**dan** — town on Lake Kinneret, perhaps same as Magdala. Mt 15:39.

Mag·**da**·la — town on Lake Kinneret, home of Mary Magdalene (see Miryam of Magdala). Mt 27:56+.

Ma·**gog** — Place from which Gog arises to make war against God's people (Ezekiel 38-39). Rv 20:8.

Ma·ha·lal·**'el** (Mahalaleel, Maleleel) —

between Adam and Noach in Messianic genealogy. Lk 3:37.

Mal·**'ah** (Melea) — in Messianic genealogy. Lk 3:31.

Mal·**ki** (Melchi) — two figures in Messianic genealogy. Lk 3:24, 28.

Mal·ki-**Tze**·dek (Melchizedek, Melchisedec) — priest of *El Elyon* ("the Most High God"), to whom *Avraham avinu* gave a tenth of the battle spoil (Genesis 14:18-20). In Psalm 110:4 he becomes the model for a new priesthood. The literal meaning of the name is, "My king is righteousness." MJ 5:6+.

mam·zer — technically, the offspring of a sexual relationship between persons forbidden by the *Torah* to marry each other (e.g., uncle and niece), but usually translated "bastard". Like that word, it can be used as a strong insult. Yn 9:34, MJ 12:8.

Ma·nah (Menna, Menan) — in Messianic genealogy. Lk 3:31.

ma·neh, pl. *ma·nim* — sum of money, 100 denarii (see glossary entry), about three months' wages for an average worker. Usally rendered "pound". Lk 19:12ff.

Ma·ra·na, ta! (Maranatha!) [A] — "Our Lord, come!" — 1C 16:22.

Mar·**ta** (Martha) [A] — sister of Miryam #6 and El'azar. The name means "lady". The masculine equivalent, *mar* ("lord" — see above, *Marana, ta!*) is used in modern Hebrew as the equivalent of English "Mr." Lk 10:38+.

Ma·shi·ach (Messiah, Christ) — literally, "anointed", "an anointed one". Transliterated into English as "Messiah". Equivalent to Greek *christos*, which also means "anointed" and comes into English as "Christ". In the *Tanakh,* kings and *cohanim* were ordained by being anointed with olive oil (Exodus 30:30, 1 Samuel 15:1, Psalm 133). The *Jewish New Testament* uses *"Mashiach"* to render Greek *messias*, which appears only twice (Yn 1:41, 4:25), and in four dramatic passages to render *christos*: Mt 16:16; Mk 8:29, 14:61; Lk 9:20.

Mat·tan (Matthan) — in Messianic genealogy. Mt 1:15.

Mat·tat (Matthat) — two figures in Messianic genealogy. Lk 3:24, 29.

Mat·ta·tah (Mattatha) — in Messianic genealogy. Lk 3:31.

Mat·tit·ya·hu (Matthew, Matthias, Mattathias) — (1) One of Yeshua's twelve *talmidim*, author of one of the Gospels, also known as L'vi (Mt 9:9+); usually rendered in English as "Matthew". (2) One of the two candidates to replace Y'hudah from K'riot as one of Yeshua's emissaries (Ac 1:23, 26); usually rendered in English as "Matthias". (3-4) Two figures in Messianic genealogy (Lk 3:25, 26); usually rendered in English as "Mattathias".

ma·tzah — unleavened bread. The "first day for *matzah*" would be the day on which, when evening comes, the *Seder* is held.

m'chi·tzah — divider which separates people into two groups, e.g., the partition separating men from women in an Orthodox synagogue. At Ep 2:14 it refers at least metaphorically to the fence which separates the inner parts of the Temple, where only Jews could enter, from the Court of the Gentiles. This *m'chitzah*, also called a *soreg*, was a stone partition about five feet high.

Me·lekh (Malchus) — slave of Kayafa the *cohen gadol*; the Hebrew word means "king". Yn 18:10.

Me·na·chem (Manaen) — "who had been brought up with Herod the governor." The name means "comforter". Ac 13:1.

me·no·rah — lamp; the *menorah* in the Temple had seven branches. MJ 9:2, Rv 1:12+.

mentsh [Y] — a good, reliable person; a real human being, energetic, moral and compassionate.1C 16:13.

me·shug·ga — crazy. Yn 10:20.

Me·tu·she·lach (Methuselah, Mathusala) — grandfather of Noach, in Messianic genealogy. Lk 3:37.

mid·rash — allegorical interpretation or homiletical application of a text. The hearer is expected to understand that the maker of the *midrash* is not expounding the plain meaning of the text but introducing his own ideas. Ga 4:24.

Mid·yan (Midian, Madian) — desert region including parts of the Sinai Peninsula and what is now southern Jordan. Ac 7:29.

Mi·kha·'el (Michael) — a ruling angel ("archangel") described at Daniel 10:21 and 12:1 as watching out for the interests of the nation of Israel, and in the New Testament as the commander of the angels contending with the Adversary, Satan. Yd 9, Rv 12:7.

mik·veh — bath or pool with a flow of fresh water; used in Orthodox Judaism to this day for ritual purification. Ti 3:5.

min·chah — the afternoon Temple sacrifice, which was accompanied by prayers. In today's Judaism the afternoon synagogue service is called *minchah* by way of commemoration. Ac 3:1, 10:30.

min·yan — quorum needed for certain public prayers; Orthodox Judaism sets it at ten men, while Conservative Judaism includes women. Ac 16:13.

Mir·yam (Mary, Miriam) — (1) The original Miryam was the sister of Moshe, but she does not appear in the New Testament. (2) Mother of Yeshua the Messiah. Mt 1:16+. (3) Miryam from Magdala (see below). (4) Mother of Ya'akov #7 and Yosef #8 (Yosi #2). Mt 27:56+. (5) Wife of Klofah. Yn 19:25. (6) Sister of Marta and El'azar in Beit-Anyah. Lk 10:39+. (7) Mother of Yochanan Mark. Ac 12:12. (8) A believer in Rome. Ro 16:6.

Mir·yam from Mag·da·la; Mir·yam, called Mag·da·lit (Mary Magdalene) — *talmidah* of Yeshua from the town of Magdala (see glossary entry). Mt 27:56+.

mitz·vah, pl. *mitz·vot* — literally: "command", "commandment"; more broadly: general principle for living, good deed. Mt 5:19+.

M'na·sheh (Manasseh, Manasses) — (1) Son of Yosef #1 and grandson of Ya'akov #1. He does not appear in the New Testament, but the half-tribe of Israel named for him does. Rv 7:6. (2) A king of Y'hudah; in Messianic genealogy. Mt 1:10.

Mo·lekh (Moloch) — false god worshipped in the ancient Near East. Ac 7:43.

Mo·she (Moses) — (1) Deliverer of Israel from Egypt, agent through whom Israel received the *Torah*. Mt 8:4+. (2) The "seat of Moshe" was not only a metaphor for the authority of the *Torah*-teachers, but an actual chair on which they sat when they taught. An example, from the third century C.E., discovered in the ruins of Korazin (see glossary entry), is on display at the Israel Museum in Yerushalayim. Mt 23:2.

Mo·tza·'ei-Shab·bat — literally, the "going-out of the Sabbath", i.e., Saturday night. By biblical and Jewish reckoning days begin at sunset; so where the text tells us that the believers met on "the first day of the week", it means Saturday night, not Sunday. Ac 20:7, 1C 16:2.

Na·'a·man (Naaman) — Syrian general healed of serious skin disease by God through the prophet Elisha (2 Kings 5). Lk 4:27.

Na·chor (Nahor) — grandfather of Avraham; in Messianic genealogy. Lk 3:34.

Nach·shon (Nahshon, Naasson) — ancestor of King David; in Messianic genealogy. Mt 1:4, Lk 3:32.

Na·chum (Nahum, Naum) — in Messianic genealogy. Lk 3:25.

Naf·ta·li (Naphtali, Nephthalim) — (1) Tribe of Israel descended from a son of the Patriarch Ya'akov. Rv 7:6. (2) The territory in *Eretz-Israel* assigned to that tribe (Joshua 19-21). Mt 4:13ff.

Nag·gai (Nagge) — in Messianic genealogy. Lk 3:25.

Na·'im (Nain) — town in the Galil where Yeshua raised a widow's son from the dead. The name means "pleasant". Lk 7:11.

Nak·di·mon (Nicodemus) — *Parush*, member of the Sanhedrin and "teacher in Israel". Though the name Nicodemus is Greek, it was hebraized to Nakdimon, and a well-known first-century Jerusalemite was named Nakdimon Ben-Gurion (*Taanit* 19b, *Genesis Rabbah* 42, etc.) Yn 3:1+.

Na·tan (Nathan) — son of King David; in Messianic genealogy. Lk 3:31.

Na·tan·'el (Nathanael) — *talmid* of Yeshua. Yn 1:45+.

Na·tze·ret (Nazareth) — town in the Galil where Yeshua grew up and lived most of his life. Mt 2:23+.

Natz·ra·ti (Nazarene), pl. *Natz·ra·tim* — In regard to Mattityahu, the *Tanakh* nowhere says that the Messiah is to be called a *Natzrati*, but Isaiah 11:2 refers to him as a *netzer* ("branch, shoot"). Since *Natzrati* means "resident of Natzeret", the name *Natzratim* (followers of the man from Natzeret) is given to the Jewish followers of Yeshua. Thus Mattityahu's "fulfillment" apparently involves a word play, although other explanations have been offered. The modern Hebrew word for "Christian" is *Notzri*, a variant of *Natzrati*. Mt 2:23, Ac 24:5.

Ne·ri — in Messianic genealogy. Lk 3:27.

Ni·ne·veh (Nineve) — capital of ancient Assyria where the prophet Yonah preached. Mt 12:41+.

No·ach (Noah) — builder of the ark, survivor of the Flood and ancestor of all mankind since then (Genesis 5-11); in Messianic genealogy. Mt 24:37+.

n'ti·lat-ya·da·yim — ceremonial handwashing prescribed by the Oral *Torah* to be done before meals and at other times in order to be ritually pure; it continues to be a norm in Orthodox Judaism. Mt 15:2+.

nu [Y] — a general-purpose word meaning variously, "Well?" "So?" "Indeed!" "I challenge you," or "If not that, then what?" — with many possible inflections and overtones. Mt 11:9+.

nud·nik [Y] — (1) a bore, (2) a pest, (3) both. Lk 18:5.

'o·lam ha·ba — the world to come, the age to come. Mt 12:32+.

'o·lam ha·zeh — this world, this age. Mt 12:32+.

O·ved (Obed) — grandfather of King David; in Messianic genealogy. Mt 1:5, Lk 3:32.

pa·ro·khet — curtain, specifically the one dividing the Holy of Holies from the rest of the Temple or Tabernacle. There were actually two such *p'rokhot* (see MJ 9:3). The first separated the Holy Place from the outer court (Exodus 26:36-37, 36:37-38), whereas the second separated the Holy of Holies from the Holy Place (Exodus 26:31-33, 36:35-36). The curtain covering the Ark of the *Torah* in a modern synagogue is also called a *parokhet*. Mt 27:51+.

Pa·rush (Pharisee) — see *P'rushim*, below.

Pe·leg (Phalec) — ancestor of Avraham; in Messianic genealogy. Lk 3:35.

Pe·retz (Perez, Phares) — grandson of the Patriarch Ya'akov; in Messianic genealogy. Mt 1:3.

Pe·sach — the feast of Passover, celebrating the Exodus of the Jewish nation from Egypt under the leadership of Moshe. It is, along with *Shavu'ot* and *Sukkot*, one of the three pilgrim festivals when Jews were to come to Yerushalayim. Mt 26:2+.

P'nu·el (Phanuel) — father of Chanah, the aged widow who blessed Yeshua in the Temple. Ac 2:36.

P'ru·shim (Pharisees), sing. *Parush* — The *P'rushim* and *Tz'dukim* were the two main components of the religious establishment in Yeshua's time. The *P'rushim* focussed on the *Torah* and what it requires of ordinary people, rather than on the Temple ritual. When the Temple was destroyed in 70 C.E., the *P'rushim* were in a position to develop their tradition into the basis for Jewish life everywhere; this tradition is the core of the *Talmud* and of modern religious Judaism. Mt 3:7+.

Rab·ba·ni — literally, "my great one", hence, "teacher". In the *Mishna* the title *Rabban* is given to Gamli'el (see glossary entry). Yn 20:16.

rab·bi — literally, "my great one", hence, a teacher. In modern Judaism a rabbi is someone ordained to determine *halakhah* (Jewish law), to judge, and to teach *Torah*. Still more recently, the term "rabbi" has come to mean a Jewish clergyman, i.e., a leader with congregational or community responsibilities. Mt 8:19+.

Ra·chav (Rahab, Rachab) — the prostitute in Yericho who hid the Israelite spies in the days of Y'hoshua; in Messianic genealogy (Joshua 2, 6). Mt 1:5+.

Ra·chel — wife of the Patriarch Ya'akov, one of the four Mothers of Israel. Mt 2:18.

Ra·mah — town in the vicinity of Yerushalayim, in the tribal portion allotted to Binyamin. Mt 2:18.

Ram (Aram) — ancestor of King David; in Messianic genealogy. Mt 1:3-4, Lk 3:33.

Ra·ma·ta·yim (Arimathea, Arimathaea) — town in the foothills *(sh'felah)* northeast of Lud and northwest of Yerushalayim. Hom of Yosef #9, who took Yeshua s body and had it buried in his own tomb. Mt 27:57+.

Re·chav·'am (Rehoboam, Roboam) — son of King Shlomo; in Messianic genealogy. Mt 1:7.

Rei·fan (Rephan, Remphan) — Babylonian god called Keivan in the *Tanakh* and corresponding to Saturn. Ac 7:43.

Rei·sha (Rhesa) — son of Z'rubavel; in Messianic genealogy. Lk 3:27.

Re·'u (Reu, Ragau) — ancestor of Avraham; in Messianic genealogy. Lk 3:35.

Re·'u·ven (Reuben) — tribe of Israel named after the first son of the Patriarch Ya'akov. Rv 7:5.

Riv·kah (Rebecca) — wife of the Patriarch Yitzchak, one of the four Mothers of Israel. Ro 9:10.

Rosh-Cho·desh — the festival, observed to this day in Judaism, celebrating the beginning of each Jewish lunar month. Co 2:16.

Ru·ach-Ha·Ko·desh — the Holy Spirit, referred to four times in the *Tanakh* as such, and many times as the Spirit of God. Mt 1:18+.

Rut (Ruth) — Moabite woman who joined the Jewish people, became the wife of Bo'az and was the great-grandmother of King David; in Messianic genealogy. Mt 1:5.

Sal·mon — ancestor of King David; in Messianic genealogy. Mt 1:4-5, Lk 3:32.

san·hed·rin — Jewish religious court. Lower *sanhedrin*s had 3 or 23 judges; the high *Sanhedrin* in Yerushalayim had 70. Mt 5:22+.

Sa·rah (Sara) — wife of Avraham, first of the four Mothers of Israel. Ro 4:19+.

Sa·tan — literally, "the Adversary", i.e., Satan, the Devil. In the *Tanakh* he is described specifically at Job 1-2 and by implication in Isaiah 14:11-15 and Ezekiel 28. Mt 4:10+.

S'dom (Sodom, Sodoma) — city near the Dead Sea destroyed by God (Genesis 19). Mt 10:15+.

Se·der — the ceremonial evening meal with which *Pesach* begins in Jewish homes. Mt 26:17+.

se·khel — intelligence, common sense, "smarts". Lk 16:8.

Se·rug (Saruch) — ancestor of Avraham; in Messianic genealogy. Lk 3:35.

Shab·bat, pl. *Shab·ba·tot* — Sabbath. Mt 12:1+.

Sha·lem (Salem, Salim) — (1) Place near Einayim. Yn 3:23. (2) Yerushalayim; see Psalm 76:3(2). MJ 7:1-2.

sha·lom — peace, tranquillity, safety, well-being, welfare, health, contentment, success, comfort, wholeness and integrity. *"Shalom!"* is a common greeting. Mt 10:12+.

Sha·lom a·lei·khem! — "Peace be upon you (plural)!" A common greeting. Mt 10:12+.

Sh·'al·ti·el (Shealtiel, Salathiel) — father of Z'rubavel; in Messianic genealogy. Mt 1:12, Lk 3:27.

sham·mash, pl. *sham·ma·shim* — attendant, servant, caretaker, deacon. Lk 4:20+.

Shap·pi·rah (Sapphira) — person who conspired to lie to the Holy Spirit. Ac 5:1+.

sha·rav — hot dry wind which blows over the Land of Israel from the deserts to the east in the spring and fall. In modern Israel it is also known by its Arabic name, *chamsin* ("fifty"), which refers to the fifty days between *Pesach* and *Shavu'ot*, the most common season for such weather. Ya 1:11.

Sha·ron, the — one of the four major geographical regions of Israel, namely, the low-lying plain near the Mediterranean Sea. The other three, which also parallel the coast, are, from west to east, the *sh'felah* (foothills), the hill country of Y'hudah and Shomron, and the Yarden Valley-Dead Sea rift. Ac 9:35.

Sha·'ul (Saul) — "also known as Paul" (Ac 13:9). Yeshua the Messiah's emissary to the Gentile world, who presented Israel's New Covenant faith in God and his Messiah in a way that does not require Gentiles to convert to Judaism. Ac 7:58+.

Sha·'ul Ben-Kish — Saul the son of Kish, Israel's first king. Ac 13:21.

Sha·vu·'ot — the Feast of Weeks, since it comes seven weeks after Passover; also called Pentecost (from Greek *pentekostos*, "fifty"), since one counts 50 days after Passover. One of the three *regalim* ("pilgrim festivals") when Jews were expected to celebrate before God in Yerushalayim; the other two are *Pesach* and *Sukkot*. Ac 2:1+.

sh·'ei·lah, pl. *sh·'ei·lot* — question. In Judaism *"sh'eilah"* can be a technical term meaning a question about *halakhah* (Jewish law) or some other aspect of the Bible or Jewish tradition. Mt 22:23+.

she·kel — a weight, variously from three to six tenths of an ounce. In Yeshua's day the half-shekel was rarely coined, so that two people could pay the Temple tax (see Exodus 30:11ff.) with a silver shekel coin. Mt 17:24.

She·lah (Sala) — ancestor of Avraham; in Messianic genealogy. Lk 3:35.

Shem (Sem) — son of Noach; in Messianic genealogy. Lk 3:36.

Shet (Seth) — son of Adam; in Messianic genealogy. Lk 3:38.

Si·la (Silas) — co-worker with Sha'ul. Ac 15:22+.

Shi·lo·ach (Siloam) — (1) A tower. Lk 13:4. (2) A pool near the city walls of Yerushalayim. The word *shiloach* means "aqueduct" (from the root *sh-l-ch*, "send"); the aqueduct, dug when Chizkiyahu was king of Y'hudah in the eighth century B.C.E., sent water from the Gichon Spring to the pool at Shiloach. One can still walk through a tunnel which formed part of the aqueduct. Yn 9:7ff.

Shim·'i (Semein) — in Messianic genealogy. Lk 3:26.

Shim·'on (Simon, Simeon) — (1) Tribe of Israel descended from the second son of Ya'akov. Rv 7:7. (2) Old man who blessed Yeshua in the Temple. Lk 2:25ff. (3) Ancestor of Yeshua the Messiah. Lk 3:30. (4) Shim'on Bar-Yochanan (Simon, son of John; Simon Barjona) — Shim'on Kefa (see below). (5) Another of Yeshua's *talmidim*, known as Shim'on the Zealot, i.e., a member of the party set on revolt against the Roman conquerors. Mt 10:4+. (6) Brother of Yeshua. Mt 13:55, Mk 6:3. (7) Person in Beit-Anyah who had had a skin disease. Mt 26:6+. (8) Cyrenian compelled to carry Yeshua's execution-stake. Mt 27:32+. (9) *Parush* in whose house Yeshua ate. Lk 7:40ff. (10) Father of Y'hudah from K'riot. Yn 6:71+. (11) Sorcerer in Shomron. Ac 8:9ff. (12) Tanner in Yafo with whom Kefa lodged. Ac 9:43+. (13) Follower of Yeshua and prophet in Antioch, called "the Black". Ac 13:1.

Shim·'on Ke·fa (Simon Peter) — one of the twelve emissaries of Yeshua (see Kefa). Mt 4:18+.

Shim·shon (Samson) — a judge of Israel (Judges 13-16). MJ 11:32.

shiv·'ah — literally, "seven". After the burial of a father, mother, brother, sister, son, daughter or spouse a Jewish mourner remains at home for seven days; this custom is called "sitting *shiv'ah*". Yn 11:20.

Sh'khem (Shechem, Sychem, Sychar) — city in the mountains of Shomron, on the southeast edge of modern Nablus (Neapolis). Yn 4:5+.

Sh'khi·nah — Divine Presence, the manifest glory of God present with men. Lk 2:9+.

Shlo·mit (Salome) — *talmidah* of Yeshua. Mk 15:40+.

Shlo·mo (Solomon) — king of Israel; in Messianic genealogy. Mt 1:6+.

Sh'ma Is·ra·el, A·do·nai E·lo·hei·nu, A·do·nai e·chad — "Hear, O Israel, the LORD *(Y-H-V-H)* your God, the LORD is one" (Deuteronomy 6:4), the central affirmation of Judaism both then and now. Together with the next verse of Deuteronomy, which enjoins loving God with everything one is and has, Yeshua called this the most important *mitzvah* in the *Torah*. Mk 12:29.

shmoose [Y] — engage in friendly gossipy chit-chat. The word is derived from Hebrew *shmu'ot*, "things heard, rumors". Lk 10:4.

Shmu·'el (Samuel) — prophet in the days of Kings Sha'ul and David. Ac 3:24+.

sho·far — ram's horn; often rendered as "trumpet". Mt 24:31+.

Sh'ol (Sheol, Hades, hell) — the place of the dead, according to the *Tanakh*. Mt 11:23+.

Shom·ron (Samaria) — region of *Eretz-Israel* in the hill country north of Yerushalayim and south of the Galil. The Samaritans, a mixed ethnic group descended from Jews deported by the Assyrians in the 8th century B.C.E. and other peoples ruled by the Assyrians, followed a religion combining pagan and Jewish elements. According to the book of Nehemiah in the *Tanakh*, they arrayed themselves against those rebuilding Yerushalayim. By the first century most Jews regarded them as pariahs. Mt 10:5+.

Sho·sha·nah (Susanna) — a follower of Yeshua. The name means "lily" or "rose". Lk 8:3.

Si·nai (Sina) — mountain in the desert between Egypt and *Eretz-Israel* where Israel received the *Torah* from God through Moshe. Ac 7:30+.

s'mi·khah — laying on of hands, hence ordination, grant of authority. Mt 21:23+.

Suk·kot — the feast of Booths (Tabernacles), celebrating the forty years when the people of Israel lived in booths or tents in the desert between Egypt and *Eretz-Israel*. It is one of three pilgrim festivals when Jews were expected to go up to Yerushalayim in Y'hudah. Yn 7:2.

Tad·**dai** (Thaddeus, Thaddaeus) — one of the twelve emissaries of Yeshua. Mt 10:3+.

talent [O] — a weight variously between 60 and 100 pounds. A talent of gold would be worth around half a million dollars at today's prices ($400/ounce). Mt 25:15+.

ta·li·ta, ku·mi! [A] — Little girl, get up! The word *talita*, being the feminine form of the word for "lamb", is therefore an affectionate diminutive (compare English "lambikin"). Mk 5:41.

Tal·**mai** — Hebrew form of Egyptian *ptolemy*, the name given to Egyptian kings during the centuries before Yeshua. In the New Testament the name is found in the form *Bar-Talmai* (Bartholomew), "son of *ptolemy*". Mt 10:3+.

tal·mid, fem. *tal·mi·dah,* pl. *tal·mi·dim* — disciple, student. The relationship between a *talmid* and his rabbi was very close: not only did the *talmid* learn facts, reasoning processes and how to perform religious practices from his rabbi, but he regarded him as an example to be imitated in conduct and character (see Mt 10:24-25, Lk 6:40, Yn 13:13-15, 1C 11:1). The rabbi, in turn was considered responsible for his

talmidim (Mt 12:2, Lk 19:39, Yn 17:12). Mt 5:1+.

Ta·**mar** (Thamar) — mother of Peretz and Zerach; in Messianic genealogy. Mt 1:3.

Ta·**nakh** — acronym formed from the first letters of the three parts of the Hebrew Bible: *Torah* ("Teaching": the Five Books of Moses or Pentateuch — Genesis, Exodus, Leviticus, Numbers, Deuteronomy); *Nevi'im* ("Prophets": the historical books [Joshua, Judges, Samuel and Kings], the three Major Prophets [Isaiah, Jeremiah, Ezekiel], and the twelve Minor Prophets); and *K'tuvim* ("Writings": Psalms, Proverbs, Job, the Five Scrolls [Song of Songs, Ruth, Esther, Lamentations, Ecclesiates], Daniel, Ezra-Nehemiah and Chronicles). Hence, the Old Testament. Rendered "scripture" or "it is written" in most translations. The reason the New Testament writers cite the *Tanakh* so frequently is that they understand it as God's authoritative Word to mankind. Mt 4:4.

Ta·**vi·ta** (Tabitha) — woman in Yafo whom Kefa raised from the dead.

Terach (Terah, Thara) — father of *Avraham avinu;* in Messianic genealogy. Lk 3:34.

t'fil·lin [A] — two black leather boxes containing scrolls with Bible passages on them (Exodus 13:1-16; Deuteronomy 6:4-9, 11:13-21). During synagogue prayers men affix one to their hand and arm and the other to their forehead, in obedience to Deuteronomy 6:8. *T'fillin* are called phylacteries in most translations. To "lay" *t'fillin* is to use them, to put them in place. Mt 23:5.

Ti·**mai** (Timaeus) — Hebrew name based on Greek *timê*, "value". Mk 10:46.

To·dah (Theudas) — There was a false Messiah with this name who promised to divide the waters of the Yarden River and lead his followers across, c. 44 C.E.; but the Todah of Ac 5:36 was the leader of a rebellion against Rome around 6 C.E.

T·'o·ma (Thomas) [A] — one of the twelve emissaries of Yeshua. Mt. 10:3+.

To·rah — literally, "teaching", but usually translated "Law" because Greek uses *nomos* ("law") to render Hebrew *Torah*. (1) The Five Books of Moses, the Pentateuch, called the Written *Torah*. Mt 5:17. (2) That plus the *Nevi'im* (Prophets) and *K'tuvim* (Writings), i.e., the whole *Tanakh*. Yn 10:34. (3) That plus additional material (the Oral *Torah*) considered in varying degree authoritative in Judaism, Ga 5:3. (4) Uncapitalized, *torah* can be understood generically as "law" or "principle". Ro 7:21ff.

To·rah-teacher — this term translates Greek *grammateus*, corresponding to Hebrew *sofer* (pl. *sofrim*), usually rendered "scribe". The first-century scribes were apparently non-ordained teachers of *Torah*. Mt 2:4+.

treif — literally "torn". Since meat torn by wild animals is forbidden under the Jewish dietary laws, *treif* means, by extension, "non-*kosher*" ("not fit" to be eaten by Jews). Ac 10:14+.

t'shu·vah — literally, "turning". In the context of behavior it means repentance, since the sinner who "does *t'shuvah*" is turning from sin to God. Mt 13:15+.

tsu·ris [Y] — troubles (from Hebrew *tzarot*). Mt 6:34+.

tzad·dik, pl. *tzad·di·kim* — righteous person. At Ac 7:52 and elsewhere "the *Tzaddik*", with the definite article, means the Messiah. Mt 10:41+.

Tza·dok (Zadok, Sadoc) — in Messianic genealogy (see also below; *Tz'dukim*). Mt 1:14.

Tzar·fat (Zarephath, Sarepta) — town near Tzidon. Lk 4:26.

Tz'du·kim (Sadducees), sing. *Tza·dok* — One of the two main components of the religious establishment in Yeshua's time, the other being the *P'rushim*. The *Tz'dukim* tended to be richer, more skeptical, more wordly, and more willing to co-operate with the Roman conquerors than the *P'rushim*. The *Tz'dukim* focused on the rituals in the Temple, so that its destruction in 70 C.E. destroyed their viability. Mt 3:7+.

tze·da·kah — literally, "righteousness", but since ancient times also used to mean "charity". Mt 6:1+.

Tzi·don (Sidon) — town on the coast north of Tzor, in what is today Lebanon. Mt 11:21+.

tzi·tzit, pl. *tzi·tzi·yot* — specially made fringes worn on the four corners of a man's *tallit*, fulfilling the *mitzvah* in Numbers 15:37-41. In ancient times, including the first century, the *tallit* was a cloak or robe included in normal male attire. After clothes stopped being made with "corners", Judaism created the modern *tallit* (prayer shawl) so that the mitzvah could be performed. Mt 9:20+.

Tzi·yon (Zion, Sion) — Mount Tziyon was originally the City of David, south of the modern Old City of Yerushalayim. Later the name Tziyon came to refer metaphorically to the Temple Mount, Yerushalayim, the people of Yerushalayim, or the peple of Israel. (The hill now called Mount Tziyon was given its name in the fourth century C.E.) Mt 21:5+.

Tzor (Tyre) — town on the Mediterranean coast of what is now southern Lebanon. Mt 11:21+.

U·ri·**yah** (Uriah, Urias) — husband of Bat-Sheva (Bathsheba) the mother of King Shlomo. Mt 1:6.

U·zi·**ya**·hu (Uzziah, Ozias) — king of Y'hudah; in Messianic genealogy. Mt 1:8-9.

Ya·'a·**kov** (Jacob, James) — The English name "James" comes from Hebrew *Ya'akov* through Greek *Iakôbos* and Late Latin *Jacomus*. (1) *Ya'akov avinu* (Jacob, our father), i.e., the Patriarch Jacob. Mt 1:2+. (2) His descendants, the House of Ya'akov, meaning the Jewish people. Lk 1:33, Ro 11:26. (3) The father of Yosef #3. Mt 1:15-16. (4) A *talmid* of Yeshua called Ya'akov Ben-Zavdai (James, son of Zebedee), brother of Yochanan #2. Mt 4:18+. (5) A *talmid* of Yeshua called Ya'akov Ben-Chalfai (James, son of Alpheus). Mt 10:3+. (6) A brother of Yeshua the Messiah who became leader of the Messianic community in Yerushalayim and is understood to be the author of the book of Ya'akov. Mt 13:55+. (7) A son of Miryam #3, called "the younger Ya'akov". Mt 27:56, Mk 15:40. (8) Father of Yeshua's *talmid* Y'hudah ben-Ya'akov (Judas, son of James). Lk 6:16+.

Ya·**fo** (Jaffa, Joppa) — port city on the Mediterranean Sea adjoining modern Tel Aviv to the south. Ac 9:35+.

Ya·'**ir** (Jairus) — synagogue president whose daughter Yeshua raised from the dead. The name means, "He will enlighten." Mk 5:22, Lk 8:41.

Ya·**khin** (Achim) — in Messianic genealogy. Mt 1:14.

Yan·**nai** (Jannai, Janna) — in Messianic genealogy. Mt 1:14.

Yar·**den** (Jordan) — river flowing from Mount Hermon in the north to Lake Kinneret and on to the Dead Sea. Mt 3:5+.

Ye·**red** (Jared) — ancestor of Noach; in Messianic genealogy. Lk 3:37.

Ye·ri·**cho** (Jericho) — one of the world's oldest cities (one tower dates from 7,000 B.C.E.), located in the Yarden River Valley east of Yerushalayim. Mt 20:29+.

Ye·ru·sha·**la**·yim (Jerusalem) — capital of *Eretz-Israel* since the days of King David. Psalm 48 calls it "the city of our God,... beautiful for situation, the joy of the whole earth." Mt 2:1+.

Ye·sha'·**ya**·hu (Isaiah, Esaias) — *Tanakh* prophet. Mt 3:3+.

ye·shi·**vah** — Jewish religious school. Ac 19:9.

Ye·**shu**·a (Jesus) — Variant of "Y'hoshua" (Joshua; see below). In the *Tanakh* nine persons and a city have the name Yeshua, usually transliterated as "Jeshua" or "Jeshuah". In the Septuagint and the New Testament the name was brought over into Greek as *Iêsous* and thence into English as "Jesus". It means *"Y-H-V-H* saves" (Mt 1:21) and is also the masculine form of *yeshu'ah* ("salvation"). (1) The Messiah of Israel, Yeshua from Natzeret. In modern Hebrew Yeshua's name is pronounced and written *"Yeshu"*, which may have been the ancient pronunciation in the Galil. However, reflecting two thousand years of conflict between the Church and the Synagogue, it is also an acronym for *Yimach sh'mo v'zikhrono* ("May his name and memory be blotted out"). Mt 1:1+. (2) A Messianic Jew in Rome, "Yeshua, the one called Justus." Co 4:11.

ye·shu·**'ah** — salvation; used in a word play on Yeshua's name at Lk 2:30.

Y'ho·sha·**fat** (Jehoshaphat, Josaphat) —

king of Y'hudah; in Messianic genealogy. Mt 1:8.

Y'ho·**shu·**a (Joshua) — leader of the people of Israel who led the conquest of *Ereiz-Israel* after Moshe's death. The name means, "*Y-H-V-H* saves, *Y-H-V-H* delivers". See also Yeshua, above. Ac 7:45, MJ 4:8.

Y'hu·**dah** (Judah, Judas, Juda, Jude) — (1) The fourth son of *Ya'akov avinu.* Mt 1:2+. (2) The tribe of Israel named after him. Rv 5:5+. (3) The southern kingdom over which various kings reigned, c. 926-586 B.C.E.; contrasted with the northern kingdom, Israel. MJ 8:8. (4) Y'hudah from K'riot, Yeshua's betrayer (see below). (5) Another emissary of Yeshua, perhaps identical with Taddai. Yn 14:22. (6) A brother of Yeshua, traditionally the author of the book of Y'hudah (Jude). Mt 13:55, Mk 6:3. (7) *Talmid* of Yeshua and son of Ya'akov #5. Lk 6:16+. (8) Y'hudah HaG'lili (see below). (9) Prophet surnamed Bar-Sabba. Ac 15:22ff. (10) Messianic Jew in Dammesek. Ac 9:11.

Y'hu·**dah** (Judea, Judah, Juda) — the portion of *Eretz-Israel* allotted to the tribe of Y'hudah. Yerushalayim was at its northern border, and it extended southward past Hevron (Hebron). Mt 2:1+.

Y'hu·**dah** of **K'**ri·**ot** (Judas Iscariot) — Yeshua's betrayer's full name in Hebrew is *Y'hudah Ben-Shim'on Ish-K'riot* (Yn 6:71), which means "Judah, son of Simon, a man of K'riot," a town some twenty miles south of Yerushalayim. Mt 10:4+.

Y'hu·**dah** Ha·G'li·**li** (Judah the Galilean, Judas of Galilee) — popular Jewish leader who led a rebellion against Rome in 6-7 C.E. and founded the party of the Zealots (Sicarii). Ac 5:37.

Y'hu·**di**, pl. *Y'hu·dim* (Jew, Judean) — in the *Jewish New Testament* the term *Y'hudi* (which means "one who praises") does not appear. As a rule, when the Greek word *Ioudaios* is used by a non-Jew, or by a Jew outside *Eretz-Israel*, it is rendered "Jew". When used by a Jew within *Eretz-Israel*, it is rendered "Judean", i.e., a resident or citizen of Y'hudah.

Yif·**tach** (Jepthah, Jephthae) — a judge of Israel. MJ 11:32.

Yir·me·**ya·**hu (Jeremiah, Jeremias, Jeremy) — *Tanakh* prophet. Mt 2:17+.

Yi·**shai** (Jesse) — father of King David; in Messianic genealogy. Mt 1:5+.

Yis·sa·**khar** (Issachar) — one of the twelve tribes of Israel, named after a son of *Ya'akov avinu.* Rv 7:7.

Yitz·**chak** (Isaac) — Second of the three Patriarchs of the Jewish people. Mt 1:2+.

Y'khan·**ya·**hu (Jeconiah, Jeconias) — king of Y'hudah, also called Y'hoyakhin (Jehoiachin); in Messianic genealogy. Mt 1:11-12.

Yo·cha·**nah** (Joanna) — wife of Herod's finance minister. Lk 8:3+.

Yo·cha·**nan** (John, Jona, Jonas) — The English name "John" is derived from Hebrew *Yochanan*, which means, "God gives grace." (1) Yochanan the Immerser (see entry below). (2) *Talmid* of Yeshua, son of Zavdai, brother of Ya'akov #4 and author of several New Testament books. Mt 4:21+. (3) Father of Kefa. Mt 16:17; Yn 21:13, 15. (4) Surnamed Mark, nephew of Bar-Nabba, co-worker with him and Sha'ul. Ac 12:25+. (5) Ancestor of Yeshua. Lk 3:27. (6) Relative of Anan the *cohen hagadol.* Ac 4:6. (7) The author of the book of Revelation (if different from #2). Rv 1:9, 22:8.

Yo·cha·nan Ben-Z'khar·yah — See Yochanan the Immerser, below. Lk 3:3.

Yo·cha·nan the Immerser (John the Baptist, John the Baptizer) — His full name is given at Lk 3:3 as Yochanan Ben-Z'kharyah (John, son of Zechariah). The Greek words *baptô* and *baptizô* mean "to immerse, to dip," so that what is dipped absorbs the character of what it is immersed in, e.g., leather in tanning solution. Mt 3:1+

Yo·dah (Joda, Juda) — in Messianic genealogy. Lk 3:26.

Yo·'el (Joel) — *Tanakh* prophet. Ac 2:16.

Yom-Kip·pur — the Day of Atonement. The Greek says, literally, "the fast", but a Jewish fast-day in the fall spoken of with the definite article can refer only to *Yom-Kippur*. Ac 27:9.

Yo·nah (Jonah) — *Tanakh* prophet. Mt 12:39+.

Yo·nam (Jonan) — in Messianic genealogy. Lk 3:30.

Yo·ram (Jehoram, Joram, Jorim) — (1) King of Y'hudah; in Messianic genealogy. Mt 1:8. (2) A second figure in the Messianic genealogy. Lk 3:29.

Yo·sef (Joseph, Josech) — (1) Son of *Ya'akov avinu*. Yn 4:5+. (2) The tribe of Israel called by his name. Rv 7:8. (3) Husband of Miryam the mother of Yeshua. Mt 1:16+. (4-6) Three different ancestors of Yeshua. Lk 3:24, 26, 30. (7) Brother of Yeshua. Mt 13:55. (8) Son of Miryam #4, same as Yosi #2. Mt 27:56. (9) Messianic Jewish member of the Sanhedrin in whose tomb Yeshua was buried; known as Yosef of Ramatayim (Joseph of Arimathea). Mt 27:57+. (10) Messianic Jew, surnamed Bar-Nabba, who worked with Sha'ul to establish the Gospel among the Gentiles. Ac 4:36.

Yo·shi·ya·hu (Josiah, Josias) — king of Y'hudah; in Messianic genealogy. Mt 1:10-11.

Yo·si (Joseph, Joses, Jose) — (1) Brother of Yeshua. Mk 6:3. (2) Son of Miryam #4. Mk 15:40. "Yosi" is sometimes a diminutive of "Yosef", as "Joe" is of "Joseph".

Yo·tam (Jotham) — king of Y'hudah; in Messianic genealogy. Mt 1:9.

yud (jot) — the smallest letter in the Hebrew alphabet. Mt 5:18.

Zak·kai (Zacchaeus) — tax collector who got saved. The name means "innocent". Lk 19:2ff.

Zav·dai (Zebedee) — father of Yochanan #2 and Ya'akov #4. Mt 4:21+.

Ze·rach (Zerah, Zara, Zarah) — son of Y'hudah; in Messianic genealogy. Mt 1:3.

Z'khar·yah (Zechariah, Zacharias) — (1) *Tanakh* prophet. Mt 23:35, Lk 11:51. (2) Father of Yochanan the Immerser. Lk 1:5+.

Z'ru·ba·vel (Zerubbabel, Zorobabel)— builder of the Second Temple, c. 520-516 B.C.E.; in Messianic genealogy. Mt 1:12-13, Lk 3:27.

Z'vu·lun (Zebulun, Zabulon) — (1) Tribe of Israel descended from a son of the Patriarch Ya'akov. Rv 7:8. (2) The territory in *Eretz-Israel* assigned to that tribe (Joshua 19). Mt 4:13, 15.

REVERSE GLOSSARY

Many names and terms familiar to readers of other translations of the New Testament do not appear in the text of the *Jewish New Testament*. The following alphabetical list of such names and terms enables you to learn what the *Jewish New Testament* uses in their place. An asterisk (*) indicates that the substitute term is used only sometimes, e.g., "lamp — *menorah**" means that sometimes *"menorah"* is used and sometimes "lamp" is used.

Aaron — Aharon
Abel — Hevel
Abia — Aviyah
Abiathar — Avyatar
Abijah — Aviyah
Abiud — Av'ichud
Abraham — Avraham
Aceldama — Chakal-D'ma
Achim — Yakhin
Aenon, Ainon — Einayim
afternoon sacrifice — *minchah*
Agabus — Agav
Ahaz — Achaz
Akeldama — Chakal-D'ma
Alphaeus, Alpheus — Chalfai
Amen — Yes; that's right; indeed*
Amminadab — Amminadav
Amos — Amotz
Ananias — Chananyah
Anna, daughter of Phanuel — Chanah Bat-P'nu'el
Annas — Anan
Apollyon — the Destroyer
apostle — emissary
Arimathea — Ramatayim
Armageddon — Har-Megiddo
Arphaxad — Arpachshad
Aser — Asher
as it is written — as it says in the *Tanakh*
atonement — *kapparah*
attendant — *shammash*
authority — *s'mikhah**
Azor — Azur
Azotus — Ashdod
Baal — Ba'al
Balaam — Bil'am
Balac — Balak
baptism — immersion
baptize — immerse

Barabbas — Bar-Abba
Barjesus — Bar-Yeshua
Barjona — Bar-Yochanan
Barnabas — Bar-Nabba
Barsabbas — Bar-Sabba
Bartholomew — Bar-Talmai
Bartimaeus — Bar-Timai
Beelzebub — Ba'al-Z'vuv
Beelzevul — Ba'al-Zibbul
Belial — B'liya'al
believe — trust, be faithful*
Benjamin — Binyamin
Beor — B'or
Berachiah — Berekhyah
Bethany — Beit-Anyah
Bethesda — Beit-Chasda
Bethlehem — Beit-Lechem
Bethphage — Beit-Pagey
Bethsaida — Beit-Tzaidah
Bethzatha — Beit-Zata
beyond the Jordan — Ever-HaYarden*
bill of divorcement — *get*
bless — make a *b'rakhah**
Blessed One, the — *HaM'vorakh*
blessing — *b'rakhah**
Boanerges — B'nei-Regesh
Boaz, Booz — Bo'az
Bosor — B'or
Caiaphas — Kayafa
Cain — Kayin
Cainan — Keinan
Calvary — Gulgolta
Cana — Kanah
Canaan — Cana'an
Capernaum —K'far-Nachum
Cedron — Kidron
Cephas — Kefa
Charran — Charan
cherubim — *k'ruvim*

Chorazin — Korazin
Christ — Messiah, *Mashiach*
Christian — Messianic
church — Messianic community, congregation
Chuza — Kuza
circumcision — *b'rit-milah**
Cleopas, Cleophas, Clopas — Klofah
coin — *shekel*, denarius*
commandment — *mitzvah* (pl. *mitzvot*)
corban — *korban*
Core — Korach
Cosam — Kosam
council — *sanhedrin*
court — *sanhedrin*
cross — stake, execution-stake
crucify — execute on a stake (as a criminal)
curtain — *parokhet*
Dalmanutha — Dalmanuta
Damascus — Dammesek
Daniel — Dani'el
daughter of — *bat-**
deacon — *shammash* (pl. *shammashim*)
devil — the Adversary, Satan; demon
disciple — *talmid*, (fem. *talmidah*, pl. *talmidim)*
dispersion — Diaspora
dividing wall — *m'chitzah*
divine presence — *Sh'khinah*
Dorcas — gazelle
Eber — Ever
Eleazar — El'azar
Eliezer — Eli'ezer
Eliakim — Elyakim
Elijah, Elias — Eliyahu
Elisabeth, Elizabeth — Elisheva
Eliseus — Elisha
Eliud — El'ichud
Elmadam, Elmodam — Elmadan
Emmanuel — Immanu'el
Emmaus — Ammaus
Emmor — Chamor
Enoch — Chanoch
Enon — Einayim
Enos — Enosh
Ephraim — Efrayim
Esaias — Yesha'yahu
Esau — Esav
Esli — Chesli
Esrom — Chetzron

Eve — Chavah
Ezekias — Chizkiyahu
faith — trust, faithfulness*
fast, the — *Yom-Kippur*
feast of dedication — *Chanukkah*
feast of tabernacles — *Sukkot*
first day of the week — *Motza'ei-Shabbat**
fringe (of garment) — *tzitzit* (pl. *tzitziyot*)
Gabriel — Gavri'el
Galilee — the Galil
Galilee of the nations — Galil-of-the-*Goyim*
Gamaliel — Gamli'el
Gaza — 'Aza
Gehenna — Gey-Hinnom
Gennesaret — Ginosar
Gentile — *Goy* (pl. *Goyim*, adj. *Goyishe*)*
Gethsemane — Gat-Sh'manim
Gideon, Gedeon — Gid'on
give to charity — do *tzedakah**
glory of God — *Sh'khinah**
God, gods — *Elohim**
Golgotha — Gulgolta
Gomorrah — 'Amora
great day (of the feast) — *Hoshanah Rabbah*
Hades — Sh'ol
Hallelujah! — *Halleluyah!*
Hamor — Chamor
Haran — Charan
Heli — Eli
hell — Gey-Hinnom, Sh'ol
Hezekiah — Chizkiyahu
Hezron — Chetzron
high priest (Jewish) — *cohen gadol* (pl. *cohanim g'dolim*)
Holy One, the — *HaKadosh*
Holy Spirit — *Ruach HaKodesh*
Hosea — Hoshea
hymn — *Hallel**
Immanuel — Immanu'el
Isaac — Yitzchak
Isaiah — Yesha'yahu
Iscariot — man from K'riot
Issachar — Yissass'khar
it is written — the *Tanakh* says
Jacob — Ya'akov
Jaffa — Yafo
James — Ya'akov
Jannai, Janna — Yannai
Jared — Yered

Jeconiah, Jechonias, Jehoiachin —
    Y'khanyahu
Jehoram — Yoram
Jehoshaphat — Y'hoshafat
Jephthah, Jephthae — Yiftach
Jeremiah, Jeremias, Jeremy — Yirmeyahu
Jericho — Yericho
Jerusalem — Yerushalayim
Jesse — Yishai
Jesus — Yeshua
Jew — Judean*
Jezebel — Izevel
Joanna — Yochanah
Job — Iyov
Joda — Yodah
Joel — Yo'el
John — Yochanan
John the Baptist — Yochanan the Immerser
Jona, Jonas — Yonah, Yochanan
Jonah — Yonah
Jonan — Yonam
Joppa — Yafo
Joram, Jorim — Yoram
Jordan — Yarden
Josaphat — Y'hoshafat
Joseph, Josech — Yosef, Yosi
Joses, Jose — Yosi
Joshua — Y'hoshua
Josiah, Josias — Yoshiyahu
jot — *yud*
Jotham — Yotam
Juda — Y'hudah, Yodah
Judah — Y'hudah
Judah the Galilean, Judas of Galilee —
    Y'hudah HaG'lili
Judas — Y'hudah
Judas Iscariot — Y'hudah from K'riot
Jude — Y'hudah
Judea — Y'hudah
Korah — Korach
Lamech — Lemekh
lamp — *menorah**
land of Israel — *Eretz-Israel*
Law — *Torah*
Lazarus — El'azar
leaven — *chametz*
leprosy — repulsive skin disease
Levi — L'vi
Levi, son of Alpheus — L'vi Ben-Chalfai
Levite — *L'vi* (pl. *L'vi'im*)

Lord — *Adonai*, sir*
Lord God Almighty — *Adonai*, God of
    heaven's armies
Lord of Sabaoth — *Adonai-Tzva'ot*
Lydda — Lud
Maath — Machat
Madian — Midyan
Mahalaleel — Mahalal'el
Majesty, the — *HaG'dulah*
Majesty on High, the — *HaG'dulah*
    BaM'romim
Malchus — Melekh
Maleleel — Mahalal'el
Manaen — Menachem
Manasseh, Manasses — M'nasheh
Maranatha — *Marana, ta!*
Martha — Marta
Mary — Miryam
Mary Magdalene — Miryam from Mag-
    dala; Miryam, called Magdalit
Mathusala — Metushelach
Mattatha — Mattatah
Mattathias — Mattityahu
Matthan — Mattan
Matthat — Mattat
Matthew — Mattityahu
Matthias — Mattityahu
Melchi — Malki
Melchizedek, Melchisedec — Malki-Tzedek
Melea — Mal'ah
Menna, Menan — Manah
Messiah — *Mashiach*
Methuselah — Metushelach
Michael — Mikha'el
Midian — Midyan
Moloch — Molekh
Moses — Moshe
Most High, the — *HaElyon*
Naaman — Na'aman
Naasson — Nachshon
Nagge — Naggai
Nahor — Nachor
Nahshon — Nachshon
Nahum — Nachum
Nain — Na'im
name, the — *HaShem**
Naphtali, Nephthalim — Naftali
Nathan — Natan
Nathanael — Natan'el
nation — *Goy* (pl. *Goyim*)*

Naum — Nachum
Nazarene, Nazorean — *Natzrati* (pl. *Natzratim*)
Nazareth — Natzeret
new moon — *Rosh-Chodesh*
Nicodemus — Nakdimon
Nineve — Nineveh
Noah — Noach
Obed — Oved
Ozias — Uziyahu
pagan — *Goy* (pl. *Goyim*)*
Paradise — Gan-Eden
Passover — *Pesach*
Passover meal — *Seder*
Paul — Sha'ul
peace — *shalom**
Peace! — *Shalom!*
Peace be upon you! — *Shalom aleikhem!*
Pentecost — *Shavu'ot*
Perez, Phares — Peretz
Peter — Kefa
Phalec — Peleg
Phanuel — P'nu'el
Pharisee — *Parush* (pl. *P'rushim*)
phylacteries — *t'fillin*
pound (coin) — *maneh* (pl. *manim*)
Power, the — *HaG'vurah*
praying — *davvening**
priest (Jewish) — *cohen* (pl. *cohanim*)
propitiation — *kapparah*
question — *sh'eilah* (pl. *sh'eilot*)*
Rabboni — *Rabbani*
Rebecca — Rivkah
Rehoboam, Roboam — Rechav'am
repent — turn from sin to God, do *t'shuvah**
Rephan, Remphan — Reifan
Reu, Ragau — Re'u
Reuben — Re'uven
Rhesa — Reisha
Righteous One, the — the *Tzaddik*
righteous person — *tzaddik**
Ruth — Rut
Sabbath — *Shabbat* (pl. *Shabbatot*)
Sadducee — *Tzadok* (pl. *Tz'dukim*)
Sala — Shelah
Salathiel — Sh'altiel
Salem, Salim — Shalem
Salome — Shlomit
salvation — *yeshu'ah**
Samaria — Shomron

Samson — Shimshon
Samuel — Shmu'el
Sapphira — Shappirah
Sara — Sarah
Sarepta — Tzarfat
Saruch — Serug
Satan — the Adversary*
Saul — Sha'ul
Saul, son of Kish — Sha'ul Ben-Kish
scribe — *Torah*-teacher
Scripture — the *Tanakh*
Sea of Galilee — Lake Kinneret
Sem — Shem
Semein — Shim'i
Seth — Shet
Sharon — the Sharon
Shealtiel — Sh'altiel
Shechem — Sh'khem
Sidon — Tzidon
Silas — Sila
Siloam — Shiloach
Simeon — Shim'on
Simon — Shim'on
Simon Peter — Shim'on Kefa
Sina — Sinai
Sion — Tziyon
Sodom — S'dom
Solomon — Shlomo
son of — *bar-, ben-**
Son of the Blessed — *Ben-HaM'vorakh*
Susanna — Shoshanah
Sychar, Sychem — Sh'khem
tabernacles — *Sukkot*
Tabitha — Tavita
tassel — *tzitzit* (pl. *tzitziyot*)
teacher — rabbi*
Terah, Thara — Terach
Thaddeus, Thaddaeus — Taddai
Thamar — Tamar
Theudas — Todah
this world — the *'olam hazeh**
Thomas — T'oma
Timaeus — Timai
tittle — stroke
troubles — *tsuris**
trumpet — *shofar*
Tyre — Tzor
unclean (food) — *treif**
unleavened bread — *matzah*
Uriah, Urias — Uriyah

Uzziah — Uziyahu
veil of the Temple — *parokhet*
voice from heaven — *bat-kol*
wash hands (ritually, before meal) — do
   n'tilat-yadayim
world to come, the — the *'olam haba**
Zabulon — Z'vulun
Zacchaeus — Zakkai
Zacharias — Z'kharyah

Zadok, Sadoc — Tzadok
Zarephath — Tzarfat
Zebedee — Zavdai
Zebulun — Z'vulun
Zechariah — Z'kharyah
Zerah, Zara, Zarah — Zerach
Zerubbabel — Z'rubavel
Zion — Tziyon
Zorobabel — Z'rubavel

Index of *Tanakh* Passages Cited
in the New Testament

This index gives the pages on which 484 *Tanakh* passages are cited 695 times in the text of the New Testament. The order in which the books of the *Tanakh* are listed and the chapter and verse numbers are those found in Hebrew editions of the Bible (and some Jewish-sponsored English ones). Where Christian editions (and some Jewish ones) have a different chapter and verse, these are given afterwards in parentheses, *e.g.*, Joel 3:1-5(2:28-32), Psalm 69:9(8). Inclusive passages are listed first, as with these five successive entries: Deuteronomy 5:17-20, 5:17-18, 5:17, 5:18, 5:19. Where a page number appears twice in a row, the *Tanakh* passage appears twice on that page.

GENESIS		GENESIS *(Continued)*		EXODUS *(Continued)*	
1:26-27	313	22:17	300, 306	6:7	242
1:27	26, 58	22:18	157	9:16	210
1:28	269	23:4	318	12:46	149
2:2	298	24:7	162, 253	12:51	173
2:7	236	25:23	210	13:2	75
2:24	26, 58, 225, 262	26:4	157	13:12	75
3:17-18	299	28:12	120	13:15	75
5:2	26, 58	32:13	306	16:18	244
5:24	306	37:11	162	16:35	173
8:21	268	37:28	162	19:5	318
12:1	162, 306	39:1-3	162	19:6	317, 317
12:3	252	39:21	162	19:12-13	309
12:7	162, 253	39:23	162	20:11	343
13:15	162, 253	41:37-44	162	20:12-13(12-16)	105
14:17-20	300	41:54	162	20:12	21, 27, 53, 58, 263
15:3	204	42:5	162	20:13-14(13-17)	215
15:4	162	45:1	162	20:13(13-16)	27, 58
15:5-6	306	47:9	318	20:13	6, 312
15:5	204, 204	47:31	307	20:13(14)	7, 201, 312
15:6	203, 204, 252, 313	48:4	162	20:13(15)	201
15:7	162			20:14(17)	207
15:13-14	162	EXODUS		21:17	21, 53
15:16	162	1:7-8	162	21:24	7
15:18-21	162	2:2	307	22:27(28)	189
17:5	204	2:11	307	24:8	303, 305
17:7	253	2:14	163	25:40	302
17:8	162	3:1-2	163	29:18	268
18:14	209	3:6-10	163	31:18	94
21:10	255	3:6	32, 62, 108, 157	32:1	163
21:12	209, 306	3:15	157, 160, 188, 191	32:6	229
22:16	300	6:6	173	32:9	164

MAP INDEX AND KEY

The following map index of 172 locations includes all New Testament place-names. Key letters A-D refer to the Map of *Eretz-Israel* in the Time of Yeshua (page 390). Key letters U-Z refer to the Map of the Eastern Mediterranean and Near East in the Second Temple Period (page 391). An asterisk (*) indicates a place in or very near Yerushalayim not shown on either map.

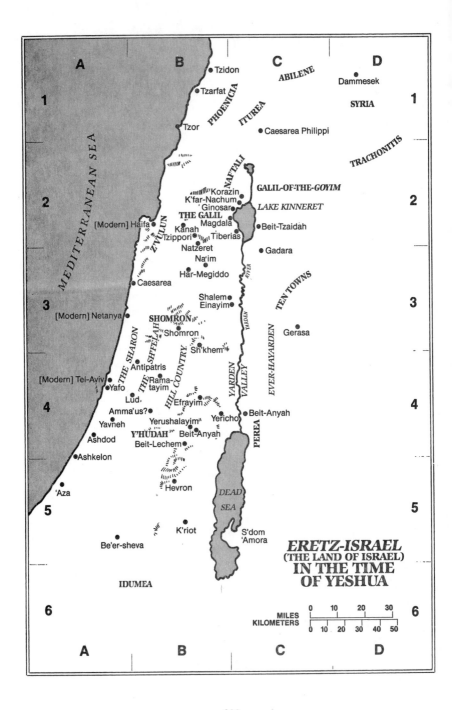

ERETZ-ISRAEL
(THE LAND OF ISRAEL)
IN THE TIME
OF YESHUA

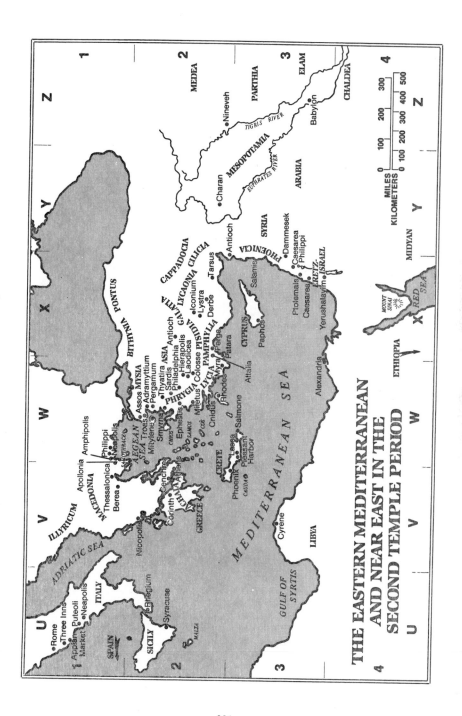

THE EASTERN MEDITERRANEAN
AND NEAR EAST IN THE
SECOND TEMPLE PERIOD

NOTES

NOTES

ABOUT THE TRANSLATOR

DAVID H. STERN was born in Los Angeles in 1935, the great-grandson of two of the city's first twenty Jews. He earned a Ph.D. in economics at Princeton University and was a professor at UCLA, mountain-climber, co-author of a book on surfing and owner of health-food stores.

In 1972 he came to believe in Yeshua as the Messiah, after which he received a Master of Divinity degree at Fuller Theological Seminary and did graduate work at the University of Judaism.

He was married in 1976 to Martha Frankel, also a Messianic Jew, and together they served one year on the staff of Jews for Jesus. Dr. Stern taught Fuller Theological Seminary's first course in "Judaism and Christianity," organized Messianic Jewish conferences and leaders' meetings, and was an officer of the Messianic Jewish Alliance of America.

In 1979 the Stern family made *aliyah* (immigrated to Israel). They now live in Jerusalem with their two children and are active in Israel's Messianic Jewish community.

Dr. Stern is the author of *Messianic Jewish Manifesto*, which outlines the destiny, identity, history, theology and program of today's Messianic Jewish movement. He also wrote *Restoring the Jewishness of the Gospel: A Message for Christians*. It consists of excerpts from the former book selected for Christians to whom the Jewishness of the Gospel is an unfamiliar idea.

The *Jewish New Testament* is the basis for its companion volume, the *Jewish New Testament Commentary*. This commentary discusses Jewish issues raised in the New Testament—questions Jews have about Yeshua, the New Testament and Christianity; questions Christians have about Judaism and the Jewish roots of their faith; and questions Messianic Jews have about their own identity and role.

The *Jewish New Testament* and the *Jewish New Testament Commentary* are available together as a boxed set and on CD-ROM. The *Jewish New Testament* has also been produced on sixteen audio cassettes. Several of Dr. Stern's books are available in other languages.

In 1998, Dr. Stern published the *Complete Jewish Bible*, his stylistically modified adaptation of an existing Jewish translation of the *Tanakh* ("Old Testament") bound together with the *Jewish New Testament*.

All these books are published by Jewish New Testament Publications, Inc. and are available through:

Messianic Jewish Resources International, *a division of The Lederer Foundation*
6204 Park Heights Avenue, Baltimore, Maryland 21215, USA
Phone: 800-410-7367, or 410-358-6471
E-mail: ledmessmin@aol.com   Fax: 410-764-1376
Internet: http://www.MessianicJewish.net